Law and Philosophy Library

Volume 121

The Law and Philosophy Library, which has been in existence since 1985, aims to publish cutting edge works in the philosophy of law, and has a special history of publishing books that focus on legal reasoning and argumentation, including those that may involve somewhat formal methodologies. The series has published numerous important books on law and logic, law and artificial intelligence, law and language, and law and rhetoric. While continuing to stress these areas, the series has more recently expanded to include books on the intersection between law and the Continental philosophical tradition, consistent with the traditional openness of the series to books in the Continental jurisprudential tradition. The series is proud of the geographic diversity of its authors, and many have come from Latin America, Spain, Italy, the Netherlands, Germany, and Eastern Europe, as well, more obviously for an English-language series, from the United Kingdom, the United States, Australia, and Canada.

More information about this series at http://www.springer.com/series/6210

Liesbeth Huppes-Cluysenaer •
Nuno M.M.S. Coelho

Editors

Aristotle on Emotions in Law and Politics

 Springer

Editors
Liesbeth Huppes-Cluysenaer
University of Amsterdam
Amsterdam, The Netherlands

Nuno M.M.S. Coelho
Faculdade de Direito de Ribeirão Preto
University of São Paulo
Ribeirão Preto, São Paulo
Brazil

ISSN 1572-4395
Law and Philosophy Library
ISBN 978-3-319-66702-7
DOI 10.1007/978-3-319-66703-4

ISSN 2215-0315   (electronic)

ISBN 978-3-319-66703-4   (eBook)

Library of Congress Control Number: 2017963135

Printed on acid-free paper

This Springer imprint is published by Springer Nature
The registered company is Springer International Publishing AG
The registered company address is: Gewerbestrasse 11, 6330 Cham, Switzerland

For Luciano de Camargo Penteado,
in memoriam

Preface

This book is the result of an interdisciplinary collaboration over many years (from 2007 onward) between ancient philosophers, legal theorists, political scientists, and historians. These scholars share an extensive reading-knowledge of Aristotle's work, some from a purely philosophical background, and good knowledge of the ancient Greek language, others from the perspective of legal and political theory.

Collaboration on this book was initiated during two workshops, one combined with a Symposium on Law and Emotion in Amsterdam (2014) and one during the IVR conference in Washington (2015). All contributions were extensively reviewed by two reviewers in 2016, as far as possible externally (double-blind), some internally (half-blind), and in a few cases in an open review. One of the reviewers is primarily an expert in ancient philosophy, while the other is an expert in contemporary legal or political theory. The reviewers were asked to express their preference on the basis of a blind overview of abstracts, and it was possible to give each reviewer one or two texts to review according to their preference. This shows that the chapters each attract their own public.

We wish to thank the following reviewers: Clifford Bates, Stefano Bertea, Enrico Berti, Giovanni Bombelli, José Britto, Edith Brugmans, Iris van Domselaar, Joao Hobuss, Samuli Hurri, Oliver Lembcke, Giuseppe Lorini, Paolo di Lucia, Saulo de Matos, Terry Maroney, Francesca Piazza, Christof Rapp, Claudio Sarra, Marlene Sokolon, Adriel Trott, Gerard Versluis, and Raphael Zillig. Complete information about the reviewing procedure has been provided to Springer, which reviewed the book as a whole with the help of two reviewers.

The book starts with a reprint of two articles, one by Terry Maroney and the other by Christof Rapp, both of which are revisions of their keynote lectures delivered at the Symposium on Law and Emotion in Amsterdam. Both papers are published after being subjected to an open peer review.[1] Together the two articles

---

[1] An open peer review of both articles can be found at http://www.paulscholten.eu/theoretical-relevance/r/law-and-emotion/.

give a good introduction to the contemporary debate around Aristotle's view on emotion. All other contributions were written as original publications for this book, with the exception of one English translation of an article by Cristina Viano which was published in French in 2011 in *Métis*.

We also wish to express our gratitude to Daniela Bonanno for her careful corrections and harmonization of the Greek language transcriptions.

Amsterdam, The Netherlands   Liesbeth Huppes-Cluysenaer
Ribeirão Preto, Brazil   Nuno M.M.S. Coelho

Contents

Contributors

Giovanni Bombelli Faculty of Law, Catholic University of Milan, Milan, Italy

Daniela Bonanno Faculty of Culture and Society, University of Palermo, Palermo, Italy

José de Sousa e Brito Constitutional Court, Lisbon, Portugal

Ian Bryan Law School, University of Lancaster, Lancaster, UK

Mateusz Franciszek Bukaty Faculty of Law, University of Lodz, Łódź, Poland

Nuno Coelho University of São Paulo, São Paulo, Brazil

University of Ribeirão Preto, Ribeirão Preto, Brazil

Emma Cohen de Lara Amsterdam University College, Amsterdam, The Netherlands

Lucia Corso Faculty of Economics and Law, Kore University of Enna, Enna, Italy

Stefano Fuselli Faculty of Law, University of Padua, Padua, Italy

Mariusz Jerzy Golecki Faculty of Law, University of Lodz, Łódź, Poland

Liesbeth Huppes-Cluysenaer Faculty of Law, University of Amsterdam, Amsterdam, The Netherlands

Misung Jang Faculty of Philosophy, Soongsil University, Seoul, South Korea

Peter Langford Law and Criminology, Edge Hill University, Ormskirk, UK

Terry A. Maroney Vanderbilt University Law School, Nashville, TN, USA

Saulo de Matos Faculty of Law, Federal University of Pará, Belém, Brazil

Daniel Simão Nascimento Pontifícia Universidade Católica of Rio de Janeiro's Nucleus of Estudies in Ancient Philosophy (NUFA), Rio de Janeiro, Brazil

Fabiana Pinho University of São Paulo, São Paulo, Brazil

University of Kiel, Kiel, Germany

Tommi Ralli Centre of European Law and Politics, University of Bremen, Bremen, Germany

Christof Rapp Faculty of Philosophy, Ludwig-Maximilian University of Munich, Munich, Germany

Ana Carolina de Faria Silvestre Southern Minas Gerais Law School and Higher Education Center in Management, Technology and Education, Minas Gerais, Brazil

Humber van Straalen University of Amsterdam, Amsterdam, The Netherlands

Cristina Viano Centre Léon-Robin, University of Paris IV-Sorbonne, Paris, France

Wojciech Zaluski Faculty of Law and Administration, Jagiellonian University, Kraków, Poland

Part I
Introduction

Chapter 1
The Debate About Emotion in Law and Politics

Liesbeth Huppes-Cluysenaer

Abstract New awareness of the cognitive role of emotions leads to new discussions in the fields of law and politics. In these new discussions Aristotle is often pointed out as a forerunner because of his theory about emotions in *Rhetoric*.

Aristotle discerns two moralities, in which the cognitive role of emotions has a different meaning: a civic morality of judicial procedure in the *Nicomachean Ethics* and a contemplative morality of theoretical study in *Politics*. In the civic morality attendance for the cognitive role of emotions means acknowledging that excellence in judges and other decision-makers is based on self-education through self-reflection. In the contemplative morality of the *Politics* the study is focused on the possibility to educate the emotions of citizens in general through laws. *Rhetoric* is about the persuasion of decision-makers in Law Courts and in the Assembly. As far as it is concerned with emotions, it is more about influencing than about educating.

1.1 Theme of the Book

There has been an explosion of emotion research in which emotions are no longer seen in opposition to reason. Instead, emotions are increasingly appreciated as being indispensable in cognitive processes because they comprise sets of perceptions and evaluations that enable judgment. Emotions are no longer set aside as mere obstacles to good judgments. At the same time, however, it is a well-known fact that emotions also often prevent people from judging carefully.

The new awareness of the important cognitive role of emotions leads to new discussions in the fields of law and politics. The question is raised for example, whether it is desirable for judges to express their emotions and what the right way would be for them to do so. Questions like this introduce new arguments into the ongoing debate in legal philosophy about legal positivism: about its rationalist ideal of the dispassionate judge who merely applies rules. Maroney, who gives an introduction to the debate (Chap. 2), describes the rationalist ideal of legal positivism as the persistent cultural script of legal theory. It can be added that there is also

L. Huppes-Cluysenaer (✉)
Faculty of Law, University of Amsterdam, Amsterdam, The Netherlands
e-mail: huppes.uva@gmail.com

© Springer International Publishing AG 2018
L. Huppes-Cluysenaer, N.M.M.S. Coelho (eds.), *Aristotle on Emotions in Law and Politics*, Law and Philosophy Library 121, DOI 10.1007/978-3-319-66703-4_1

a persistent cultural script of Jurisprudentialism in legal theory, which is opposed to the rationalist ideal of legal positivism.

Maroney refers to Nussbaum as one of the first philosophers to not only call attention to the cognitive relevance of emotions, but to also attribute the origin of this view to Aristotle's theory on emotions in Rhetoric. With this reference to Aristotle, the theme of "law and emotion" also gives rise to a debate about what Aristotle exactly wrote about emotions in law and politics, and more particularly, how these ideas are related to Aristotle's view on virtue ethics. Rapp (Chap. 3) deals specifically with the issue of whether the references to Aristotle, made by Maroney in her elaboration of the righteously angry judge, are correct interpretations.

Aristotle's ideas about virtue as elaborated in his *Nicomachean Ethics* have not long ago also attracted new attention in legal philosophy, as well as in business ethics, computer ethics, criminal justice ethics and the like. Virtue ethics has become very fashionable in these fields over the last ten to twenty years. In these fields it is readily acknowledged that it is not enough to teach students a set of rules, but that it is necessary for them to develop a certain moral disposition: a virtuous way of understanding, feeling and acting.[1] To refer to Aristotle for this insight, to a text so far away from contemporary society, could also be characterized as a way to circumvent the difficult question of how such a virtuous practice in law or business is compatible with contemporary political ideals and practices.

The new interest in emotions in law and politics is specifically oriented towards contemporary political issues. Thus it is important to note that there are two attacks on legal positivism, both of which refer to Aristotle: one to *Nicomachean Ethics* and the other to *Rhetoric*. The theme of this book is the relation between these two views in both Aristotle's work and in contemporary legal and political theory.

1.2   Practice and Theory

One of the important exponents of the virtue-centered approach, Solum, was interested above all in the flourishing and maintenance of a purely jurisprudential approach. He argued for a depoliticization of law in legal decision-making—for turning away from considerations of welfare, efficiency, autonomy or equality[2]— and for aiming instead at strengthening the influence of legal excellence in legal decision-making. Solum emphasized that in the end a judicial decision rests on a personal view: this is the way I—the judge—see it. He stated that it was widely acknowledged that no criterion could be provided for sorting out errors of judges, not even for clear errors.[3] The fact that no such criterion can be defined makes it impossible to justify decisions conclusively with an appeal to rules.

---

[1] These sentences are borrowed from the very useful comments of one of Springer's reviewers on an earlier version of this chapter.

[2] Solum (2013), p. 2/3.

[3] Ibid., p. 27.

Maroney advocates a new specialism in the legal discipline. She wants to replace the jurisprudential excellence for which Solum argued with the rationalism of legal-neuroscience and legal-psychology. This new specialism in law should be developed by scholars who analyze and discuss cases in which emotions on the part of the judge have played a role in order to establish the appropriateness of certain emotions and for prescribing ways to display them. Once it is clear which emotions are appropriate, judges can be taught to (not) have or at least (not) display such emotions. Solum's statement can be extended, however, to this new specialism of emotions in law and politics. Is there a criterion for sorting out clear cases of (in)appropriateness?

The views of Maroney and Solum agree in rejecting the idea that the practice of law and politics can be understood as an application of rules. Both claim that legal theories which ignore emotions are misguided. Their views differ, however, in the way they conceive of the relation between theory and practice. In the view of Solum practice has the final word and in the view of Maroney theory has the last word. Both views can be traced back to Aristotle, the first to his elaboration of civic morality, the second to his elaboration of contemplative morality.

1.3 Multidisciplinarity

Rapp (Chap. 3) writes that he doesn't like the idea of an angry judge and wants reason to remain the ultimate authority in legal decisions. Rapp could thus be called a legal positivist. He depicts himself, however, explicitly as a legal philistine who knows nothing at all about the legal discipline. At the same time Rapp, as a translator of Aristotle's *Rhetoric* and specialist in ancient philosophy, calls Aristotelians, such as Maroney, hotheaded in their attempt to use Aristotle's writing about emotions in the context of contemporary judicial decision-making.

In this way Rapp acknowledges the importance of collaboration between legal, political or psychological theorists, such as Maroney, and ancient philosophers/translators such as himself, to properly interpret Aristotle's texts for use in current times. Such collaboration is the main characteristic of this book. Rapp says that he expresses a view similar to Aristotle's when he writes that reason should remain the ultimate authority in legal decision-making. By saying that he is a legal philistine, he excuses himself for the fact that he does not understand the enormous difference between the meaning of reason in legal positivism and in a virtue-centered approach as proposed by Solum. Similarly, when Solum calls himself a neo-Aristotelian,[4] he indicates with the prefix *neo* that he cannot appreciate the enormous gap between the biological approach of Aristotle and modern biology,[5] nor the enormous differences in institutional setting between ancient Athens and the contemporary United States.

Aristotle's works on emotion and the role of emotion in contemporary legal and political theory are explored in this book from the perspective of different disciplines.

---

[4]Ibid., p. 1.
[5]Ibid., p. 8/9.

Rapp agrees with Maroney that Aristotle is the forerunner of the new attention for emotions. He criticizes Maroney's claim, however, that Aristotle propagates that a judge should be righteously angry. He argues that Aristotle's ethics concern an individual moral agent and that Aristotle's theory of emotions in *Rhetoric* is directed at speaking before hundreds of judges in law courts or in the Assembly.

Rapp's view is supported in many chapters of the book. Nonetheless, Rapp's view leaves open the question of whether a contemporary judge can be conceived as an individual moral agent in Aristotelian terms.

1.4 Cognition, Moral Agency and Legitimation

What Aristotle means with the term individual moral agent is the most important question underlying the chapters of this book. Can an individual who freely chooses its goals be a moral agent in Aristotelian terms? What does it mean to have appropriate emotions? Appropriate for whom? Does appropriate in fact mean the same as rational? These questions connect the three subdivisions of chapters: Cognition (Chaps. 4–8), Moral agency (Chaps. 9–15) and Legitimation (Chaps. 16–22).

The chapters each have their own approach and it is best to read each on its own merits. It is also interesting to focus on the themes that connect the different contributions.

1.4.1 Cognition

In the part *Cognition* the authors compare the new interest in emotions to Aristotle's view of cognition and to his ontology. Aristotle conceived the world as continuous as opposed to being divided into species. This means that in his view the world cannot be known through the lens of concepts and that action is the primary source of knowledge of the world. Consequently knowledge was situated in individual practices in Aristotle's view.

The discussions about Aristotle's view of cognition have in the past mostly been focused on Descartes's rejection of Aristotle's theory that living beings have a soul. Specific for the discussion on cognition in this book is the focus on Aristotle's view on language. This view was rejected in the Middle-Ages, most prominently in the nominalism of Ockham.[6] The medieval understanding of language formed the basis for the development of enlightened science and for the building of nations with their own national languages. Aristotle's texts were therefore mostly interpreted in the frame of this conception of language.

---

[6]Aristotle's view is certainly also rejected by Scholastic Realism, and this realism has played an important role in the way, for example, Peirce has salvaged the Medieaval view on language for current times. See Oleksy (2015).

Today's interest in the role of emotions in cognitive processes, however, brings a new emphasis on individual action as the primary source of knowledge of the world. This makes it possible to de-construct widely accepted interpretations of Aristotle's works. If, for example, Aristotle saw the world as continuous rather than divided into species, he cannot have believed that living beings were oriented towards the completion of their species-specific growth. Nor can Aristotle have attributed truth value to taxonomic systems, or to any other systematic approach.

The focus of Aristotle's view on language is specifically relevant in the context of globalization. Aristotle's view concerns the gap between an abstract view of the world as continuous and a concrete appreciation of the world in the context of actual individual practices. The view on language that developed in the Middle-Ages was foundational for the development of the concept of nation: the idea of collective practice.

The part on cognition can be summarized as follows:

- Aristotle's concept of rationality implies in all its aspects the continuous force of emotions (Chap. 4).
- Aristotle's view on perception presupposes an 'en-souled' moral agent, while the current view projects general knowledge about stimuli and automatic responses on certain individual contexts of action by understanding acts as determined by programs (Chap. 5).
- Aristotle's view on law is based on a functional language in which the individual understanding of a proper end plays a crucial role, while in current times a nominalist view prevails in which individuals attempt to align with the will of an authority (Chap. 6).
- Aristotle's concept of reasoning is not based on the truth of formal syllogisms, but on Enthymemes, i.e., the commonplaces[7] (topics) which are expected to be acceptable to the discussants in a given context (Chap. 7).
- Aristotle's concept of rationality is dialogical, which implies a civic morality of legal procedure, while the current view of rationality is categorical and replaces civic morality with rule-application (Chap. 8).

1.4.2 Moral Agency

Even within the virtue-centered approach, most authors would find it strange to re-introduce Aristotle's biological view into the field of ethics.[8] Attention to the

---

[7]"That a deduction is made from accepted opinions—as opposed to deductions from first and true sentences or principles—is the defining feature of dialectical argumentation in the Aristotelian sense." in Rapp (n.d.). In this volume authors mostly speak of common place(s) instead of commonplace(s) to clarify that topos does not refer to generally existing common opinions, but to an opinion which is thought to be accepted by the parties in an actual debate.

[8]See for example Solum (2013), p. 27.

cognitive role of emotions, however, brings a reconsideration of Descartes's rejection of Aristotle's theory that living beings have a soul. Will such a reconsideration of an 'en-souled' moral agent (Chap. 5) lead to changes in ethical theory? Brito (Chap. 9) rejects such an inference. But is it possible to rhyme a virtue-centered approach with the concept of a free individual capable of choosing its own goals who does not feel a natural attraction to live virtuously? Is the conclusion of Brito that Aristotle is inconsistent in his qualification of killing out of anger not caused by his explicit rejection of the 'en-souled' moral agent? Viano (Chap. 10) does not see an inconsistency in Aristotle's qualification, because she sees the emotion of anger as a natural reaction to a wrong.

Aristotle's conception of moral agency is concerned with the exertion of entrusted authority over others, such as the master of a household or in an office of the city-state. Cognition and political authority are connected in moral agency. It concerns decisions about the interests of others in the light of what is conducive to the common good. For an individual who has no other concern than him or herself the warning and welcoming signals of emotions suffice. This is different when an individual has decision-making power over others. The individual then needs the comparative skills by which similarities can be perceived and by which rules can be formulated about what is conducive to the common good. To be able to exert authority it is crucial to understand what the dignity of an office is and to have the capacity to maintain this despite continuous countervailing pressures.

The part on moral agency can be summarized as follows:

- There is a remarkable inconsistency in Aristotle's view on killing out of anger (Chap. 9).
- Seen from the perspective of the importance of honor in Athens, an angry reaction to a perceived slight was in a certain sense morally obligated. In this perspective Aristotle's view on killing out of anger is not inconsistent (Chap. 10)
- For a judge, indignation is more appropriate than anger because it presupposes existing standards of merit and discerns relations which deviate from these standards (Chap. 11).
- To cultivate the right emotions at the right time, the individual should primarily educate him/herself. This attitude can be transferred to a professional practice in which a person has to take decisions that do not concern his or her own life (Chap. 12).
- Consequentialist theorists struggle with the warning emotion of feeling dirty, which can/should be felt by people in certain situations even if they believe they have done what is best (Chap. 13).
- Chesterton's theory of the mean depicts the subject as merely the incorporation of a struggle between two opposing forces. This theory is definitely different from the Aristotelian approach (Chap. 14).

1.4.3 *Legitimation*

Central to the virtue-centered approach is the acknowledgment that no criterion can be provided for sorting out errors of judges. This acknowledgment is an inference from Aristotle's view on language. This means that once people are aware of the under-determinateness of natural language, a justification for judicial decisions by reference to rules can no longer be experienced as conclusive. How is it then possible to prevent a completely arbitrary exercise of power? What is then the function of law?

Aristotle studied politics partly within the framework of civic morality and partly within the framework of contemplative morality. In his civic morality the function of law was primarily to create strict procedures for the regulation of public discussion.

Very important from a contemporary point of view are Aristotle's ideas about contemplative morality which concerned the question of how to preserve the constitution that lays down these strict procedures. Aristotle saw contemplative morality as the work of theorists who lead lives that are removed from the daily practice of politics and business. He characterized their research as a part of zoology and contributed to it with his comparison of constitutions. This is an inquiry into the influences that preserve and destroy particular kinds of constitutions and lead to good or bad administration in states. Aristotle's contemplative morality triggers the new attention for emotions in law and politics with the question: which emotions are foundational for a well-organized state?

The part on legitimation can be summarized as follows:

- Aristotle's conception of practical wisdom leads to the exclusion of slaves from political life (Chap. 15).
- What exactly is the incapacity of the "apolis" of Aristotle, who cannot be part of a household and by this is also unfit for political life? (Chap. 16)
- Aristotle gives many examples of characteristics the presence of which can be too much or too little to contribute to political life (Chap. 17).
- The attribution to Aristotle of the belief that humans can only develop their excellences fully by participating in the juries of Law Courts or in the Assembly is disputable (Chap. 18).
- The orator has to cultivate certain emotions in an audience to instill an attitude oriented toward following the rule of law (Chap. 19).
- Political friendship is oriented at utility according to Aristotle and creates the legal agreement needed for the maintenance of the city-state. At the same time, however, political friendship aims at the moral good of living well together and acting in an honorable way (Chap. 20).
- An impartial spectator, who is not involved in a specific process of judgment, but rather in the whole decision-making process, is needed to make an intervention now and then in the judicial process to enhance its rationality (Chap. 21).

References

Oleksy, Mateusz W. 2015. *Realism and Individualism: Charles S. Peirce and the Threat of Modern Nominalism*. Amsterdam: John Benjamins Publishing.

Rapp, Christof. n.d. Aristotle's *Rhetoric*. Edited by Edward N. Zalta. *The Stanford Encyclopedia of Philosophy*. http://plato.stanford.edu/archives/spr2010/entries/aristotle-rhetoric/.

Solum, Lawrence. 2013. Virtue Jurisprudence: Towards an Aretaic Theory of Law. In *Aristotle and the Philosophy of Law Theory, Practice and Justice*, ed. Liesbeth Huppes-Cluysenaer and Nuno M.M.S. Coelho, 1–32. Dordrecht and New York: Springer. http://public.eblib.com/choice/publicfullrecord.aspx?p=1083709.

Chapter 2
Judicial Emotion as Vice or Virtue: Perspectives Both Ancient and New

Terry A. Maroney

Abstract Is emotion a judicial vice or a judicial virtue? While Western post-Enlightenment norms insist on the former, contemporary psychology suggests the latter—or perhaps it suggests that either could be true. This view is illuminated and given texture by the Aristotelian tradition. This chapter explores historical, philosophical and scientific perspectives that converge around the view that emotion is a vital source of judicial wisdom. At the same time, judicial emotion can sometimes operate as a vice. The chapter situates this more nuanced position on judicial emotion within the broader frame of law and emotion studies, demonstrates how most scholars within that movement either explicitly or implicitly adopt an Aristotelian philosophy, and uses the case of anger to demonstrate the value of an Aristotelian virtue approach to the emotional element of judicial behavior and decision-making.

2.1 Introduction

Is emotion a judicial vice or a judicial virtue? While Western post-Enlightenment norms insist on the former, contemporary psychology suggests the latter- or, at least, it suggests that either could be true, or that sometimes it is one and sometimes the other. This more realistic and nuanced view of judicial emotion is illuminated and given texture by the Aristotelian tradition.

This chapter has before been published in open access for the Digital Paul Scholten Project. Maroney, "Judicial Emotion as Vice or Virtue." http://www.paulscholten.eu/research/article/judicial-emotion-as-vice-or-virtue-2/. It is largely adapted from my prior writings on the topic, to which the reader is directed for a more in-depth analysis. See Maroney (2011b); Maroney (2011a), p. 1485; Maroney (2012), p. 1207.

T.A. Maroney (✉)
Vanderbilt University Law School, Nashville, TN, USA
e-mail: terry.maroney@vanderbilt.edu

© Springer International Publishing AG 2018
L. Huppes-Cluysenaer, N.M.M.S. Coelho (eds.), *Aristotle on Emotions in Law and Politics*, Law and Philosophy Library 121, DOI 10.1007/978-3-319-66703-4_2

Exploration of the role of emotion in judicial behavior and decision-making forms an important part of the larger law and emotion movement within interdisciplinary scholarship. The movement is based primarily in the United States but is gaining significant traction elsewhere, particularly Europe, the United Kingdom, and Australia. This chapter briefly describes the contour of that movement. Importantly, much law and emotion scholarship relies—either implicitly or explicitly—on Aristotelian concepts of the emotions. The Aristotelian perspective is particularly useful in analyzing judicial emotion. This chapter uses the case of anger to demonstrate that utility. A virtue perspective illuminates the normative variability not just of anger but of judicial emotion more generally.

2.2   Aristotelian Thought Within Law and Emotion Scholarship

Much of the exploration of the role of emotion in law—particularly that subset that explicitly identifies itself with the law and emotion movement—has been Aristotelian (whether explicitly or implicitly) in its approach.

2.2.1   Some Background on Law and Emotion

Law and emotion interact on multiple levels. Events that call for a legal response—violent crime, property theft and damage, environmental destruction, and infringements on personal liberty, just to name a few—evoke powerful emotional responses among those immediately affected and in the public at large. The people who implement those legal responses—police, legislators, lawyers, judges, and jurors—experience emotions of their own. Law sometimes varies according to the existence, sincerity, and depth of emotion: in determining whether a search or seizure was unreasonable under the U.S. Constitution, for example, the extent to which the person searched was frightened or humiliated is relevant; a similar inquiry is at the heart of the law of workplace sexual harassment. Sometimes law has to put a price on it, as in determinations of emotional damages. People even have emotions about law itself, or about particular laws, feelings that range from revulsion to reverence.[1]

A distinct body of scholarship exploring this constellation of interactions between law and emotion began to emerge in the United States in the mid-1980s, trailing slightly behind the explosion of emotion research in psychology and disciplines as diverse as history, sociology, and neuroscience. As in the intervening decades emotion research has grown exponentially in the social sciences, hard

---

[1]Maroney (2015).

sciences, and humanities, so too has law and emotion scholarship. It gained significant traction by the late 1990s, a progress marked by the 1999 publication of *The Passions of Law*,[2] and has expanded rapidly since that time. Happily, the scholarship is no longer limited to the United States. Recent years have seen the publication of journals devoted to law and emotion in the United Kingdom;[3] the convening of conferences in Germany and the Netherlands;[4] and the rollout of empirical studies in Sweden and Australia,[5] just to name a few high points in the increasing internationalization of this developing field.

The field's diversity is rooted in a set of common perspectives and commitments. Abrams and Keren helpfully propose that law and emotion scholarship seeks to illuminate the affective features of legal problems; investigate these features through interdisciplinary analysis; and integrate resulting understandings into practical, normative proposals, helping law to be more responsive to the emotions that inflect its operation.[6] As emotion shapes law and law shapes emotion, legal theory and practice ignore emotion at its peril.[7]

Perhaps most fundamentally, law and emotion scholarship positions itself in opposition to the widespread and caricatured view of emotion that permeates Western legal theory—a view that reason and emotion are separable and exist in an oppositional relationship to one another. This view underlies the common supposition that law ought to admit only of reason and, therefore, that part of the work of law is to heavily police its boundaries so as to exclude and neuter emotion.[8] Virtually all modern scholars of the emotions, whatever their disciplinary home, reject those underlying views. Law has been more stubborn. A major part of the task of law and emotion scholars therefore has been to find a language with which to persuade traditional legal theorists to understand emotions as something other than irrational, epiphenomenal, idiosyncratic, stubborn, and mysterious.

---

[2]Bandes (1999).

[3]Schweppe and Stannard (2013).

[4]"Criminal Law and Emotions in European Legal Cultures: From the 16th Century to the Present," *Max Planck Institute for Human Development*, May 2015, https://perma.cc/X5E4-WBNK; "Aristotle: Law, Reason, and Emotion," *University of Amsterdam*, November 2014, https://perma.cc/K638-GL45.

[5]Anleu et al. (2015).

[6]Abrams and Keren (2010).

[7]Bandes and Blumenthal (2012), pp. 161–181.

[8]Maroney (2006), p. 119.

2.2.2 Aristotle's Theory of the Emotions and Contemporary Appraisal Theory

Scholars have found this language in two primary sources: first, contemporary affective psychology, and second, Aristotle. These ancient and new accounts of human nature, different as they are on many levels, converge in at least one aspect: the idea that emotions both contain and rely on thoughts and judgments about the world. Those thoughts and judgments are not all emotions are—emotions also carry physiological and motivational aspects—but thoughts and judgments are a necessary part of emotion.

A contemporary affective psychologist would refer to this aspect of emotion as a "cognitive appraisal." A cognitive appraisal is a set of perceptions and evaluations, distinctive sets of which underlie any given emotion.[9] For example, as cogently articulated by the great psychologist Richard Lazarus, fear reflects perception of "an immediate, concrete, and overwhelming physical danger"; guilt attends self-evaluation of having "transgressed a moral imperative"; sadness indicates a belief that one has "experienced an irrevocable loss"; and so on for every emotion.[10] Thus, emotion embodies thought, often complex thought, and those thoughts can be evaluated just like any others. That is, using for a moment the example of guilt, we may judge both whether the event really occurred as the guilty person believes it did, and whether her actions actually transgressed a moral imperative.

As legal scholars have been quick to note, this fundamental notion—that emotions contain and rely on evaluative thoughts—is deeply Aristotelian. The most prominent advocate of this view within law has of course been Martha Nussbaum. Nussbaum, particularly in *Upheavals of Thought: The Intelligence of Emotions*,[11] has offered an interpretation of Aristotle that centers on the object-directed, thought-driven nature of emotion. Emotions are not, as legal theory long has held, "unthinking, opposed to reason in some very strong and primitive way," just "mindless surges of affect"; rather, emotions embody beliefs about states of the world.[12] A similar account has been explicitly adopted by other prominent legal theorists, most notably former Judge Richard A. Posner, who has defended emotion's role in law on that basis.[13]

Aristotle, to be sure, recognized that emotion is something distinctive; it cannot be collapsed into other forms of thinking and reasoning. But he did not denigrate it simply because it is emotion. Rather, for Aristotle emotion could be either virtuous

---

[9]Ortony et al. (1988) and Oatley and Johnson-laird (1987).

[10]Lazarus (1994), pp. 164–165, table 1.

[11]Nussbaum (2001); see also Kahan and Nussbaum (1996); Deigh (2008), pp. 12 and 142 (reflecting modern philosophical consensus that thought is "an essential element of an emotion").

[12]Nussbaum (1996), pp. 23–25. *See also* Nussbaum (2001).

[13]Posner (2010); Posner (2001), pp. 226–228.

or non-virtuous, depending on whether it reflects a correct way of viewing the world and one's place in it. As the philosophers Cheshire Calhoun and Robert C. Solomon therefore have asserted:

> Aristotle, in his *Rhetoric*, developed a strikingly modern theory of emotion that stands up to the most contemporary criticism.[14]

Legal scholars have come to rely on this cognitive view of emotion for a number of purposes. Rhetorically, it forces emotion's denigrators to find new justifications for its outlaw status, and highlights emotion's kinship with traditionally valued forms of legal reason. Normatively, it offers a tool with which to judge the propriety of any given emotion within legal judgment. For example, Nussbaum argues that the distinctive cognitive underpinnings of disgust render it an illegitimate basis for law, for disgust felt toward another human being both reflects and expresses a morally inappropriate dehumanization, as if that person were feces or a slug. Disgust at those objects, she argues, is appropriate; disgust with a human is not, at least as a basis for law, because it disturbs law's baseline assumption of equality among humans.[15] Dan Kahan, on the other hand, argues that the cognitive structure of disgust can reflect a morally proper judgment not of persons but rather of the evils we often impose on one another, and therefore could find a place in law.[16] Thus, as this debate reflects, recognizing an emotion's cognitive element does not answer difficult questions of its legal normativity. However, recognizing that element allows us to argue coherently and with specificity in terms that are highly accessible to law.

2.3 Emotion as a Judicial Virtue

The growing acceptance of an emotional element in law has been hard-won and has benefitted greatly from the contribution of Aristotelian thought. But perhaps nowhere has such progress been more difficult, or as challenging to traditional notions of law, than in the context of judging. And perhaps nowhere is Aristotelian thought as crucial.

---

[14]Calhoun and Solomon (1984a), p. 3. See also Solomon (1990), p. 253.

[15]Nussbaum (1999), pp. 20–21; Nussbaum (2004).

[16]Kahan (1999), p. 63.

2.3.1   The Persistent Cultural Script of Judicial Dispassion

Accepting a legitimate role for emotion in judicial behavior and decision-making is challenging because it runs so squarely into what I have called the "persistent cultural script of judicial dispassion."[17] Insistence on emotionless judging is a cultural script of unusual longevity and potency. Thomas Hobbes declared in the mid-1600s that the ideal judge is "divested of all fear, anger, hatred, love, and compassion."[18] Nearly 300 years later, the German jurist Karl Wurzel classified "dispassionateness of the judge" as a fundamental tenet of Western jurisprudence. Indeed, he wrote, lawyers were "the first and the most emphatic in insisting on the absence of emotional bias," because "absence of emotion is a prerequisite of all scientific thinking," and judges, more so than other scientific thinkers, regularly are "exposed ... to emotional influences."[19] Just a few years ago, the nomination of U.S. Supreme Court Justice Sonia Sotomayor turned into a firestorm over the mere suggestion that she might bring to the bench a capacity for empathy.[20]

This fact that hostility to judicial emotion enjoys a long pedigree does not make it correct, either as an account of what judges actually do or as an aspiration for what they ought to do. It is, for one thing, entirely unrealistic; judges are human and inevitably feel emotions in response to their work. While we tell them to "put those feelings aside," that is a very difficult thing for humans to do, and the effort to suppress emotion often does more harm than good.[21]

More radically, even were it realistic for judges always to put their emotions aside we would not actually want them to. Indeed, the great U.S. Supreme Court Justice William J. Brennan, Jr. launched the law and emotion movement with a strong declaration to that effect. Brennan wrote that in the modern era "the greatest threat to due process principles is formal reason severed from the insights of passion." Passion—which he defined as "the range of emotional and intuitive responses to a given set of facts or arguments, responses which often speed into our consciousness far ahead of the lumbering syllogisms of reason"—does not "taint the judicial process, but is in fact central to its vitality," preventing law from devolving into the agent of an "alien" and sterile bureaucracy.[22]

Brennan was correct in perceiving emotion's value even though he was vague on articulating the features of emotion that give it that value. Briefly stated, those features are the following: emotions reflect reason, enable reason, and are educable. That emotions reflect reason is a core finding of appraisal theory. Further, as contemporary psychology and neuroscience have convincingly demonstrated, without a normal capacity for emotion human beings become incapable of practical reason. Finally, emotions are educable because they can respond to reason: if we

---

[17]Maroney (2011b).

[18]Hobbes (1904), p. 203.

[19]Wurzel (1921), pp. 286–428.

[20]Maroney (2011b), p. 636.

[21]Maroney (2011a), p. 1490.

[22]Brennan (1988).

change the way we think about things, the emotions that attend those things change. Such change is often not easy, but neither is training in formal logic. The fact that humans find something hard does not mean it is beyond our capacity. It may instead signal need for a skill that can be trained and practiced.[23]

Contemporary understandings of emotion, then, compel the same conclusion as was promoted by many of the early-twentieth century American Legal Realists[24] and their contemporary, the Dutch scholar Paul Scholten[25]: judicial emotions are not only inevitable but valuable. That emotions are valuable does not, of course, mean they are invariably reliable guides; no one attempts to make that case. Nor could one make such a case while taking seriously the cognitive theory of emotions, as emotions can reflect inaccurate beliefs or bad values. Their value is variable. That variation is nicely captured through the lens of Aristotelian virtue.

2.3.2 Judicial Emotion Through the Lens of Aristotelian Virtue: The Case of Anger

To illustrate the utility of an Aristotelian virtue frame when evaluating judicial emotion I turn to the specific emotion of anger. As Aristotle wrote in the *Nicomachean Ethics*, emotion is virtuous if felt

> at the right times, with reference to the right objects, towards the right people, with the right motive, and in the right way. (*EN* 1106b20, trans. R. McKeon)[26]

The same is true of judicial anger. Anger is an important example not just because it so nicely illustrates the value of a virtue approach but also because it is so pervasive. Anger is a common, perhaps the most common, emotion that judges feel in the course of their work.[27] Judges regularly are confronted with highly angering stimuli: lawyers who lie, pander, or are incompetent; litigants and witnesses who defy or insult; evidence of the harm people do to one another; frustrating situations they are powerless to fix; intransigent colleagues; and so on. Indeed, courts frequently acknowledge that anger is a regular staple of the judicial diet, such that even highly trained and professional jurists will sometimes give voice to it, including in ways they might later regret. In the words of one court, trials "are not conducted under the cool and calm conditions of a quiet sanctuary or an ivory tower," and the pressures of the job "can cause even conscientious members of the bench ... to give vent to their frustrations by displaying anger and partisanship."[28]

---

[23]Maroney (2011a).

[24]Maroney (2011b), p. 652.

[25]For an exploration of Scholten's work and legacy, see http://www.paulscholten.eu/.

[26]Aristotle (1941), p. 958.

[27]Maroney (2012), p. 1226.

[28]United States v. Nazzaro, 472 F.2d 302 (2d Cir. 1973).

The relevant question therefore is not whether judges ought to get angry, but under what circumstances such anger is appropriate to experience and express.

2.3.2.1 Seneca and Aristotle on Anger

To get at this question it is instructive to examine an important contrast between Seneca and Aristotle.[29]

Though Seneca and Aristotle may be positioned as extreme opposites on the issue of anger, they in fact agreed on what anger is. They agreed that anger is an emotion that is directed at persons who culpably have inflicted harm on someone or something within one's zone of care, and that it predisposes one to pursue punishment or correction of the wrong. They agreed, further, that making such a complex evaluative judgment requires the exercise of reason.[30]

However, in his *De Ira*—the first known work devoted entirely to anger—Seneca argued that anger's dependence on reason did not redeem the emotion, for he believed it to be grounded in the wrong use of reason. First, Seneca advocated that the cognitive judgments underlying anger represent false valuations of the world and one's place in it. Affronts to one's pride, for example, should not arouse anger, because one should not be prideful.[31] Second, Seneca argued that the thinking underlying anger necessarily reflects illogic and weakness.[32] Third, he posited that anger depends on a free-will choice to yield to the feeling. Though the ability to make such a choice stems from humans' status as rational agents, the consequences of so choosing are irrational. Once yielded to, anger—which Seneca called "the most hideous and frenzied of all the emotions"[33]—vanquishes the reason on which its existence depends. Anger in this quintessentially Stoic view therefore is a mistake in all instances.

In contrast, in the Aristotelian view anger can be entirely good and proper. Aristotle held that one *should* value one's own safety, dignity, and autonomy, just as one should care about the safety, dignity, and autonomy of others. One should feel a strong impulse to respond to affronts to those goods, for only thus are those

---

[29]Maroney (2012), pp. 1219–1224.

[30]Averill (2012), p. 83 (quoting (AD 40-50/1963) Seneca (1928), *De Ira*, p. 115: "Wild beasts and all animals, except man, are not subject to anger; for while it is the foe of reason, it is nevertheless born only where reason dwells."). See also Anderson (1964), p. 153; Potegal and Novaco (2010).

[31]Gillette (2010), p. 7.

[32]Averill (2012), p. 85 (quoting Seneca, *De Ira*, p. 267: "No mind is truly great that bends before injury. The man who has offended you is either stronger or weaker than you: if he is weaker, spare him; if he is stronger, spare yourself.").

[33]Ibid., 83 (quoting Seneca, *De Ira*, p. 107).

goods appropriately valued and the world set right.[34] Anger is in this view "commingled with, if not equivalent to, justice itself."[35]

As Aristotle therefore wrote in the *Nicomachean Ethics*, anger may be felt both too much and too little, and in both cases not well (*EN* 1106b20). As Averill has asserted, by this Aristotle did not intend to define virtuous anger as "an algebraic mean between two set quantities," but rather as a response that is well-calibrated to the nature of the offense, the qualities of the offender, and the prospects for corrective action.[36] For example, to be enraged with a person who has violated one's mother is virtuous, as not to feel rage would signify an inadequate valuation of one's mother.[37] Thus, Aristotle wrote:

> they are thought to be fools who fail to become angry at those matters they ought. (*EN* 1126a4, trans. R. McKeon)

While the Stoic position against anger has rhetorical appeal, it is fatally flawed insofar as it in no way reflects lived human experience. Not even Seneca appears actually to have believed his hard line; his real target was violence and cruelty, not anger per se.[38] The Aristotelian account similarly condemns needless violence and cruelty but does not in the same stroke condemn all anger. That account instead invites us to dissect, educate, and shape this fundamental human experience through the power of our reason. The superiority of the Aristotelian account is further evidenced by the number of allies it claims, both ancient and contemporary.[39] For example, the early Christian theologian St. Thomas Aquinas defined anger much as Aristotle had—a judgment "by which punishment is inflicted on sin"—and maintained that, while it can be turned to bad ends, it is an indispensable aspect of justice.[40] That account is strongly embraced by virtually all contemporary

---

[34]Calhoun and Solomon (1984b).

[35]Potegal and Novaco (2010), p. 18. Plato, too, took the position that anger was "a natural, open response to a painful situation." *Ibid. See also* Averill (2012), p. 77 (explaining that, to Plato, anger became "allied with reason to protect the individual from wrongs perpetrated by others").

[36]Averill (2012), p. 97.

[37]Ibid. (all philosophers but Seneca agreed that one sometimes has "not only the right but the *obligation* to become angry"); Calhoun and Solomon (1984b) (quoting Aristotle, *Rhetoric* using the translation by Solomon) (anger is directed at persons who harm "those whom it would be a disgrace not to defend—parents, children, wives, subordinates").

[38]Seneca made his case against anger easier by focusing only on its most extreme manifestations, while Aristotle examined a much broader spectrum. Averill (2012), p. 85 (quoting *Seneca, De Ira*) ("[If] anger suffers any limitation to be imposed upon it, it must be called by some other name—it has ceased to be anger; for I understand this to be unbridled and ungovernable.").

[39]Though Plato and Aristotle held differing views of emotions generally, their views on anger's redeeming qualities are surprisingly harmonious. Plato asserted that anger can be allied either with the rational portion of the *psychē*, as when it helps protect the individual from wrongdoing, or with the irrational portion, as when loss of control leads to rash deeds. See Averill (2012), pp. 77–78; *see also* Smith (1880), p. 93 ("[T]he violation of justice is injury," and "is the proper object of resentment, and of punishment, which is the natural consequence of resentment.").

[40]Averill (2012), pp. 87–90. Lactantius distinguished between uncontrollable rage and just anger, writing that the latter "ought not be taken from man, nor can it be taken from God, because it is both useful and necessary for human affairs." Ibid., p. 87 (quoting Lactantius, *De Ira Dei*).

philosophers of emotion and underpins virtually all of modern affective science.[41] The Aristotelian view is the superior one with which to evaluate judicial anger.

2.3.2.2 Judicial Anger Through an Aristotelian Lens

When judicial anger meets the Aristotelian measure of virtue it may be characterized as *righteous*.[42] The opposite also holds true: when judicial anger is not righteous, it is a form of vice. To discern righteousness we first ask whether the anger is *justified*—in Aristotle's terms, whether it is felt:

> with reference to the right objects, towards the right people, with the right motive. (*EN* 1106b20, trans. McKeon)

The justification inquiry is logically precedential, as when anger is unjustified no experience or expression of it is proper. If the anger is justified, we ask whether its *manifestation* comports with the expectation that judges be fair and dignified—in Aristotle's terms, whether it is shown:

> at the right times, and in the right way. (*EN* 1106b20, trans. McKeon)

Some examples, grounded in research into actual cases,[43] are helpful to flesh out this account.

Judicial anger is justified if it rests on accurate premises; is relevant to the judicial task; and reflects worthy beliefs and values. The first criterion is the simplest. If a judge is angry at a lawyer for having lied to him, for example, it matters whether the statement actually was untrue, whether the lawyer believed it to be untrue, and whether the lawyer intended to mislead. The judge's assessment of the truth status of any of these questions might be literally wrong. This is precisely what happened in one case, in which a judge harshly penalized a lawyer for falsely representing that certain information had been ordered sealed by another judge; she turned out to be correct. An appeals court righted the wrong, but the lawyer already had been made to suffer the brunt of the mistaken judge's wrath.[44] Other examples include a judge who became enraged at a group of jurors for (he thought) defying orders to appear, and ordered them jailed and strip-searched; they in fact had obeyed mistaken instructions to wait in the wrong courtroom.[45] Judges, of course,

---

[41]Deigh (2008), pp. 12 and 142 (reflecting modern philosophical consensus that thought is "an essential element of an emotion"); Maroney (2011b), p. 644.

[42]For a fuller exploration of the concept of righteous judicial anger, see generally Maroney (2012).

[43]The research from which these examples and assertions are drawn, all of which are from the United States, is described in Maroney, "Angry Judges." That research does not pretend to be comprehensive—such an undertaking would be impossible, given the sheer number of cases heard in the U.S. legal system, most of which are unreported and unnoticed by anyone other than the parties. The examples are nonetheless instructive and reveal important patterns.

[44]*In re* McBryde, 117 F.3d 208, 213 (5th Cir. 1997).

[45]*In re* Sloop, 946 So. 2d 1046 (Fla. 2007).

make mistakes. The fact of a mistake does not necessarily impugn her qualifications or character, particularly if it is an honest one, but it does rob her anger of justification.

The more difficult cases are those requiring that we evaluate the anger's underlying premises not for their accuracy but for their propriety. In these instances, we ask not whether the judge is angry for no reason, but whether she is angry for no *good* reason.

The triggers for a judge's anger might, for example, be irrelevant—that is, not tethered to legally or morally salient features of the case before her. A judge might find cause for anger with a litigant when she is really mad at his lawyer. Even if the lawyer is the recognized target, the judge might find fault with some current, relatively blameless act because she is seething over some earlier misstep by that lawyer. Indeed, occasional statements by judges in unguarded moments suggest that such irrelevant anger, anger that lives on and finds outlet in ways disconnected from its original trigger, does have an impact on judicial behavior.[46]

Perhaps the most important inquiry, though, is whether the anger reflects the sort of beliefs and values that are proper for a judge in a democracy. A judge ought not, for example, be angry at persons for doing things they have a legal right or obligation to do. Consider cases in which trial judges express anger at lawyers and litigants for having successfully appealed their rulings. Appeal is a legal entitlement, and appellate success indicates adequate grounds, but a judge might nonetheless take umbrage at the suggestion that he was wrong and resent having been called out as wrong.[47] Similarly, judges sometimes became enraged at defense attorneys for making proceedings more difficult and protracted, even though in many of those instances that is the advocate's job. Indeed, in many cases not complicating the proceedings would be a dereliction of a defense lawyer's duties.[48] Anger in that instance shows that the judge has chosen to disrespect an obligation the law commands him to respect.

Judges sometimes also take great offense at people who talk back in a manner they perceive as challenges to their authority.[49] These anger triggers can also come bundled together. In a recent case that drew enormous publicity, a state-court trial judge angrily confronted a defense attorney who was asserting his client's right to a speedy trial. The attorney, though acting well within his legal rights, spoke to the judge in a rather obnoxious manner. The judge—in open court, with many people

[46]See e.g., "Former Judge Newton Reprimanded by Court," *Florida Bar News*, June 15, 2000, https://perma.cc/WBQ9-QGUR (reporting a judge made "threatening and abusive" comments to a lawyer who had filed a recusal motion, saying "judges can make or break attorneys" and "clients come and go, but you have to work with the same judges year in and year out. You better learn who your friends are.").

[47]Anderson v. Sheppard, 856 F.2d 741 (6th Cir. 1988); Tollett v. City of Kemah, 285 F.3d 357 (5th Cir. 2002).

[48]United States v. Nazzaro, 472 F.2d 302 (2d Cir. 1973); Harrison v. Anderson, 300 F. Supp. 2d 690 (S.D. Ind. 2004).

[49]Shaw v. State, 846 S.W.2d 482, 485–86 (Tx. Ct. App. 1993).

watching—expressed a wish to hit the lawyer with a rock; cursed him; and challenged him to a fight in the hallway, leading to a hallway confrontation during which blows may have been exchanged.[50] Such anger is unjustified, and therefore not righteous, because it signifies that the judge places too great a value on his personal pride, wrongly measures that pride by shows of servility, and places undue emphasis on always being correct. Similarly, the judge who ordered jurors jailed (as a result of which they were strip-searched) for allegedly defying orders to appear was not just operating on mistaken premises, but reacting in a shockingly extreme fashion to a perceived affront.

In contrast, a judge is perfectly justified in being angered at affronts to justice. Indeed, one might argue that Aristotle would see an obligation for the judge to be angry. Consider cases in which judges have caught government officials, including police officers, in lies on the witness stand.[51] Such lies can lead to wrongful prosecution and conviction in ways that are difficult to detect and correct. It would be unvirtuous not to be angered at such behavior, because it corrupts the judicial process itself and therefore is an affront to a public good that lies within the judge's obligation to protect.

Further, at criminal sentencing it often is appropriate for the judge to feel and express anger at the harm the defendant has done to the community. Expressing anger vividly demonstrates to victims and their survivors that they are within the judge's zone of care. It communicates, in a way that other demonstrations could not, that they are members of the valued community. It also demonstrates judicial respect for the defendant. As one feels anger only where a human agent has chosen to inflict an unwarranted harm, showing anger reveals the judge's assessment that the defendant is a fellow human possessed of moral agency. By using his or her authoritative position to send moral messages to the wrongdoer, the judge frees others in society from feeling a need to do so themselves, including through vigilante action. The judge who imposed a 150-year-long sentence on the disgraced financier Bernard Madoff, for example, has openly embraced a role for emotion in sentencing.[52] That judge functioned as the mouthpiece of our collective anger at Madoff for the extraordinary harms he caused. Such judicial anger is virtuous because justice relies upon it. As Solomon has written, one cannot

have a sense of justice without the capacity and willingness to be personally outraged.[53]

Finally, we come to manifestation. As Aristotle cautioned, anger ought not be manifested either too violently nor too weakly (*EN* 1105b24). Even justified anger

---

[50]Inquiry Concerning Judge John C. Murphy, Before The Hearing Panel Of The Judicial Qualifications Commission of the State Of Florida, S. Ct. Case No.: SC14-1582, File NO.: 14-255, May 19, 2015. "The Florida Supreme Court permanently removed this judge from the bench following this incident." Inquiry Concerning a Judge, No. 14-255, Re: Judge John C. Murphy, Florida Supreme Court, Dec. 17, 2015.

[51]Weiser (2008), p. B1.

[52]Weiser (2011), p. A1; Chin (2011), p. 1561.

[53]Solomon (1990), p. 42.

can be unvirtuous if expressed in a way that detracts from the dignity of the court, misdirects public attention from the parties and issues, or otherwise is demonstrably excessive. Returning to the example above of the judge, who threatened and physically fought with the defense attorney, entertain the notion that at least a portion of that anger was justified. In fact, the judicial conduct board that reviewed this incident concluded on the basis of good evidence that the defense attorney was acting consistently with his reputation of being incompetent, obnoxious, and unreliable; in contrast, the judge was well-respected and liked.[54] To the extent that the judge's anger was responding to a bona fide attempt by the defender to provoke him, it may have been at least partially justified. But no amount of justification could overcome the extremity of the response, which has resulted in very professional serious consequences for the judge. Similarly, in a civil case an appeals court was required to overturn a highly competent judge's imposition of extreme sanctions after losing patience with lawyers who were in fact acting badly.[55]

Even justified anger, then, must be well-regulated to be virtuous. Emotion regulation is the mechanism by which humans "fine-tune" our emotional responses to serve situational demands.[56] Regulating one's emotions is labor, and often very difficult labor at that.[57] But judges can and do learn to be strategic about how and when they show their anger, a skill they can improve with mindful effort.[58] Doing so encourages them to take the time necessary to examine the reasons behind their anger; determine whether it is justified; decide whether a public good is served by communicating it; and then choose to communicate it in a way that, to use an American expression, throws off more light than heat. This is something that great judges actually do, and something all good judges can learn to do. Indeed, in recent years this author has collaborated frequently with judicial groups in the United States to foster greater emotional-regulation skill throughout the judiciary.

2.4 Conclusion

Aristotle provided us with a theoretical framework within which to welcome judges' inevitable emotions. By testing those emotions for virtue, both in the reasons they reflect, the purposes for which they are expressed, and the manner in which they are expressed, we can separate the righteous from the non-righteous. This is as true of other emotions, such as sorrow and joy, as it is for anger.

---

[54]Inquiry regarding Judge John C. Murphy, Florida Judicial Qualifications Commission (2015).

[55]Sentis Group v. Shell Oil, 559 F.3d 888 (8th Cir. 2009).

[56]Maroney (2011a), p. 1504 and n. 117 (citing Vandekerckhove et al. 2008, p. 3).

[57]Maroney (2011a), p. 1494; Anleu and Mack (2005), p. 612.

[58]A humorous account of one judge's efforts in this regard may be found at O'Brien (2003), p. 251.

To be sure, a judge may both experience and express unjustified anger without being a bad judge; indeed, even excellent judges, being fallible humans, will do so. But one mark of true excellence is the ability to introspect about justification, recognize one's failings, and take corrective action—whether that be apologizing, otherwise making amends, or resolving to process similar situations differently in the future. One marker of a consistently bad judge, in contrast, is a pattern of unjustified anger, robustly expressed, with little or no introspection or change. Most judges will fall somewhere in the middle, meaning they have capacity to develop this particular virtue.

Cultivating this sort of virtue is not easy. Indeed, we should expect it to be hard.[59] As Aristotle wrote:

> [I]t is not an easy task to delineate how, at whom, at what, and for how long one should anger, nor at what point justifiable anger turns to unjustifiable. He who swerves a bit toward excess of anger is not to be blamed [, but] [h]ow far and how much one has to swerve before he becomes ... blameworthy is not easy to specify. (*EN* 1126b1, trans. McKeon)

Difficulty signifies challenge rather than certain defeat. The Aristotelean model provides theoretical tools with which to imagine righteous judicial anger–and, indeed, righteous judicial emotion more generally–and practical tools with which to achieve it.

References

Abrams, Kathryn, and Hila Keren. 2010. Who's Afraid of Law and the Emotions? *Minnesota Law Review* 94 (6): 1997.

Anderson, William S. 1964. *Anger in Juvenal and Seneca*. Berkeley: University of California Press.

Anleu, Sharyn Roach, Stina Bergman Blix, and Kathy Mack. 2015. Researching Emotion in Courts and the Judiciary: A Tale of Two Projects. *Emotion Review* 7 (2): 145–150.

Anleu, Sharyn Roach, and Kathy Mack. 2005. Magistrates' Everyday Work and Emotional Labour. *Journal of Law and Society* 32 (4): 590–614.

Aristotle. 1941. *The Basic Works of Aristotle*. Edited and translated by Richard McKeon. New York: Random House.

Averill, James R. 2012. *Anger and Aggression: An Essay on Emotion*. Berlin: Springer. (original print 1982).

Bandes, Susan A., ed. 1999. *The Passions of Law*. New York: New York University Press.

Bandes, Susan A., and Jeremy A. Blumenthal. 2012. Emotion and the Law. *Annual Review of Law and Social Science* 8 (1): 161–181. https://doi.org/10.1146/annurev-lawsocsci-102811-173825.

Brennan, William J., Jr. 1988. Reason, Passion, and the Progress of the Law. *Cardozo Law Review* 10: 3.

---

[59]Lerner and Tiedens (2006), pp. 115 and 132 ("[A]ngry decision-makers may then, as Aristotle suggested long ago, have a difficult time being angry at the right time, for the right purpose, and in the right way.").

Calhoun, Cheshire, and Robert C. Solomon. 1984a. Introduction. In *What Is an Emotion?: Classic Readings in Philosophical Psychology*, ed. Cheshire Calhoun and Robert C. Solomon. New York: Oxford University Press.

———. 1984b. What Is an Emotion? In *What Is an Emotion?: Classic Readings in Philosophical Psychology*, ed. Cheshire Calhoun and Robert C. Solomon, 44–52. New York: Oxford University Press.

Chin, Denny. 2011. Sentencing: A Role for Empathy. *University of Pennsylvania Law Review* 160: 1561.

Deigh, John. 2008. *Emotions, Values, and the Law*. Oxford and New York: Oxford University Press. http://public.eblib.com/choice/publicfullrecord.aspx?p=415269.

Gillette, Gertrude. 2010. *Four Faces of Anger: Seneca, Evagrius Ponticus, Cassian, and Augustine*. Lanham, MD: University Press of America.

Hobbes, Thomas. 1904. *Leviathan, or the Matter, Forme & Power of a Commonwealth, Ecclesiasticall and Civill*. Edited by A. R. Waller. Cambridge: Cambridge University Press.

Kahan, Dan M. 1999. The Progressive Appropriation of Disgust. In *The Passions of Law*, ed. Susan A. Bandes, 63. New York: New York University Press.

Kahan, Dan M., and Martha C. Nussbaum. 1996. Two Conceptions of Emotion in Criminal Law. *Columbia Law Review* 96: 269–374.

Lazarus, Richard S. 1994. Universal Antecedents of the Emotions. In *The Nature of Emotion: Fundamental Questions*, ed. Paul Ekman and Richard J. Davidson. New York: Oxford University Press.

Lerner, Jennifer S., and Larissa Z. Tiedens. 2006. Portrait of the Angry Decision-maker: How Appraisal Tendencies Shape Angers Influence on Cognition. *Journal of Behavioral Decision-making* 19 (2): 115.

Maroney, Terry A. 2006. Law and Emotion: A Proposed Taxonomy of an Emerging Field. *Law and Human Behavior* 30: 119–142.

———. 2011a. Emotional Regulation and Judicial Behavior. *California Law Review* 99 (6): 1485. https://doi.org/10.15779/Z38XQ3J.

———. 2011b. The Persistent Cultural Script of Judicial Dispassion. *California Law Review* 99 (2): 629. https://doi.org/10.15779/Z38K98M.

———. 2012. Angry Judges. *Vanderbilt Law Review* 65 (5): 1207.

———. 2015. A Field Evolves: Introduction to the Special Section on Law and Emotion. *Emotion Review* 8: 3–7. https://doi.org/10.1177/1754073915601356.

———. 2016. *Judicial Emotion as Vice or Virtue: Perspectives Both Ancient and New*. 2nd Edition. Amsterdam: Digital Paul Scholten Project. http://www.paulscholten.eu/research/article/judicial-emotion-as-vice-or-virtue-2/.

Nussbaum, Martha C. 1999. Secret Sewers of Vice: Disgust, Bodies, and the Law. In *The Passions of Law*, ed. Susan Bandes, 367. New York: New York University Press.

———. 2001. *Upheavals of Thought: The Intelligence of Emotions*. Cambridge and New York: Cambridge University Press.

———. 2004. *Hiding from Humanity Disgust, Shame, and the Law*. Princeton, NJ: Princeton University Press. http://search.ebscohost.com/login.aspx?direct=true&db=sih&jid=8W03&site=ehost-live.

———. 1996. Emotion in the Language of Judging. *St. John's Law Review* 70 (1): 4.

O'Brien, Gregory C., Jr. 2003. Confessions of an Angry Judge. *Judicature* 87: 251.

Oatley, Keith, and P.N. Johnson-laird. 1987. Towards a Cognitive Theory of Emotions. *Cognition and Emotion* 1 (1): 29–50. https://doi.org/10.1080/02699938708408362.

Ortony, Andrew, Gerald L. Clore, and Allan Collins. 1988. *The Cognitive Structure of Emotions*. Cambridge and New York: Cambridge University Press.

Posner, Richard A. 2001. *Frontiers of Legal Theory*. Cambridge, MA: Harvard University Press.

———. 2010. *How Judges Think*. Cambridge, MA: Harvard University Press.

Potegal, Michael, and Raymond W. Novaco. 2010. A Brief History of Anger. In *International Handbook of Anger*, 9–24. New York: Springer.

Schweppe, JennIfer, and John Stannard. 2013. What Is So 'Special' About Law and Emotions? *Northern Ireland Legal Quarterly* 64 (1): 1–9.

Seneca, L. Annaeus. 1928. *Moral Essays.* Translated by John William Basore. Cambridge, MA and London: Harvard University Press and Heinemann.

Smith, Adam. 1880. *The Theory of Moral Sentiments to Which Is Added, a Dissertation on the Origin of Languages.* Edited by Dugald Stewart. London: G. Bell & Sons. http://books.google.com/books?id=TfM9AQAAMAAJ.

Solomon, Robert C. 1990. *A Passion for Justice: Emotions and the Origins of the Social Contract.* Reading, MA: Addison-Wesley.

Vandekerckhove, Marie, Christian Von Scheve, Sven Ismer, Susanne Jung, and Stefanie Kronast. 2008. *Regulating Emotions: Culture, Social Necessity, and Biological Inheritance.* Hoboken, NJ: Wiley.

Weiser, Benjamin. 2008. Police in Gun Searches Face Disbelief in Court. *New York Times,* May 12, 2008, B1.

———. 2011. Judge Explains 150-Year Sentence for Madoff. *New York Times,* June 28, 2011, A1. Accessed November 14, 2015.

Wurzel, Karl Georg. 1921. Methods of Juridical Thinking. In *Science of Legal Method; Select Essays by Various Authors,* ed. Ernest Bruncken and Layton Bartol Register, translated by Ernest Bruncken. Modern Legal Philosophy Series, IX. New York: Macmillan. http://catalog.hathitrust.org/Record/001624693.

Cases

Anderson v. Sheppard, 856 F.2d 741 (6th Cir. 1988).

Harrison v. Anderson, 300 F. Supp. 2d 690 (S.D. Ind. 2004).

Inquiry Concerning Judge John C. Murphy, Before The Hearing Panel Of The Judicial Qualifications Commission of the State Of Florida, S. Ct. Case No.: SC14-1582, File NO.: 14-255, May 19, 2015.

Inquiry Concerning a Judge, No. 14-255, Re: Judge John C. Murphy, Florida Supreme Court, Dec. 17, 2015.

McBryde, 117 F.3d 208, 213 (5th Cir. 1997).

Sentis Group v. Shell Oil, 559 F.3d 888 (8th Cir. 2009).

Shaw v. State, 846 S.W.2d 482, 485–86 (Tx. Ct. App. 1993).

In re Sloop, 946 So. 2d 1046 (Fla. 2007).

Tollett v. City of Kemah, 285 F.3d 357 (5th Cir. 2002).

United States v. Nazzaro, 472 F.2d 302 (2d Cir. 1973).

Chapter 3
Dispassionate Judges Encountering Hotheaded Aristotelians

Christof Rapp

Abstract It has traditionally been assumed that a judge should pass judgement in a rather dispassionate state of mind. More recently, this traditional assumption has been challenged by authors who claim that emotions such as compassion, indignation or anger are not only indispensable, but can even play a beneficial and important role in judicial decision-making. Thus the old ideal of the impassionate judge is challenged by the new ideal of the rightly compassionate, rightly indignant or even rightly angry judge. Some supporters of this new ideal of an emotionally engaged judge invoke Aristotle for the idea that a judge should feel the right emotions in the right way. This paper argues that although there are passages in Aristotle that might be understood as implying such views, Aristotle's account of the right emotions of a virtuous person does not lend support to an ideal of passionate judges. On the contrary, the author points to contexts in which Aristotle seems to be rather concerned about the possibility of judges who pass their judgement in an emotional state. It is entirely justified to regard Aristotle as an ally in the promotion of the idea that emotions, rather than being blind, obstructive impulses, are intrinsically connected with our thoughts, judgements and wishes. The impact of these ideas, however, must be assessed against the background of Aristotle's account of character virtues.

This chapter has before been published in open access for the Digital Paul Scholten Project. Rapp, Christof. 2016. Dispassionate Judges Encountering Hotheaded Aristotelians. Amsterdam: Digital Paul Scholten Project. http://www.paulscholten.eu/research/article/dispassionate-judges-encountering-hotheaded-aristotelians-2/.

Ch. Rapp (✉)
Faculty of Philosophy, Ludwig-Maximilian University of Munich, Munich, Germany
e-mail: Ch.Rapp@lmu.de

© Springer International Publishing AG 2018
L. Huppes-Cluysenaer, N.M.M.S. Coelho (eds.), *Aristotle on Emotions in Law and Politics*, Law and Philosophy Library 121, DOI 10.1007/978-3-319-66703-4_3

27

3.1   An Amateurish Case for the Ideal of Dispassionate Judges

It might be in order to begin this paper with an admission of the author's completely pedestrian convictions on legal issues. In case I am ever brought before the court I ardently hope that the jurors or judges I meet there won't have negative feelings for me. At least I hope that, in case they do have such feelings, I won't be judged and sentenced on the basis of them. In fact, I even assume that I have a sort of right to have the decision-making of the jurors or judges not be driven by their personal feelings, as this could violate my right for an impartial treatment. Admittedly, there might be situations in which I hope for the jurors' and judges' *favorable* feelings and for their compassion or empathy, for example when I plead for mercy. These favorable feelings seem to add the proverbial 'human touch' to the allegedly 'sterile' legal system, so that I am more inclined to accept such favorable feelings in the law court than the negative ones. On reflection, however, I would not want to endorse a system in which jurors and judges are generally expected to form favorable judgements in accordance with their favorable feelings, since, after all, I would not like the opposing party benefiting from the jurors' or judges' feelings; nor would I like to see compassionate, favorable sentences for culprits who do not deserve them. All things considered then, I expect to be better off with dispassionate jurors and judges and am relieved to find myself in agreement with a longstanding tradition of legal theory.[1]

As a legal philistine I was thus nonplused to learn that this same longstanding tradition has recently come under pressure. It is being challenged by a trend that has already pervaded much of the humanities and the social sciences. This trend is centered on the idea that for a long time the emotions have been systematically neglected and underestimated, as they were mainly taken to be strong, mysterious, and irrational impulses that have nothing but distorting effects on our lives. However, more recent research in different fields converges in saying that emotions are intimately connected with our thoughts, are directed at objects and are apt to express our evaluative judgements. For this reason, or so the founding story of this movement goes, it is high time that we reconsider and reassess the role of emotions in all fields that have been oblivious to their emotional dimension. From the outside it seemed that law schools were like a calm resilience to this movement, but recent juridical publications with titles such as 'The Passions of Law', 'Emotion and the Law', 'Angry Judges', etc. clearly indicate that times have changed.[2]

---

[1]In the United States of America, I take it, the support of 'emphatic' or otherwise emotion-guided decision-making of judges is sometimes (misleadingly) associated with a certain political position; this became obvious during the Judiciary Committee hearings on the nomination of Sonia Sotomayor for the Supreme Court in July 2009. The political debate may have intensified the corresponding scholarly debate. The author of this paper does not connect his position with any political affiliation. 'Empathic politics', if one likes this expression or the corresponding denotatum, can be implemented by both detached and emotionally engaged decisions-makers.

[2]See Bandes (1999), Bandes and Blumenthal (2012), and Maroney (2012).

3.2   The Emotional Approach in Legal Studies

It is the juridical side-branch of the general *emotional turn* that this paper will be concerned with. In general, scholarship on the relation between law and emotion has a wide range of possible topics. It can deal, e.g., with the public emotions that are evoked by legal decisions or with the emotions of the litigants during a judicial hearing. Or it can deal with the emotions by which a culprit was motivated to commit a crime; often such emotions have to be acknowledged as mitigating factors. Also, the law and emotion scholarship can deal with the emotions of the victims; in some cases they are crucial for defining the type and severity of a crime. All this is certainly interesting and pertinent[3]; however, this paper will focus on the more specific question of whether it is acceptable for the emotions of jurors and judges[4] to play a role or not. Due to intuitions like the ones already mentioned in Sect. 3.1 above, one might tend to think that the forensic decision-makers should ideally pass their judgements in an entirely impassionate state of mind. However, it has recently been objected that judges will inevitably become emotionally engaged. Also, since emotions are directed at objects and are dependent on thoughts, they can be directed at appropriate or inappropriate objects and can derive from true or mistaken thoughts; accordingly emotions can be assessed as appropriate or inappropriate, so that the traditional ideal of the impassionate judge might be understood as recommending the exclusion of only inappropriate feelings. Finally, if emotions are like judgements or are intimately connected with judgements, certain emotions might even support the decision-making of the judge. If compassion, for example, is seen as a kind of awareness of mitigating factors, it might help the judge to take account of such pertinent factors in her sentence.[5] Or take anger: if it is always directed at persons who have voluntarily caused harm to someone else, one might think that it is often appropriate for judges to feel anger when dealing with criminals who actually have inflicted harm on innocent people. The idea might be, then, that it is not only acceptable for a judge to feel and express the due amount of anger, but that her anger, being directed at harms and acts of injustice, actually helps her arrive at a correct judgement.[6]

  This is, roughly, the set of ideas that is put forward by legal scholars in order to challenge the traditional ideal of the dispassionate judge.[7] My attention was excited by the idea that there are (among other things) philosophical reasons, most notably suggestions made by the Greek philosopher Aristotle, that urge us to think that the old ideal of the dispassionate, emotionally neutral judge must be overcome. And

---

[3]For a state-of-the-art article on this subject see Bandes and Blumenthal (2012).

[4]I include jurors to accommodate different legal systems. At any rate, my interest is in those participants of a trial that are supposed to make judgements and verdicts.

[5]See Nussbaum's plea for compassion in Nussbaum (2001), chap. 8, and in Nussbaum (2004), 20–22, 48–49, 52–56.

[6]This overview is inspired by ideas that Maroney put forward in this volume Maroney (2018).

[7]I use this formula of the "impassionate judge" with reference to Maroney (2011).

this is the claim that will be discussed in the course of this paper: Does it actually follow from Aristotle's account of emotions or from anything else that Aristotle says that an (appropriately) angry or otherwise emotional judge is better than a dispassionate one? This is, I take it, a crucial question, since leading supporters of the current attack on the old ideal of dispassionate judges present themselves as Neo-Aristotelians who are merely applying uncontested premises of Aristotelian philosophy to the contemporary legal debate. One could have the impression, then, that it is above all Aristotle's philosophy that lends support to the ideal of the 'emotional judge'. It will be argued that, although Aristotle is justly mentioned as a predecessor of the current rehabilitation of emotions in general, and although Aristotle's ethical theory actually distinguishes between appropriate and inappropriate emotions, the status of the judge or juror is not really comparable to the situation of a virtuous agent in Aristotle's moral philosophy. Admittedly, there is room for scholarly disagreement about the relation between reason and emotions in Aristotle's moral psychology. The idea, however, that Aristotle would favor an emotional judge over a sober, emotionally neutral and deliberate decision-maker would require an extreme and, to my mind, implausibly anti-intellectualist reading of some of his main tenets. It seems that, in spite of all current enthusiasm about Aristotle's account of emotions, Aristotle wants to assign a more restricted role to the emotions. At any rate, it is not an uncontested fact about the history of ancient philosophy that Aristotle would favor the idea of emotional judges. It rather takes— or this is my claim—hotheaded Aristotelians to find support for this kind of thesis.

3.3   Judges Getting Angry

Let us suppose that, contrary to a long standing tradition that has tended to denounce emotions, emotions are nor just mysterious, irrational, distorting impulses, but are crucially connected with our thoughts, beliefs, judgements or evaluations. Let us further suppose that it is in general good for human beings to have emotions and not to suppress or ignore them. Further, let us suppose that due to their relation to thoughts, beliefs, judgements or evaluations, the emotions we have might be either appropriate or inappropriate, and that there is nothing wrong with having emotions of the appropriate sort. Finally let us suppose or rather emphasize that jurors and judges are also human beings.[8] It seems to follow quite naturally, then, that there is nothing objectionable in the idea that jurors and judges, being themselves human beings, should feel the emotions that are connected with the judgements they pass. In particular, there is nothing objectionable about this idea, if we are speaking of emotions of the appropriate sort. A quite candid development of such views has been given by Terry Maroney in a series of papers. The present

---

[8]Need a reference? See Maroney (2012), p. 1210: "One of the most enduring lessons of the early-twentieth-century legal realists, though, is that judges are human first."

paper will take her claims as paradigmatic of Neo-Aristotelian approaches to the question of the emotions of a judge. In the present section I want to specify some of her claims.[9]

Maroney points out that judicial anger is ubiquitous and inevitable. The focus on anger is not meant to exclude other judicially salient emotions, but anger is the "quintessentially judicial emotion". Maroney sketches several different circumstances in which judges tend to get angry. They are not only angry at criminals and litigants, but also at lawyers, witnesses, colleagues, etc. If judicial emotion is inevitable, the traditional ideal of the dispassionate judge seems to be misguided. Indeed she calls this old ideal a "dangerous myth".[10] Quite generally, Maroney concludes from this inevitability that judges should not exert themselves trying to avoid or suppress their emotions, but should rather work on their emotion regulation, which includes the distinction between appropriate and inappropriate emotions as well as the correct way of dealing with the effects and articulations of one's anger. Indeed, her papers offer practical tools for the successful regulation of judicial anger. The new model she wants to suggest is the model of a *righteously angry judge* (RAJ), who is angry for good reasons and expresses her anger in an agreeable way. Righteously angry judges, she says, deserve our approval rather than our condemnation.[11]

That judges have many occasions in their professional lives to get angry with good reasons, and that they may therefore welcome any profound guidance for dealing with this anger, sounds very plausible. That judicial anger is a literally ubiquitous and inevitable phenomenon is a different claim; but this might be an empirical matter. From a philosophical point of view the decisive question is whether the emotionally made judgements are actually thought to be good or even better and whether the emotional judge is actually a better judge than the dispassionate one. And if this claim is actually made, the philosopher would be interested to know why this is so: What are the advantages of emotions in judicial judgements? How can emotions help the judge to form better judgements?

Maroney is actually quite cautious with regard to this latter sort of claim. The main interest of her RAJ model seems to lie in the careful exposition of factors that can make judicial anger inappropriate, irrelevant and thus objectionable. This seems convincing, since whoever wants to become a righteously angry judge, has to exclude these disqualifying aspects of her (judicial) anger. Also, this kind of rational assessment of instances of emotional reactions actually seems to derive from the Aristotelian take on emotions. But once again: Is it better to be an angry judge than a dispassionate one? It seems that Maroney would answer this question

---

[9]The following discussion is mainly based on Maroney (2012). Although the main purpose of my current paper is a critical discussion of some of her views (insofar as they make use of the alleged evidence from Aristotle), I hasten to acknowledge that my paper is also parasitic on her work, as it is the primary source for my knowledge of the pertinent legal debate.

[10]See Maroney (2012), p. 1213.

[11]See Ibid., p. 1215.

in the affirmative. For example, she repeatedly says, as already quoted, that the righteously angry judge deserves our approval. She also says that the judge *must not* deny or suppress her anger.[12] Indeed, there seems to be no reason to suppress anger, if "to act on anger is in large part to act on reasons"[13] and if emotions are "critical to substantive rationality".[14] The attempt to extinguish emotions would "needlessly consume cognitive resources."[15] Anger is indeed said to be "a legitimate basis for judicial action".[16] It seems, then, that Maroney would favor an angry judge (provided that she is angry for good reasons and in the right way). But why is it that such an emotional judge would be favorable?

Apart from the fact that emotions are human and inevitable and that it is therefore of little use to attempt to avoid or to extinguish them, Maroney mentions several benefits of the RAJ model. Since she sometimes takes the perspective of practicing judges, she also includes benefits *for the judges* themselves; e.g. that disclosure of one's anger makes it far easier to live with it.[17] This sounds plausible again, but is not the kind of advantage or benefit we are looking for, as we are looking for reasons of why judgements that are informed by emotion are supposed to be the superior ones. In another context Maroney mentions the thoroughly convincing point that judges can draw lessons from the previous experience of anger, for example by identifying recurrent triggers and by evaluating their relevance for their work.[18] This is not a personal benefit for the judge, like the previously mentioned one, but a benefit that aims at the improvement of a judge's professional performance. Analyzing the reasons for previously experienced anger a judge can improve her future judgements. I am fine with this. But is there also an advantage for a particular judgement, if it is conducted in a state of righteous anger? Here are some hints provided by the RAJ model that might help to answer this question:

(i.) Anger facilitates judgement.[19]

a. Anger facilitates judgement by narrowing and focusing attention.[20]
b. Given the wearying nature of the job, anger helps the judge to stay attentive.[21]

(ii.) Anger motivates responsive action.[22] /Anger facilitates actions necessary to carry out the desire to assign punishment.[23]

---

[12]Ibid., p. 1284.
[13]Ibid., p. 1223.
[14]Ibid., p. 1216.
[15]Ibid., p. 1279.
[16]Ibid., p. 1214.
[17]Ibid., p. 1277.
[18]Ibid., p. 1277.
[19]Ibid., pp. 1262 and 1272.
[20]Ibid., pp. 1262 and 1272.
[21]Ibid., p. 1264.
[22]Ibid., p. 1262.
[23]Ibid., p. 1209.

(iii.) Anger carries expressive benefits; it is a potent communicative device.[24] Its expression communicates with unusual clarity, conveying the underlying judgement and underlining its seriousness.[25]

(iv.) More generally, emotions signal that an event is of particular importance.[26]

This is meant to be a fair compilation of ideas I found in Maroney's texts. Do they help us to understand why the judicial judgement improves under the influence of anger?

3.4 Some Quick and Dirty Comments

Frankly, I cannot find a particularly strong reason among (i.) to (iv.) for thinking that the judgement that is formed under the influence of anger is the better one. To begin with, I cannot really see from Maroney's argument in what sense anger *facilitates* the judicial judgement (i.). In fact, the only support explicitly given for this claim is (i.a), i.e. that anger narrows and focuses our attention. Well, this is certainly right. If anger helps us to focus our attention on the pertinent points, this might be an advantage. But why do professional judges need this kind of support? Is it only through anger and other emotions that we can focus our attention? This would be weird. If the mathematics professor grades her students' papers she passes judgements on her students' work and must focus her attention on the particular calculations, but cannot rely on any particular emotion. Why, then, does the judge need this emotional support? One kind of support is explained in (i.b): the judges' job is wearying; anger helps them "to keep attention from sagging".[27] I am unsure what that means. That anger helps them not to fall asleep? Why can't they do with a cup of strong coffee? And isn't it particularly tiring to indulge in one's anger? Or is this meant to say that anger helps them not to become cynics? I take *this* point. That they still get angry indicates that they have not yet surrendered or that they are not mentally retired. However, this again would be a benefit for the judge's own person, not for the particular judgement.

Idea (ii.) draws on the generally accepted view that emotions are apt to motivate certain actions. As anger is connected with the wish to impose punishment or to get restitution, anger may well be said to motivate us to carry out the actions that are required for punishment. I am not sure, however, whether the point is that anger motivates the judge to pass a judgement or whether it is that anger motivates us to go beyond the mere judgement and to carry out actions that actually lead to the required punishment. In the latter case, the benefit would not concern the judgement itself, but only certain consequences that could follow from the judgement. Also I

---

[24]Ibid., p. 1263.

[25]Ibid., p. 1272.

[26]Ibid., p. 1216.

[27]Ibid., p. 1264.

wonder what other actions a judge has to take. Isn't it the judge's first and foremost task to arrive at a sentence? In both the former and the latter cases one could wonder why the judge is expected to need this additional boost. Take the example of a bus driver. As a bus driver, she is most probably motivated to perform the inherent goals of her profession, i.e. bus driving, well. Or take the math professor again. As a math professor she will certainly be motivated to perform the inherent goals of her profession, i.e. teaching math or carrying out research, well. If one of them occasionally happens to lack the required motivation for the inherent goals she may remind herself of, as it were, external incentives, e.g. the approval of her colleagues, the monthly payroll, etc. Why is it that of all various professions it is the judge who needs additional anger-based motivation for doing what she is supposed to do?

Idea (iii.) concerns communication and how a judge gets across her assessments and decisions. Again, I think the point is well taken. However, it is not about the quality of the judgement itself. Also, if a judge happens to be a skilled actor, feigned anger and indignation could do the same job (think of all the gifted TV judges, whose feigned anger has as much impact as the sincerely felt anger of hard working real life judges).

According to idea (iv.) emotions signal importance. Right. Still, this is not sufficient to justify the claim that the quality of a judgement might be improved by the impact of anger, as emotions in general only signal what is important *for us*, which would render an emotionally formed judgement as partial. It might be more important for a particular judge to sentence convicted rapists than convicted robbers, but this difference in personal preferences shouldn't lead to disproportionate attention or unequal treatment.

Reviewing these ideas I haven't come across a really good reason for thinking that a judicial judgement that is formed by righteously angry judges is somehow superior (although there were reasons for thinking (a) that judges who adhere to their anger are better off and (b) that there are beneficial concomitants of angrily formed judgements). Perhaps the chief point of the RAJ model is that, since emotions are inevitable, judges should accept that they find themselves in emotional states of mind, and so should not attempt to get rid of their emotions, but sincerely try to make the best of them. Still, one cannot help but thinking that there is a more ambitious project in the background—and that this has to do with the appearance of good old Aristotle.

3.5 How Aristotle Comes In

Aristotle is mostly invoked in support of the two following ideas: first, emotions can and, indeed, should be defined with reference to the objects they are directed at, and second, it is not bad to have emotions, though one should avoid having inappropriate emotions. Important early representatives of the philosophy of emotions actually drew on some of Aristotle's ideas.[28]

It is, above all, Martha C. Nussbaum who carries a considerable responsibility for the presence of Aristotle in parts of the current legal debate. Nussbaum has published widely and profoundly on ancient accounts of emotions; in particular, she often compared the Aristotelian and the Stoic account of emotions. In principle, she seems to appreciate both camps for their acknowledgement that emotions are deeply entangled with beliefs or judgements, but in the end she favors Aristotle's more permissive and welcoming attitude to emotions. In Nussbaum (2001)[29] she formulates an 'Aristotelian account' of emotions that derives from exegetically plausible claims about Aristotle, but also goes (partly intentionally) beyond Aristotle in one or another respect. As a successful author and publicly visible intellectual she contributed immensely to the dissemination of the ancient philosophers' contributions to more complex and more ambitioned accounts of emotions. As a professor of law she also managed to implement her 'Aristotelian account' of emotions into certain debates within legal studies. In various publications (e.g. Nussbaum 2001, 2004[30]) she makes a case for the presence of certain emotions in public life and in law, while denying a legitimate place for certain other emotions, like disgust, in the same realm.

If one understands Aristotle's account of emotions along the lines of Nussbaum's 'Aristotelian account', it is tempting to invoke Aristotle for defending the phenomenon of judicial anger and for motivating the RAJ model. When Maroney in the above mentioned papers tries to articulate criteria for good reasons for anger and for the correct manifestation of anger in our behavior she again and again refers to "Aristotle's counsel" that one ought to be angry "at the right times, with reference to the right objects, towards the right people, with the right motive, and in the right way."[31] She is aware that Aristotle's counsel was directed to human beings generally and not to judges specifically.[32] But, as judges are human beings too, she takes herself to be on the safe side when applying this counsel also to judges. According to Aristotle, she points out, a judge is not only justified to being angry at certain crimes or affronts, but a judge is in fact obligated to be angry.[33] She also points out that in the 'Aristotelian account,' appropriate or virtuous anger is equivalent with

---

[28]See e.g. Kenny (1963) and Lyons (1980).

[29]See Nussbaum (2001), chap. 8; Nussbaum (2004), 20–22, 48–49, 52–56.

[30]Maroney (2012).

[31]See Ibid., p. 1250.

[32]See Ibid., e.g. p. 1210.

[33]See in this volume Maroney (2018).

justice; she even dares to say that "in the Aristotelian view" anger *is* justice.[34] She recommends seeing judicial anger "through the lens" of Aristotle's theory of virtue, which seems to imply that the righteously angry judge judges in the virtuous way. And since virtuous judging is certainly preferable to vicious judging it seems to follow from Aristotle's account that it is preferable to form judicial judgements in states of (righteous) anger. In this general picture, driven by a somehow hotheaded version of Aristotelianism, it seems to be suggested that the deeper reasons for why righteously angry judgements are preferable to dispassionate ones (the kind of reasons we were unable to find during the discussion of Sect 3.4 above) are to be found in Aristotle's philosophy. We will examine this suspicion in the following sections.

3.6   Aristotle and Angry Judges: A Mismatch?

Before we start browsing Aristotelian philosophy for hints to the ideal of the angry judge, it might be useful to address some preliminary concerns.

To begin with, the formula that according to Aristotle the judge should feel anger for the right reasons and should deal with her anger in the right way (see Sect. 3.5 above), bears a significant ambiguity. Aristotle himself, to be sure, never applies the formula of having emotions in the right way etc. to judges in particular. In any case, leaving aside this minor mismatch, the formula applied to judges could either mean (a) that whoever acts as judge should feel anger at the case at hand and should feel it for the right reasons and in the right way, or it could mean (b) that *if* a judge happens to feel anger, it should be for the right reasons and in the right way. As we will see below in Sect. 3.7, Aristotle's account of virtues, from which this formula is taken, provides a rationale for the claim given in reading (b), while it is much more difficult to find an Aristotelian theorem that would correspond to claim (a). If, however, one wishes to ground a preference for angry judgements in Aristotelian virtue ethics, one would need to presuppose reading (a), not (b).

A related point is this. Maroney's account is based on the claim that judicial anger is ubiquitous and inevitable. Reading (a) in the previous paragraph would square well with this ubiquity claim, while the claim in reading (b) is much more limited. Frankly speaking, I find it hard to imagine that Aristotle thought of emotions as a ubiquitous phenomenon. For example, Aristotle says in the

---

[34]See Maroney (2012), e.g. pp. 1221 and 1284. The source of this idea remains obscure to me. She quotes Potegal and Novaco (2010) for the claim that "the idea of justified anger becomes commingled with, if not equivalent to, justice itself." The mentioned authors make such a claim in a section that is dedicated to "Aristotle and afterward", but they do not claim to quote or to interpret Aristotle by saying this. Rather they refer to a rhetorical trope that is used in "classical Athens". And not even the reference to this trope in question rests on an examination of ancient texts, but is taken from an author by the name of D. S. Allen.

Nicomachean Ethics[35] that young people usually follow their passions or emotions and are at this stage not able to follow reason (*EN* 1095a4–9). This sounds to me as if the emotion-driven stage of life is something that we should overcome rather sooner than later. Once we are grown up, we should be able to structure our lives in accordance with reason and should no longer follow emotional impulses. Here is another example: Aristotle describes emotions in *De Anima*[36] as episodes that involve extraordinary bodily changes (*DA* 403a5–6, 16–18, 31f). Anger is connected with the boiling of the blood in the region around the heart. Such bodily conditions, he says in Rhetoric,[37] are exhausting and thus have definite limits in time (*Rhet.* 1382a7). On this account, a job in which we are expected to produce episodes of anger on a regular basis would be extremely unhealthy. Aristotle once reports a case in which people who poured all their anger into the sentencing of culprit A on the one day, were too exhausted to be angry with culprit B on the next (*Rhet.* 1380b10–14). These are not decisive reasons, but together they suggest a picture in which the experience of anger and other strong emotions is rather limited to very specific situations.

Another preliminary worry. *Human beings should have emotions in the right way. Judges are human beings. Judges should have emotions in the right way.* This sounds like a safe conclusion. Nevertheless we never find anything like this in Aristotle. Why is this so? Well, when Aristotle speaks about the conditions under which a person is thought to be virtuous, his paradigm case is a moral agent who makes decisions concerning her own life and then acts on them (for example *EN* 1105a28–33). What is decisive is the good practical decision (*prohairesis*), which involves both practical reason and the virtues of the non-rational part of the soul (which, on Aristotle's account, is also responsible for the emotions). It is due to the latter part that the virtuous persons desire the right virtuous goals. The *prohairesis* is always directed at things that are possible for the agent to do and that lie in the future. If the *prohairesis* is good, it singles out the option that makes the best contribution to the agent's life as a whole. A judge, by contrast, does not make decisions that are expected to concern her own life or her own happiness directly. For the most part she has to deal with questions concerning other people and what they have done in the past. If she tries to convict someone of a crime, she mostly has to deal with factual questions of the past. Whereas in the decisions of moral agents the non-rational part of the soul determines the goals of the virtuous conduct, there are no practical goals that the judge as judge could realize. Therefore the judge does not make *prohaireseis*, practical decisions in the technical sense, and hence does not have to rely on the non-rational part of soul—at least not in the same way in which the paradigmatic moral agent does. Since the judge is not herself about to undertake certain actions (apart from the formation of the just judgement or sentence), the question of her motivation does not occur. In all these respects the

---

[35]*Nicomachean Ethics* (Ethica Nicomachea), edition used: Aristotle (1984b).

[36]*On the soul* (De Anima), edition used: Aristotle (1984c).

[37]*Rhetoric*, edition used: Aristoteles (2002).

situation of the judge is different from the moral agent who makes practical decisions and who is the subject of Aristotle's formula that one should have emotions in the right way.

Furthermore, Aristotle's reflections on the role of judges are deeply influenced by the Athenian legal system of his time, in which it was common not to have a single (professional) judge, but some hundred democratic jurors. This is the kind of judge that the litigants of Aristotle's time were facing. Thinking of an assembly of, say, five hundred jurors, Aristotle was not worrying about whether all of them were virtuous or not. For Aristotle, virtue is a difficult thing to achieve; examples of virtuous people are rather rare, they certainly do not show up in groups of five hundred. When Aristotle speaks in his *Rhetoric* about the judges or jurors that are to be addressed by a judicial speech, he takes it for granted that they are uneducated, easily distractible, and unable to follow complex arguments. He hence favors a legal system in which they have to decide as little as possible. That the majority of the democratic judges could or should be virtuous in the sense of his virtue theory would be an unrealistic idea for him.

The next worry concerns the "quintessential judicial emotion" of anger itself. Aristotle defines anger as a desire, accompanied by pain, for revenge (or what we take to be revenge) for an undeserved insult (or what we take to be an undeserved insult) that was directed against oneself or those near to one (*Rhet.* 1378a31–3). The Greek word that is translated by "insult" implies acts of contempt, spite or belittling; such acts manifest someone's opinion that the affected person is worthless. Sometimes an injustice or harm can be meant to belittle or humiliate the victim; but in general the pertinent kind of insult is not the same as injustice. Very often acts of belittlement have little to do with justice or injustice; for example, Aristotle takes forgetfulness about names as a type of insulting behavior (*Rhet.* 1379b34–7). Such behavior hurts because it aims at violating our self-esteem. Our anger reflects the fact that we think of ourselves as valuable persons who deserve to be treated with the due respect. This is also Aristotle's justification of anger: it is legitimate, as it is legitimate to have the appropriate amount of self-esteem; and if someone tends not to get angry when being insulted, this can indicate a lack of self-esteem (which may have other negative consequences, as Aristotle thinks). This is the Aristotelian notion of anger. When, by contrast, someone somewhere suffers a harm or injustice, that won't affect our self-esteem. This is why Aristotelian anger cannot be the quintessential judicial emotion that is required by the RAJ model. In a monograph that explores our emotional attitudes to justice, Robert Solomon writes:

> Aristotle tells us that anger takes as its occasion a sufficient offense to oneself or one's friend. I think that we can safely expand that to include any offense to a person or persons with whom we can empathize.[38]

Maroney[39] refers to this remark approvingly. Of course, one can expand or replace Aristotle's quite narrow notion of anger. The only problem is that this

---

[38] Solomon (1990), p. 253.

[39] See Maroney (2012), p. 1219, footnote 64.

expansion or replacement results in a notion of anger that is no longer Aristotle's notion and that, hence, cannot be justified by reference to Aristotle or by the strategy that Aristotle adopts. Aristotelian anger is not concerned with all sorts of injustice. In general, it seems to me that Aristotelian *indignation* would be the better candidate for accounting for the judges' emotional experience, as indignation is more generally directed at wrongdoing and injustice of all kind. Still, Aristotle's notion of indignation would also be too narrow, as it is only stirred by the well-being of wrongdoers.[40]

Accordingly, the connection between anger and justice that the RAJ model presupposes cannot be mapped onto the Aristotelian theory. If we look more closely into Aristotle's account of character virtues it is remarkable that only a few virtues are defined by reference to emotions (e.g. courage, mildness), whereas other virtues are determined without any reference to particular (named) emotions (*EN* 1107a27 ff.). Justice is not among the virtues that are defined by emotions. The fifth book of Aristotle's *Nicomachean Ethics* is entirely dedicated to justice, but makes no attempt to identify the specific emotions connected with this virtue. Anger does not play a role at all.

3.7 Aristotelian Emotions and Virtue Theory

It is quite common to appeal to Aristotle for the idea that it is by no means wrong or bad to have emotions, but that it might even be good or required to have them, provided that they are the right or the appropriate emotions. This is often tentatively contrasted with the view of the Stoics who take *apatheia*, the absence of affections or emotions as an ideal and hence tend to think that it is always bad to have (these particular) emotions. All these elements are also crucial for the model of the righteously angry judge. The main impact of the Aristotelian account hence seems to be the distinction between appropriate and inappropriate emotions, and this distinction leads us into the ambit of Aristotle's theory of virtue, for it is the virtuous person who is expected to have the right emotions.

For Aristotle, a character virtue is a relatively stable trait or disposition of the non-rational part of the human soul. In order to acquire them, it is helpful if people live in well-ordered cities with good laws (for example *EN* 1196b31–32); it is also crucial that parents, teachers or parental friends make them do the right things, because it is through doing the right things and getting accustomed to it that people become virtuous.

Long term dispositions of our character can be good or bad. Virtues are the good or right type of character traits; once we have them, they help us getting things right, i.e. to do the right things and to have the right emotions. Both right actions and right

---

[40]This is why I would also resist the temptation to turn Aristotelian indignation into a general "sense of injustice", as Nussbaum (2001), does at p. 312.

emotions flow from the same attitude or disposition the character virtues consist in. A disposition that brings about bad actions and inappropriate emotions could never be called a 'virtue'. It is crucial, then, for the virtue theorist to focus on the good sort of character disposition.[41] How are *good* or *right* character dispositions to be distinguished and defined? Well, these are the dispositions by which we do the right actions and have the right feelings. But how should 'right actions' and 'right feelings' be defined? Well, they are the ones that are not failures—and wherever there is a continuous scale, Aristotle says, failure can come in two forms, either as deficiency or as excess. Hence the range that defines the right actions and feelings must be somehow in between, i.e. between actions and feelings that fail in the direction of deficiency and actions and feelings that fail in the direction of excess. This is why Aristotle calls virtue of character a mean (*mesotês*). It is a disposition for getting things right, which is equivalent to saying that it is a disposition for hitting the mean between the failure of the deficient and the failure of the excessive kind. Essentially the same idea can be expressed in the following way. Getting things right, i.e. doing the right things and having the right emotions, is a quite demanding undertaking: we can fail to get things right, when we do something in the wrong place (taking care of one's personal hygiene: in principle, right/doing it in the classroom, wrong) or at the wrong time (personal hygiene again: in principle, right/during office hours, wrong) or with the wrong persons (sexual reproduction: in principle, right/with the neighbor's spouse, wrong) or with the wrong instruments (playing cops and robbers: in principle, okay/using real guns, not okay) or in the wrong way (helping an old lady cross the street: in principle right/doing it violently, wrong), etc. If we want to do an action right having the right emotions, we must succeed with respect to each of these parameters. Doing something at a time when we should not is a failure of the excessive kind; not doing it when we should, is a failure of the deficient kind. Doing something with a person with whom we should not, is a failure of the excessive kind, not doing it with a person with whom we should, is a failure of the deficient kind, etc. All this is summed up by Aristotle with respect to emotions in the following famous formulation:

> For instance, both fear and confidence and appetite and anger and pity and in general pleasure and pain may be felt both too much and too little, and in both cases not well; but to feel them at the right times, with reference to the right objects, towards the right people, with the right aim, and in the right way, is what is both intermediate and best, and this is characteristic of excellence. (*EN* 1106b18–23, trans. W. D. Ross/revised by J. O. Urmson)[42]

Once again, this quotation shows that the famous 'doctrine of the mean' is not different from the requirement that we should have the emotions at the right time, with reference to the right objects, etc., but that these latter requirements are just a

---

[41]The following account of Aristotelian virtues is based on Rapp (2006).

[42]Incidentally, all these parameters together define the appropriateness of an emotional response. Maroney uses this formula in order to distinguish between factors that make an episode of anger legitimate and other factors that only concern the right manifestations of that emotion.

way of spelling out what it means for an emotion to be right or appropriate, and that the virtue is a mean or hits the mean precisely in that it brings about these right or appropriate emotions (and the corresponding actions).

In the contemporary movement of virtue ethics it became a commonplace that the virtuous person does the right things with the right motivation and that this idea derives from Aristotle. We are now in a position to rephrase this commonplace by saying that for Aristotle a virtuous person does the right actions with the right motivation because it is due to her virtuous disposition that she does the right actions. And it is the same firm virtuous disposition that brings about the right emotional responses. This is not to say that the virtuous person is always motivated by emotions; it only says that if we do the right action and have the right emotional attitude towards this same course of action, this derives from the same virtuous attitude or disposition. If a person does the right thing, while having adversary desires or while feeling reluctant to do this right thing, this is an indication that the person has not or not yet acquired the kind of disposition that is definitive of a character virtue.

Let us now briefly address some possible ramifications of the sketched account:

- Does the virtuous person always have *moderate* emotions? No. This is a later theory (called '*metriopatheia*'), probably deriving from a misinterpretation of Aristotle's doctrine that the virtue is a mean. What Aristotle says and requires is that the virtuous person has the *right* or *appropriate* emotions.
- Are all actions accompanied or even motivated by emotions? No, sometimes (perhaps, often) the required appropriate emotion in a given situation might be a zero-emotion, i.e. it might be appropriate not to have any emotion (Correspondingly, there might be situations in which it is appropriate to have maximally strong emotions). Not even virtuous actions are always motivated by emotions. The requirement is that the virtuous person acts for non-contingent reasons and that she does not have competing desires, i.e. desires that would conflict with the aim of the virtuous action.
- Is it, according to Aristotle, in general good or beneficial for an agent to decide and to act in accordance with the appropriate emotions? Of course, this is better than deciding and acting in accordance with inappropriate emotions. However, Aristotle's point seems to be a weaker one: *if* we undergo episodes of emotions or *if* we find ourselves in situations that usually trigger our emotions, we should have the appropriate, not the inappropriate ones.
- Does Aristotle's theory aim at the regulation of emotions? In one sense *yes*, in another sense *no*. On the one hand the virtuous person has appropriate or, if you like, perfectly 'regulated' emotions. On the other hand, if we associate 'emotion regulation' with the curing of symptoms, this notion would not match the core issue of Aristotle's account, for the appropriate emotions are rather thought to be an effect of the good and virtuous state of this particular part of the soul. Aristotle does not aim to offer tips for how to deal with inappropriate emotions.
- Here is another, related point. A virtuous person is likely to have the appropriate emotions in different kinds of situation. She can rely on her emotional responses

without 'controlling' or 'regulating' them, as her emotions flow from a firm character disposition. By contrast, a non-virtuous person can never rely on having the right emotions. For her, having the right emotions is, of course, still better than having the wrong ones. However, since she cannot rely on having the appropriate emotional responses, she cannot just follow her emotions, but has to rationally check or control her impulses. In sum, Aristotle is not interested in good or bad emotions as such, but only in the good emotions that indicate and flow from a good character.

How does all this relate to the RAJ model? Aristotle's interest in appropriate emotions cannot be separated from his interest in character virtues. Without this framework the "Aristotelian counsel" that one should have emotions for the right reasons and in the right ways makes little sense. From the point of view of Aristotle's virtue ethics, it is by no means required that everything we do or judge, must be accompanied or driven by emotions; it is only required that the virtuous person must not fail with respect to her emotional reactions. Also, occasionally having the right emotions does not make someone virtuous; it is the other way around, that being virtuous makes someone reliably have the appropriate emotions. If one has to regulate or to alter one's emotional reactions in a particular situation (as the judge in the RAJ model does) this would be a clear indication that one has not yet acquired the corresponding virtues.[43] Further, not virtue-based, but occasionally appropriate emotions are not a real relief of burden; they provide no reliable, reason-independent guidance for the judge, as one would have to make sure from case to case (by rational—emotionless—examination, I suppose), that one's emotions are actually appropriate. Requiring, on the other hand, that all judges become virtuous persons in the Aristotelian sense would be an over-demanding and unrealistic move. This would also include a holistic approach, according to which one could not be a good judge without being a fully virtuous person in one's private life. This is a consequence, I suppose, that would not even be welcomed by the Neo-Aristotelians among law theorists.

3.8   Aristotle and the Alleged Rationality of Emotions

As we have seen in the earlier sections of this paper, the RAJ model rests on the assumption that became part of the predominant contemporary view that emotions are not just opposed to reason, but are themselves 'cognitive' or 'rational'. According to an influential interpretation of Aristotle this is a view that Aristotle would share.[44] In his *Rhetoric* he acknowledges that persuasion is not always and exclusively a matter of providing conclusive arguments, but can also be a matter of

---

[43]In fact, what Maroney describes as the regulation of judicial emotions is far more reminiscent of the techniques suggested by post-Aristotelian thinkers, like the Stoics and the Epicureans.

[44]See the references to Martha C. Nussbaum's work above.

the emotional state that the audience happens to be in. Hence, he decides to consider how one can modify the emotional state of an audience, since this may make a considerable difference in how people judge and how they respond to an argument. In the second book of the *Rhetoric* Aristotle therefore introduces about fourteen different types of emotions. He introduces each emotion by giving a general definition and then goes on to explicate for what reason, with which kind of people and in which state of mind we feel emotions of this type. The aspiring orator who uses Aristotle's book is obviously expected to use this material in the following way. If he wants to bring his audience into a state of fear or anxiety (for example, if he wants an assembly to spend more money on military buildup), he has to convince the audience of the existence of real threats or dangers, e.g. that there are well-armed enemies and that they are about to attack them. Also he has to point out that they are in a state in which they have reasons to be anxious, e.g. in the state of being unprotected and vulnerable, etc. In sum, orators try to alter the people's thoughts and beliefs in such a way that they will be prone to a particular kind of emotion. Aristotle does not tell us very much about the philosophical background theory he adopts; nor does he claim that emotions always include beliefs or full-blown judgements. However, it is clear that he presupposes something like a strong covariance between our thoughts or beliefs on the one side and our emotions on the other.

All this makes Aristotle a natural ally in the attempt to overcome the picture that emotions are just irrational and destructive impulses. If emotions are thought to be responsive to certain thoughts, beliefs or judgements and if the latter are thought to be cognitive efforts or, generally speaking, efforts that require our capacity for reasoning, one might think that emotions themselves have to be regarded as 'cognitive' or, in a sense, 'rational'. This is how philosophers came to speak of 'cognitive' theories or accounts of emotions. And indeed, it seems much more challenging and worthwhile to explore emotions if we think of them as 'cognitively rich' phenomena that are intimately connected with our thoughts and convictions. Since Aristotle was the first to systematically demonstrate how different emotions are connected with different thoughts he might well be seen as the originator of the family of 'cognitive' accounts of emotions and as the initiator of this more challenging research program for the exploration of emotions. Adopting such a cognitive theory of emotions one might indeed think that it is somehow misleading to see a sharp contrast between emotions and reason. And this is indeed what approaches like the RAJ model need and what they can find in Aristotle.

All this is correct as far as it goes. However, from an Aristotelian point of view it is in a sense ambiguous to say that emotions are 'cognitive' or 'rational' and to say that they are no longer opposed to reason. We came to label such accounts of emotions as 'cognitive' because they rely on the idea that emotions are somehow dependent on certain cognitive or intellectual efforts. This does not mean, however, that the emotions themselves become rational in the sense that it is rational to have such an emotion. For example, an episode of fear in a dark cellar might derive from the (irrational) thought or belief that this cellar is inhabited by undead souls; but the connection of this emotion with a thought does not render it rational. Or an episode of anger can derive from the judgement that we have not been treated with the due respect. Again, the judgement, albeit an intellectual effort does not render the emotion rational, as it might simply be wrong to think that we actually deserve this kind of respectful treatment. One might distinguish hence between 'cognitive' and 'rational'. An emotion might be called 'cognitive' as it comes about through certain cognitive or intellectual efforts and has an impact on other cognitive achievements, but this does not yet imply that such an emotion is 'rational'.[45]

Also, the parlance of the 'cognitive' character of emotions is sometimes misleading in another sense, for emotions are often connected with evaluative but not discerning or recognizing judgements. Evaluative judgements may also involve a considerable intellectual effort: evaluations might be simple or complex; often it takes the consideration of multiple aspects to reach at a decent evaluation. However, in evaluative judgements we do not claim to know what a piece of reality is objectively like; we rather state our attitude towards or our appraisal of this piece of reality. So even if emotions are seen as 'cognitive' or as 'judgements', this does not yet imply that they tell us what the world is like, but rather tell us how we and other people see and assess the world.

Aristotle would endorse this caveat, since after all, he assigns in *Politics*[46] emotions to the non-rational part of the soul (*Pol.* 1254b8). In my understanding this does not preclude the possibility of collaboration, as it were, between the non-rational and the rational part of the soul. Aristotle often emphasizes that there is a non-rational part of the soul that is able to 'listen' to what the rational part of the soul says, so that the non-rational part of the soul must in a sense be responsive to reason and to the reasons that the rational part of the soul provides. Furthermore, Aristotle often refers to the phenomenon that emotions can impair our judgements and bring about irrational effects (for example *Rhet.* 1354a24–26, b10–11). For example, emotions do not follow the same principles of mutual exclusion as judgements do; we cannot be angry with one person, Aristotle says, (*Rhet.* 1387b14–15, 1380a31–33) and feel pity with another person at the same time, although it would be possible at the same time to hold the opinion that the one person has insulted us and the opinion that another person deserves our pity. For Aristotle, emotions are intrinsically connected with extraordinary bodily alterations. The resulting bodily conditions may continue even after the occasion or reason for a particular episode of emotion is gone; in other cases our body may not be in the condition to undergo the physiological alterations that are typically connected with a type of emotion. Also, we can form judgements and initiate episodes of thinking whenever we fancy, but we cannot decide here and now to have a certain emotion; for example, we can form the judgement that a certain challenge is not too difficult to handle, but whether or not we feel the corresponding

---

[45] Martha C. Nussbaum made the same important distinction, but preferred to speak of 'rational in a normative' (what we called 'rational') and 'rational in a descriptive sense' (what we called 'cognitive'). See Nussbaum (1996), p. 320, footnote 4.

[46] *Politics*, edition used: Aristotle (1984a).

emotion of confidence depends on our character traits, i.e. on whether we became accustomed in the long run to handling situations of this type, on whether our experience with such challenges were pleasant or unpleasant, etc. There are many reasons, then, for thinking our rational judgements and our emotions may differ, even though emotions are in principle covariant with our thoughts and judgements.

These latter, deflationary remarks are not meant as a direct argument against the RAJ model (as this model does not claim that *all* occurrences of anger are equally rational); but they are meant to explain why Aristotle might have been less enthusiastic than certain Neo-Aristotelians about the alleged 'rationality' of emotions and, in general, about the idea of transferring genuine tasks of reason and reasonable judgements to the emotions. If, on this account, our emotional reactions are rational it is because they have been trained to be in line "with what reason says". Well-trained emotions motivate us to do the things that rational deliberation takes to be good, they can push us in the right direction when there is no time for deliberation; but reason remains the ultimate authority. To present the RAJ model in its strongest form, one would have to claim that there are elements in the judicial judgement (in the judgement itself and not only in its concomitants) that either can *only* be handled by the emotion of anger or can *better* be handled by anger than by reason. In its strongest form it would require anger to be a sort of "feeling for injustice" that is able to detect injustice even in regions where rational examination would remain insensitive. Some of the appeals to Aristotle (see Sect. 3.5 above) seem to attribute such views to him, but that would certainly ask too much of Aristotle's account of emotions.

3.9   Angry Judges in Aristotle's *Rhetoric*

The discussion of the previous sections suggested that there are certain mismatches between Aristotle and the RAJ model. However, this might be due to the kind of evidence that we have considered so far. Perhaps Aristotle's *Rhetoric* is a better source for RAJ-related themes, as it includes plenty of material on the emotions. A special section of the *Rhetoric* is dedicated to the judicial speech, which is meant to address judges or jurors. We have good reasons to expect, then, that the *Rhetoric* will include pertinent material.

The first chapter of this book, however, starts with a great disappointment for the supporter of the RAJ model. For Aristotle claims here straightforwardly that

> ... one must not warp the judge by leading him to anger, envy or pity; for that would be similar to someone who is about to use a straightedge, but crooks it beforehand. (*Rhet.* 1354a24–26, trans. G. A. Kennedy)[47]

---

[47]Translation used: Aristotle (1991). For my translation in German: Aristoteles (2002). For a general overview Rapp (2010).

The crooked straightedge or rule is a strong image. It means that the judge is supposed to be like the straightedge for justice and injustice. By arousing emotions like anger (!), envy or pity in the judge, however, one deprives the judge of just this function, i.e. of her status as authority in discerning and measuring justice and injustice. This implies in turn that it is in virtue of one's emotionally unimpaired reasoning capacity that the judges perform their function well. It seems, then, that Aristotle's statement amounts to a view that is straightly opposed to the RAJ model. True, Aristotle obviously is thinking of non-pertinent emotions and not of the righteously felt anger of RAJ; still he makes a general claim and does not provide an exception for righteously felt emotions (which could be used as an *argumentum e silentio*: Had he been interested in acknowledging the possibility of righteously emotional judges, this would have been the right place to mention it).

Some commentators tend to downplay this passage and treat it as something like a unique outburst on Aristotle's part.[48] I don't think that this is a tenable move, as this passage squares very well with some other tenets that seem to be important for him. For example, he several times alludes to the question of whether it is better to be ruled by laws or by a personal ruler. A point that he makes in favor of the 'rule of law', is that laws, as opposed to human beings, have no passionate part of the soul (*Pol.* 1286b17–18). In a similar vein he says that the rule of law is like a divine and or well-reasoned governance, while someone who wants particular human beings to rule, also accepts that a brutish element gains influence, as *thumos*—meaning rage, temper, anger—seduces even the best human beings (*Pol.* 1287a28–32). When it comes to laws, justice and judicial judgements, Aristotle wants to be on the safe side and, hence, tries to diminish the risk of emotionally colored decisions.

This is not quite encouraging for the friends of RAJ. Here is a possible move they could make to get Aristotle on their side. Although Aristotle in *Rhetoric* I.1 criticizes other rhetoricians for focusing on the arousal of passions or emotions in their audience, he later acknowledges that the arousal of emotions can be a useful means of persuasion. At first glance this does not seem to be reconcilable with the idea that emotions corrupt the judges' judgements and with the criticism of previous rhetoricians. This tension provides material for an almost endless scholarly debate, and it seems that more than one solution is feasible. For example, it has been suggested that the orator only deals with the emotion of the audience in order to calm down already existing excitements. Or it is has been argued that emotions in the rhetorical context are innocuous whenever they are aroused in the right way, e.g. by referring the audience to actually outrageous characteristics of the case at hand. The defender of the RAJ model would have to argue that Aristotle recommends that the aspiring orator only arouse *righteous* emotions in the *right* way, so as to improve the judgements of the jury. This is not a completely implausible suspicion. However, it is not very likely that this is Aristotle's main concern. Here are a few hints to the effect that the *Rhetoric* does not really care about the righteousness of emotions.

---

[48] See for example Barnes (1995), p. 263.

In the *Rhetoric* Aristotle never mentions the difference between righteously felt and corrupting emotions; he deals with emotions like anger and fear that can be appropriate and inappropriate, but he equally equips the orator with material for arousing envy, which Aristotle thinks can never be good. He says that the art of rhetoric is merely concerned with what is persuasive and he gives hints to the effect that emotions are to be included, since the persuasion of a public audience does not only depend on arguments, but also on the emotional state the audience happens to be in. He seems to be proud that his technique allows bringing

> those who through anger or enmity are on the other side of the case over to whatever feeling he chooses. (Rhet. 1382a18–19, trans. G. A. Kennedy)

Hence, the general purpose of the rhetorical arousal of emotions is probably not to arouse the *appropriate* emotions of a *virtuous* person—after all, Aristotle is, as already indicated (see Sect. 3.6 above) not very optimistic about the moral excellence of a public mass audience. Aristotle just noticed that certain emotions make it more likely that an audience will accept a certain position, thesis or sentence: If one happens to be in a favorable mood, then he or she will be more inclined to come to a favorable judgement or to assent to a favorable proposal, whereas if one is in a hostile mood, then one will rather assent to an unfavorable proposal or sentence, etc. Aristotle's comments on the purpose of the rhetorical arousal of emotions actually do not go much deeper than that. When the Aristotelian rhetorician arouses the emotions in the audience, he will do so in order to make it more likely that the audience will accept the conclusion he suggests. End of story. By contrast, one will look in vain in the *Rhetoric* for hints to the effect that the angry juror will make better judgements.

3.10   Conclusion

Don't get me wrong. This paper is not meant to censure an incorrect or pretentious use of an elevated historic philosopher. If scholars make use of ancient philosophers in order to come up with interesting new ideas or even with innovative research programs, these new ideas, theories or research programs should be assessed as independent projects and not as exegetical contributions.

What I am interested in is rather the phenomenon that from time to time certain readings of ancient philosophers—often readings that were originally shaped by certain modern debates and interests—get somehow canonized as 'standard readings' and then exert a considerable influence on ongoing debates. For a certain period of time it becomes even difficult to voice concerns about these standard readings or to differentiate them—although the ancient texts might not be as straightforward as the new 'standard reading' suggests. The canonized idea that underlies the Neo-Aristotelian approach to law theory consists roughly in the thought that since Aristotle assigned all these wonderful attributes to emotions he can be used as a patron for all sorts of emotion-friendly accounts. Before the emotional turn had reached the classics and philosophy departments Aristotle was not seen like this. When e.g. Robert C. Salomon, one of the great initiators of the new philosophy of emotions, in 1977[49] started to dispel what he called the myth of "reason versus the passions", he still mentioned Aristotle as one of the bad guys, i.e. as an originator of the objectionable myth that reason and passion are opposed. And there is some truth in his intuition. But as long as people are under the spell of the new and fashionable standard reading they tend to ignore all aspects that could threaten the current standard view.

There is something else that is somehow trivial to note, but still strikes me as pertinent. If Neo-Aristotelians say things like "this is, after all, what Aristotle said" or "this is Aristotle's counsel", they use Aristotle as an authority. Of course they don't do it the naïve and indiscriminate way in which e.g. some medieval Aristotelians made use of him. They rather refer to selected aspects of his philosophy and to smart contemporary ('standard') readings. Still, saying that *Aristotle said it* is *per se* never a good argument (especially if he did not even say it). Often such references have the purpose to cover gaps in one's own argument. And revealing such gaps is always a worthwhile rational endeavor.

References

Aristoteles. 2002. *Rhetorik.* Translated by Christof Rapp. Berlin: Akademie Verlag.

Aristotle. 1984a. Politics. In *The Complete Works of Aristotle: The Revised Oxford Translation,* ed. Jonathan Barnes and trans. B. Jowett. Princeton, NJ: Princeton University Press.

———. 1984b. Nicomachean Ethics. In *The Complete Works of Aristotle: The Revised Oxford Translation,* ed. Jonathan Barnes and trans. W. D. Ross and J. O. Urmson. Princeton, NJ: Princeton University Press.

———. 1984c. On the Soul. In *The Complete Works of Aristotle: The Revised Oxford Translation,* ed. Jonathan Barnes and trans. J. A. Smith. Princeton, NJ: Princeton University Press.

———. 1991. *On Rhetoric: A Theory of Civic Discourse.* Translated by George A. Kennedy. New York: Oxford University Press.

Bandes, Susan A., ed. 1999. *The Passions of Law.* New York: New York University Press.

Bandes, Susan A., and Jeremy A. Blumenthal. 2012. Emotion and the Law. *Annual Review of Law and Social Science* 8 (1): 161–81. https://doi.org/10.1146/annurev-lawsocsci-102811-173825.

Barnes, Jonathan, ed. 1995. *Cambridge Companion to Aristotle.* Cambridge: Cambridge University Press.

Kenny, Anthony. 1963. *Action, Emotion and Will.* London: Routledge & Kegan Paul.

Lyons, William. 1980. *Emotion.* Cambridge and New York: Cambridge University Press.

Maroney, Terry A. 2011. The Persistent Cultural Script of Judicial Dispassion. *California Law Review* 99 (2): 629–81. https://doi.org/10.15779/Z38K98M.

———. 2012. Angry Judges. *Vanderbilt Law Review* 65 (5): 1207–86.

———. 2018. Judicial Emotion as Vice or Virtue: Perspectives Both Ancient and New. In *Aristotle on Emotions in Law and Politics,* ed. Liesbeth Huppes-Cluysenaer and Nuno M.M.S. Coelho. Dordrecht: Springer.

---

[49]Solomon (1990).

Nussbaum, Martha Craven. 1996. Aristotle on Emotions and Rational Persuasion. In *Essays on Aristotle's Rhetoric*, ed. Amelie Rorty, 303–23. Berkley: University of California Press.

———. 2001. *Upheavals of Thought: The Intelligence of Emotions*. Cambridge and New York: Cambridge University Press.

———. 2004. *Hiding from Humanity Disgust, Shame, and the Law*. Princeton, NJ: Princeton University Press.

Potegal, Michael, and Raymond W. Novaco. 2010. A Brief History of Anger. In *International Handbook of Anger*, 9–24. New York: Springer.

Rapp, Christof. 2006. What Use Is Aristotle's Doctrine of the Mean. In *The Virtuous Life in Greek Ethics*, ed. Burkhard Reis, 99–126. Cambridge: Cambridge University Press.

———. 2010. *Aristotle's Rhetoric*. Edited by Edward N. Zalta. Spring 2010 Edition. The Stanford Encyclopedia of Philosophy. http://plato.stanford.edu/archives/spr2010/entries/aristotle-rhetoric/.

Solomon, Robert C. 1990. *A Passion for Justice: Emotions and the Origins of the Social Contract*. Reading, MA: Addison-Wesley.

Part II
Cognition

Chapter 4
Emotion and Rationality in Aristotle's Model: From Anthropology to Politics

Giovanni Bombelli

Abstract This contribution clarifies and further elaborates the complex nature of the relationship between emotion and reason in Aristotle's philosophy. A lexical-conceptual analysis of key-concepts in *De Anima* (sensation, affection, fear/pity, appetite/desire and impulse) highlights Aristotle's view on the role of emotions in cognitive processes. Aristotle's assumption of continuity between mind and body (ontological continuity) and his view on the cognitive relevance of emotion (teleonomy) are foundational for his complex model of reason merging biological and cognitive processes (circular anthropology). The interaction between evaluative levels and emotive factors in cognitive processes as conceived by Aristotle is fundamentally different from the modernist Cartesian perspective, but is surprisingly modern when compared with particular contemporary perspectives.

4.1 Introduction

Within the modern-contemporary debate *emotion* has frequently been understood as connected to a primitive instinct and has consequently been opposed to *reason*.[1] Aristotle has a different outlook. His philosophy represents a pre-Cartesian and organicist anthropological model.[2] This is based on an *ontological principle of continuity* (=OPC), in which the realms of nature *are connected to each other:* they

---

[1]Sidgwick (1966), p. 482. More recently Campos et al. (1989), p. 395: emotions "are *processes of establishing, maintaining, or disrupting the relations between the person and the internal or external environment*" (emphases in the text). Furthermore Keltner and Gross (1999), pp. 468–470: the authors define "emotions as episodic, relatively short-term, biologically based patterns of perception, experience, physiology, action and communication that occur in response to specific physical and social challenges and opportunities.[...][F]unctions are a certain sort of consequence of goal-directed action.[...]Functional accounts most generally assume that emotions are adaptations to the problems of social and physical survival" (the authors emphasize the implications of a functional account of emotion).

[2]Frede (1992b), pp. 93–94: "[T]he conception of the soul which Descartes adopts in place of an Aristotelian notion itself historically is a descendant of a conception Aristotle rejects; and

G. Bombelli (✉)
Faculty of Law, Catholic University of Milan, Milan, Italy
e-mail: giovanni.bombelli@unicatt.it

© Springer International Publishing AG 2018
L. Huppes-Cluysenaer, N.M.M.S. Coelho (eds.), *Aristotle on Emotions in Law and Politics*, Law and Philosophy Library 121, DOI 10.1007/978-3-319-66703-4_4

are distinct but not separated because there is a *continuum*, i.e. an *analogy*, underlying vegetable, animal and human life.[3] This analogical model of reality *determines* how people can know reality according to Aristotle: *his ontology determines his epistemology.* Accordingly reason and instinct are not opposite but intertwined. In Aristotle's view emotion is *cognitively relevant* and implies different forms of knowledge.

We will focus on three points.

Firstly we will draw a short survey of the circular anthropological model elaborated in *De Anima* (On the Soul).[4] This work offers both the general horizon underlying the Aristotelian perspective and some crucial notions closely related to the concept of emotion. Secondly we will give an analysis of some key concepts to analyze some aspects of emotion. This analysis shows the crucial role of what we would *currently* call emotion. It is a sort of *fil-rouge* within Aristotle's philosophy and shows a theoretical continuity from ontology to the anthropological level up to the legal-political sphere. Finally we will sketch the feasibility of Aristotle's theory in view of a post-Cartesian model of human identity by understanding it as a new inclusive psychology between biology and philosophy.

4.2 A Circular Anthropology

De Anima provides the conceptual framework of Aristotle's anthropology.[5] A *circular*, neither pyramidal nor linear, anthropological scheme emerges from the typologies of the soul (*psuche*) described in *De Anima* (*DA* 414b 20–415a 12). Due to the presence of their similar forms of soul (nutritive, sensitive and appetitive) human beings are placed *in continuity* with other living beings and both are assumed to be provided with a sentient capacity ascribable to their soul, which implies in some way their capacity to understand.[6] Their development (i.e. their

---

Descartes' notion shares with the conception Aristotle rejects precisely the feature Aristotle is objecting to. The conception Aristotle rejects is a Platonist conception."

[3]Lloyd (1996), pp. 138–139: "Aristotle's concept of analogy plays several distinctive and important roles in his metaphysics and his zoology especially.[...]The two principal uses of analogy he makes are[...]the metaphysical and the zoological."

[4]Edition used: *The Complete Works of Aristotle: The Revised Oxford Translation*, edited by Jonathan Barnes.

[5]Oksenberg Rorty (1992a), p. 7: "The scope of *De Anima* is much broader than that of either contemporary philosophy of mind or contemporary philosophical psychology. It is a metaphysical inquiry[...], a philosophical psychology[...], an investigation of the teleologically organized functions that are common to living bodies." (and the footnote 1: "Because it carries many post-Cartesian connotations, "mind" is not a felicitous translation of Aristotle's *nous*").

[6]MacIntyre (1999), p. 8: "[There are human] resemblances to and commonality with members of some other intelligent animal species." (see also the chapter 3 entitled *The Intelligence of Dolphins*).

growth process) pursues a certain goal and tends to satisfy a purpose/goal (*telos*), which is seen as the *form* or the *peculiar organization* of each living entity.

In this circular anthropological view the biological level is intrinsically *meaningful* and cannot be reduced to a dynamics of automatic self-preservation. It is important to understand the crucial concept of soul as something quite different from a static unity. The soul is to be conceived as a *dynamic and inner force.*

In the opening lines of De Anima Aristotle states:

the soul is in some sense the principle (*arche*) of animal life. (*DA* 402a 7, trans. Smith)

And proceeds then with the fundamental notion of affections (*pathe*). Some affections are specifically human, while

others are considered to attach to the animal owing to the presence of a soul. (*DA* 402a 9, trans. Smith)

This involves the definition of soul:

whether soul is divisible or is without parts and whether it is everywhere homogeneous or not. (*DA* 402b 1–2, trans. Smith)

The important point here for us is that affections have always a *structural connection with the body*, being aimed at a purpose. To the question whether all affections are affections of the complex body-soul, Aristotle remarks that

thinking (*to noein*) seems the most probable exception; but if this too proves to be a form of imagination (*phantasia*) or to be impossible without imagination, it too requires a body (*soma*) as a condition of its existence.[. . .]It seems that all affections of soul involve a body [. . .], in all [. . .]there is a concurrent affection of the body.[7] (*DA* 403a 8–19, trans. Smith, Greek words added by GB)

The distinction between ensouled (*empsuchon*) entities and realities without soul (*apsuchon*) is introduced by Aristotle (*DA* 403b 26) in the context of movement (*kinesis*) and especially sensation (*aisthesis*), with a reference to the pre-Socratic debate about the interwovenness of movement[8] and knowledge. This enables him to point out a *close correspondence* between the human soul and the natural/material elements.

On one hand he identifies the soul with the concept of thought or mind of his days.[9] He explicitly refers to Democritus:

---

[7]A point related to the enmattered accounts (*logoi enuloi*) (*DA* 403a 25): as regards this topic I completely agree with the analysis proposed by Stefano Fuselli in this volume: Fuselli (2018); See also Everson (1997), pp. 96–102 and 236 about the relation between soul and living body (especially DA 424a 17–25 with the idea of ratio) with a criticism of the Cartesian perspective.

[8]Witt (1992), pp. 171–78: "[S]ouls do not undergo the same kind of motion that material substances (or organism) do[. . .].[G]iven [Aristotle's] *analysis of motion*[. . .]it makes no sense to say that the soul moves" (emphases in the text; pp. 181–182 for the nexus perception/motion).

[9]Wilkes (1992), pp. 116–22: "[*psyke*]is theoretically superior to the mind [because] it provides a better framework within which contemporary study should proceed.[. . .]Aristotle paid absolutely no attention to consciousness *per se*"; Hardie (1976), p. 405 (in a non-Cartesian perspective): "[Aristotle] affirms in his own idioms, and never doubts, that animal behavior is accompanied by

soul (*psuche*) and thought (*nous*) are[...]one and the same thing, and[...]must be one of the primary and indivisible bodies. (*DA* 405a 9–10, trans. Smith, Greek words added by GB)

Other authors (i.e. Thales, Critias) confirm the role played by three elements within the soul: movement, sensation and incorporeality (*asomaton*) (*DA* 405b 11). With his criticism of theories based on a simple union of soul and body (*DA* 406a 1 and ff.) Aristotle underlines that

each body seems to have a form (*eidos*) and a shape (*morphe*) of its own. (*DA* 407b 24, trans. Smith, Greek words added by GB)

On the other hand Aristotle criticizes the theories of soul as a harmony. The soul cannot be conceived according to him as a composition of parts (*sunthesis ton meron*) or, symmetrically, as a ratio of mixture (*logos tes mixeos*). If this would be the case there would be many souls distributed throughout the whole body: in fact

every one of the bodily parts is a mixture of the elements, and the ratio of mixture is in each case a harmony, i.e. a soul[10] (*DA* 408a 17-19, trans. Smith)

This discussion highlights a decisive point: the soul encompasses the *totality-unity* of the human being. Aristotle develops this idea in various ways.
Firstly it is:

doubtless better to avoid saying that the soul pities or learns or thinks, and rather to say that it is the man who does this with his soul. (*DA* 408b 14–15, trans. Smith)

Accordingly

[t]hinking, loving, and hating are affections not of thought, but of that which has thought, so far as it has it. (*DA* 408b 25–26, trans. Smith)

Furthermore he criticizes Xenocrates, and the elementarist theories, because they are unable to explain

the affections and actions of the soul[...]. [...][I]t is not easy even to make a guess on that basis. (*DA* 409b 15–18, trans. Smith)

In addition Aristotle says about the comparison plants and animals that

it appears that plants live, and yet are not endowed with locomotion or perception, while a large number of animals are without discourse of reason. (*DA* 410b 23–24, trans. Smith)

Apart from the complexity of the Aristotelian concept of life,[11] there is the question of the unity underlying the soul and its possible extension to other living beings according to OPC:

---

consciousness and that human conduct and human planning is prompted and guided by consciousness."

[10]Witt (1992), pp. 178–179: "In rejecting the *harmonia* theory, Aristotle is rejecting the idea that the soul could be defined as being a composition of the four elements or a ratio of their mixture".

[11]Matthews (1992), p. 187 who highlights seven acceptations: thinking, perception, local movement and rest, movement (with respect to nutrition and decay and growth or self-nutrition), touch, appetite (or desire and passion and wishing), reproduction.

It seems that the principle (*arche*) found in plants is also a kind of soul (*psuche*); for this is the only principle which is common to both animals and plants; and this exists in isolation from the principle of sensation, though there is nothing which has the latter without the former.[12] (*DA* 411b 27–30, trans. Smith, Greek words added by GB)

The basic doctrine of act and potency (*DA* 412b 9–10), according to which everything, which actually exists is to be understood as the development of a potentiality or possibility, represents the condition of the unity-inseparability-continuity between the soul and the body:

the soul may not be the actuality (*entelecheia*) of its body in the same way as the sailor is the actuality of the ship.[13] (*DA* 413a 8–9, trans. Smith, Greek words added by GB)

Once again there is here neither a real separation between soul and body nor a functional relation[14] as in the modern-Cartesian perspective, which also entails a separation between soul (mind) and body.[15] Aristotle's model cannot be understood

---

[12]I agree with the analysis developed by Lloyd (1992), p. 143; furthermore Lloyd (1996), pp. 67–103 for the idea of fuzzy natures in Aristotle's theory.

[13]Tracy (1982), p. 112: "The sentence at 413a 8-9 marks the end of Aristotle's sketch of the soul as "first act", substantial form or entelechy of the body – its "static" aspect- and introduces the subsequent discussion[. . .]of the soul's dynamic function as efficient cause of all "second acts," the organic reactions involved in nutrition, sensation, appetition, local motion, and even intellectual cognition." The relation pilot-boatman-soul is also discussed in Descartes (2006), pt. V.

[14]"[W]hat has soul in it differs from what has not in that the former displays life. Now this word has more than one sense, and provided any one alone of these is found in a thing we say that thing is living – viz. thinking or perception or local movement and rest, or movement in the sense of nutrition, decay and growth. Hence we think of plants also as living, for they are observed to possess in themselves an originative power through which they increase or decrease in all spatial directions; they do not grow up but not down – they grow alike in both, indeed in all, directions; and that holds for everything which is constantly nourished and continues to live, so long as it can absorb nutriment. This power of self-nutrition can be separated from the other powers mentioned, but not they from it – in mortal beings at least. The fact is obvious in plants; for it is the only psychic power they possess. This is the originative power the possession of which leads us to speak of things as *livings* at all, but it is the possession of sensation that leads us for the first time to speak of living things as *animals*" (*DA* 413 a 21-413b 3, emphases in the text, trans. Smith).

[15]Damasio (1994), pp. xii–xiii and 70 who criticizes the Cartesian separation: "[C]ertain aspects of the process of emotion and feelings are indispensable for rationality[. . .]Both "high-level" and "low-level" brain regions[. . .]cooperate in the making of reason. The lower levels in the neural edifice of reason are the same ones that regulate the processing of emotions and feelings[. . .].[. . .][T]here appears to be a collection of systems in the human brain consistently dedicated to the goal-oriented thinking process we call reasoning, and to the response selection we call decision-making, with a special emphasis on the personal and social domain. This same collection of systems is also involved in emotion and feeling, and is partly dedicated to processing body signals"; DeSousa (1997), pp. XV and 333: "Despite a common prejudice, reason and emotion are not natural antagonists. On the contrary [w]hen the calculi of reason have become sufficiently sophisticated, they would be powerless in their own terms, except for the contribution of emotion.[. . .]The ideal of emotional rationality is *adequate emotional response*." (emphases in the text; see also chapter 7).

in a functionalistic manner, as for instance the computational scheme of input-output of the Turing machine in mental functionalism.[16]

Aristotle faces a different set of issues. In a teleological-hylomorphic view the mind is not isolated and the bodily reactions, as well as thoughts and ideas, are not the simple probabilistic output of a mental state. The OPC entails a fluid scheme: the soul circularly represents the completion and articulation of the *specific* goal *within* the body.[17] This can be further elaborated through the concepts of matter and faculty.

Aristotle offers a twofold notion of matter (*hule*): the organic, i.e. *essentially* ensouled, and the material elements which are only *accidentally* ensouled. Accordingly the soul's parts can be conceptually divided but *not separated* (*DA* 413b 29):

> it is plain that soul is an actuality or account (*logos*) of something that possesses a potentiality (*dunamis*) of being such.[18] (*DA* 414a 27–29, trans. Smith, Greek words added by GB)

---

[16]Putnam (1975), pp. 362–385; Fodor (1978), pp. 201–202 in a more problematic manner: "[S]ome of the most systematic[. . .]kinds of mental events may be among those about whose etiology cognitive psychologists can have nothing at all to say.[. . .][T]he mere fact that creative mental processes are *mental* processes does not ensure that they have explanation in the language of psychology under *any* of their description." (emphases in the text); Crane (2003), p. 231: "[O]ur investigations into the mechanical mind have[. . .]yielded one broad and negative conclusion: there seems to be a limit to the ways in which we can give *reductive* explanations of the distinctive features of the mind" (emphasis in the text).

[17]Code and Moravcsik (1992), pp. 129–138 on teleology and non-teleology underlying Aristotle's framework; Everson (1997), pp. VII–VIII, 5 and ff. about the incompatibility functionalism-teleology in order to understand Aristotle "in his own terms" and some references to Descartes and to the contemporary debate; Burnyeat (1992), p. 16: "[The Putnam-Nussbaum functionalist thesis] fails to notice that Aristotle's conception of the material or physical side of the soul-body relation is one which no modern functionalist could share[. . .]."; Nussbaum and Putnam (1992), pp. 55–56: "[W]e can have non-reductionism and the explanatory priority of the intentional without losing that sense of the natural and organic unity of the intentional with its constitutive matter that is one of the great contributions of Aristotelian realism."; Cohen (1992), p. 72: "The apparent success of the functionalist seems to me to depend on whether the apparent role of *psyke* as efficient cause can be satisfactorily explained away. I am not convinced that it can be."; Kafetsios and LaRock (2005), pp. 639–40, 642–43, 647–50, and 654: "[Different from functionalism]Aristotle [includes] as part of his analysis of the essence of cognition and emotion the *biological* material and the characteristic operations associated with it[. . .].[Aristotle's theory of cognition and emotion is based][. . .]on the integration of form and matter (hylomorphism) and the hierarchical organization of the biological world.[. . .][For Aristotle] the soul is organized-organizer of biologically based organisms.[. . .][T]he material type plays *an essential role* in defining the nature of a substance and its peculiar activities." (emphases in the text). In this volume I partially disagree with Brito's position within which teleonomy and functionalism are substantially put on the same level and assimilated, Brito (2018). See also hereinafter the last paragraph.

[18]Whiting (1992), pp. 88–89: "Aristotle does not distinguish potentiality as capacity from potentiality as matter[. . .].[T]he sort of potentiality Aristotle associates with *energeia* proper can exist simultaneously with its own actualization."

The basic faculty of even plants is the nutritive faculty (*to threptikon*), while the perceptual faculty characterizes other living beings. The presence of the appetition/desire (*orexis*) implies the desire (*epithumia*) and its multiple articulations:

all animals have one sense at least[...]and whatever has a sense has the capacity for pleasure and pain and therefore has pleasant and painful objects present to it, and wherever these are present, there is desire (*epithumia*), for desire is appetition (*orexis*) of what is pleasant. (*DA* 414b 3–6, trans. Smith, Greek words added by GB)

Hence:

[i]t is now evident that a single definition (*eie logos*) can be given of soul only in the same sense as one can be given of figure. (*DA* 414b 19–21, trans. Smith, Greek words added by GB)

This means that Aristotle develops a *formal model* of soul. In his attempt to formulate a common definition of soul the OPC underlying Aristotle's model emerges:

It is true that a common definition (*logos*) can be given for a figure which will fit all figures without expressing the peculiar nature of any figure. So here in the case of soul and its specific forms[...][W]e must ask in the case of each order of living things, what is its soul, i.e. what is the soul of plant, man, beast.[19] (*DA* 414b 26–33, trans. Smith, Greek words added by GB).

Among the faculties the nutritive soul plays a central role. It is

found along with all the others and is the most primitive and widely distributed power of the soul, being indeed that one in virtue of which all are said to have life (*to zen*). (*DA* 415a 24–26, trans. Smith, Greek words added GB)

The soul aims at reproduction. This should not be understood as a mere functional dynamic but as *a complex organization* which constitutes the universal goal of all living beings.

The concepts of purpose/goal (*telos*) and good (*agathos*) should be interpreted in terms of the already mentioned *continuum* as remarked in *Ethica Nicomachea* (Nicomachean Ethics)[20]:

If [..] there is some end of the things we do[and]desire for its own sake [...], and if we do not choose everything for the sake of something else [...] clearly this must be the good and the chief good.[21] (*EN* 1094a 18–22, trans. Ross and Urmson)

This means that the soul is conceived as a cause (*aitia*) in the self-increasing, autopoietic and spontaneous but not mechanistic process underlying all living beings:

---

[19]Everson (1997), pp. 3–4: according to Everson Aristotle does not define the concept of soul (*psuche*) because it is based on a capacity for activity.

[20]Edition used: *The Complete Works of Aristotle: The Revised Oxford Translation*, edited by Jonathan Barnes.

[21]Furthermore: "the function of man is an activity of soul in accordance with, or not without, rational principle." (EN 1098a 7–8, trans. Ross and Urmson).

It is manifest that the soul is also the final cause [because] is the cause of nutrition and growth. (*DA* 415b 15; *DA* 416a 10, trans. Smith)

Furthermore:

[T]he psychic power [...] may be described as that which tends to maintain whatever has this power in it of continuing such as it was [...] [T]he first soul ought to be named the reproductive soul.[22] (*DA* 416b 18–26, trans. Smith)

4.3 Analysis of Some Key-Concepts

Through a lexical-conceptual analysis we will consider some key-concepts: sensation (*aisthesis*), emotion (*pathos*), fear (*phobos*) and pity (*eleos*), appetition/desire (*orexis*) and impulse (*thumos*). This approach makes it possible to elaborate some fundamental notions of the *continuum* knowledge-rhetoric-drama-politics which play a key-role in the debate about the relation between emotion and rationality.[23] The goal is to highlight the *cognitive* role, which emotion plays in Aristotle's anthropology *as the articulation of a biological structure*.

Aristotle develops a specific model of the material (or natural, biological) dimension of nature. Unlike the Cartesian-modern mechanistic perspective matter is perceived as *structurally* finalistic. This means that natural objects are not only understood as a composition of mere physical (material) elements but that attention is being paid to an essence, that is to say an inner organization of the properties of these objects.[24]

---

[22]Maturana and Varela (1980), especially pp. 59–134 for a similar notion of autopoietic and spontaneous processes (although in a mechanistic and not teleological manner: see also hereinafter); Lloyd (1996), p. 104 and ff.: "One thing that emerges from[the]study of Aristotle's treatment of spontaneous generation and metamorphosis is the robustness of his views on nature."

[23]Leighton (1982), p. 168: "Aristotle is quite able to call upon the notion of emotion when needed, and related notions when they are needed. By this ability to wield the features that distinguish these notions, by his sensitivity to the different notions and their place, we see an extremely subtle philosopher at work."

[24]Frede (1992b), pp. 94–95, 99, and 104–105 about the concept of essence as a formal organization; for the similar concept of *homeostasis* as a dynamic process related to the equilibrium of the organisms Damasio (1994), p. 135; Damasio (2010), pp. 55–60; and Damasio (2003), pp. 166–169. Furthermore Damasio (1994), p. 139; Damasio (2010), pp. 89 and ff. for the complex nature of emotion which is based on a mental evaluation and a dispositional response placed *between* brain and body: emotion (or feeling) is the *experience* of these changes similarly to Aristotle's soul; Everson (1997), pp. 9 and 11: in a non-Cartesian perspective within Aristotle's theory "particular acts of perception and nutrition require explanation in material terms[...] [Aristotle distinguishes]different determining relations[...]as different relations[...]rather than relations between property – or event-types which are then instantiated by token substances or events[...][A] method for the explanation of natural changes, including what we would call mental changes, which can provide a proper role for the determination of a substance's changes by the changes undergone by its material parts".

4.3.1 Sensation (Aisthesis)*: A Complex Structure*

Sensation (*aisthesis*) or perception, including common sense, has a paramount role in Aristotle's conceptual architecture.[25] At the beginning of the *De Anima* Aristotle highlights the twofold nature of sensation according to the ontological scheme of act and potency:

> We use the word "perceive" (*aisthanesthai*) in two ways, for we say that what has the power (*dunamis*) to hear or see, "sees" or "hears", even though it is at the moment asleep, and also that what is actually seeing or hearing, "sees" or "hears". Hence "sense" too must have two meanings, sense potential, and sense actual. Similarly "to be a sentient" means either to have a certain power or to manifest a certain activity. (*DA* 417a 10–14, trans. Smith, Greek words added by GB)

Aristotle also distinguishes different objects of sensation: we focus here on hearing and touch. With regard to the first one the voice is to be understood not only in its material or immediate physical dimension but also as structurally "oriented" to a goal:

> Voice is a kind of sound characteristic of what has soul in it (*empsuchon*) nothing that is without soul (*apsuchon*) utters voice, it being only by a metaphor (*homoioteta*) that we speak of the voice [. . .]of what (being without soul) possesses the power of producing a succession of notes [. . .]. The metaphor is based on the fact that all these differences are found also in voice. Many animals are voiceless[. . .]. This is just what we should expect, since voice is a certain movement of air.[. . .]Voice is the sound made by an animal, and that with a special organ. (*DA* 420b 5–14, trans. Smith, Greek words added by GB)

Moreover:

> Voice[. . .] is the impact of the inbreathed air against the windpipe, and the agent that produces the impact is the soul resident in these parts of the body. Not every sound[. . .] made by an animal is voice [. . .]; what produces the impact must have soul in it and must be accompanied by an act of imagination (*phantasia*), for voice is a sound with a meaning (*ti semantikon*), and is not the result of any impact of the breath[. . .]; in voice the breath[. . .] is used as an instrument[. . .]. This is confirmed by our inability to speak when we are breathing[. . .]. (*DA* 420b 28–421a2, trans. Smith, Greek words added by GB)

The notion of metaphor[26] highlights that the use of language generates from a sort of physical-instinctive or *biological* basis. It *incorporates* a *symbolic* meaning

---

[25]Lloyd (1996), pp. 126–137: "Aristotle's doctrine of perception plays a key role at the intersection of a number of his deepest concerns" (I agree with Lloyd's analysis which encompasses knowledge and ethics); Everson (1997), pp. 4–5: sensation is "the clearest example of an Aristotelian explanation of the mental behavior of material beings and [is] a test-case for the application of the principles of Aristotelian physics to the study of the mind."; Hamlyn (1959), pp. 6 and 16: "[Aristotle tries]to develop a new [transitional]view of aesthesis"; Gregoric (2007), p. 28: "Aristotle's account of the perceptual capacity of the soul is considerably longer and more worked out than his account of the other capacities. This is hardly surprising, given the internal complexity of this capacity."

[26]Lloyd (1996), pp. 205–222 who underlines the multiple variations of the concept of metaphor and some certain deep-ambivalences within Aristotle's outlook.

or, by Aristotelian lexicon, imagination (*phantasia*).[27] The same thing stands for
the sense of touch and its relevant role among the senses. It entails a process which
goes beyond the physical dimension:

> To the question whether the organ of touch lies inward or not (i.e. whether we need look any
> farther than the flesh), no indication can be drawn from the fact that if the object comes into
> contact with the flesh it is at once perceived.[28] (*DA* 422b 33–423a 2, trans. Smith)

Once again the pair act-potency emerges in order to understand the physical
dimension as a teleological/aware process:

> for all sense-perception is a process of being so affected; so that that which makes
> something such as it itself actually is makes the other such because the other is already
> potentially such. (*DA* 424a 1–3, trans. Smith)

The objectivity of tactile presentation seems to imply a complex circle between
the theory of the relation between sense and knowledge and the model of scientific
explanation.[29] More widely sensation, which is peculiar to animals and not to
plants, involves an evaluative teleonomy: the idea of good.[30] Sensation is an
articulated function or part of the *formal model* of the soul:

> a sense is what has the power of receiving into itself the sensible forms (*eide*) of things
> without the matter.[31] (*DA* 424a 18–19, trans. Smith, Greek words added by GB)

As Aristotle suggests sensation should be understood as a sort of conscious
proportion based on a perceptual selection:

> Since it is through sense that we are aware that we are seeing or hearing, it must be either by
> sight that we are aware of seeing, or by some sense other than sight. [T]he sense that gives
> us this new sensation must perceive both sight and its object[...] [E]ither there will be two

---

[27]Frede (1992a), pp. 279, 282, and 294 who emphasizes the problems of a unified concept of
imagination and its role as synthesizer: "all *phantasiai* are motions in the soul caused by sense-
perceptions"; White (1985), especially pp. 483–488, about the nexus between soul and imagination and then the close interaction among sensation, imagination and (human) thought; Watson
(1982), pp. 100, 106, 108, and 113: "There is no general agreement among scholars that Aristotle
had a unified concept of *phantasia*"; Watson underlines the relation between sensation, imagination and thinking and concludes: "[Aristotle's *phantasia* was] a deliberate and stubborn correction
of Plato." See also hereinafter about Aristotle's theory of language.

[28]Everson (1997), pp. 78–89: starting from the paradigmatic nature of the sense of touch (including a comparison between plants and animals) Everson underlines the *potency* within the sensible
knowledge.

[29]Freeland (1992a), p. 228 and ff. about a comparison with contemporary models based on neural
cells, the relevance of inter-subjectivity in the Aristotelian theory of perception (with the priority
of touch) and the role of *dynamic forces* within the natural bodies; Lloyd (1996), p. 127 and ff.:
"The fundamental mode of perception is touch"; Damasio (2000), pp. 25–26: touch is a specific
kind of wordless because the "consciousness begins as the feeling of what happens when we see or
hear or touch."

[30]Everson (1997), p. 13 and chapter 1 about the *cognitive* role of perception which is based on a
definitional circle.

[31]See also *DA* 424a 34–35; furthermore the previous references to plants and the mentioned notion
of *enmattered accounts*.

senses both percipient of the same sensible object, or the sense must be percipient of itself. [...][W]e must somewhere assume a sense which is aware of itself. (*DA* 425b 12–17, trans. Smith)

From this point of view there is a proportion (*sumphonia*) or ratio (*logos*), that is to say a sort of circular relation, between each sense and its proper and direct object (i.e. the voice, the hearing and what is heard: see especially the passage *DA* 426a 27-30)[32] The idea of ratio is closely connected to common sense (*koine aisthesis*)[33] underlying all Aristotle's anthropology.[34] Therefore there is a close *relationship between* sensation and soul and there is a ratio between thinking and sensation. Thinking and understanding represent a sort of sensation and, vice versa, *sensation is a form of knowledge*[35]:

There are two distinctive peculiarities [of] the soul – 1) local movement and 2) thinking, understanding, and perceiving. Thinking (*noein*) and understanding (*phronein*) are regarded as akin to a form of perceiving (*aisthanesthai*); for in the one as well as in the other the soul discriminates and is cognizant of something which is. Indeed the ancients go so far as to identify thinking and perceiving [...]. (*DA* 427a 17–22, trans. Smith, Greek words added by GB).

Aristotle insists on the existence of a circle between sensation, image and imagination:

imagination (*phantasia*) must be a movement (*kinesis*) resulting from an actual exercise of a power of sense. (*DA* 429a 1–2, trans. Smith, Greek words added by GB)

So

there is nothing outside and separate in existence from sensible spatial magnitude, the objects of thought are in the sensible forms,[...]both the abstract objects and all the states

---

[32]Furthermore *DA* 426a 30-426b 3 about the sense as a ratio.

[33]Gregoric (2007), p. 125 who offers a survey about the Aristotelian occurrences of this locution and concludes: "I am inclined to think that the phrase "common sense" has not[...]crystallized into a technical term with Aristotle"; Everson (1997), chap. 4, especially p. 157: "[E]ven the perception of a proper sensible of an individual sense requires the exercise of the common capacity for the perception of perception and so the activity of the controlling organ as well as that of the relevant primary sense organ"; Hamlyn (1968), pp. 195 and 208: "[Within *De Anima* the locution "common sense"] is used explicitly to deal with perception of the *koina*, the so-called common-sensible.[...]Aristotle does speak of a common *sense*, but only in connection with the perception of the *koina*" (emphases in the text).

[34]Gregoric (2007), pt. III, p. 205. The author underlines the multiple functions of the common sense: he opposes common sense (*koine aisthesis*) *and* rationality but admits the *cognitive* role of the common sense ("high-order non-rational power").

[35]According to Fortenbaugh (2002), p. 68 also in animals. In a partially different perspective Sorabji (1993), p. 7 who wants to show "what a crisis was provoked when Aristotle denied reason to animals" (see also the Part I).

and affections of sensible things. [...] [I]mages are like sensuous contents except in that they contain no matter. (*DA* 432a 3–19, trans. Smith)

Concerning the question about the relation between imagination and the *cognitive* dimension of sensation, Aristotle states in *De Sensu et Sensibilibus* (On Sense and Sensibilia)[36]:

> [t]he activity of sense-perception (*aisthanesthai*) in general is analogous, not to the process of acquiring knowledge (*manthanein*), but to that of exercising knowledge already acquired (*theorein*).[37] (*SS* 441b 22–23, trans. Beare, Greek words added by GB)

Imagination has thus according to Aristotle a twofold *cognitive* role: in the *synthesis* of sense-perceptions and in *applying thought to objects*. It is a two-fold link *between* the sensible and the intelligible.[38] The crucial point is the *double* nature of sensation: sensation is placed *between* soul and body in so far as it is the outcome of their close interaction. Furthermore in *De Somno et Vigilia* (On Sleep)[39]:

> [S]ince the exercise of sense-perception does not belong to soul or body exclusively, then (since the subject of actuality is identical with that of potentiality, and what is called sense-perception, as actuality, is a movement of the soul through the body) it is clear that it is not an affection of soul exclusively, and that a soulless (*apsuchon*) body has not the potentiality of perception. (*Somn.* 454a 7–11, trans. Beare, Greek words added by GB)

Within Aristotle's outlook sensation-perception is not a rudimentary reaction. According to some scholars it is a "half-way house between [reason and thought]".[40] This is also confirmed by Aristotle's treatment of memory in *De Memoria et Reminiscentia* (On Memory and Recollection)[41]:

> [N]ot only human beings and the beings which possess opinion or intelligence, but also certain other animals, possess memory. If memory were a function of the thinking parts, it would not have been an attribute of many of the other animals, but probably, in that case, no

---

[36]Edition used: *The Complete Works of Aristotle: The Revised Oxford Translation*, edited by Jonathan Barnes. About this topic: Schofield (1992), p. 256: the Aristotelian imagination is "a loose-knit, family concept"; Everson (1997), pp. 157–186 concerning the relation between the sensation and imagination (the *capacities* of the perception), the nexus between perception and thought, the activity of the senses as a whole, the common sense as a perceptual awareness and the relation between imagination and perception; Damasio (1994), pp. 147–148 for some contemporary analogies: "Receiving a comprehensive set of signals about the body state in the appropriate brain regions is the necessary beginning but is not sufficient for feelings to be felt. [Similarly to images] a further condition for the experience is a correlation of the ongoing representation of the body with the neural representations constituting the self. A feeling about a particular object is based on the subjectivity of the perception of the object, the perception of the body state it engenders, and the perception of modified style and efficiency of the thought process as all of the above happens."

[37]Everson (1997), pp. 1–2 who underlines the relation between the *De Anima*, *Little Physical Treatises* and *Physics* regards the point here discussed.

[38]Frede (1992a), pp. 282 and 292 concerning the nature of practical and theoretical thinking.

[39]Edition used: *The Complete Works of Aristotle: The Revised Oxford Translation*, edited by Jonathan Barnes.

[40]Sorabji (1992), p. 195, moreover 196 and ff.

[41]Edition used: *The Complete Works of Aristotle: The Revised Oxford Translation*, edited by Jonathan Barnes.

mortal beings would have had memory; [...] it is not an attribute of them all, just because all have not the faculty of perceiving time. (*Mem.* 450a 14–19; see also 450b 25–27, 452b 23–24, 453a 6–14, trans. Beare).

Hence:

> [Memory] is the having of an image, related as a likeness to that of which it is an image; and [...]it is a function of the primary faculty of sense-perception, i.e. of that faculty whereby we perceive (*aisthanometha*) time.[42] (*Mem.* 451a 16–17, trans. Beare, Greek words added by GB)

The circular scheme underlying Aristotle's model in the relation between sensation and thinking[43] has an important implication for the connection between sensation and practical judgment:

> To perceive then is like bare asserting or thinking (*noein*); but when the object is pleasant or painful, the soul makes a sort of affirmation or negation, and pursues or avoids the object. To feel pleasure or pain is to act with the sensitive mean (*aisthetike mesotes*) towards what is good or bad as such. Both avoidance and appetite when actual are identical with this: the faculty of appetite and avoidance are not different, either from one another or from the faculty of sense-perception; but their being *is* different. (*DA* 431a 8–18, emphasis in the text, trans. Smith, Greek words added by GB)

The role played in moral agency by the irrational dimension (i.e. the senses) is treated by Aristotle in the *Nicomachean Ethics* in the context of the debate about virtue:

> There seems to be also another irrational element (*alogos*) in the soul[...]which in a sense, however, shares in a rational principle.[...][T]he irrational element (*alogon ditton*) [is]twofold. For the vegetative element in no way shares in reason (*logos*), but the appetitive (*epithumetikon*) and in general the desiring element (*orektikon*) in a sense shares in it, in so far as it listens to and obeys it. (*EN* 1102b 13–31, trans. Ross and Urmson, Greek words added by GB)

The concept of moral agency is thus developed by Aristotle in close relation to his formal model of the *biological fundament*:

---

[42]See also Mem. 449b 25–30. Annas (1992), pp. 297 and 311: "[Aristotle's outlook] is[...]more like that of the modern psychologist than of the modern philosopher[...].[This perspective]raises issues relevant to philosophy of mind[...][and]marks the boundaries for a developing empirical psychology."; Lang (1980), pp. 379, 387, and 393: "[Different from Plato]Aristotle's shift to a positive relation between body and soul enables sensible objects to serve as the origin of sensation *and* to provide the content of mental images" (emphasis in the text); Sorabji (2006), p. xxiii: "It is the *existence* of time, not the *perception* of it, that[...]introduces a requirement of *counting*, and even this is only[...]the *possibility* of counting." (emphases in the text); Wedin (1988), pp. 136–141: "[Aristotle construes]imagination[...]as what supplies certain items essential to thought, namely, devices for [re]presentation.[...]There simply is no such thought to be intuited, grasped, or touched apart from the image. Thus, images really are essential for thought."

[43]Schiller (1975), pp. 285 and 295–296: "[Aristotle's outlook]suggests a fruitful approach to the analysis of the concept of sense perception.[...][H]is attempt to account for awareness ultimately breaks down.[...][Anyway] he clearly grasped the complexity of the phenomenon of perception [...]."

The faculty of thinking (*to noetikon*) then thinks the forms (*eide*) in the images, and as in the former case what is to be pursued or avoided is marked out for it, so where there is no sensation and it is engaged upon the images it is moved to pursuit or avoidance.[44] (*DA* 431b 2–4, trans. Smith, Greek words added by GB)

All faculties are related to each other and, in particular, the nutritive faculty and the sensitive one. *Both faculties* are placed, in an indefinable way, *between reason and unreason*:

the nutritive faculty[...]belongs both to plants and to all animals, and the sensitive[...] cannot easily be classed as either irrational (*alogon*) or rational (*logon echon*); further the imaginative, which is[...]different from all, while it is very hard to say with which of the others it is the same or not the same, supposing we determine to posit separate parts in the soul; and lastly the appetitive, which would seem to be distinct both in definition and in power from all hitherto enumerated. It is absurd (*atopon*) to break up the last-mentioned faculty: for wish (*boulesis*) is found in the calculative part and desire and passion in the irrational; and if the soul is tripartite appetite (*orexis*) will be found in all three parts. (*DA* 432a 28–432b 7, trans. Smith, Greek words added by GB)

Appetite in the sense of desire, as an inclination or disposition, and reason (*logos*), as an intellective dimension, represent in interaction with each other the interwoven reasons for movement and moral agency (including animals).[45] Imagination (*phantasia*) is a sort of thinking[46] and thinking symmetrically represents an *intermediate level* between body and soul (as their equator[47]). And as every inclination moves from an image and tends to a goal (from an ethical perspective: good or pleasure[48]), and animals have an inclination, hence animals possess *some kind of imagination*. After all each animal has an unique motor, represented by its faculty of appetite (*orektikon*) (*DA* 433a 22). In On Sense and Sensibilia Aristotle reaffirms this close relation between body and soul:

[The most important attributes of animals are manifestly] attributes of soul and body in conjunction, e. g., *sensation, memory, passion, appetite* and *desire* in general, and, in addition, *pleasure* and *pain* [they belong to all animals].[...]Sensation must[...]be attributed to all animals as such, for by its presence or absence we distinguish between what is and what is not an animal. (*SS* 436a 6–11; 436b 11–12, emphases in the text, trans. Beare)

---

[44]"[T]he soul is analogous to the hand; or as the hand is a tool of tools, so thought is the form of forms and sense the form of sensible things." (*DA* 432a 1–2, trans. Smith).

[45]See the capital (*DA* 433a 9 and ff.).

[46]Sorabji (1992), pp. 197–198: "Propositions are[...]involved in *phantasia*, which in Aristotle's *De Anima* is perceptual and post-perceptual appearance"; Sorabji (2006), pp. XIV–XX about the distinction between imagination and image and thinking as an image which involves soul and body: "The picture-like thing is in the soul as well as the body[...]". About the circle imagination-image see also (*DA* 431a 16-431b 2; 432a 3–14).

[47]Sorabji (2006), p. XX who develops this image.

[48]Annas (1980), p. 285 starting from Nicomachean Ethics 7 and 10: "The accounts in Books 7 and 10[...]agree in the thesis that pleasure is not a bad thing. In the good life it is something to be pursued, not shunned"; Wilkes (1980), p. 355: "[T]he ethical demand[...]is[...]to cultivate to the utmost the excellences required by the life chosen by each man as being best for himself."

As a matter of fact

inasmuch as an animal is capable of appetite it is capable of self-movement; it is not capable of appetite without possessing imagination; and all imagination is either calculative (*logistike*) or sensitive (*aisthetike*). In the latter all animals partake. (*DA* 433b 28–30, trans. Smith, Greek words added by GB)

In conclusion:

[s]ensitive imagination[...]is found in all animals. (*DA* 434a 6, trans. Smith)[49]

4.3.2   Emotion (Pathos): Linguistic Dimension

Emotion (*pathos*) represents another relevant concept, which nowadays is mostly translated by the word emotion.[50] In the modern-Cartesian model, passion (i.e. emotion or also affection) is the opposite of reason and is interpreted in a mechanistic or functionalist way.[51] The Aristotelian emotion (*pathos*) is closely interconnected with the rational sphere *as a whole*. Beyond its conceptualization explained in De Anima, emotion appears also in a linguistic perspective, especially in *Ars Rethorica* (Rhetoric)[52] and in *De Interpretatione* (On Interpretation).[53]

With regard to the *Rhetoric* we can refer to a decisive passage about the relation between emotion and public discourse:

Goodwill (*eunoia*) and friendliness of disposition (*philia*) must form part of our discussion of the emotion (*ta pathe*). The emotions are all those feelings that so change men as to affect their judgments (kriseis), and that are also attended by pain or pleasure. Such are anger, pity, fear and the like, with their opposites. We[...]have to say about each of them under three heads [...]:[i.e. the emotion of anger] we must discover what the state of mind of angry people is, who the people are with whom they usually get angry, and on what grounds they get angry with them. (Rhet. 1378a 19–26, trans. Rhys Roberts, Greek words added by GB)

---

[49]See also the following lines in the Aristotelian text about the finalistic dimension of faculties of the body of animals.

[50]The words emotion and *pathos* are treated in the text as the same. It will be explicitly indicated when a modern use of the concept is made.

[51]Descartes (1978), pp. I:331–344: "There is nothing in which the defective nature of the sciences which we have received from the ancients appears more clearly than in what they have written on the passions[...]. [Passions are] perceptions, feelings, or emotions of the soul which we relate specially to it, and which are caused, maintained, and fortified by some movement of the spirits" (quotation from Descartes' *The Passions of the Soul*).

[52]Edition used: *The Complete Works of Aristotle: The Revised Oxford Translation*, edited by Jonathan Barnes.

[53]Edition used: *The Complete Works of Aristotle: The Revised Oxford Translation*, edited by Jonathan Barnes.

Beyond the extensive expositions throughout the entire rhetoric,[54] there is a cognitive dimension underlying the argumentation, which is connected to emotion.[55] This dimension entails a *political-social function*, especially in relation to value judgments and the public-pedagogic role played by rhetoric (similarly to theatre) within the Greek context. Accordingly, and once again unlike the modern-contemporary perspective,[56] the political importance of passions such as impulse (*thumos*) and friendship (*philia*) should be emphasized as well as their cognitive-evaluative role *as complex value judgments and rational elements* (especially pity and fear).[57]

More widely the relation between emotion and public discourse also refers in a general sense to language, specifically to the circle emotion-soul-language.[58] Aristotle's inquiry implies the entire semantic family connected to emotion (*pathos*) and especially the concept of affections (*pathemata*), which is elaborated in terms of symbols, affection and soul:

> Now spoken sounds are symbols (*sumbola*) of affections (*pathemata*) in the soul, and written marks symbols of spoken sounds. And just as written marks are not the same for all men, neither are spoken sounds. But what these are in the first place signs (*semeia*) of – affections of the soul – are the same for all; and what these affections are likenesses of – actual things – are also the same. (*DI* 16a 3–8, trans. Ackrill, Greek words added by GB)

The important point here is the relation between symbols and affections, which is based on convention (usual translation for *kata suntheken*) as developed in *De Interpretatione* (DI 16a19–16b5). Through this conception of a convention (*kata suntheken*) Aristotle elaborates an articulated model of language (starting from the scheme offered in *De Anima* 427a17–432a13).

Aristotle's position is different from the conventionalist approach[59] in respect of (1) the *nature* of the relation between symbols and affections and (2) the *intersection* between emotion and affections. There is in the view of Aristotle no symmetrical correspondence between the symbol and the affections: the former is not a mere container of the latter. On the contrary it takes the shape of a *structural*

---

[54]I agree with the analysis developed in this volume by: Rapp (2018).

[55]Fortenbaugh (2002), pp. 11–12 who discusses the nexus between emotion and cognition starting from Plato and Aristotle; Koziak (2000), p. 15: "In the *Rhetoric*, Aristotle identifies three aspects of an emotion-a thought or belief, a feeling of pain or pleasure, and a desire for some event, action, or situation".

[56]Campos et al. (1989), p. 400 with any ambiguities. Furthermore see the footnote 1.

[57]Nehamas (1992), p. 297: "the nonrational parts[. . .]are still to be distinguished from reason", but "all desire, rational and nonrational, involves both thought and evaluation", with the discussion about the concepts of wish (*boulesis*), impulse (*thumos*) and appetite (*epithumia*); Gross (2006), pp. 40–41: according to Aristotle's *Rhetoric* "passions condition our very ability to evaluate the world.[. . .]For Aristotle it would be untenable to distinguish[. . .]between emotions that are socially constituted and those that are not." (Gross explicitly refers to Damasio).

[58]Irwin (1982), p. 266: "[There is a connexion]between Aristotle's views on signification and his other philosophical interests. Inquiry into words and their signification is part of inquiry into the world and the real essences in it."

[59]Coseriu and Narr (1975), p. I:80.

synthesis. The relation encompasses a twofold and interlaced dimension: a biological, in some way emotive, factor (the sound or voice) and a *symbolic, and meaningful, element*: see furthermore in *Poetica* (Poetics) (1456a 32 and ff.).[60] This scheme has an important implication.

The affection, or its apparent passive articulation, is for Aristotle not a mere mental reflex produced by the physical voice and expressed by linguistic signs. He sees it as the outcome of a very complex *and (also) emotive and symbolic* interpretation of reality. Hence, in the light of Aristotle's model of sensation, emotion has a *cognitive* role. In the linguistic process the emotive and reflexive moment are closely interwoven (somehow language is common to all animals). That's why his model, in opposition to the current conventionalist interpretation, should be understood as a *symbolic* model: far more than the mere linguistic sign, it is the biological-emotive affection (voice) which is intrinsically and linguistically symbolic.[61]

We should also take into account the political-legal horizon underlying the Aristotelian doctrine of language explained in *Politica* (Politics)[62]:

> [T]hat man is more of a political animal than bees or any other gregarious animals is evident. Nature [...] makes nothing in vain, and man is the only animal who has the gift of speech (*logos*). And whereas mere voice is but an indication (*semeion*) of pleasure or pain, and is therefore found in other animals (for their nature attains to the perception of pleasure and pain and the intimation (*semainein*) of them to one another, and no further), the power of speech is intended to set forth the expedient and inexpedient, and therefore likewise the just (*to dikaion*) and the *unjust (to adikon)*. And it is a characteristic of man that he alone has any sense of good (*agathos*) and evil (*kakos*), of just and unjust, and the like, and the association (*koinonia*) of living beings who have this sense makes a family and a state. (*Pol.* 1253a 7–18, trans. Jowett, Greek words added by GB)

The Aristotelian argumentation, based on his crucial model of nature,[63] implies a concept of language, which is a *combination* of a biological/emotive level and a rational/mental dimension, and which is *structurally* oriented to the political relation (also in a communitarian perspective).[64]

---

[60]Edition used: *The Complete Works of Aristotle: The Revised Oxford Translation*, edited by Jonathan Barnes.

[61]Lo Piparo (2003), pp. 187–193. Lo Piparo criticizes the traditional (linear or semiotic) interpretation which is based on the binary or denotative relation between the linguistic sign and the meaning (objects, reality) and on a semiotic notion of symbol. According to Lo Piparo Aristotle's linguistic theory relies on a dynamic and threefold scheme (vocal units, logical-cognitive operations, natural-linguistic systems): the vocal units and the script (*grammata*) are the typical human physical signs of language, i.e. the symbolic correlation between the articulations of the human voice and the logical-cognitive operations of the soul. This relation is expressed through the various linguistic-natural systems, that is to say the natural languages.

[62]Edition used: *The Complete Works of Aristotle: The Revised Oxford Translation*, edited by Jonathan Barnes.

[63]Lloyd (1996), p. 184 and ff. for the complex idea of nature in Politics also compared to Hume's perspective.

[64]Bombelli (2013), pp. 275–287.

4.3.3 Pity (Eleos) and Fear (Phobos)

The circle between emotion, language and politics also plays an important role in *Poetics*.[65] As is well known drama played a great role within the Greek context: through the reinterpretation of myth[66] it was a *public space* closely connected to political-representative systems.[67] Emotions and their necessary stimulation through drama were considered to be the *political* conditions of the *polis* which could guarantee social cohesiveness.[68]

According to the scheme developed in *Rhetoric*, Aristotle underlines the *necessity* to arouse emotions *in order to obtain an imitation* (*mimesis*):

> Epic poetry and tragedy, as also comedy, dithyrambic poetry[...]are all[...]modes of imitation (*mimesis*). [...][T]hey differ[...]in three ways[...]: means[...], objects[...], manner of their imitations. (*Poet.* 1447a 14–17, trans. Bywater, Greek words added by GB)

We focus on some passages of *Poetics* starting from the relation between learning and pleasure. In general

> to be learning something is the greatest of pleasures (*Poet.* 1448b 13–14, trans. Bywater)

After all:

> [t]he marvellous[...]is a cause of pleasure[and we tell a story with additions]in the belief that we are giving pleasure to our hearers. (*Poet.* 1460a 18, trans. Bywater)

In this way we can understand the *cognitive* dimension underlying tragedy[69] and the central role of catharsis (*katharsis*). The fundamental passage:

> [Tragedy] is the imitation (*mimesis*) of an action that is serious and [...] complete in itself; in language with pleasurable accessories, each kind brought in separately in the parts of the work; in a dramatic, not in a narrative form; with incidents arousing pity (*eleos*) and fear (*phobos*), where with to accomplish its catharsis(*katharsis* of such emotions.[...]

---

[65]Koziak (2000), pp. 132–133 who underlines the relation between poetics and politics; in a similar line Fortenbaugh (2002), pp. 18–22.

[66]Vernant (1992), p. 33: "Greek tragedy is strongly marked of characteristics: tension between myth and the forms of thought peculiar to the city, conflict within[...] the domain of values[...]. [...][T]he play startlingly reveals that the divine intervenes even in the course of human action."

[67]Sommerstein et al. (1993), p. 12: "[Tragedy and comedy]were performed in the same thoroughly public, civic external setting."

[68]Freeland (1992b), pp. 125–126: Freeland identifies "three central assumptions of the *Poetics*": aesthetic naturalism, moral realism and an account of literary tragedy "as a naturally occurring phenomenon with intrinsic necessary properties and a specific aim": hence "Aristotle's teleology of plot presupposes an active, responsible hero who has a definite social context."; Blundell (1992), p. 155: "[Ē]thos and *dianoia* [i.e. character and intellect]form two of the essential "parts" of tragedy, following only plot in significance. Their presence and importance follow directly from the definition of tragedy as the imitation of *praxis*."

[69]Oksenberg Rorty (1992b), pp. 2–3 about the contrast between Aristotle's outlook and the-Dionysian origins; Nussbaum (1992), pp. 273 and ff. for the relation between rhetoric, the cognitive value of fear and pity, the Homeric roots and a comparison with Plato; Woodruff (1992), p. 87 concerning the cognitive power of emotions.

'[L]anguage with pleasure accessories'[means]with rhythm and harmony; and[…]'the kinds separately'[means]that some portions are worked out with verse only, and others in turn with song. (*Poet.* 1449b 24–31, trans. Bywater, Greek words added by GB)

The question what catharsis exactly means is notoriously difficult. Still it is a very relevant concept because it involves the role of emotion. Leaving other interpretations aside,[70] the important point here is the political-civic relevance of emotion and its direct connection with friendship (*philia*) (*Poet.* 1453b 19–22), which is based on intellectual clarification and emotional rectification.[71] One could emphasize the moral value of the tragic emotion *as a judgment*[72] or, according to a different perspective, the *cognitive* role of emotion as a form of understanding.[73] Within this conceptual horizon we can appreciate the Aristotelian definition of emotion:

[F]or the finest form of tragedy, the plot must be not simple but complex;[…]it must imitate actions arousing fear and pity, since that is the distinctive function of this kind of emotion (*mimesis*). […] There are three forms of plot to be avoided. A good man must not be seen passing from good fortune to bad, or bad man from bad fortune to good. The first situation is not fear-inspiring or piteous, but simply odious to us. The second is the most untragic that can be; it has no one of the requisites of tragedy; it does not appeal either to the human feeling (*philantropon*) in us, or to our pity, or to our fears. Nor[…]should an extremely bad man be seen falling from good fortune into bad. (*Poet.* 1452b 31–1453a 2, trans. Bywater, Greek words added by GB)

---

[70]Lear (1992), p. 334 who highlights the key-concept of *pathos* as emotional possibility and criticizes the interpretation of catharsis as a mere purification of the emotions; Janko (1992), p. 341 about the relation between catharsis and virtue and the continuity underlying representation and catharsis; Koziak (2000), pp. 143–147: according to Koziak catharsis means "to coax the *thumos* to react habitually well in political situations".

[71]Oksenberg Rorty (1992b), pp. 12–17: "[Pity]involves an affective understanding of the proper domain of *philia*[…][related to the] common civic project (*koinonia*)[…][Catharsis is]a cognitive term, referring to an intellectual resolution or clarification that involves directing emotions to their appropriate intentional objects.[…]When pity and fear are appropriately felt[…]according to the *logos* and the measure that is appropriate to them, they can play their natural psychological and civic functions[…].[Hence]the distinction between intellectual clarification and emotional rectification is[…]spurious and tendentious.[…]The distinction between theory and practice is a distinction between types of activities – both of them cognitive – as characterized by their methods and aims[…]towards a larger, common civic *philia*."; Koziak (2000), pp. 134–138; Belfiore (1992), pp. 44 and ff.; 70–ff., 82, 181, 226, 246, and chapters 8–10; Nussbaum (2001), pp. 388–394.

[72]Freeland (1992b), pp. 122–125 *contra* cognitivist and emotivist interpretations.

[73]Halliwell (1992), pp. 241–256: "[pleasure, understanding, emotion]form an interlocking set of elements in Aristotle's interpretation [of representational art]" which is based on two types of aesthetic pleasure: the first one is "*mediated* through the artist's skilled accomplishment", the second one is "*restricted* to the material and sensual properties of the artifact[…]. [E]motion and recognition[…][are]somehow *fused* in aesthetic experience" (emphases in the text, with a parallelism between *Politics*, *Rhetoric* and *Poetics* in stark contrast to the Kantian line); Nussbaum (2001), pp. 383–388: according to Nussbaum pity and fear are irrational but valuable sources of recognition; Nussbaum (1992), pp. 281–287 and 308 who condemns the idea of catharsis as a homeopathic purification.

Consequently

not every kind of pleasure should be required of a tragedy, but only its own proper pleasure. (*Poet.* 1453b 10–11, trans. Bywater)

Moreover:

There should be nothing improbable among the actual incidents. If it be unavoidable, however, it should be outside the tragedy. (*Poet.* 1454b 6–7, trans. Bywater)

Tragedy aims at taking out a *good* human feeling, which should always be understood in the light of the public role of drama within the *polis*:

in their reversals of fortune[and] in their simple plots, the poets[…]show wonderful skill in aiming at the kind of effect they desire – a tragic situation that arouses the human feeling in one. (*Poet.* 1456a 20–23, trans. Bywater)

The Aristotelian persistence in emphasizing the relation between language (i.e. public discourse), thought and emotion is very significant, in the way he highlights it in *Rhetoric* and in *De Interpretatione* and extends this to the pragmatic sphere. In addition this paramount passage:

As for the thought (*dianoia*), we may assume what is said of it in our Art of Rhetoric[…]. The thought of the personages is shown in everything to be effected by their language – in every effort to prove or disprove, to arouse emotion (*to pathe paraskeuazein*) (pity, fear, anger, and the like), or to maximize or minimize things.[…][T]heir mental procedure must be on the same lines in their actions likewise, whenever they wish them to arouse pity or horror, or to have a look of importance or probability. The only difference is that with the act the impression has to be produced by the speaker, and result from his language. What, indeed, would be the good of the speaker, if things appeared in the required light even apart from anything he said? (*Poet.* 1456a 34–1456b 8; see also 1458a 18 and ff., 1460b 1 and 1461b 13–16, trans. Bywater, Greek words added by GB)

To sum up. Tragedy and, more widely, the *pedagogic* role played by drama (including its emotive bases) play an important role in guaranteeing the political-legal cohesiveness.[74] In this context we can understand the theoretical continuity between drama-theatre and friendship (*philia*) and its political-legal relevance.[75] For the political animal friendship is not a superficial social homogeneity, but a sort of pre-theoretic and sympathetic sense of affiliation (emotive or pre-rational dimension) which should be cultivated: a civic friendship.[76]

The Greek (Aristotelian) notion of friendship (*philia*) should therefore not be confused with the modern and contemporary concept of friendship. The former

---

[74]Golden (1992), p. 381: "Aristotelian comic theory requires the representation of action that is "ridiculous" and that such action evokes[…]a form of "indignation" whether or not that indignation is accompanied by laughter."

[75]Fortenbaugh (2002), p. 32 who distinguishes "political and ethical psychology" and "[the] biological psychology familiar to readers of the *De Anima*": Aristotle develops the implicit dichotomy of Plato's *Laws* (see also chapters 2 and 3).

[76]Cooper (1980), p. 302.

expresses the ontological and structural origin of a human/communitarian relationship, whereas the latter involves a mere sentimental-subjective relation.

Two aspects of friendship (*philia*) ask for specific attention. Firstly, it can develop only within a communitarian horizon (household, village, political community) according to a circular scheme: there is no community (*koinonia*) without friendship. Secondly friendship is intrinsically political in so far as it is the theoretical-sociological basis for political obligation. This connection between community and friendship (*Pol.* 1280b 30–1281a 11; 1295a 25–1296a 19) implies a conjunction with happiness (*eudaimonia*) and education (*paideia*).

Happiness represents anthropological flourishing,[77] or the universal ideal of human perfection including its emotive (and only apparently irrational) profile.[78] As it develops *only* within the community, or more precisely the political community (*polis-koinonia*), it cannot be compared to the modern notion of happiness *as a mere individual right to pursue the complete personal satisfaction*. The pedagogic model extensively drawn in *Politics* VIII as well as in *Rhetoric* synthesizes the Hellenic tradition and forms the logical outcome of Aristotle's philosophy. Because human relations develop only within the community it is philosophically, politically and legally legitimated to impose a public education of emotion (*Pol.* 1337a 11–22, 35–36).[79]

On this level we can grasp the flexibility of the concept of community as a *formal* notion. Community (*koinonia*) is a sort of *tension* between a historical-empiric dimension and a theoretical level: it is a *descriptive* model in so far as it identifies the historical political context as a whole, but, *at the same time*, it represents a *normative-dynamic* form (the community *as it ought/should be*), which in turn is based on complex concepts of nature and being.[80]

The principle of ontological continuity involves therefore an ambiguous view on the community and its emotive bases: community can be the dynamic political-legal framework to enhance personal and collective identity or happiness (*eudaimonia*) and, *at the same time*, can transform into a platonic-totalitarian structure which controls emotion through education (*paideia*).[81] Perhaps that's why only human beings, being endowed with emotion, can live within the community: they are neither the beast nor the god (*Pol.* 1253a 27–29).

---

[77] Albeit it is vulnerable: Nussbaum (2001), chap. 11 for the nexus between the tragic action and the Greek concept of happiness (*eudaimonia*).

[78] Fortenbaugh (2002), p. 63.

[79] Newman (1950), I, pp. 369–374.

[80] About the pair stagnation and movement, or rest and dynamics, within a political-legal horizon *Pol.* 1252a 1-1255a 2; in a hermeneutic perspective Gadamer (1972), Part II, chap. 2; Newman (1950), I, pp. 18–21 and 48.

[81] Bombelli (2013), pp. 327–340 with particular attention to the relation between community and education.

The important point for us is philosophical-legal. Friendship (*philia*) as an *emotive dimension* represents the condition of the *political-legal stability*.[82] Different from the modern and pivotal idea of rational contract, as a foundation of political obligation, Aristotle founds politics in a complex semantic area (drama, friendship) closely related to emotion.[83]

4.3.3.1 Intermezzo

Hitherto we have considered some aspects of emotion in an anthropological perspective, namely knowledge (sensation) and language with its projections in the public space (rhetoric and drama) and the political reflexes of this. We now have to look more closely into the relation between emotion and the pragmatic sphere (moral agency). Two categories are important here: impulse (thumos) and appetition/desire (orexis). Although the former represents the premise of the latter, indicating a fundamental inclination and motor of desire, we will firstly consider the desire and later the concept of impulse, which appears to be conceptually wider in the light of its political-legal relevance.

4.3.4 Desire (Orexis)

In some way Aristotle elaborates the first Greek conceptualization of appetition/ desire (*orexis*) in its close connection with other concepts as impulse (*thumos*) and appetite (*epithumia*). According to the dynamic Aristotelian model appetition/ desire (*orexis*) is to be understood fundamentally as a goal-oriented activity, underlying the whole of nature.[84] Appetitition/desire (*orexis*) is a fundamental energy or movement: energy/activity (*energeia*) is the Greek way to express its

---

[82]Koziak (2000), pp. 104 and 111–125: "Aristotle does not hope merely to replace disagreeable emotions with rational behavior, but to stimulate citizens to feel more affection[and]to become more reasonable with the aid of this emotion" (with regard to the relation between middle class and the political role of friendship).

[83]Bombelli (2015), pp. 1086 and 1098 about the nexus between friendship, community and justice; Bombelli (2016), pp. 24–27 for a contextualization of Aristotle's outlook within Greek literature.

[84]Nussbaum (2001), p. 275: through the word appetition/desire (*orexis*) Aristotle "selects (or, very probably, invents) a word well suited to indicate the common feature shared by all cases of goal-directed animal movement.[...][*Boulēsis, thumos*, and *epithumia* are all forms of *orexis* and[...] some *orexis* is involved in every animal movement"; Charles (2011), pp. 84–86 (about De Motu Animalium): "[Aristotle applies the term "desire" (*orexis*)] more widely than to sensual desire alone[...]"; Pearson (2011), pp. 111–113: "*epithumia* is pleasure-based, whereas *boulēsis* is good-based in a narrower sense of "good" than that in which all desires (*orexeis*) are good-based[...].[T]he faculty of desire (*to orektikon*) is the part of us in virtue of which we are moved to intentional action[...]."; Segvic (2011), pp. 176–177: starting from Nicomachean Ethics 1139b 4–5 "choice is characterized as "desiderative understanding" (*orektikos nous*) or "rational desire" (*orexis*

fluid character. It connects different levels of reality and it is possible to distinguish at least three closely interwoven dimensions: ontological, teleological and moral-practical.

Firstly appetition/desire (*orexis*) appears (similarly to other concepts: i.e. thinking as image/appearance (*phantasma*)) as an *intermediate* between potency and act. It is described as a *tendency* or *inclination*. For instance:

> The pleasure proper to a worthy activity is good and that proper to an unworthy activity bad; just as the appetites for noble objects are laudable, those for base objects culpable. But the pleasures involved in activities are more proper to them than the desires; for the latter are separated both in time and in nature, while the former are close to the activities, and so hard to distinguish from them that it admits of dispute whether the activity is not the same as the pleasure. (*EN* 1175b 26–34, trans. Ross and Urmson)

This point must be understood in the light of the distinction between potential and actual existence outlined in *Physica* (Physics)[85]:

> Being is spoken of in many ways [. . .], the infinite is in the sense in which [. . .] one thing after another is always coming into existence. For of these things too the distinction between potential and actual existence holds. (*Phys.* 206a 21–24, trans. Hardie and Gaye)

Secondly appetition/desire (*orexis*) should be considered *in a finalistic perspective*. Accordingly it is a little different from the concept of impulse (*thumos*) and is, in some way, related to appetite (*epithumia*) as stated in *Metaphysica* (Metaphysics)[86]:

> [E]ven if one has a rational wish, or an appetite (*epithumia*), to do two things or contrary things at the same time, one cannot do them; for it is not on these terms that one has the potentiality (*dunamis*) for them, nor is it a potentiality for doing both at the same time, since one will do just the things which it is a potentiality for doing. (*Met.* 1048a 20–24, trans. Ross, Greek word added by GB)

The finalistic value of appetition/desire (*orexis*) also emerges in a very relevant political meaning because

> [l]ike the sailor, the citizen is a member of a community. Now, sailors have different functions [. . .]; and while the precise definition of each individual's excellence applies exclusively to him, there is, at the same time, a common definition applicable to them all. For they have all of them a common object, which is safety in navigation. (*Pol.* 1276b 20–27, trans. Jowett)

Thirdly appetition/desire (*orexis*) implies a *moral level*. It encompasses an implicit moral evaluation involving a fundamental aspiration (inclination, appetite, desire) to a *good*. We can now grasp the different degrees of the emotive (and practical) aspect and the difference between impulse (*thumos*) and appetition/desire

---

dianoetikē), which comes closer to suggesting that choice is a state of the soul that is *sui generis*, and not merely a combination of a desire and a belief."

[85]Edition used: *The Complete Works of Aristotle: The Revised Oxford Translation*, edited by Jonathan Barnes.

[86]Edition used: *The Complete Works of Aristotle: The Revised Oxford Translation*, edited by Jonathan Barnes.

(*orexis*). The former is the undetermined impulse underlying the human behavior, the latter is the movement directed or oriented to a *qualified* goal (i.e. a good):

> each man desires what is good. (*EN* 1162b 12, trans. Ross and Urmson)

Aristotle develops the idea of appetition/desire (*orexis*) as a basis of moral agency in other passages, which are dedicated to the achievement of rewards. For instance:

> it is possible to desire (*oregesthai*) small honors as one ought, and more than one ought, and less, and the man who exceeds in his desires is called ambitious (*EN* 1107b 27–29, trans. Ross and Urmson, Greek word added by GB)

Furthermore:

> [f]or the unduly humble man, being worthy of good things, robs himself of what he deserves, and seems to have something bad about him from the fact that he does not think himself worthy of good things, and seems also not to know himself; else he would have desired the things he was worthy of, since these were good. (*EN* 1125a 19–23, trans. Ross and Urmson)

Once again

> where there is excess and defect, there is also an intermediate; now men desire honor both more than they should and less (*EN* 1125b 19–20, trans. Ross and Urmson)

And also

> one is a liar because he enjoys the lie itself, and another because he desires reputation or gain. (*EN* 1127b 15–16, trans. Ross and Urmson)

More generally those who desire honor from good men, and men who know, are aiming at confirming their own opinion of themselves (*EN* 1159a 21–23) as well as some communities aim at wealth or victory or the taking of a city that they seek (EN 1160a 17–18) or, with reference to democracy, many are more desirous of gain than of honor. (*Pol.* 1318b 16).

In conclusion. There is a structural ambiguity involved in the concept of appetition/desire (*orexis*), which has *an emotive and cognitive implication*.[87] Appetition/desire (*orexis*), perhaps emotion as a whole, represents a sort of *intermediate level between the empiric-material and the teleological-cognitive dimension*.[88]

---

[87]Nussbaum (2001), pp. 276–282: "The connections among *orexis*, cognition, and motion are logical or conceptual".

[88]See the fundamental and previously quoted *EN* 1102b 13–31, which synthesizes the interaction between reason and emotion.

4.3.5 Impulse (Thumos)

Impulse (*thumos*), sometimes translated with spirit or passion or spiritedness, has a close relation with desire and appetite. It can be considered as a (biological) dynamic phenomenon which underlies every form of emotion: the *genesis* of the movement produced by appetite (*epithumia*), which is literally a form of impulse (*thumos*), the appetition/desire (*orexis*) and, in a wider sense, the sensation (*aisthesis*).

The notion of impulse (*thumos*) is very complex, dating back to the archaic era.[89] Within Aristotle's theory impulse covers a wide semantic field[90] and has a twofold and interwoven tendency: *cognitive-theoretical and practical-political.*

Impulse, being the linguistic root of wonder (*thaumazein*), could be understood as a sort of emotive puzzlement. In other words emotion, hence a *physical* and in some way a genetic factor, seems to be the *condition* or premise for theoretical activity: accordingly it is a *form of knowledge* (in the sense of perception). In the Metaphysics Aristotle establishes this point when he states that

> it is owing to their wonder (*thaumazein*) that men both now begin and at first began to philosophize. (*Met.* 982b, 12–13, trans. Ross, Greek words added by GB)

In a practical perspective we can distinguish at least three concepts of impulse: impulse as anger, as an aggressive force or spiritedness (both according to Plato) and, finally, the Aristotelian innovation of impulse as the general capacity of emotion. In the latter meaning impulse has also a relevant political role.[91] Given its connection with the complex dimension of friendship (*philia*),[92] it represents the *condition* for the political bond and for its possible destruction as

---

[89]If we cautiously accept the position expressed in Koziak (2000), p. 38: "[*Thumos*] is the key to understanding[the] philosophical psychology of politics [in Homer, Plato and Aristotle]"; furthermore Bombelli (2016), pp. 10–11, 16, and 23–27 for the relation between Greek literature and the Aristotelian perspective.

[90]Berns (1984), pp. 345–346: "[Aristotle does not provide a] thematic analysis of spiritedness.[...] Spiritedness manifests itself most conspicuously in anger and courage [and fear and hope] seem to be the primary passions of spiritedness.[...]Not only is spiritedness the temperamental condition of political freedom, but in social and political life it is the indispensable temperamental basis for the fight against injustice."; Lord (1991), pp. 52, 59–60, and 72: "[T]he "spiritedness"[...]is central to Aristotle's analysis of civic solidarity and political rule.[...]. [P]olitical society[...] comes into being through a discontinuous act[...][and]the human soul uniquely combines reason with "spiritedness"[...].[...][Spiritedness provides]a critical link between man's biological and psychological nature and the structures of human society.[It]is one of the features of classical political philosophy[...]."

[91]Sokolon (2006), especially Part III concerning the Aristotelian relation between emotion and the political community as the specific horizon of impulse (*thumos*); Koziak (2000), p. 2: "Aristotle's treatment of *thumos*[...]represents a theory of political emotion available to contemporary challenges to rationalistic explanations of political community."

[92]Nussbaum (2001), pp. 359–361 about the vulnerability of friendship (*philia*): "[T]he best sort of love between persons is highly vulnerable to happenings in the world."

well,[93] given the *tensional nature* of the community. The unity in the political community (*polis-koinonia*) develops on the basis of a dialectics between intelligence (*dianoia*) or rationality (*logos*) and a combination of opposite factors (*Pol.* 1327b 36–1328a 15), based on emotions (i.e. friendship, impulse) which, at the same time however, *could* destroy the political unity.

Different from the current view that emotion brings disorder, Aristotle sees emotion as a fundamental condition for political obligation, which is actualized at the moment that a specific political community (*polis-koinonia*) is constituted (*Pol.* 1253a 29–31). Only in this perspective we can appreciate the radical difference between Greece and other nations as suggested in an important passage:

> Having spoken of the number of the citizens, we will proceed to speak of what should be their character.[...]Those who live in a cold climate and in Europe are full of spirit (*thumos*), but wanting in intelligence (*dianoia*) and skill; and therefore they retain comparative freedom, but have not political organization, and are incapable of ruling over others. Whereas the natives of Asia are intelligent and inventive, but they are wanting in spirit, and therefore they are always in a state of subjection and slavery. But the Hellenic race, which is situated between them, is likewise intermediate in character, being highspirited (*enthumon*) and also intelligent. Hence it continues free, and is the best-governed of any nation, and, if could be formed into one state, would be able to rule the world. (*Pol.* 1327b 19–32, trans. Jowett, Greek words added by GB)

The *combination* rationality and emotion not only marks the *decisive boundary* between freedom and slavery but represents also the *condition* of political life.[94] The well-balanced relation between reason *and* emotion allows the passage from the immediate or disordered (chaotic) relations to the legal-political dimension and makes political community (*polis-koinonia*) possible:

> And clearly those whom the legislator will most easily lead to excellence may be expected to be both intelligent and courageous (*thumoeideis*). (*Pol.* 1327b 36–38, trans. Jowett, Greek words added by GB)

Similarly to friendship (*philia*) there is a sort of *pre-theoretic* (emotive) disposition underlying the political-legal structure:

> passion (*thumos*) is the quality of the soul which begets friendship and enables us to love.[95] (*Pol.* 1327b 40–1328a 1, trans. Jowett, Greek words added by GB)

---

[93]Koziak (2000), p. 110: "With Aristotle's final word on the best regime, *thumos* in its most complex sense loses its meaning of one emotion or of one drive or instinct, becoming instead the soul's capacity for emotion."

[94]About this point I share the perspective offered by Nuno Coelho's contribution in this volume. Coelho (2018).

[95]Berns (1984), pp. 346–348: "Aristotle refers to spiritedness as rising more powerfully against intimates and friends[...]than it does against those it does not know.[...]There is[...]a [common] substratum to both friendship and enmity-care.[...]*Thumos*, or spiritedness, would then be the source of those feelings directed primarily to the care for one's own[...].[...]The love of one's own and its spiritedness[...]reach fulfillment when together they are shaped and disposed by reason as material for virtue. One's own and the cherishable come together[...]in the friendship of the virtuous."

Finally we can grasp the relation between impulse and friendship: the former should be placed within the horizon of a *common friendship* also in the light of the problematic relation with non-Greek peoples. This scheme symmetrically confirms the emotive nature of friendship as a basis of the political community (*koinonia*):

> [F]riendly feeling towards anyone [is] wishing for him what you believe to be good things not for your own sake but for his, and being inclined, so far as you can, to bring these things about. (*Rhet.* 1380b 35–1381a 1, trans. Rhys Roberts)

In a recapitulatory passage the structural and dialectic role of impulse (*thumos*) emerges:

> notably the spirit (*thumos*) within us is more stirred against our friends and acquaintances than against those who are unknown to us, when we think we are despised by them[. . .]. The power of command and the love of freedom are in all men based upon this quality, for passion (*thumos*) is commanding and invincible. (*Pol.* 1328a 1–8, trans. Jowett, Greek words added by GB)

4.4 A Recap and Some Remarks

The previous analysis highlights the central role of emotion within Aristotle's model, including the relation with rationality, and its wide semantic field. Starting from this framework we can better grasp the *theoretical continuity* underlying Aristotle's theory according to the conceptual line ontology, anthropology and political-legal level. The ontological (i.e. natural) dimension represents a platform based on a sort of *continuum* among all living beings. They are characterized by some inner forces (sensation, cause, goal etc.) which, in different manners and degrees, belong to the area of emotion: *emotion as a structurally goal-oriented dimension*.

Accordingly on the anthropological level we can appreciate the *flexible* role of emotion and its nexus with reason as regards to many dimensions: knowledge, language and practical sphere (i.e. moral agency and politics). Aristotle's theory of knowledge entails a circular scheme grounded in the pair sensation (*aisthesis*) and emotion (*pathos*). All the knowledge-processes, the apparent primitive level of the sensation and the more complex forms, reveal a close connection between emotion and reason. Emotion plays a *cognitive* role which implies, although in a problematic manner, the couple consciousness-awareness. Language, including its public or political projections (rhetoric, drama), confirms this conceptual framework. It relies on an emotive (genetic?) origin with regard both to the close linguistic level, the symbolic concept of affections (*pathemata*) elaborated within the *De Interpretatione*, and to the degrees distinguished within the *Rhetoric*. But the emotive dimension connotes also moral agency. The practical sphere arises from a sort of blending of emotion and reason grounded in the sequence impulse (*thumos*)-appetition/desire (*orexis*), including the role of appetite (*epithumia*): impulse (*thumos*), as the genetic origin of all behaviors, is also underlying the emotions and hence the dynamics of appetition/desire (*orexis*). Emotion has a social-political projection: the conceptual continuity impulse (*thumos*)-friendship (*philia*) is the inescapable horizon of the cohesiveness within political community (*polis-koinonia*).

We can shortly reconsider some points introduced at the beginning.

Firstly Aristotle's theory presents a *twofold principle of ontological continuity*: the analogy among the degrees of nature, which is confirmed in *Meteorologica* (Meteorology)[96] 389b 28 e ss.,[97] and the anthropological continuity mind-body, which allows for the question whether there is a real distinction between on the one hand emotion, feeling, and desire and on the other rational decision or both have to be understood in terms of a continuum. Secondly we can grasp the *cognitive relevance* of emotion. When considered along all its gradients emotion plays a crucial role on many levels (knowledge, moral action, language, politics) in order to elaborate a comprehension of reality. Thirdly a complex model of reason (*logos*) emerges, which includes legal/political reasoning. Unlike the modern (i.e. Cartesian) perspective, reason (mind) should be understood as a combination of evaluative factors and an emotive dimension well synthesized and formulated with the help of an irrational element (*alogon ditton*) which in the case of the desiring element (*orektikon*) shares in reason (*logos*) (*EN* 1102b 23–32). Within this framework Aristotle elaborates his model of knowledge encompassing the entire relation man-world.

4.5   Some Concluding Remarks About the Feasibility of Aristotle's Theory in View of a Post-Cartesian Model of Human Identity

We can now better appreciate the complexity of Aristotle's outlook and, in some way, the unexpected modernity of the Aristotelian anthropology and his theory of emotion.[98] It is possible to shortly suggest some analogies between Aristotle's

---

[96]Edition used: *The Complete Works of Aristotle: The Revised Oxford Translation*, edited by Jonathan Barnes.

[97]Lloyd (1996), pp. 158–159 on the importance of the pair potentiality-actuality and its application to the "form-matter dichotomy [which is highlighted by]the intelligible matter of mathematical entities and the genus in relation to its differentiae [or similarly the investigation about]what *connects* [animals]as all members of the multifarious animal kingdom, and the recognition of their *variety* [in the light]of proportional analogies" (emphases in the text).

[98]Wilkes (1992), pp. 123–125: "Aristotle is in advance of many contemporary "cognitive scientists" in understanding that both the "dialectician" and the "student of nature" can contribute to the study of human competences[...][with reference to] the sheer *possibility* of so-called 'multiple realizability'[...][or]at best 'variable realizability': form sets very substantial constraints on matter, and on the organization of matter.[...][W]e *should* return from the mind to the *psyke* [but]indirectly and without realizing it we have in fact been doing so for some time" (emphases in the text).

nexus emotion-reason and contemporary research in the cognitive neuroscience of emotion, even though the latter starts from a different conceptual framework.[99] Damasio's model, mentioned in the previous paragraphs, which focuses on the dynamic relation between reason and feeling, as well as its notions of representation (i.e. touch), image and homeostasis as an autopoietic organization, confirms the theoretical legitimacy of a organicist or holistic (i.e. Aristotelian) anthropology, especially also of the conception of a *continuum* among low levels and high levels of nature based on a wide model of consciousness.

Similar perspectives are provided by Humberto Maturana, Francisco Valera and Gerald Edelman with Giulio Tononi. These authors try to conceptualize the human identity, including emotion, within a model of embodiment of mind. They even start from some concepts which are in some way related to the Aristotelian framework: perception, autopoiesis, consciousness and embodied mind. Aristotle's doctrine of perception, including his theory of self-organizing entities, can be compared to the biology of cognition and to the concept of *autopoiesis* elaborated by Humberto Maturana and Francisco Varela who move from the question: "*What is cognition as a function? What is cognition as a process?*"[100] The authors state that a cognitive system "is a system whose organization defines a domain of interactions in which it can act with relevance to the maintenance of itself":[101] living systems, including all organisms, are cognitive systems and living is to be understood as a process of cognition. This perspective implies a problematic neurophysiology of cognition (i.e. the explication of self-consciousness and linguistic domain)[102] The observer is conceived as a living system and "any understanding of cognition as a biological phenomenon must account for the observer and his role in it".[103] Although the authors sometimes present a less deterministic perspective,[104] they understand,

---

[99]For a similar perspective Kafetsios and LaRock (2005), especially pp. 640 and 650–654: "[Aristotle supports]an integrative view of affect and cognitive processes of emotion.[. . .]For Aristotle[. . .]emotion is a complex, yet unified, form-matter activity.[. . .][R]ecent developments in the cognitive neuroscience and social-cognitive neuroscience research[support]the Aristotelian thinking of emotion.[. . .]Aristotle's commitment to the hierarchical organization embedded in the biological world intimates a biologically based psychology that bears affinities with emotion research in cognitive neuroscience. [For Aristotle]the human body exhibits many levels of living organization[. . .]because of the causal activity of form.[. . .][F]orm is understood to be a metaphysical principle of life embedded in and expressed at various levels of organizational complexity in the world of biological entities."

[100]Maturana and Varela (1980), p. 7, emphases in the text.

[101]Ibid., p. 13, See also pp. 22–26 and 29–38 for the concept of representation and the model of thinking, natural language and memory.

[102]Ibid., pp. 42 and 45.

[103]Maturana and Varela (1980), p. 49: the living organization is "a circular organization which secures the production or maintenance of the *components*[. . .].[Accordingly]a living system is an homeostatic system [and] living systems are a subclass of the class of circular and homeostatic systems" (original emphasis: see also pp. 50–51).

[104]Maturana and Varela (1980), pp. 57–58. In particular "The ultimate truth on which a man bases his rational conduct is necessarily subordinated to his personal experience[. . .]."

however, self-organizing entities as living machines, or as autopoietic homeostatic machines (similar to Damasio's homeostasis).[105]

The rejection of teleonomy plainly differentiates Maturana-Varela's perspective from Aristotle's.[106] Nevertheless the proximity to the Aristotelian perspective is perceived, when the Authors point to the unavoidable embodiment of autopoiesis.[107] An autopoietic system is defined as a *unity* through its autopoietic organization, that is to say as a topological unity which encompasses interactions.[108] In other words: living systems embody living organizations. Similar to Aristotle the concept of unity is the sole necessary condition for the existence of autopoietic systems in any given domain.[109] At the same time the assumption of the plasticity of ontogeny, and the problem of maintaining unity within the process of reproduction, cause these authors to speak about second and third order autopoietic systems. This is once again in conformance with the Aristotelian idea of the intersection of levels of nature.[110] There are therefore some *epistemological* and *cognitive* issues, which ask for attention.

Similarly to the Aristotelian concept of organization, the authors remark that "the phenomena generated through interactions of autopoietic unities must be explained in the domain of interactions of the autopoietic unities through the relations that define that domain."[111] This epistemological perspective implies the possibility to compare human societies to biological systems: a complex horizon which, as the authors acknowledge, involves ethical and political implications.[112] On a cognitive level an autopoietic system can interact in a closed linguistic domain, for instance through recursive interactions with its linguistically generated states. This implies that there is a universal logic for *all* phenomenological domains linked to the relations between the unities underlying the domain.[113]

---

[105]It is based on a network of process of production: Ibid., pp. 78–79 and 82 (the concept of autopoiesis *"is necessary and sufficient to characterize the organization of living systems"*: emphases in the text).

[106]Ibid., pp. 85–87.

[107]Ibid., pp. 88 and ff.

[108]Ibid., p. 94 (different from autocatalytic processes). Furthermore Freeman (2000), especially pp. 7, 10, 15, 129, 154, and 211. The nuclear thesis: "a neural basis for goal-oriented actions[...]is common to both humans and other animals". Nevertheless "[h]uman intentionality is not optimally productive and effective until it has been acculturated through a long educational process, by which the capacity emerges for cooperative social action[and]knowledge."

[109]Maturana and Varela (1980), p. 96.

[110]Ibid., p. 111.

[111]Ibid., p. 117.

[112]Ibid., p. 118.

[113]Ibid., p. 123: "Autopoietic systems define the world in which they can exist in relation to their autopoiesis, and some interact recursively with this world through their descriptions, it being impossible for them to step out of this relative descriptive domain through descriptions. This demands an entirely new cognitive outlook: there is a space in which different phenomenologies can take place; one of these is autopoiesis: autopoiesis generates a phenomenological domain, this is cognition" (see also pp. 121–122).

Maturana-Valera's outlook can be compared to Edelman-Tononi's theory which is concerned with the question whether consciousness is a "philosophical paradox or a scientific object."[114] Concerning consciousness there is a particular problem between ongoing unity and endless variety.[115] The comparison between the concepts of consciousness and brain enables Edelman-Tononi to functionally conceive consciousness as an extraordinarily differentiated dimension based on information (i.e. reduction of uncertainty) and complexity which implies a neural complexity as a statistical measure.[116] The dynamic core hypothesis relies in this theory on the idea that a group of neurons directly determine the conscious experience as part of a highly differentiated cluster, characterized by interactions and high values of complexity. Unlike theories which depart from the idea of a mere correlative consciousness i.e. an (undetermined) group of neurons, this perspective explains some important points through the assumption of consciousness-specific neural processes[117]: the problem of *qualia* (i.e. the specific quality of subjective experience) and the relation between conscious and unconscious within an high-order consciousness (definition of self, language and nature of thinking).[118]

Edelman-Tononi's position of a qualified realism is problematically based on the idea of embodiment[119] and fluctuates between a mechanistic approach and a sort of finalistic (Aristotelian?) view. While high order consciousness is based on neural changes, the self (as a conscious subject) develops beyond the biological dimension i.e. in the environment of social and affective relationships, which leads via a continuous refinement of phenomenological experience to the emergence of superior capacities.[120] After all and despite the neuro-scientific advances these authors still cannot explain the complexity of thinking.[121] Therefore, Edelman-Tononi's outlook appears to be distant from Aristotle's position, in spite of the similarity of their questions and some ambiguities in their theory. Nevertheless Edelman-Tononi's perspective suggests some issues (high-order consciousness, the role of

---

[114]Edelman and Tononi (2000), p. 3.

[115]Edelman and Tononi (2000), p. 51 with an explicit reference to Aristotle's position.

[116]Ibid., p. 125.

[117]Ibid., pp. 139–140.

[118]Ibid., pp. 164–170 and ff.

[119]Ibid., p. 207: "[T]here is no judge in nature deciding categories except for natural selection[...], consciousness is a physical process embodied in each unique individual[...]this embodiment can never be substituted for by a mere description. Our embodiment is the ultimate source of our descriptions and provides the base of how we know – the proper concern of the branch of philosophy known as epistemology.[...][E]pistemology should be grounded in biology, specifically in neuroscience.[...][Hence three consequences]: being is prior to describing[...], selection is prior to logic[...]in the development of thought, doing is prior to understanding."

[120]Ibid., p. 193: "Three mysteries [ongoing awareness, the self, the construction of stories/plans/fictions] can be clarified if not completely dispelled by considering a combined picture of primary and higher-order consciousness."

[121]Ibid., p. 200.

social interactions, the complexity of thought) and especially the model of embodied mind,[122] which can be compared to the Aristotelian framework.

The authors here discussed start all from non-Aristotelian premises: the absence of teleonomy in Maturana's model and the pair information-complexity in Edelman's theory. Nevertheless they highlight the current plausibility of some Aristotelian arguments: the multiple levels of consciousness, the complex nature of cognitive processes, the self-organization in living entities and the crucial concept of embodied mind pertaining to the dynamic relation between the physical (material) dimension and the mind (or consciousness).

In conclusion. Is the Aristotelian position a useful (albeit problematic) post-Cartesian perspective within the current neuro-scientific and political-legal debate? The Aristotelian anthropology, including the model of emotion, represents a sort of *ante litteram* neuro-scientific (even though ontologically based) framework concerning human identity. It could lead to a new inclusive psychology placed between biology and philosophy, according to some scholars a "new alliance" among the different levels of nature,[123] and a new model of politics and law. In a *political-legal perspective* we grasp the differences but also the analogies between Aristotle's position and some current approaches which, despite the different horizons, take into account again some decisive political-legal issues.[124]

References

Annas, Julia. 1980. Aristotle on Pleasure and Goodness. In *Essays on Aristotle's Ethics*, Major Thinkers Series, ed. Amélie Rorty, vol. 2, 285–299. Berkeley: University of California Press.
———. 1992. Aristotle on Memory and the Self. In *Essays on Aristotle's De Anima*, ed. Martha Craven Nussbaum, 297–311. Oxford and New York: Oxford University Press.
Aristotle. 1984a. Metaphysics. In *The Complete Works of Aristotle: The Revised Oxford Translation*, ed. Jonathan Barnes and trans. W. D. Ross. Princeton, NJ: Princeton University Press.
———. 1984b. Meteorology. In *The Complete Works of Aristotle: The Revised Oxford Translation*, ed. Jonathan Barnes and trans. E. W. Webster. Princeton, NJ: Princeton University Press.
———. 1984c. Nicomachean Ethics. In *The Complete Works of Aristotle: The Revised Oxford Translation*, ed. Jonathan Barnes and trans. W. D. Ross and J. O. Urmson. Princeton, NJ: Princeton University Press.
———. 1984d. On Interpretation. In *The Complete Works of Aristotle: The Revised Oxford Translation*, ed. Jonathan Barnes and trans. J. L. Ackrill. Princeton, NJ: Princeton University Press.
———. 1984e. On Memory. In *The Complete Works of Aristotle: The Revised Oxford Translation*, ed. Jonathan Barnes and trans. J. I. Beare. Princeton, NJ: Princeton University Press.

---

[122]Lakoff and Johnson (2010), pp. 561–563: "Your body is not[...]a mere vessel for a disembodied mind. [...][C]ognitive science shows that our minds are not[...]disembodied[and] explains why we *think* that our minds are disembodied." (emphasis in the text: see also the entire Part IV).

[123]Prigogine and Stengers (2005), para. 8.

[124]Maturana and Varela (1980), p. XXIV.

————. 1984f. Sense and Sensibilia. In *The Complete Works of Aristotle: The Revised Oxford Translation*, ed. Jonathan Barnes and trans. J. I. Beare. Princeton, NJ: Princeton University Press.

————. 1984g. On Sleep. In *The Complete Works of Aristotle: The Revised Oxford Translation*, ed. Jonathan Barnes and trans. J. I. Beare. Princeton, NJ: Princeton University Press.

————. 1984h. On the Soul. In *The Complete Works of Aristotle: The Revised Oxford Translation*, ed. Jonathan Barnes and trans. J. A. Smith. Princeton, NJ: Princeton University Press.

————. 1984i. Physics. In *The Complete Works of Aristotle: The Revised Oxford Translation*, ed. Jonathan Barnes, trans. R. P. Hardie and R. K. Gaye. Princeton, NJ: Princeton University Press.

————. 1984j. Poetics. In *The Complete Works of Aristotle: The Revised Oxford Translation*, ed. Jonathan Barnes and trans. I. Bywater. Princeton, NJ: Princeton University Press.

————. 1984k. Politics. In *The Complete Works of Aristotle: The Revised Oxford Translation*, ed. by Jonathan Barnes and trans. B. Jowett. Princeton, NJ: Princeton University Press.

————. 1984l. Rhetoric. In *The Complete Works of Aristotle: The Revised Oxford Translation*, ed. Jonathan Barnes and trans. W. Rhys Roberts. Princeton, NJ: Princeton University Press.

Belfiore, Elizabeth S. 1992. *Tragic Pleasures: Aristotle on Plot and Emotion*. Princeton, NJ: Princeton University Press.

Berns, Laurence. 1984. Spiritedness in Ethics and Politics: A Study in Aristotelian Psychology. *Interpretation A Journal of Political Philosophy* 12 (2–3): 335–348.

Blundell, Mary W. 1992. Ēthos and Dianoia Reconsidered. In *Essays on Aristotle's Poetics*, ed. Amélie Rorty, 155–175. Princeton, NJ: Princeton University Press. Princeton Paperbacks.

Bombelli, Giovanni. 2013. *Occidente e "figure" comunitarie. I Un ordine inquieto: koinonia e comunità "radicata". Profili filosofico-giuridici*. Naples: Jovene.

————. 2015. Aristotle on Justice and Law: Koinonia, Justice and Politeia. In *Human Rights, Rule of Law and the Contemporary Social Challenges in Complex Societies (Proceedings of the XXVIth World Congress of Philosophy of Law and Social Philosophy)*, ed. Marcelo Galuppo, Mônica Sette Lopes, Karine Salgado, Lucas Gontijo, and Thomas Bustamante, 1080–1101. Belo Horizonte: Initia Via.

————. 2016. Emotion, Reason and Political-Legal Bond: Ideas from Greek Literature. Edited by Carla Faralli, Jeanne Gaaker, Marcelo Campos Galuppo, Maria Paola Mittica, and Ana Carolina De Faria Silvestre Rodrigues. *DOSSIER The Harmonies and Conflicts of Law, Reason and Emotion: A Literary-Legal Approach. Proceedings of the Special Workshop on "Law and Literature" Held at 27th IVR World Conference Washington, D.C. 27 July–1 August 2015* 9: 9–31.

Brito, José de Sousa e. 2018. Aristotle on Emotions in Ethics and in Criminal Justice. In *Aristotle on Emotions in Law and Politics*, ed. Liesbeth Huppes-Cluysenaer and Nuno M.M.S. Coelho. Dordrecht: Springer.

Burnyeat, Myles F. 1992. Is an Aristotelian Philosophy of Mind Still Credible? A Draft. In *Essays on Aristotle's De Anima*, ed. Martha Craven Nussbaum and Amélie Rorty, 15–26. Oxford and New York: Oxford University Press.

Campos, Joseph J., Rosemary G. Campos, and Karen C. Barrett. 1989. Emergent Themes in the Study of Emotional Development and Emotion Regulation. *Developmental Psychology* 25 (3): 394–402. https://doi.org/10.1037/0012-1649.25.3.394.

Charles, David. 2011. Desire in Action: Aristotle's Move. In *Moral Psychology and Human Action in Aristotle*, ed. Michael Pakaluk and Giles Pearson, 75–93. Oxford: Oxford University Press.

Code, Alan, and J. Moravcsik. 1992. Explaining Various Forms of Living. In *Essays on Aristotle's De Anima*, ed. Martha Craven Nussbaum and Amélie Rorty, 129–145. Oxford and New York: Oxford University Press.

Coelho, Nuno M.M.S. 2018. How Emotions Can Be Both an Impediment and a Base for Political Well-Being. In *Aristotle on Emotions in Law and Politics*, ed. Liesbeth Huppes-Cluysenaer and Nuno M.M.S. Coelho. Dordrecht: Springer.

Cohen, Marc S. 1992. Hylomorphism and Functionalism. In *Essays on Aristotle's De Anima*, ed. Martha Craven Nussbaum and Amélie Rorty, 57–73. Oxford and New York: Oxford University Press.

Cooper, John M. 1980. Aristotle on Friendship. In *Essays on Aristotle's Ethics*, Major Thinkers Series, ed. Amélie Rorty, vol. 2, 301–340. Berkeley: University of California Press.

Coseriu, Eugenio, and Gunter Narr. 1975. *Die Geschichte Der Sprachphilosophie von Der Antike Bis Zur Gegenwart: Eine Übersicht. 2., Überarb. Aufl. Vol. I. Tübinger Beiträge Zur Linguistik; 11*. Tübingen: s.n..

Crane, Tim. 2003. *The Mechanical Mind: A Philosophical Introduction to Minds, Machines, and Mental Representation*. 2nd ed. London and New York: Routledge.

Damasio, Antonio R. 1994. *Descartes' Error: Emotion, Reason, and the Human Brain*. New York: Putnam.

———. 2000. *The Feeling of What Happens: Body and Emotion in the Making of Consciousness*. London: Vintage.

———. 2003. *Looking for Spinoza: Joy, Sorrow, and the Feeling Brain*. 1st ed. Orlando, FL: Harcourt.

———. 2010. *Self Comes to Mind: Constructing the Conscious Brain*. 1st ed. New York: Pantheon Books.

Descartes, René. 1978. *The Philosophical Works of Descartes*. 2 Vols. Reprinted, Vol. I. Cambridge: Cambridge University Press.

———. 2006. *A Discourse on the Method of Correctly Conducting One's Reason and Seeking Truth in the Sciences*, Oxford World's Classics. Oxford and New York: Oxford University Press.

DeSousa, Ronald. 1997. *The Rationality of Emotion*. Vol. 1. Paperback ed., 5. Print. Bradford Books. Cambridge: MIT Press.

Edelman, Gerald M., and Giulio Tononi. 2000. *A Universe of Consciousness: How Matter Becomes Imagination*. 1st ed. New York: Basic Books.

Everson, Stephen. 1997. *Aristotle on Perception*. Oxford and New York: Clarendon Press and Oxford University Press.

Fodor, Jerry Alan. 1978. *The Language of Thought*, The Language and Thought Series. Hassocks: Harvester.

Fortenbaugh, William W. 2002. *Aristotle on Emotion: A Contribution to Philosophical Psychology, Rhetoric, Poetics, Politics, and Ethics*. 2nd ed. London: Duckworth.

Frede, Dorothea. 1992a. The Cognitive Role of Phantasia in Aristotle. In *Essays on Aristotle's De Anima*, ed. Martha Craven Nussbaum and Amélie Rorty, 279–295. Oxford and New York: Oxford University Press.

Frede, Michael. 1992b. On Aristotle's Conception of the Soul. In *Essays on Aristotle's De Anima*, ed. Martha Craven Nussbaum and Amélie Rorty, 93–107. Oxford and New York: Oxford University Press.

Freeland, Cynthia. 1992a. Aristotle on the Sense of Touch. In *Essays on Aristotle's De Anima*, ed. Martha Craven Nussbaum and Amélie Rorty, 226–248. Oxford and New York: Oxford University Press.

———. 1992b. Plot Imitates Action: Aesthetic Evaluation and Moral Realism in Aristotle's Poetics. In *Essays on Aristotle's Poetics*, ed. Amélie Rorty, 111–132. Princeton, NJ: Princeton University Press. Princeton Paperbacks.

Freeman, Walter J. 2000. *How Brains Make Up Their Minds*. London: Phoenix.

Fuselli, Stefano. 2018. Logoi Enuloi. Aristotle's Contribution to the Contemporary Debate on Emotions and Decision-Making. In *Aristotle on Emotions in Law and Politics*, ed. Liesbeth Huppes-Cluysenaer and Nuno M.M.S. Coelho. Dordrecht: Springer.

Gadamer, Hans-Georg. 1972. *Wahrheit Und Methode. Grundzüge E. Philos. Hermeneutik*. 3rd ed. Tübingen: Mohr.

Golden, Leon. 1992. Aristotle on the Pleasure of Comedy. In *Essays on Aristotle's Poetics*, ed. Amélie Rorty, 379–386. Princeton, NJ: Princeton University Press. Princeton Paperbacks.

Gregoric, Pavel. 2007. *Aristotle on the Common Sense*, Oxford Aristotle Studies. Oxford and New York: Oxford University Press.

Gross, Daniel M. 2006. *The Secret History of Emotion: From Aristotle's Rhetoric to Modern Brain Science*. Chicago: University of Chicago Press.

Halliwell, Stephen. 1992. Pleasure, Understanding, and Emotion in Aristotle's Poetics. In *Essays on Aristotle's Poetics*, ed. Amélie Rorty, 241–260. Princeton, NJ: Princeton University Press. Princeton Paperbacks.

Hamlyn, David M. 1959. Aristotle's Account of Aesthesis in the De Anima. *Classical Quarterly* 9 (1): 6–16.

Hamlyn, David W.W. 1968. Koine Aisthesis. Edited by Sherwood J. B. Sugden. *Monist* 52 (2): 195–209. https://doi.org/10.5840/monist196852238.

Hardie, William F.R. 1976. Concepts of Consciousness in Aristotle. *Mind* 85 (339): 388–411.

Irwin, Terence H. 1982. Aristotle's Concept of Signification. In *Language and Logos: Studies in Ancient Greek Philosophy Preented to G.E.L. Owen*, ed. Gwilym E.L. Owen, Malcom Schoefield, and Martha C. Nussbaum, 241–266. Cambridge and New York: Cambridge University Press.

Janko, Richard. 1992. From Catharsis to the Aristotelian Mean. In *Essays on Aristotle's Poetics*, ed. Amélie Rorty, 341–358. Princeton, NJ: Princeton University Press. Princeton Paperbacks.

Kafetsios, Konstantinos, and Erick LaRock. 2005. Cognition and Emotion: Aristotelian Affinities with Contemporary Emotion Research. *Theory & Psychology* 15 (5): 639–657. https://doi.org/10.1177/0959354305057267.

Keltner, Dacher, and James J. Gross. 1999. Functional Accounts of Emotions. *Cognition & Emotion* 13 (5): 467–480. https://doi.org/10.1080/026999399379140.

Koziak, Barbara. 2000. *Retrieving Political Emotion: Thumos, Aristotle, and Gender*. University Park: Pennsylvania State University Press.

Lakoff, George, and Mark Johnson. 2010. *Philosophy in the Flesh: The Embodied Mind and Its Challenge to Western Thought*. New York: Basic Books. Nachdr.

Lang, Helen S. 1980. On Memory: Aristotle's Corrections of Plato. *Journal of the History of Philosophy* 18 (4): 379–393. https://doi.org/10.1353/hph.2008.0252.

Lear, Jonathan. 1992. Katharsis. In *Essays on Aristotle's Poetics*, ed. Amélie Rorty, 315–340. Princeton, NJ: Princeton University Press. Princeton Paperbacks.

Leighton, Stephen R. 1982. Aristotle and the Emotions. *Phronesis* 27 (2): 144–174. https://doi.org/10.1163/156852882X00104.

Lloyd, Geoffrey E.R. 1992. Aspects of the Relationship between Aristotle's Psychology and His Zoology. In *Essays on Aristotle's De Anima*, ed. Martha Craven Nussbaum and Amélie Rorty, 147–167. Oxford and New York: Oxford University Press.

———. 1996. *Aristotelian Explorations*. Cambridge and New York: Cambridge University Press.

Lo Piparo, Franco. 2003. *Aristotele E Il Linguaggio: Cosa Fa Di Una Lingua Una Lingua*, Percorsi. Vol. 48. Rome: GLF editori Laterza.

Lord, Carnes. 1991. Aristotle's Anthropology. In *Essays on the Foundations of Aristotelian Political Science*, ed. David Kevin O'Connor and Richard Bodéüs, 49–73. Berkeley: University of California Press.

MacIntyre, Alasdair C. 1999. *Dependent Rational Animals: Why Human Beings Need the Virtues*. Chicago, IL: Open Court.

Matthews, Gareth B. 1992. De Anima 2. 2-4 and the Meaning of Life. In *Essays on Aristotle's De Anima*, ed. Martha Craven Nussbaum and Amélie Rorty, 185–193. Oxford and New York: Oxford University Press.

Maturana, Humberto R., and Francisco J. Varela. 1980. *Autopoiesis and Cognition: The Realization of the Living*, Boston Studies in the Philosophy of Science. Vol. 42. Dordrecht and Boston: D. Reidel.

Nehamas, Alexander. 1992. Pity and Fear in the Rhetoric and the Poetics. In *Essays on Aristotle's Poetics*, ed. Amélie Rorty, 291–314. Princeton, NJ: Princeton University Press. Princeton Paperbacks.

Newman, William L. 1950. *The Politics of Aristotle*. Oxford: Clarendon Press.

Nussbaum, Martha Craven. 1992. Tragedy and Self-Sufficiency: Plato and Aristotle on Fear and Pity. In *Essays on Aristotle's Poetics*, ed. Amélie Rorty, 261–290. Princeton, NJ: Princeton University Press. Princeton Paperbacks.

———. 2001. *The Fragility of Goodness: Luck and Ethics in Greek Tragedy and Philosophy*. Rev. ed. Cambridge and New York: Cambridge University Press.

Nussbaum, Martha Craven, and Hilary Putnam. 1992. Changing Aristotle's Mind. In *Essays on Aristotle's De Anima*, ed. Martha Craven Nussbaum and Amélie Rorty, 27–56. Oxford and New York: Oxford University Press.

Oksenberg Rorty, Amélie. 1992a. De Anima: Its Agenda and Its Recent Interpreters. In *Essays on Aristotle's De Anima*, ed. Martha Craven Nussbaum and Amélie Oksenberg, 7–13. Oxford and New York: Oxford University Press.

———. 1992b. The Psychology of Aristotelian Tragedy. In *Essays on Aristotle's Poetics*, ed. Amélie Rorty, 1–22. Princeton, NJ: Princeton University Press. Princeton Paperbacks.

Pearson, Giles. 2011. Aristotle and Scanlon on Desire and Motivation. In *Moral Psychology and Human Action in Aristotle*, ed. Michael Pakaluk and Giles Pearson, 95–117. Oxford: Oxford University Press.

Prigogine, Ilya, and Isabelle Stengers. 2005. *La nouvelle alliance: métamorphose de la science*. 2nd ed. Paris: Gallimard. Folio/Essais 26.

Putnam, Hilary. 1975. *Mind, Language, and Reality*, His Philosophical Papers. Vol. 2. Cambridge and New York: Cambridge University Press.

Rapp, Christof. 2018. Dispassionate Judges Encountering Hotheaded Aristotelians. In *Aristotle on Emotions in Law and Politics*, ed. Liesbeth Huppes-Cluysenaer and Nuno M.M.S. Coelho. Dordrecht: Springer.

Schiller, Jerome P. 1975. Aristotle and the Concept of Awareness in Sense Perception. *Journal of the History of Philosophy* 13 (3): 283–296. https://doi.org/10.1353/hph.2008.0442.

Schofield, Malcolm. 1992. Aristotle on the Imagination. In *Essays on Aristotle's De Anima*, ed. Martha Craven Nussbaum and Amélie Rorty, 249–277. Oxford and New York: Oxford University Press.

Segvic, Heda. 2011. Deliberation and Choice in Aristotle. In *Moral Psychology and Human Action in Aristotle*, ed. Michael Pakaluk and Giles Pearson, 159–185. Oxford: Oxford University Press.

Sidgwick, Henry. 1966. *The Methods of Ethics*. New York: Dover Publications.

Sokolon, Marlene K. 2006. *Political Emotions: Aristotle and the Symphony of Reason and Emotion*. DeKalb: Northern Illinois University Press.

Sommerstein, Alan H., Stephen Halliwell, Jeffrey Henderson, and Bernhard Zimmermann, eds. 1993. *Tragedy, Comedy, and the Polis: Papers from the Greek Drama Conference: Nottingham, 18-20 July 1990*, Le Rane/Collana Di Studi E Testi. Vol. 11. Bari: Levante Editori.

Sorabji, Richard. 1992. Intentionality and Physiological Processes: Aristotle's Theory of Sense-Perception. In *Essays on Aristotle's De Anima*, ed. Martha Craven Nussbaum and Amélie Rorty, 195–225. Oxford and New York: Oxford University Press.

———. 1993. *Animal Minds and Human Morals: The Origins of the Western Debate*. London: Duckworth.

———. 2006. *Aristotle on Memory*. 2nd ed. Chicago: University of Chicago Press.

Tracy, Theodore. 1982. The Soul/Boatman Analogy in Aristotle's De Anima. *Classical Philology* 77 (2): 97–112. https://doi.org/10.1086/366689.

Vernant, Jean P. 1992. Myth and Tragedy. In *Essays on Aristotle's Poetics*, ed. Amélie Rorty, 33–50. Princeton, NJ: Princeton University Press. Princeton Paperbacks.

Watson, Gerard. 1982. Φαντασία in Aristotle, De Anima 3. 3. *Classical Quarterly* 32 (1): 100–113.

Wedin, Michael V. 1988. *Mind and Imagination in Aristotle*. New Haven, CT and London: Yale University Press.

White, Kevin. 1985. The Meaning of Phantasia in Aristotle's De Anima, III, 3–8. *Dialogue* 24 (3): 483–505. https://doi.org/10.1017/S0012217300040348.

Whiting, Jennifer. 1992. Living Bodies. In *Essays on Aristotle's De Anima*, ed. Martha Craven Nussbaum and Amélie Oksenberg Rorty, 75–91. Oxford and New York: Oxford University Press.

Wilkes, Kathleen V. 1980. The Good Man and the Good for Man in Aristotle's Ethics. In *Essays on Aristotle's Ethics*, Major Thinkers Series, ed. Amélie Oksenberg Rorty, vol. 2, 341–357. Berkeley: University of California Press.

———. 1992. Psuchē versus the Mind. In *Essays on Aristotle's De Anima*, ed. Martha Craven Nussbaum and Amélie Rorty, 109–128. Oxford and New York: Oxford University Press.

Witt, Charlotte. 1992. Dialectic, Motion and Perception: De Anima Book I. In *Essays on Aristotle's De Anima*, ed. Martha Craven Nussbaum and Amélie Rorty, 169–183. Oxford and New York: Oxford University Press.

Woodruff, Paul. 1992. Aristotle on Mimēsis. In *Essays on Aristotle's Poetics*, ed. Amélie Rorty, 73–95. Princeton, NJ: Princeton University Press. Princeton Paperbacks.

Chapter 5
Logoi enuloi. Aristotle's Contribution to the Contemporary Debate on Emotions and Decision-Making

Stefano Fuselli

Abstract It seems natural to refer to Aristotle when reflecting on the role of emotion in decision-making in the legal field. Yet today study of the relationship between emotion and decision-making is carried out not only from a psychological, sociological, or rhetorical-argumentative perspective, but also via research on neural processes. Cognitive neuroscience has shown that emotions are components of the neural processes that underlie cognition and decision-making. This paper is an analysis of whether it is possible to trace a relationship between this new approach and Aristotle's approach to the emotions. In this perspective Damasio's theses are of main interest. By moving from Damasio's antidualistic programme to Aristotle's *De anima*—the work which lies closest to the domain of contemporary neuroscience—the paper also aims to show whether the latter can still provide useful tools for dealing with issues arising from the neuroscientific approach.

5.1 Introduction

In the last decades, the scientific interest for emotions and their role in affecting our cognitive and practical processes has been considerably increasing[1] and special attention has been directed to their role in moral judgment or to their social function.[2] In the legal field, studies have been published concerning, e.g., their impact on the jury decision-making, or on the social alarm caused by crimes, or on the perception of just and deserved punishment, or about their role in aggressive or crime-oriented personalities.[3]

---

[1]Lerner et al. (2015).

[2]See e.g. Nussbaum (2001), Haidt (2001), Prinz (2006), and Hauser (2006).

[3]See e.g. Bornstein and Wiener (2006). Therefore, it is not surprising that in the past decade "law and emotion" has been an "emerging field"—Maroney (2006)—and nowadays it has become the

S. Fuselli (✉)
Faculty of Law, University of Padua, Padua, Italy
e-mail: stefano.fuselli@unipd.it

© Springer International Publishing AG 2018
L. Huppes-Cluysenaer, N.M.M.S. Coelho (eds.), *Aristotle on Emotions in Law and Politics*, Law and Philosophy Library 121, DOI 10.1007/978-3-319-66703-4_5

Even if the scientific interest for the topic has recently developed considerably, the discussion itself about the role of emotions in decision-making processes, including the legal and the judicial, is far from being something new. In fact, Aristotle himself has offered in his *Rhetoric* a wide treatment of emotions as "modes of persuasion" (*pisteis*) (*Rhet.* 1356a2).[4] However, what is undoubtedly new is that the phenomenological basis of the discussion has changed, under the influence of the cognitive neuroscience and its research tools, as well as of its categories. Nowadays, the study of emotions is carried out not only from a psychological point of view, but also through the research on neural processes.[5]

A considerable contribution to the discussion has been given at first by the development of neuroimaging tools and techniques. Through these means, scholars have tried to evaluate to what extent brain activity is affected by emotion-eliciting stimuli.[6] For example, some scholars have argued that neuroimaging has brought evidence to support the connection between emotional stimulus and increased punitiveness in jurors.[7] Whilst, the idea that emotions influence or even cloud the sharpness of critical reasoning is a traditional view, what is certainly innovative in this tradition of studies is the method of the inquiry, which is done by analysing the brain activity.

On the other side, some theories outlined by neuroscientists seem to be wide and more innovative than the results of empirical research. In fact, scholars like LeDoux, Panksepp, Freeman, Gazzaniga[8] have argued that emotions are components of the neural processes on which cognition and decision-making are based. That is, not only are not emotions a handicap for good decision-making, but they are also necessary in performing a situation-appropriate judgment.

This approach to emotions is also interesting from another point of view. It keeps up with the anti-dualistic and anti-Cartesian program developed by neuroscience.[9] That is, emotions would give one of the clearest evidences for the psychophysical unity of the human being whose mind is an embodied one.

Among the neuroscientists dealing with emotions, Antonio Damasio is probably the scholar who more than anyone else has systematically outlined a theoretical frame where emotions have a central place, insofar he makes emotions his guiding thread in exploring both the cognitive and the decision-making processes and the processes through which one's self and consciousness are built.

---

theme of an international congress of philosophy of law. For further details on law and emotions scholarship see in this volume Maroney (2018).

[4]Rhetoric, edition used: *The Complete Works of Aristotle: The Revised Oxford Translation*, edited by Jonathan Barnes.

   I agree with the grounding idea of the approach to emotions in Aristotle's *Rhetoric* provided in this volume by Cohen de Lara (2018).

[5]Critical to this approach, Bennett and Hacker (2003), pp. 199–223.

[6]See Greene's classical discussion (Greene et al. 2001). For a critical evaluation of Greene's approach see e.g. Berker (2009) and Pardo and Patterson (2013).

[7]Salerno and Bottoms (2009).

[8]LeDoux (1996), Panksepp (1998), Freeman (2000), and Gazzaniga (2005).

[9]For a criticism of the neuroscientific approach to mind-body problem see Bennett and Hacker (2003).

In general, Damasio's contribution appears to be under many aspects innovative and fruitful. However, the most particular aspect is the role emotions are supposed to have for the good functioning of reason. One of the most intriguing—but also problematic—aspects of Damasio's approach is given by the entanglement of many levels. He always provides a wide perspective on his empirical findings, which deals with anthropological and philosophical issues. From this point of view, e.g., the possible relationships between neurobiology and legal field are outlined not only by reference to decision-making, but also to the development of justice systems.[10]

In this paper, I will firstly analyse Damasio's theory. My purpose is not to criticise his methodological or epistemological premises,[11] but to highlight some internal problems of his claims. I intend to show that the questions arising from his approach need a different theoretical level of inquiry. Moving from this point on, I will turn to Aristotle's approach to emotions in *De anima*—the work that lies the closest to the domains of contemporary neuroscience—in order to show which could be its contribution to the contemporary debate.[12] My aim is not to provide a comprehensive reconstruction of Aristotle's theory of emotion,[13] but rather to use some Aristotelian concepts concerning emotional phenomena as reading keys for the issues on the table.

According to Aristotle, psychical phenomena, like perception, imagination, desire, emotion, thinking, are affections of the soul (*pathe tes psuches*) (*DA* 403a3). The affections of the soul are characterised as enmattered forms (*logoi enuloi*) (*DA* 403a25),[14] intelligible structures inseparable from the matter which they are forms of, and therefore concrete signs of the psychophysical unity of the living-being. It is my view that the idea of enmattered forms can offer the different level of inquiry mentioned above in order to understand the role of emotions in decision-making processes.

Putting in relationship two perspectives which are so far from each other in time and culture could raise some doubts about methodological legitimacy of this approach. However, Damasio himself provides the grounds for this kind of

---

[10]Damasio (2010), p. 292. For possible outcomes of Damasio's theory for decision-making in the legal field see f.i. Bennett and Broe (2007); Pettys (2007); Di Giovine (2009), pp. 130–138; Fuselli (2014), pp. 81–126.

[11]For an overview of the criticism of Damasio's theory, see Mezzalira (2011).

[12]For possible relationships between Aristotle and other neuroscientists, see in this volume Bombelli (2018), sec. 5. However, in my opinion the notion of autopoiesis used by some modern (neuro)biologists lacks the specific trait of the Aristotelian idea of the living being, that is the notion of soul as its actuality (entelecheia).

[13]As it has been pointed out, in the *Corpus Aristotelicum* there is no independent tractation of emotions, Rapp (2002), p. 545.

[14]English translations of "*logoi*" in this context are not uniform; e.g., Barnes: "enmattered accounts" (Aristotle 1984); Lawson-Tancred: "formulae in matter" (Aristotle 1986); Smith: "enmattered formulable essence" (Aristotle 1931). For translations in other languages, see, e.g. Jannone-Barbotin: "des formes engagées dans la matière" (Aristote 1966); Theiler: "materiegebundene Begriffe" (Aristoteles 1994); Movia: "forme contenute nella materia" (Aristotele 2001); Rapp: "in der Materie befindliche Begriffe" (2002, p. 551). By using "forms", I follow the French translation provided by Jannone-Barbotin and the Italian by Movia.

approach. In fact, he suggests that the ancient Greeks referred to what the neurologists today call *mind* using the word *psuché*,[15] usually translated as *soul*. The *soul* is precisely the object of Aristotle's inquiry in *De Anima*. The extent to which these two different perspectives can have a dialogue needs to be examined. Emotions are a good means of testing it out.

5.2   Organism as Integrated Unity

To offer a comprehensive account of Damasio's theory of emotion would require a longer tractation than the length of this paper allows for, and it is not necessary for the issue at stake here. The best way to proceed, then, is to have a guiding thread. This guiding thread is provided by Damasio himself whose explicit premise is the idea that organism is an integrated unity which interacts with the environment as a whole, an "ensemble".[16] According to Damasio, every kind of dualism and separation—between mind and brain and between mind and body—is an abstraction which hinders the understanding of brain and mind processes.[17]

In this integrated unity, the body has a central role, because the surviving of the organism is the main goal of both brain and mind. The biological function of the brain is to manage all the necessary processes, and therefore it is "imbued" from the start of life with the required "knowledge".[18] The activity of neural circuits from which the mind arises is primarily oriented to provide basic representations of the states of the organism and to monitor the states of organism in action.[19]

Therefore, on the one hand, the mind depends on the brain, namely on the representations of the body which happen in the brain.[20] In fact, the first and the most important of the mind activities is transforming the neural maps of the bodily modifications into mental images which allow to manipulate and integrate more easily the information coming from the neural maps.[21] However, on the other hand, if the main goal is the survival and the wellness of the organism, then the mind exists both *because* there is a body, which provides the topics for the mind, and *for* the body, insofar the mind is acting for its living.[22] This is the reason why, in Damasio's view, the mind is properly "embodied" and not just "embrained".[23]

---

[15]Damasio (1999), p. 30. On the relationship between our use of "mind" and Aristotle's use of "soul" see Caston (2006), p. 317.

[16]Damasio (2005), p. xx.

[17]"(…) the mind exists in and for an integrated organism", Ibid. On this topic see Johnson (2006).

[18]Damasio (2003), p. 205.

[19]Damasio (2005), p. 226.

[20]Damasio (2003), p. 192.

[21]Ibid., pp. 207–208.

[22]"The mind had to be first about the body, or it could not have been", Damasio (2005), p. xx.

[23]Ibid., p. 118.

The notion of organism as integrated unity should also explain the arising of consciousness. Consciousness provides the possibility of connecting the automated life regulation with the "processing of images".[24] Therefore, integration is stronger in a conscious organism like ours.

5.3   Emotion and Feeling

In analysing emotion and feeling, Damasio draws a distinction between them.[25] This distinction is sometimes more stressed—it is said to be an ontological one, concerning their essence[26]—sometimes less—it is said to be introduced for methodological reasons.[27] However, the issue at stake is that emotion and feeling are primarily body-centred like all other brain and mental events. Their basic common goal is the survival (and the wellness) of the organism as integrated unity.

From a strictly physiological point of view, *emotion* does not appear to be very different from other organic processes. It can be understood as one of those automated unconscious biological dispositions necessary to the organism's survival.[28] At its basic level, emotion is part of the homeostatic regulation, this is to say of those physiological reactions and processes which avoid the loss of the integrity of the organism. Its biological function is twofold: producing a specific reaction to a given situation (e.g. flight in case of danger) and regulating the internal states which prepare for the specific reaction.[29]

Thus, in its *"essence"* emotion is nothing but "the collection of changes in body state that are induced in myriad organs by nerve cell terminals"[30] activated by certain stimuli. Therefore, emotion reflects a body state in stereotyped patterns of response like other biological dispositions[31] and the emotive state does not need to be conscious. The six universal or primary[32] or innate[33] emotions are common not only to all human beings, but also to many animals. In all organisms where they can be found, they appear in typical attitudes involving body posture, or face musculature, or behaviour. This is the reason why it is characteristic for emotions to be publicly

---

[24]Damasio (1999), p. 24.

[25]For a discussion see Panksepp (2003). For an overview of Damasio's classifications see Barile (2013).

[26]Damasio (2010), p. 109.

[27]Damasio (1999), p. 37.

[28]Damasio (2005), pp. 114–118.

[29]Damasio (1999), pp. 53–54.

[30]Damasio (2005), p. 139.

[31]Damasio (1999), p. 55, Table 2.1. For a critical discussion see Lenzen (2004).

[32]They are "happiness, sadness, fear, anger, surprise, or disgust", Damasio (1999), p. 50.

[33]Damasio (2005), p. 133.

observable and perceivable by an external observer,[34] regardless of their type: background emotions,[35] primary emotions or even social or secondary emotions.[36]

However, although emotions are similar to other biological devices, they can extend their effects to a higher level. In fact, because they connect external stimuli to the homeostatic internal values, they are inseparable from the idea of avoiding and pursuing something which could be dangerous or favourable. Moreover, in their social function they are also inseparable not only "from the idea of reward or punishment" but also "of good and evil".[37] From this point of view, emotions seem to be in the middle of two different kinds of devices, "sandwiched between the basic survival kit (. . .) and the devices of high reason."[38]

According to Damasio, *feeling* stands on another level when compared to emotional reaction. On the one hand, it is based on emotion. If emotion is a collection of changes in body state, feeling an emotion means to experience it as the effect of an emotion-inducting event.[39] Therefore, the term feeling "should be reserved for the private, mental experience of an emotion".[40] On the other hand, feeling is involved in the structure of self and consciousness. This is the case of "background feelings"[41]—like fatigue, wellness, tension—which reflect the general body state as it is perceived by the organism.[42] It is also the case of "*primordial feeling*", which is the primitive feeling of existing, of being alive.[43]

Like emotions, feelings have a specific biological function. They force the mind to pay attention to the body state, they "let us *mind the body*"[44] and in so doing they help the organism to find a solution to the problem which induced the automatic emotional response.[45] Therefore, they have an evident cognitive function, they are "*as cognitive as any other perceptual image*",[46] and have a central role in decision-making.

The clearest example of their influence is given by what Damasio calls the *somatic marker*. In situations which call for a choice, it could happen that before analysing the pros and cons of the different options, the image of the possible bad outcome of one option comes to mind like a lightning and that causes an unpleasant gut feeling. This is a *somatic* or bodily state, which *marks* this mental image and assists us in our decision. In fact, when we are called for a choice, images of

---

[34]Damasio (1999), p. 42.

[35]Ibid., p. 52.

[36]Damasio (2005), p. 134.

[37]Damasio (1999), p. 55.

[38]Ibid., p. 54.

[39]Ibid., p. 282.

[40]Ibid., p. 42.

[41]Ibid., p. 286.

[42]Damasio (2005), p. 151.

[43]Damasio (2010), p. 185.

[44]Damasio (2005), p. 159.

[45]Damasio (1999), p. 284.

[46]Damasio (2005), p. 159.

"myriad" options and possible outcomes "are activated".[47] Therefore, deciding needs the mechanisms of *basic attention*, and of *basic working memory*, and the complex of *basic values* for the homeostatic regulation.[48] The somatic marker activates basic attention and basic memory by marking the images of the different options according to those basic values. Acting as a sort of "biasing device",[49] the somatic marker forces our attention to focus on the possible bad (or good) outcome acting like an automated warning signal. It reduces the number of (good or bad) interesting options, assisting us in our deliberative process. Therefore, the decision-making is faster, sharper and more efficient.

Feeling can be not only about emotion, but also about feeling itself: feeling feelings, feeling that we are feeling has to do with self and consciousness.[50] Having this kind of conscious feeling extends the possibilities of the organism by enabling it to react in flexible and innovative ways to the stimuli.[51] In particular, occurring in an autobiographical setting, conscious feelings enlighten the temporal dimensions—the past, the now and the anticipated future—involved in decision-making processes.[52]

Comprehensively, emotion and feeling are integrated in the "loop of reason",[53] that is to say they are "indispensable for rationality".[54] On the one hand, they are necessary in decision-making processes. Patients with neurological damages which make difficult this integration offer concrete evidence of the problems caused by the separation of affects and reason, in particular for the personal and social dimension of reasoning.[55] On the other hand, they are structurally involved in the construction of a conscious mind, which can act creatively and go beyond the pure biological dimension.[56]

5.4 The "Crown Jewel"

As mentioned above, Damasio himself seems to ground the distinction between emotion and feeling on two different kinds of reasons. On the one hand, they are *methodological* reasons, that is "the purpose of investigating these phenomena".[57]

---

[47]Ibid., p. 196.

[48]Ibid., p. 197.

[49]Ibid., p. 174. For an overview of the reactions to this hypothesis, see Dunn et al. (2006). For a more detailed discussion, see also Colombetti (2008).

[50]Damasio (1999), p. 280.

[51]Damasio (2003), p. 177.

[52]Ibid., p. 178.

[53]Damasio (2005), p. xi.

[54]Ibid., p. xvii.

[55]Ibid., p. 10.

[56]Damasio (2010), p. 287.

[57]Damasio (1999), p. 37.

However, state of emotion, state of feeling and state of feeling made conscious are comprehensively *affective phenomena* and represent "three stages of processing along a continuum".[58] On the other hand, the distinction seems to be *ontological* due to their *essence*. In his latest book, emotions are said to be "complex, largely automated programs of *actions*", whereas feelings "composite *perceptions* of what happens in our body and mind when we are emoting".[59] This ambiguity in the meaning of the distinction can be seen as a clue that something is problematic in Damasio's theory of affects. To shed light onto this problematic aspect, it is helpful to consider some features of emotion and feeling emerging from of his analysis.

One first relevant aspect that has to be mentioned concerns the relationship between emotion and the other biological devices. Although the body emotional states are stereotyped, they are by far more various than the drives or the startle responses. Damasio argues that it is "not accurate" to say that regulatory reactions like emotions proper are inevitably stereotyped.[60] On the one hand, their taxonomy evidences that their devices become increasingly sharper and more specific[61]; on the other hand, they are shaped by experience.[62]

Over time, automated reactions occurring as a result of innate emotions decrease; at the same time, and correspondingly, social emotions and emotions induced by punishment and reward increase. Moreover, as human beings we categorise the situations and connect the conceptual categories we form mentally with the neurological apparatus we use to trigger emotions.[63]

This variety of forms seems to be connected in a certain way with a sort of generalising reactivity so that "certain *sorts* of objects or events tend to be system-atically linked to a certain *kind* of emotions more than to others".[64] On the one hand, emotions are inducted by some *kinds* of images[65]; on the other hand, they act for the appropriate direction of attention by providing "an automated signal" concerning the organism's past experience.[66] Therefore, the 'stiffness' which causes emotions to be stereotyped is somehow counterbalanced by their typologising the meaning of every single event, its relevance for the organism, thus inducing the adequate behaviour. Although emotional responses are stereo-typed, in association with feelings they enable the organism to take some distance from the 'here and now' anticipating the future consequences of actions and remembering the past outcomes.[67]

---

[58]Ibid.

[59]Damasio (2010), p. 109.

[60]Damasio (2003), p. 52.

[61]Damasio (1999), p. 342.

[62]Ibid., p. 57.

[63]Damasio (2003), p. 146.

[64]Damasio (1999), p. 56. My emphasis.

[65]Ibid., p. 69.

[66]Ibid., p. 143.

[67]Damasio (2003), p. 147.

The second relevant aspect is the pervasiveness of emotional phenomena. Emotion is completely pervading and affecting the integrated unity of the organism in everyday experience.[68] This does not mean that emotion is only a consequence of such a unity, but that it acts on the organism as an indivisible whole, as an *in-dividuum*. On the one hand, the emotional process entails "a global change in the state of the organism"[69]; on the other hand, "emotional responses target *both* body proper and brain".[70]

The third relevant aspect is that the affective phenomena—i.e. emotion and feeling—seem to provide a globalising and mediating function. At a more general level, the systems concerned with emotion and feeling, attention and working memory "constitute the source for the energy of both external action (movement) and the internal action (thought animation, reasoning)".[71] But even if one considers the more detailed level of brain structures and their functioning, emotions and feelings "provide the bridge between rational and non-rational processes, between cortical and subcortical structures".[72]

Thus comprehensively, emotion is richer than all other automated devices and is not limited to an impulsive dimension like drives and reacting to pain and pleasure. Although emotional responses are stereotyped, they enable the organism to take some distance from the 'here and now'. Instead of being engaged by a particular drive, the organism finds in emotion a means for the appraisal of the environment and for providing an adequate adaptive reaction.[73] Therefore emotions are "the crown jewel of automated life regulation",[74] although feelings alone are to be found at top of the homeostatic regulation.

5.5 The Need of Forms: From Damasio to Aristotle

As shown above, Damasio ascribes emotions to actions, feelings to perceptions. This could be considered an ontological distinction grounded on their essence. However, he argues that those actions that are emotions are complemented "by a *cognitive* program that includes certain ideas and modes of cognition".[75] The point in question is that insofar as emotions are "actions accompanied by ideas and certain modes of thinking"[76] complemented by a cognitive program, they are not only motions carried out in our body, but they have already got in themselves the

---

[68]The term used is "pervasiveness", Damasio (1999), p. 58.

[69]Ibid., p. 67.

[70]Ibid., p. 288.

[71]Damasio (2005), p. 71.

[72]Ibid., p. 128.

[73]Damasio (2003), p. 54.

[74]Ibid., p. 34.

[75]Damasio (2010), p. 109.

[76]Ibid., p. 110.

conditions for the grafting of cognitive elements. Perhaps one may argue that the action side in emotions is widely predominant. Yet, this is not the issue at stake here. The central concern here is that such actions are emotions just *because of* their intrinsic referring to cognitive aspects by which they are complemented. If—on another level—reason can control even only modestly what Damasio calls "the pervasive tyranny of emotion",[77] there is in emotion itself something which reason can (or must) clasp.

Even if we consider the distinction between emotion and feeling as a methodological one, the problem seems to persist. As a stage along the continuum of affects, emotion contributes to the mediative activity between rational and non-rational processes, between body and mind; therefore, it is itself part of that unitary source of energy for external and internal actions. Therefore, defining emotion as a "combination"[78] or a "*collection*"[79] of changes or processes seems to provide a far too narrow perspective, because emotion is *not only* a product of changes, *but* it is *also* the necessary condition for these changes to be organised and shaped in some way. The same problem appears from another perspective too. Emotions are said to be the product of two possible kinds of triggers: bodily sensations and mental images.[80] This is the point in question. If both circumstances, the bodily and the mental, can induce the same phenomenon (i.e. occurring of emotion) a disposition or a readiness is necessary which is in itself and by itself *already* receptive (even if only potentially) to the two different kinds of triggering. That means that emotion needs to have already in itself the conditions for unifying both the bodily and the mental aspects, the non-rational and rational aspects.

These difficulties could be seen as clues that Damasio's aim to overcome the Cartesian dualism has not been really achieved. Reversing the *cogito ergo sum* into "We are and then we think, and we think only inasmuch as we are"[81] is not the same as walking on new ground. If the relationship between being and thinking is a causal one, then it is unfair to reproach Descartes "for having persuaded biologists to adopt, to this day, clockwork mechanics as a model for life processes".[82] In fact, using the working hypothesis that "mental events are equivalent to certain kinds of brain events"[83] foreshadows a reductionist outcome which preserves the grounding hypothesis of Descartes' dualism, according to which the only way of seeing the mind as something other than the body (i.e. the brain) is viewing it as a different and opposite substance.[84] What Damasio tends to underestimate is that living beings

---

[77]Damasio (1999), p. 58.

[78]Damasio (2005), p. 139.

[79]Ibid., p. 145. My emphasis.

[80]Damasio (1999), p. 56.

[81]Damasio (2005), p. 248.

[82]Ibid.

[83]Damasio (2010), p. 16.

[84]On this topic, see Chiereghin (2004), pp. 189–196. For different critical perspectives about Damasio's Cartesianism see, f.i., Kirkebøen (2001) and Teixeira (2002).

have an organising principle which is not added to the matter but is intrinsic to it, that is an intelligible form in themselves.

Although Damasio's analysis is rich, and his overviews and perspectives are powerful and innovative, they seem to require another level of inquiry. From this point of view, the issues arising from his theoretical frame make fruitful the comparison with the different perspective provided by Aristotle's theory of affections of the soul (*pathe tes psuches*). According to Aristotle, affections like anger or courage—just as appetite or sensation—have a double character, because it seems not to be "the case in which the soul can act or be acted upon without involving the body" (*DA* 403a6–7).[85] Therefore they can be defined in different ways: a physicist (*phusikos*) would describe their material condition, the dialectician (*dialektikos*) the "form and essence" (*DA* 403b1–2).[86]

In my opinion, what is lacking in the theory of emotions provided by the '*physicist*' Damasio is precisely the attention to what Aristotle calls form and essence, that is an organising and determining principle, which offers the conditions of possibility of the thing it is the form of, and the conditions for approaching it. Looking at the *De anima* could offer an important contribution to focusing on the character of *source of energy* that Damasio ascribes to emotion, and on the kind of activity that goes on in emotion.

5.6 Emotions as *logoi enuloi*

As it is well known, the grounding idea of Aristotle's inquiry about the soul is that the soul is not separable from the body (*DA* 413a4). The soul is the form or the essence of a living body. That is, it is what distinguishes a living body from any other kind of body and it is the organising principle of that array of capacities and activities which are specific of a living body (*DA* 412a27–412b9).

This is the reason why the affections of the soul—like appetite, imagination, sensation, perception[87]—are associated with the body, because every state of the soul is a concurrent state of the body (*DA* 403a6–7). However, this is also the reason why affections of the soul are enmattered forms (*logoi enuloi*) (*DA* 403a25)[88]; that

---

[85]*De Anima* (On the soul), edition used: *The Complete Works of Aristotle: The Revised Oxford Translation*, edited by Jonathan Barnes.

[86]I am following here the Italian translation provided by Movia: "la forma e l'essenza", Aristotele (2001), p. 61.

[87]As it is well known, the word *pathe* is not specific for emotions only, but it can be used for all that can happen to a subject, all that someone can be affected by, Rapp (2008), p. 48. On the meaning of *pathe* in *De Anima*, see Oksenberg Rorty (1992), Leighton (1996), and Polansky (2007).

[88]See above note 14. For a different reading, see Barnes (1979), p. 36. In this volume see also Brito (2018). The fact that the expression *logoi enuloi* is not used elsewhere by Aristotle seems to me to highlight the peculiarity of the *pathe* and the way they are a unity of form and matter. This is the reason why I do not agree on this point with de Sousa e Brito.

is, they are not forms which are added to the matter, but forms which have their own collocation in matter and are intrinsic (*en*) to the matter (*hule*).[89] Therefore, explaining them requires both the physicist and the dialectician.

Emotions like anger, gentleness, fear, pity, courage, joy, love or hatred are types of the above mentioned affections (*DA* 403a16–19).[90] Hence, emotions are enmattered forms inasmuch as they are affections of the soul.

One first clear meaning of this characterisation is that emotions have both bodily and cognitive aspects.[91] So, e.g., anger is not only a body state alteration, like the boiling of the blood around the heart, but also the idea of having been unjustly injured and the desire of revenge (*DA* 403a30–403b1). This is also the reason why Aristotle says that emotions are followed by pain and pleasure (*EN*[92] 1105b21–23; *Rhet.* 1378a20–21)[93] and that emotions can arise also by thinking or imagining something pleasant or fearful (*MA*[94] 701b18–22). Yet the implication of this characterisation can be also explored taking into account Aristotle's general explanation for generating movement and action in animals which are capable of locomotion, like human beings.

Appetite (*orexis*) plays the main role in causing movement. In its elementary shape, the movement of a living being is always for avoiding or pursuing something, which appears unpleasant or pleasant (*DA* 432b28–29). Therefore, appetite requires the faculty of feeling and distinguishing between pleasure and pain.

The organism acquires this kind of information through sensation, the sensitive faculty, because each sense can distinguish between pleasure and pain (*DA* 414b4–6). In general,

> To feel pleasure or pain is to act with the sensitive mean towards what is good or bad as such. (*DA* 431a10–11, trans. J. A. Smith)

Thus, something becomes pursuable as good or avoidable as bad for appetite as a consequence of a sensation.

However, actual sensation needs a sensible object being here and now (*DA* 417b25–26). Therefore, desire—which acts according to pleasure or pain—is only

> influenced by what is just at hand (*DA* 433b8–10, trans. J. A. Smith)

---

[89]On this kind of relationship see Aubenque (1957).

[90]According to Nussbaum and Putnam (1992), p. 44, in those passages (*DA* 403a5–19), "Aristotle is actually treating emotion as a type of perception, a selective cognitive awareness of an object or objects in the world".

[91]Oksenberg Rorty (1992), p. 8. About the reasons why that twofold character of emotions cannot be understood as the product or result of two different components, see Rapp (2008), p. 52.

[92]Nicomachean Ethics, edition used: *The Complete Works of Aristotle: The Revised Oxford Translation*, edited by Jonathan Barnes.

[93]With the well known exception of hate (*Rhet.*, 1382a13). This could be seen as a clue that the field of emotion is wider than the field of the (bodily) pain-pleasure. On the different possibilities to understand the relationship between emotion and pleasure or pain sensation, see Rapp (2008), p. 49.

[94]Movement of Animals, edition used: *The Complete Works of Aristotle: The Revised Oxford Translation*, edited by Jonathan Barnes.

And is incapable of projecting into the future what here and now immediately appears good or bad as a consequence of an actual sensation.

The faculty by means of which the subject calculates and deliberates for the future by reference of what is present is the faculty of thinking. By contrast with the immediate impulsivity of appetite, the faculty of thinking is what advises us to resist to the present drive looking at the future (*DA* 433b7–8). The rational faculty is able to do it because images in thinking soul take the place of direct sensations (*DA* 431a14–15). Hence, the subject can act even only on the ground of images (e.g. of something good in the future) as if it actually had a sense-perception (*DA* 431b6–8).

However, this kind of independence of intellect from the immediacy of sensations, gained by replacing them with images, seems to have a cost. Images are like sense-perceptions, but they are "somehow non-committing".[95] When

> we merely imagine we remain as unaffected as persons who are looking at a painting of some dreadful or encouraging scene. (*DA* 427b23–24, trans. J. A. Smith)

It is my view that this is the crucial point which allows to grasp the nature of emotions and affects as enmatterd forms. If emotions are followed by pain and pleasure, we can assume that they are able to qualify the images according to the dyad pain and pleasure to such an extent that the thinking faculty can use those images for outlining action choices which are attractive, visible, appreciable or significant for appetite. On the one hand, by providing 'reasons' for desires and drives, emotions prepare them for being evaluated and managed by the practical intellect; on the other hand, they give 'flesh' and 'matter'—that is the concrete attractiveness or repulsiveness of what is pleasant or painful—to the deliberations of the thinking soul.

This can be indirectly confirmed by what Aristotle says about incontinence, distinguishing the one caused by anger (*thumos*) from the one caused by desire (*epithumia*). Whereas desire obeys only pleasure and pain, "anger seems to listen to reason (*logos*) to some extent", but mishearing it

> as do hasty servants who run out before they have heard the whole of what one says, and then muddle the order; (*EN* 1149a24–29, trans. W. D. Ross/J. O. Urmson)

Or like a dog barking before knowing who is knocking at the door. So, if on the one side, reason (*logos*) or imagination (*phantasia*) inform us that we have been insulted, on the other side, anger moves

---

[95]Frede (1992), p. 282. The reason for it could perhaps be that imagination (*phantasia*) itself "is presentational or representational rather than discriminating or evaluative", Polansky (2007), p. 433. Something like that could also be seen as the reason why humans can act according to imagination (*phantasia*) when their mind is eclipsed by passions. On the other hand, imagination (*phantasia*) is said to have a central role in the movement of animals (*MA* 700b17–18), inasmuch it can arouse the appetite (*orexis*) (*MA* 701a4–6). In discussing the issue, Nussbaum (1978), p. 261, suggests that imagination "is the animal's awareness of some object or state of affairs, which may well prove to be an object of desire". We can perhaps comprehensively say, that images move, insofar they are emotionally qualified or acting (see *MA* 701b16–702a5). As Schofield (2011), p. 131, points out "the psychological aspect of the psychophysical reaction prompted by *phantasia* and thinking – representing 'the pleasant or fearful' as they do in the cases Aristotle imagines – is emotion, something notable by its absence in the discussion so far, and particularly in the practical syllogism passage."

reasoning as it were that anything like this must be fought against. (*EN* 1149a33–34, trans. W. D. Ross/J. O. Urmson)

Thus, in the general frame of animals' biological functions, emotions and affects have a key role in acting, especially for those animals which, like human beings, have

a sense of time. (*DA* 433b7, J. A. Smith)

They shape the communication between the articulated mediated temporality of intellect and the punctual here-and-now immediacy of appetite.

Affects make it possible to extend to the whole time spectrum the discrimination between pleasure and pain; to activate it even when there are no more sensations (like in remembering the past); or to postpone it in resisting to a present sensation, because of the prevision of something good or bad in the future; or to reawaken it in an apparently neutral present situation. Affects and emotions allow appetite to be managed in the whole time spectrum, thus connecting it with images and the calculating practical intellect. At the same time, they give a punctual dimension—the here and now of pleasure and pain sensations—to the images and to the calculations of intellect, allowing them to communicate with the appetite.

5.7 Emotion as Mediation

To sum up: by means of their being followed by pleasure and pain, emotions provide the bridge between two kinds of temporality, the one of the appetite, which is the present only, and the one of the intellect, which is articulated and differentiated. Emotions activate the conditions for passing from the one to the other enabling their concord in the deliberated action. As we have seen, they are inseparable from the body. At the same time, emotions are not only body state, but also forms, that is enmattered forms. Therefore, on the one hand, they are an organising principle and not a mere effect; on the other hand, they provide a mediation which integrates the different faculties and activities of the organism acting as a whole. These two features need to be analysed.

For the first, looking at the temporal dimension involved in emotional processes can clarify why the mediation provided by emotion is *not only* a product of changes, *but* also the principle which provides the conditions for these changes to be organised and shaped in a certain way. Inasmuch they are enmatterd forms, emotions are neither mere body affections, changes in body state, nor the effects of such changes. At the same time, they are not present without those changes; that is they can only occur *in* and *through* the body.[96] In the first book of the *De Anima*, we are told that the physicist (*phusikos*) would define anger as "the boiling of the blood or warm substance" (*DA* 403a31–403b1) surrounding the heart. More in

---

[96]Adamos (2001), p. 228, argues that emotions cannot be only mind states because they always imply a physiological state change.

general, passions like blind courage or fear involve bodily affections, painful or pleasant, accompanied by heating or chilling of a part or of the whole body (*MA* 702a2–5). That is, emotions involve those bodily changes or alterations which are suitable to *prepare* the organic parts for the movements.

The beginning of emotion activity in and through the body is a sort of getting ready for movement, preparing oneself for movement corresponding to a certain direction. In this 'preparing itself for', the organism is completely active in its wholeness and unity, and is affected only by itself, by its own activity without being affected by external triggers.

This 'preparing itself for' implies a change, which brings into light the conditions for the different time articulations. In 'preparing itself for', the view of the '*after*' (the 'not yet' the organism is preparing for) and the effects of the '*before*' (the 'no more' which has already been) are collected and synthesised in the punctuality of the '*now*'.[97] At the same time however, none of these time articulations remains fixed, because they flow into one another. 'Preparing itself for' implies transforming the 'now' (the moment of preparing itself for) into the 'before' (the necessary antecedent) of everything that comes 'after' (the end the organism is preparing for). So the 'now', extending itself to the next coming, has changed into an 'already been', into a 'no more', and the 'not yet' has already been advanced to the 'now'.

As regards the second feature of emotions, the kind of mediation they provide can be clarified considering that they have a certain kind of independence from sensible stimuli and sensations. In fact, emotions might not occur even if there is a strong or obvious stimulus; but they may occur even if there are very small or obscure causes, if the body is in a state of tension. Sometimes, however, it can also happen that we feel an emotion like fear without the occurrence of the usual causes of it (*DA* 403a19–24). The independence from sensible stimulation is more evident when emotions occur because of having some opinions or beliefs (*DA* 427b21–23). Therefore, emotions are not only the consequence of stimuli coming from the environment or from the organism's external world by means of the senses, because they can have their origin in something which is not a sensation, like opinions. Although they can occur only in and through the body and its physical matter, they get some autonomy from it.

If we look closer at the way in which the mediation between appetite and intellect occurs, we can notice that in a certain way, emotions stop both of them. On the one hand, they arrest the immediate impulsivity, diversifying it and deferring it by means of their articulated cognitive structure. On the other hand, they put a stop to the analysing and calculating activity of the intellect. Emotions do not mediate by interposing their activity (like a third 'genus') between the activities of

---

[97]The structure of this *preparing itself for* seems to be similar to that of the instantaneous present (*nun*) which is "an extremity of the past (no part of the future being on this side of it) and again of the future (no part of the past being on that side of it): it is, as we maintain, a limit of both." (*Phys.* 233b35–234a3, trans. R. P. Hardie and R. K. Gaye) Edition of *Physics* used is *The Complete Works of Aristotle: The Revised Oxford Translation*, edited by Jonathan Barnes.

intellect and appetite. Their function does not seem to be that of adding something, but rather that of removing something by limiting the activity of intellect and appetite. In so doing, emotions shape a discontinuity in their way of acting and provide the conditions for their mutual concord.

The change occurring by means of emotion puts a stop to the movements characterising both intellect and appetite in their specificity and separateness. Therefore this change is the occurrence in which both faculties find their own principle and they also find in each other what they both lack. Each of them can appreciate the contribution of the other faculty only by means of such a discontinuity of its own activity; each of them can enrich through the relationship with the other only by means of its own stopping and keeping a distance from itself.

5.8   Emotion and Decision-Making

The richness and the fullness of emotion cannot be understood without considering its intrinsic and constitutive negative behaviour towards everything it deals with. It's mediating function (which enables it to pervade quite completely the different organism's systems, processes and faculties), its specific cognitive role, its performance in decision-making, it's devastating strength (which oft brings to naught even the best intentions), can be seen as consequences or, more appropriately, occurrences of a discontinuity.

Having such strong emotions, which implies stopping moving, perceiving, reasoning or even forming images for a moment, is quite a common experience. Emotion arrives on the scene putting suddenly a stop to the acting of those faculties through which the organism normally explores the environment, analyses circumstances, processes and combines information. In cases which could be devastating like being paralysed with fear, it turns out that the drive towards outside, which characterises even the simplest organism, suffers a kind of recoil and turns on itself.

On the other hand, the accordance among the different faculties can become particularly flowing by means of positive emotions. It is a very common experience that a strong joy can provide such a burst of enthusiasm that the agent can also perform far beyond his/her own expectations.

Extreme emotional phenomena bring into light what is acting at the beginning of emotion as its principle. As we have seen above, in his 'preparing itself for', the organism is completely active in its wholeness and unity, and is affected only by itself, by its own activity. Emotion shapes an act in which the highest fulfilment of acting on itself by a feeling organism—the point where the organism feels how it is affected by its own activity and accords with itself—is at the same time its getting ready to feel the world. The different ways of self-feeling become different ways of concord with the world and different ways to prepare itself for the world. In so acting, emotion provides the conditions for something else than mere appetizing and calculating, that is reasonable deciding and acting.

This is the reason why affects play a crucial role when a decision must be taken about what has to be done, choosing between alternatives. In the second book of *Rhetoric*, Aristotle says that the orator has to distinguish in each emotion three aspects which are: the state of mind when experiencing a certain emotion; who are the people for whom an emotion is usually felt; on what grounds it is usually experienced. Then, he warns us that the lack of one of these aspects makes the arousing of a given emotion impossible (*Rhet.* 1378a23–28). Emotion enriches the mere appetite with complex cognitive structures, which orient the decision about the concrete given situation.[98] Each emotion shapes an indissoluble net of relationships which foreshadows some connection possibilities that only certain objects, circumstances and situations can saturate. Judging and deciding is the way to determine them.

Somebody could think that emotions, like judgments of value, have a propositional content, but one might properly say—with a play on words—that emotions do not have any *pro*positional content but a *pre*positional one, that is they shape connection forms like prepositions, which are not yet articulated judgments, but are necessary for formulating them.[99] They are reasons (*logoi*) sufficient to move our appetite (giving a direction and some conditions like 'for', 'against', 'with', 'by', and so on), but in too hasty a way (not properly according to a reasoning but only as if it were doing it), because of the lack of other elements and contents.

Although emotions are on such a pre-predicative level, which is, however, necessary for a certain kind of predication, they have an informative content. This does not mean that they provide the content of a statement or that they are themselves a sort of statement. Rather, they offer the connection forms which shape the way in which we evaluate our relationship to the world and act according to it.

5.9 Conclusion: Managing Emotion in Juridical Experience

Scholars have long recognised legal reasoning and judicial decision-making as having a particular kind of rationality. Admitting that the different aspects contributing to a good reasoning and a good decision-making harmonise by means of the 'space' opened by emotion does not imply supporting emotivism or irrationalism. Trying to understand the rationality which leads jurists in their daily activities without considering the contribution of affects or making affects the ultimate criteria are the consequence of the same abstract view of the human being. Practical

---

[98]According to Fortenbaugh *Rhetoric* makes clear the relationship of emotion to reasoned argumentation (Fortenbaugh 1975, p. 17). On the cognitive structure and function of emotion in *Rhetoric*, see also Cooper (1996), Frede (1996), Nussbaum (1996), and Striker (1996). For an overview and a discussion of this topic, see Rapp (2002).

[99]About the reasons why emotion is not like a judgement, see Rapp (2008), pp. 56–57.

rationality[100] is an embodiment of the unity of the agent, who is choosing, deciding, acting like a whole. None of its dimensions or faculties—appetite, reason or affects—can lack without causing an idle knowledge or a mere impulsive motility. For the same reason, none of them can replace the others.

Moving from this point on, it is possible to outline the range of the contribution of emotion to juridical experience. Emotion can be so violent as to inhibit the choosing and deliberating faculties themselves. It is as if the subject were overridden by the disproportionate width of his own possibilities, to such an extent that any concrete acting seems inadequate. Such a paralysis, far from occurring infrequently, brings into light that emotion cannot contain a fitting limit in itself, and therefore it cannot be subjected to the analysing, balancing processes, needed for rational decision-making. On the one hand, analysing can only carry out its practical function in the space opened by emotion; on the other, it sets a different level of organisation in which discussing, examining and balancing of reasons—processes which also involve limiting, defining—are needed. An action choice or a decision grounded only on emotional triggers would be unable to deal with the critical checking, which can never lack in legal and juridical experience.

All this leads to recognise which kind of discourse is fit for the rational decision-making in the juridical field: it is a discourse which from the beginning and for all its extension can deal with the unity of levels necessary for each concrete decision. Traditionally this kind of discourse has been called *rhetoric* and it has been considered useful to decision-making in judicial contexts too. Since rhetoric exists in order to predispose an audience to take a certain decision (*Rhet.* 1377b21), it has to deal with everything useful in allowing someone to make a decision about what needs to be done, on the basis of reasons which are not only communicable in a certain cultural context, but also more preferable than others from a concrete point of view and more defendable on a logical level.

The emotional drive and force of rhetoric are actually 'informative' for the person who has to decide, insofar they provide the necessary elements in order to form the kind of knowledge which grounds an appropriate decision. Firstly, they 'inform' because they make appreciable a difference, i.e. a *form*, through which something stands out from a fuzzy background and distinguishes itself, positively or negatively, from anything else. Secondly, they 'inform' because they organise the concurrency of theoretical and practical faculties, necessary for decision-making by helping our attention focus on a specific point. Finally, they 'inform' because they make possible the sharing of the 'emotional mark' through which something becomes an element for those processes which nourish the practical reason, such as perceiving, memorising, processing. In so doing, they shape the form of a common evaluation perspective, making it explicit, checkable and questionable.

---

[100]Of course, the adjective 'practical' is not used here with the Aristotelian technical meaning.

References

Adamos, Maria Magoula. 2001. Aristotle on Emotions and Contemporary Psychology. In *Aristotle and Contemporary Science*, ed. Dēmētra Sphendonē-Mentzou, Jagdish N. Hattiangadi, and David Martel Johnson, vol. 2, 226–235. New York: P. Lang.
Aristote. 1966. *De l'âme*. Texte établi par A. Jannone. Traduction et notes de E. Barbotin. Paris: Les Belles Lettres.
Aristotele. 2001. *L'anima*. Introduzione, traduzione, note e apparati di Giancarlo Movia. Milan: Bompiani.
Aristoteles. 1994. *Über die Seele*. Übersetzt von Willy Theiler. Berlin: Akademie Verlag.
Aristotle. 1931. *De Anima*. In *The Works of Aristotle*. Vol. 3. Translated by John A. Smith. Translated into English under the Editorship of W. D. Ross. Oxford: Clarendon Press.
———. 1984. *The Complete Works of Aristotle: The Revised Oxford Translation*. Princeton, NJ: Princeton University Press.
———. 1986. *De Anima (On the Soul)*. Translated, with an Introduction and Notes by Hugh Lawson-Tancred. Penguin Classic. London: Penguin.
Aubenque, Pierre. 1957. La définition aristotélicienne de la colère. *Revue Philosophique de La France et de L'étranger* 156: 300–317.
Barile, Emilia. 2013. *Pensare Damasio. Due o tre cose che so di lui*. Milan: FrancoAngeli.
Barnes, Jonathan. 1979. Aristotle's Concept of Mind. In *Articles on Aristotle, 4. Psychology and Aesthetics*, ed. Jonathan Barnes, Malcom Schofield, and Richard Sorabji, 32–41. London: Duckworth.
Bennett, Hayley, and G. A. (Tony) Broe. 2007. Judicial Neurobiology, Markarian Synthesis and Emotion: How Can the Human Brain Make Sentencing Decisions? *Criminal Law Journal–Sidney* 31: 75–90.
Bennett, Maxwell R., and Peter M.S. Hacker. 2003. *Philosophical Foundations of Neuroscience*. Malden, MA: Blackwell.
Berker, Selim. 2009. The Normative Insignificance of Neuroscience. *Philosophy & Public Affairs* 37: 293–329.
Bombelli, Giovanni. 2018. Emotion and Rationality in Aristotle's Model: From Anthropology to Politics. In *Aristotle on Emotions in Law and Politics*, ed. Liesbeth Huppes-Cluysenaer and Nuno M.M.S. Coelho. Dordrecht: Springer.
Bornstein, Brian H., and Richard L. Wiener. 2006. Emotion in Legal Judgment and Decision-Making. *Law and Human Behavior* 30: 115–248.
Brito, José de Sousa e. 2018. Aristotle on Emotions in Ethics and in Criminal Justice. In *Aristotle on Emotions in Law and Politics*, ed. Liesbeth Huppes-Cluysenaer and Nuno M.M.S. Coelho. Dordrecht: Springer.
Caston, Victor. 2006. Aristotle's Psychology. In *A Companion to Ancient Philosophy*, ed. Mary Louise Gill and Pierre Pellegrin, 316–346. Malden, MA: Blackwell.
Chiereghin, Franco. 2004. *L'eco della caverna. Ricerche di filosofia della logica e della mente*. Padua: Il Poligrafo.
Cohen de Lara, Emma. 2018. Aristotle's Rhetoric and the Persistence of the Emotions in the Courtroom. In *Aristotle on Emotions in Law and Politics*, ed. Liesbeth Huppes-Cluysenaer and Nuno M.M.S. Coelho. Dordrecht: Springer.
Colombetti, Giovanna. 2008. The Somatic Marker Hypotheses, and What the Iowa Gambling Task Does and Does Not Show. *British Journal for the Philosophy of Science* 59 (1): 51–71. https://doi.org/10.1093/bjps/axm045.
Cooper, John M. 1996. An Aristotelian Theory of the Emotions. In *Essays on Aristotle's Rhetoric*, ed. Amélie Oksenberg Rorty, 238–257. Berkeley: University of California Press.
Damasio, Antonio R. 1999. *The Feeling of What Happens. Body and Emotion in the Making of Consciousness*. Orlando, FL: Harcourt.
———. 2003. *Looking for Spinoza. Joy, Sorrow and the Feeling Brain*. Orlando, FL: Harcourt.

―――. 2005. *Descartes' Error. Emotion, Reason and the Human Brain*. New York: Penguin Putnam.

―――. 2010. *Self Comes to Mind: Constructing the Conscious Brain*. New York: Pantheon.

Di Giovine, Ombretta. 2009. *Un diritto penale empatico? Diritto penale, bioetica e neuroetica*. Turin: Giappichelli.

Dunn, Barnaby D., Tim Dalgleish, and Andrew D. Lawrence. 2006. The Somatic Marker Hypothesis: A Critical Evaluation. *Neuroscience and Biobehavioral Reviews* 30: 239–271. https://doi.org/10.1016/j.neubiorev.2005.07.001.

Fortenbaugh, William W. 1975. *Aristotle on Emotion. A Contribution to Philosophical Psychology, Rhetoric, Poetics, Politics and Ethics*. London: Duckworth.

Frede, Dorothea. 1992. The Cognitive Role of *Phantasia* in Aristotle. In *Essays on Aristotle's De Anima*, ed. Martha Craven Nussbaum and Amélie Oksenberg Rorty, 279–295. Oxford: Clarendon Press.

―――. 1996. Mixed Feelings in Aristotle's *Rhetoric*. In *Essays on Aristotle's Rhetoric*, ed. Amélie Oksenberg Rorty, 258–285. Berkeley: University of California Press.

Freeman, Walter J. 2000. *How Brains Make Up Their Minds*. New York: Columbia University Press.

Fuselli, Stefano. 2014. *Diritto Neuroscienze Filosofia. Un itinerario*. Milan: FrancoAngeli.

Gazzaniga, Michael S. 2005. *The Ethical Brain: The Science of Our Moral Dilemmas*. New York: Dana Press.

Greene, Joshua D., R. Brain Sommerville, Leigh E. Nystrom, John M. Darley, and Jonathan D. Cohen. 2001. An fMRI Investigation of Emotional Engagement in Moral Judgment. *Science* 293 (5537): 2105–2108. https://doi.org/10.1126/science.1062872.

Haidt, Jonathan. 2001. The Emotional Dog and Its Rational Tail: A Social Intuitionist Approach to Moral Judgment. *Psychological Review* 108: 814–834.

Hauser, Marc D. 2006. *Moral Minds: How Nature Designed Our Universal Sense of Right and Wrong*. New York: HarperCollins.

Johnson, Mark. 2006. Mind Incarnate: From Dewey to Damasio. *Daedalus* 135: 46–54.

Kirkebøen, Geir. 2001. Descartes' Embodied Psychology: Descartes or Damasio's Error? *Journal of the History of the Neuroscience* 10: 173–191.

LeDoux, Joseph. 1996. *The Emotional Brain. The Mysterious Underpinning of Emotional Life*. New York: Simon & Schuster.

Leighton, Stephen R. 1996. Aristotle and the Emotions. In *Essays on Aristotle's Rhetoric*, ed. Amélie Oksenberg Rorty, 206–237. Berkeley: University of California Press.

Lenzen, Wolfgang. 2004. Damasios Theorie Der Emotionen. *Facta Philosophica* 6: 269–309.

Lerner, Jennifer S., Ye Li, Piercarlo Valdesolo, and Karim S. Kassam. 2015. Emotion and Decision-Making. *Annual Review of Psychology* 66: 799–823. https://doi.org/10.1146/annurev-psych-010213-115043.

Maroney, Terry A. 2006. Law and Emotion: A Proposed Taxonomy of an Emerging Field. *Law and Human Behavior* 30: 119–142.

―――. 2018. Judicial Emotion as Vice or Virtue: Perspectives Both Ancient and New. In *Aristotle on Emotions in Law and Politics*, ed. Liesbeth Huppes-Cluysenaer and Nuno M.M.S. Coelho. Dordrecht: Springer.

Mezzalira, Selene. 2011. Intenzionalità e azione nel mondo delle emozioni. Damasio e i suoi critici: rilevanza filosofica di un dialogo scientifico. *Verifiche* 40: 153–199.

Nussbaum, Martha C. 1978. Essay 5: The Role of *Phantasia* in Aristotle's Explanations of Actions. In *Aristotle's De Motu Animalium*. Text with Translation, Commentary and Interpretative Essays by Martha Craven Nussbaum, 221–269. Princeton, NJ: Princeton University Press.

―――. 1996. Aristotle on Emotions and Rational Persuasion. In *Essays on Aristotle's Rhetoric*, ed. Amélie Oksenberg Rorty, 303–323. Berkeley: University of California Press.

―――. 2001. *Upheavals of Thought. The Intelligence of Emotions*. Cambridge: Cambridge University Press.

Nussbaum, Martha C., and Hilary Putnam. 1992. Changing Aristotle's Mind. In *Essays on Aristotle's De Anima*, ed. Martha Craven Nussbaum and Amélie Oksenberg Rorty, 27–56. Oxford: Clarendon Press.

Oksenberg Rorty, Amélie. 1992. *De Anima*: Its Agenda and Its Recent Interpreters. In *Essays on Aristotle's De Anima*, ed. Marta Craven Nussbaum and Amélie Oksenberg Rorty, 7–13. Oxford: Clarendon Press.

Panksepp, Jaak. 1998. *Affective Neuroscience. The Foundations of Human and Animal Emotions.* Oxford: Oxford University Press.

———. 2003. Looking for Spinoza: Joy, Sorrow, and the Feeling Brain. *Neuropsychoanalysis* 5: 201–215.

Pardo, Michael S., and Dennis Patterson. 2013. *Minds, Brains, and Law. The Conceptual Foundations of Law and Neuroscience.* Oxford: Oxford University Press.

Pettys, Todd E. 2007. The Emotional Juror. *Fordham Law Review* 76: 1609–1640.

Polansky, Ronald. 2007. *Aristotle's De Anima.* Cambridge: Cambridge University Press.

Prinz, Jesse J. 2006. The Emotional Basis of Moral Judgements. *Philosophical Explorations* 9: 29–43.

Rapp, Christof. 2002. Vorbemerkung zu Kap. II 2-11: Die, Emotionen. In *Aristoteles, Rhetorik, übersetzt u. erläutert v. Christof Rapp, 2.er Halbband*, 543–583. Berlin: Akademie Verlag.

———. 2008. Aristoteles: Bausteine für eine Theorie der Emotionen. In *Klassische Emotionstheorien. Von Plato bis Wittgenstein*, ed. Hilge Landweer and Ursula Renz, 45–67. Berlin and Boston, MA: de Gruyter.

Salerno, Jessica M., and Bette L. Bottoms. 2009. Emotional Evidence and Jurors' Judgments: The Promise of Neuroscience for Informing Psychology and Law. *Behavioral Sciences & the Law Special Issue: The Neuroscience and Psychology of Moral Decision-Making and the Law* 27 (2): 273–296. https://doi.org/10.1002/bsl.861.

Schofield, Malcom. 2011. *Phantasia* in *De Motu Animalium*. In *Moral Psychology and Human Action in Aristotle*, ed. Michael Pakaluk and Giles Pearson, 119–134. Oxford: Oxford University Press.

Striker, Gisela. 1996. Emotions in Context: Aristotle's Treatment of the Passions in the *Rhetoric* and His Moral Psychology. In *Essays on Aristotle's Rhetoric*, ed. Amélie Oksenberg Rorty, 286–302. Berkeley: University of California Press.

Teixeira, Francisco. 2002. A propósito de "O Sentimento de Si": (Ou o erro de Damásio). *Revista Portuguesa de Filosofia* 58 (1): 161–184.

Chapter 6
Aristotle's Functionalism and the Rise of Nominalism in Law and Politics: Law, Emotion and Language

Saulo de Matos

Abstract This article explores the language of law and politics in Aristotle's ethical writings and the difference between Aristotle's teleological model and the nomological model of Christian ethics, especially in the case of Ockham. Nomological politics and law are only possible when based on authority, that is, on a communicative theory between sender and addressee, according to which the intention of the sender is somehow contingent.

The nomological approach clearly represents a nominalistic metaphysical view on social reality, since legal and political concepts become completely contingent if their content depends only on the will of an authority. In contrast to nomological politics, the Aristotelian or teleological view is based on a non-authoritative interpretation of the function argument. The function argument hinges above all on grasping the final cause of an action. The core of grasping law and politics in Aristotle's model consists in the cognitive task of identifying the goal or the end of law. This end of actions is holistic, in the sense that it aims to present a permanent continuum between desire and reason, even in the case of social actions. Whereas emotions do not play a significant role in the nomological approach, they are pivotal in identifying the proper end of the individual and political action according to the Aristotelian model.

The presentation and publication of this article would not be possible without the financial support of the program "Apoio a Eventos no Exterior" of the Coordenação de Aperfeiçoamento de Pessoal de Nível Superior (CAPES), and the "Programa de Apoio ao Doutor Pesquisador" (PRODOUTOR) of the Federal University of Pará.

S. de Matos (✉)
Faculty of Law, Federal University of Pará, Belém, Brazil
e-mail: saulomdematos@hotmail.com

© Springer International Publishing AG 2018   113
L. Huppes-Cluysenaer, N.M.M.S. Coelho (eds.), *Aristotle on Emotions in Law and Politics*, Law and Philosophy Library 121, DOI 10.1007/978-3-319-66703-4_6

6.1   Introduction: Two Premises

The central aspect of language is its representational character. By language, I mean both natural languages, like Portuguese or German, and invented languages, like mathematics or logic. In order to grasp phenomena of the world, we use language. *Language usage* means the use of concepts (or mental terms) and propositions in order to communicate thoughts. Each language is a model of representation, in the sense that it entails a given grammatical structure or compositional rules and a body of representational units, i.e. linguistic meanings. For instance, in the case of Aristotle's theory of predication, each proposition is an instance of the form *S is P*—or an equivalent form and reduced to that—and pretends to be an observation of facts in the world.[1] Because of the representational character of language, when one uses a given language or model to grasp or represent the world, the product of this action, i.e. a given representation, is of course itself constituted through this language. In this sense, the model of language is constitutive regarding the content of the world.[2] Aside some special cases, a meaningful sentence S represents the world as being a certain way.[3]

Therefore, law and politics are created through the use of language. If one understands law and politics as the actions of selecting certain social facts in order to justify specific legal contents, that is to say, in order to represent the world in some way on the basis of a given model of language, it is clear that the kind or model of language elected will be decisive to the comprehension of what law and politics are. In my view, modern practices of law and, to a certain extent, politics—for the sake of this paper, I will use sometimes *law* for both practices of law and politics, because the difference between these two practices is contingent or based on some unnecessary features of modern law and modern politics—are based on a grammar of claims, privileges, powers and immunities in the Hohfeldian sense.[4] It is possible to regard the birth of this way of understanding the world through the social rights movement and, consequently, the welfare rights movement, such as in the women's rights movement and students' rights movement, although one can already find a primitive language of rights in the writings of Ockham.[5] Because of this fact, human rights or the language of human rights, for instance, are so important for ethical issues in our society, both in constructing social actions and in resolving social conflicts.

Nevertheless, one can understand this changing of normative language in a broader sense. Since the scope of this paper consists in reflecting about emotions as a constitutive element of the action of grasping law and politics in Aristotle's

---

[1]Angioni (2009), p. 17.

[2]"A model is the counterpart at the metaphysical level of a method of interpretation at the epistemic level." (Greenberg 2004, p. 178).

[3]Soames (2012), p. 1.

[4]Hohfeld (1917), p. 710.

[5]Edmundson (2004), pp. 7–10; *Vide* Wellman (1985); de Matos (2015).

ethics, I will claim that this modern language of rights and powers modified our view on the role emotions play in grasping the end or goal (*telos*) of legal and political practices.[6] According to Anscombe, although this language of rights and powers was intensively developed during the twentieth century by means of social movements, the very concept of this *nomological* approach has its origin in Christianity:

> The ordinary (and quite indispensable) terms 'should', 'needs', 'ought', 'must' – acquired this special sense by being equated in the relevant contexts with 'is obliged' or 'is bound', or 'is required to', in the sense in which one can be obliged or bound by law, or something can be required by law. How did this come about? The answer is history: between Aristotle and us came Christianity, with its law conception of ethics. For Christianity derived its ethical notions from the Torah.[7]

Some exceptions and details aside, *law ethics,* or the *nomological approach to ethics,* is based on the Christian concept of freedom, that is, the idea that an action can only be considered free if it is according to reason and, additionally, in accordance with moral norms (or principles) that guide human will.[8] Upon regarding ethics in such a nomological way, modern jurisprudence normally entertains concepts like *autonomy, authority, rules, efficiency,* whereas there is usually no place for concepts like *virtue, excellence* or *emotions.*[9]

What is called law ethics[10] or imperativistic ethics,[11] I will call nomological language of ethics, in order to stress the rationality behind the use of a language of rights and duties. This nomological approach to ethics has been premised on the idea (not always explicitly defended) that practical reason is about finding rules for actions. This is the case for individual and social actions (law and politics). Yet, without considering individual actions, the understanding and validity of these rules for social actions depend on an authority, like the Parliament, the Government or God.

Based on that nomological approach, which regards ethics as an enterprise of finding rules for actions, there is clearly a nominalistic metaphysical view on social reality. For the sake of this article, I will call this idea *nominalism* in law and politics, because legal and political concepts become completely contingent if their content depends only on the will of an authority—with the exception of God.[12] Certainly, *nominalism* is a much broader metaphysical problem; but the basic claim of nominalism consists in the contingency of human knowledge in contrast, for instance, with the discussion on the universal and essential character of some concepts and propositions, that is to say, the necessity of a given knowledge.[13]

---

[6] About the relation between means and ends regarding law: von der Pfordten (2013), pp. 27–31.

[7] Anscombe (1958), p. 5. See too: Gadamer (1999a).

[8] Schopenhauer (1977).

[9] Solum (2013), p. 2.

[10] Anscombe (1958), p. 5.

[11] Gadamer (1999a), p. 55.

[12] See von der Pfordten (2009).

[13] Maritain (2001), pp. 47–49.

Therefore, the epistemological debate on the will of an authority, as fundamental criterion for grasping the content of law, is an important part of a nominalistic view in the field of ethics.

I conclude that nomological politics and law are only possible on the basis of authority, to wit, of a communication theory between sender and addressee, according to which the intention of the sender is somehow contingent. I will argue that this modern conception of practical reasoning has its root in Ockham's reception of Aristotle's most fundamental thesis in the field of politics, namely the function argument. On the basis of authority, i.e. this nomological approach, emotion has no significant role, in the sense that it is not part of a discourse on justice. Therefore, if emotions should play a role in law and politics, it is necessary to rethink the Aristotelian view on ethics. In other words, it must be based on a non-authoritative interpretation of the function argument. Thus, my conclusion is a plaidoyer *ex negativo* for taking emotions seriously in law and politics.

6.2   Functionalism

"Function" or "functional" is an essential notion to explain reality and, since Aristotle, it has been a central concept in ancient philosophy. Aristotle repeatedly supports the so-called function argument, one of the most influential and controversial claims in ethics.[14] The *locus classicus* of this claim is in the passages below:

> So also no hand of bronze or wood or constituted in any but the appropriate way can possibly be a hand in more than name. For like physician in a painting, or like a flute in a sculpture, it will be unable to perform its function. Precisely in the same way no part of a dead body, such I mean as its eye or its hand, is really an eye or a hand. (PA, 140b35–141a4, trans. W. Ogle)
>
> For if a piece of wood is to be split with an axe, the axe must of necessity be hard; and, if hard, must of necessity be made of bronze or iron. Now exactly in the same way the body, since it is an instrument – for both the body as whole and its several parts individually are for the sake of something – if it is to do its work, must of necessity be of such and such a character, and made of such and such materials.[15] (PA, 642a9–14, trans. W. Ogle)

There are many ways to clarify the passages above. In light of the goal of this study, the functionalistic way to explain is the following. An axe is primarily characterized by its office—chopping—whereas a hand is characterized by its office—grasping. Axes and hands that cannot be used in their respective ways (functions) are just names, but no longer an axe or a hand.[16] In order to be

---

[14]"Aristotle develops his conception of happiness with one of the most famous arguments in all of moral philosophy – the function argument." (Solum 2013, p. 7). See also Murphy (2006), p. 29.

[15]Parts of Animals, edition used: *The Complete Works of Aristotle: The Revised Oxford Translation*, edited by Jonathan Barnes.

[16]Murphy (2006), p. 29 calls this form of argument the canonical form of explanation within natural law jurisprudence.

something, the thing must perform its respective goal or office, and it must be constituted to properly fulfill its goal or office. Form and material of objects are evaluated based on their proper end or telos.[17] It is possible to write this argument in the following form, which I call function, or *ergon*, argument:

Function Argument
P1. It is the office of Xs to φ.
P2. Only things that are Y are constitutionally able to φ.
C1. Nothing is an X unless it is Y.

In this manner, function argument is a type of teleological explanation.[18] Following Bombelli,[19] one can conceive functionalism either in a finalistic-teleological manner or in a mechanistic-sociological, way. As a consequence of the dominance of the nominalistic view nowadays, functionalism in law is usually regarded as the sociological question on the social purpose of law.[20] However, teleological functionalism presupposes that the relation between means and ends is not a given, i.e. the realization of an end is part of the realization of a means, and a given end cannot be known before the realization of the action.[21] Mechanistic functionalism, by contrast, bases itself on the autopoietic character of the relation between means and ends. Accordingly, we can describe actions based on a contingent system or a causal relation between inputs and outputs, the purpose of which should be taken as known. In order to have a mechanistic functionalism in *ethics*, one has to read the telos, or goal, of human actions through a fully contingent causal relation between means and ends as part of a descriptive system, according to which it would be very difficult to speak about the essence of human action and its undeterminability. As I will explain below, one can understand this mechanistic functionalism as an explanation based on an efficient-causal account, whereas the teleological functionalism is rooted on a final-causal explanation.[22]

As Huppes-Cluysenaer[23] precisely stated, Aristotle's model of scientific reasoning is natural history or descriptive taxonomies. He uses pictures, for instance, of birds, to produce definitions or words. In that sense, he develops the classical method of conceptual analysis through the basic idea of *genus proximum et differentia specifica* in order to represent the difference between species through words or definitions. Therefore, the best way to grasp Aristotelian scientific reasoning consists in putting together theory of meaning and theory of extension, or scientific method and ontology.[24]

---

[17]Against this view: Nussbaum and Putnam (1992), p. 20.

[18]Charles (2000), p. 309.

[19]Bombelli (2018).

[20]For instance: Atienza (2001), pp. 157–184.

[21]de Matos (2012), pp. 96–97.

[22]See also Nussbaum and Putnam (1992), p. 36.

[23]Huppes-Cluysenaer (2013), p. 37.

[24]Ibidem.

Instead of being just a structural-linguistic analysis, functionalism is a theory about how language can fully satisfy its function of referring *objectively* to the world and give us the best explanation of facts and situations. It is a subset of a theory of predication as a theory about two subjects. On the one hand, it refers to the objective structures by which phenomena occur in the world. On the other hand, it relates to the linguistic-logical structures through which we grasp phenomena and refer to them.[25] In Aristotelian terms, a proposition always has to be in the form "S is P", and, additionally, it must objectively make a claim. Therefore, the affirmation "S is P", such as "Socrates is human", is actually a claim that this state of affairs exists objectively in the world.

The objectivity of a proposition referring to a state of affairs hinges on Aristotle's metaphysical claim about the essence of things (*ousia*). According to Aristotle, objects in the world have an essence (*ousia*), which consists of their elements or characteristics. Decisively, these elements determine what objects are and what always and necessarily falls into the object's being. A definition is a complete statement of an object's elements or characteristics.[26] For example:

> That is the nature of living beings – to be forms embodied in ever-changing matter. By the same token, the organization characteristic of the species has the best claim to be the essential nature, or what-is-it, of the thing, since it is what must remain the same so long as that thing remains in existence. If it is no longer there, the identity of the thing is lost, and the thing is no more.[27]

If the essence is lost, the thing becomes a mere name, and ceases to exist. Through the function argument, therefore, we can grasp the essence of objects or, in other words, explain the necessary proprieties of a certain object. Yet, it is clear that the taxonomic method of *genus proximum et differentia specifica* cannot be the only one used to identify the essence of an object, due to the lack of a specific criterion to differentiate necessary and contingent properties.[28] To this effect, Aristotle believed it was necessary to introduce another criterion, i.e. efficient and final causes:

> But we can inquire why man is an animal of such and such a nature. Here, then, we are evidently not inquiring why he who is a man is a man. We are inquiring, then, why something is predicable of something; that it is predicable must be clear; for if not, the inquiry is an inquiry into nothing. E. g. why does it thunder? – why is sound produced in the clouds? Thus the inquiry is about the predication of one thing of another. And why are certain things, i.e. stones and bricks, a house? Plainly we are seeking the cause. And this is the essence (to speak abstractly), which in some case of a house or a bed, and in some cases in the first mover, for this is also is a cause. But while the efficient cause is sought in the case of genesis and destruction, the final cause is sought in the case of being also. (Met., 1041a19–30, trans. W. D. Ross)

---

[25] Angioni (2009), p. 20.

[26] Ibidem, p. 30.

[27] Nussbaum and Putnam (1992), p. 32.

[28] Angioni (2009), p. 39.

The introduction of the metaphysical notions of efficient and final causes is the fundamental Aristotelian way to explain particular elements of a definition.[29] The efficient cause explains the origin of a given phenomenon as, for example,

> What is eclipse? Deprivation of light. But if we add 'by interposition of the earth', this is the formula which includes the cause. (Met., 1044b13–15, trans W. D. Ross)

The final cause explains the proper goal of something as in the example above of a hand or an axe. Although functionalism can deal with the two explanatory causes of a phenomenon, this paper focuses on the final cause, since it is relevant in the field of ethics. Aristotle's functionalism in ethics has to do, above all, with the final cause explanation, because of its necessary character as a practical science.[30]

In this manner, functionalism can be understood as the *lógos* behind the relation between means and ends in law and politics. It depends on practical truth, that is, truth in accordance with desires. Desires entail moral excellences and sentiments or emotions that are, according to Aristotle, a necessary part of practical deliberation. Even though emotion is usually defined as an irrational aspect of action because of its necessary corporal dimension, in contrast with the rational dimension of action, it is also true that emotions play a decisive role in identifying the *ethos* of a political community. *Ergo*, emotions involve cognitive appraisals:

> Another way of putting this point, to which I shall often return, is that all the major emotions are 'eudaimonistic', meaning that they appraise the world from the person's own viewpoint and the viewpoint, therefore, of that person's evolving conception of a worthwhile life. (...) But the ones who will stir deep emotions in us are the ones to whom we are somehow connected through imagining of a valuable life, what I shall henceforth call our 'circle of concern'. If distant people and abstract principles are to get a grip on our emotions, therefore, these emotions must somehow position them within our circle of concern, creating a sense of 'our' life in which these people and events matter as parts of our 'us', our own flourishing.[31]

In conclusion, in order to present one of the central definitions of this study in a precise way, it is possible to differentiate between finalism and functionalism. *Finalism* is the broadest concept, according to which grasping something means identifying the properties of an object with reference to some values, or ends, which are independent of the subject or objective. A Neo-Kantian, like Gustav Radbruch, can be regarded as a finalist in the sense that human knowledge is the result of the reference to a priori values, namely truth, beauty, good and justice.[32] In this sense, one can speak about an idealistic finalism, as in the case of Radbruch. In contrast to this idea, I use the term *functionalism* to stress the function argument at the heart of Aristotle's teleology in the field of practical philosophy. Albeit both idealism and functionalism explain facts on the basis of a reference to ends or values, function argument presupposes the idea that these ends or values are intrinsic to the social

---

[29]Charles (2000), pp. 274–309.

[30]Varela (2014), pp. 82–83.

[31]Nussbaum (2013), p. 11.

[32]Radbruch (2003), p. 9. See also Schröder (2012), pp. 349–350.

practices, in the sense that each practice has a proper office to be fulfilled. The realization of its function cannot be separated from the practice itself; in other words, form and material must be regarded as a continuum. Although it can be the case that one can observe some conceptual influence of Aristotle's teleological metaphysics and physics on practical philosophy, I assume that the Aristotelian question on human good is independently developed from theoretical aspects.[33]

6.3   Practical Truth and Functionalism in Law and Politics

6.3.1   Practical Truth

Functionalism, function argument or *ergon* argument is a practical reasoning related to a special concept of truth. In the present case, it relates to the concept of practical truth.[34] However, practical truth, as a term or a name, is mentioned only once in Aristotle's entire corpus[35]:

> The excellence of a thing is relative to its proper function. Now there are three things in the soul which control action and truth – sensation, thought, desire. (...) What affirmation and negation are in thinking, pursuit and avoidance are in desire; so that since moral excellence is a state concerned with choice, and choice is deliberate desire, therefore both reasoning must be true and the desire right, if the choice is to be good, and the latter must pursue just what the former asserts. Now this of intellect and of truth is practical. (EN, 1139a21–30, trans. W. D. Ross/J. O. Urmson)

In order to understand this, it is necessary to look at Aristotle's project regarding practical science. The passage above clearly presents Aristotle's model of practical reason as a relation between thought and desire. According to Aristotle, the human soul entails two essential dimensions that can be presented or regarded as the duality between ethos and logos (*EN* 1139a2). By reaffirming the difference between *lógon échon* (rational) and *álogon* (irrational), the first one, i.e. rational thought (*lógos*), will be once again divided between theoretical and practical thought (*EN* 1139a8–11). Theoretical thought consists in a reason about things whose principles cannot be otherwise, whereas practical thought has things whose principles can be otherwise as its object. Theoretical thought and practical thought can be differentiated in the following way: theoretical thought would be the act of reasoning about things of which the principles cannot be otherwise; and, in contrast, practical thought would reason about things in which the principles can be otherwise. In this sense, Aristotle's ethical writings aim to present the specific character of practical thought, which is knowledge about praxis—things whose principles can

---

[33]Gadamer (1999b), p. 353.

[34]In order to understand the relation between truth and falsity and being and not-being, see: Aristotle (1984a), 1050b10–1052a12. I thank Liesbeth Huppes-Cluysenaer for this comment.

[35]Olfert (2014), p. 205.

be otherwise—and, therefore, it demands a special kind of reasoning, namely *phronesis*.[36] *Phronesis* is not just sagacity. Rather, *Prohairesis* is, indeed, the proper deliberative action designed to unify thought and desire.[37] Consequently, practical science has to do with a special kind of necessity, i.e. a *conditional necessity*.[38]

Practical truth is the product of practical reasoning or deliberation—*phronesis*. The complex concept of practical truth entails two simple concepts: truth and practical. *Truth* presupposes the human capacity of evaluating the veracity or falsity of certain statements or thoughts.[39] According to Aristotle,

> The function of both the intellectual parts, then, is truth. Therefore, the states that are most strictly those in respect of which each of these parts will reach truth are the excellences of the two parts. (*EN*, 1139b10–13)

Practical specifies the kind of truth that is in agreement with right desires (*EN* 1139a30). If practical truth can be seen as a distinctive kind of truth that relates to things whose principles can be otherwise, i.e., with praxis, and, therefore, with practical reasoning and practical wisdom, it is then possible to say that practical truth is a sort of real union between universal and particular. In other words, practical truth about universal or unqualified good and particular good for a particular person when all particular circumstances are taken into account.[40] Nevertheless, due to the fact that practical truth is based on the idea of virtue, in the sense of constancy of behavior, and not apodictic law, that is to say, *conditional necessity*, it is important to note that the universality in ethics is not the same as the one in theoretical philosophy and, furthermore, in physics.

In short, functionalism represents a method or way to grasp necessary and sufficient characteristics—specifically, the essences—of objects in the world through its final cause. Indeed, the first definition of Aristotle's functionalism, which is laid down in *Nicomachean Ethics*, appears as an *ergon* argument:

> Every skill and every enquiry, and similarly every action and rational choice, is thought to aim some good, and so the good has been aptly described as that which everything aims. (EN, 1094a1–3, trans. W. D. Ross/J. O. Urmson)[41]

---

[36]Gadamer (1998), p. 4. Technical knowledge is, of course, another kind of practical wisdom, although it seems not to be the primarily goal of Aristotelian ethics.

[37]Aristotle (1984b), p. 1139a30.

[38]Varela (2014), p. 83.

[39]Olfert (2014), p. 210.

[40]Olfert (2014), p. 219.

[41]Socrates and Plato of course, employed the same structure of means and ends by thinking on the essence of justice, love, beauty, and so on: "Socrates advances his own example of knowledge of the good only as an illustrative introduction to the general question of what knowledge is. As early as the *Phaedo* a teleological cosmology is postulated, which, to be sure, is not worked out. Similarly, in the *Seventh Letter*, we find the extension of knowledge about arete to knowledge about the whole reality (344b). And, in the final analysis, the *Timaeus* is the mythical exposition of the unelaborated postulate of the *Phaedo* – even if, strictly speaking, the Socratic question is no longer mentioned there at all. One sees that Aristotle is extending a Platonic line of thought in his teleological physics and metaphysics." (Gadamer 1986, p. 96).

6.3.2 Functionalism in Law and Politics

In Aristotelian ethics, function argument hinges above all on grasping the final cause of an action. Because the object of ethics is human action, or in other words, the relation between actions and their ends, law and politics as social actions are part of the ethical consideration. In a functional approach, law and politics are linked as means and end.

As I stated above, emotions play an important role in identifying the proper end of the individual and political action. While emotions are closer to desire than reason as an action's part, and, consequently, more irrational, he treats emotion equally as a special kind of perception, a cognitive awareness of an object:

> This view that emotions are more animal, more bodily, than perceiving is actually a view unknown in the ancient world, though common enough in modern times. If ancient thinkers make any distinction of the sort, it goes the other way: animals are always considered perceiving creatures, but frequently denied the emotions.[42]

The absence of a nomological approach to ethics, i.e. law and politics, in the case of Aristotle allows a more integrative way of thinking about the proper goals of human action that are not necessarily rules or norms.[43] I will show this difference in the next section, especially on the basis of Ockham's ethics.

The core of grasping law and politics in Aristotle's final cause method consists in the cognitive task of identifying the goal or the end (*telos* or *skopos*) of law. This end of actions is holistic, in the sense that it aims to present a complete union between desire and reason. According to Aristotle, in the field of practical reasoning, there are two possible relations between means and ends. The first relation is téchne:

> Among things that can be otherwise are included both things made and things done; making and acting are different (for their nature we treat even the discussions outside our school as reliable); so that the reasoned state of capacity to act is different from the reasoned state of capacity to make. Nor are they included one in the other; for neither is acting making nor is making acting. (...) All art is concerned with coming into being, i.e. with contriving and considering how something may come into being which is capable of either being or not being, and whose origin is in the maker and not in the thing made. (*EN*, 1140a1–13, trans. W. D. Ross/J. O. Urmson)

The second relation between means and ends is called *phronesis*:

> Now no one deliberates about things that cannot be otherwise nor about things that it is impossible for him to do. Therefore since knowledge involves demonstration, but there is no demonstration of things whose first principles can be otherwise (for all such things might actually be otherwise), and since it is impossible to deliberate about things that are of

---

[42]Nussbaum and Putnam (1992), p. 47.

[43]This thesis of course needs more explanation. See, for instance, another opinion in the study of Daniel Nascimento in this book. Nascimento (2018). I will, however, follow Liesbeth Huppes-Cluysenaer's ("Reasoning against a Deterministic Conception of the World") view on Aristotle's concept of free action.

necessity, practical wisdom cannot be knowledge nor art; nor knowledge because that which can be done is capable of being otherwise, nor art because action and making are different kind of things. It remains, then, that it is true and reasoned state of capacity to act with regard to the things that are good or bad for man. For while making has an end other than itself, action cannot; for good action itself is its end. (*EN*, 1140a30–1140b5, trans. W. D. Ross/J. O. Urmson)[44]

Both reasons are practical and they have as objects actions that can be otherwise. Accordingly, such things can have principles that change depending on the situation. They are therefore situational knowledge. While *techne* means knowing how to make things, *phronesis* consists in knowing how to decide or how to act. Regarding the product of technic, there is a distance between maker and product. By contrast, the product of *phronesis* is related to the agent. In this regard, technic can be taught, whereas moral as *phronesis* cannot. Desires and, therefore, sentiments, are thus an essential part of a practical reasoning in the sense of *phronesis*, because of the lack of determinacy regarding its end.

6.4   Function Argument in Aquinas' and Ockham's Political Writings

Aristotle's functionalism does not fit so easily into modern law and politics, if one assumes that authority does not play a central role in his practical reasoning, and, consequently, that there is no clear communication theory as a basis for understanding law.[45] In other words, it is difficult to engage with desires (emotions) as part of the justification of action, when actions are usually justified based on compliance to norms or authority. Thus, the existence and justification of authority as someone or something legitimizing actions foster in law and politics a different role for emotions than the one proposed by Aristotle, although I am not denying that emotions can play a role even in a kind of law ethics. I will try to briefly show this problem through the works of two Aristotelian philosophers: Thomas of Aquin and William of Ockham. Following Finnis,[46] I will take for granted the fact that one can identify an autonomous social philosophy in Aquinas' writings. I will consider Ockham as an Aristotelian philosopher due to the fact that he has adopted the function argument as an explanation for law and politics, albeit he does not seem to call for a holistic approach to good. Both Aquinas and Ockham tried to interpret Aristotle's politics in order to fit into Christian legalistic ethics.[47] Finally, I will concentrate my analysis on two writings, namely *De regimine principum* and *Breviloquium de principatu tyrannico*, because both texts were written in order to

---

[44]I will not discuss the difference between external and internal or intrinsic ends. See *EN*, 1094a1.
[45]Greenberg (2011).
[46]Finnis (1998), p. 21.
[47]Horn and Scarano (2002), pp. 91–105.

give advice to kings and popes. Consequently, they are the best example of an Aristotelian practical science, that is to say, the reflection on social praxis in order to identify the proper end of political community.

6.4.1 Aquinas' De regimine principum

One of the most important contributions of Aquinas' opera rests on its first reception and systematization of Aristotle's practical philosophy, and especially Aristotle's politics. Aquinas' political writings do a systematic presentation and development of Aristotelian politics, both of which were key to the modern reflection on the relation between temporal and eternal powers. This study focuses on his work *De regimine principum* (*On kingship*), where Aquinas tried to answer the three fundamental issues in political philosophy: the foundations of State as a political community, the justification for the transmission of power, and the reasoning for political actions as a whole.

The debates on political justice demonstrate a theoretical *continuum* from Antiquity to the Middle-Ages. This is quite clear. From Antiquity to Middle-Ages, the Platonic theory guided the justification for action and the concept of justice as virtue prevailed, in contrast to the concept of political justice (that came to dominate after the Middle-Ages). Yet, both periods—Antiquity and the Middle Ages—contrast in some points with each other, especially regarding political and ethical discussions. The main difference was the justification of political action based on the concepts of individual—in the case of Ockham—and God. In this sense, the justification for actions began to be considered as a kind of *adaequatio* of human action to the will of God, and no longer as a concept or image of a good citizen. In fact, *adaequatio* as a model of justification seems to be the central concept for understanding Christian ethics.[48] Nevertheless, this new approach to ethics was mediated through Aristotle; that is, new concepts of individual or God's will were integrated and developed through Aquinas' interpretation of Aristotle's writings. This new development of ethics and politics would later give rise to modern political philosophy, or to law ethics.

Aquinas adopted the function argument as basis of his political thought. Accordingly, the justification for political action necessarily entails the representation of its final cause or end, and its efficient cause. Both Aquinas and Aristotle, agree that the final end is best understood as holistic. Furthermore, pursuant to Aquinas' conceptual model, each concept has an end: law in a similar way as horse can only be regarded as law on the basis of the gradual fulfillment of its proper end, although other conditions can exist.[49]

---

[48]Ibidem, p. 91.

[49]Murphy (2006), p. 2.

In *quaestio* LVII (*de iure*) of *Summa Theologica*, Aquinas deals with the question concerning the nature of justice (*iustitia*) and the article inquires whether law can be regarded as an object of justice.[50] He claims that there is a difference between *iustitia*, *ius*, and *lex*. Whereas *iustitia* is a type of idea, i.e., a mental representation, *ius* is the realization or the real product of the idea of *iustitia*:

> For this reason justice has its own special proper object over and above the other virtues, and this object is called the just, which is the same as right.[51]

Lex, however, means a kind of rule or criterion for human actions, i.e., *ratio juris*, and it should not be mistaken for *ius*.

On the basis of this difference, Aquinas presents the difference between natural and positive law (*ius naturale et ius positivum*). Natural law means the capacity to halt both the good and the right, the distinction of which is based on nature. Indeed, the human being has a dual nature: it has an animal nature and a rational or human nature. According to Aquinas, however, natural law is a consequence of the rational nature of the human being. It arises from the special inclination of human nature and it is called *ius gentium*.[52] *Ius gentium* is a form of natural law, because it entails sentences that are valid as consequence from the general principles of natural law.

The rightness of an action can also be justified through a contract, which may be either private or public. In the case of a private contract, an action can be judged as to whether or not it is in agreement with a determination of two persons, for example. On the other hand, in a public contract, an action may be regarded as right according to the determination of the people (*ex condicto publico*) or of the ruler (*vel cum hoc ordinat princeps*). The ruler is a person who cares and represents the interest of the people:

> ... this is decreed by the prince who is placed over the people, and acts in its stead ...[53]

Therefore, one can see a possible relation between the political action and the will of the people. Furthermore, positive law must be deduced from natural law, but its deduction occurs, above all, *per modum determinationis*, i.e., through approximation.

The inquiry on the political community's existence is, at the same time, a question about the political community's justification. Function argument plays an important role because Aquinas claims the existence of a hierarchy of ends or principles and of a final end which can justify political actions.[54]

---

[50]Aquinas (1952).

[51]Ibidem, Pars II II:Quaest. LVII, Art. 1, Respondeo, translation mine. "Et, proper hoc, specialiter iustitiae, prae aliis virtutibus, determinatur secundum se obiectum, quod vocatur iustum. Et hoc quidem est ius."

[52]Schilling (1930), p. 29.

[53]Aquinas (1952), Pars II II:Quaest. LVII, Art. II, Respondeo, translation mine. "vel cum hoc ordinat princeps, qui curam populi habet, et eius personam gerit."

[54]Schilling (1930), p. 38.

Each action, or everything that occurs in order to achieve an end, must deliberate about the means that bring about said end. Thus, each action presupposes a relation between means and ends, although the end can be external or internal to the action. For instance, a ship can be driven into many directions by the wind, but it must be guided to a port in order to fulfill its function. The human action is like a ship. Every human being has an end, to which her whole life and actions must be driven, since she acts according to her reason, and this can only be acting towards an end.[55] In other words, the human soul is able to identify the perfect good through its reason and to desire it through its will. Whereas the helmsman, i.e., his will drives the ship to the harbor, it is the reason which drives human action to its goal:

> So, too, in the individual man, the soul rules the body; and among the parts of the soul, the irascible and the concupiscible parts are ruled by reason.[56]

The end of each human action consists necessarily in the happiness that can be achieved by reason.

Two elements give rise to a political society: natural instinct and reason.[57] Aquinas states that reason and language are decisive for justifying the political community's existence.[58] On the one hand, the human being is the only creature that can think from general principles to the knowledge of particulars. On the other hand, it is impossible for a human being to achieve all technical knowledge needed in order to be alive in nature. He needs, therefore, more persons. Language gives human beings the possibility of communicating emotions and knowledge.

If it is natural for human beings to live in society, then it must be something that guides them. Political community should be regarded as an artifact created in order to realize the social nature of the human being. Therefore, her goal consists in providing the material conditions for being alive and attaining happiness or the good life. According to Aquinas, the first end of each political community is called *bonum commune*, i.e. the common good.[59] The second end of each political community is maintenance of peace.[60] According to him, these ends are not a proper decision of the government or the political community, but rather they belong to the nature of political community, i.e., they are part of the natural law. Nevertheless, there is a sphere of freedom where the political community can decide how to realize (execute) these principles.[61]

The collective and individual good can only be regarded connectedly. According to Aquinas, although each individual could theoretically strive for her own good, it is necessary to have something that guides the individuals to a common good. The

---

[55] Aquinas (1949), p. 3.

[56] Ibidem, p. 6.

[57] Schilling (1930), p. 65.

[58] Aquinas (1949), pp. 4–5.

[59] Ibidem, p. 7.

[60] Ibidem, p. 12.

[61] Ibidem, p. 19.

government has this function: a government exists in order to drive society through the adequate means to the end of common good and, secondarily, peace.

Thomas of Aquin developed the function argument to adequate Aristotle's functionalism to an imperativistic ethics, which would later be considered the foundation of modern law and morality. The fundamental step towards adequacy consists in developing the concept of common good, and the idea of a hierarchy of ends. In the case of law and politics, this idea would later give rise to the necessity of an authority, such as the government. The existence of an authority on the basis of legal and political actions changes the way in which their language is developed. Nevertheless, in contrast with Ockham, emotions can play a decisive role by identifying the proper decision in the case of a political action, although Aquinas is clearly more rationalist than Aristotle regarding human action.

6.4.2 Ockham's **Breviloquium de principatu tyrannico**

Whereas it is possible to notice a kind of *continuum* between functionalism in Aristotle and Aquinas, the same cannot be said of Ockham.[62] *Breviloquium de principatu tyrannico* is a form of political theology, due to the fact that Ockham still justifies political actions by referring to a systematic interpretation of the New and Old Testaments. Ockham argues for a possible separation between temporal and spiritual powers, and for the legitimacy of these powers to natural rights and liberties, that is to say, the justification of political authority towards individuals:

> The anguish I feel is greater because you do not take the trouble to inquire with careful attention how much such tyranny wickedly usurped over you is contrary to God's honor, dangerous to the Catholic faith, and opposed to the rights and liberties given to you by God and nature; and worse, you reject, hinder, and condemn those who wish to inform you of the truth.[63]

Based on the refusal of a mimetic theory of reality, he acknowledges the linguistic capacity of individuals to create concepts or representations of the world. Concepts—e.g. *justice* or *beauty*—do not have an *in abstracto* meaning, but rather an *in concreto* meaning—i.e. as an attribute to something. Therefore, *justice* is only meaningful as *just* or *unjust* if concerning some state of affairs.

According to Ockham, the object of ethics is the free, rational and human action. Aristotle's difference between reason and desire is still preserved.[64] The intention or will is the decisive aspect when evaluating an action as good or bad, i.e., as

---

[62]About Ockham's final cause: Culleton (2011), pp. 135–151.

[63]Ockham (1992), p. 3, trans. John Kilcullen. "non minori autem affligor angustia, quia, quam sit divino honori contrarius, fidei periculosus catholice, iuribus et tyrannicus principatus, super vos nequiter usurpatus, vana sollicitudine inquirere non curatis, et, quod deterius est, vos de veritate informare volentes abicitis, confunditis et ipsos iudicatis." (Ockham 1944, I, p. 15).

[64]Adams (1999), p. 257.

justified. Ockham presupposes a certain freedom of human will regarding the execution or not of an action. Even an action in accordance with the direct command of God should be executed pursuant to freedom of will.[65]

However, freedom of will can only be understood within Ockham's ethical system. He makes a difference between positive and pre-positive ethics. Positive ethics assume an authority, and its knowledge is built up on human and sacred laws. To be justified, human action—free and rational action—must correspond to the will of an authority, which is the source of the laws, such as God or the Government. The pre-positive ethics consists in the knowledge about human, free and rational action that is built up on natural and empirical knowledge. But, in both cases, freedom remains a question on the *adaequatio* of human action towards rules or principles.

Furthermore, this *adaequatio* is based on three possible kinds of will.[66] First, one can wish what another would wish with another's will. As an example, when God gives a command to St. Peter. Second, one can wish what another person would wish that she had wished. The decision for a new pope after the death of St. Peter is an example of this kind of will. Third, one can wish what another person would wish in a similar way. For example, the decision for a new Government or king is of this kind. This gives rise to a modern communication theory in the sense that ethics starts to be seen as a conversation between senders and addressees of commands.

Ockham's nomological approach towards law and politics is even stronger than Aquinas', because the most important aspect of an ethical justification turns out to be individual rational will. In this context, ethics is regarded in a wholly modern way, i.e., as an imperativistic or normative science that focuses on understanding the correctness of principles or rules, based on the individual rational choice. Functionalism or justification regarding the final end of human action comes to be regarded as the search for rules or principles that are given either by an authority or by means of evident principles of experience—empirical knowledge. Emotions come to be secondary in virtue of the prevalence of a rational legitimacy model based on individual action, even in the case of law and politics.

6.5   Conclusion

Modern law and politics are nomological (law or imperativistic ethics), and, therefore, nominalist. The nomological approach to ethics, especially social ethics, entails three elements. First, it assumes a language or tongue of rights and duties. Second, this language of rights and duties refers to an authority that is the basis of its legitimacy. Third, there must be a communication theory at the foundation of the relation between authority and addressees of the commands, i.e., actions must be

---

[65]Ockham (1944), IV, c. 1.

[66]King (1999), p. 237.

justified on the basis of their adequacy towards rules given by some authority. Emotions can have a role within this model, but only a secondary one, such as in the case of improving obedience to law, and never in a cognitive capacity. This relation between actions and norms is fundamental.

In contrast with this nomological approach, Aristotle's view on ethics is based on the function argument, i.e., a method to grasp the essence of objects or, in other words, to explain the necessary properties of a certain concept, and in an integrative approach to human action as a union between desire and reason. The notions of efficient and final causes are decisive for comprehending this way of understanding the world. Whereas efficient cause explains the origin of a given phenomenon, final cause sheds light on the proper goal of something or of an action. Above all, Aristotle's functionalism in law and politics takes the final cause concept to heart.

It is, of course, difficult to grasp Aristotle's project of practical reasoning as a deliberative action of mediation between desire (emotion) and reason, i.e., universal ends and situational indeterminacy. Through the reception of Aristotle's ethics by the political works of Aquinas and Ockham, I tried to show that the cognitive role of emotions has gradually come to play a secondary role or, in Ockham's work, none at all, by grasping and building ends of actions. Emotions that should play a role by mediating universal and particular are then replaced by a communication theory of rights and duties.

References

Adams, Marilyn McCord. 1999. Ockham on Will, Nature, and Morality. In *The Cambridge Companion to Ockham*, ed. Paul Vincent Spade. Cambridge and New York: Cambridge University Press.

Angioni, Lucas. 2009. *Introdução à teoria da predicação em Aristóteles*. São Paulo: UNICAMP.

Anscombe, G.E.M. 1958. Modern Moral Philosophy. *Philosophy* 33 (124): 1–19.

Aquinas, Thomas. 1949. *On Kingship, to the King of Cyprus*. Translated by G. B. Phelan. Westport, CT: Hyperion Press.

———. 1952. *Summa Theologiae. Vol. Pars II II*. Turin: Marietti.

Aristotle. 1984a. Metaphysics. In *The Complete Works of Aristotle: The Revised Oxford Translation*, ed. Jonathan Barnes and trans. W. D. Ross. Princeton, NJ: Princeton University Press.

———. 1984b. Nicomachean Ethics. In *The Complete Works of Aristotle: The Revised Oxford Translation*, ed. Jonathan Barnes and trans. W. D. Ross and J. O. Urmson. Princeton, NJ: Princeton University Press.

Atienza, Manuel. 2001. *El sentido del derecho*. Barcelona: Editorial Ariel.

Bombelli, Giovanni. 2018. Emotion and Rationality in Aristotle's Model: From Anthropology to Politics. In *Aristotle on Emotions in Law and Politics*, ed. Liesbeth Huppes-Cluysenaer and Nuno M.M.S. Coelho. Dordrecht: Springer.

Charles, David. 2000. *Aristotle on Meaning and Essence*. Oxford and New York: Clarendon Press and Oxford University Press.

Culleton, Alfredo. 2011. *Ockham e a lei natural*. Florianópolis: Editora da UFSC.

de Matos, Saulo. 2012. O Conceito de Direito Na Filosofia Moral Gadameriana. *Revista de Estudos Constitucionais, Hermenêutica E Teoria Do Direito* 4 (1): 90–101.

———. 2015. *Zum normativen Begriff der Volkssouveränität: rechtsphilosophische und verfassungstheoretische Versuche der Legitimierung des politischen Handelns*. Baden-Baden: Nomos.

Edmundson, William A. 2004. *An Introduction to Rights*. Cambridge and New York: Cambridge University Press.

Finnis, John. 1998. *Aquinas: Moral, Political, and Legal Theory*. Vol. 430. New York: Oxford University Press.

Gadamer, Hans-Georg. 1986. *The Idea of the Good in Platonic-Aristotelian Philosophy*. Translated by Christopher Smith. New Haven, CT: Yale University Press. https://www.worldcat.org/title/idea-of-the-good-in-platonic-aristotelian-philosophy/oclc/12584472&referer=brief_results.

———. 1998. *Nikomachische Ethik VI*. Klostermann: Frankfurt.

———. 1999a. Aristotle and the Ethics of Imperatives. In *Action and Contemplation: Studies in the Moral and Political Thought of Aristotle*, ed. Robert C. Bartlett and Susan D. Collins, 53–68. Albany: State University of New York Press.

———. 1999b. *Gesammelte Werke 3: Neuere Philosophie I*. Tübingen: Mohr.

Greenberg, Mark. 2004. How Facts Make Law. *Legal Theory* 10: 157–198.

———. 2011. Legislation as Communication? Legal Interpretation and the Study of Linguistic Communication. In *Philosophical Foundations of Language in the Law*, ed. Andrei Marmor and Scott Soames, 217–264. Oxford and New York: Oxford University Press.

Hohfeld, Wesley Newcomb. 1917. Fundamental Legal Conceptions as Applied in Judicial Reasoning. *Yale Law Review* 26 (8): 710–770.

Horn, Christoph, and Nico Scarano. 2002. *Philosophie der Gerechtigkeit: Texte von der Antike bis zur Gegenwart*. Suhrkamp: Frankfurt.

Huppes-Cluysenaer, Liesbeth. 2013. Reasoning Against a Deterministic Conception of the World. In *Aristotle and the Philosophy of Law Theory, Practice and Justice*, ed. Liesbeth Huppes-Cluysenaer and Nuno M.M.S. Coelho, 33–58. Dordrecht and New York: Springer.

King, Peter. 1999. Ockham's Ethical Theory. In *The Cambridge Companion to Ockham*, ed. Paul Vincent Spade, 227. Cambridge and New York: Cambridge University Press.

Maritain, Jacques. 2001. *Elementos de filosofia: II, A ordem dos conceitos*. Translated by Ilza das Neves. Rio de Janeiro: Livraria AGIR.

Murphy, Mark C. 2006. *Natural Law in Jurisprudence and Politics*. Cambridge, UK and New York: Cambridge University Press.

Nascimento, Daniel Simao. 2018. Rhetoric, Emotions and the Rule of Law in Aristotle. In *Aristotle on Emotions in Law and Politics*, ed. Liesbeth Huppes-Cluysenaer and Nuno M.M.S. Coelho. Dordrecht: Springer.

Nussbaum, Martha Craven. 2013. *Political Emotions: Why Love Matters for Justice*. http://public.eblib.com/choice/publicfullrecord.aspx?p=3301331.

Nussbaum, Martha Craven, and Hilary Putnam. 1992. Changing Aristotle's Mind. In *Essays on Aristotle's De Anima*, ed. Martha Craven Nussbaum and Amélie Rorty, 30–60. Oxford: Clarendon Press. http://public.eblib.com/choice/publicfullrecord.aspx?p=3052875.

Ockham, Wilhelm. 1944. *Wilhelm von Ockham Als Politischer Denker Und Sein Breviloquium de Principatu Tyrannico*. Edited by Richard Scholz. Leipzig: K.W. Hiersemann.

Ockham, William. 1992. *A Short Discourse on the Tyrannical Government over Things Divine and Human, but Especially over the Empire and Those Subject to the Empire, Usurped by Some Who Are Called Highest Pontiffs*. Edited by Arthur Stephen McGrade. Translated by John Kilcullen. Cambridge, UK and New York: Cambridge University Press.

Olfert, C.M.M. 2014. Aristotle's Conception of Practical Truth. *Journal of the History of Philosophy* 52 (2): 205–231.

Radbruch, Gustav. 2003. *Rechtsphilosophie*. Heidelberg: Müller.

Schilling, Otto. 1930. *Die staats- und soziallehre des heiligen Thomas von Aquin*. Munich: M. Hueber.

Schopenhauer, Arthur. 1977. *Über die Freiheit des menschlichen Willens: Über die Grundlage der Moral: kleinere Schriften II*. Zürich: Diogenes.

Schröder, Jan. 2012. *Recht als Wissenschaft: Geschichte der juristischen Methodenlehre in der Neuzeit (1500-1933)*. Munich: C.H. Beck.

Soames, Scott. 2012. *Philosophy of Language*. Princeton, NJ: Princeton University Press.

Solum, Lawrence. 2013. Virtue Jurisprudence: Towards an Aretaic Theory of Law. In *Aristotle and the Philosophy of Law Theory, Practice and Justice*, ed. Liesbeth Huppes-Cluysenaer and Nuno M.M.S. Coelho, 1–32. Dordrecht and New York: Springer. http://public.eblib.com/choice/publicfullrecord.aspx?p=1083709.

Varela, Luis Enrique. 2014. *Filosofía práctica y prudencia: lo universal y lo particular en la ética de Aristóteles*. Buenos Aires: Remedios de Escalada: Biblos; Universidad Nacional de Lanús.

von der Pfordten, Dietmar. 2009. About Concepts in Law. In *Concepts in Law*, ed. J.C. Hage and Dietmar von der Pfordten, 17–34. Dordrecht and New York: Springer. http://public.eblib.com/choice/publicfullrecord.aspx?p=478131.

———. 2013. *Rechtsphilosophie: eine Einführung*. Munich: C.H. Beck.

Wellman, Carl. 1985. *A Theory of Rights: Persons Under Laws, Institutions, and Morals*. Totowa, NJ: Rowman & Allanheld.

Chapter 7
On *Logos*, *Pathos* and *Ethos* in Judicial Argumentation

Fabiana Pinho

Abstract The chapter endeavors to present what is known in the legal literature as a rhetorical approach to law. The contribution may be understood as a preface to a broader research agenda, which proposes a conceptual framework to analyze legal argumentation in an international context. The point of departure is that law may be considered as a rhetorical practice. The chapter will justify the theoretical premise that analytical categories from the Aristotelian rhetoric can be useful in understanding the discourse in international courts. To achieve this the paper has been divided into three main parts. In the first section, Aristotle's rhetorical categories *logos*, *pathos* and *ethos* are defined in accordance with a rhetorical empirical method elaborated by the legal philosophers from the School of Mainz. In the second section, the core of this rhetorical empirical method is outlined following K. von Schlieffen's work on the analysis of judicial decisions. Finally, as a simple illustration of the rhetorical approach, two decisions on human dignity from the International Court of Justice (ICJ) are examined, taking these two examples as a *topos*, which in turn, reinforces the case for problem-oriented reasoning in the practice of international law.

7.1 Introduction

This paper aims to present and discuss what has been known in the legal literature as a rhetorical approach to law. The point of departure is that law can be considered as a kind of rhetorical practice. The paper will be concerned mostly with justifying such a theoretical premise. It will explain how analytical categories from Aristotle's *Rhetoric*[1] can be useful in understanding the evolution of the discourse produced by international courts. This contribution should be understood as a preface to a broader research agenda. Building on Aristotle's philosophy and its development

---

[1] Aristotle (1984a). Edition used: Jonathan Barnes. *The Complete Works of Aristotle*.

F. Pinho (✉)
University of São Paulo, São Paulo, Brazil

University of Kiel, Kiel, Germany
e-mail: fabiana.o.pinho@gmail.com

© Springer International Publishing AG 2018
L. Huppes-Cluysenaer, N.M.M.S. Coelho (eds.), *Aristotle on Emotions in Law and Politics*, Law and Philosophy Library 121, DOI 10.1007/978-3-319-66703-4_7

by the School of Mainz, it proposes a conceptual framework to analyze legal argumentation at the international level.

In order to achieve this goal, the paper will be divided into three main sections. In the first section, the rhetorical categories of logos, pathos and ethos[2] are defined in accordance with the interpretation of Aristotle's view by the legal philosophers from the School of Mainz. Although these rhetorical categories of Aristotle's works are well known and have long been discussed by scholars, they carry special features when part of a rhetorical empirical method for the analysis of judicial decisions. Thus, on the one hand these rhetorical categories preserve their original function—that is, logos, which builds arguments in an enthymematic structure, pathos, which aims to cause some emotional impact on the audience and ethos, which appeals to the speaker's authority to obtain the audience's consent. On the other hand, the rhetorical empirical method specifies which source of law or kind of legal justification matches with these classical rhetorical categories.

In the second part, the core of the rhetorical empirical method is outlined, following K. von Schlieffen's work on the analysis of judicial decisions. As a member of the "Mainzer Schule", K. von Schlieffen builds on Ottmar Ballweg's contributions to analytical rhetoric and develops her own approach towards the theoretical conclusions of Theodor Viehweg's seminal work, "Topic and Jurisprudence". While avoiding a deeper discussion about the rhetorical nature of law, the rhetorical empirical method is presented as a useful instrument in identifying the function of rhetorical categories in judicial argumentative constructions. To set the stage for that method, the tools from the Aristotelian rhetoric become key in strengthening the view that the structure of legal argumentation is not a "systematic", but rather a "problematic reasoning" and that common place (topos) plays a fundamental role during the entire argumentative process in courts.

Finally, as a simple illustration of the rhetorical approach, two decisions from the International Court of Justice (ICJ) on human dignity are examined in accordance with the Aristotelian categories, stated in the previous section, and with the rhetorical empirical method on the analysis of judicial decisions. Based on the topical nature of human dignity,[3] this part investigates when and how human dignity is molded into the categories of logos, pathos or ethos in the ICJ's legal discourse. These cases, as relevant precedents in international law, allow us to emphasize how argumentative moves, captured by the categories of logos, pathos and ethos, shape judicial argumentation. This, in turn, reinforces the case for a problem-oriented reasoning in the practice of international law.

---

[2]Some Greek terms will be used as theoretical terms and will not be translated. The translation common place instead of commonplace is used for theoretical reasons.

[3]Bornscheuer (1976).

7.2 Aristotle's Rhetorical Categories

Even today there is not a consensus among scholars in Greek philosophy regarding the exact contours of Aristotle's rhetoric. This same lack of agreement occurs in respect to the content of the rhetorical categories and their role in producing persuasive discourses in the realm of argumentation.[4] While avoiding taking sides or furthering discussions regarding the place of rhetoric in Aristotle's work, this paper adopts from the outset a deliberate definition for rhetoric and rhetorical categories—logos, ethos and pathos[5] (see Sects. 7.2.1–7.2.3)—to guide the reflections presented below.

Narrowing the gap between rhetoric and dialectics, Aristotle defines rhetoric as a dialectical discipline based on plausible arguments intended to persuade the audience of a discourse that, in principle, may address any contended issue. Taken as an intellectual craft, the Aristotelian rhetoric can also be understood as the art of finding plausible means to achieve the persuasion of a specific audience (*Rhet.* 1354a). Accordingly, the conception of rhetoric adopted, though not undisputable, is clearly distinct from the vulgar notion of rhetoric as mere oratory or a skill to deceptively convince an audience through any available means.[6] For the scholars affiliated with the School of Mainz ("Mainzer Schule")—including Katharina von Schlieffen, proponent of the method for rhetorical analysis of judicial decisions—a discourse of rhetoric aims to achieve the most plausible legal decision through a process of dialogical argumentation.[7]

Conclusions achieved by a rhetorical reasoning, always comprising a range of possible decisions to be argued, can be evaluated only as more or less plausible, in correspondence to the degree of plausibility of the supporting premises of an argument. In the Aristotelian tradition, those premises are named common places (topoi) (*Rhet.* 1403a17–18). The traditional Greek terminology will be maintained throughout this paper for the sake of precision. The characteristics and function performed by the common places (topoi) in the rhetorical-dialectical discourse, particularly as premises to the judicial argumentation, will be further explained later (see Sect. 7.3.1). For now, it should be noted only that the quality of truth about those premises pertains to a different kind of reasoning, called here demonstrative

---

[4]Braet (1992).

[5]About the role of emotions in legal reasoning, see in this volume: Maroney (2018) and Silvestre (2018).

[6]In this volume a different view about the purpose of rhetoric in Aristotelian work is supported by Cohen de Lara. She argues that content, either moral or political, are not a subject matter that belongs to rhetoric. In her view, learning rhetoric means merely to gather persuasion skills. Something else cannot be required from this art of delivering effective discourses. Cohen de Lara (2018). However, as already said, in accordance with the rhetorical approach to law of the School of Mainz, we are in favor of a rhetoric in which meanings are really important in shaping the most plausible decision. In other words, not only convincing matters, but particularly the plausibility of contents built during the whole argumentation process.

[7]Bayer (1975).

or apodictic. Structured under the tenets of formal logic, the demonstrative reasoning does not allow for plausible conclusions but for true ones, taking the form of propositions produced through valid inferences (*Top.* 100a20–101a1).[8]

Accordingly, the distinctive nature of the premises underlying the rhetorical and demonstrative reasoning bears also on the kind of questions posed for each of these patterns of rationality. On the one hand, demonstrative reasoning deals with questions which discussants would answer pointing to the certainty and determinacy of propositions from which necessarily indisputable results derive. Rhetorical-dialectical reasoning, on the other hand, tackles questions with recourse to the verisimilitude or probability of propositions, which are commonly accepted by discussants, but from which only more or less plausible opinions can be built (*Top.* 105b30–106a1). Following the theoretical approach of the School of Mainz, legal reasoning is assumed to be a constitutive element of a rhetorical practice. Hence, the typical rationality of jurists is considered to be aporetic in nature, not apodictic.

In addition to the general characteristics mentioned above, which distinguish rhetoric from a demonstrative reasoning founded on formal syllogism, there are two specific aspects of rhetorical legal reasoning which become relevant here. The first is the possibility that a dialectical interaction between parties in a lawsuit contributes to the construction of arguments supporting the most plausible decision to a legal case. The second aspect is that shared meanings concerning law, although preexistent to concrete legal discourses, are often actively redefined by the dialogue between parties. This can be revealed through analytical use of the rhetorical categories: logos, pathos and ethos (*Rhet.* 1356a20–25). In such a dialogical struggle, persuasion results from identifying which is the soundest of all of the legal arguments that, varying in their degree of plausibility, determine the range of possible decisions to a case.

7.2.1 Logos

In Aristotle's work, the category of logos held a prominent position among the means of persuasion of rhetoric. For the purposes of the empirical rhetorical method, such a category expresses argumentative appeals to the reason of the participants in legal discourse. It can be formalized as a rhetorical enthymeme, (*Rhet.* 1357a10–1357b20) so characterized for having at its base a rhetorical syllogism, built on the notion of common place (topos).[9] Enthymemes, visualized in legal discourse from the perspective of logos, produce what can be narrowly defined as *arguments*.[10]

These arguments, as specific means of persuasion, are not structured with the same kind of propositions as those utilized in formal syllogisms: a major premise,

---

[8]Aristotle (1984b). Edition used: Jonathan Barnes. The Complete Works of Aristotle.

[9]van Zantwijk (2011).

[10]Sobota (1994).

indicating normative elements from the law, and a minor premise, including factual elements from the case under analysis. Also, conclusions from enthymematic arguments are not automatic conclusions derived from a logical superposition of major and minor premises. Hence, contrary to arguments derived from formal syllogism, the enthymeme begins with the selection of plausible premises and ends with merely a range of possible decisions, characterized by the same degree of plausibility.

An enthymematic structure of arguments comprises propositions that support one another, amounting to an argumentation that contributes to the formulation of the most plausible decision—see Sect. 7.3.2 about "tree of supporting arguments" ("Stützungsbaum").[11] In the diagram below, the enthymematic structure of arguments is summarized and compared to the structure of arguments from formal syllogism. It is easy to see the difference between the rationality patterns that inform each of those structures. While inductive reasoning reinforces the problematic character of enthymemes, as it builds arguments from the legal problem, the deductive reasoning underscores the systematic aspect that defines the logical syllogism, because the legal system is taken as starting point for resolving the case.

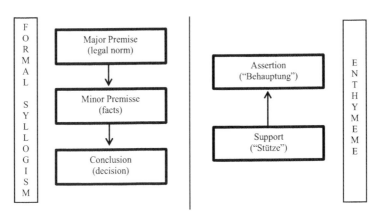

Structure of formal syllogism and enthymeme

To analyze legal decisions by the empirical-rhetorical method, K. von Schlieffen distinguishes several different ideal-types of argument that would represent the argumentative dimension represented by the category of logos.[12] Together, these argument types, utilized as analytical tools, become a catalog of argumentative persuasive means. They are summarized below:

---

[11]von Schlieffen (2005), p. 422.

[12]von Schlieffen (2008), pp. 1820–1821.

Components of *Logos* in legal reasoning

Type	Definition
Codification argument	Codified norms ("This is so because norm xy says it must be so")
Principles argument	Principles of law, including the special rules of interpretation of legal texts
Common sense argument	Rules of every-day life, maxims of common sense
Conclusions	Sentences which contains conclusions (The end of ideas and thoughts)

7.2.2 *Pathos*[13]

While the category of logos aims to reach the discussant's reason via arguments, the category of pathos aims at the emotions of the participants (*Rhet.* 1356a). This pathetical effect can be achieved in different ways, from the voice tone adopted by a speaker to the use of certain gestures or body language during the speech. In rhetorical analysis of judgments, however, these elements of non-verbal communication cannot be captured. For this reason, rhetorical empirical analysis of the presence of pathos in legal argumentation is restricted to the verbal elements, which are consolidated in the text.[14]

In this verbal or written level of communication,[15] the category of pathos is manifested by the figures of speech. These figures do not aim at building an argument—in the sense explained above—but at provoking an emotional impact on the addressee of the speech. Even though legal language is normally supposed to be objective and to some extent neutral, this rhetorical empirical method provides tools to detect the pathetical mechanisms in judicial argumentation. The detection of these figures in legal discourse pertains mainly to the analysis of the stylistic choices that were made in composing the text. It involves the choices of vocabulary, the strength of a verb, and even the way in which the punctuation in the text is used.

Pathos is not present in most methods for analysis of judicial decisions and is considered as an irrational persuasive mean. This may have been caused by the fact that the role of pathos is not clearly expressed in the argumentative processes, in comparison with the role of logos. This impression, however—as well as some other biases against the use of emotional effects in courts—breaks down when confronted with the rhetorical analysis of the judicial decisions of German courts on delicate matters. This empirical research carried out by K. von Schlieffen shows that judges more frequently use persuasive speech based on pathos than we would have imagined. Furthermore, these pathetical resources are invoked even more

---

[13]About the role of emotions in legal reasoning, see also in this volume: Maroney (2018) and Silvestre (2018).

[14]von Schlieffen (2008).

[15]Schirren (2009).

when needed to support an important claim, which could not count on an easy acceptance if its relevance would have to be justified on a rational basis only.

In the rhetorical empirical method proposed by K. von Schlieffen, analysis of the category of pathos is carried out through the use of 37 subspecies of figures which go back to the rhetorical figures of the ancient doctrines.[16] According to K. von Schlieffen, some common examples of these figures found by the rhetorical empirical method in legal decisions are emphasis (exclamatio), hyperbola (exaggerations) or brevitas (ellipsis and zeugma), metaphors, metonymies, tautologies, antithesis.[17] The identification of these figures is especially important when employing the rhetorical empirical method in quantitative analysis, in order to construct the *rhetorical Seismograms*[18] (see Sect. 7.3.2 below).

The analysis of the impact of pathos in law, specifically in the adjudication process, can sound somewhat self-contradictory, when it is assumed that law is a rational process of impartial deliberation. This paper, however, considers pathos as an analytical category meant to detect emotional aspects that could, in fact be part of judicial justification. However, as affirmed by C. Rapp[19] in this volume, some legal philosophers have been trying to give extra attention to the role of emotions in legal decision-making, even transforming it into a totally emotional process. This would not be a problem in itself, if these legal scholars had not evoked an interpretation of Aristotle's work, stating that emotion is undeniably present in processes of legal decision-making. As highlighted by C. Rapp, one must take care when asserting that law is emotion, since, in fact, the standard opinion about Aristotle's view on this matter has indicated, until recently, another kind of relationship between law and emotion.

7.2.3   Ethos

As the rhetorical method proposes, the category of ethos is defined formally as not containing a genuine argument—according to the above definition (see Sect. 7.2.1)—nor does it aim at the emotions of the participants in the discourse with the help of rhetorical linguistics constructions.[20] In the category of ethos persuasive means are gathered which convey aspects of morality, either linked to the reputation of the speaker (*Rhet.* 1356a), or linked to values socially constructed by custom and tradition.[21] Even though the category of ethos in Aristotle's work is nearly always bound to the speaker's reputation or speaker's moral authority, in judicial

---

[16]Sobota (1994), p. 158.

[17]Ibid., p. 159.

[18]Sobota (1992).

[19]In this volume Rapp (2018).

[20]Sobota (1994), p. 158.

[21]Sprute (1991).

discourse this category of ethos appears in some other ways. The reason for this lies in the attempt to transform law into a completely objective enterprise, which has been in progress since the Enlightenment era.

In doing so, legal actors seldom support their position by means of subjective features. Neither can the judge expressly justify a decision based on his/her own reputation or moral attributes, nor are the parties allowed to sustain their defense or accusation on a subjective basis. The ideal consists in extracting the answer to a legal problem from a hypothetically neutral system of norms, which barely corresponds to the tense real conflict, at the bottom of the problem. In this context—with the exception of expert opinions, which occasionally are used in a legal process to reinforce a certain position by invoking the reputation of a renowned person—the persuasive means usually rely on the *authority of law* and on the *authority of an important document or text* as well as on *some legal sources* able to create law.

Assertions like "the *democratic law* says that...", or "the *constitution, our magna Charta,* allows no other way to solve this issue" or even "it is not possible, because the *spirit of the norm* was not shaped in this way" are very common in legal discourse. Even though these assertions are not bound to a specific person, and cannot be definitively connected to the speaker's morals and reputation, these statements indeed are meant to carry some authority and, in so doing, to have an effect in the argumentation process. Taking into account these objectification efforts as notorious legal phenomena, K. von Schlieffen classifies the following persuasive means in the category of ethos[22]:

Components of *Ethos* in judicial reasoning

Authority argument	Example: "This is so, because this or that court has said it is so"
Text argument	Example: "This is so because the text says so"
The mentioning of the sources	Example: quotations, footnotes with references to the academic system of law and its rules of accuracy

Furthermore, it must be said that the analyses undertaken so far with the rhetorical empirical method have used the decisions of the German domestic courts as their source. However, international law when compared to national law has certain other specific characteristics. The most relevant one for analysing International Court decisions with the rhetorical empirical method is the fact that customary law is a very significant normative source at the international level. The normativity of customary law arises from established practices among international actors and it does not depend on their consolidation in formal documents such as international treaties. Since most customs rest on values shared by practitioners and on the recognition of tradition, the means of persuasion in judicial decisions of international courts which are based on customary law should be classified in our view as part of the category of ethos.

---

[22]Sobota (1994), p. 158.

7.3 Rhetorical Empirical Analysis of Judicial Decisions

Continuing the tradition by T. Viehweg and scholars of the School of Mainz ("Mainzer Schule"),[23] K. von Schlieffen formulated the original version of the empirical method for rhetorical analysis. This method assumes that law should be understood as a rhetorical practice,[24] which moves the analytical focus to the construction of legal decisions through a structured argumentative process. In fact, the empirical rhetorical method of analysis reveals an argumentative structure very different from the idea commonly held by the participants in legal discourse: it is not built on a syllogistic basis and the final decision does not come automatically from a systematic chain of inferences. On the contrary, rhetorical empirical analysis points to the existence of several argumentation nests ("Argumentnester"), each one grounded on a common place (topos) as a starting point for legal reasoning which has developed in a problem-oriented way.

7.3.1 Problematic Thinking and the Role of Topos in Judicial Discourse

The discussion about the role that common places (topoi) play in the argumentative construction of judicial discourses affects the debate concerning the kind of reasoning employed in courts. Of course, this debate is nuanced and has been of great concern for the philosophy of law and for legal theory. In turn, this chapter proposes to face the dichotomy between systematic thinking ("Systemdenken") and problematic thinking ("Problemdenken") and to investigate the function of the common places (topoi) in legal reasoning.[25] Such a dichotomy was also T. Viehweg's departing point when he claimed that law is an argumentative practice and stated that, until the seventeenth century, this argumentative character had been indisputable.[26]

Viehweg's proposal to restate topics as the prevailing mode of thinking about the law, presented in "Topics and Jurisprudence", is based on the meaning he attributes to the different ways in which problem and system establish and guide legal reasoning. When facing a practical question, which has to be legally solved, the premises that guide the solution must be chosen from the perspective of the definition of the problem. As said above (cf. Sect. 7.2), those premises are neither true nor necessary. When interpreting the law, several premises are available, which are all considered acceptable by authoritative legal interpreters. One of these is then chosen as a departing point to the argumentative process.

---

[23]Sobota (1991), pp. 275–278.
[24]von Schlieffen (2008), p. 1811.
[25]Hartmann (2014).
[26]Viehweg (1974).

In doing so, legal argumentations, particularly those developed in courts, can be understood as forms of *situational problematic thinking*.[27] The reference to situational context points to the fact that the litigants actively contribute to the construction of the meanings that constitute the specific legal discourse. Because legal discourse is situational, the problematic thinking employed by legal arguers does not support the notion of a preexistent legal system which is logically organized to be complete and coherent and by which thus any problem of a possible normative gap or contradiction is prevented. Problematic thinking on the contrary centers the legal argumentation on a particular disputed issue. This is methodologically relevant in cases, which arise in a fragmented international order because the legal problem is then a safe starting point to determine the most plausible solution.

This situational, problem-oriented, argumentative process develops through dialogue with reference to the different persuasive means—based on logos, pathos and ethos. It brings a way of thinking which more adequately explains the construction of arguments in an international order characterized by the fragmentation of normative sources.[28] In a fragmented international order, the ideal of a complete and coherent legal system collapses. Therefore order is much easier to realize when an answer in litigation is not thought to originate automatically from a set of rules and dogmatic categories, but rather from the efforts placed into discourse by participants attempting to find a plausible solution in an argumentative process.

Once the typical mode of thought about law is framed as a dialogical reasoning, the premises, which are able to provide legal arguments, can be understood as common places (topoi). In short, a common place (topos) is a point of view, the content of which, despite not being completely defined beforehand, is more or less accepted by the members of a community. Along with the development of argumentative practice, participants to the legal discourse in fact actively contribute to the (re)construction of normative meanings. For that reason, the common place (topos) can also be seen as a formula that embodies updated and prevailing content of legal concepts, which, in turn, are constantly transformed by the very argumentative practice that once consolidated their (contingent) meaning.

From the perspective of the category of logos, structured as a rhetorical enthymeme, the common place (topos) is the starting point for the organization of reasoning. As said before (cf. Sect. 7.2.1), it is precisely because a common place (topos) is the basis for several types of reasoning that these can be qualified as enthymematic reasoning. In order to argue in the law with the support of an enthymeme, several alternative premises are always available, among which a choice must be made, which lead to different possible legal decisions. During the construction of the enthymeme however, elements which are typical of apodictic reasoning (demonstrative) take part in the argumentative process as well. Legal doctrine and interpretive statements produced by academic jurists are therefore also relevant to the topical dimension of the legal discourse as revealed by the category of logos.

---

[27]Horn (1966) and Rodingen (1972).

[28]Koskenniemi (2006) and Koskenniemi and Leino (2002).

That legal reasoning reflects problematic thought does not mean that one can identify the most plausible premises and conclusion only from the perspective of the concrete problem, or that accumulated knowledge derived from legal practice and developed in previous cases is not relevant. Problematic thought opposes systematic thought, especially in relation to the beginning and end of the argumentative practice. Once the premises are selected from the possible alternatives and the expected solution is proposed, the reasoning employed by legal arguers cannot dispense with doctrine. Indeed, the system of rules and legal concepts derived from the doctrinal work contributes to the construction of arguments, which drive the dialogue between parties in court to the most plausible solution of a problem.

The topical aspects of law are mostly recognized in legal arguments, such as revealed by the category of logos. The presence of common place (topos) in legal discourse is, however, also expressed in other persuasive means which are framed by the categories of pathos and ethos. This occurs because a defining characteristic of the common place (topos) is that such a notion carries—besides the shared meanings of the law—social values, moral parameters, authoritative customs of a given community, and emotional strategies to affect the participants of the legal discourse (cf. Sect. 7.2). These multiple aspects of legal argumentation as explained by the topical approach warrant that some important concepts in law, such as human dignity, are qualified as common place (topos). This concept is the focus of the latter part of this chapter (see Sect. 7.4.1).

7.3.2   Rhetorical Empirical Method

As a member of the School of Mainz, K. von Schlieffen also states that legal decisions are not simple deductions from a pre-established system of legal norms, but rather come from a complex exercise that involves discovering arguments in problem-oriented reasoning.[29] In doing so, the formal syllogistic schema consisting of a major premise (abstract rule), a minor premise (facts) and a conclusion (legal decision) does not fit in with the analytical categories used to perform the rhetorical empirical method. On the contrary, this method, which is essentially built on the views of T. Viehweg and O. Ballweg, combines the classical categories from Aristotle's *Rhetoric* and is meant to reveal the sophisticated structure of an argumentative process towards a final decision.

From a problem-oriented point of view—to which the rhetorical approach to law belongs—the contribution of K. von Schlieffen with this method of analysis for judicial decisions has a comparative advantage: on the one hand, this rhetorical method can highlight the moves taken by the participants in court on dialogical basis. In doing so, it becomes clear which strategies have been chosen in a litigation to support a particular position and how the decision-maker has tried to justify his/her final decision. On the other hand, this kind of rhetorical analysis reinforces the

---

[29]Ballweg (1984) and Ballweg (1989).

decision-making process as a disputation towards the most plausible decision. This way, the method emphasizes the plurality of starting points available to the parties—here more precisely designed as common places (topoi)—and the large chance of a plausible conclusion which is not solely derived from a system of legal rules.

The empirical rhetorical method, however, was not intended to teach how the rhetorical categories should be manipulated in order to construct enthymematic reasoning and produce plausible decisions. This method rather serves a strict analytical purpose. K. von Schlieffen's theoretical proposal has a clear descriptive character. It shows that the argumentative process is not a normative one, and suggests how argumentation in courts can be explained by abstract parameters. Indeed, the method provides analytical tools, molded as the categories of logos, pathos and ethos, to determine: (1) how these rhetorical notions explain the influence of specific arguments in the formulation of a judicial decision; (2) in which frequency these notions are employed in the argumentative constructions which lead to the formulation of such judicial decisions.

This twofold proposal aligns two different approaches to the analysis of judicial decision-making: a qualitative and a quantitative one. In the qualitative approach, the argumentative chain built during the argumentative process and expressed in the structure of the justification of the decision is relevant. Because the starting points of an argumentative process normally begin with different points of view—here better called common places (topoi)—this argumentative structure resembles a tree with branches. This is why the expression of this argumentative process in the form of a diagram is called a "tree of supporting arguments" ("Stützungsbaum"). In a broader perspective, this tree diagram can be seen as a visual representation of the dialectical rhetorical construction of a decision-making process.

As previously stated, the common places (topoi) represent the departing points of an argumentative process in courts. Argumentative moves are based on the choices of each participant to the litigation, who presents assertions ("Behauptung") in a progressive manner. The successive assertions ("Behauptung") find support ("Stütze") in the previous ones and are also supposed to work as a support to further additional assertions connected to the original common place (topos). These combinations among assertions and supports shape enthymemes, as explained above (see Sect. 7.2.1), classified by K. von Schlieffen in the category of logos. Because the enthymemes are the core of a judicial decision and intended to appeal to the participants' practical rationality, the trees of supporting arguments are usually dominated by this rhetorical category. However, also pathos and ethos can be marked by this analytical method, when they change the argumentation course or even when they work to reinforce the previous or later assertion. An example of a tree of supporting arguments is presented in this chapter (see Sect. 7.4.2).

In turn, the quantitative approach utilizes the same analytical rhetorical categories—logos, pathos and ethos—as a unit of measurement for another diagram, called rhetorical "Seismogramm". In this case, the occurrence of the rhetorical categories are calculated per cluster of 1000 words, and then plotted on a graph. From the data produced by the empirical-rhetorical method,[30] especially through

---

[30]Sobota (1996).

quantitative analysis, the most important finding of K. von Schlieffen and other authors is that, contrary to the common wisdom about the law, a judicial decision is usually not formulated with recourse to arguments based on logos only.[31]

7.4 The Rhetorical Categories in the International Judicial Argumentation

7.4.1 *Human Dignity as Topos in International Law*

From the very beginning, it is relevant to take human dignity as a common place (topos)—regardless of any doctrinal discussion concerning a principle, a legal rule or an undetermined concept—because such an approach reveals decisive implications for the development of the legal discourse. Taking human dignity as a common place (topos) also implies the theoretical acceptance of a model of legal argumentation centered on the notion of *problem*, that is, a contested question to be settled by a practical decision. This problem-oriented model of argumentation also implies a form of problematic reasoning characterized by the features exposed above. In this sense, from a rhetorical view, the common place (topos) of human dignity can provide *arguments* as well as other *persuasive means* that guide the dialogue between the arguers towards the most plausible solution of their legal case (see also Sect. 7.3.1).

Because the concept and function of the common place (topos) was not yet fully exposed in Aristotle's work, philosophers have been trying to identify its constitutive elements, to devise qualification criteria and to propose a classification. Of course, several proposals have been made in that respect, and this paper adopts only one of them to justify the characterization of human dignity as an argumentative common place (topos): the theoretical approach of L. Bornscheuer.[32] Such a proposal offers advantages because the author takes the common place (topos) not only as an abstract notion at the foundation of a dialogical reasoning, but also as a comprehensive discursive framework covering moral and political aspects, such as consolidated values and social practices in a given community.[33] In this way, common place (topos) is not only a formal piece pertaining to a kind of reasoning, but it is also seen as a repository of meanings established by the participants in a broader discourse.

In this way, human dignity is considered to be a common place (topos) because this legal concept displays four characteristic elements: habituality ("Habitualität"), potentiality ("Potentialität"), intentionality ("Intentionalität") and symbolicity ("Symbolizität").[34] It is true that human dignity has a prominent role in the political organization of western societies since the Christian era in moral, as well as in religious, political and/or legal discourse. However, it became especially relevant

---

[31]von Schlieffen (2005).

[32]Bornscheuer (1976).

[33]Ibid., p. 20.

[34]Ibid., p. 91.

during the twentieth century, and through successful codification of human rights law in international treaties and documents, these four elements have even further clarified the topical nature of human dignity.[35]

The *habituality* ("Habitualität") element underscores the common place (topos) as a pattern of conscience internalized by a community, accordingly expressed by the linguistic and behavioral habits of its members.[36] This characteristic indicates how the self-understanding of societies is determined by traditions and conventions. The common place (topos) would thus gather both in its form and content the consolidated habits of a given society. Regarding human dignity, in particular, the *habituality* element has become quite evident after World War II. Since then, the basis of the self-understanding of international society has been moving progressively from the paradigm of "state sovereignty" to the paradigm of the "dignity of individuals." This has had concrete implications for the discourse and behavior of individuals, institutions and international actors in general.[37]

The *potentiality* ("Potentialität") element refers to the common place (topos) as a standpoint that can be employed in several discussions as part of distinct argumentative strategies.[38] Accordingly, discussants utilize the same common place (topos) to construct distinct arguments, which promote different perspectives on the same problem. It means that, *a priori*, there is no limitation for the use of a particular common place (topos) as a source of argumentation in a debate. Particularly in judicial discourses produced by legal argumentation in hard cases, one can see how the *potentiality* of the common place (topos) of human dignity manifests itself. In those cases there would be room for two or more plausible, though opposing, arguments based on the same common place (topos).

The *intentionality* ("Intentionalität") element points to the fact that despite the implications of the *potentiality* element, a common place (topos) can only be employed to produce *specific* argumentative effects in a dialectical rhetorical debate.[39] In fact, the characteristic of *intentionality* presupposes both *potentiality* and *habituality* of the common places (topoi), but it goes further. The common place (topos) cannot be understood as only a standard that is socially consolidated by tradition and linguistic conventions, or as a simple standpoint applicable to any discussion. In addition to this, a common place (topos) comprises a specific *understanding horizon* ("Verständnishorizont") that is determined by specific social values and practices.[40] This means, for example, that nowadays there is no room for arguments derived from human dignity to defend legal entitlements that privilege one particular ethnic group over another. This is the case, because the argumentative construction of human dignity during the last century acknowledges egalitarianism as a legal value, and any deviation from this principle of equality would lead astray from the horizon of understanding of that common place (topos).

[35]Marhaun (2001).
[36]Bornscheuer (1976), p. 96.
[37]Peters (2014).
[38]Bornscheuer (1976), p. 99.
[39]Ibid., p. 102.
[40]Ibid.

Finally, the *symbolicity* ("Symbolizität") element expresses the fact that when employed by a particular discussant in a particular discussion, the common place (topos) takes the most appropriate form to benefit this particular group in society.[41] Indeed, there is no fixed set of common places (topoi) that is used by every social group because each of those groups argues about a common place (topos) in its own specific way. This aspect becomes evident in the context of the common place (topos) of human dignity. Although philosophers have been known for their efforts to determine the meaning of human dignity for many years, the meaning assigned to that concept in a philosophical discussion is not precisely the same as the meaning that emerges in cases adjudicated by a constitutional court. This does not mean, however, that the common place (topos) of human dignity has diverging semantic contents when utilized by philosophers and judges, but that the meanings employed by different groups cannot be exactly the same.

Once the four characteristics explained above have been presented, the common place (topos) can be identified in both static and dynamic dimensions. A common place (topos) can be said to be static because it results from social practices at a determined historical moment which contribute to the formulation of possible meanings and, in the final analysis, to the understanding horizon. In this way, it would be possible to identify, at a given moment, the core meaning of human dignity and it could give an impression of a stable meaning of human dignity. A common place (topos) can also be said to be dynamic as representing a virtually infinite source of arguments which, during the course of a debate, can lead to a shift in socially accepted meanings. It's meaning will depend on the moves of participants in a rhetorical dialectical discourse and their capacity to construct binding normative meanings in a collective enterprise. Thus, the notion of common place (topos) conveys both stability and transformation, and the perception of its ambivalent character is clarified by the analysis of common places (topoi) in the legal discourse.

Concerning the rhetorical categories, human dignity can emerge in legal discourse as a rational basis for arguments *stricto sensu*—framed by the category of logos—and as source of moral knowledge or emotional impact—framed respectively by the categories of ethos and pathos—regarding particular persuasive means. In each of these topical dimensions of human dignity, the content of human dignity is always culturally and historically determined and, at the same time, likely to be consolidated, expanded or modified by the participants of the legal discourse. To illustrate how these rhetorical categories are combined in judicial argumentation, two cases from the International Court of Justice (ICJ) will be explored in the next section. It will be also an opportunity to understand how an analysis of problematic bases is performed.

7.4.2 Rhetorical Analysis at International Court of Justice (ICJ)

As mentioned in the introduction, this section aims to provide an example of how analysis based on the rhetorical empirical method works. In this analytical task it could

---

[41]Ibid., p. 103.

also be noted which role the rhetorical categories—logos, ethos and pathos—play in shaping the argumentation process at the international level as well as the position of common place (topos) as a starting point in problematic reasoning in court. Most importantly, the examination of the selected cases will demonstrate the way in which a consolidated understanding of several international rules was completely modified by presenting different arguments in two cases adjudicated at ICJ.

This example, built on the "Vienna Convention on Consular Relations cases", is even more relevant, because no amendments in the words of the rule involved in the controversy have occurred. The change in the ICJ's interpretation was carried out simply due to argumentative efforts in the Court, which combined the new possibilities of constructing meaning built by the international community on the basis of the use of the common place of human dignity. References to human dignity by the ICJ, even after the creation of specialized international courts responsible for enforcing human rights law, were not merely incidental. In several cases brought before the Court there was a direct employment of the common place (topos) of human dignity, or correlated concepts such as humanity, by litigants and judges.

As stated above, this paper is concerned with two cases adjudicated by the ICJ from 2001 and 2004, known as the "Vienna Convention on Consular Relations cases": *Germany v United States of America - LaGrand Case* and *Mexico v United States of America*. The common facts pertaining to those cases are: the US prosecuted and sentenced to death citizens from foreign countries (Germany and Mexico) without either (1) informing the defendants of their right to consular assistance provided by the Vienna Convention on Consular Relations, or (2) officially notifying the Consulate of those countries so that foreign authorities could offer adequate legal assistance to their citizens during the judicial proceedings in US courts.

To recap the guidelines for this chapter: transformations affecting the content of legal rights do occur in judicial argumentation by contribution of parties, who advance arguments grounded in the topical dimensions of the law, as explained by the rhetorical categories. For that reason, analysis of the legal discourse represented in ICJ cases will be focused on the identification of argumentative movements that reveal how it was possible in this Court to make some advance in promoting international human rights law.[42]

Accordingly, with recourse to the rhetorical empirical method a diagram is presented below (see inserted image two), displaying the tree of supporting arguments ("Stützungsbaum") regarding the common place (topos) of human dignity employed in the cases *Germany v United States of America - LaGrand Case* and *Mexico v United States of America*. The relevant arguments in those two cases were analyzed together because the argumentation movement presented in *Mexico v United States of America* includes previous developments which originated from *Germany v United States of America*.

---

[42]Bedi (2007), pp. 49–51.

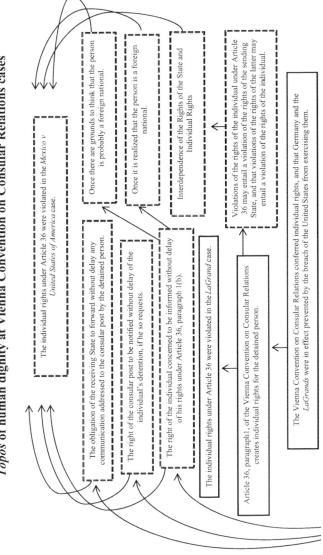

Topos of human dignity at Vienna Convention on Consular Relations cases

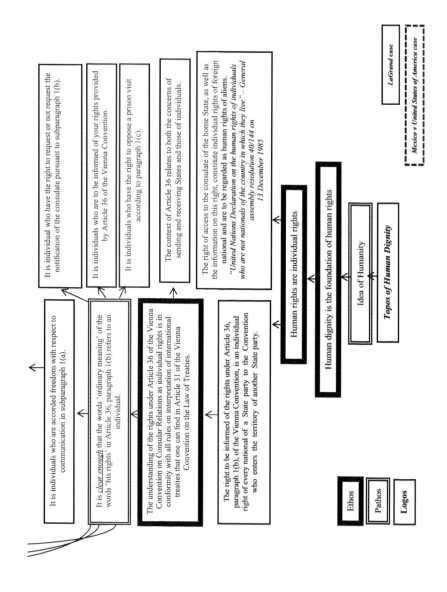

7.5 Conclusions

Taken as a rhetoric practice, the discursive character of law is not merely instrumental but constitutive. In an argumentative struggle, rights are created, modified and extinguished as a consequence of the dialogical argumentation produced between discussants who, to reinforce their positions, treat the topical aspects of the legal discourse framed by the rhetorical categories of logos, pathos and ethos. This means that the participants to the legal discourse employ common places (topoi) as comprehensive frameworks, which incorporate meanings emerging from consolidated social practices, so that plausible normative contents can support their arguments.

In such an argumentative process, litigant parties, on the one hand, adopt consolidated social meanings to argue about the law and, on the other hand, contribute to the permanent reconstruction of those normative meanings. By analyzing the ICJ two cases, it was clear how the problem-oriented argumentation process based on common place (topos) works. In the *Vienna Convention on Consular Relations cases* the common place (topos) of human dignity was the starting point for the judicial discourse. The litigants and the ICJ judges, employed the concept of human dignity in accordance with the shared meanings of the international community to construct arguments via dialectical-rhetorical reasoning to claim that Art. 36 of the Vienna Convention in fact states individual rights.

Although the Vienna Convention dates back to 1961, it was not until these cases were adjudicated that Art. 36 was claimed to create rights of citizens or that this treaty provision could be interpreted to integrate the normative corpus of existing international human rights law. Before the *Vienna Convention on Consular Relations cases*, States were considered to be the privileged actors in the international order, who were responsible for implementing the legal assurance of consular assistance to foreign citizens subject to prosecution and judicial proceedings outside the defendant home country. In deciding the Vienna Consular Relations cases, the ICJ built on the common place (topos) of human dignity by using rhetorical categories in order to change the prevailing reading of Art. 36. The Court justified its interpretation with recourse to normative meanings consolidated by the practice of international law during the twentieth century.

Since the post-WWII era, the content of the common place (topos) of human dignity has been molded to progressively empower the individual, who has become the epicenter of international law, replacing the state as the main origin of normative concerns. In this new paradigm, the privileged place granted to the individual in international law has certainly been influenced by the semantic transformation of the notion of human dignity in the international community. In the ICJ decisions, these new meanings were brought to the Court by different argumentative strategies enabling the judicial discourse's participants to contribute to modifying the consolidated understandings at that time about the legal effects of Art. 36 of the Vienna Convention on Consular Relations.

As a final remark, it must be highlighted that the ICJ's judicial arguments recognize that Article 36 of the Vienna Convention creates, in fact, not only individual rights, but also human rights. Additionally, the argumentative process that was meant to justify the existence of such legal rights, as derived from that international treaty, has as its starting point the common place (topos) of human dignity. This means that such interpretive development resulted from a previous reformulation of the moral content of the common place (topos) of human dignity, which was made possible through the arguments produced in a dialectical rhetorical reasoning promoted in the Court. The rhetorical categories played a central role in this process. It is the task of a rhetorical approach to law to reveal how and to what extent it occurs.

References

Aristotle. 1984a. Rhetoric. In *The Complete Works of Aristotle: The Revised Oxford Translation*, ed. Jonathan Barnes and trans. W. Rhys Roberts. Princeton, NJ: Princeton University Press.
———. 1984b. Topics. In *The Complete Works of Aristotle: The Revised Oxford Translation*, ed. Jonathan Barnes and trans. W.A. Pickard-Cambridge. Princeton, NJ: Princeton University Press.
Ballweg, Ottmar. 1984. Rhetorik Und Res Humanae. In *Gedächtnisschrift Für Peter Noll*, ed. Robert Hauser, Jörg Rehberg, and Günter Stratenwerth, 13–26. Zürich: Schulthess.
———. 1989. Entwurf Einer Analytischen Rhetorik. In *Rhetorik Und Philosophie*, ed. Helmut Schanze and Josef Kopperschmidt, 229–247. Munich: Wilhelm Fink Verlag.
Bayer, Wolfgang. 1975 Plausibilität Und Juristische Argumentation. Mainz.
Bedi, Shiv. 2007. *The Development of Human Rights Law by the Judges of the International Court of Justice*. Oxford: Hart Publishing.
Bornscheuer, Lothar. 1976. *Topik: Zur Struktur Der Gesellschaftlichen Einbildungskraft*. Frankfurt: Suhrkamp.
Braet, Antoine C. 1992. Ethos, Pathos and Logos in Aristotle's Rhetoric: A Re-Examination. *Argumentation* 6 (3): 307–320.
Cohen de Lara, Emma. 2018. Aristotle's Rhetoric and the Persistence of the Emotions in the Courtroom. In *Aristotle on Emotions in Law and Politics*, ed. Liesbeth Huppes-Cluysenaer and Nuno M.M.S. Coelho. Dordrecht: Springer.
Hartmann, Nicolai. 2014. Diesseits von Idealismus und Realismus. In *Studien zur Neuen Ontologie und Anthropologie*, ed. Gerald Hartung and Mathias Wunsch, 19–66. Berlin and Boston, MA: Walter de Gruyter.
Horn, Dieter. 1966. *Rechtssprache und kommunikation: grundlegung einer semantischen kommunikationstheorie*. Berlin: Duncker & Humblot.
Koskenniemi, Martti. 2006. *From Apology to Utopia: The Structure of International Legal Argument*. Cambridge: Cambridge University Press.
Koskenniemi, Martti, and Päivi Leino. 2002. Fragmentation of International Law? Postmodern Anxieties. *Leiden Journal of International Law* 15 (3): 553–579. https://doi.org/10.1017/S0922156502000262.
Marhaun, André. 2001. *Menschenwürde und Völkerrecht. Mensch, Gerechtigkeit, Frieden*. 1st ed. Tübingen: Medienverlag Köhler.
Maroney, Terry A. 2018. Judicial Emotion as Vice or Virtue: Perspectives Both Ancient and New. In *Aristotle on Emotions in Law and Politics*, ed. Liesbeth Huppes-Cluysenaer and Nuno M.M.S. Coelho. Dordrecht: Springer.

Peters, Anne. 2014. *Jenseits der Menschenrechte: Die Rechtsstellung des Individuums im Völkerrecht*. Heidelberg: Mohr Siebeck.

Rapp, Christof. 2018. Dispassionate Judges Encountering Hotheaded Aristotelians. In *Aristotle on Emotions in Law and Politics*, ed. Liesbeth Huppes-Cluysenaer and Nuno M.M.S. Coelho. Dordrecht: Springer.

Rodingen, Hubert. 1972. Ansätze Zu Einer Sprachkritischen Rechtstheorie. *ARSP: Archiv Für Rechts-Und Sozialphilosophie/Archives for Philosophy of Law and Social Philosophy* LVIII: 161–183.

Schirren, Thomas. 2009. Figuren im Rahmen der klassischen Rhetorik. In *Rhetorik und Stilistik*, ed. Ulla Fix, Andreas Gardt, and Joachim Knape, vol. 31. Berlin: Walter de Gruyter.

Silvestre, Ana Carolina de Faria. 2018. Rethinking Legal Education from Aristotle's Theory of Emotions and the Contemporary Challenges of the Practical Realization of Law. In *Aristotle on Emotions in Law and Politics*, ed. Liesbeth Huppes-Cluysenaer and Nuno M. M. S. Coelho. Dordrecht: Springer.

Sobota, Katharina. 1991. System and Flexibility in Law. *Argumentation* 5 (3): 275–282. https://doi.org/10.1007/BF00128811.

———. 1992. Rhetorisches Seismogramm—Eine Neue Methode in Der Rechtswissenschaft. *JuristenZeitung* 47 (5): 231–237.

———. 1994. Logos, Ethos, Pathos: A Quantitative Analysis on Arguments and Emotions in Law. In *Retorik & Rätt—sett Genom Tio Författarens Ögon*, 155–171. Uppsala.

———. 1996. Argumente Und Stilistische Überzeugungsmittel in Entscheidungen Des Bundesverfassungsgerichts. In *Rhetorik. Ein Internationales Jahrbuch*, Juristische Rhetorik, ed. Joachim Dyck, Walter Jens, and Gert Ueding, vol. 15, 115–136. Tübingen: Niemeyer.

Sprute, Jürgen. 1991. Ethos Als Überzeugungsmittel in Der Aristotelischen Rhetorik. In *Rhetorik Zwischen Den Wissenschaften. Geschichte, System, Praxis Als Probleme Des "Historischen Wörterbuchs Der Rhetorik"*, Rhetorik-Forschungen, vol. 1, 281–290. Tübingen: Niemeyer.

van Zantwijk, Temilo. 2011. Das Enthymem: Fragmentarische Ordnung Und Rhetorische Wahrscheinlichkeit. *Rechtstheorie* 42 (4): 437–453.

Viehweg, Theodor. 1974. *Topik Und Jurisprudenz Ein Beitrag Zur Rechtswissenschäftlichen Grundlagenforschung*. 5th ed. Munich: Beck.

von Schlieffen, Katharina G. 2005. Zur Topisch-Pathetischen Ordnung Juristischen Denkens: Resultate Empirischer Rhetorikforschung. In *Die Sprache Des Rechts: Recht Verhandeln. Argumentieren, Begründen Und Entscheiden Im Diskurs Des Rechts*, 405–448. Berlin and New York: Walter de Gruyter.

———. 2008. Rhetorik Und Stilistik in Der Rechtswissenschaft. In *Rhetorik Und Stilistik. Ein Internationales Handbuch Historischer Und Systematischer Forschung*, Handbücher Zur Sprach- Und Kommunikationswissenschaft, ed. Ulla Fix, Andreas Gardt, and Joachim Knape, vol. 2, 1811–1833. Berlin and New York: De Gruyter.

Cases

Germany v United States of America.
Mexico v United States of America.

Chapter 8
Religion of Humanity: A Shift from a Dialogical to a Categorical Model of Rationality

Liesbeth Huppes-Cluysenaer

Abstract The chapter describes the three religions of humanity, of Rousseau, Kant and Comte, to which Nussbaum refers in her book *Political Emotions* and which she hopes to revitalize. These three religions can be compared to the contemplative morality of Aristotle, which concerns the well-being of the citizens at which legislation and education are aimed.

Aristotle, however, pays greater attention to the civic morality of the enforcement of law than to the contemplative morality. From Aristotle's model of rationality (dialogical) it can be concluded that much interpretation has to be done to conclude that a conflict can be narrowed down to a decision about the application of a specific rule. This interpretation requires extensive institutional arrangements, regulated by a judicial procedure. Only when such a judicial procedure is in place there can be political organization and a debate about the good and the bad in actual practice.

Enlightenment generated a different (categorical) model of rationality and transformed the state by taking technical practice as a model for political organization. It recognized contemplative morality only and downgraded civic morality to obedience to rules. In this way Enlightenment thinking endangers social coherence and political debate.

8.1 Introduction

The renewed interest of legal theorists in Aristotle's work was initially focused on his *Nicomachean Ethics*. In it emotions pertain to virtuous actions of individual adjudicators.[1] Nussbaum's book *Upheavals of Thought*[2] has recently triggered a

---

[1]Best known in this respect Solum (2013).

[2]Nussbaum (2001). See in this volume for an overview of the new attention to emotions in Law and Politics Maroney (2018).

L. Huppes-Cluysenaer (✉)
Faculty of Law, University of Amsterdam, Amsterdam, The Netherlands
e-mail: huppes.uva@gmail.com

© Springer International Publishing AG 2018   155
L. Huppes-Cluysenaer, N.M.M.S. Coelho (eds.), *Aristotle on Emotions in Law and Politics*, Law and Philosophy Library 121, DOI 10.1007/978-3-319-66703-4_8

new interest in the role of emotions in Aristotle's *Rhetoric*. In her subsequent book *Political Emotions*[3] Nussbaum further clarified her interest in the ways in which speakers in the Athenian Law Courts and Assembly tried to influence the emotions of their audience. Nussbaum closes the chapter about *Teaching Patriotism* as follows:

> (. . .) a nation that pursues goals that require sacrifice of self-interest needs to be able to appeal to love of the nation, in ways that draw on symbol and rhetoric, emotional memory and history (. . .) If people interested in relief of poverty, justice for minorities, political and religious liberty, democracy, and global justice eschew symbol and rhetoric, fearing all appeals to emotion and imagination as inherently dangerous and irrational, people with less appetizing aims will monopolize these forces, to the detriment of democracy and of people.[4]

Nussbaum thus focuses in *Political Emotions* on the emotions that are foundational for contemporary liberal society. She believes that these emotions have to be cultivated among the public by using rhetorical means. Nussbaum refers in this respect to Comte as the founder of contemporary liberalism.[5] Comte developed a religion of humanity to coach individual persons to sacrifice their self-interest in favor of the collective.[6] Nussbaum appears to do the same, but differs from Comte by being less anti-religious and by emphasizing the need for a vigorously critical public culture. These two latter elements enable her to connect Comte's ideas with the heritage of the Enlightenment as elaborated in the religion of humanity postulated by Rousseau and Kant.

The religion of humanity of Rousseau and Kant aimed to develop a set of civic legal rules necessary for collective life in a state. Rousseau compared this set of rules with the dogmas of religion.[7]

Book seven of Aristotle's *Politics*[8] (*Pol.* 1323a14–1337a7) also concerns such a set of rules. Aristotle called this contemplative morality and as such distinguished it from civic morality, which he discusses in the *Nicomachean Ethics*. According to an earlier publication by Nussbaum,[9] Aristotle can be seen as a forerunner of the liberal social democracy.

The religion of humanity of Comte is different from that of Rousseau and Kant. Comte saw it as the worship of the human mind, with its great products of music and poetry. In book eight of *Politics* (*Pol.* 1337a7–1342b35) Aristotle also aims at public education in music and poetry. Aristotle's *Rhetoric* can be interpreted as

---

[3]Nussbaum connects here the moral psychology of compassion she had developed in Upheavals of Thought with the normative political philosophy she had already developed in her capabilities approach. See Nussbaum (2013), p. 449.

[4]Ibid., p. 256.

[5]Nussbaum emphasizes that Mill was a great admirer of Comte and introduced his works in England. She also refers to Tagore as great admirer.

[6]Nussbaum (2013), p. 20.

[7]Rousseau (1988), IV, p. 8.

[8]Edition used: Aristotle (1932).

[9]Nussbaum (1988) and Mulgan (2000).

treating public speech in the Law Courts and Assembly as a sort of theatre for cultivating civic emotions in the audience.

The author of this chapter agrees with Nussbaum that Aristotle can be seen as a forerunner of our liberal social democracy. It is argued, however, that for Aristotle contemplative morality was a supplement to civic morality.

Aristotle's civic morality touches on the essence of individual self-realization and is closely connected with the sphere of law-enforcement, where debate about the good and the bad is strictly regulated by a judicial procedure. In the Enlightenment, civic morality was reduced to the mere application of rules, however.

The chapter will provide an explanation of how Aristotle's view on civic morality is inherently connected with his dialogical model of rationality and how in the Enlightenment a different—categorical—model of rationality developed. In this new model of rationality the civic morality of individual self-realization in office was replaced by the contemplative morality of individual self-realization in critical public speech.

The difference between the old Aristotelian and the new enlightened rationality has long been concealed because Aristotle's physics—his zoology, which includes his political science—was incorrectly interpreted as aimed at creating a taxonomic classification system. However, before the end of the eighteenth century classification systems such as the system produced by Linnaeus were not generated. They are typically products of the new enlightened rationality and are founded on a belief in fixed species with a common nature: natural categories. Aristotle's teleology is then interpreted in terms of these fixed classes represented by ideal images.[10] Aristotle, however, explicitly rejected natural categories and representations with ideal images. His rationality is not founded on a belief in common natures, but on individual differences. Only on the level of contemplative morality—as an abstract theoretical approach—did Aristotle ascribe meaning to common natures. And even though Aristotle called this theoretical approach the best thing in life, he believed that abstract insights should not determine practice. In reverse, the enlightened view holds that language determines how individuals think and are likely to implement common ideas. The idea of individual agency is replaced by the idea of collective agency.

In the next section, Aristotle's zoological concept of natural law will first be explained. Aristotle conceived the interactions between living beings in terms of a range of possibilities between two contrary functions. This makes the approach dialogical. Attention will then be paid to the implications of this zoological concept of natural law for the Aristotelian concept of civic morality, specifically the crucial roles of subjective authority, office and judicial procedure. In the subsequent section Aristotle's concept of contemplative morality and public education will be compared with the enlightened view. Finally the three Religions of Humanity of Rousseau, Kant and Comte will be analyzed.

---

[10]See Burns (2011), p. 47/48; Hart (1961), p. 186; Cooper (1987), p. 243/244.

8.2   Aristotle's Zoology

8.2.1   *Diversity and Functionality*

Aristotle sees his study of animals (zoology) as a part of physics; his comparison of constitutions in *Politics* is part of this study of animals.[11] (*Pol.* 1290b25) A new understanding of Aristotle's zoology was introduced by Pellegrin at the end of the twentieth century. Pellegrin criticized the old interpretations which assumed that Aristotle, similar to Plato, aimed at classification.[12] Such a taxonomic approach did not develop until the end of the eighteenth century, with Linnaeus, according to Pellegrin.[13] Neither Plato nor Aristotle aimed at classification and systematic unification.

Plato surely did aim at rigorous definition. Pellegrin explains that Aristotle believed that Plato's method of definition was inadequate to cover the abundant diversity of nature and that his own functional method was much more adequate to this task. Aristotle deemed Plato's definitions, which create divisions among different species and subspecies, useful as a cognitive strategy, but not as containing relevant knowledge about the world.[14]

According to Aristotle animals can be perceived from different points of view. None of these different views has exclusive value. To give an example: a whale can be seen as a fish when one takes habitat as a point of departure, and as a mammal from the view of propagation, while the perspective of locomotion may lead to a different qualification. One may wonder why for so long whales were not classified as mammals since Aristotle clearly was perfectly aware of the many similarities between whales and human beings or horses.[15] As Pellegrin clarifies, Aristotle did not believe that the classification "mammals" was the true one, because he simply did not believe in a true nature of species.

Not the appearance of animals was relevant in Aristotle's view, nor their immediately given attributes, but the functions of attributes which are life-supporting for specific animals in specific environments. In such a type of inquiry, species are overlapping groupings.[16]

---

[11]See Pellegrin (1986), pp. 120–122.

[12]Gotthelf and Lennox (1987), p. 288.

[13]Pellegrin (1986), p. 45. Compare also in this volume Bombelli (2018).

[14]Ibid., pp. 21–40.

[15]See Romero (2012).

[16]Pellegrin (1986), p. 119.

8.2.2   *Zoological Method, Subject and Predicate*

The differentiation between subject and predicate is foundational for Aristotle's zoological method, as clarified in *Metaphysics*.[17]

> For it seems impossible that any universal term can be substance. First, the substance of an individual is the substance which is peculiar to it and belongs to nothing else, whereas the universal is common; for by universal we mean that which by nature appertains to several things. (...) Again, substance means that which is not predicated of a subject, whereas the universal is always predicated of some subject. (*Met.* 1038b10–18, trans. Tredennick)

Now Aristotle asks: In what sense of substance is the term animal used in the sentence: An animal can be two-footed and terrestrial? (*Met.* 1039b5) Aristotle explains that substance is of two kinds: (1) the concrete thing that can be destroyed, and (2) the abstract formula that is or is not, independent of generation and destruction. In the sentence above, the term animal indicates substance in the latter sense, e.g., of abstract formula. In their minds people can think abstract formulae as things with a separate existence, even though in the real world these abstract formulae cannot exist apart: these abstract formulae—such as animal—have an analytical, but not an empirical existence.[18] Concrete substances on the other hand, do have existence, but cannot be defined (*Met.* 1041a). At this level of particular things, there can only be knowledge through contact (*Met.* 1051b26).

Aristotle attacked Plato for creating an intermediate world between these two meanings of substance: the world of symbols or images (*Met.* 987b ff., again 1040b25ff., again 1059b5 ff.). Plato's approach is confusing, claimed Aristotle, because it creates a sort of concrete existence of abstract formulae. This is the reason that Plato cannot explain variability and change.

> Now since that which is composed of something in such a way that the whole is a unity; not as an aggregate is a unity, but as a syllable is – the syllable is not the letters, nor is BA the same as B and A; nor is flesh fire and earth; because after dissolutions the compounds *e.g.*, flesh or the syllable, no longer exist; but the letters exist, and so do fire and earth. Therefore the syllable is some particular thing; not merely letters, vowel and consonant, but something else besides. (...) It would seem however, that this "something else" is something that is not an element, but is the cause that *this* matter is flesh and that matter a syllable, and similarly in other cases. And this is the substance of each thing, for it is the primary cause of its existence. (...) not an element but a principle. (*Met.* 1041b10, trans. Tredennick)

Aristotle's zoological method studied abstract formulae as contrary potentialities: white as the complete existence of colour contrary to black as the total privation of colour. With respect to the particular substances he differentiated between elements and something which is the source of change and growth in the

---

[17]Edition used: Aristotle (1933).
[18]I disagree here with Cooper (1987), p. 243, who ascribes a counterfactual way of thinking to Aristotle.

attributes. This source, which exists within the particular substance, is the potency to enact abstract formulae (such as colour), which then become part of the real world in the measure and form in which they are enacted by it. Outside particular substances, the totality of all the potentialities of the real world has a separate existence in an unmovable mover, which exists permanently, e.g., in God.[19] (*Met.* 1054a–1057b35) Next to mathematics and physics there is therefore a third speculative science: the theory of science, metaphysics or theology (*Met.* 1064b15–20).

8.2.3   *Theory and Religion*

Metaphysics pertains to teleology, i.e., events which come about in the course of nature as a result of thought. In processes of learning, healing, walking, jumping, aging or maturing, abstract formulae (today understood as programs[20]) have existence by being enacted in particular things.

In each enactment, thought refers to the full potentiality of certain specific abstract formulae—all the operations which these formulae could enable—and in this sense the formulae have complete reality in the thinking particular.[21] (*Met.* 1065a30–b30) Formulae have this reality as contrary potentialities, however, which then become actually existent to a certain degree at the moment of enactment (*Met.* 1065b25).

Aristotle believed that nature is characterized by a continuous diversity of concrete individual substances that are in continuous movement. The more one looks with precision, the less things will turn out to be the same. In a general and abstract analogical sense, however, one can treat species and genus as if they are particular substances (*Met.* 1070a 32 ff.). Only species of the same genus can be compared as a difference in genus indicates difference in matter.

> But what is different from something is different in some particular respect, so that that in which they differ must be the same sort of thing; *i.e.*, the same genus or species. For everything which is different differs either in genus or in species – in genus such things as have not common matter and cannot be generated into or out of each other, e.g. things which belong to different categories; and in species, such things as are of the same genus (genus meaning that which is predicated of both the different things alike in respect of their substance). (. . .) For whereas things which differ in genus have no means of passing into

---

[19]See for Aristotle's concept of God (*Met.* 1072a27–33, 1072b4–22, 1074b32–35).

[20]See Mayr (1974) for a reference to Aristotle's teleonomic programs and the way the world has been blinded to this idea. See especially also section 7 about Kant's "as if solution" in the Critique of Judgment and the added explanatory comment of Pittendrigh (referring to Rosenblueth et al. 1943) that in the "newly – emerging computer period it was possible to design and build machines that had ends or purposes without implying that the purposes were the cause of the immediate operation of the machine." See further about teleonomy in this volume Bombelli (2018) and de Matos (2018).

[21]Compare in this volume Fuselli (2018).

each other, and are more widely distant, are not comparable, in the case of things which differ in species the contraries are the extremes from which generation takes place. (*Met.* 1054b25–1055a10, trans. Tredennick)

Bogen and Young[22] describe how Aristotle's teleological approach solved some of the problems concerning measurement, which had been discovered by Plato.

> To see how this applies to due measures, imagine that you are an ancient Greek physical trainer who prescribes foods and exercises to maintain the fitness of a runner. You should know the maximal and minimal weights for normal human beings. You should know what intermediate weight range is healthy for humans, and appropriate for athletes like the one you are training. This knowledge will allow you to decide whether she weighs too much or too little. If you also know how much pasta is required to maintain weight in the proper range, you will be able to find out whether her diet includes too much or too little, and if necessary, how her pasta intake should be changed to remedy an excess or defect in weight.
>
> At *Categories* 6, 5b24ff, Aristotle observes that what counts as many people in a village would not qualify as many people in Athens, and that what counts as many people in a house is less than what counts as many people in a theater. Thus a group of people is not many or few relative to the number of people who were actually in the house, the theater, the village, or the city at any particular time. Instead, *many* and *few* are understood—depending on what is appropriate for the relevant context—*as many for a house* (or *theater*, or *village*, etc.) These magnitudes are determined, not by the populations, but by the capacities of the relevant places. Aristotle's use of Sortal Comparisons to explain quantitative contraries is analogous to this: magnitudes are fixed by appeal to the abilities (e.g., for growth) that are characteristic of kinds of individuals, rather than the magnitudes that have actually been attained by the members of the kinds.
>
> The idea that natural kinds are distinguished from one another to an important extent by the capacities of their normal members is, of course, central to Aristotelian biology.[23]

8.2.4 The Dialogical Good

Aristotle's teleology is thus a method to establish "the good" of each action by comparing it in many ways with many factors.

> And that science is supreme, and superior to the subsidiary, which knows for what end each action is to be done; *i.e.* the Good in each particular case and in general the highest Good in the whole of nature. (...) its acquisition might justly be supposed to be beyond human power (...) As Simonides says, "God alone can have this privilege", and man should only seek the knowledge, which is within his reach. (*Met.* 983a1–5, trans. Tredennick)

According to Aristotle thought is a force, which makes living things move. This moving force of thought is conceived by Aristotle as a force of attraction which is blindly exerted by the unmoved mover (God). Humans feel this attraction in their capacity to apprehend the real nature of the things with which they are in direct contact (*Met.* 1051b26). It is a cognitive and appreciative perception, which moves people from without by being attracted and from within by feeling desire to reach

---

[22]Bogen and Young (2014).

[23]Ibid., p. 57.

out for it. Aristotle explains in the *Nicomachean Ethics*[24] that desire and the reasoning capacity thus cooperate.[25] (*EN* 1102b13–1103a4).

The true nature of individuals is their "life," the inner determinedness of their desires as informed by their life experiences. Their inner determinedness exhibits their character, their virtue.

Pellegrin clarifies that Aristotle's zoological method is a combination of induction and deduction because an intuition of the innate nature of individual animals contributes to an understanding of the functions of their attributes, while at the same time the study of their attributes contributes to the understanding of their true innate nature.[26]

The natural order of all these things with their innate determinedness is very complex:

> (...) and the system is not such that there is no relation between one thing and another; there is a definite connexion. Everything is ordered together to one end; but the arrangement is like a household, where the free persons have the least liberty to act at random, and have all or most of their actions preordained for them, whereas the slaves and the animals have little common responsibility and act for the most part at random. (*Met.* 1075a18–25, trans. Tredennick)

Scientific study can help to get a clear picture of some relations, but as a whole reality is so complex that reasoning about the world will have a topical character.[27] Reasoning will always be dialogical, which means that it will concentrate on a few specific issues which are thought relevant by the specific participants in a specific dialogue. The dialogical concept of scientific knowledge is best captured by the way a teacher orders his or her materials to introduce students to the most difficult details of the discipline.

8.2.5 Laws

Zoological research is the highest thing in which a person can engage. It is legislative knowledge which should be assembled and taught to citizens (*EN* 1180a33–1180b18). In a state intelligence should rule. Laws—written or

---

[24]Edition used: Barnes (1984).

[25]Elaborated in this volume in Fuselli (2018). Jurisprudentialist legal theorists emphasize this capacity for direct apprehension as the source for the practical wisdom of judges. See in this volume Silvestre (2018).

[26]Pellegrin (1986), pp. 123 and 147–148.

[27]See for further explanation Pinho (2018).

unwritten—work to the extent to which they are interpreted and implemented in the acts of individuals.

There are two ways in which laws work. First, they work from within as educated desire or virtue. It is clear, however, that many people are not susceptible to this working. They have to be controlled by commands and punishment.

> For these do not by nature obey the sense of shame, but only fear, and do not abstain from bad acts because of their baseness but through fear of punishment; living by passions they pursue their own pleasures (...) and have not even a conception of what is noble and truly pleasant, since they have never tasted it. What argument would remould such people? (...) For he who lives as passion directs will not hear argument that dissuades him, nor understand it if he does. (...) But it is difficult to get from youth up a right training for excellence if one has not been brought up under right laws. (*EN* 1179b10–33, trans. Ross/ Urmson)

The second way in which laws have influence in the state is through education by teachers who have studied political life from the outside. A proper education is better than listening to the speeches before the law courts or Assembly.[28] (*EN* 1181b4) Proper education guides through habituation and instruction. The study of laws guides and instructs practitioners who have to deal with conflicts and offenders.[29]

In politics—different from other disciplines—the practitioners do not give lectures about their own professional knowledge. Political science is zoological research, which is performed at a distance from active political life. To be a zoological researcher is really to have a different type of life.[30] (*EN* 1178a22 ff. and also *Met.* 982a4 ff.) Therefore, theoretical study is also a morality: a contemplative morality in which theoretical wisdom is acquired. There is, however, a definite connection between the theoretical wisdom of contemplative morality and the practical wisdom of civic morality. Only those practitioners who have experience can really use collections of laws and connect abstract theoretical insights with their own experience.

> laws are as it were the works of the political art; how then can one learn from them to be a legislator, or judge which are best? Even medical men do not seem to be made by a study of text-books. (...) Surely then, while collections of laws, and of constitutions also, may be serviceable to those who can study them and judge what is good or bad and what enactments suit what circumstances, those who go through such collections without a practised faculty will not have the right judgement (unless it be spontaneous), though they may perhaps become more intelligent in such matters. (*EN* 1181b6–11, trans. Ross/ Urmson)

---

[28]See Natali (2013), p. 97 about the collection of proverbs Aristotle was working on. These could well function as the overall premise of an argument in *Rhetoric*. "This activity of learned research, of collecting the most widely varying facts, such as this collecting of the proverbs, the popular maxims, and the sayings of the ancients, for instance, will remain one of Aristotle's distinctive traits."

[29]Practitioners will be foremost the authorities of the magistracies which regulate daily life.

[30]Natali (2001), pp. 174–175.

8.3   Civic Morality: Aristotle's Subjective Authority

8.3.1   Office

Personal freedom or personal virtue and happiness are **not** the key-features of Aristotle's ethics.[31] Personal freedom is the freedom of slaves and animals who can act at random (*Met.* 1075a18–25). The key-figure in Aristotle's ethics is not simply the individual moral agent, but the office-holder: the authority (*EN*, 1140b7 and 1141b24ff). Office-holders are those who manage a household or the state and who as a result have to take care of the interests of others. Aristotle's ethics concerns the daily political administration, in which laws are given and implemented, so to speak, by manual labourers (*EN* 1141b29). Aristotle sees the relation between the office-holder and his clerks as similar[32] to the relation of the master craftsman to his artisans or of the master of a household to his wife, children and slaves. The master knows more and is wiser; the artisan has more experience with certain particularities. Good management brings both together: it enacts commands and takes care that these are carried out in conformity with the specific details of the situation.

The different offices are described in *Politics* (*Pol.* 1321b4 ff.). In the practice of an office-holder such as a harbour-guardian, for example (*Pol.* 1321b27), two different types of practical knowledge can be distinguished analytically, while in fact they are intermingled: craft and practical wisdom.[33] Zoological theoretical wisdom (contemplative morality) is the background of both, but is rather smoothly connected with craft, while there is a real gap in its connection with political practical wisdom.

Crafts are the source of laws of a different type from the natural laws which are formulated by zoology. The rules of craft are based on experience, while the natural laws of zoology are purely theoretical or philosophical. When acting as craftsmen, individual agents perceive similarities and become aware of causal relations such as that many patients recover after receiving a certain treatment. In a technical practice of craft the product demonstrates as it were the validity of the rule. Nevertheless, every patient is different and also every medical doctor is different. This means that even these cognitive rules always consist of rough approximations and have to be adjusted to the specific details of the situation in which they are applied.[34]

---

[31]The statement that free choice is essential for Aristotle's view is wrong in my opinion, when applied to something like a personal life-plan. See for an example of this type of discussion, Mulgan's critical argument versus Nussbaum in Mulgan (2000), specifically section 7.

[32]Compare the passage of *EN* 1141b29 with *Met.* 981a30.

[33]See Natali (2001), p. 24, who explains that for Aristotle the demarcation between both was not very sharp such as in the modern conception of the difference between praxis and technique.

[34]This aspect of variability is absent in Broadie (1987), p. 47 and because of this she elaborates her "craftsmen analogy" in the context of "the massive constancy that is nature's hallmark."

Practical wisdom, however, does not have this demonstrative aspect of craft. It is oriented towards living well. Practical wisdom is formed in the practice of individual agents, to whom by law, tradition or lot the task is assigned to take care of the interests of others. These agents perform these tasks as an office holder, and this means that the deliberations and decisions in such a practice are political. When conflicts arise as part of the enforcement of such decisions, this can lead to the use of public force. Practical wisdom is treated by Aristotle in the context of offices (magistracies) and not in the context of lawsuits.

8.3.2 Deliberation and the Act

Magistrates deliberate. Deliberation is not deductive, demonstrative reasoning as in mathematics. Deliberation concerns the mental organization required to make the body ready to act. It involves reasoning that goes on for some time and is slow. This reasoning can be tacit. In *Physics*[35] Aristotle gives the example of spiders that build their web (*Phys.* 199a20–25). When deliberation happens in words it does not formulate opinions but says what must be done. Deliberation is not having opinions but is choosing how to act (*EN* 1143a13–25). People are by nature endowed with judgement (the faculty of being considerate), understanding (the faculty of having relevant opinions about what other people think about practical matters) and comprehension (the faculty to give a good assessment of the practical situation). These faculties are further developed during people's lives on the basis of experiences and are therefore to be found in refined form in elderly people. These states of mind have meaning in themselves and are resources for deliberation.

The capacity to act differs from deliberation. Here a comparison with the art of medicine can be made (*EN* 1143b25). To be learned in medicine (to know the rules for curing certain illnesses) does not constitute a physician. It is the act of curing a particular person which does this. Medical knowledge is nothing more than a form of cleverness until it is acted out in the successful curing of specific people. In the sphere of medicine, the act (administering this drink) can be separated from the result (fever is gone). In the sphere of practical wisdom this is not possible (*EN* 1140b4). The practical intuition of living well is needed to act adequately in a specific situation. This intuition makes itself known by attraction, i.e., as an internal feeling, and cannot be judged externally such as the question whether the fever is gone. Practical wisdom is formed as a subjective intuition: different judges will judge differently and will perceive the same case differently.

---

[35]Edition used: Barnes (1984).

8.3.3   Subjective Authority

Aristotle criticizes Socrates (*EN*, 1144b 18) for not noting the analytical distinction of two sides of the decision: (1) the decision as the final step in the mental activity of the deliberation, and (2) the decision as the act of an authority which has consequences for people's lives. Socrates believes that the latter is implied by the first. Aristotle agrees, but by perceiving his decision as an act, the judge takes responsibility for the consequences of it. By acknowledging the decision as an act, the judge makes the formulated decision part of his own life. He therefore not only has to *think* that the decision is right, he also has to *feel* it as right. This is a purely subjective feeling that is only indirectly aimed at a personal good. Directly it aims at a common good, but by feeling it as a personal responsibility to take the right decision it makes one happy when done right.[36] In the end practical wisdom is not the capacity to think, but the enactment of thought and in this sense an act of faith: not a form of knowledge, but of virtue.[37]

8.3.4   The Judicial Procedure: Separation Between Formal and Substantial Decisions

The judicial procedure in Athens is described in the Athenian Constitution[38] and involved:

1. Office-holders who legislated, judged and executed. They were like kings for the time of their appointment and were limited to their specific assignment. By regular inspection or as soon as a politically relevant issue arose—a complaint of corruption or inadequacy concerning enactments or decisions—the case had to be brought to level 2 by a complaint.[39] (*Ath. Const.* 43, the Sovereign Assembly juncto *Pol.* 1298a1–10).

---

[36]See Scholten (2014), p. 502 (http://www.paulscholten.eu/dutch-english/#section_28) for an exposition of this same idea of the decision as an act, not written as an exposition of Aristotle's ideas but as the general accepted method of civil law in the Netherlands in 1931.

[37]Natali (2001), pp. 12–13.

[38]Edition used: Barnes (1984).

[39]Blackwell (2003) writes that "The democratic government of Athens rested on three main institutions, and a few others of lesser importance. The three pillars of democracy were: the Assembly of the Demos, the Council of 500, and the People's Court." This ignores completely the relevance of the magistracies and their function for practical wisdom. It suggests that practical wisdom is acquired by deliberation in the Assembly and Law-courts, but voting is not the same as decision-taking in a situation of responsibility. Blackwell describes participation in the Council as follows: "Although participation in the Council was paid, and considered an office, it also seems to have been considered an unexceptional part of a citizen's life, rather than a part of a political career." On the whole Blackwell has no eye for the intellectual challenge of the Council's tasks.

2. The tasks of the Council.[40] The Council had no final jurisdiction (*Ath. Const.* 45). It took preliminary cognizance of all matters brought before the Assembly. The Assembly could not vote on any issue unless it had first been considered by the Council. When the Assembly condemned someone to imprisonment or death or inflicted a fine, the sentence had to be brought before the Law Court. The Council had no power of decision other than over how to bring into procedure the issues belonging to its tasks (*Ath. Const.* 43). The Council's practice therefore involved decisions of a very specific nature: decisions about decisions.[41] This is a decision in a purely formal practice: the enforcement of the decision-making procedure described in the Constitution.
3. The Assembly of all citizens and the Law Courts (mostly 201 or 401) had the power of decision over the substance of all issues brought before them by the Council.

The interaction between these three steps was orchestrated by the Council. Crucial in the interaction between the first and the second step was that through regular inspection a framework for the tasks developed. This forced office-holders to think in more general terms about their decisions and the inspector to think in a more general way about the criteria for inspection. Crucial in the interaction between step two and three was the instruction of the courts and the formulation of the charge: the Council had to answer for example a question such as, "is this a fine, a confiscation or a compensation for damage?" to determine to which court the case should be brought. Also the formulation of the question subjected to a vote in the Assembly was a problem of instruction. This was the task of the Proedroi.[42] Because all participants in the judicial procedure were appointed for a short term, there was a need to make protocols (habits) for the transfer of tasks. The 50 Prytanes, who each month functioned as an executive committee for the council, had meals together in the period that they were on duty. This gave ample room for serious discussions about the instruction problems that were encountered. All Athenian citizens had to do duty in the Council twice in their life. In this respect the Council was the most important democratic institution in Athens.

---

[40]Nearly all magistrates who were concerned with the ordinary routine of administration were elected by lot (*Ath. Const.* 43). The same passage informs that the Council of 500 was elected by lot, 50 from each tribe; that each tribe held the office of Prytanes in turn (ordered by lot) for 36, respectively 35 days; that the 50 of the tribe that held the Prytane-office messed together in that period and were paid for their maintenance; that these 50 convened daily meetings of the Council, and four times in their period the meetings of the Assembly; that it was their duty to draw up the program of the business of the Council and to decide what subjects were to be dealt with on each particular day and where the sitting was to be held; that they also drew up the program for the meetings of the Assembly.

[41]This feature of a separation between the formal and substantial decision has always been pointed out by Romanists as the peculiar strength of Roman Civil Law. See for example Gardini (2015).

[42]Blackwell (2003).

8.3.5 Partnership in the Perception of Good and Bad

Aristotle believed that partnership in the perception of good and bad makes a household and a city-state and that the judicial procedure regulates this partnership (*Pol.* 1253a17 and 1253a39). This partnership is enacted in the Council. It is contemplative morality at work: education/cultivation of political emotions.

Discussions in the Council were about instruction. They concerned the qualification of acts. To qualify an act in a particular way means to establish that it belongs to a certain kind or species of acts. A certain kind of acts comprises a whole range of acts. An act with characteristics beyond the limits of this range would belong to another kind. The discussions in the Council were therefore zoological discussions of a practical kind. Zoology is oriented towards the understanding of "the ratio" to which phenomena conform: their function.[43]

In two chapters of this volume, one by Brito and the other by Viano, Aristotle's view on self-defense is discussed.[44] These chapters show that legal thought about homicide was fully developed in Athens and was more or less comparable with the current treatment in criminal law.[45] The ancient legal theory differentiated between unwillful and willful homicide and more specifically between unwillful homicide as a mistake in the exercise of honorable acts or merely as an act by mistake, willful homicide by anger or by a cherished resentment, and finally rightful killing in self-defense. Aristotle added a new aspect to this discussion by relating the act of self-defense to the feelings aroused in the one who pleads self-defense by the one who had attacked him. This new aspect clarifies how in Aristotle's view acts should be qualified in relation to the actual and potential inner determinedness of the acting subject: a concept of moral responsibility.

The Council's instruction will have been reflected in the rhetoric in the Law Courts and Assembly. Legal theory creates a great variety of possible interpretations for each case. Every possible interpretation holds a shift in perspective. From each perspective the distribution of moral responsibility is different and from each perspective the relevance of facts is different. Mollification of feelings results from the fact that different interpretations are possible and that each perspective opens up different angles of doubt.[46] It is clear that in the end a choice has to be made. If the outcome of the vote shows a narrow victory by one side, this is in fact a sign that the treatment was careful and that by this the honor of both sides is saved. It is then through understanding the need for a choice that the law can be abided and that the losing party can accept its lot. Persuasion by rhetorical means should therefore not be understood in terms of rationality, but as molding and courting the public.

---

[43]Pellegrin (1987), p. 122.

[44]Viano (2018) and Brito (2018).

[45]See Fletcher (1998) for a treatment of the current theory. See also the comparison between the current and Athenian theory in this volume by Brito (2018) who is critical of Aristotle's view.

[46]Compare in this volume Nascimento (2018) and Cohen de Lara (2018).

The vote by the multitude is praised by Aristotle[47] as a way to draw the poor and badly educated citizens into the political process.

> For it is not safe for them to participate in the highest offices (for injustice and folly would inevitably cause them to act unjustly in some things and to make mistakes in others), but yet not to admit them and for them not to participate is an alarming situation, for when there are a number of persons without political honors and in poverty, the city then is bound to be full of enemies. It remains therefore for them to share the deliberative and judicial functions. For this reason Solon and certain other lawgivers appoint the common citizen to the election of the magistrates and the function of calling them to audit, although they do not allow them to hold office singly. For all when assembled together have sufficiently discernment, and by mingling with the better class are of benefit to the state, just as impure food mixed with what is pure makes the whole more nourishing than the small amount of pure food alone. (*Pol.* 1281b30–35, trans. Rackham)

8.3.6 Pure Theory

The Athenian Constitution begins with a narrative about the history of Athens. From this it becomes clear that the political partnership of the city-state originated in a revolt by the poor people who were held in debt-slavery by a few powerful families. The revolt resulted in the deadlock that both parties were equal in power, until Solon drafted a new constitution with a judicial procedure that created an armed peace.

> When he had completed his organization of the constitution in the manner that has been described, he found himself beset by people coming to him and harassing him concerning his laws, criticizing here and questioning there, till as he wished neither to alter what he had decided on nor yet to be an object of ill will by remaining in Athens, he set off for a journey to Egypt, with the combined objects of travel and trade, giving out that he should not return for ten years. (. . .) The mass of the people has expected him to make a complete redistribution of all property, and the upper class hoped he would restore everything to its former position. . . .. (*Ath. Const.* 11, trans. Kenyon)

Solon spread tasks evenly over the tribes, always assigning responsibilities for a short period and always organizing that the inspectors themselves would be inspected, forcing people to cooperate, to have meals together, while at the same time keeping offices apart, households apart, responsibilities apart and organizing competitive games between tribes, forcing all people to participate in some way by using in many cases the appointment by lot.[48]

Law enforcement by the Council could easily fuel the ongoing conflict between the two parties.

---

[47]See in this volume also Coelho (2018).

[48]"The law enacts that anyone who does not serve as Arbitrator when he has arrived at the necessary age shall lose his civil rights. . ." (*Ath. Const.* 53, trans.).

Aristotle described how the constitution was endangered by the continuous attempts to redistribute power in Athens.[49] Such proposals had to be brought before the Council, which then had to bring them before the Assembly in the way indicated by the existing rules.[50] Aristotle wrote that one should not think that such a redistribution of power could have legitimacy simply by majority vote in accordance with the existing rules. Such changes can only keep the political partnership in order when they show understanding of custom and tradition (*Pol.* 1281a13–1281b15; 1292a1–40). Custom and tradition refer here to a type of law which antedates the state and the constitution: a pre-law. The literature discusses the question whether Aristotle refers with this pre-law to natural law or to positive law.[51] In a certain sense it is both, but at the same time it is neither of these two because it indicates another level.

One could think that Aristotle refers here to the understanding which grows by participating in the political partnership: an understanding of the forces which traditionally and actually are to be pacified by a given constitution at a given place: in Athens the powerful families and the citizenry. In this case it is both natural and positive law.

At the same time, however, this pre-law could be seen as the subject of Aristotle's comparative study of constitutions i.e., as the zoological external study of natural laws (*Pol.* 1332a35). In that case it is the pure theory of a political education which pertains not only to Athens, but to all possible constitutional states.

---

[49]Compare in this volume Bonanno and Corso (2018).

[50]Blackwell (2003). Laws were passed through a process called nomothesia or "legislation." Each year the Assembly met to discuss the current body of laws. Any citizen could propose a change in the laws, but could only propose the repeal of a law if he suggested another law to replace the repealed law. If the Assembly decided to change the laws, a board of "Nomothetai" or "legislators" was selected to review and revise the laws. The process of legislation was like a trial, with advocates speaking in defense of the existing laws, and others speaking against the existing laws. The Nomothetai would vote on changes, and any changes that passed were published on inscriptions near the statues of the Eponymous Heroes and read aloud at the next meeting of the Assembly. The Nomothetai also undertook an annual review of all existing laws to make sure that none contradicted others and that none were redundant.

[51]See for a recent discussion of these opinions Bates (2013), p. 62/64. It is interesting here to draw a parallel with the concept of fundamental laws developed by Ulrik Huber (1636–1694) as described in van Nifterik (2016): "Proper laws must be "given" and "announced." (Huber *DJC* I.3.5.13) Tacit laws obviously are not; they are so to say implicit in the idea of political power." As concerned express fundamental laws Huber emphasized that they too so to say antedate the state and the ruler, since they lay the fundament thereof; fundamental laws are the *constitutiones* (*DJC* I.3.5.21) or "grondwetten" (*HR* II.i.7.21).

8.4 Political Education

8.4.1 Aristotle's View on Political Education

At the end of *Nicomachean Ethics* Aristotle prepared the ground for education in legislative or political science, which he elaborated in book seven and eight of *Politics*. Aristotle explains why the subject of legislation has always been left unexamined (see above Sect. 2.5) and announces that he is going to undertake the examination. On the basis of a collection of constitutions, Aristotle wanted to study what sort of influences preserve and destroy states or particular kinds of constitutions, and what things cause good or bad administration in states (*EN* 1181b15–20).

Many authors have noticed that book seven of *Politics* seems to stand in contradiction with the earlier chapters and some have concluded that it seems to be written for the new colonies of Macedon in Asia Minor.[52] Before turning to the historical context of the conquest of Macedon over Athens, it should be noted that pure zoological theory which compares the different constitutions of Greece necessarily proceeds on a meta-level in its view of the democracy in Athens. It is an abstract view in which it is taken for granted that different societies in different circumstances will have different constitutions.[53] While Aristotle believed that Athens had the best constitution because it created a partnership in the perception of good and bad (*Pol.* 1253a17), he also believed that Athens' constitution was adjusted to a specific situation and that on a more abstract level the function of a constitution should be defined as establishing peace and leisure (*Pol.* 1333a31ff.).

By taking historical context into account, this meta-view can be elaborated. Aristotle had spent some time in Athens during which he studied at the school of Plato. He left and spent some time at the court in Macedon, later to return to Athens after the conquest of Macedon. Thus, by the time Aristotle set up his own school in Athens, Philippus of Macedon had forced most Greek city-states into an alliance. Although Macedon did not take part in the new League of Greek city-states, Philippus was accepted as the head who would determine its external policy. Philippus' League was not only aimed at the prosecution of the war against Persia, but also at the protection of the constitutions of its members against revolutionary forces from within.[54]

---

[52]Kelsen (1937) and Samaras (2007).

[53]"But since, just as with all other natural organisms those things that are indispensable for the existence of the whole are not parts of the whole...(....) Hence although states need property, the property is not part of the state. (...) for as each set of people pursues participation in happiness in a different manner and by different means they make for themselves different modes of life and different constitutions. (...) And we must also further consider how many there are of these things referred to that are indispensable for the existence of a state; for among them will be the things which we pronounce to be parts of a state, owing to (the function for LHC) which their presence is essential. We must therefore consider the list of occupations that a state requires: for from these it will appear what the indispensable classes are." (*Pol.* 1328a24–1328b4, trans. Rackham).

[54]Kelsen (1937), section 4.

It seems probable that Philippus admired the Greek city-states, but at the same time observed the military threat of Persia and the incapacity of the Greek city-states to cooperate and band together against the Persian threat. The city-states waged war among themselves and some even made alliances with Persia. It seems likely that Philippus invited one of the great thinkers of his time to advise him and that in this context Aristotle made his comparison of Greek constitutions. Aristotle designed in book seven the type of empire which since then survived in the West until a completely new type of state—the unity state—came into existence.

Not elaborated in book seven, but foundational for the dialogical rationality of Aristotle and for the type of empire he designed, is his rejection of the unity state. In Aristotle's view, only composite things can move. This assumption is the basis for the complex relationship between practice and theory in his teaching. When a state is understood as consisting of autonomous constituent units, all power at the top is limited by the constitutions of its units. In an empire there will be different peoples with different types of constitutions and also peoples who have no judicial self-organization and will be despotically ruled (*Pol.* 1261a15–30).

Book seven can be read as an advice to the emperor:

The units in which a judicial order and a partnership in the perception of good and bad can exist are necessarily small:

> But in order to decide questions of justice and in order to distribute the offices according to merit it is necessary for the citizens to know each others's personal characters, since where this does not happen to be the case the business of electing officials and trying law-suits is bound to go badly; haphazard decision is unjust in both matters, and this must obviously prevail in an excessively numerous community. Also in such a community it is easy for foreigners and resident aliens to usurp the rights of citizenship, for the excessive number of the population makes it not difficult to escape detection. It is clear therefore that the best limiting principle for a state is the largest expansion of the population with a view to self-sufficiency that can well be taken in at one view. (*Pol.* 1326b14–25, trans. Rackham)[55]

Different classes are indispensable in a state, but only one class is part of the state. This is the class that is susceptible to reason and consists of three sub-classes according to age. The young have the tasks which involve violence, the middle age is for the councillors and old age is for priests (*Pol.* 1329a30). Different virtues are important for the state, such as love of wisdom in times of leisure, fortitude and courage in business and justice and temperance in both. While theory (love of wisdom) is most important, it at the same time drives people to be arrogant and insolent. Therefore it is good that councillors have had experience with activities in their youth that come with violence and also that the knowledge of the wise in later life can only have effect in society when it is enacted and enforced by people of middle age with the help of younger people who are courageous and can use violence (*Pol.* 1333a17–1334b4).

A well-organized state takes care—by way of political education—to form good habits for family life in order to raise strong children that are susceptible to reason.

---

[55]The same argument returns in Rousseau (1772), p. 12.

Furthermore, no citizen should be ill-supplied with means of subsistence (*Pol.* 1329a34).

It seems accurate to see in book seven the first signs of a social democratic liberalism as Nussbaum does,[56] and at the same time aspects of medieval Catholicism as Mulgan[57] does. The interplay between the contemplative morality of old age, which is alienated from practical and economic interests (*Pol.* 1324a14) and the civic morality of the practice of law enforcement could be compared with the division of roles between a church and civil government.

8.4.2 Intermediate Conclusion

Contemplative morality establishes a general, purely theoretical approach which aims at gaining insight into the primary function (telos) of humanity and state. Crucial for the difference between Aristotle's view and the enlightened view is the Enlightenment belief that descriptions of reality in general terms correspond to reality. This means that it is assumed to be self-evident which things or events conform to a description in general terms. According to Aristotle such a correspondence is merely approachable in crafts. The belief in an inner orientation towards a very abstract telos is replaced in the Enlightenment by the belief in an inner orientation towards goals, which can be envisaged as the statues of Plato[58]: craftsmen's goals in the view of Aristotle. The speculative, philosophical theory of teleology is replaced by the technical rationality of the craftsmen. The religion of humanity becomes the project to describe the world in terms of craftsmen's goals. These descriptions are thought better to be made by people who are alienated from practice. These descriptions of the world are the laws. The office-holders become equal to the artisans: they simply limit themselves to law-application.

One of the most pernicious problems facing the religion of humanity is that some people do not want to merge telos and craftsmen's goals: the representatives of dialogical rationality do not want this. In the next part of this essay our attention will focus on the development of counterfactual reasoning. This form of reasoning acknowledges on the one hand the distinction between telos and craftsmen goals by presenting technical rationality as a cognitive strategy, but is unfaithful on the other hand to this acknowledgment by degrading practice into rule-application.

---

[56]Nussbaum (1988).

[57]Mulgan (2000).

[58]In the famous allegory of the cave in Plato's Republic, the people in the cave think that the shadows of statues are real.

8.4.3 Enlightened View on Political Education

The first European Industrial Revolution, based on waterpower, started in the twelfth century according to Gimpel.[59] As the Greeks and Roman already had watermills, it is not the invention of the watermill which is remarkable, but the massive way in which it became incorporated in the social/economic life in the Middle-Ages. It thus offered a very good substitute for the slave labor employed by the Greeks and Romans. Monasteries in France and manors in England played an important role in spreading this program of mechanization.

Economic growth in the Middle-Ages was thus the result of long term cooperation for economic goals between different property-owners, for example, to distribute the water-use of different towns along the same river. Economic cooperation required alternative roles between free men as ruler and ruled in terms of interests rather than political power, as craftsmen and business men instead of office-holders. Crafts have, as already observed by Aristotle, a specific position in epistemology—between theory and practice—due to the concrete goals aimed for. Craft is a domain in which stable concepts naturally arise and have great value. This faculty to produce stable concept by orientation towards utility was also observed by Aristotle, who took the common sense categories of experienced people such as sea-faring people as the starting point for his zoological research.[60]

A new rationality developed hand in hand with the cooperation between free men for common economic aims in Europe. It is a technical rationality, with its own developing technical conception of law, morality, politics and metaphysics. This new rationality developed in opposition to the overwhelming influence of dialogical reason. Along with Positivism this technical rationality had its finest hour: the development of taxonomic classification systems.

Both rationalities, the dialogical and the categorical, have the same problems concerning the choice between democracy and meritocracy. The difference between both rationalities is that technical rationality is bound to specific interests and is not fit for long term perspectives with a broad scope. Technical rationality thus endangers the institutionalizations which are necessary for long term relations. The technical rationality breaks existing institutionalizations down, but by doing this it also emancipates and realizes social mobility. Both rationalities are opposed to and naturally conflict with each other. In the end, however, both are needed.

Arendt was the first to conceptualize the difference between the Ancient (dialogical) and Modern (categorical) conception of public life. She argues that modern times discovered the social realm between private individuals and public authority as a public space of communication and as the arena in which individuals could shine and become famous. According to her, the Ancients were familiar with this

---

[59]Gimpel (1977).

[60]Pellegrin (1986), pp. 45/46 and 120. As a cognitive strategy says Pellegrin (25).

function of public space in the period before Socrates.[61] She opposes her conception of public life as an—in origin Pre-Socratic—sphere of communication to the way Plato and Aristotle have legalized political life. Her opposition between a legal and a communicative conception of political life is, however, merely applicable for the enlightened view on politics, in which civic morality is downgraded into rule-application. The opposition is therefore certainly correct for the Enlightenment, but not for the Ancient world. From Solon on political life was completely determined by a judicial procedure. It was through this procedural form that the discussion about the good and the bad was made possible. As will be clarified below the true political arena of the Enlightenment is indeed not the formalized juridical sphere of decision-making, but the sphere of public communication, which develops as a side effect of the traffic of economic information.[62] In the Enlightenment the political arena has not the function to solve conflicts, but to create a common appreciation of craftsmen's goals. Opinion-leaders are like the orators in the law courts, who mold and court emotion to shape the masses into a unity with a shared opinion. However, different from these orators, they aim at will-formation concerning general interests instead of jurisdiction in a particular case.[63]

8.4.4   Categorical Rationality

Enlightenment is the process in which dialogical rationality is replaced by categorical rationality.

Categorical rationality developed in the Middle-Ages with a heated debate about the meaning of universals (Aristotle's abstract formula of Sect. 2.2).

The first step in this debate had already been taken with the shift from Aristotle's God to the Christian God. Aristotle's Unmoved Mover had in its mind the very abstract genus-form pertaining to, for example, **both** humans and horses.[64] (*Met.* 1054b27–1055a8) The Christian God, however, had created humans and horses separately. The change towards the Christian God also replaced the zoological research of Aristotle with Bible-exegesis. The new categorical rationality originated in these linguistic analyses and started with the reception of the ideas of Avicenna.[65]

---

[61]She glorifies the agonal spirit of that period: "the passionate drive to show one's self in measuring up against others that underlies the concept of politics prevalent in the city-states." Arendt (1998), p. 194.

[62]Habermas (1989), Chapters 7 and 8.

[63]Compare Drosterij (2008).

[64]Pellegrin (1986), p. 55.

[65]See Comte for his reference to "Islamic or Arabic influence" in Comte (1975a), p. 11. See for a general overview of the discussion Klima (2016).

Avicenna introduced the idea that species-forms have existence apart from their existence in particulars: the common natures or natural categories. This resulted in a heated debate between nominalists and realists: the first believing in a natural existence of universals in the minds of people, enabling them to recognize natural kinds; the latter believing in an existence of universals in reality enabling people to recognize the essential—permanent—characteristics of species. And of course there were the conservatives who rejected this new idea of a separate existence of common natures. This chapter focuses on the distinction between conservatives and progressives and is not interested in the distinction between nominalists and realists.

In order to create taxonomic classification systems, the natural categories had to become disconnected from a directing inner force in individual living things.[66] This was achieved by Descartes, whose work meant a definitive break with Aristotelianism. It is remarkable that the conservative Protestants in the Dutch republic who rejected this new philosophy,[67] the anti-Cartesians, are characterized in recent research as fully Aristotelian and followers of the interpretation of Aquinas.[68] These religious conservatives rejected Cartesianism for primarily ethical reasons. The religious conservatives reasoned that Descartes' theory in fact introduced the idea that God was the only effective external motor, imparting motion upon the clockwork of nature.[69] Only by accepting the Aristotelian view in which individual living things are composites of form and matter, could the understanding of moral human action be preserved.[70]

The new philosophy therefore went into full swing when a new categorical **collective** morality was developed. This was developed by humanists, who analyzed the common nature of Man.

When at the end of the eighteenth century this humanist analysis of the common nature of Man was merged with the conception of individuals as disconnected from an inner directing force, a new enlightened interpretation of Aristotle's teleology developed. In this new enlightened interpretation the individual finds its essential nature in the collective directing force of society. This directing force is economically interpreted: the possession of property.

The substantive idea about the common drive of living things is the ordering principle in a taxonomic classification system. For Linnaeus this ordering principle was sexuality. His classification method was thought to be strictly scientific. The common nature was first formulated hypothetically and was thought to be corroborated by the logical quality of the order that could be realized by it.

---

[66]Pellegrin (1986), pp. 45 and 163.

[67]Israel (1995).

[68]van Ruler (1991). See also van Ruler (1995) and Douglas (2015).

[69]van Ruler (1991), p. 79.

[70]Ibid., p. 88. Similar to Aquinas Voetius elaborates the idea of secondary causality, which concurs with God's primary causality.

The summit of this classification method was realized in legal theory by the Begriffsjurisprudenz as developed by Savigny. At first sight Savigny followed completely the same method as Aristotle. The difference, however, is that he believed in the existence of common natures and a common directing force.[71] As a result his conclusion is the reverse of what Aristotle had in mind.

Savigny elaborated how concepts can be derived from the comparison of cases, in which by Einfühlung (empathy) is discovered the way in which the cases conform to reason. Savigny viewed his method for the genealogy of concepts as simultaneously historical (substantive) and systematic (formal): historical because the spirit which belongs to all people motivates their action and gives orientation to their perception and judgment; systematic, because this spirit can be described in its manifestation with the help of the comparison of cases. By this combination of form and matter at the level of the natural category humanity, the system becomes perfect and moralism refers not to an individual moral agent, but to a common essence of the people of a nation, or all people. The spirit was designated as Volksempfindung by Savigny. His method brought moral perfectionism and nationalistic culturalism into law.[72]

8.5 Three Religions of Humanity

Hobbes is the first author to make the analysis of the common nature of humanity politically relevant. He refers to Aristotle[73] when he explains why human beings cannot live in peaceful cooperation as ants do. Man is doomed to an endless fight for economic and political dominance by virtue of his rational capacities. At the same time, however, reason can teach Man how to achieve peace. For this men have to create a real unity of them all, in one and the same person. This is envisaged by Hobbes as a social contract between all citizens, who, driven by their rational insight, agree to be fully obedient to the king (or council) who by the course of events has come to power, and is thus God's lieutenant on earth. Hobbes is thus the first to give the state a moral function: the state has to repair the moral deficit of reason.

Rousseau follows the same path as Hobbes concerning the ideas of a social contract and the moral function of the state. He elaborates these ideas into the concept of the legislative state. The set of state-laws is seen by him as a positive divine law. These state-laws are the core of what Rousseau calls a civil religion.

---

[71]Pellegrin (1986), p. 123. Pellegrin calls the method of Aristotle moriology, referring to it as a research of parts. See also Steel (2010). To emphasize the normative assumption, implied in the taxonomic method of Begriffsjurisprudenz, I used the name normative inductivism in my thesis Huppes-Cluysenaer (1995), p. 164.

[72]von Savigny (1973).

[73]Hobbes (1986), II, pp. 17 and 225.

This moral legislative state is a new phenomenon which changed the tradition of law profoundly.[74]

8.5.1 Rousseau

Rousseau compares the set of general state-laws which manifest the collective self with the dogmas of a religion. The general laws are the sentiments of sociability, without which it is impossible to be a good citizen and a faithful subject.[75] Rousseau's social contract unites people in a metaphysical person. This metaphysical collective person has a mind (the collectivity of individuals as sovereign), a body (all individuals as subjects) and acting-power (the prince, the government, which is a democracy, an oligarchy or a monarchy).[76] Rousseau's civil state has collective agency, which replaces the agency of individual persons. Different peoples will have different sets of general laws, which manifest different national characters with a different moral virtuousness. In essence these sets of laws are all manifestations of the same common nature of human beings.

8.5.1.1 State of Nature

There is ambivalence in Hobbes' elaboration of the moral theme of the state of nature. Hobbes describes the state of nature partly as the cooperation of ants and partly as the behavior of the citizens of his time. The following quotation clearly refers to the dialogical rationality of his days, which Hobbes rejects

> Whereas Man is then most troublesome, when he is most at ease: for then it is that he loves to shew his Wisdome, and controule the Actions of them that governe the Commonwealth.[77]

The same ambivalence can be found in Rousseau's elaboration of this moral theme. Different from Hobbes, Rousseau believes that a true non-competitive state of nature, a life similar to that of an ant or bee, is possible for man. He depicts it as a life without political organization and with anarchical freedom.[78] At the same time Rousseau describes the emergence of the civil state from the state of nature as a passage from a badly organized civil state, which degrades man beneath the original state of nature, into a well-organized civil state.

---

[74]Compare Kelsen (1941), p. 93.

[75]Rousseau (1988), IV, p. 8.

[76]Ibid., III, p. 1.

[77]Hobbes (1986), II, pp. 17 and 226.

[78]Rousseau (1772), pp. 1–2. Compare with Aristotle *Pol.* 1327b20–1328a19 and in this volume Coelho (2018).

> This passage from the state of nature to the civil state produces a most remarkable change in man, (...) Although in this state he denies himself several of the advantages he owes to nature, he gains others so great - his faculties are exercised and developed, his ideas are extended, his feelings are ennobled, his whole soul is so uplifted - that if the abuse of this new condition did not often degrade him beneath the condition from which he emerged, he would constantly have to bless the happy moment that tore him away from it forever, and made a stupid and shortsighted animal into an intelligent being and man.[79]

The first view, which concerns the passage from a non-competitive state of animal life into the morally uplifted life in a civil state, describes what the individual can gain morally from the sacrifice of its autonomy. The argument is that man, when he began to use his reason, became conscious and clever, but also lost the simplicity he had before. The enforcement of general state-laws can help him to do morally consciously the good things he would unconsciously have done in a pre-rational life.

The second view, which concerns the passage from a badly organized state into a well-organized state, describes what the individual can gain politically in terms of civil freedom. It concerns nation-building and makes a multitude able to speak with one voice.[80] In the words of Rousseau:

> Although it is easy, if you wish, to make better laws, it is impossible to make them such that the passions of men will not abuse them as they abused the laws which preceded them. (...). Solve this problem well, and the government based on your solution will be good and free from abuses. But until then you may rest assured that, wherever you think you are establishing the rule of law, it is men who will do the ruling.
>
> There will never be a good and solid constitution unless the law reigns over the hearts of the citizens; as long as the power of legislation is insufficient to accomplish this, laws will always be evaded. But how can hearts be reached? That is a question to which our law-reformers, who never look beyond coercion and punishments, pay hardly any attention; and it is a question to the solving of which material rewards would perhaps be equally ineffective. Even the most upright justice is
>
> Insufficient, for justice, like health, is a good which is enjoyed without being felt, which inspires no enthusiasm, and the value of which is felt only after it has been lost. How then is it possible to move the hearts of men, and to make them love the fatherland and its laws? Dare I say it? Through children's games; through institutions which seem idle and frivolous to superficial men, but which form cherished habits and invincible attachments.[81]

In this second view, which is concerned with nation-building, the religion of humanity plays an important role in the cultivation of emotions. In the first view, the religion of humanity plays an important role in creating obedient people: by becoming a member of a nation one becomes a morally better person through fear for punishment by positive law. These two concepts of law are different: children's games which reach the heart (second view) and the dogma's of a civil religion (first view). The relation between these two concepts of law is constitutive for Rousseau's civil state.

---

[79]Rousseau (1988), I, p. 8.

[80]See Drosterij (2008). Nation-building brings about a change in the focus of political theory: from jurisdiction to will-formation.

[81]Rousseau (1772), p. 2.

8.5.1.2   The Sacrifice

A good example of the difference between governing in the traditional manner and
Rousseau's proposed legislative form of governing can be found in the 'reglement'
(regulation) made as advice by Grotius (1583–1645) at the invitation of the Dutch
Staten-Generaal, when many Portuguese Jews arrived in the Netherlands as refugees.
A modern law would treat religion in general as the relevant category. Grotius,
however, was asked to make a reglement for a specific group of Jews who had
their own church organization. The reglement was a proposal for an agreement to be
made with this group. The group was very rich and the reglement was designed to
prevent competition between the towns. When the proposal was discussed and the
number of permitted synagogues was accepted in general, the advice to prevent
ghetto's was left to each city to decide for itself.[82] The total rejection of this system
of agreements and privileges is needed to enter into Rousseau's civil state.

> Anyone who dares to undertake the founding of a people should feel himself capable of
> changing human nature, so to speak, of transforming each individual, who by himself is a
> perfect and solitary whole, into part of a greater whole from which this individual receives
> in a way, his life and his being (. . .) He must, in a word, take away man's own forces in
> order to give him new ones, which are alien to him and which he cannot use without the
> help of others. The more inactive and impotent these natural forces are, and the greater and
> more enduring the acquired ones are, the more solid and perfect the institution is as well, so
> that if each citizen is nothing and can do nothing except through all the others and if the
> force acquired by the whole is equal or superior to the sum of the natural forces of all the
> individuals, it can be said that the legislation has reached the highest level of perfection it
> can attain.[83]

The individual has to be transformed. This transformation makes the individual
part of a whole powerful enough to guide him in his moral choices when he
deviates. This transition would make the individual a slave unless it is conceived
as an act of self-organization. Rousseau is well aware of the metaphysical, counterfactual nature of his reasoning when he presents this transition as an act of self-
organization:

> Laws are properly speaking only the conditions of civil association. The people who are
> subject to the laws should be their author; defining the conditions of the society is solely a
> function of those who form the association, but how will they define them? Will it be by
> common accord, by sudden inspiration? Does the body politic have an organ for declaring
> its will? Who will give it the foresight necessary to formulate decisions on this basis, and to
> announce them in advance, or how will it make these decisions in time of need? How would
> a blind multitude, which often does not know what it wants because it rarely knows what is
> good for it, carry out on its own as great and difficult an undertaking as that of creating a
> system of legislation? (. . .)[84]

---

[82]Information based on a lecture by M. de Wilde in Amsterdam, not on reading the document
(de Wilde 2017).

[83]Rousseau (1988), II, p. 7.

[84]Ibid., II, p. 6.

The problem is thus that the social spirit, which is the result of the sacrifice, will have to preside over the will to make the sacrifice. This is the religious aspect of Rousseau's view of the state.

> That is what has forced the fathers of nations in every age to take recourse to divine intervention and to credit the gods with their own wisdom, so that the people, bound by the laws of the state as by those of nature, and recognizing the same power in the formation of the city as in the creation of man, might freely obey and docilely bear the yoke of public felicity. In order to lead by divine authority those who could not be moved by human prudence, the lawgiver places the decision of this sublime reason which rises above the understanding of the vulgar herd, in the mouth of the immortals.[85]

The enlightened person does not need religion, because he or she will reason—similar to a natural scientist—that a natural power forms the city in the same way as it forms humankind in general, and that state-laws will conform to this formative power. This is a categorical rationality, in which the world is thought of in terms of a craftsman's rationality: as a perfect design. The actual world consists of manifestations of this design. It is a determinist view. What then is the sacrifice?

The rationality of Rousseau is still akin to the dialogical rationality by virtue of the fact that he sees the individual as autonomous. An autonomous individual understands freedom as a commission to be virtuous and to take care of one's soul. This freedom is connected with existential feelings of doubt and is different from the freedom of liberalism.[86]

In Ancient dialogical rationality this concept of freedom is developed in parental relations and in the context of office (Described in Sect. 3 as a civic morality pertaining to the decision as an act in combination with a contemplative morality at work in the Council).

Individual autonomy is no longer connected with office in the enlightened view of Rousseau. In his view the sphere of office becomes restricted to the obedient execution of the laws of the Sovereign people. For Rousseau the act of transformation is in itself the manifestation of individual autonomy. The act of transformation is stage-set as a battle against the bad world in which the citizen is driven by egoism. The public sphere is not a sphere of rational discussion, but a communicative sphere in which the act of transformation can be celebrated as a moral act. For the enlightened person the act of transformation is an act of eloquence in the world of letters and speech which contributes to the expression of a public collective morality. It is contemplative morality at work—akin to the communication in the Council in Athens—but not part of a judicial procedure. For the simple person the act of transformation is participating in the rituals of a civil religion.[87] Rousseau's eloquence is revealed in the passage below, in which he manifests his own autonomy and morality by attacking the evilness of his fellow citizens.

---

[85]Ibid., II, p. 7.

[86]Drosterij (2008), p. 137.

[87]Rousseau (1988), IV, p. 8.

If we have laws, it is solely for the purpose of teaching us to obey our masters well, to keep our hands out of other people's pockets, and to give a great deal of money to public scoundrels. If we have social usages, it is in order that we may know how to amuse the idleness of light women, and to display our own with grace. If we assemble, it is in the temples of a cult which is in no sense national, and which does nothing to remind us of the fatherland; it is in tightly closed halls, and for money, to see play-actors declaim and prostitutes simper on effeminate and dissolute stages where love is the only theme, and where we go to learn those lessons in corruption which, of all the lessons they pretend to teach, are the only ones from which we profit; it is in festivals where the common people, forever scorned, are always without influence, where public blame and approbation are inconsequential; it is in licentious throngs, where we go to form secret liaisons and to seek those pleasures which do most to separate, to isolate men, and to corrupt their hearts. Are these stimulants to patriotism? Is it surprising that ways of life so different should be so unlike in their effects, and that we moderns can no longer find in ourselves anything of that spiritual vigor which was inspired in the ancients by everything they did? (...) Today, no matter what people may say, there are no longer any Frenchmen, Germans, Spaniards, or even Englishmen; there are only Europeans. All have the same tastes, the same passions, the same manners, for no one has been shaped along national lines by peculiar institutions. All, in the same circumstances, will do the same things; all will call themselves unselfish, and be rascals; all will talk of the public welfare, and think only of themselves; all will praise moderation, and wish to be as rich as Croesus. They have no ambition but for luxury, they have no passion but for gold; sure that money will buy them all their hearts desire, they all are ready to sell themselves to the first bidder. What do they care what master they obey, under the laws of what state they live? Provided they can find money to steal and women to corrupt, they feel at home in any country.[88]

8.5.1.3 Religion and Tolerance

Rousseau distinguishes four types of religion: (1) of man, (2) of the citizen, (3) of the priest and (4) civil religion. The religion of the citizen and civil religion (2 + 4) are both adequate according to Rousseau, because they teach the citizen to adore the laws of the city: the so-called positive divine law.[89] In such a religion, to serve the state means to serve God, and to acknowledge the prince and the magistrates means to serve the pontiff and the priests. Such religions are imperial cults as was historically the use—for example, in Rome. According to Rousseau, the religion of the priest and the religion of man are both inadequate. The religion of the priest (3)—Roman Catholicism—is absurd because it acknowledges two sets of positive divine laws.[90] The religion of man (1) refers to dialogical rationality in its Christian form. Rousseau rejects it because instead of making Man obedient to the state it makes Man independent of the state:

(it is) holy, sublime, and true, men, as children of the same God, all acknowledge each other as brothers...(...) But (...) this religion has no particular relation to the body politic, it

---

[88]Rousseau (1772), pp. 4–5.

[89]Rousseau (1988), III, p. 8. See also II, 7, footnote 9.

[90]This duality can be read in terms of a civic and contemplative morality.

leaves to the laws only the force that they have in themselves, without adding any force to them, and because of this one of the chief bonds of particular societies remains ineffective.

(. . .) Provided he has no reason to reproach himself, it matters little to him whether all goes well or badly here below. If the state is flourishing, he hardly dares to enjoy the public happiness.[91]

Rousseau strips his own civil religion (4) of the errors of the theocratic religion of the citizen (2), which created superstition and empty ceremonials and above all made people intolerant by making their own religion exclusive. Rousseau acknowledges religion as a necessary constructive part of the state on two conditions: that its laws are not in opposition to the positive divine law and that it accepts that its church cannot be exclusive. The best religion is civil religion (4), the religion of those who are rational:

a purely civil profession of faith, the articles of which are for the sovereign to determine, not precisely as religious dogma's, but as sentiments of sociability, without which it is impossible to be a good citizen or a faithful subject. Without being able to obligate anyone to believe them, the sovereign can banish from the state anyone who does not believe them; it can banish him not for being impious but for being unsociable (. . .) The dogma's of the civil religion should be simple, few in number, and precisely enunciated, without explanations or commentaries. The existence of a powerful, intelligent, beneficent, prescient, and provident divinity, the life to come, the happiness of the just, the punishment of the wicked, the sanctity of the social contract and the laws: these are the positive dogma's. As for the negative dogma's I limit them to one alone: this is intolerance; it is part of the cults we have to exclude. Those who distinguish between civil and theological intolerance are mistaken in my opinion. (. . .) Wherever theological intolerance is allowed, it is impossible for it not to have some civil effect, and once it does, the sovereign is no longer sovereign. (. . .) Now that there is no longer and can no longer be an exclusive national religion, all those which tolerate others must be tolerated, insofar as their dogma's are in no way contrary to the duties of a citizen. But whoever dares say, outside the church, no salvation, should be driven from the state. . ..[92]

Seen from the focus of this chapter, the most important aspect of Rousseau's religion of humanity is its rejection of the religion of man. With this he rejects civic morality which is the crucial sphere for acquiring a virtuous character in the dialogical rationality. Civic morality is elaborated by Aristotle as a sphere of epistemological doubt (similar to Plato) and moral doubt (weakness of will, different from Plato). Both doubts are foundational for toleration in the sense of moderation.

Epistemological doubt is rejected in categorical rationality. Moral doubt becomes with Rousseau the essence of the collective communicative sphere. While the contemplative morality at work in the Council was primarily based on epistemological doubt, the contemplative morality at work in the public communal life of Rousseau is primarily based on moral doubt.

---

[91]Rousseau (1988), III, p. 8.

[92]Ibid., III, p. 8.

8.5.1.4   The Democratic Spirit: Critical Culture

Rousseau believes that a national virtuous character is formed with the help of children's games. This is reminiscent of the discussion which Plato starts in *Laws*.[93] In it he compares the constitution of Sparta with the methods Athens used to teach young people what it means to drink too much, for example. In Athens certain festivities were established where youngsters find out what for them personally the meaning is of "drinking too much," while in Sparta certain strict rules were implemented with punishment. Plato explains that in the Spartan system rules are not willed from within and will only work when actually enforced. Aristotle actually agrees with Plato's argument when he explains that Sparta's constitution is only adequate in a military regime and is unfit for times of leisure (*Pol.* 1324b95–10). Rousseau follows the model of Sparta,[94] while at the same time he understands that to reach the hearts of people, you can better use games. In other words the government should execute like a Spartan, while the legislator should be educated to be sovereign like an Athenian. Rousseau acknowledges two forms of publicity: a regulated publicity for execution and a free democratic publicity for the self-creation of a nation.

Shklar describes Rousseau's concept of law as moralistic, exhibiting a non-cultural, a-theoretical ideal of the life of a Swiss peasant. She sees Rousseau's project in this respect as one of disciplining. By depersonalizing dominion, Rousseau moralized the obedience of the slaves and the poor.[95] Such a description is adequate as an analysis of the deeper forces in the era in which Rousseau lived, but as also Shklar notes, such a description does not fit very well with the existential nature of Rousseau's work. Shklar describes how Rousseau presented himself to the reading public of his days as the son of a watchmaker, how he showed his own personal life as anti-establishment, spoke against luxury, denounced the pseudo-morality of the ruling classes, coined and advertised political pity and social solidarity. She concludes that his democracy was not designed to promote a long conversation, compromise or social change, but to reassert the unity of townsmen.[96]

Rousseau's sovereign collectivity should be understood against the background of the rise of a public sphere of communication. Habermas gave a seminal description of the liberating effect of this "public sphere in the World of Letters".[97] In this public communication people learned to experience their common nature. They experienced how their own most intimate feelings were mirrored in the feelings of the heroes of books. By reading these books about the lives of others they could enlarge their world in scope and depth at the same time.

---

[93]Plato (1970).

[94]Rousseau (1988), II, p. 7.

[95]Shklar (1978), pp. 263–268.

[96]Ibid.

[97]Habermas (1989), section 7.

It therefore seems better to conclude that Rousseau uses the unattractive picture of Sparta to be able to describe "the bad world" as bad and at the same time attractive. If the good world was attractive, there would be no moral public discussion. By framing the collective public discussion as a moral discussion about egoism and altruism Rousseau put his new legislative civil state in continuity with the debate in Athens which was framed as a debate between the poor and the rich, and not, for example, as a debate about drinking rules. Thus Rousseau put the democratic spirit in the center of the civil state and elaborated it—specifically in his educational works—in the same way as in Athens: as the insight that a life spent in luxury in one's own social group is degrading and boring and that the intellect should feel itself continuously invited to look at the same world from different points of view. The best way to achieve this is to force people to a certain extent to have actual contacts as equals with each other.

Similar to Aristotle, Rousseau concludes that:

> Practically all small states, no matter whether they are republics or monarchies, prosper merely by reason of the fact that they are small; that all the citizens know and watch over one another; that the leaders can see for themselves the evil that is being done, the good they have to do; and that their orders are carried out before their eyes.[98]

Nation-building was specifically necessary in Rousseau's days to make it possible for the technical rationality of the categorical rationality to fully develop. It created the unity which could set and discuss collective goals. While a rational approach would tend to become cosmopolitan and lose connection with the hearts of the people, Rousseau's sentimental approach organized the idea of a concrete manifestation of the common nature of human beings in the form of a nation.

8.5.2 Kant

8.5.2.1 Epistemology

Kant's point of view is primarily epistemological. Many of the themes of Rousseau return in Kant's work, but what he adds is an epistemological take. Kant defines Enlightenment as follows:

> Enlightenment is man's emergence from his selfimposed nonage. Nonage is the inability to use one's own understanding without another's guidance. This nonage is selfimposed if its cause lies not in lack of understanding but in indecision and lack of courage to use one's own mind without another's guidance. (...) It is more nearly possible, however, for the public to enlighten itself; indeed, if it is only given freedom, enlightenment is almost inevitable. There will always be a few independent thinkers, even among the selfappointed guardians of the multitude. (...) a public can achieve enlightenment only slowly. A revolution may bring about the end of a personal despotism or of avaricious tyrannical

---
[98]Rousseau (1772), p. 12.

oppression, but never a true reform of modes of thought. New prejudices will serve, in place of the old, as guide lines for the unthinking multitude.

This enlightenment requires nothing but *freedom* (...): freedom to make public use of one's reason in all matters[99]

Similar to Rousseau, Kant still takes an autonomous individual as his point of departure and believes that each individual is commissioned to be oriented towards a virtuous life. Similar to Rousseau, Kant believed that the individual can be uplifted and become enlightened by being a participant in a collective process. Similar to Rousseau, Kant viewed the concept of general law as the key by which this process will naturally come about when people use their reason. Kant differs from Rousseau by not taking desire as his point of departure, but reason. He formulates the Categorical Imperative, which requires the individual to use his reason to formulate the rules (maxims) which would entitle everybody to the same behavior as his own and to conclude that he has to comply with such rules. This way each individual is not only his own legislator and at the same time a legislator for all, but also his own law-enforcer.

Similar to Rousseau, Kant thus requires from the individual a moral use of personal freedom, conditioned by faith, to choose to be part of the collective process. Different from Rousseau, Kant takes the bourgeois state as point of departure. His main focus is epistemological and not emotional and moral as Rousseau's view.

Kant saw and supported the shift from a dialogical to a categorical rationality. He studied all aspects of the categorical rationality and understood its close relation to crafts, as elaborated above in Sect. 4.3. Kant also understood the specific epistemological position of crafts as intermediate between theory and practice.

Kant elaborated all this in his Kritik of Judgment, in which he explains that there is a gap between theory and practice—indicated by Aristotle as originating from the need to talk and think in categories about a world which is infinitely diverse—and that this gap has to be bridged by a moral attitude of reason i.e., to have faith.

Faith is the moral attitude of Reason as to the belief in that which is unattainable by theoretical cognition. It is therefore the permanent principle of the mind to assume as true (...) that which it is necessary to presuppose as condition of the possibility of the highest moral final purpose.[100]

This faith concerns the assumption needed to establish the unity of all empirical principles under higher ones, and hence their systematic subordination.

The reflective Judgment, which is obliged to ascend from the particular in nature to the universal, requires on that account a principle that it cannot borrow from experience, because its function is to establish the unity of all empirical principles under higher ones, and hence to establish the possibility of their systematic subordination. Such a transcendental principle, then, the reflective Judgment can only give as a law from and to itself. (...) This principle can be no other than the following: (...) particular empirical laws, in respect

---

[99]Kant (1784).

[100]Kant (1992), p. 409.

of what is in them left undetermined by these universal laws, must be considered in accordance with such a unity as they would have if an Understanding (although not our Understanding) had furnished them to our cognitive faculties, so as to make possible a system of experience according to particular laws of nature. Not as if, in this way, such an understanding must be assumed as actual (. . .) The purposiveness of nature is therefore a particular concept, a priori, which has its origin solely in the reflective Judgment. For we cannot ascribe to natural products anything like a reference of nature in them to purposes.[101]

In this way Kant lays the foundation for the rise of classification systems in the moral attitude of reason. As Bernard says, Kant explains the categorical rationality *as if* nature is a work of design of God.[102] This way he explains how people can think that their understanding approximates truth, while at the same time he refuses to accept its truth in any other way than as a faith. The point of view of Kant is therefore counterfactual and religious. This is important in relation to Kant's conception of critical discussion, because in this area Kant attributes consequences to truth claims, as if these claims rest on beliefs which are attainable by theoretical cognition.

8.5.2.2   Critical Discussion

the public use of one's reason must be free at all times, and this alone can bring enlightenment to mankind. On the other hand, the private use of reason may frequently be narrowly restricted without especially hindering the process of enlightenment. By "public use of one's reason" I mean that use which a man, as *scholar*, makes of it before the reading public. I call private use that use which a man makes of his reason in a civic post that has been entrusted to him. (Italics Kant)[103]

Kant elaborates the idea of a public discussion by scholars and the distinction between public and private use of reason in a short essay, entitled *Der Streit der Fakultäten*,[104] He defines his subject as:

to handle the entire content of learning (really, the thinkers devoted to it) by *mass production*, so to speak – by a division of labor, so that for every branch of the sciences there would be a public teacher or *professor* appointed as its trustee, and all of these together would form a kind of learned community called *university* (or higher school). (italics by Kant)[105]

Kant distinguishes between scholars proper and members of the "intelligentsia" who are instruments of the government, i.e., invested with an office for a purpose which is different from the progress of science. The latter have been educated at the university and use their learning in a civil practice. Kant calls them "businessmen"

---

[101]Ibid., p. 17.

[102]Bernard (1992), pp. xxv–xxxvii.

[103]Kant (1784).

[104]Kant (1979).

[105]Ibid.

or "technicians of learning." As tools of the government they (clergymen, magistrates and medical doctors) must be kept under strict control of the government because they deal with uneducated people and exercise authority over them.

The scholars who are incorporated in the universities are divided into two groups. First, there are three faculties—theology, jurisprudence and medicine—which Kant calls the higher faculties because their teachings are in the interest of the government. Next to these higher faculties is the lower faculty of philosophy, which consists of the department of historical knowledge (history, geography, philology, and the humanities, along with all the empirical knowledge contained in the natural sciences) and a department of pure rational knowledge (pure mathematics and pure philosophy, the metaphysics of nature and morals). The technicians of learning are subjected to the censorship of the faculties and the teachings of the faculty professors of the higher faculties are sanctioned by the government. All three higher faculties base the teachings which the government entrusts to them on *writings*, according to Kant. The theology-professors teach the bible, the legal professors teach the statutes as promulgated by the authority. About the professors of medicine who are entrusted with medical regulations, Kant says the following:

> Although medicine is an art, it is an art that is drawn directly from nature and must therefore be derived from a science of nature. (...) Unlike the other higher faculties, however, the faculty of medicine must derive its rules of procedure not from orders of the authorities but from the nature of things themselves so that its teachings must have also belonged originally to the philosophy faculty, taken in its widest sense.[106]

The lower faculty of philosophy may use its own judgment about what is taught. In relation to the higher faculties, the faculty of philosophy has the function to control them and in this way be useful to them, since truth is the main thing and governments should understand that truth should never be driven away or silenced. It is important, however, that the intelligentsia, which is in direct contact with the public, stay outside the public discussion. Free public discussion should be limited to a learned community devoted to the sciences:

> The philosophy faculty can, therefore, lay claim to any teaching, in order to test its truth. The government cannot forbid it to do this without acting against its own proper and essential purpose; and the higher faculties must put up with the objections and doubts it brings forward in public, though they may well find this irksome (...) Only the businessmen of the higher faculties (clergymen, legal officials, and doctors) can be prevented from contradicting in public the teachings that the government has entrusted to them (...).[107]

Kant concludes that the higher faculties (as the right side of the parliament of learning) support the government's statutes in opposition to the left side:

> But in as free a system of government as must exist when it is a question of truth, there must also be an opposition party (the left side), and this is the philosophy faculty's bench. (...) This conflict is quite compatible with an agreement of the learned and civil community in

---

[106]Ibid.

[107]Ibid.

maxims which, if observed, must bring about a constant progress of both ranks of the faculties toward greater perfection,(...)[108]

Kant's view on free public discussion demands that all restrictions on the freedom of public judgments by the lower faculties be removed and this in the end will make the lower faculty the highest because it will offer better means for the Government to achieve its ends.

8.5.2.3 Kant's Religion of Humanity

Different and new in Kant is that he solved the existing dilemma between rationalism and empiricism that had prevented science from steady growth and political status. With his critical analysis he was foundational for the theory of science in making explicit the important assumptions of science. In the same way as Hume's skepticism gave empiricism its full swing, Kant's counterfactual reasoning legitimized the categorical rationality and thus gave science political force.

When Kant reasons that the philosophy faculty can lay claim to any teaching in order to test its truth, he not only assumes something which is unattainable by theoretical cognition i.e., an approximation of truth, but also something which is unattainable by practical reason, i.e., the conclusion that truth is equivalent to the morally good. These claims are attributed by him to the universities.

Acting should be in obedience to the rules reason teaches. For the law faculty and the theology faculty this means acting according to writings. The jurists should be cured from their dialogical attitude with its emphasis on judicial practice:

> the biblical theologians do not join in the jurist's complaint that it is all but vain to hope for a precisely determined norm for the administration of justice (ius certus); for they reject the claim that their dogma lacks a norm that is clear and determined for every case.[109]

Those who are entrusted with an office have, according to Kant, only the duty to obey and are not allowed a claim to epistemological doubt. Practical wisdom is exchanged for obedience to the will of the Government.

The vigorously critical public culture of Kant is not about right and wrong in any moral sense, but about true or false. Epistemological doubt in this sphere of science is acknowledged by Kant in all its rigour and then rubbed away in counterfactual reasoning.

In the Kritik of Judgment Kant makes a distinction between theoretical philosophy and technical practice, between physical law and precepts.

> All technical practical rules (...) so far as their principles rest on concepts, must be reckoned only as corollaries to theoretical Philosophy. For they concern only the possibility of things according to natural concepts, to which belong not only the means which are to be met with in nature, but also the will itself (as a faculty of desire and consequently a natural faculty) so far as it can be determined conformably to these rules by natural motives.

---

[108]Ibid.
[109]Ibid.

However, practical rules of this kind are not called laws (like physical laws) but precepts; because the will does not stand merely under the natural concept, but also under the concept of freedom, in relation to which its principles are called laws. These with their consequences alone constitute the second or practical part of Philosophy.[110]

But what sense does it make to distinguish between the counterfactual "real (objective) purposefulness reasoning" of theoretical philosophy and the real purposes of a technical practice? With Aristotle it would be a distinction between a general contemplative morality and the responsibility of an individual agent with an office, whose acts can be judged by their results as far as these acts are technical. What Kant wins with his counterfactual reasoning is the introduction of "objective collective practice," as if such an abstraction has agency, as if individuals can think about their own acts in terms of categorical imperatives that are ethically and technically informed. Similar to the way Rousseau turned the moral field of practice into an imperial cult, Kant turns the epistemological field of practice into an imperial cult: the idea of objective collective practice establishes unfounded general legitimate claims of authority where it should acknowledge subjective authority.

8.5.3   Comte

Nussbaum refers to Comte. Comte's elaboration of the religion of humanity gives a rather outdated impression, however. Nussbaum's reference is nevertheless consequent and relevant. Comte has—different from Rousseau and Kant, and in conformity with the modern mind—a typically liberal individual in mind and tries to set up a religion of humanity according to the principles of social science. It is in a certain sense telling that the philosophies of Rousseau and Kant are much more appealing than the philosophy of Comte, because—given the fact that these philosophies are still full of religious concepts—one would have expected otherwise.

8.5.3.1   Positivist Science

Science Comte is known as the first to develop a science for the social world: sociological positivism. His positive science represents an organic view and is therefore in a way very similar to Aristotle's view. It is a neo-Aristotelianism which is adapted to the categorical approach of modern science. Comte's approach is not yet empirical and sociological qua method. This is later developed by Durkheim, who further elaborated Comte's theory.

Positivism After the defeat of Napoleon there was the need to restore order. In France many people wanted simply to restore the "ancien régime," which refers to

---

[110]Kant (1992), p. 8.

the reign of Louis XVI. Comte set out to elaborate a plan for restoration oriented towards progress guided by political scientists (called publicists). His third essay in 1822 is called *Plan of the Scientific Operations Necessary for Reorganizing Society*.[111] In his first essay *Separation of Opinions from Aspirations* in 1819 the plan was in essence already set out in the separation of three powers, based on a distinction between spectator and actor (the latter subdivided in collective and individual). Comte states that:

> (. . .) rulers, even when honest, are by their position more disqualified from gaining a just and elevated view of general politics, since a continual preoccupation with details incapacitates for correct theory.[112]

If publicists wish to have large political conceptions, they should rigorously refrain from political office.

Comte discerns three separated powers: (1) The public should indicate the end, its own wishes. (2) The scientific politicians—publicists (spectators)—should consider the means to realize these, and (3) The rulers should realize them. When politics enters the rank of a positive science, the public should and must accord the same confidence to publicists that it now concedes to astronomers and physicians in medicine, etc. The public should be exclusively entitled to point out the end and aim of the work.[113]

8.5.3.2   Comte's Three Stages of Development: Theological, Metaphysical and Positive

Comte sees the metaphysical construction of the social by Rousseau merely as a transition phase between the theological Roman Catholic feudal system and the scientific or positive state.[114] He attributes the downfall of the theological state to the progress of the sciences of observation, enabled by Arabic thought. The downfall created the reformist philosophy of the eighteenth century. This philosophy had a hostile negative attitude towards government—the "ancient régime"—but because of this attitude could not contribute to its abolishment. A positive organic principle was needed to escape from the vicious circle in which society was kept by the metaphysical philosophers.[115]

Comte's anti-metaphysics expressed an anti-legal approach, which closely matches Kant's ideas about a critical public culture and the left side of government. Roscoe Pound[116] quotes Timasheff, who wrote that sociology was born in a state of

---

[111]Comte (1975a).

[112]Comte (1975b).

[113]Ibid., p. 8.

[114]Comte (1975a), p. 29.

[115]Ibid., p. 9.

[116]Pound (1945), p. 304.

hostility to law. Timasheff thought that the developmental theories of early sociol-ogists had difficulty to incorporate law because they saw law as something arbitrary and disturbing—in the words of Spencer a "hardened form of custom," "the rule of the dead over the living"—rather than as expressing organic development.[117] However, those who saw law as an organic development, like von Savigny (Sect. 4.4), developed law as a closed taxonomic model. Every conception of law which understands legal practice as rule-application will produce rules of the dead. When a civic morality is interpreted in these terms, it will always be superseded by new insights of the left side of government.

Comte was able to understand society in a dynamic way by viewing it as a combined activity towards one of two possible aims: conquest or production. The first step for social reorganization should be to choose for the positive aim of industrialization.[118]

Reorganization should not be left to practitioners (who apply rules), but taken up by theorists (who let themselves be inspired by goals). The degree of civilization in a society can be measured according to Comte by looking to the degree of separation between theory and practice (spectator and actor) and the subsequent harmonization: division of labor and combination of efforts.

This separation was realized in the theological stage:

> By the definitive establishment of Christianity, the separation of theory and practice was systematically and completely effected in relation to the general action of society (...) It was vivified and consolidated by the creation of a spiritual power, distinct and independent of the temporal power, which maintained towards the latter the natural attitude of a theoretical towards a practical authority, modified of course by the special character of the ancient system (ancient régime LHC). This great and beautiful conception was the principal cause of the admirable vigor and consistency that distinguished the feudo-Catholic system during its flourishing period. The superficial and negative philosophy of the last century misconceived its importance.[119]

To restore spiritual power, attention should be turned away from constitutional principles of the negative reformist philosophy. What was needed was the work of savants to observe and investigate. Individuals should not be considered, but rather classes and the ensemble of the scientific corps should guide the general theoretical work.

Spiritual power thus being confided to the hands of the savants, temporal power will belong to the heads of industrial works, who will organize the administrative

---

[117]Timasheff (1939), pp. 45 and 46. About Comte Timasheff writes: "Prophesying the disappear-ance of law, he expressed the opinion that law had played a useful part during the transitory period of revolution, because it helped to dissolve the previous social system. That Comte's attitude was not accidental is corroborated by the fact that another great sociological system, born almost simultaneously with his, comprised an analogous prophesy of the disappearance of law with the advance of society: for K. Marx, law was one of the "super structures" characteristic of the "bourgeois" order and was to "wither away" together with the State, after the establishment of classless society."

[118]Ibid., p. 20.

[119]Ibid., p. 22.

system according to the principles established by the savants.[120] Only savants will have the capacity to win back the people who mistakenly believe in the social contract philosophy and think to be the supreme judge of political conceptions. Only savants will be capable to establish the needed European power:

> It is clear that scientific men alone constitute a really compact and active body, all of whose members throughout Europe have a mutual understanding and communicate easily and continuously among themselves. This springs from the fact that they alone, in our days, possess common ideas, a uniform language, a general permanent aim. (. . .) The industrial classes (. . .) are still too much influenced by the hostile inspirations of a savage patriotism . . .[121]

8.5.3.3 Comte's Religion of Humanity

Comte believed that man's selfishness has to be turned into altruism in order to reach a higher type of existence. At the same time—similar to Rousseau's rejection of the religion of man[122]—he believed that total altruism would dissolve society.[123] Comte's religion of humanity refers not to a state of nature as a metaphysical counterfactual view based on the philosophical analysis of the common nature of man, but rather as actual uniformity of functions and classes. Religion is defined by Comte as:

> that state of complete harmony peculiar to human life, in its collective as well as in its individual form, when all parts of life are ordered in their natural relations to each other. . .[124]

The necessary subordination of every organism to the environment in which it is placed is the great principle of religion and at bottom the primary notion of sound biology.

> (. . .) to regulate or to combine mankind, religion must in the first instance place man under the influence of some external power, possessed of superiority so irresistible as to leave no sort of uncertainty about it.

Humans have in common with animals that the surrounding circumstances furnish food, excite affection as the vital power to desire this food and provide the rationality to find out how to get it. This vegetative existence is the primary basis of all higher types of life.[125] The higher type is not essential for living and therefore a great number of races lack it, but some form is found in all social existence.[126] Religion has the function to create harmony and unity.[127]

---

[120]Ibid., pp. 23–26.

[121]Ibid., p. 28.

[122]See for the social unsociability in Kant: Kant (1784, 1970).

[123]Comte (1975c), p. 408.

[124]Comte (1975d), p. 393.

[125]Ibid., p. 396.

[126]Ibid., pp. 396–398.

[127]Ibid., p. 398. And Comte (1975c), p. 399.

Many elements of Aristotle's contemplative morality return in Comte. For a spiritual power, at the root of its influence are the renunciation of wealth and rank. Spiritual power is morally and intellectually superior even though in fact wealth and position prevail in society. The organ of social sympathy should abstain from political action. Moral power should not be imperative, but should provide a high standard via a rational system of education and should thus maintain the breadth of view and the sense of duty that are so apt to be impaired by the ordinary course of daily life.

But all of these elements adapt Aristotle's view to modern industrial society. Each generation in a society produces a surplus that is used to facilitate and maintain the next generation. The leaders of industry take care of this and are therefore the temporal chiefs of modern society. The spiritual task—the progress of society—is borne by the scholars who propagate this priesthood. In family life the priests are supported by the women who have a strongly sympathetic nature and who are the original source for all moral influence in the family due to the passive character of their life. In political life they are assisted by the working men, who are

owing to their freedom from practical responsibilities and their unconcern for personal aggrandizement, are better disposed than their employers to broad views and to generous sympathies, and will therefore naturally associate themselves with the spiritual power. It is they who will supply the principal basis of the true public opinion, as soon as they are enabled by positive education, which is specially framed with a view to their case to give greater definiteness to their aspirations.[128]

The philosophic priesthood is in turn the systematic guardian of the interests of the workingmen against the governing class. As a result of the common system of education also the noblest members of the governing class will offer assistance as a sort of new chivalry. The modern capitalist ought to be regarded simply as a public functionary, responsible for the administration of capital and the direction of industrial enterprise. In distributing wages the prevailing principle should be: that the man can support his wife and that the active class supports the speculative class of the savants.

Comte designed a worship of the new enlightened humanity. It no longer has to project the source of a high standard of existence in a supernatural force, but can entrust this task to social science. For this worship Comte created a calendar in which the names of the saints are replaced by names of philosophers, for example January 1st (the month called Moses) is the day of Prometheus, January 16th of Lao-tzu, January 28th is Mohammed, March 28th (the month called Aristotle) of Plato. Comte places feeling before intellect, love before doctrine, art above science, the worship before doctrine.

At the first stage of human development, religion consisted of fetishism i.e. in worship of *materials* and nothing more. Comte's positive religion is a systematization of this instinctive practice of the early childhood of the human race. In positive religion *results* are worshipped and nothing more. In primitive as well as in positive religion there is a natural correlation between worship and daily life. While in theologism and even in polytheism the temporal world is separated from the divine, positivism does not need such constructions and acknowledges only the

---

[128]Comte (1975e), p. 384.

temporal world. The Supreme power which is adored by positivism is nature. Humanity should learn to know the forces of nature and prosper by using them in conformity with its own appetites. Morality and science are one.[129]

8.6 Conclusion

According to Aristotle only individual agency can be moral. Such agency is moral when the individual accepts the offices demanded and makes itself accountable for the unjustifiable harm it inevitably inflicts on others by virtue of such offices. This civic morality is at the core of Aristotle's ethical theory and anthropology. Learning one's own deepest personal desires and acting well are intertwined.

Next to this civic morality, Aristotle acknowledges a contemplative morality. This morality is theoretical. It takes a comparative point of view and thus operates at a meta-level. There are philosophers—such as Aristotle himself—who devote their lives to theoretical knowledge. They formulate general theories about the world and these can be of great value. At the same time these theories are impractical. Only when they are incorporated in the ideas of people with practical experience in law enforcement can they be of value for the state. Aristotle emphasized that the class that should play a leading role in the state should comprise not only the roles of civic morality such as military service and counseling, but also the role of contemplation and should keep apart from business and labor.

In the Enlightenment morality not only became restricted to contemplative morality, but this contemplative morality was conceived as the attainment of concrete technical goals, representing the general will of the people. The enlightened view contemplated the world as an intelligent design, the purposefulness of which is subject to human understanding. Aristotle rejected such a belief (*EN* 1141a20–b20). Kant accepted it as a belief. Only on the basis of such a belief could Kant propose that contemplative morality should have practical meaning.

The criticism of categorical rationality and its assumption of a natural order, which started in the second half of the nineteenth century, has not been addressed here. This chapter limits itself to conclude that in the period that followed there have been many careful analyses about the unattainability of the claims of categorical rationality, but that these have always been accompanied by the wish to save Enlightenment ideals. For current times, Peirce's pragmatic solution has been the most influential. He translated the idea of common natures into a belief in uniform behavior: the objective reality of habits, i.e., the existence of social rules.[130] This social foundation for categorical rationality has been elaborated in the realistic theory of science of neopositivism, as well as in the interpretative discursive theories.

---

[129]Comte (1975f), pp. 461–464.
[130]Oleksy (2015), p. 20.

Two aspects of Enlightenment thinking specifically were saved: (1) The conception of the state as a collective person, which can set common goals and can turn politics into a common enterprise instead of the armed peace of a judicial procedure; (2) The rejection of office as a sphere of personal authority and responsibility by reorganizing the context of justification into an open communicative public discussion, instead of a strictly regulated law court.

This chapter is motivated by the belief that globalization is the cause of the present political crisis because it undermines the idea of "we, the people" that is foundational for the idea of a common project and democratic justification. The author of this chapter judges the chances for a revitalization of these ideas on a global level as defended by Nussbaum, as low, and on a provincial backwards level of "exit" as unattractive.

Thus it is argued that there is a need for the differentiation acknowledged in dialogical rationality. This need will force a reappraisal of the concepts of civic morality and armed peace. In this context it is a comforting thought that both opposing rationalities are in agreement on social democratic values.

References

Arendt, Hannah. 1998. *The Human Condition*. 2nd ed. Chicago: The University of Chicago Press.

Aristotle. 1932. *Politics (Loebedition)*. Translated by H. Rackham. Loeb Classical Library. London and New York: W. Heinemann and G.P. Putnam's Sons.

———. 1933. *Metaphysics (Loebedition)*. Translated by Tredennick Hugh. Loeb Classical Library. Aristotle in 23 Volumes, 17 and 18. Cambridge, MA and London: William Heinemann Ltd. and Harvard University Press.

———. 1984a. Nicomachean Ethics. In *The Complete Works of Aristotle: The Revised Oxford Translation*, ed. Jonathan Barnes and trans. W. D. Ross and J. O. Urmson. Princeton, NJ: Princeton University Press.

———. 1984b. Physics. In *The Complete Works of Aristotle: The Revised Oxford Translation*, ed. Jonathan Barnes and trans. R. P. Hardie and R. K. Gaye. Princeton, NJ: Princeton University Press.

———. 1984c. Constitution of Athens. In *The Complete Works of Aristotle: The Revised Oxford Translation*, ed. Jonathan Barnes and trans. F. G. Kenyon. Princeton, NJ: Princeton University Press.

Barnes, Jonathan, ed. 1984. *The complete works of Aristotle: the revised Oxford translation*. Vol. 2. Princeton, NJ and Guildford: Princeton University Press.

Bates, Clifford Angell. 2013. Law and the Rule of Law and Its Place Relative to Politeia in Aristotle's Politics. In *Aristotle and the Philosophy of Law: Theory, Practice and Justice*, ed. Liesbeth Huppes-Cluysenaer and Nuno M.M.S. Coelho, 59–75. Dordrecht and New York: Springer. https://doi.org/10.1007/978-94-007-6031-8.

Bernard, J.H. 1992. Introduction. In *Kant's Kritik of Judgment*, ed. J.H. Bernard. London: Macmillan. http://books.google.com/.

Blackwell, C. W. 2003. Athenian Democracy: A Brief Overview. http://www.stoa.org/projects/demos/article_democracy_overview?page=all.

Bogen, James, and Charles M. Young. 2014. Contrariety and Change: Problems Plato Set for Aristotle. *International Journal of Scientific Research and Innovative Technology* 1 (4): 45.

Bombelli, Giovanni. 2018. Emotion and Rationality in Aristotle's Model: From Anthropology to Politics. In *Aristotle on Emotions in Law and Politics*, ed. Liesbeth Huppes-Cluysenaer and Nuno M.M.S. Coelho. Dordrecht: Springer.

Bonanno, Daniela, and Lucia Corso. 2018. What Does Nemesis Have to Do with the Legal System? Discussing Aristotle's Neglected Emotion and Its Relevance for Law and Politics. In *Aristotle on Emotions in Law and Politics*, ed. Liesbeth Huppes-Cluysenaer and Nuno M.M.S. Coelho. Dordrecht: Springer.

Brito, José de Sousa e. 2018. Aristotle on Emotions in Ethics and in Criminal Justice. In *Aristotle on Emotions in Law and Politics*, ed. Liesbeth Huppes-Cluysenaer and Nuno M.M.S. Coelho. Dordrecht: Springer.

Broadie, Sarah. 1987. Nature, Craft and Phronesis in Aristotle. *Philosophical Topics* 15 (2): 35–50.

Burns, Tony. 2011. *Aristotle and Natural Law*. London: Bloomsbury.

Coelho, Nuno M.M.S. 2018. How Emotions Can Be Both an Impediment and a Base for Political Well-Being. In *Aristotle on Emotions in Law and Politics*, ed. Liesbeth Huppes-Cluysenaer and Nuno M.M.S. Coelho. Dordrecht: Springer.

Cohen de Lara, Emma. 2018. Aristotle's Rhetoric and the Persistence of the Emotions in the Courtroom. In *Aristotle on Emotions in Law and Politics*, ed. Liesbeth Huppes-Cluysenaer and Nuno M.M.S. Coelho. Dordrecht: Springer.

Comte, Auguste. 1975a. Plan of the Scientific Operations Necessary for Reorganizing Society (Third Essay 1822). In *Auguste Comte and Positivism: The Essential Writings*, ed. Gertrud Lenzer. New York: Harper & Row.

———. 1975b. Separation of Opinions from Aspirations (First Essay 1819). In *Auguste Comte and Positivism: The Essential Writings*, ed. Gertrud Lenzer. New York: Harper & Row.

———. 1975c. Sociological Inquiry into the Problem of Human Life; (and Therein) the Positive Theory of Material Property (Vol II, of Système de Politique Positive (1851-1854) Chapter 2). In *Auguste Comte and Positivism: The Essential Writings*, ed. Gertrud Lenzer. New York: Harper & Row.

———. 1975d. The General Theory of Religion, or the Positive Theory of Human Unity (Vol II, of Système de Politique Positive (1851-1854), Chapter 1). In *Auguste Comte and Positivism: The Essential Writings*, ed. Gertrud Lenzer. New York: Harper & Row.

———. 1975e. The Religion of Humanity (Vol I, Chapter Six of Système de Politique Positive (1851-1854)). In *Auguste Comte and Positivism: The Essential Writings*, ed. Gertrud Lenzer. New York: Harper & Row.

———. 1975f. The Worship: Système de Politique Positive (1851-1854). In *Auguste Comte and Positivism: The Essential Writings*, ed. Gertrud Lenzer. New York: Harper & Row.

Cooper, John M. 1987. Hypothetical Necessity and Natural Teleology. In *Philosophical Issues in Aristotle's Biology*, ed. Allan Gotthelf and James G. Lennox, 243–274. Cambridge: Cambridge University Press.

de Matos, Saulo. 2018. Aristotle's Functionalism and the Rise of Nominalism in Law and Politics: Law, Emotion and Language. In *Aristotle on Emotions in Law and Politics*, ed. Liesbeth Huppes-Cluysenaer and Nuno M.M.S. Coelho. Dordrecht: Springer.

de Wilde, Marc. 2017. Offering Hospitality to Strangers: Hugo Grotius's Draft Regulations for the Jews. *Tijdschrift Voor Rechtsgeschiedenis* 3/4 (forthcoming).

Douglas, Alexander X. 2015. *Spinoza and Dutch Cartesianism: Philosophy and Theology*. Oxford: Oxford University Press.

Drosterij, Gerard. 2008. Politics as Jurisdiction: A New Understanding of Public and Private in Political Theory. s.n. https://pure.uvt.nl/portal/files/1027677/drosterij_pol_as_jurisdiction.pdf.

Fletcher, George P. 1998. Subject Versus Object. In *Basic Concepts of Criminal Law*, ed. G. P. Fletcher, 43–58. Oxford University Press. https://books.google.nl/books?hl=nl&lr=& id=eCa55NQ8UpIC&oi=fnd&pg=PR9&dq=G.+ Fletcher+Basic+Concepts+of+Criminal+Law&ots=O8MIvzr7Rn& sig=se4sMHVtAvUrxjCEaYPNDIduVeg.

Fuselli, Stefano. 2018. Logoi Enuloi. Aristotle's Contribution to the Contemporary Debate on Emotions and Decision-Making. In *Aristotle on Emotions in Law and Politics*, ed. Liesbeth Huppes-Cluysenaer and Nuno M.M.S. Coelho. Dordrecht: Springer.

Gardini, Marco. 2015. *Case Based Reasoning and Formulary Procedure: A Guard against Individual Emotions.* 1st ed. Amsterdam: Digital Paul Scholten Project. http://www.paulscholten.eu/research/article/case-based-reasoning-and-formulary-procedure/.

Gimpel, Jean. 1977. The Medieval Machine: The Industrial Revolution of the Middle Ages. Reprint ed. New York: Penguin Books.

Gotthelf, Allan, and James G. Lennox, eds. 1987. *Philosophical Issues in Aristotle's Biology.* Cambridge: Cambridge University Press.

Habermas, Jürgen. 1989. *The Structural Transformation of the Public Sphere: An Inquiry into a Category of Bourgeois Society.* Cambridge, MA: MIT Press.

Hart, H.L.A. 1961. *The Concept of Law.* Oxford: Clarendon Press.

Hobbes, Thomas. 1986. *Leviathan.* Edited by C. B. Macpherson. Harmondsworth: Penguin Books.

Huppes-Cluysenaer, E. A. 1995. Waarneming en theorie: naar een nieuw formalisme in empirische wetenschap en rechtswetenschap. s.n.

Israel, Jonathan I. 1995. *The Dutch Republic: Its Rise, Greatness and Fall, 1477-1806.* Oxford: Clarendon Press.

Kant, Immanuel. 1784. What Is Enlightenment. Translated by Mary C. Smith. Accessed October 31, 2016. http://www.columbia.edu/acis/ets/CCREAD/etscc/kant.html.

———. 1970. On the Common Saying: 'This May Be True in Theory, but It Does Not Apply in Practice'. In *Kant's Political Writings*, ed. Hans Siegert Reiss and trans. H. B. Nisbet. Cambridge: Cambridge University Press.

———. 1979. *The Conflict of the Faculties—Der Streit Der Fakultäten.* Translated by Mary J. Gregor. New York: Abaris Books.

———. 1992. *Kant's Kritik of Judgment.* Translated by J. H. Bernard. London: Macmillan. http://books.google.com/.

Kelsen, Hans. 1937. The Philosophy of Aristotle and the Hellenic-Macedonian Policy. *Ethics* 48 (1): 1–64.

———. 1941. The Law as a Specific Social Technique. *University of Chicago Law Review* 9: 75–98.

Klima, Gyula. 2016. The Medieval Problem of Universals. In *The Stanford Encyclopedia of Philosophy*, ed. Edward N. Zalta. Stanford, CA: Stanford University, Metaphysics Research Lab. https://plato.stanford.edu/archives/win2016/entries/universals-medieval/.

Maroney, Terry A. 2018. Judicial Emotion as Vice or Virtue: Perspectives Both Ancient and New. In *Aristotle on Emotions in Law and Politics*, ed. Liesbeth Huppes-Cluysenaer and Nuno M.M.S. Coelho. Dordrecht: Springer.

Mayr, Ernst. 1974. Teleological and Teleonomic, a New Analysis. In *Methodological and Historical Essays in the Natural and Social Sciences*, 91–117. Boston, MA: Reidel.

Mulgan, Richard. 2000. Was Aristotle an 'Aristotelian Social Democrat'? *Ethics* 111 (1): 79–101.

Nascimento, Daniel Simao. 2018. Rhetoric, Emotions and the Rule of Law in Aristotle. In *Aristotle on Emotions in Law and Politics*, ed. Liesbeth Huppes-Cluysenaer and Nuno M.M.S. Coelho. Dordrecht: Springer.

Natali, Carlo. 2001. *The Wisdom of Aristotle.* Albany: SUNY Press.

———. 2013. *Aristotle, His Life and School.* Edited by D. S. Hutchinson. Princeton, NJ: Princeton University Press.

Nussbaum, Martha C. 1988. Nature, Function, and Capability: Aristotle on Political Distribution. In *Oxford Studies in Ancient Philosophy*, 145–184. https://www.google.nl/webhp?sourceid=chrome-instant&ion=1&espv=2&ie=UTF-8#q=Martha+Nussbaum,+%E2%80%98%E2%80%98Nature,+Function,+and+Capability:+Aristotle+on+Political+Distribution,%E2%80%99%E2%80%99+Oxford+Studies+in+Ancient+Philosophy,+suppl.+vol.+(1988),+pp.+145%E2%80%93+84,&*

————. 2001. *Upheavals of Thought: The Intelligence of Emotions*. Cambridge and New York: Cambridge University Press.

————. 2013. *Political Emotions: Why Love Matters for Justice*. http://public.eblib.com/choice/publicfullrecord.aspx?p=3301331.

Oleksy, Mateusz W. 2015. *Realism and Individualism: Charles S. Peirce and the Threat of Modern Nominalism*. Philadelphia: John Benjamins Publishing.

Pellegrin, Pierre. 1986. *Aristotle's Classification of Animals: Biology and the Conceptual Unity of the Aristotelian Corpus*. Berkeley: University of California Press.

————. 1987. Logical Difference and Biological Difference. In *Philosophical Issues in Aristotle's Biology*, ed. Allan Gotthelf. Cambridge: Cambridge University Press.

Pinho, Fabiana. 2018. On Logos, Pathos and Ethos in Judicial Argumentation. In *Aristotle on Emotions in Law and Politics*, ed. Liesbeth Huppes-Cluysenaer and Nuno M.M.S. Coelho. Dordrecht: Springer.

Plato. 1970. *The Laws*. Translated by Trevor J. Saunders. Harmondsworth: Penguin Books.

Pound, Roscoe. 1945. Sociology of Law, Chapter XI. In *Twentieth Century Sociology*, ed. Georges Gurvitch and Wilbert Ellis Moore. New York: Philosophical Library.

Romero, Aldemaro. 2012. When Whales Became Mammals: The Scientific Journey of Cetaceans from Fish to Mammals in the History of Science. https://doi.org/10.5772/50811.

Rosenblueth, Arturo, Norbert Wiener, and Julian Bigelow. 1943. Behavior, Purpose and Teleology. *Philosophy of Science* 10 (1): 18–24. https://doi.org/10.1086/286788.

Rousseau, Jean-Jacques. 1772. Considerations on the Government of Poland and on Its Proposed Reformation. https://www.files.ethz.ch/isn/125482/5016_Rousseau_Considerations_on_the_Government_of_Poland.pdf.

————. 1988. On Social Contract. In *Rousseau's Political Writings: New Translations, Interpretive Notes, Backgrounds, Commentaries*, ed. Alan Ritter and Julia Conaway Bondanella. New York: W.W. Norton.

Samaras, Thanassis. 2007. Aristotle's Politics: The City of Book Seven and the Question of Ideology. *Classical Quarterly (New Series)* 57 (1): 77–89.

Scholten, Paul. 2014. *General Method of Private Law. Chapter 1 of Volume I (General Part) of Mr. C. Asser's Manual for the Practice of Dutch Civil Law*. Preprint, 1st ed. Translated by Liesbeth Huppes-Cluysenaer, Termorshuizen, and Cassandra Steer. Amsterdam: Digital Paul Scholten Project. http://www.paulscholten.eu/research/article/english.

Shklar, Judith N. 1978. Jean-Jacques Rousseau and Equality. *Daedalus* 107 (3): 13–25.

Silvestre, Ana Carolina de Faria. 2018. Rethinking Legal Education from Aristotle's Theory of Emotions and the Contemporary Challenges of the Practical Realization of Law. In *Aristotle on Emotions in Law and Politics*, ed. Liesbeth Huppes-Cluysenaer and Nuno M. M. S. Coelho. Dordrecht: Springer.

Solum, Lawrence. 2013. Virtue Jurisprudence: Towards an Aretaic Theory of Law. In *Aristotle and the Philosophy of Law Theory, Practice and Justice*, ed. Liesbeth Huppes-Cluysenaer and Nuno M.M.S. Coelho, 1–32. Dordrecht and New York: Springer. http://public.eblib.com/choice/publicfullrecord.aspx?p=1083709.

Steel, Daniel. 2010. What If the Principle of Induction Is Normative? Formal Learning Theory and Hume's Problem. *International Studies in the Philosophy of Science* 24 (2): 171–185.

Timasheff, Nicholas S. 1939. *An Introduction to the Sociology of Law*. Cambridge, MA: Harvard University Committee on Research in the Social Sciences.

van Nifterik, G. 2016. Ulrik Huber on Fundamental Laws: A European Perspective. *Comparative Legal History* 4 (1): 2–18. https://doi.org/10.1080/2049677X.2016.1176351.

van Ruler, J.A. 1991. New Philosophy to Old Standards: Voetius' Vindication of Divine Concurrence and Secondary Causality. *Nederlands Archief Voor Kerkgeschiedenis/Dutch Review of Church History* 71 (1): 58–91.

————. 1995. *The Crisis of Causality: Voetius and Descartes on God, Nature, and Change*. Leiden and New York: E.J. Brill.

Viano, Cristina. 2018. Ethical Theory and Judicial Practice: Passions and Crimes of Passion in Plato, Aristotle and Lysias. In *Aristotle on Emotions in Law and Politics*, ed. Liesbeth Huppes-Cluysenaer and Nuno M.M.S. Coelho. Dordrecht: Springer.

von Savigny, Friedrich Carl. 1973. Vom Beruf unsrer Zeit für Gesetzgebung und Rechtswissenschaft. In *Thibaut und Savigny: ihre programmatischen Schriften*, ed. H. Hattenhauer. Munich: Vahlen.

Part III
Moral Agency

Chapter 9
Aristotle on Emotions in Ethics and in Criminal Justice

José de Sousa e Brito

Abstract Aristotle completes his phenomenological description in the *Rhetoric* with a complex scientific theory in *De anima*, where he considers the physiological aspect of emotions. This complex theory as well as the criminal law of Athens constitute the basis of Aristotle's theory about the influence of emotions on moral responsibility, and their regulation by criminal law. Aristotle follows Plato when in principle he accepts moral responsibility for actions committed under the influence of an emotion. In accordance with Athenian criminal law Aristotle elects to punish such actions as involuntary and therefore does not apply his own analysis of intentional action (*prohairesis*), which would consider the actions as resulting from deliberation and therefore intentional. This despite the deliberation being perturbed by the emotion, in particular by the physiological part of the emotion.

9.1 Introduction

Emotions influence belief, motivate action, reveal and mould character, and if uncontrolled, they may be reasons for blame and for more or less punishment for the actions they motivate. Therefore they are treated in the rhetorical, psychological and ethical works of Aristotle. If we want to understand what Aristotle says about them in ethics and in criminal justice we have to depart from the psychological facts they consist in, which are the basis of the ethical and the legal reasons and which are mainly studied in the *Rhetoric* and in the *De anima*.[1] Criminal justice is not based on reason (and facts) alone, as ethics is, but also on convention.[2] The conventional part of criminal justice comes from Athenian law and explains some strange inconsistencies we find in Aristotle.

---

[1] Edition used: for Rhetoric and De Anima (On the Soul): *The Complete Works of Aristotle: the Revised Oxford Translation*, edited by Jonathan Barnes.

[2] See Nicomachean ethics (*EN*, 1134b 18–19 and *MM*, 1194b 30–1195a 1–5) Edition used: *The Complete Works of Aristotle: The Revised Oxford Translation*, edited by Jonathan Barnes.

J.d.S.e. Brito (✉)
Constitutional Court, Lisbon, Portugal
e-mail: josesousabrito@yahoo.com

© Springer International Publishing AG 2018
L. Huppes-Cluysenaer, N.M.M.S. Coelho (eds.), *Aristotle on Emotions in Law and Politics*, Law and Philosophy Library 121, DOI 10.1007/978-3-319-66703-4_9

9.2   The Dialectical Definition of Emotion in the *Rhetoric*

In the second Book of the *Rhetoric* Aristotle deals extensively with emotions. The Greek word is *pathos* traditionally translated by "passion." So, the medieval philosophers, Descartes and Hume, and many others, did write their treatises on "passions", clearly under the influence of Aristotle. I shall use here "emotion" and "passion" indifferently. Aristotle begins by explaining why the study of emotions is important to rhetoric. Rhetoric is the art of persuading someone of some judgement. However, forming a certain judgement can be influenced by emotions as well as by arguments.

> When people are feeling friendly and placable – says Aristotle – they think one sort of thing; when they are feeling angry or hostile, they think either something completely different or the same thing with a different intensity: when they feel friendly to the man who comes before them for judgement, they regard him as having done little wrong, if any; when they feel hostile, they take the opposite view. (*Rhet.*, 1377b30–1378a2, trans. W. Rhys Roberts)

The orator should therefore study the emotions in order to obtain from his audience, in deliberative assemblies or lawsuits, the judgements he seeks about himself or about someone else (1377b28). That is enough for Aristotle to give a definition of emotion in general, which does not aim at being a scientific one and so getting at the essence of an emotion, but only to be useful for the orator. Within such a scope it is a dialectic definition not an epistemic one. Aristotle says that

> emotions are those feelings that so change men as to affect their judgements, and that are also attended by pain or pleasure. (*Reth.*, 1378a19–20, trans. W. Rhys Roberts)

In the following 13 emotions are studied in detail: anger (*orge*), calm (*praotes*), friendship, friendly feeling (*philia, to philein*), hate (*misos*), fear (*phobos*), confidence (*tharsos*), shame (*aischune*), kindness (*charis*), pity (*eleos*), indignation (*nemesan*), envy (*phthonos*), emulation (*zelos*), and contempt (*kataphronesis*). It may seem strange that Aristotle does not treat that form of desire which is the appetite (*epithumia*), especially the sexual appetite (*concupiscentia*, in the Latin translation), which he refers to as emotion in the *Nicomachean Ethics* (1105b21), in the *Eudemian Ethics*[3] (1220b13) and in *De anima* (403a7). Since this emotion is of lesser utility for the orator confronting his audience, this could perhaps explain the omission.[4] The list of emotions in the *Nicomachean Ethics* refers to joy (*charan*) as

---

[3]Edition used: *The Eudemian Ethics*. Translated by Anthony Kenny.

[4]Cooper (1999), p. 420, note 26 suggests a conjectural explanation, that the fact in *Reth.*, 1370a18–1370b29 Aristotle explains what *epithymia* is by way of telling us what pleasure is and what gives pleasure to different people, may explain why he omits to discuss *epithymia* as a *pathos* in Book II of the *Rhetoric*. But in the same context he treats also of other emotions, like anger, and this did not impeach their systematic study in Book II.

a real contrary of envy in the same situation, and not as *Schadensfreude* in the envious person,[5] and also to longing (*pothos*). However, no list or study of emotions in Aristotle pretends to be complete.

In his analysis of each particular emotion Aristotle follows almost uniformly a scheme he explains with respect to anger as the first emotion he studies. He begins with a dialectic definition he considers acceptable in view of the usage of the word:

> anger may be defined as a desire accompanied by pain, for a conspicuous revenge for a conspicuous slight at the hands of men who have no call to slight oneself or one's friends. (*Rhet.*, 1378a30–33, trans. W. Rhys Roberts)

This definition is explained afterwards to make clear, at first, what the state of mind of angry people is, secondly, who the people are with whom they usually get angry, and thirdly on what grounds they do get angry with them (*Rhet.*, 1378a22–23).

9.3 The Scientific Definition of Emotion in *De Anima*

In *De Anima* Aristotle makes clear that the definitions of emotions, and the concepts and relations that constitute their study in the *Rhetoric*, are not suitable to psychology, which is conceived by Aristotle as a part of natural science, i.e., of physics, because they do not give us the essence of the emotions, as it is to be expected from science. They are mere dialectic definitions, not only in the sense that they presuppose to be adequate since they correspond to the use of language of both the orator and his audience, but also in the sense that they remain in the intellectual sphere. At such a level, even if they would describe correctly the language games that apply to each emotion, they leave aside an essential element, which is its existence in the body. In an exclusive regard to this latter element, anger could also be defined as the boiling of the blood or warm substance surrounding the heart (*De an.*, 403a30–403b1). However, such a material definition of anger would also be insufficient, not only because the same physiological reaction may exist without feeling anger (403a21–22), but also because it leaves aside the way anger is thought by who feels it. A scientific description of anger has to include both elements, so that

> anger should be defined as such and such a movement of such and such a body (or part or faculty of a body) by this and that cause and for this or that end. (*DA* 403a25–27, trans. J. A. Smith)

---

[5] See Aristotle (1970), 133.

The same would apply to every emotion: they are thoughts that exist in matter (*en hule*)[6] whenever they exist, being inseparable from body, necessarily corporal and necessarily thought.[7]

The discussion about the ways to define emotion is part of an argument that seeks to demonstrate that the soul cannot be separated from the body and that involves the entire psychology of Aristotle. It can, however, be separated from such an argument and the whole dimension of any emotion that it reveals is most relevant to ethics and to criminal justice.

9.4   Kinds of Desire and Parts of the Soul

Going now from psychology to ethics, the meeting point of the emotions or passions with the moral action is desire. Aristotle distinguishes three kinds of desire (*orexis*): appetite (*epithumia*), temper (*thumos*) and volition (*boulesis*).[8] Appetite and temper are caused by the emotions. Anger typically causes temper to seek vengeance. Volition is intellectual desire as it is proposed by the rational part of the soul, the intellect (*nous*). However, every desire proposes the end of an action, which may be incompatible with others or not realizable. It is by means of deliberation that the ends are weighed in the face of the means at disposal, followed by the choice or decision of a certain action or omission. The emotions contribute in this way to moral action, which is action that can be praised or censured in consequence of its being rational or not. We shall see that things are not so linear, since there are actions without deliberation.

This theory of the two parts of the soul, the one rational, the other irrational, where appetite and temper are located and which should be governed by the first, was received from Plato, who in the fourth book of the *Republic*[9] lets Socrates defend it against two erroneous theories. The first was earlier espoused by Socrates in the *Meno* (77a3–78b2) and in the *Protagoras* (355b3–359a1), and it says that reason is the only source of action. Therefore the actions of the incontinent man, who is driven by appetite instead of reason, and of the angry one, who is driven by temper instead of reason, could only be explained by mistake or ignorance of what is good as the reason for action. The other is explored in Greek tragedy, especially

---

[6]See Aristote (1966). With Jannone, I prefer this reading of *De an.*, 403a25 to *enuloi*, which has no attestation whatsoever in Aristotle.

[7]For a fuller treatment of this, see in this volume Fuselli (2018), section 6.

[8]*EE*, 1123a26–27 and 1225b24–26; De an. 414b2, 432b5–6 and 432a22–26. I am following the translation of these words by Kenny in his edition of *The Eudemian Ethics*. I am following also his translation of the Books which are common to *Nicomachean Ethics* and *Eudemian Ethics* (*EN* V, VI and VII = *EE* IV, V and VI), which are quoted by its Bekker edition (*EN* 1129a3–1154b34).

[9]See *Resp.* 439 d4–e3 on the conflict between appetite and reason. Plato adds a third part of the soul, temper (*thymos*), which sometimes reinforces the rational part in its conflict with the appetitive one, sometimes not.

in Euripides. Passion is presented there as a kind of irresistible madness. In Hippolytus[10] Phaedra tries to choose prudence against the sexual appetite that drives her to Hippolytus. But Aphrodite is stronger:

> Aphrodite, if she streams upon us in great force, cannot be endured. (443, trans. David Kovaks)

Medea[11] is taken by anger when she comes to know that Jason, who brought her from her motherland by swearing his love to her and is the father of her children, married the daughter of the king of Corinth. She decides to kill the children, and says:

> I know well what pain I am about to undergo, but my temper[12] overbears my calculation. (1078–1079, trans. David Kovacs)

Against the earlier Plato and against Euripides, Aristotle refers, as Socrates did in the *Republic* (439a c1–d2), to the cases of weakness of the will (*akrasia*) of the incontinent man. And so he says in the *Nicomachean Ethics*:

> "we praise the rational principle of the continent man and of the incontinent, and the part of their soul that has such a principle, since it urges them aright and towards the best objects; but there is found in them also another natural element beside reason, which fights against and resists it" and so "the impulses of the incontinent people move in contrary directions." (*EN* 1102b14–21, trans. W. D. Ross and J. O. Urmson)

Therefore we are dealing with different desires, namely volition and appetite, moving in contrary directions to do and not to do something, and not with error or ignorance. Besides, Aristotle says in the *Eudemian Ethics* that the incontinent man

> suffers force contrary to reason, but he seems to feel less pain, because appetite is for what is pleasant and he follows gladly. So the incontinent man's condition is closer to voluntariness than to force, because he suffers no pain. (*EE* 1224a36–38, trans. Anthony Kenny)

Aristotle has a lot more to say about weakness of the will and we shall return to it later.

9.5 Athenian Law on Homicide and Plato's Proposal

If we want to understand Aristotle's texts about voluntary action we have to have in mind Athens' law on involuntary homicide, which is attributed to Draco. The law uses indifferently the words *me hek pronoias*, without malice aforethought (i.e. without previous intent), and *akon* (involuntary). In contrast, the words *hekousios phonos*, voluntary homicide are usual in ordinary language and in orators

---

[10]Euripides (1996).

[11]Euripides (1994).

[12]For *thymos*, instead of "wrath."

lawyers like Antiphon.[13] Whereas voluntary homicide was heard by Areopagus and punished with death, involuntary homicide was heard by another court, the Palladium, and was punished by exile, unless it was pardoned unanimously by the family of the victim. When legal justification is pleaded, as when a man takes an adulterer in the act, or kills another by mistake in battle or in an athletic contest, the prisoner is tried in the court of Delphinium.[14] There was no written law nor settled jurisprudence about voluntary homicide and so the concepts were defined through discussion in court. Homicide committed under the influence of extreme emotional disturbance was discussed by the orators, and will receive a systematic treatment by Plato and by Aristotle, who builds here, as almost always, upon Plato.

Plato held in *Laws*,[15] regarding his utopian republic of Magnesia, that in cases of homicide done in anger, those committed after deliberation should be punished as voluntary, but those committed suddenly without deliberation, although voluntary, should be punished as involuntary (*Laws*, 866d6–867c1). Since Plato is proposing legislation for a utopian city, he is not bound to choose, according to Draco's law, between voluntary and involuntary homicide, having to call involuntary a voluntary homicide that deserves to be punished like an involuntary one, and is able to propose a new kind of homicide:

> Thus murders done in passion are difficult to define,—whether one should treat them in law as voluntary or involuntary. The best and truest way is to class them both as resemblances, and to distinguish them by the mark of deliberate intent or lack of intent, and to impose more severe penalties on those who slay with intent and in anger, and milder penalties on those who do so without intent and on a sudden. (867b1–b7, trans. Bury)[16]

9.6 Aristotle on Voluntary and Involuntary Homicide and on Prohairesis

Aristotle's point of departure are the concepts and distinctions of Athenian law, even if he does not find them precise enough and proposes new ones. He certainly refers to Draco's law when in the *Eudemian Ethics* he praises the legislators who

---

[13] See Gernet (2001), pp. 352–361. Maschke (1968), pp. 28–63 and MacDowell (1963). The text of Draco's law (IG I 104. 10–20) has been edited by Stroud (1968), p. 5 and was translated with commentary in Gagarin (1981), pp. xvi–xvii and 30–64, Carawan (1998), pp. 33–45 and 68–98 and Phillips (2013), pp. 44–84, with reference to later developments. On Antiphon (1923, 1997) and Carawan (1998), pp. 171–389.

[14] Aristotle, *Ath. Pol.* 57, 3; Editions used: Aristotle (2002) and Aristoteles (1990). See also Rhodes (1993).

[15] Editions used: Plato (1926) and Platon (1994–2011).

[16] On homicide out of anger in Laws; see also the translation of Schöpsdau in Platon (1994–2011), III, pp. 314–323 and in this volume Viano (2018).

classify items as being voluntary (*hekousia*), or involuntary or premeditated (*hek pronoias*) and adds

> their classifications may not be accurate in detail, but they have got hold of the truth to a
> certain extent. (*EE* 1226b 36–1227a2, trans. Anthony Kenny)

He not only accepts the conceptual classification, but he also agrees with the different legal treatment. In a parallel place of the Magna Moralia[17] he says that

> a few legislators, even, appear to distinguish the voluntary act from the act done by choice
> (*ek prohaireseōs*) as being something different, in making the penalties that they appoint
> for voluntary acts less than those that are done by choice. (*MM* 1189b 4–7, St. G. Stock)

The *Magna Moralia* substitutes the legal concept of premeditation by the Aristotelian concept of *prohairesis*, which I translate by "choice". It is indeed this concept that explains, according to Aristotle, the different legal treatment. The explanation is given in the book on justice, of which there is only one version that is common to the *Eudemian Ethics* and the *Nicomachean Ethics* and to which the quoted passage of the *Eudemian Ethics* refers for a fuller study of these matters (*EE* 1227a 2–3).

Now in the book on justice we find that

> a man acts unjustly or justly if he does the appropriate acts voluntarily. When his action is
> not voluntary, it is neither unjust nor just except coincidentally, in the sense of doing things
> that simply happen to be just or unjust. An unjust action, and a just one, is marked off by
> being voluntary or not; for if it is voluntary it attracts blame and is at the same time an
> unjust action, but if there is no element of voluntariness then an outcome may be unjust
> without being an unjust action. (*EN* 1135a16–23, trans. Anthony Kenny)

By voluntary Aristotle means

> "something within his power that a man does knowingly" (1135a24). We shall return to the
> Aristotelian definition of voluntary. But now it matters to mark the difference between
> voluntary and by choice: "of our voluntary acts we do some with, and some without, choice;
> there is choice when we have deliberated beforehand, and otherwise there is no choice."
> (*EN* 1135b8–12; also *EE* 1226b32–36, trans. Anthony Kenny)

This distinction is then applied to actions due to anger or other passions:

> when a man acts with awareness, but without deliberation, his act is an injustice. The
> actions I mean are those that are due to anger or other passions that are necessary or natural
> to human beings. When people do such harmful and wrongful acts, they do act unjustly and
> their deeds are unjust, yet this does not mean that they are themselves unjust or wicked,
> since the injury does not originate in depravity. But when a man inflicts an injury out of
> choice, then he is an unjust and depraved man. Hence acts done out of rage are rightly
> judged as unpremeditated; the originator of the mischief is not the man enraged but the
> person who provoked the rage. (*EN* 1135b19–27, trans. Anthony Kenny)

Here Aristotle is referring to the distinction in the law of Athens between voluntary homicide with and without premeditation, but he extends it to unjust

---

[17]Edition used: *The Complete Works of Aristotle: The Revised Oxford Translation*, edited by Jonathan Barnes.

acts in general, and applies it to acts committed out of anger, at first, and to every act due to passions afterwards: in acts due to passions the act is voluntary but is not done by choice, because there is then no deliberation and consequently no choice nor premeditation. Secondly he applies to the same set of acts the distinction between an unjust act and an unjust man: in acts due to passions the act is unjust but not the man who does it, since he is not acting out of depravity but out of passion. Thirdly, he tells us that the action that was caused by temper is not originated by the enraged man but by the person who provoked the rage. Anyone of these theses meets serious difficulties.

Let's consider first the last thesis, which denies that the enraged person does originate (*archei*) the mischief. This seems to contradict that the action is voluntary, since Aristotle defines voluntary action as that of which man is the source (*arche*) and controller (*EE* 1223a5). The contradiction disappears only if we forget the technical meaning of the words and make them signify simply that the action caused by temper was first caused by the man who provoked rage, who so initiated a set of voluntary actions: the provocation and the provoked enraged action.

The distinction between unjust action and unjust agent explains the lesser blame in criminal law of the instant action caused by anger (*EN* 1111b 9–10) in comparison with the premeditated action. Aristotle follows the Platonic doctrine (*Gorgias* 478d 4–7) of punishment as a cure for wickedness, and therefore depending upon the wickedness of the agent who has to be cured, i.e. recuperated for society through punishment.[18] The malice aforethought that characterizes the premeditated action allows for a judgement upon the character (*ethos*), revealing the injury in the agent more than the injury in his action. If this is the Aristotle's doctrine, how do we understand what he says in the same book on justice about corrective justice:

> it makes no difference whether a good man has cheated a bad man, or a bad man a good one, nor whether adultery has been committed by a good or a bad man: the law looks only to the degree of injury[19], and treats the parties as equal, inquiring only who was the wrong doer and who was wronged, who caused the harm and who suffered it. (*EN*, 1132a 2–6, trans. Anthony Kenny)

This passage seems to adopt a mere objective conception of crime, which would be incompatible with the Platonic doctrine referred to above. Ross[20] thinks that corrective or rectificatory justice is that of the civil, not that of the criminal court, which seems at odds with the listing of crimes falling under such justice in *EN* 1131a6–9. And Dirlmeier[21] concludes that Aristotle, by considering here the moral

---

[18] On Plato's and Aristotle's theories of punishment see Brito (2010), pp. 315–316 (Plato) e 314, note 25 (Aristotle).

[19] In Aristoteles (1956), *Nikomachische Ethik* one reads "according to injury and to damage" where the text only has "according to damage" (*pros tou blabous*). The context, however, shows that the law treats indeed 'according to injury and to damage', an idiomatic expression used by Plato (1926), 862b6 (*pros tē adikian kai blabēn*), as Burnet noted in The Ethics of Aristotle, edited by him.

[20] In his translation of the Nicomachean Ethics in Aristotle, *The Works of Aristotle*, note at 1132a2.

[21] Op. cit., p. 409.

status of the agent as irrelevant, departs radically from Plato, even though this might seem shocking. It seems to me that Aristotle departs indeed from Plato, but not so much. If the judge has to treat people equally when determining the degree of punishment, he cannot take into account the whole previous life of the criminal man. This would be conspicuous from the point of view of Plato, who indeed aims at a complete therapy of the criminal man, but only at a special prevention concerning the character revealed by the crime: that which makes the act unjust (its culpability in today's terminology): In Aristotle's words:

> good conduct and its opposite cannot exist without both thought and character. (*EN* 1139a34–35, trans. Anthony Kenny)

However Ross rightly sees that the discussed passage is located in a treatment of rectificatory justice, which is about the interactions between parties, inquiring who caused the harm and who suffered it. Therefore Aristotle thinks, here, about the amount of damage and its reparation, not about culpability and its punishment.

Greater difficulties meet Aristotle's justification for not punishing as if done by choice in the case of temper and punishing instead as involuntary action. Aristotle works with his concept of choice (*prohairesis*) and he says that there is no choice in an act committed under the influence of extreme emotional disturbance. However, in order to justify a different punishment it would be enough to demonstrate that character is less involved in temper than in choice or in premeditation, because of instant action and of the physiological element in passion. In the criminal law of many contemporary states homicide, which otherwise would be murder, is punished as manslaughter, if committed under the influence of extreme emotional disturbance, with a punishment that may be closer to that of involuntary or negligent homicide. Similarly, Plato had already proposed in his utopic penal code of Laws a new kind of homicide in case of temper.[22] Remaining within the limits of Athenian law, Aristotle could only define anew the limits of involuntary and voluntary homicide, but he did not have to give an inaccurate description of the facts. Homicide out of violent emotion or temper or under extreme emotional disturbance is intentional or out of choice, but the intention is weaker or less prolonged than in the case of premeditation, and that is a good reason for less punishment. In contrast, Aristotle leans towards approximating the concepts of choice and premeditation, which he sometimes uses as synonyms (*EE* 1226b32–36), following the literal suggestion of the word *prohairesis:*

> even the name seems to suggest that it is what is chosen before other things. (*EN* 1112a16–17, trans. W. D. Ross and J. O. Urmson)

The temporal priority of choice over action is required by the phenomenology of action, even if it is not expressed by most translations: "*electio*" (William of Moerbeke's Latin translation of Aristotle's texts as used by Aquinas)[23] "choice"

---

[22]See above note 5.

[23]Aquinas (1964), *passim.*

(Ross), "Entscheidung" (Dirlmeier), "decision" (Gauthier), "resolution" (Kenny),[24] with exception of the German "Vorsatz". However, against Aristotle, it should be said that, in spite of the fact that the strongest choice is premeditated or afore-thought, there is previous intent in every case of choice, including instant choice under extreme emotional disturbance. Aristotle recognizes that

> when reason or appearance announces an insult or a slight, temper rears up at once, as if reasoning that one must take arms against anything of the sort,(...) accordingly, temper does in a manner follow reason. (*EN* 1149a33–b1, trans. Anthony Kenny)

In a similar way, in the case of incontinence

> there is present a universal premise forbidding tasting, and another saying "every sweet thing is pleasant and this is sweet" (this premise being operative), and when desire is present, then it says, "avoid this" but desire drives on; because each part of the soul is capable of sending us in motion. So it turns out that incontinent behaviour is in a manner the effect of reason and belief, and one that is not in itself contrary to right reasoning but only coincidentally: what opposes right reasoning is not the belief but the desire. (*EN* 1147a31–b3, trans. Anthony Kenny)

We have therefore in every case the scheme of syllogism, which characterizes deliberation, although in some cases with imperfect syllogisms, since they do not conclude with an action. That derives from Aristotle's own analysis of choice as

> deliberate desire of things in our own power. (*EN* 1113a10–11, trans. W. D. Ross and J. O. Urmson)

Prohairesis is the most accomplished form of control over actions and the results of them. But Aristotle recognizes that such a control exists also in every voluntary action, those done by choice being only some of a kind.

9.7   Moral Action, Omission and Negligence

The *Eudemian Ethics* arrives at the concept of voluntary action through a classification of sets of cases, by means of concepts obtained by successive differences, i.e., by division (*dihairesis*). The first division is based on Aristotle's criterion of moral action, according to which there is a moral action whenever it is voluntary. An act is voluntary if it occurs or not because it is in our power, if it depends on us (*eph'emin*), if we are the source or first cause (*arche*) or the controller (*kurios*) of its existence. Only when we have in this sense the control of a state, that it comes into existence or not, are we responsible (*aitios*) for it. The text says:

> of the actions of which man is the source and controller – of those at least where he is in control of whether they occur or not- it is clear they admit of occurring or not, and that it is in his power whether their occur or not. But for what is in his power to do or not to do, he

---

himself is responsible, and if he is responsible for something, then it is in his power. (*EE* 1223a4–9, trans. Anthony Kenny)

Now, says Aristotle, it is clear that blame and praise, vice and virtue have to do with the kind of actions of which man is the source and controller, and so with moral action. Aristotle does not speak of moral action, but simply of action. I do, to make the point that only in relation to such acts it is meaningful to use moral qualifiers such as blame, etc. Those actions that are not in the human power such as to prophesize, to act under hypnosis or irresistible force, belong to another category. Such actions cannot be morally qualified, they are non-moral actions. Using a different terminology, they are not actions at all.

Such a concept of voluntary action applies both to actions and omissions. It implies indeed the power to act or to omit. According to Aristotle

> where it is in our power to act it is also in our power not to act, and *vice-versa*; so that, if to act, where this is noble, is in our power, not to act, which will be base, will also be in our power, and if not to act, where this is noble, is in our power, to act, which will be base, will also be in our power. (*EN* 1113b7–11, trans. W. D. Ross and J. O. Urmson)

In a famous example,[25]

> we ascribe the wreck of a ship to the absence of the pilot whose presence was the cause of its safety.[26] (*Phys* 195a11–14, trans. R. P. Hardie/R. K. Gaye)

Aristoteles could certainly add: and if he does it deliberately, he acts by choice. The same concept applies also to cases of self–induced intoxication or of mistake, if there is negligence. So

> we punish a man for his very ignorance, if he is thought responsible for the ignorance, as when penalties are doubled in the case of drunkenness; for the moving principle is in the man himself, since he had the power of not getting drunk and his getting drunk was the cause of his ignorance. And we punish those who are ignorant of anything in the laws that they ought to know and that is not difficult, and so too in the case of anything else that they are thought to be ignorant of through carelessness; we assume that it is in their power not to be ignorant, since they have the power to take care. (*EN* 1113b30–1114a3, trans. W. D. Ross and J. O. Urmson)

Aristotle introduces here an important element that completes his negative characterization of the voluntary action as the one that is done without mistake or duress:

---

[25]Loening (1967), p. 253 questions if this saying comes authentically from Aristotle, considers *EN* 1113b7–11 a confusion that can only be explained by a lack of precise observation' and accounts for *EE* 1226b30 as originating in Eudemos and not in Aristotle. All this because Loening departs from a subjective theory of negation (held by Sigwart 1924, p. 155 and others, against Aristotle) according to which "the omissions do not exist in the reality but only in our representation or in our judgement." (p. 246).

[26]The phrase is identical to *Met.* 1013b12–15, where it is translated by Ross as: "we impute the shipwreck to the absence of the steersman, whose presence was the cause of safety." Editions used for Physics and Metaphysics: *The Complete Works of Aristotle: the Revised Oxford Translation*, edited by Jonathan Barnes.

since what is done under compulsion or by reason of ignorance is involuntary, the voluntary would seem to be that of which the moving principle is in the agent himself, he being aware of the particular circumstances of the action.[27] (*EN* 1111a22–24, trans. W. D. Ross and J. O. Urmson)

Now the action in a state of drunkenness has been in the power of the agent in a moment anterior to its beginning, and the action done by mistake is still voluntary if it was in the power of the agent to avoid the mistake through due care. The voluntary divides into action and omission, by choice and by negligence.

9.8 The Cases of Weakness of the Will (*Akrasia*)

In the actions by choice, where the deliberation can be analyzed through the scheme of the practical syllogism, the emotions can interfere by causing avoidable error in the formulation or in the choice of the premises, as happens with the intemperate, who thinks that is better to act in accordance with appetite than in accordance with duty, by doing what is the best thing to do. His action is certainly done by choice. The intemperate is defined as

a person who pursues excessive pleasures and does so out of choice, for their own sake and not at all for any further consequence. (*EN*, 1150a19–21, trans. Anthony Kenny)

The emotions can instead impede the choice that results from a correct deliberation[28] in the cases of *akrasia*, i.e. incontinence or weakness of the will, where an end is chosen which is known to be bad. So it is that

some men after deliberating fail, because of passion, to keep to the conclusions of their deliberation. (*EN*, 1150b19–20, trans. Anthony Kenny)

There is another kind of incontinence when

others because of their failure to deliberate are driven by their passion. (*EN*, 1150b20–21, trans. Anthony Kenny)

We have already referred to the peculiarities of the deliberation in these cases, where the conclusions arrived at are in a way not conclusive because they are not followed by the actions according to the deliberation. Aristotle says that in these cases the agent has in a sense and has not at the same time knowledge of the conclusion, remaining half way, and compares with the actions of a man asleep, mad or drunk. He says:

---

[27]The same qualification should be made to the passage of *EE*, 1226b30–32: "if someone does or refrains from doing something that is in his power to do or not to do, of his own accord and not in error, he acts or refrains voluntarily (*hekōn*)" trans. Anthony Kenny.

[28]Aristotle dedicates to *akrasia* the entire book VII of the *Nicomachean Ethics* (= book VI of the *Eudemian Ethics*). For a comprehensive treatment see Kenny (1979), pp. 155–166.

now this is just the condition of people under the influence of passions: manifestly, attacks of rage; desires for sex, and other similar passions alter our bodily condition and even drive some people crazy. It is clear that incontinent people must be said to be in a condition similar to such cases [of a man asleep, or crazy, or drunk]. (*EN*, 1147a14–19, trans. Anthony Kenny)

The question is then whether the force of the emotion can still be opposed and controlled or is absolute and irresistible. In the first case, which should be more frequent, the action is "voluntary" (although "involuntary" in a legal sense that we have found in Aristotle), and also by choice or with malice aforethought (however eventually with diminished culpability) for contemporary law. In the second case, there is no moral action. Here may be discussed the cases of Phaedra and of Medea. Aristotle seems to hesitate when he refers to common opinion on the example of the tragedians, but as we have seen he finally follows Plato and blames the action.

I would, however, suppose that Aristotle would in doubtful cases be inclined to hear the opinion of the physiologist, since

the explanation of how the error is dissolved and the incontinent man regains possession of his knowledge is the same as in the case of the man drunk or asleep. It is nothing peculiar to this condition and we must listen to what the physiologists say about it. (*EN*, 1147b5–8, trans. Anthony Kenny)

If the physiologists know better how the incontinent dissolves the error originated by his passion, then they should also know what the state of the incontinent is like, when he is dominated by passion.

References

Anscombe, G.E.M. 1981. *From Parmenides to Wittgenstein*. Minneapolis: University of Minnesota Press.

Antiphon. 1923. *Antiphon, Discours*. Edited and Translated by Louis Gernet. Paris: Les Belles Lettres.

———. 1997. *The Speeches*. Edited by Michael Gagarin. Cambridge: Cambridge University Press.

Aquinas, Thomas. 1964. *In decem libros Ethicorum Aristotelis ad Nicomachum expositio*. Edited by Raimondo M. Spiazzi. 3rd ed. Turin: Marietti.

Aristote. 1966. *De l'âme*. Edited by A. Jannone. Translated by E. Barbotin. Paris: Les Belles Lettres.

———. 1970. *L'Éthique à Nicomaque*. Translated by René Antoine Gauthier and Jean Yves Jolif. 2nd ed. Louvain: Publications Universitaires; Paris: Béatrice-Nauwelaerts.

Aristoteles. 1956. *Nikomachische Ethik*. Translated by Franz Dirlmeier. Berlin: Akademie-Verlag.

———. 1990. *Staat der Athener*. Translated by Mortimer Chambers. Berlin: Akademie Verlag.

Aristotle. 1900. *The Ethics of Aristotle*. Edited by John Burnet. London: Methuen.

———. 1908–1952. *The Works of Aristotle*. Translated under the editorship of W. D. Ross and J. A. Smith. Oxford: Clarendon Press.

———. 1984a. "Magna Moralia." In *The Complete Works of Aristotle: the Revised Oxford Translation*. Edited by J. Barnes. Translated by St. G. Stock. Princeton, NJ: Princeton University Press.

———. 1984b. "Metaphysics." In *The Complete Works of Aristotle: The Revised Oxford Translation*. Edited by J. Barnes. Translated by W. D. Ross. Princeton, NJ: Princeton University Press.

————. 1984c. "Nicomachean Ethics." In *The Complete Works of Aristotle: The Revised Oxford Translation.* Edited by J. Barnes. Translated by W. D. Ross and J. O. Urmson. Princeton, NJ: Princeton University Press.

————. 1984d. "On The Soul." In *The Complete Works of Aristotle: The Revised Oxford Translation.* Edited by J. Barnes. Translated by J. A. Smith. Princeton, NJ: Princeton University Press.

————. 1984e. "Physics." In *The Complete Works of Aristotle: The Revised Oxford Translation.* Edited by J. Barnes. Translated by R. P. Hardie and R. K. Gaye. Princeton, NJ: Princeton University Press.

————. 1984f. "Rhetoric." In *The Complete Works of Aristotle: The Revised Oxford Translation.* Edited by J. Barnes, Translated by W. Rhys Roberts. Princeton, NJ: Princeton University Press.

————. 2002. *The Athenian Constitution.* Translated by Peter John Rhodes. London: Penguin.

————. 2011. *The Eudemian Ethics.* Translated by Anthony Kenny. Oxford: Oxford University Press.

Brito, José de Sousa e. 2010. "Strafzwecke im Rechtsstaat." *Festschrift für Winfried Hassemer.* Edited by Felix Herzog and Ulfrid Neumann. Heidelberg: C. F. Müller.

Carawan, Edwin. 1998. *Rhetoric and the Law of Draco.* Oxford: Clarendon Press.

Cooper, John M. 1999. *Reason and Emotion: Essays on Ancient Moral Psychology and Ethical Theory.* Princeton, NJ: Princeton University Press.

Euripides. 1994. "Medea." In *Cyclops, Alcestis, Medea.* Edited and translated by David Kovacs. Cambridge, MA: Harvard University Press.

————. 1996. "Hippolytus." In *Children of Heracles, Hippolytus, Andromache, Hecuba.* Edited and translated by David Kovacs, Cambridge, MA: Harvard University Press.

Fuselli, Stefano. 2018. "Logoi Enuloi. Aristotle's Contribution to the Contemporary Debate on Emotions and Decision-Making." In *Aristotle on Emotions in Law and Politics.* Edited by Liesbeth Huppes-Cluysenaer and Nuno M. M. S. Coelho. Dordrecht Heidelberg, New York and London: Springer.

Gagarin, Michael. 1981. *Drakon and Early Athenian Homicide Law.* New Haven: Yale University Press.

Gernet, Louis. 2001. *Recherches sur le développement de la pensée juridique et morale en Grèce (étude sémantique).* Paris: Ernest Leroux, 1917. Paris: Albin Michel.

Kenny, Anthony. 1979. *Aristotle's Theory of the Will.* London: Dukworth.

Loening, Richard. 1967. Geschichte der strafrechtlichen Zurechnungslehre, 1. *Die Zurechnungslehre des Aristoteles.* Jena: Fischer, 1903. Reprint. Hildesheim: Olms.

MacDowell, Douglas M. 1963. *Athenian Homicide Law in the Age of the Orators.* Manchester: Manchester University Press.

Maschke, Richard. 1968. *Die Willenslehre im griechischen Recht: Zugleich ein Beitrag zur Frage der Interpolationen in den griechischen Rechtsquellen.* Berlin: Stilke, 1926; Reprint. Darmstadt: Wissenschaftliche Buchgesellschaft.

Phillips, David D. 2013. *The Law of Ancient Athens.* Ann Arbor: University oif Michigan Press.

Plato. 1926. *Laws.* Edited and Translated by Robert Gregg Bury. Cambridge, MA: Harvard University Press.

Platon. 1994–2011. *Nomoi (Gesetze).* Translated by Klaus Schöpsdau. Göttingen: Vandenhoeck & Ruprecht.

Rhodes, Peter John. 1993. *A Commentary on the Aristotelian Athenion Politeia.* Oxford: Clarendon Press.

Stroud, Ronald S. 1968. *Drakon's Law on Homicide.* Berkeley: University of California Press.

Viano, Cristina. 2018. Ethical Theory and Judicial Practice: Passions and Crimes of Passion in Plato, Aristotle and Lysias. In *Aristotle on Emotions in Law and Politics,* ed. Liesbeth Huppes-Cluysenaer and Nuno M.M.S. Coelho. Dordrecht Heidelberg, New York and London: Springer.

von Sigwart, Christoph. 1924. *Logik.* Tübingen: Verlag der Laupp'schen Buchhandlung, 1873. 4th ed. Tübingen: Mohr.

Chapter 10
Ethical Theory and Judicial Practice: Passions and Crimes of Passion in Plato, Aristotle and Lysias

Cristina Viano

Abstract This paper analyzes and compares the opinions of Plato and Aristotle about the crimes of passion, particularly in the case of murders caused by anger in response to an outrage (*hubris*). The act of *hubris* was certainly the most serious form of injustice which a citizen could encounter, an intolerable crime, which would compromise his raison d'être as a member of the community of men. For this reason Attic law considered it in certain cases—like rape and adultery—legitimate for the victim or his relatives to kill the perpetrator of the outrage. The opinions of Plato and Aristotle concerning the moral and juridical gravity of outrages concur, just as they both approve of the legitimacy of certain killings in response to such crimes. Their appreciation of anger however is very different and bears witness to a radical disagreement. For Plato the violence of anger is above all a danger for collective life and should be eliminated, while Aristotle gives more room for justification and for psychological satisfaction. The famous speech of Lysias *On the Murder of Eratosthenes*, which precisely treats the issue of a killing provoked by an outrage, illustrates that Aristotle shows more insight into the *esprit des lois* of his time than Plato.

This article was published in French in Viano, 2011 "Théorie Éthique et Pratique Judiciaire: Passions et Délits Passionnels Chez Platon, Aristote et Lysias," 101–121. I want to thank Liesbeth Huppes-Cluysenaer and Peter Langford for the English translation and the Journal *Mètis* for giving me the permission to publish the article in English as a chapter of this volume.

This research started in October 2005, during my stay at the Center for Advanced Studies in Humanities of Edinburgh, which I have to thank for its cordial hospitality. Different versions of this text have already been presented: in 2005 at Rethimnon, on the occasion of the colloquium "Emotions over Time" and in 2006 at São Paulo, during the colloquium "Ação e responsabilidade moral em Aristóteles". I want to thank especially David Konstan, Jocelyne Wilhelm and Marco Zingano for their remarks.

C. Viano (✉)
Centre Léon-Robin, University of Paris IV-Sorbonne, Paris, France
e-mail: cristina.viano@wanadoo.fr

© Springer International Publishing AG 2018
L. Huppes-Cluysenaer, N.M.M.S. Coelho (eds.), *Aristotle on Emotions in Law and Politics*, Law and Philosophy Library 121, DOI 10.1007/978-3-319-66703-4_10

10.1   Passion, Actions and Criminal Law

In the beginning of book III of the *Nicomachean Ethics*,[1] when he addresses the notion of a voluntary act, Aristotle shows the direct link which exists between moral reflection and the practical authority to decide criminal cases:

> Since excellence is concerned with passions and actions, and on voluntary passions and actions praise and blame are bestowed, on those that are involuntary forgiveness, and sometimes also pity, to distinguish the voluntary and the involuntary is presumably necessary for those who are studying excellence and useful also for legislators with a view to the assigning both of honours and of punishments. (*EN* 1109b33–35, trans. Ross/Urmson)

Criminal law is indeed one of the most philosophical domains of the law, because it directly concerns human actions and passions. The passions play a causal role by inciting criminal actions, while at the same time they play an instrumental role during the trial as persuasive means to influence the judges in court. We have only fragmentary information about the crimes of passion and the evaluation of passions in Attic law, as is the situation with all the other aspects of this law. Basically our sources are the testimonials not only of the poets, orators and historians, but also of the philosophers, particularly Plato and Aristotle, who of course address this theme from a "philosophical" perspective, by linking it directly to their theories of ethics, politics and psychology. Plato and Aristotle and also certain orators such as Demosthenes and Lysias, are even regarded as the major theorists of juridical thought of the IVth century BC through their engagement in a political-theoretical project of understanding law and justice.[2]

In this text I will analyze and compare the opinions of Plato and Aristotle concerning the crimes of passion; the way they think morally and juridically about emotions, particularly in the case of those crimes in which one can see how the most exemplary passion reacts against the most exemplary form of injustice, namely, in murders caused by anger in response to an outrage (*hubris*). The act of *hubris* was certainly the most serious form of injustice which a citizen of the city-state (*polis*) could encounter, an intolerable crime, which would, at the same time, compromise his private and public identity, his honour and his reputation, even his *raison d'être* as a member of the community of men. For this reason Attic law considered it in certain cases—such as rape and adultery—legitimate for the victim or his relatives to kill the perpetrator of the outrage. As will be seen, the opinions of Plato and Aristotle concerning the moral and juridical gravity of outrages concur, in the same way that they both approve of the legitimacy of certain killings in response to such crimes. Their appreciation of anger, however, is very different and indicates a radical disagreement.

---

[1] Edition used: for translation: *The Complete Works of Aristotle: The Revised Oxford Translation.* Edited by Jonathan Barnes.

[2] See Ober (2005), particularly p. 407 ff.

I would like to ask the following question: which relationship can be established between the ethical thoughts about anger of these two philosophers and the practice of the courts? I will pay attention in this respect to the famous speech of Lysias On the murder of Eratoshenes which precisely treats the issue of a killing provoked by an outrage.

10.2   Plato, *The Laws*, Book IX

Plato offers us a complete array of his principles of criminal law in book IX of *The Laws*. As correctly observed by Saunders, the Platonic criminal code is a mix of innovation and radical conservatism.[3] It comprises a very complex construction in which the same object is often subjected to different criteria of classification; here I will restrict myself to the essential aspects.

The whole juridical construction of Plato is based, in a paradoxical way, on the theory of involuntary injustice (860d). According to this theory every unjust act is involuntary and brought about by ignorance, because acting well makes people happy, while acting badly makes them unhappy. In the Platonic criminal law the distinction between voluntary (*hekousion*) and involuntary (*akousion*) has a meaning which is independent from the unjust act (*adikia*) and is derived from another level, namely, from the caused damage (*blabe*). According to this view the law should provide punishment for injustice and compensation for damage. But, as nobody willingly does wrong, Plato situates the cause of the unjust act in a psychical error, in a pathology of the soul which is normally curable but in the severe cases incurable. The function of the punishment decreed by law is precisely to *cure*, which means to root out the negative passion in a way that the individual will be no longer a danger for society and for himself, or simply by removing him in the cases in which cure is impossible.

The degree of responsibility for crimes is determined by criteria which are in essence psychological. Plato starts by distinguishing between three causes for faults: impulsive desire (*thumos*), pleasure (*hedone*) and ignorance (*agnoia*). This classification concerns the passions that dominate within the soul. As ignorance is essentially a deficiency or rational illusion, impulsive desire and pleasure are the true effective causes of crimes; they are described by the Athenian as the two opposite *forces* (*rhomai*) acting in the soul and difficult to master:

> Doubtless in the course of conversation you make at least this point to each other about the soul: one of the constituent elements (whether 'part' or 'state' is not important) to be found

---

[3]Saunders (1991), Introd., p. 2. See also Gernet and Diès (1951), Vol. I, p. 205, who define the penal code by Plato as the work of a reformer and jurist. See Brisson and Pradeau (2006), Vol. I, p. 17 regarding the problem of assessing the innovative character of the measures proposed by Plato in the *Laws* in relation to the Athenian legislation.

in it is 'impulsive desire' (thumos), and this innate impulse, unruly and difficult to fight as it is, causes a good deal of havoc by its irrational force. (. . .) We say Pleasure wields her power on the basis of an opposite kind of force; she achieves whatever her will desires by persuasive deceit that is irresistibly compelling. (*Leg.*, 863a–b, trans. Saunders slightly modified)

In this description Plato hesitates to characterize *thumos* as either a passion or constitutive part of the soul.[4] I prefer to translate *thumos* by impulsive desire because anger designates rather the passion (*pathos*), while the impulsive desire can designate the irascible part of the soul as well as its passion. Aristotle will be the first to distinguish clearly between *thumos* as a faculty of the soul and *thumos* as a passion, thus defining anger (*orge*) with the help of the distinction of potency and act. When Aristotle uses the term *thumos* sometimes also to designate both the impulsive desire and the anger (which frequently happens in the *Rhetoric*, where the use of language is deliberately less precise), this can also be attributed to the fact that anger can be seen as the paradigmatic passion of *thumos*. It is also clear that Plato characterizes *thumos* in a negative way, particularly by its irrational violence. The desire of pleasure is characterized, on the contrary, by the trickery without violence.

In a following section (864c), Plato distinguishes three types of unjust acts, which correspond to the psychical state of the perpetrator: (a) anger and fear; (b) pleasure and desire; (c) ignorance. To this should be added two categories which play a role in the application of laws and which correspond to the manner in which the crimes are committed: (1) acts which are violent and are publicly committed (*biaion kai sumphanon*); (2) acts which are committed in secrecy, in the shadow and by fraud (*meta skotous kai apates lathraios*).

All these elements, the psychical states, on the one hand, and the way the crimes are committed, on the other, become merged in the establishment of criteria to classify crimes, especially homicides. Plato classifies them according to their degree of gravity: (a) involuntary (*akousia*), (b) by anger (*thumou*), (c) voluntary (*hekousia*). A separate class is constituted by the homicides of which the author is exempted from the crime (*katharos en to nomo*).

The involuntary homicides (a), often violent acts, are accomplished without premeditation, for example, killing a friend in a fighting or in war, or, to give another example a physician kills his patient by accident when he gives him a potion meant to cure him. The voluntary homicides (c) (869e) are premeditated and committed out of pleasure, sensual desires or envy.

The killings incited by anger (b) are difficult to classify (*chalepoi diorizein*) (867b). They form in fact an intermediate level between voluntary acts and involuntary acts (*metaxu de pou tou te hekousiou kai akousiou*) (867a), or to be more exact they form an intermediate level in a twofold sense, because there are two kinds of them and each kind has a tendency to orient itself toward one of the two

---

[4]Laks (2005), pp. 91–92, interprets this hesitation of Plato as a sign that in *Laws* Plato did not completely reject his thesis of the division of the soul, defended in *Republic*, and that he conceives the human being as one and divided at the same time.

sides but without identifying with the one or the other. Plato distinguishes in fact (b.1) homicide without deliberate intention (*aprobouleutos*) (866e), followed by repentance and accomplished by someone whose anger suddenly bursts out with a violent act, from (b.2) premeditated homicide (*meta epiboules*) (867a) committed by someone who outraged by offensive words or dishonorable acts (*propelakisthentes* [by *propelakizo*] *logois kai atimois ergois*) guards his anger and pursues his revenge by killing much later and without regret. The crimes of the first type are less severe and resemble the involuntary crimes. Those of the second type are more severe and resemble the voluntary crimes. The penalty for them, is longer (3 years of exile instead of the 2 years attributed to the crimes committed by involuntary anger) and is needed to punish them and to cure the harmful passion of anger. In cases which are incurable, the perpetrator will be banned forever and will be punished by death when he tries to come back. Plato dedicates a long analysis to killings imposed by anger, especially those between parents. It will be noted that this passion is always considered as a negative one. In a similar manner, there is no acceptance at all of vengeance as a psychological compensation.[5] It is only when treating the punishment for voluntary homicide, that Plato refers to the archaic usage to entrust the murderer to the family of the dead to enable them to exercise their right of vengeance.

By considering anger as an independent category in the classification of homicides Plato seems to have introduced a novelty[6] into Attic law, which until then had restricted itself to accentuating in a very general way the difference between voluntary and involuntary crimes. The attention devoted to the emotional factor in the context of criminal law is that which is new in Plato. As we will show the importance of anger will be amplified by Aristotle, who will accentuate its irresistibility and unpremeditated character and who will highlight, contrary to Plato, the positive nature of a right reaction to an offence.

Concerning the homicides of which the authors are exempt from crime (d), the following circumstances create their legitimacy:

So much, then, for the law on that sort of murder. In the following conditions, however, it will be right to regard the killer as innocent: (a) If he catches a thief entering his home at night to steal his goods, and kills him, he shall be innocent. (b) If he kills a footpad in self defence, he shall be innocent. (c) If anyone sexually violates a free woman or boy, he may be killed with impunity by the victim of the violence or by the victim's father or brothers or sons. (d) If a husband discovers his wedded wife being raped and kills the attacker, the law will regard him as innocent. (e) If a man kills someone while saving the life of his father (provided the latter is not committing a crime), or while rescuing his mother or children or brothers, or the mother of his children, he shall be completely innocent. (*Leg.*, 874 b–e, trans. Saunders)

---

[5]In the *Protagoras*, Plato excludes vengeance from punishment because one cannot erase the past: "But he who desires to inflict rational punishment does not retaliate for a past wrong which cannot be undone; he has regard to the future, and is desirous that the man who is punished, and he who sees him punished, may be deterred from doing wrong again." (324b, trans. Jowett).

[6]Saunders (1991), p. 225.

The first, the second and the last case refer in essence to cases of legitimate defence against aggression to one self or ones immediate family, but the third and the fourth case appear to be cases of anger, which is provoked "by acts that harm the honour (*atimois ergois, cf.* 866c)". It concerns sexual abuse (*cf. hupo te tou hubristhentos bia*), rape and adultery, of which Plato underlines the element of violence (*cf. biazetai*). This list complies with the cases provided by the Athenian laws on homicide and adultery based on the ancient sources.[7] In fact, compared with the Athenian law, Plato puts more emphasis on the component of violence in such sexual crimes, while the law seems to pay more attention to the severity of the *hubris*, the infringement of honour which these acts imply.[8] Although anger is evidently the psychical driving force of the reaction to these sexual crimes, Plato says nothing here about anger or about the notion of vengeance. Therefore, it is not the psychological state of the perpetrator that explains the legality of the killing, but the circumstances which arose for the perpetrator and, above all, the high degree of injustice caused by the offence committed against him.

10.3 Aristotle

Aristotle elaborates and systematizes the legal theories of Plato about passions and crimes. As with Plato, Aristotle takes his point of departure in the distinction between the voluntary and involuntary and in the *Nicomachean Ethics*, book V, 10 he classifies human actions according to the psychical states of humans. But his conception of moral responsibility and his appreciation of passions, particularly of anger, are very different and are based on completely different anthropological, psychological and metaphysical principles.

It is a pity that Aristotle does not offer us a systematic exposition of his thoughts about law in general or about penal law, as Plato had in book XI of the *Laws*. In his work one does not find a general and conclusive definition of the law or of crimes but analyses of different aspects of these notions seen from different points of view and closely connected to the social and political reality of his time.[9] As a result of these partial and open definitions, Aristotelian legal thinking has been considered to be akin to modern legal thought.[10]

The main source for the Aristotelian ideas concerning the function of passions in criminal law is the *Rhetoric*, where Aristotle in his exposition of its use in court analyzes the passions in their double meaning of motives for unjust acts (I, 10) and

---

[7]*Ibid.*, p. 243.

[8]In fact, there were public actions for outrage (*graphê hubreôs*), for adultery (*graphe moicheias*) and private actions for violence (*dikê biaion*). The Law of Draco accepted the legitimacy of this type of killing. See Cantarella (2005), p. 22.

[9]*Cf.* Drago (1963), p. 68.

[10]*Cf.* Cairns (1949), p. 92 ff.

technical means to influence the judges in court (II, 2–11). In particular the long analysis in the book II of the role of passions as "technical means of persuasion" (*pisteis entechnoi*) in a subjective and moral sense, extends far beyond a purely technical treatment. It offers us the most comprehensive examination of the complex mechanisms of action and reaction of basic emotions that we can find in the Aristotelian corpus.

I will, therefore, begin to summarize the fundamental aspects of the Aristotelian conception of anger as a cause of action, by undertaking an analysis of book II of the *Rhetoric* and of the *Nicomachean Ethics*. I want to start with the analysis of two passages of the *Nicomachean Ethics* in which Aristotle's treatment of legal concepts and situations is, in my view, essential for his form of reasoning.

10.3.1   The Portrayal of Anger in the "Rhetoric of Passions"

In book II of *Rhethoric* anger (*orge*) is the passion which is addressed first and foremost. Aristotle defines it as follows:

> Anger may be defined as a desire accompanied by pain, for a conspicuous revenge for a slight at the hands of the men who have no call to slight oneself or one's friends. If this is a proper definition of anger, it must always be felt towards some particular individual, e.g. Cleon, and not man in general. It must be felt because the other has done or intended to do something to him or one of his friends. It must always be attended by a certain pleasure – that which arises from the expectation of revenge. (*Rhet.* 1378 a 31–b 1, trans. Rhys Roberts)

In this definition, anger manifests itself clearly as a reactive emotion, in particular to a form of provocation which expresses an evident disdain. To have disdain means to belittle certain things *peri to mêdenos axion*). In human relationships, publicly denying the value of someone means to assert his inferiority and thus to endanger his position in society.[11]

The different forms of belittling (*oligoria*) are: contempt (*kataphronesis*)), spite (*epereasmos*), outrage (*hubris*), disrespect (*atimia*, which is a form of *hubris*. *Hubris* deserves special attention:

> Outrage is also a form of slighting, since it consists in doing and saying things that cause shame to the victim, not in order that anything may happen to yourself, or because anything has happened to yourself, but simply for the pleasure involved. (Retaliation is not insolence, but vengeance) The cause of the pleasure thus enjoyed by the insolent man is that he thinks himself greatly superior to others when ill-treating them. (*Rhet.* 1378 b 23, trans. Rhys Roberts)

---

[11]Konstan (2003), pp. 118–119, draws attention to two fundamental aspects, which characterize the anger: the perception of contempt and the desire for vengeance. He emphasizes that the equality defended in the Athenian courts was completely centered on the protection of the reputation and property of individuals.

Somewhat later (1383 b 12) shame is defined as "a pain or a commotion brought about by vices in the past or future, that seems to lead to a loss of reputation (*eis adoxian*)".[12]

In the Greek world, as stated above, *hubris* means the most serious form of injustice, it is the paradigmatically unjust act, it is even that which is the opposite of law[13] and the leading cause of the ruin of the political community. In *Politics* V, *hubris* is analyzed accordingly as one of the causes of the destruction of tyranny.[14]

In the *Rhetoric*. Aristotle provides the legal definition of *hubris*:

> It is choice that constitutes wickedness and wrong-doing, and such names as outrage or theft imply choice as well as the mere action. A blow does not always amount to outrage, but only if it is struck with some such purpose as to insult the man struck or gratify the striker himself. (*Rhet.* 1374 a 11, trans. Rhys Roberts)

This passage shows that the intention is decisive for the qualification (*epigramma*, 1374 a 1) of a crime as *hubris*. According to Fisher,[15] the *focal meaning* of the Greek notion of *hubris*—legally and politically as well as morally—is well expressed by the definition Aristotle provides in his *Rhetoric* of the deliberate insult.

We have seen that an outrage can consist in acts and in words.[16] In relation to the acts, there is a list of examples of *hubris* in *Politics* (1311 a 36–b36) which consists primarily of attacks against a person. (*cf.* 1311 b 6: *eis to soma*) in the first place rape and adultery, but also castrations, beatings, physical abuse and corporal punishment. The appeasement of the anger brought about by the vengeance is the calmness (*praotes*) of a return to the normal state. In the *Nicomachean Ethics* the calmness or "mildness of character" is a virtue, which corresponds to the passion of anger (*peri orgas*, IV, 11, 1125 b 26). It has to establish the mean between irritability and indifference. Actually, as Aristotle himself admits, it is not correct to speak of mildness of character, because there is no name for the right middle in relation to anger and the term *praotês* indicates rather the rare situation in which anger is absent (cf. 1125 b 28: *pros ten elleipsin*). Aristotle therefore emphasizes often in the *Nicomachean Ethics* that anger as a desire for vengeance is natural and positive (*cf. anthropokoteron gar to timoreisthai, cf* 1126 a 13). We can conclude

---

[12]In the *Nicomachean Ethics*, Aristotle considers shame, as with self-respect (*aidôs*), rather as a passion than as a virtue in the strict sense: "And if shamelessness – not to be ashamed of committing base acts – is bad, that doesn't mean that it is a virtue to be ashamed when one commits base acts." invert: (1128 b 32–33, Trans. Ross/Urmson). This passage gives also a good example of the different roles of self-respect and shame: self-respect has the function to inhibit bad behavior, while shame looks back to it with regret.

[13]Paoli (1950), p.140, n. 28.

[14]The word *hubris* receives here the general meaning of excess and designates the typical attitude of the tyrant driven by an excess of desire and with pleasure as his sole purpose: the wealth for which he manifests an insatiable desire is actually the means to procure all kinds of pleasure. This excess causes anger in the governed and is thus one of the main causes of revolts against tyranny.

[15]Fisher (1992).

[16]In *Pol.* 1311 a 32–36, *hubris* is described as consisting of many varieties (*polumerês*).

therefore that the right attitude towards anger i.e. the one which is according to rules, against the right individuals and because of the right reasons, the one which obeys to reason, is not criticized, but is, on the contrary, considered to be virtuous and laudable (*cf. apainetes*, 1126 b 4), while indifference to a provocation is seen as a defect and as showing the attitude of a slave (cf. 6 in 1126).

Aristotle shows us therefore a positive opinion about anger and vengeance. Let us turn now to anger as the cause of an unjust act.

10.3.2 Unjust and Voluntary

In the *Nicomachean Ethics*, V, 10 Aristotle states that the unjust act can be characterized as voluntary. It is exactly on the basis of its voluntary nature that an act is characterized as just or unjust (1135 a 20). Aristotle defines the voluntary as follows:

> By the voluntary I mean, as has been said before, any of the things in a man's own power which he does with knowledge, i.e. not in ignorance either of the person acted on or of the instrument used or of the end that will be attained (e.g. whom he is striking, with what, and to what end) each such act being done not incidentally nor under compulsion. (*EN* 1135 a 23–27, trans. Ross/Urmson)

The classification of harmful acts (*blabai*) made by Aristotle is based on psychic states (1135 b 8 ff.) and differentiates between:

(a) involuntary acts (*akousia*) i.e. wrong acts (faults, mistakes), which have ignorance as cause (the principle of action can be inside or outside the doer);
(b) voluntary acts (*hekousia*) i.e. unjust acts

However

> (b.1) "When he acts with knowledge but not after deliberation, it is an act of injustice – e.g. the acts due to anger or to other passions necessary or natural to man; for when men do such harmful and mistaken acts they act unjustly, and the acts are acts of injustice, but this does not imply that the doers are unjust or wicked; for the injury is not due to vice.

> (b.2) But when a man acts from choice, he is an unjust and a vicious man." (*EN* 1135 b 19–25, trans. Ross/Urmson)

Aristotle resolves the uncertainty which Plato had about the question whether anger is voluntary or involuntary by classifying it as a voluntary act without deliberation. Within that context, the individual who commits an injustice in the grip of anger is not himself unjust. Aristotle accentuates this aspect of anger in the end more specifically by the following explanation:

> Hence acts proceeding from anger are rightly judged not to be done of premeditation (ouk ek pronoias); for it is not the man who acts in anger but he who enraged him that starts the mischief. Again, the matter in dispute is not whether the thing happened or not, but its injustice; for it is apparent injustice that occasions anger. (*EN* 1135b26–29, trans. Ross/Urmson modified)

This passage is rather surprising because it seems to be in contradiction with the voluntary character of an action performed by anger. From an ethical point of view, one could understand this displacement of the operating principle in the case of an unjust act which was forced on the actor by anger in a metaphorical sense: focusing solely on the deliberation, one could say that the principle (*arche*) of the act is in the person who has provoked the anger in him who has reacted to this by committing himself an unjust act voluntarily but without deliberate intention. But one can also interpret this passage in a juridical sense and assume that Aristotle refers here to the context of criminal law, especially to the judgement (*cf. krinetai*) about the nature of an act of aggression (like murder), committed out of anger in reaction to an injustice which had been deliberately inflicted.[17] According to Stewart,[18] the one who has provoked the anger could be the accuser (*diokon*), while the one who acted under the influence of anger, could be the accused (*pheugon*). Even when it can be admitted that a person acts out of an impulse of sudden anger and thus without premeditation, the question to be answered by the court is whether the harm he did, could be justified: had the provocation he actually suffered or could have considered to have suffered been serious enough to justify the assault? Aristotle indeed adds (*eti*) that the "dispute" (*amphisbeteitai*) is not about the facts of the case but about the rightness or justness of the act (*peri tou dikaiou*). By contrast, Aristotle refers to lawsuits about business affairs, in which the parties argue to ascertain if the harm actually has occurred:

> For they do not dispute about the occurrence of the acts – as in commercial transactions where one of the parties *must* be vicious – unless they do so owing to forgetfulness; but, agreeing about the fact, they dispute on which side justice lies (whereas a man who has deliberately injured another cannot help knowing that he has done so), so that the one thinks he is being treated unjustly and the other disagrees. (*EN* 1135 b 29–1136a1, trans. and it. Ross/Urmson)[19]

The verb *amphisbetein* is a juridical term, the *amphisbetountes* are the opposing parties in a lawsuit. In the classification of the different criminal courts in *Politics* we find the same expression concerning confessed crimes:

> The sixth (court LHC) tries cases of homicide, which are of various kinds, premediated, involuntary, and cases in which the guilt is confessed, but the justice is disputed. (...) The

---

[17]See, for example, Saunders (1991), p. 225, n. 24: "Is a report of jurisprudential opinion, common opinion, or legal practice, and what relevance it has to homicide law in particular".

[18]Stewart (1892), vol. I, p. 506.

[19]The last lines of this passage are obscure: how can these three figures be identified: the one who states that he has been wronged (A), the one who denies this (B) and the one who has acted by premeditation (C). The ancients envision the moment of the trial and identify A with the challenger and B with the impetuous actor. The majority of the modern readers, in contrast, think of the moment of action and identify A with the impetuous actor and B with the challenger. Others identify the challenger B with C, while there are also people that think that C is not a challenger, but someone who deliberately commits an unjust act. See, on this point Natali (2009), p. 497, n. 512.

different kinds of homicide may be tried either by the same or by different courts. (*Pol.* 1300b 25–31, trans. Jowett)

The question is to establish whether a certain killing is legal or not. The preceding passage explains in ethical and psychological terms how anger which is provoked by an unjust act functions as a ground for exculpation. But what kind of injustice is here at stake? Since anger is the main issue here, the provocation should consist in a form of contempt, and *hubris* is a very serious form of contempt.

In the *Constitution of Athens* LVII, 3, 1. Aristotle explicitly furnishes the example of the killing in case of adultery as a form of legitimate killing

> When the homicide is acknowledged, but legal justification is pleaded, as when a man takes an adulterer in the act (hoion moichon labôn) (...) the prisoner is tried in the court of Delphinium. (trans. Kenyon)[20]

10.3.3 Lack of Control of the Impulsive Desire (Thumos)

In the *Nicomachean Ethics* VII, 7, 1149a 24–b 25 reference to the legal meaning of *hubris* is made in my view when Aristotle presents four arguments[21] to prove that the lack of control (*akrasia*) is less shameful (*hetton aischra*)[22] in the case of impulsive desire (thumos) than in the case of sensual desire (*epithumia*). The first argument pertains to the way the *thumos* functions in relation to reason: it somehow listens to reason, while the sensual desire does not listen to it at all (*EN* 1149 a 24–b 2). The second argument is about the fact that the impulsive desire is much more "natural" than the *epithumia*, which is orientated to excess and that which is not necessary (*EN* 1149 b 2–13). The third relating to the fact that there is no malice or cunning in the impulsive desire which operates always openly (*ouk epiboulos...alla phaneros*), while cunning is typical for the sensual desire and a sign of the presence of injustice (*EN* 1149 b 13–20). Finally, the fourth argument comprises the element of *hubris* and is formulated in this manner:

> Further, no one commits wanton outrage with a feeling of pain, but everyone, who acts in anger acts with pain, while the man who commits outrage acts with pleasure. If then those acts at which it is most just to be angry are more unjust, the incontinence which is due to appetite is the more unjust [than the incontinence due to impulsive desire (C.V.)]; for there

---

[20]The tribunal Delphinium was seated in the Temple of Apollo Delphinios, outside the walls of Athens. It was chaired by the Archon Basileus, who established whether a murder had occurred by mistake and for a just cause, as in the case of adultery (*cf.* Demosthenes *in Aristocratem* XXIII, p. 74). On the origins of this tribunal and the cults that were linked to it, *cf.* Todd (2007).

[21]The Anonymous Commentator in Heylbut (1892), p. 432, 12, characterizes the argument as *epicheirêma*. It is a dialectical argument in contrast to the *philosophêma*, which is a scientific argument. See Aristotle, *Top.* VIII, 11, 162 a 15: *epicheirêma de sullogismos dialektikos.*

[22]Shame (*aischune*) is the *pathos*, which one experiences when one has done wrong. See *Eth. Nic.* IV, 15, 1128 b 22. Therefore *aischron* has a moral meaning which is negative in a general sense.

is no wanton outrage involved in impulsive desire. (*EN* 1149 b 23–23, trans. Ross/Urmson modified)

This passage is difficult; much ink has been spilled on it and it continues to be the subject of heated discussions, as, for example during the *Symposium Aristotelicum*, dedicated to book VII of the *Nicomachean Ethics*.[23]

Firstly the argumentative structure of it is not easy to follow. Demonstration is developed on different levels and not all premises are made explicit.[24] The main problem is to understand the focal meaning of this argument: what is the decisive reason why the lack of control of the impulsive desire (*thumos*) is less grave than the lack of control of the sensual desire? One could accentuate (1) the factor of the pain, which accompanies acts in anger or (2) the factor of the gravity of *hubris*, which is absent when people act in anger. But which meaning should be accorded here to the word *hubris*?[25]

One could think that also this argument calls to mind a juridical situation[26] analogous to the one referred to above i.e. the qualification of an offence which is committed under the influence of anger in reaction to the suffering of a severe injustice, i.e. to an act of *hubris*.[27] But it is possible to take a step further and to treat *hubris* straightforwardly as a legal act (comparable to *graphe hubreos*: public outrage). By attributing to *hubris* the meaning of a crime, it becomes possible to understand the argument in this following way: the lack of control of the impulsive desire (*thumos*) is less severe than the lack of control of the sensual desire (*epithumia*) because it is never the origin of a crime of *hubris*, which is the worst of all injustices. The pain which accompanies acts which are done in anger is the guarantee or even the incontrovertible sign, that there is no *hubris* involved in these acts, because this would, on the contrary, always lead to the involvement of pleasure.[28]

If this hypothesis is correct, our passage could, as with the previous one, provide the ethical interpretation of a situation which is often discussed in court, in which

---

[23]Venice, July 2005. For the proceedings see Natali (2009).

[24]See the intelligent and precise analysis in Fisher (1992), pp. 15–17.

[25]Another problem concerns the implication of *hubris* for the sensual desire (*epithumia*). Fisher pays attention to the fact that Aristotle seems a little uncertain when he treats the relation between *hubris* and psychical and physical pleasures. If *hubris* consists in the pleasure of being superior, it could be said that it is primarily a mental pleasure. It can also originate in sexual acts or in drunkenness, however, although it is to be expected that Aristotle will consider the *hubris* in these cases as a frequent *companion* of excessive pleasures and as the essential component of some of them. Ibid., p. 17, footnote 15.

[26]The third argument also seems to be "legal" and refers to the distinction between criminal acts which are committed openly and the ones which are done secretly (*EN* V 5, 1131 a 1 and Plato, *Leg.* IX, 864c).

[27]S. Broadie thinks that the second part of this argument suggests that anger is the pre-eminent response to a perceived prior aggression, caused by a lack of control of sensual desire. Aristotle (2002), p. 396.

[28]See the definition of anger in Aristotle, Rhetoric II 2, 1378 b 23.

the judge has to decide about the legal nature of a crime caused by anger at an outrage. From the perspective of the *Rhetoric*, where the passions are described as the "reasons which change the judgments of people" (*di' hosa metaballontes diapherousi pros tas kriseis*)[29] and are used as technical instruments of persuasion, it is easy to imagine how the orator recalls the details of the outrage to change the minds of the judges by exciting their anger towards the one who committed the offence of *hubris* and, simultaneously, through sympathy their indulgence towards the accused.[30] The offence for which the accused is tried could very well be a homicide. In such a case, the orator for the defence might very well try to achieve the acquittal of the killer, by showing that the act actually was a case of legitimate homicide, because it was, as with the killing an adulterer, the reaction to a grave case of *hubris*.

I would like to focus attention now upon a concrete example of a "crime of honour", that can demonstrate very effectively the situation to which Aristotle refers, in which the judge has to decide about the justness of an attack (in fact a killing) inflicted by the one who was outraged in reaction to his challenger.

10.3.4 A Case of a "Crime of Honour": Lysias, On the Murder of Eratosthenes

One of the most famous orations of Lysias is *On the Murder of Eratosthenes*, in which the Athenian Euphiletos, who has killed the lover of his wife, tries to put forward a defence for his act in court. I have called it a "concrete" situation, because this oration is a plea that Lysias has written, meant to be pronounced by Euphiletos in his defence before court. As is well known, there were no lawyers at this period nor professional jurists. The parties therefore entrusted the drafting of pleas to speech writers (*logographes*) such as Lysias. As also the judges were no experts, these speechwriters (*logographes*) had not only the task of making a persuasive oration, but also compiling a real: "dossier", which contained the text of the laws and even their interpretation.[31] The speechwriter (*logographe*) wants to attain his goal i.e. achieving the acquittal of his client and convincing the jurors by the combination of the presentation of the facts and the power of his persuasion. This brings us fully within the context of book I and II of the *Rhetoric* of Aristotle.

The story of Euphiletos is rather straightforward. Euphiletos, an honorable citizen of Athens, discovers that his wife has a relation with a young *playboy*, Eratosthenes, which had lasted already for a long time and which he had never surmised. After having surprised the man together with his wife in his own house,

---

[29]Ibid., 1378 a 19.

[30]Ibid., 1378a30–1388a28.

[31]Compare Maffi (2005), pp. 1278–1279.

he kills him on the spot, invoking a law of Draco on adultery that permits the insulted husband to kill the guilty party when caught in the act.

The parents of the killed man maintain, on the contrary, that the homicide took place with premeditation (*phonos ek pronoias*); that Euphiletos has attracted Eratosthenes with a trick to his house with the help of a slave. Euphiletos had the killed Eratosthenes after having kept him with force in the house when he was trying to flee from it.

This oration is considered one of the masterpieces of Lysias. The reasoning is not one of a very tight logic, but is very efficacious: it is a sequence of simple observations, clear and skillfully designed to refute the accusations of the opposing party and to justify the accused by reference to the laws.[32] This plea based upon a "crime of honour" is also one of the most important testimonies of the Attic law regarding adultery (*moicheia*). There are, in fact, two laws on adultery at stake here: the Areopagean law on homicide (which was engraved, like all *nomoi phonikoi*, in a stele of the Areopagus, and went back to the old laws of Draco), which establishes impunity for killing in certain circumstances like catching one's wedded wife in close embrace (*epi damarti*) with an adulterer, that is to say in the act,[33] and the law which pertains specifically to adultery (*nomos moicheias*), which authorizes the homicide of an adulterer caught in the act.[34] The essence of the defence speech of Euphiletos is summarized at its opening (§4–5):

> But I take it, sirs, that what I have to show is that Eratosthenes had an intrigue with my wife, and not only corrupted her but inflicted disgrace upon my children and an outrage on myself by entering my house; that this was the one and only enmity between him and me; that I have not acted thus for the sake of money, so as to raise myself from poverty to wealth; and that all I seek to gain is the requital accorded by our laws I shall therefore set forth to you the whole of my story from the beginning; I shall omit nothing, but will tell the truth. For I consider that my own sole deliverance rests on my telling you, if I am able, the whole of what has occurred. (trans. Lamb)

The most important arguments for the defence are: the legality of the act of Euphiletos and the lack of premeditation. The latter is indeed one of the essential characteristics of the type of homicide, which can be admitted by law. It will be clear that the adultery is presented, above all, as a unilateral act of outrage (*hubris*) committed by Eratosthenes against Euphiletos, not only involving the seduction of his wife, but also implying the dishonour of the children and especially the violation of the house (*oikos*).[35] The latter will actually be the central issue of the defence speech of Euphiletos: the violation of the house (*oikos*), the ruining of its order by a

---

[32]On the skill and ability to synthesize of Lysias, see L. Gernet in Lysias (1924), vol. I, p. 27 and Cooper (2007), p. 214.

[33]See Aristotle, *Constitution of Athens*, LVII, 3, 1 Démosthène XXIII (*in Aristocratem*). Like remarked by Paoli (1950), n. 13, and Cantarella (2005), p. 22, adultery comprises all extramarital affairs, not only with one's wife, but also with one's mother, sister, daughter and concubines. Only prostitutes are excluded.

[34]See Demosthenes, Against Neera (59), 87.

[35]See, for a clear and exhaustive analysis of the Attic law on adultery Paoli (1950).

foreign element that enters the house like a thief and seduces the housewife, stealing her from her spouse and creating bastards, thus constituting the prelude to the corruption of the whole city. Adultery affects therefore not only the private sphere, but also the public order and, by killing Eratosthenes, Euphiletos did not only seek justice in relation to his own personal interest, but in relation to the interest of the city as a whole.

Here, we have a "political" explanation for the exceptional seriousness (*cf. deinotate hubris*, §3; *to megiston ton adikematon*, §45) of the crime of adultery as the paradigmatic case of *hubris*.

But what is the role played by passions in this story? From the perspective of our inquiry one of the most interesting aspects of this oration is exactly that no word is said about passion as the motivation for the homicide. Euphiletos explicitly excludes hatred (*echthra*) and the desire for wealth, and says that the "requital accorded by our laws" (*kata tous nomous timoria*, §4) has been his sole motive. His defence against the accusation of premeditation is limited to the presentation of the facts and the circumstances. It is also remarkable that there is even no mention of emotional factors on the side of the adulterer: the main purpose of the seducer is never presented as a sensual pleasure, but as the deliberate will to outrage the ruler of the house.

As for the spouse, from a legal point of view, she plays a completely passive role in the matter: she was simply seduced. There is also no psychological interpretation to explain the gravity of the hubris. Should it be concluded that the emotional factor in this case of homicide is deliberately neglected for some moral reason? Or is it a choice of rhetorical strategy?

The role of *pathos* as an instrument to persuade an audience is also ambiguous in another sense here. Euphiletos undeniably aims to produce an emotional effect. From the beginning onwards he appeals to the sympathy and indignation of the judges:

> I should be only too pleased, sirs, to have you so disposed towards me in judging this case as you would be to yourselves, if you found yourselves in my plight. For I am sure that, if you had the same feelings about others as about yourselves, not one of you but would be indignant at what has been done. (trans. Lamb, §1)

But somewhat further he states that those who try to incite anger in the judges with lies and devices (*orgas tois akouousi. . .paraskeuazousi*) had better first read the text of the law (§28). But what kind of sentiment should one incite in the judges? And about what exactly?

The fundamental sentiment which is invoked by Euphiletos in his appeal to the judges is the indignation about what has happened to him personally. Although in the language of oratory *aganaktein* is considered as a synonym for *orge* and *thumos*,[36] this form of indignation/anger is accorded a special meaning. In fact, in relation to the manner, in which Aristotle describes it in the *Rhetoric*, anger appears as an individual *pathos* aroused by a form of injustice that affects one's own person

---

[36] Allen (2000), pp. 52 and 349, note 6.

or those who are closest, such as friends or family, who one considers to be part of oneself. The indignation of the judges, however, concerns an injustice which has affected another person, a citizen similar to them, whose misery only interests them as far as it could have happened in the same way to themselves. The anger of the judge has, therefore, to be different from that of personal anger, a kind of indirect emotion of the second degree. It is closer—without, however, seeking to identify it with one of them—to the three emotions *eleos* (pity), *nemesis* (indignation), *phthonos* (envy) described by Aristotle in his *Rhetoric* (II, 8–10), which deal with failures and undeserved success that concern the others.

We saw that it was the main strategy of the speech of Lysias to convert a private case of adultery into a public offence towards the community. Because of this the anger incited in the judges becomes a type of extended and transformed individual anger, which as a result has turned into a "civic anger" against the injustice.[37]

It is therefore possible to see here, in the example of a defence speech for a case relating to what could be called a crime of honour, that the appeal to the anger of the judges can be described as a well-known and perfectly legitimate form of practice relating to the role of the judge. But this form of proceeding makes use of the public legitimation of the passion of an individual person[38] and thus of the transformation of a private case into a political case, concerning the whole city and its safeguard.[39]

The silence about the individual *pathos* of anger as the motive for crime seems to be a rhetorical strategy. The aim of this strategy is not to censure the emotional component of the crime's motivation, but to show its legitimacy by placing emphasis on the absence of premeditation, which is a principal characteristic of crimes triggered by *thumos*.

10.3.5 Anger: Negative Pathos or Civil Pathos?

We have seen that, according to both Plato and Aristotle, anger plays an important role as one of the causes of criminal acts, but that their appreciation of this passion is diametrically opposed. In Plato's view, anger is a negative and violent passion, which should be "cured" as a psychical pathology. For Aristotle, anger is not an illness to be taken care of, but much more a capacity of the soul, an innate desire for

---

[37]Konstan (2006), p. 68.

[38]Allen (2003) explains the fundamental importance of the appeal to the anger of the judges by the fact that this emotion referred in reality to a very important moral value which formed an inherent part of the definitions of law and justice. Allen (2000) summarizes this situation well in *The World of Prometheus*, p. 62: "The practice of punishing transformed a moment of anger into a moment of justice. The movement from the anger to justice or from the personal to the political occurred as a negotiation of honor and of status roles within the community".

[39]See, for example, Lysias, *Against Eratosthenes*, in which Lysias transforms a private law suit in a public one, by presenting his personal enemy Erathostenes as the one who is responsible for all the crimes of Thirty Tyrants.

vengeance and recovery of self-esteem, which reacts to injustice and has to be controlled and tamed in order to make a moral use of it. For Aristotle, it is even possible to speak of virtue in the context of anger, but the true measure of this virtue has a greater tendency towards the excess than to the default.

Concerning the responsibility for acts in anger, we have seen that Aristotle resolves the uncertainty Plato had regarding the voluntary or involuntary character of this passion (*pathos*) and that made him classify these acts as voluntary without deliberation. Aristotle thinks that the individual person who commits an unjust act driven by anger is not an unjust person himself. As a result of this Plato and Aristotle have a different opinion concerning the gravity of criminal acts which are driven by anger. Certainly, there is substantial agreement between them about homicides which are justified by the law and in relation to the extreme gravity of outrage, but for Aristotle there is room for justification of anger and for the psychological satisfaction, which the individual experiences from vengeance, while for Plato the violence of anger is above all a danger for collective life and should therefore be eliminated. Plato gives anger no role in the explanation of the legality of the homicide. It is legal because the law recognizes the seriousness of the circumstances.

The importance of circumstances and the juridical qualification of the responsibility for acts triggered by anger together with the mitigation of the gravity of a lack of control over *thumos* in the *Nicomachean Ethics* is very significant. If Aristotle uses juridical arguments in an ethical argument, the reason for this is that Aristotle sees a close relationship between these two domains. Moreover, if in the *Nicomachean Ethics* the "discipline" of ethics is still "under construction" as is its vocabulary, it is quite normal that Aristotle seeks to articulate his concepts with the use of different choices of language, especially those which belong to domains that are closely connected. According to the Aristotelian 'architectonic' therefore, legislation is a function of politics, and politics involves ethics and is, in a certain sense, similar to it. If ethics is for Aristotle the basis of the science of the legislator[40] and if the passions are the prime matter of the Aristotelian ethics, it is clear that according to Aristotle the moral evaluation of the different passions has to play a fundamental and foundational role in the lengthy process of the establishment of laws.

> Next, laws are made after long consideration, whereas decisions in the courts are given at short notice. (*Rhet.* 1354 b1 trans. Rhys Roberts)

The question remains if these two different views regarding the emotional element of anger as cause of the criminal act, offered by Plato and Aristotle, can both be traced to the judicial practice in Greece or if one of them prevails. In other words, could anger be considered in certain cases as a mitigating circumstance or would it always be an aggravating one? And is the appeal to the anger of the judges in defence speeches always used as a normal and perfectly legitimate way of

---

[40] *Cf. Eth. Nic.*, I, 1, 1094 a 25 suiv.

undertaking such things or is it seen as a dubious practice? To answer these questions in an exhaustive way a more complete inquiry of the works of the orators would be needed. Still, it seems to me that the example of the oration of Lysias concerning a paradigmatic case of killing because of adultery shows an essential aspect of the "bon usage" of anger in a judicial context. This is not only so when Lysias—as Aristotle does in the beginning of the *Rhetoric*[41]—argues against those, who try to convince the judges through manipulating them by an exclusive appeal to their passions, but also when he makes an appeal to a specific form of anger, public and partial, concerning an injustice suffered by a citizen.

The recognition of vengeance as a crime's motivation and the transfiguration of the individual emotion into a civil emotion make it possible to integrate anger in a positive manner into legality. Moreover, the fundamental importance of the appeal to the anger of the judges in court can only be explained by the fact that this emotion reflects a moral value of high importance, which is already an inseparable part of the definitions of law and justice. From this position the positive connotation anger has for Aristotle seems to reflect much better the "esprit des lois" of his time, than the negative view on it of Plato.

References

Allen, D.S. 2000. *The World of Prometheus. The Politics of Punishing in Democratic Athens.* Princeton, NJ: Princeton University Press.

———. 2003. Angry Bees, Wasps, and Jurors: The Symbolic Politics of *Orgê* in Athens. In *Ancient Anger: Perspectives from Homer to Galen*, ed. S. Morton Braund and G. Most, 76–98. Cambridge: Cambridge University Press.

Aristotle. 1999. *Etica Nicomachea*. Trad., introd. e note di Carlo Natali. Rome: Laterza.

———. 2002. *Nicomachean Ethics*. Edited and translated by C. J. Rowe and S. Broadie. Oxford: Oxford University Press.

---

[41]In the first pages of the *Rhetoric* (I, 1, 1354 a 11 ff.), Aristotle criticizes actually the exclusive importance attached by the "technographes" of his time to the appeal to passions to the detriment of the true "body of persuasion", namely, the demonstration (*enthymeme*). Here, he considers the *pathos* as accessory evidence. But later in I.2 he sees the appeal to emotions as technical evidence and devotes nearly the whole of book II to them. Many interpretations are given to explain the contrast between I.1 and I.2. For example, Fortenbaugh (2006), who chooses for a "developmental explanation" according to which Aristotle would have moved from an idealistic, Platonic position to a more practical rhetorical view, which sees the passions as "remedial measures", adapted to the sensibility of a mediocre audience (*see* III, 14, 1415 a 34–35). He quotes specifically the defense speech by Euphiletos in *On the murder of Eratosthenes* of Lysias, to show that Aristotle's view reflects in fact an ambivalence in the use of the appeal to the passions already present in the rhetoric of his time: "Apparently the position Aristotle adopts in *Rhetoric* I,1 is not only ideal and Platonic; it is also a reflection of both actual judicial procedure and the artful practice of the *logographos*" (p. 392) and somewhat further about the call to the feelings of judges: "That too is Aristotelian. It illustrates in a single passage what Aristotle has in mind when he speaks of a remedial proem derived from an attempt to create goodwill and to arouse anger" (p. 402).

————. 2014a. Constitution of Athens. In *The Complete Works of Aristotle: The Revised Oxford Translation*, ed. J. Barnes. Princeton, NJ: Princeton University Press.

————. 2014b. Nicomachean Ethics. In *The Complete Works of Aristotle: The Revised Oxford Translation*, ed. J. Barnes. Princeton, NJ: Princeton University Press.

————. 2014c. Politics. In *The Complete Works of Aristotle: The Revised Oxford Translation*, ed. J. Barnes. Princeton, NJ: Princeton University Press.

————. 2014d. *Rhetoric*. In *The Complete Works of Aristotle: The Revised Oxford Translation*, ed. J. Barnes. Princeton, NJ: Princeton University Press.

Brisson, L., and J.-F. Pradeau. 2006. Introduction. In *Les lois. Livres I à VI Livres I à VI*, ed. Platon. Paris: Flammarion.

Cairns, H. 1949. *Legal Philosophy from Plato to Hegel*. Baltimore, MD: Johns Hopkins Press.

Cantarella, E. 2005. Adultère (Grèce). In *Dictionnaire de l'Antiquité*, ed. J. Leclant. Paris: Presses Universitaires de France.

Cooper, C. 2007. Forensic Oratory. In *A Companion to Greek Rhetoric*, ed. I. Worthington. Oxford: Blackwell.

Demosthenes. 1959. Contre Midias. Contre Aristocrate. In *Plaidoyers politiques*, trans. J. Humbert and L. Gernet. Paris: Les Belles Lettres.

————. 2010. *Speeches 50-59*. Translated by V. Bers. Austin: University of Texas Press.

Drago, G. 1963. *La giustizia e le giustizie. Letture del libro quinto dell'Etica a Nicomaco*. Milan: Marzorati.

Fisher, N.R.E. 1992. *Hybris: A Study in the Values of Honour and Shame in Ancient Greece*. Aris & Phillips: Warminster.

Fortenbaugh, W.W. 2006. On the Composition of Aristotle's Rhetoric. In *Aristotle's Practical Side on His Psychology, Ethics, Politics and Rhetoric*, ed. W.W. Fortenbaugh, 399–412. Leiden: Brill.

Gernet, L., and A. Diès. 1951. Introduction. In *Les Lois: Livres I-II [-III-VI]*, ed. Platon and trans. E. Des Places. Paris: Les Belles Lettres.

Heylbut, G., ed. 1892. *Eustratii et Michaelis et anonyma in Ethica Nicomachea commentaria*. Berlin: Reimer.

Konstan, D. 2003. Aristotle on Anger and the Emotions: The Strategies of Status. In *Ancient Anger: Perspectives from Homer to Galen*, ed. S. Morton Braund and G. Most, 99–120. Cambridge: Cambridge University Press.

————. 2006. *The Emotions of the Ancient Greeks: Studies in Aristotle and Greek Literature*. Toronto: Toronto University Press.

Laks, A. 2005. *Médiation et coercition, Pour une lecture des 'Lois' de Platon*. Lille and Villeneuve-d'Ascq: Presses Universitaires de Lille and Presses universitaires du Septentrion.

Lysias. 1924. *Discours*. Edited and translated by L. Gernet. Paris: Les Belles Lettres.

————. 1930a. Against Eratosthenes. In *Lysias with an English translation*, ed. W.R.M. Lamb. Cambridge, MA and London: Harvard University Press and Heinemann. (Loeb).

————. 1930b. On the Murder of Eratosthenes. In *Lysias with an English Translation*, ed. W.R.M. Lamb. Cambridge, MA and London: Harvard University Press and Heinemann. (Loeb).

Maffi, A. 2005. Loi (Grèce). In *Dictionnaire de l'Antiquité*, ed. Jean Leclant. Paris: Presses Universitaires de France.

Natali, C., ed. 2009. *Aristotle Nicomachean Ethics, Book VII, Symposium Aristotelicum*. Oxford: Oxford University Press.

Ober, J. 2005. Law and Political Theory. In *The Cambridge Companion to Ancient Greek Law*, ed. M. Gagarin and D. Cohen. Cambridge: Cambridge University Press.

Paoli, U.E. 1950. Il reato di adulterio [*moicheia*] nel diritto attico. *Studia et documenta historiae et iuris* 16: 132–182.

————. 1970. *The Laws of Plato*. Translated by Trevor J. Saunders. Harmondsworth: Penguin Classics.

Saunders, T.J. 1991. *Plato's Penal Code: Tradition, Controversy, and Reform in Greek Penology.* Oxford: Clarendon Press.

Stewart, J.A. 1892. *Notes on the Nicomachean Ethics of Aristotle.* Oxford: Clarendon Press.

Todd, S.C. 2007. Introduction to Lysias I, Concerning the Killing of Eratosthenes. Defence Speech. In *A Commentary on Lysias, Speeches 1-11*, ed. S.C. Todd, 43–62. Oxford: Oxford University Press.

Viano, C. 2011. Théorie éthique et pratique judiciaire: passions et délits passionnels chez Platon, Aristote et Lysias. In *Mètis. Anthropologie des mondes anciens*, Dossier: *Émotions.* vol. 9, 101–121. Athens-Paris: Daedalus.

Chapter 11
What Does Nemesis Have to Do with the Legal System? Discussing Aristotle's Neglected Emotion and Its Relevance for Law and Politics

Daniela Bonanno and Lucia Corso

Abstract Aristotle defines *nemesis* (*to nemesan* = from the verb *nemesao*) as the emotional reaction of someone with a noble character at unmerited good fortune. That another's good fortune is a central element of *nemesis* can also be inferred by the contraposition Aristotle proposed between nemesis and pity, which is pain at undeserved bad fortune. The modern concept of *indignation*, commonly used as a translation for the word *nemesis,* refers to outrage at *a general form* of injustice, and usually a serious one.

The authors intend to remain faithful to the original meaning of the term and to explore the impact it can have with respect to law. In contrast to the existing literature, which especially during the 1960s, discredited the narrow conception of indignation as defined in Aristotelian terms and interpreted indignation in terms of negative emotions such as envy or resentment, they argue that this emotion has a central position in legal reasoning and legal thought. *Nemesis* is that emotion which creates a strong conceptual bond between *rectificatory justice* (*to diorthotikon dikaion*), which today we may define as typical of legal reasoning, and *distributive justice* (*to dianemetikon dikaion*), typical of the moral and political realm. The concept of individual desert is presented as the juncture between the moral, the legal and the political fields.

D. Bonanno: Research financed by the A.v. Humboldt Foundation - Bonn.

D. Bonanno (✉)
Faculty of Culture and Society, University of Palermo, Palermo, Italy
e-mail: daniela.bonanno@unipa.it

L. Corso
Faculty of Economics and Law, Kore University of Enna, Enna, Italy
e-mail: lucia.corso@unikore.it

11.1   Introduction

In the *Rhetoric*[1] (1386b 8–16) Aristotle defines *nemesis*[2] as the emotional reaction felt by a noble character in the event of unmerited good fortune. *Nemesis* is inserted by Aristotle in a network of emotions, which are connected to each other by complex relationships of contraposition, symmetry and complementarity. The term *nemesis* is commonly translated by the modern concept of indignation, which usually refers to *a general form* of injustice. Departing from the Aristotelian account of emotions related to *nemesis* such as shame, pity, envy and emulation, this paper will examine the role of *nemesis* in its reflection on justice. Secondly, it will take into consideration similarities and differences between the ancient *nemesis* and the modern notion of indignation, by exploring its importance in political thought. The aim of this article is to demonstrate how fruitful the original meaning of the Aristotelian *nemesis* could be, showing its possible application in the legal field and its importance for legal reasoning.

11.2   Nemesis Defined in Aristotelian Terms

11.2.1   Nemesis as a Moral Emotion

Aristotle's attitude towards emotions in the normative discourse is ambivalent. On the one hand, he often hints that specific emotions such as anger (*orge*), envy (*phthonos*) and compassion (*eleos*) may lead to excess or misjudgment[3] (*Rhet.* 1354a1, 24–25), on the other hand, some emotions seem morally appropriate and convenient so that emotional comportment is a moral achievement.[4]

Several of the emotions discussed in the *Rhetoric* appear in the definition of a list of moral virtues in the *Nicomachean Ethics* as a mean between two vices: courage (*andreia*) is a mean between fear (*phobos*) and confidence (*tharros*) (*EN* 1107a33–b4); gentleness (*praotes*) is a mean between irascibility (*orgilotes*) and spiritlessness (*aorgesia*) (1108a3–9); shame (*aidos*), fear of bad reputation, is a mean between shamelessness and being ashamed of everything (*EN* 1108a31–35). Indignation (*nemesis*), pain at unworthy good fortune (*EN* 1108b 3–4 and *Rhet.* II 1386b 11–13), is also described as a *mesotes*, a mean between the vices of envy, feeling pain at everybody's good fortune, and *epichairekakia*, feeling pleasure at everyone's bad fortune (a sort of *Schadenfreude* as a German would say). *Nemesis* figures also in the *Rhetoric* in antithesis to pity (*eleos*). Both are termed emotions proper of

---

[1] Edition used: Aristotle (1926).

[2] He uses the infinitive *to nemesan* of the verb *nemesao*, derived from the noun *nemesis*.

[3] Nussbaum (1996), pp. 318–319. On this particular attitude, see also Gastaldi (1995).

[4] Sherman (1993), p. 2.

a noble character (1386b10–11). Thus, while some emotions must be trained and calibrated,[5] other emotions are fit for moral discourse. *Nemesis* is one of them. It is an emotion which one shall (*dei*) have and in this respect it can be defined as a moral emotion.

11.2.1.1 Nemesis and Aischune

In the *Rhetoric*, Aristotle introduces *nemesis* under the section dedicated to *aischune,* or shame, which is that pain or disturbance regarding that class of evils, in the present, past, or future, which we think will discredit us (*Rhet.* 1383b 14–16). After examining the inner disposition from which shame arises, Aristotle analyses the circumstances, which promote its insurgency. Shame arises before the intransigent individual, the man capable of indignation who is supposed not to be indignant (*ou nemesan*) with others for what he does himself, while he is indignant (*nemesa*) with them for what he does not do himself (*Rhet.* 1384b 2–4).

In contemporary discourse, the tie between shame and indignation is not so obvious. In fact it can happen that shame arises before any kind of authority regardless of its moral character[6] or, on the contrary, that individuals who trigger indignation do not feel ashamed. Aristotle thinks differently: Aristotelian indignation is above all the third party perspective, a sort of impartiality that does not suppose a full personal involvement.[7] It is often translated into English as the "righteous indignation". When defined in relation to shame, Aristotelian indignation seems to be a broad emotion, which is aroused at any act of injustice either actual or perceived. Something similar seems to emerge from the *Eudemian Ethics* (*EE*) where Aristotle says that what the ancients called *nemesis* consists of being pained at [others'] faring ill or faring well contrary to desert, and being pleased at the same states when they are merited (*EE* 1233M6–34).[8] In such broad terms, *nemesis* recalls the concept of indignation provided by Martha Nussbaum as anger triggered by unfairness.[9]

11.2.1.2 Nemesis and Eleos

However, in the *Rhetoric* (1386b9–1387b20), Aristotle defines the feeling of *nemesis* (*to nemesan*) in much narrower terms. Captured in its opposition to pity (*eleos*), it describes the specific emotional reaction to unmerited fortune. While

---

[5]Hardie (1975); Sherman (1993); Hutchinson (1995), esp. pp. 213–232; Shields (2002).

[6]Haidt (2003).

[7]As told by Aristotle: "if a virtuous man does not obtain what is suitable for him, we feel indignant" (*Rhet.* 1387a 11, trans. J. H. Freese).

[8]Konstan (2006) Ch. V, Envy and Indignation.

[9]Nussbaum (2004), p. 75.

feeling pity (*to eleein*) expresses pain for an unmerited misfortune, *to nemesan* refers to unmerited fortune. Both *eleos* and *nemesis* are related to desert while the last one is even ascribed to the gods (*Rhet.* 1386b 2–3). This explains the third party perspective, which *nemesis* conveys.

Today we tend to place indignation inside the broader emotion of anger, but Aristotle's *nemesis* is much narrower.[10] While anger is a

> a longing, accompanied by pain, for a real or apparent revenge for a real or apparent slight, affecting a man himself or one of his friends, when such a slight is undeserved. (*Rhet.* 1378a31–33, trans. J. H. Freese)

Aristotelian indignation differs under three aspects. First, unlike anger, indignation does not require any closeness with the victim of the undeserved slight and it lacks anger's partiality.[11] Second, unlike anger it is not triggered by undeserved suffering but by undeserved fortune so that while anger implies that a harm has occurred, Aristotelian indignation is independent of any harm. Third, Aristotelian indignation is not necessarily tied to any desire to act, like for example the emulation (*zelos*), which will be discussed later. While anger is an emotion accompanied by a conspicuous desire to revenge and therefore has a strong motivational force, we know little about the effects of indignation, at least according to Aristotle. It seems to be more appropriate when looking for a good judgment rather than for taking the correct action.

In a typical Aristotelian style, the bond between pity and indignation is confirmed also at an empirical level. Both emotions are proper of the same kind of individual—the same moral character—so that people capable of experiencing pity are also capable of becoming indignant.

11.2.1.3   Nemesis and Envy

Aristotle stresses the importance of the unmerited acquisition of fortune. People who suffer from the joy or fortunes of others similar to them are not indignant. They are rather envious. In fact, *nemesis* is not envy (*phthonos*). *Phthonos* is envy of the fortune of people in identical conditions (*isos kai homoios*).

> It is equally clear for what reason, and of whom, and in what frame of mind, men are envious, if envy is a kind of pain at the sight of good fortune in regard to the goods mentioned; in the case of those like themselves; and not for the sake of a man getting anything, but because of others possessing it. For those men will be envious who have, or seem to have, others "like" them. (*Rhet.*, 1387b–6, trans. by J. H. Freese)

---

[10]In this respect, it is meaningful that even the scholars of the ancient world often analyze *nemesis* within the semantic field of the wrath: see Cairns (2003), esp. pp. 35–39; Scheid-Tissinier (2007), p. 180; and Scheid-Tissinier (2012).

[11]On the importance of the distance and proximity in the arousal of the emotions, see Ginzburg (1998).

All three emotions, envy, pity and indignation, are other-oriented. They all concern prosperity or misfortune that have occurred to other people and they are not aroused by a process of identification with the other.

11.2.1.4 Nemesis and Zelos

Another other-oriented emotion, which is different from envy, even if it is also addressed at people in similar social conditions, is the emulation, i.e. the pain caused by goods, which are possible to obtain (*Rhet.* 1388a33–b30). Pain does not arise from the fact that others possess such goods, but from the fact that people, who are in same social conditions (birth and reputation etc.) as those who own these goods, do not own them. According to Aristotle, *zelos* is a virtuous emotion and typical of virtuous men (*epieikes esti* [. . .] *kai epieikon*). *Zelos* works as a stimulus to act and reach goods that one believes to be worthy. Although in this case Aristotle does not speak of merit, it is evident that the consciousness of his own desert is the basis for a proper push to emulation. *Nemesis* and *zelos* are therefore complementary emotions: both are positive, other-oriented and based on a consideration of the individual desert.[12]

11.2.1.5 Nemesis as a Moderate Emotion

Nemesis is moderate. It is capable to counterbalance not solely envy and malice but also excessive pity. In fact, indignation implies a characteristic trait of the person, who experiences it. Solely ambitious men are disposed to be indignant. On the contrary men of servile disposition who are not ambitious are not prone to be indignant for they do not think to be worthy of anything.

> Men are prone to indignation, first, if they happen to deserve or possess the greatest advantages, secondly, if they happen to be virtuous and worthy, for they both judge correctly and hate what is unjust. And those who are ambitious and long for certain positions, especially if they are those which others, although unworthy, have obtained. And, in general, those who think themselves worthy of advantages of which they consider others unworthy, are inclined to be indignant with the latter and because of these advantages. This is why the servile and worthless and unambitious are not inclined to indignation; for there is nothing of which they think themselves worthy. (*Rhet.* 1387b 4–15, trans. by J. H. Freese)

Anger, like indignation, is also a mean between two excesses, irascibility and excessive compliance. Both hot-tempered individuals who are too quick to get angry and sulky individuals who tend to repress their emotion are not inclined to make good judgements. The same applies to indignation. Individuals who lack

---

[12]On the relationship between *envy, nemesis and zelos*, see Gastaldi (1990), pp. 28–30 and more recently, Castelli (2015).

indignation, because of their servile disposition, may be inclined to excessive indulgence.

11.2.1.6 Merit

What makes Aristotelian indignation a moral emotion is among other things its strict tie with the concept of merit. The other's prosperity excites the indignant solely when undeserved.

> [. . .] for instance, no good man would be pained at seeing parricides or assassins punished; we should rather rejoice at their lot, and at that of men who are deservedly fortunate; for both these are just and cause the worthy man to rejoice, because he cannot help hoping that what has happened to his like may also happen to himself. And all these feelings arise from the same character and their contraries from the contrary. (*Rhet.*, 1386 b 4–5, trans. by J. H. Freese)

Nemesis is a complex emotion which cannot be reduced to a bodily event and a material process, such as "a ferment of the blood or heat which is about the heart."[13] (*DA* 403a31–b1) but implies a cognitive framework. Unlike other emotions which often have non rational variants as the cases of anger (*orge*) (*Rhet.* 1369a4–5) and desire (*epithumia*) (*EN* 1149a21–b2), *nemesis* seems to assume that rules of certain moral and social codes have been internalized. It cannot be understood outside a conception of the good concerning the appropriateness of a given condition. In line with the Aristotelian way of arguing in practical reason, such a concept of good cannot be established in general terms, but requires a particular context. Aristotelian indignation is excited when the standards of correspondence and appropriateness are violated. But these standards could be captured solely within a specific context. For instance, Aristotle explains, it is appropriate for the brave man, not the just man, to have fine weapons. It is appropriate for men of good families, not for parvenus, to make distinguished marriages. Similarly, it is appropriate for the inferior to respect the superior rather than objecting the hierarchy, such as when a musician contends with a just man, as justice is better than music (*Rhet.*, 1387a–b).

Since the standards of correspondence and appropriateness are ingrained into experience, it may happen that indignation is aroused by an *apparent cause of injustice*. Also common places may excite the indignant. Thus, Aristotle clarifies that because what is long established seems akin to what exists by nature; therefore we feel more indignation at those possessing a given good if they have as a matter of fact only just got it and the prosperity it brings with it. This explains why

> [. . .] the newly rich cause more annoyance than those who have long possessed or inherited wealth. The same applies to offices of state, power, numerous friends, virtuous children, and any other advantages of the kind. And if these advantages bring them some other advantage, men are equally indignant; for in this case also the newly rich who attain to

---

[13] Aristotle (1907).

office owing to their wealth cause more annoyance than those who have long been wealthy; and similarly in all other cases of the same kind. (*Rhet.*, 1387b, trans. by J. H. Freese)

11.2.1.7 Nemesis and Ploutos

In the *Rhetoric*, *nemesis* is not addressed towards any form of injustice and it is not triggered by any unjustified or unexpected fortune. It is aroused by undeserved fortune, but in the Aristotelian vocabulary merit is strictly tied to action that is under human control. *Nemesis* does not directly refer to courage, beauty or virtue, since these are traits, which are held by nature (*Rhet.* II 9, 1387b). It is not elicited by moral luck[14] and is rather triggered by the sight of wealth (*ploutos*) and power (dunamis), and, and especially by the knowledge that power is acquired through wealth rather than virtue.

> For if indignation is being pained at the sight of good fortune that is apparently undeserved, in the first place it is clear that it is not possible to feel indignation at all good things; for no one will be indignant with a man who is just or courageous, or may acquire any virtue for one does not feel pity in the case of opposites of those qualities, but men are indignant at wealth, power, in a word, at all the advantages of which good men are worthy. [And those who possess natural advantages, such as noble birth, beauty, and all such things.]. (*Rhet.*, 1387a 9–15, trans. by J. H. Freese)

Having as a target predominantly material goods and power, Aristotelian indignation has a strong social function as it encourages a reflection regarding the right distribution of wealth and honor.

11.2.1.8 Nemesis in Synthesis

Let's recapitulate Aristotle's idea of indignation. *Nemesis* is an emotion elicited by the sight of underserved good fortune, which mediates between envy, malice and excessive compassion. It is proper of a noble character, that is of an individual not solely capable of moral actions but who also perceives himself as worthy of respect and of those goods, which have been unduly acquired by others. Aristotelian indignation implies a natural sense of the proper order in society and more specifically is aroused by the violation of the principle that the bad suffer and the good man prosper.[15] Being ingrained into a general feeling of how things go in the world, it tends to have a conservative strand. Aristotelian indignation is a reaction especially addressed against sudden changes, such as the revolt of the inferior against the superior; the sudden entrance of the newly rich into the political arena; the transgression of given borders as when the musician claims to know better than the wise man about issues of justice. Aristotelian indignation in other words has an

---

[14]Williams (1981) and Nagel (1979).
[15]Burger (1991), p. 127.

almost preservative dimension. Contemporary moral biologists would argue that it is functional in keeping order, but Aristotle makes a more ambitious claim, tying indignation to justice.

11.2.2 Aristotle's Nemesis and the Idea of Justice

Aristotle makes two claims about *nemesis*, which have normative implications. First, *nemesis* contributes to justice as natural virtue (*EE* 1234a 31). Second, *nemesis* is a proper emotion to elicit in the judges (*Rhet.*, 1387b 18–20).[16] The conceptual tie between nemesis and justice is "merit". The idea of merit is central in the discussion contained in Book V of *EN* where justice in the complete and whole sense, *dikaiosyne*, is defined

> that moral disposition which renders men apt to do just things, and which causes them to act justly and to wish what is just. (*EN* 1129a 7–10, trans. Rackham)

After having made a distinction between justice in the complete or whole sense, and justice in a particular sense (*EN* 1129a 30–1130b10), Aristotle specifies that the latter shall be subdivided into one which is exhibited in the distribution of honor, property and anything else which is divisible among those who share in the commonwealth and the other which is called rectificatory justice (*EN* 1131b 25–1133b28), that involves predominantly the resolution of disputes and the righting of wrongs in the subpolitical and private social relations among individuals. In each realm, fairness means equality in some sense, but not necessarily simple equality or arithmetic equality. Distributive justice (*EN* 1131a–b) (*dianemetikon dikaion*) is the realm where merit could matter the most. Calculations of the just results need to be informed by a principle of proportionality where equal individuals obtain equal goods and unequal individuals obtain unequal goods. The calculation cannot be done without reference to the idea of merit. Many modern and contemporary rights-orientated philosophers, such as Rawls, believe that distributive justice is not a matter of rewarding virtue or moral desert but to provide a fair framework of rights where individuals can pursue their own values.[17] Aristotle puts things differently. Justice consists in giving people what they deserve and a just society is one that enables human beings to realize their highest nature and to live a good life.

---

[16]According to Maroney (in this volume) anger is the most appropriate emotion to support the judgement. In her opinion, anger is the "quintessentially judicial emotion", Maroney (2018). More convincing is the position of Rapp (also in this volume), who more prudently suggests that *nemesis* could be a better candidate to explain the emotional experience of the judge. He proposes to revise the myth that according to Aristotle "an emotional judge" would be better than a "dispassionate" one. Rapp (2018).

[17]Scheffler (2000), p. 965.

An individual who seeks more than his fair share of various goods has the vice of greediness (*pleonexia*), and a just individual is one who has rational insight into his own merits in various situations and who habitually (and without having to make heroic efforts to control contrary impulses) takes no more than what he merits, no more than his fair share of good things.[18] However, there is no agreement on the exact definition of merit. Democrats identify it with the status of freemen, supporters of oligarchy with wealth (or noble birth) and supporters of aristocracy with excellence (*EN* 1132a 25).

To capture the content of merit it is necessary to refer to the teleological way of reasoning in ethics and politics. Because the goal (*telos*) of the state and political community is the good life, those citizens who contribute most to the purpose of the community are the ones who should be most rewarded.[19] We can speculate that Aristotle is making reference to the financial contributions (*ta eisenechthenta*), (*EN* 1131b 31)[20] which wealthy citizens used to make through the system of liturgies, sustaining the cost for the organization of choruses, religious feasts, public banquets, or the trierarchies in classical Athens. Often the indicted in a criminal trial would use his monetary contribution to the *polis* as a means of defense (Lysias, VII 31; XXV 12; XXX 26). However, the idea of merit shall not be limited to patrimonial contributions. Politics shall be mostly accessible to virtuous men, for these are the most inclined to deliberate and argue about the right and the wrong, the just and the unjust. *Nemesis* is elicited when political offices are not distributed on the basis of honor and virtue but on the basis of wealth.

Aristotle intends merit as a standard of appropriateness and convenience (*harmotton*) so that the individual's place in society is determined by where one best fits. Flutes need to be given to the best flute players because flutes are made to be played well and such a distribution would foster excellence the most (*Pol.* 1282b). *Nemesis* is excited when the best flutes are given to the wealthiest or to those people who crave for admiration regardless of their merits.

11.2.3 Nemesis and Rectificatory Justice

The second kind of justice plays a rectificatory part in transactions between man and man (*EN*, 1131a 5–10). This form of justice, Aristotle explains, has a different specific character from the former. In the second dimension equality in the simple or arithmetic sense prevails, and the rule is equality before the law-the same treatment of all persons, regardless of differences in character or achievement or need. Apparently merit does not seem to matter:

---

[18] Slote (2002).

[19] Sandel (2009), p. 295.

[20] Cf. also Adkins (1960), pp. 195–219.

> For it makes no difference whether a good man has defrauded a bad man or a bad one a
> good one, nor whether it is a good or a bad man that has committed adultery; the law looks
> only at the nature of damage, treating the parties as equal, and merely asking whether one
> has done and the other suffered injustice, whether one inflicted and the other has sustained
> damage. (*EN* 1132a, 2–6, trans. by Rackham)

The judge called to adjudicate these kind of controversies shall be impartial, a kind of mediator capable to reestablish the perfect equality among the parties. This is the reason why the judge is called *dikastes*, for his task is to divide in equal parts (*dicha*). *Dichastes* is the one who adjudicates by dividing in equal parts (*EN* 1132a 30).

If merit is not relevant to rectificatory justice why would *nemesis* be a proper emotion for making good judgement, as the *Rhetoric* emphatically states? Aristotle does not say it explicitly, however, we can make the hypothesis that some kind of merit is in a way relevant also in legal adjudication. The equalization made by the judge is, in fact, a form of distribution:

> Hence the unjust being here the unequal, the judge endeavors to equalize it: inasmuch as
> when one man has received and the other has inflicted a blow, or one has killed and the
> other been killed, the line representing the suffering and doing of the deed is divided into
> unequal parts, but the judge endeavors to make them equal by the penalty or loss he
> imposes, taking away the gain. (*EN* 1132a 6–10, trans. by H. Rackham)

Although legal reasoning does not require an in depth judgement on the appropriateness or convenience of the gain, it still implies an attitude which chastises the unmerited good fortune, the undeserved gain. The debtor who does not comply with the terms of the agreement is similar to the thief. They both have acquired an unmerited position with regards to the moral order. The law does not relieve the judge from the task to rebuke the unmerited gain. It does only exonerate him from an in depth judgement on the moral appropriateness of the gain. It is not the role of the judge to establish whether the debtor is good man and therefore whether he really deserves a portion of the wealth of the creditor. However, defaults in payments of a debt, unlawful appropriations of other possessions and even assaults or homicides amount to the acquisition of an unmerited position of advantage. Penalties and damages are the means to equalize, that is to bring the distribution to the correct standard:

> Hence Justice in involuntary transactions is a mean between gain and loss in a sense: it is to
> have after the transaction an amount equal to the amount one had before it. (*EN*
> 1132b20–25, trans. by H. Rackham)

Perhaps *nemesis* was an emotion which could contribute to the *gnome dikaiotate*, the most just understanding, on whose basis the Athenian *dikastai* swore to judge before entering the court (Demosthenes, *Against Aristocrates*, 96–97). This is why, as the Eudemian Ethics states, nemesis is an emotion which contributes to justice (*dikaiosune*), as envy (*phthonos*) leads to injustice (*adikia*) and shame (*aidos*) to wisdom (*sophrosune*).[21]

---

[21]According to Burger (1991), *nemesis* is the psychological horizon acting as the background of the Aristotelian reflection on justice; it is the *pathos* motivating justice in the human soul. For this

11.3 Aristotelian Nemesis and Indignation in Contemporary Discourse: Differences and Similarities

The Aristotelian definition of *nemesis* as pain at unmerited fortune is an aspect of a broader conception where indignation is intended as an emotional reaction elicited by what is perceived as unfairness and injustice. There is, however, a more significant difference between the Aristotelian treatment of emotions and the contemporary analyses of the indignation. The recent interest in emotions, and in social emotions in particular, has mostly an explanatory intent while the normative aspect seems less relevant. In the vein of Hume and other moral sentimentalists, emotions are scrutinized not with the aim of advancing a set of justifications for collective action but mostly to explain social, political or legal behavior.[22] This approach, favoured in prevalence by cognitive psychologists, sociologists and political scientists, has had the merit to offer detailed analyses of social emotions but has neglected their normative forces.

Indignation has attracted particular attention especially in virtue of some recurring features. First, indignation is commonly interpreted as referring to a complex emotion where the moral and social dimensions prevail over the natural. Anger, for example, may be elicited by a form of goal blockage; similarly, disgust has a non-moral primordial form, called core disgust, which is best described as a guardian of the mouth against potential contaminants. Indignation, however, implies a cognitive framework and a certain degree of internalization of moral and social norms. Second, unlike shame or embarrassment which are self-focused, indignation is turned outward to others and is commonly classified within the "other critical" moral sentiments, a cluster of related but distinguishable emotional reactions to the moral violations of others. Haidt groups all variants of indignation under the other-condemning family, while Izard refers to them as the hostility emotions. Third, indignation is elicited by a various array of norms violations. The recent literature on social norms has stressed the centrality of the hostility emotions, and of indignation, in explaining punishment and norm enforcement.[23] Indignation is reputed central to the act of blaming.[24]

---

reason, Burger claims: "as a psychological dimension behind the institutional-mathematical analysis of justice [. . .], it is not mere accidental but essential that *nemesis* remain hidden. It is a prerequisite for any sustainable political community that the desire for nature itself to punish the bad be converted into confidence in the law and satisfaction through it" (p. 131). This assumption seems to be based on two observations: first of all, the absence of "piety" in the *EN*, which appears instead in the *Rhetoric* as an emotion counterbalancing the *nemesis*; secondly, on the problematic status of the latter. *Nemesis* is in fact inserted by Aristotle among the ethical virtues, while not being a virtue at all and then it apparently disappears from the discussion. Even if quite stimulating, the *argumentum e silentio* does not seem sufficient to validate this thesis.

[22] Viola (2014).

[23] Dubreuil (2010b).

[24] Strawson (1962), p. 1.

Despite the agreement on some general traits of indignation, the analyses of the emotion differ at least under three aspects concerning its content, its causes as an intentional state, and its function from an evolutionary perspective. With regards to the content, departing from the narrow Aristotelian conception, Rozin et al. (1999) suggest that indignation comes in three variants: contempt, anger and disgust. More in particular the authors argue that each variant is seen as a response to violations of three different moral codes called, respectively, the ethics of community in the case of contempt, autonomy in the case of anger, and divinity in the case of disgust. For example, while indignation/anger is linked to unjustified insults, transgressions and rights violations against the self or to those close the self, indignation/disgust is a moral emotion through which actions and events that remind us that we are animals—such as sex, dirt, eating—are highly regulated, hidden, or condemned.[25] Indignation/contempt on the other hand is often linked to hierarchy and a vertical dimension of social evaluation.

The idea of defining indignation as an umbrella concept under which anger, contempt and disgust can be grouped, has several detractors. Dubreuil for example states that while indignation is elicited by judgments about unfairness, anger is triggered by unexpected harm.[26] Righteous anger, Dubreuil argues, obtains when the two mechanisms are triggered in concert. While unfairness in itself only motivates weak forms of punishment, the visceral emotion of the righteous anger motivates strong punishment, but is only elicited by unexpectedly unfair behavior. Nussbaum strongly objects the assimilation between indignation on the one hand and contempt and disgust on the other and claims that while the first may be a useful emotion to be mastered by a judge, the latter shall be banned from legal reasoning. Other authors have defined indignation as the reaction of the impartial third party observing something's getting away with norm violation.[27] Such a definition implies the hypothesis of an altruistic judgmental attitude not necessarily tied to any harm which would make indignation more similar to empathy than to anger and which is sometime expressed as altruistic anger[28]; while other theorists have blurred the line between indignation and envy, stating that the first is solely a revised reaction of the latter.[29]

Regarding the causes of indignation as an intentional state, Sunstein and Kahneman argue that the emotion can be explained in two quite different ways: by referring to reasons, or to psychological causes. In the first case, indignation is triggered by the reason, which has caused the negative judgement. The categorization of the action provides a reason for indignation, a reason that the observer expects other objective observers to endorse.[30] According to the other view,

---

[25] An example may be given by the law on purity contained in the *Leviticus*.

[26] Dubreuil (2010a), p. 26.

[27] Vromen (2012), pp. 174–175.

[28] Mouchiroud and Zenasni (2013), p. 394.

[29] Elster (2007), p. 159.

[30] Sunstein (2009), p. 407; Kahneman and Sunstein (2007), p. 2.

indignation is not tied to reasons. It is similar to fear of spiders, where one does not fear spiders because they are dangerous, one just fears them. The perception of dangerousness is not the reason for the fear or even its cause; both the fear and the perception are symptoms of an uncontrolled reaction to spiders.

Let's finally turn to the social function of indignation. It is now widely accepted that emotions exist to motivate social behavior. Anger and indignation direct others to desist from what they are doing not to face punishment. Moral emotions are regulators of moral actions directed toward vice-ridden persons.[31] Haidt argues that indignation is functional to assist individuals in their effort to cooperate by creating a fire alarm against untrustworthy people:

> In endless hours of gossip people work together to catch cheaters, liars, hypocrites, and others who are trying to fake the appearance of being reliable interaction partners.[32]

It has also a preserving function, aiming at protecting the social order against sudden changes. Other authors have suggested broader explanations, such as the need of humans to distance themselves from their animal origins or the need to preserve a hierarchical order within society.[33]

Aristotle's *nemesis* differs from the contemporary analyses under all three aspects above, i.e. content, cause and function. First, *nemesis* is not the emotional reaction towards anything or anyone, which is perceived as a threat for social integrity, as moral evolutionists assume. It is triggered by a special kind of disapproval, that is the transgression of the principle that goods shall be appropriate and convenient for the individual acquiring them. Unlike most moral emotions involved in the act of blaming, *nemesis'* target is not a behavior or a character but a state of affair. Indignation is elicited by an inappropriate distribution. It may, obviously, be aroused also in connection with certain conducts as when a politician gains power not because of her virtue but because of her wealth. In the Aristotelian picture, however, the emotion is mainly addressed against the result of the conduct—the unmerited gain—rather than the conduct itself.

Second, Aristotle would reject the close alternative prospected by Sunstein and Kahneman according to which either indignation has a cause in a reason or it results from a psychological impulse. If people feel indignant when the newly rich come into power it means that the acquisition of power through wealth is wrong. Emotions may help to reach an objective moral truth. Although a discussion on Aristotle's concept of practical reason would lead us too far, it could be argued that the contribution of emotions in moral discernment is strictly tied to a properly functioning subjectivity of a moral agent. The virtuous individual is able to experience the proper emotions and grasp the moral truth.[34]

---

[31]Weiner (2006), p. 96.

[32]Haidt (2003), p. 860.

[33]Rozin et al. (1999).

[34]Fitterer (2008).

Third, *nemesis* has a moral function which is not limited to social integrity, but is mostly related to social order. Social order, for Aristotle, has a moral dimension and it is not simply tied to survival. Such an order implies that the bad suffers and the good prospers, but it also demands that a certain natural design is maintained. Nemesis is an emotion, which gives assistance to justice: it helps citizens to judge people in power as well as it helps the judge to fairly adjudicate among the parties of a legal proceeding.

To sum up, on the one side, *nemesis* seems to be similar to the modern notion of indignation under the following aspects: first, it is fundamentally other-oriented; secondly, it implies a cognitive framework and finally it presumes a certain degree of internalization of social and moral rules. On the other side, it differs, as mentioned above, in terms of content, cause and function.

11.4   Pain at Unmerited Good Fortune in Politics

That emotions play a role in political discourse is an opinion thousands of years old.[35] There is no agreement, however, on their normative force. Spinoza for example argues that commands which arouse the indignation (*indignatio*) of many persons can hardly be part of the law of the commonwealth; and explains that indignation is the "guidance of Nature", which causes citizens to join together in resistance.[36] Hume defines indignation as the innate emotion aroused by violence and injury, which leads us to action. Kant ties indignation to self-respect.[37]

The bad reputation of indignation has, however, superseded the good one. Seneca claims that indignation is that sort of anger which springs from too high an opinion of one's virtues (*a nimio sui suspectu*) and consequently creates an irrational, disproportionate view of other's faults (*De Ira* V 7). Following Seneca, the satirist Juvenal adds that indignation, with its hypocrisy and self-assertion often becomes self-indulgence. The indignant judge childishly enjoys taking vengeance on some criminals; and even when the angry man lacks the power to carry through its vengeful designs, he still indulges himself in the desire (*cupiditas*) for punishment and self-expression.[38]

In Nietzsche's description, indignation/resentment is a mixture of rancor and envy. The person of *resentment*, Nietzsche claims, is neither sincere, nor naive, nor honest and frank with himself. His soul looks obliquely at things; his spirit loves hiding places, secret passages and back doors, everything hidden strikes him as his

---

[35]Nussbaum (2013).

[36]Spinoza (n.d.), ch. III, p. 9.

[37]Kant (1963), p. 12.

[38]Anderson (2014), p. 337.

world, his security, his balm; he knows all about being silent, not forgetting, waiting, belittling oneself for the moment, humbling oneself.[39] The indignant man is "he who perpetually tears and lacerates himself with his own teeth [and ...] is the more ordinary, more indifferent, and less instructive case. And no one is such a liar as the indignant man."[40] Although departing from the explicit terms of Nietzsche, such a view has not disappeared. The idea that indignation is a middle class attitude mostly based on rancor rather than on a natural sense of justice has remained popular, at least until the 1960s. In 1964 Harold Lasswell edited a new edition of Ranulf's study which defined indignation a middle class emotion,[41] while Adorno et al. tied the inclination towards indignation to an authoritarian personality.[42]

In recent years, indignation has gained a new popularity in political discourse both at a descriptive and at a normative level. From a descriptive point of view, indignation helps to explain citizens' behavior and ponder affection for people in power. Aristotle's analysis illuminates on its inherent ambivalence and therefore results particularly helpful for a political analysis.

In political discourse, Aristotelian *nemesis* follows two opposite trajectories. On the one hand, indignation expresses a more or less explicit suspicion towards new entrants into politics. It is the feeling of the old bureaucracy in power or the traditional parties' ruling class towards neophytes; of the elderly towards the young; of the incumbent towards the opponent. Under this respect it is a "top-down"[43] emotion where a conservative dimension prevails. On the other hand, however, indignation follows the opposite direction and signals a good degree of disaffection of citizen for individuals in power. Indignation is not excited by crimes committed by common people or by old time criminals, for in these cases the emotional reaction to the act of injustice is anger or contempt or disgust, but not *nemesis*. *Nemesis* is elicited by misconduct of powerful people, exploitation, corruption of public officers. The emotion, as Aristotle correctly grasped, does not simply amount to anger before any kind of unfairness but it is more specifically directed against excess, hubris, arrogance and especially transgressions of a special role in society. This is why we may feel angry at a pedophile but feel indignant when the abuse is committed by a teacher or a spiritual guide.

From a normative point of view, the idea that good fortune needs to be based on some kind of moral justification seems to have retained its relevance today. It is true that in democratic regimes access to public office is mostly the result of elections rather than merit, and contemporary economic theories do not reject excessive accumulation for the sake of distribution. However, the normative force of *nemesis* shall not be underestimated. Contemporary political and economic debates cannot ignore the issue of desert. This is why *nemesis* retains its importance also in the

---

[39]Nietzsche (1994), I, p. 21.

[40]Nietzsche (1998), II, p. 26:21.

[41]Ranulf (1938).

[42]Adorno et al. (1950).

[43]Cf. Konstan (2006), p. 125.

normative domain. Democratic theorists are engaged in the analyses of the proper procedures—districting, voting laws, primaries—through which selecting the best candidates. Economic theorists rarely neglect moral issues and base accumulation on peculiar forms of merit, such as capability to take risks, intelligence, financial intuitions and so forth.

Most of contemporary constitutions try to accommodate the wishes of *nemesis*. Article 97 of the Italian Constitution provides that access to public offices shall be the result of a public selection based on the merit. Article 34 provides that deserving students shall be assisted with grants or vouchers to families. In order to reduce unmerited suffering, the government provides for a system of welfare (article 38) and to pursue such a goal the Republic shall remove those social and economic obstacles which impede the full development of the human being (article 3, 2 Const.).

Article 21 of the European Convention of Human Rights provides that the judges (of the European Court of Justice) shall be of high moral character and must either possess the qualification required for appointment . . . or be jurisconsults of recognized competence. Similarly Article III section I of the US Constitution provides that judges shall hold their office during good behavior.

In other words, the feeling of pain at unmerited good fortune not solely is able to explain some common dynamics in politics, but can have a normative function as well. We may speculate about the specific content of merit, Aristotle argues, but we can rarely neglect it when allocating power and resources.

11.5 Nemesis and Legal Reasoning

Nemesis' contribution to legal reasoning seems more troubling. First, the role played by emotions in law is still subjects of strong debates; second, even acknowledging the emotional aspect of legal judgement, *nemesis*, intended as pain at undeserved good fortune, seems not appropriate for legal adjudication. We will try to defeat both kinds of objections.

The first argument against the role of *nemesis* in legal discourse is common to most moral emotions and states that indignation may be, actually often is, irrational and may lead to wrong moral, political or legal decisions. The cognitive emptiness of the indignant may result in "puzzling outcomes, in both politics and law," such as moral dumbfounding.[44] Sunstein and Kahneman have extensively written on the negative impact of indignation on legal adjudication and have blamed indignant jurors for excessive punitive damages awards; distorted risk calculation and group polarization. Indignation is often associated with penal populism, i.e. a generalized craving for severe punishments and strict criminal rules combined with a strong suspicion against due process guarantees.

---

[44]Kahneman and Sunstein (2007), p. 2.

Critiques of the sort of Sunstein and Kahnemann's are commonly rebutted both at an empirical and a normative level. Empirically, it is argued, emotions cannot be suppressed even in a legal trial, for the judgement could not be based solely on cognitive reasons.[45] The effort should, if anything, be addressed to regulate the emotions rather than neglecting them.[46] The normative reply, which has been gaining credit and extension in the last 30 years with regards to most social emotions,[47] argues that indignation is the natural basis of the act of blaming without which no legal judgement may be delivered.[48] Rather than saying with Aristotle that indignation counterbalances malice, envy and excessive compassion, it could be argued that indignation is the strongest natural devise against apathy and indifference and that therefore its normative significance cannot be underestimated. If human beings were not endowed with an emotion elicited by the sight of unfairness, irrespective of any harm suffered, normative systems, including legal systems, would collapse. The third party perspective makes indignation, as wittily Aristotle grasped, the best suited among the emotions for making a normative judgement. It is true that indignation may have some downfalls: it lacks a strong motivational force, especially when experienced in solitary, and it may be elicited by an apparent cause of unfairness, as when we confuse what appears to have been always what it is with what is real. But indignation is not envy or rancor or resentment. It cannot simply be explained as the unconscious desire to project inner negative qualities to others object of condemnation. Following Aristotle, indignation is an authentic emotion from which we may infer the existence of a natural disposition towards justice.

The second argument against the relevance of indignation in legal reasoning may be specifically addressed at the narrow definition of Aristotle as pain at unmerited fortune. The judge adjudicating a case shall deliver a *prima facie* judgement on the unmerited gain. However, it could be argued that legal reasoning is mainly rooted on the blame of harmful behavior, such as the breach of a promise or violence, and of the antisocial dispositions that stand behind the illegal conducts, such as greediness, disloyalty, and aggressiveness. The wrongful distribution of wealth and honor seems to be recessive in this picture.

Attributing to the Aristotelian *nemesis* some weight in legal reasoning implies a different vision of law, where laws are not simply intended as defenses against human vulnerability to a wide variety of harms,[49] but shall be conceived as a normative system intended to achieve a certain moral order. Laws, it is true, are means to give or confirm temporary situations of advantage, however, they are at the same time a tool to question and overturn the contingent order. *Nemesis*, Aristotle argues, tends to replicate nature, so that old time riches look more

---

[45]Such a reply is common to most legal realists; see Ratnapala (2009), pp. 108–109.

[46]Maroney (2011a).

[47]Among others: Maroney (2011b), Bandes (2009), and Henderson (1993).

[48]Smith (2013), p. 27.

[49]Nussbaum (2004), pp. 6–7.

deserving that new ones. It makes suspicious towards radical changes. The *dikastes* shall not indulge in inquiring whether the creditor initially deserved the property he lent; and no legal judgement is required on the legitimate original title of the dispossessed. Law, unlike politics, comes into the scene of moral behavior when most of human interactions have taken places: when transactions have been performed and when cooperation had already displaced its effects. This is not, however, the end of the story. For law, with its proceedings, its oratory and mostly with its emotions, is able to subvert the pre-legal order. These changes are slow, because the legal system is endowed with viscosity; but they are unavoidable.

With such a background the role of the Aristotelian *nemesis* becomes more clear. Aristotle was keen to preserve an analytic approach and by distinguishing distributive and rectificatory justice he clarified that politics and law are separate matters. The strictly legal *nemesis* is functional to the preservation of the order, which the legal system has endorsed: the unmerited gain shall be equalized through adjudication regardless of the worth of the winning party. However, Aristotle was fully aware that the distinction between politics, law and morality could not be absolute. In-depth judgements on the authentic merit of some acquisition cannot be totally expelled. Law cannot be indifferent to moral shades and cannot treat in the same manner voluntary and involuntary misconducts. This was especially true in ancient Greece, where trials resembled public dramas and the parties could appeal to the emotions of the jurors. Distributive and rectificatory justice, although separated from a theoretical point of view, would commonly overlap.[50] This is why the indicted could demur in his defense that his contribution to the *polis* had been extensive and hope for an acquittal (Lysias, *supra*) and this is why the judge could appeal to the broader field of equity (*epieikeia*) when the case was not resolved with the help of the law.[51]

> And it is equitable to pardon human weaknesses, and to look, not to the law but to the legislator; not to the letter of the law but to the intention of the legislator; not to the action itself, but to the moral purpose (*prohairesis*); not to the part, but to the whole; not to what a man is now, but to what he has been, always or generally; to remember good rather than ill treatment, and benefits received rather than those conferred. (*Rhet.*, 1374b 17–18, trans. by J. H. Freese)

While law implies a pre legal social order, it is apt to modify it through forensic rhetoric and legal techniques. Eliciting citizens' emotions, *nemesis* above all, is a tool towards this aim. *Nemesis* is an evidence of the connection between law and politics, between law and morality.

---

[50]Viola and Zaccaria (2003), p. 77.

[51]About the contribution of the *epieikeia* to the Athenian justice, Harris (2013).

11.6   Law and Unmerited Fortune: The Double Face of Indignation

Indignation, in its narrow variant depicted by Aristotle, is a two-faced Janus. On the one hand, the indignant resists to social changes. *Nemesis* is elicited when the proper role of the office-holder is transgressed. Under this respect, *nemesis* resembles the definition of contempt provided by Rozin et al. where the emotion is elicited by the violation of a moral code implying a communitarian ethics. Being linked to hierarchy, *nemesis* has a conservative function. It supervises the proper distinction among different logic of actions. For example, while flute-players may excel in music, they shall not claim a special position in politics because music and justice have different criteria of excellence. In contemporary discourse, we could say that actors and showmen as well as successful business men are not necessarily the best suited to hold political offices, because the goal of politics is much broader than the specific aims of show business and entrepreneurship. *Nemesis* is the natural disposition to resist changes and forces citizens to think twice about social movements pervaded by excessive enthusiasm and optimism. *Nemesis* carries the wisdom of viscosity against social hysteria. So intended, *nemesis* has a dark side which resides in the prejudicial defense of privilege against equality and innovation or worst in the snobbish haughtiness resisting social upgrades. On the other hand, *nemesis* may lead to the opposite consequences. It requires a self-conscious attitude, which makes the citizen confident of his political opinion and fosters a continuous engagement. *Nemesis* opens the way to political participation and strengthens the sense of entitlement on public affairs. Being mostly directed at prosperous people, people who have acquired prosperity undeservedly, *nemesis* activates a vigilant eye on political office holders and in general on individuals which bear public responsibility. *Nemesis* carries on an incessant battle towards equalization.[52] This second face of *nemesis* is in some way the opposite of the first. Here *nemesis* is the legitimating force for civil disobedience, the vehement protest against excess and hubris. It is not surprising that recent protest social movements such as *Indignados*, *Occupy Wall Street* or No-Tav (in Italy) make frequent reference to the emotion of indignation to chastise the undeserved acquisition of power (*ploutos and dunamis* combined) of their target enemies.[53] Although it may be argued that anger rather than Aristotelian indignation is in place here, it shall be stressed that *Aristotle's nemesis* provides legitimacy to some forms of protests. Not only anger or envy motivates social protests. Aristotle's analysis may suggest that also a reflection on the unmerited good fortune may offer a normative tool for political opposition.

---

[52]Shields (2002).

[53]Abrams (2011), p. 588.

We could reformulate our thoughts with an example coming from the US Supreme Court. In the infamous decision *Plessy v. Ferguson*[54] upholding the constitutionality of state laws requiring racial segregation in public facilities, *nemesis* was at work on both sides of the battle. *Nemesis* was the feeling of the whites who perceived the mixed train carriages as a form of contamination. It was therefore the emotional basis of the doctrine "separate but equal". However, *nemesis* was also the sentiment underlying the challenge of Homer Plessy and of all the black people who were forced to experience the humiliation of being distanced from the white seats. It was such a feeling which would have been vindicated more than 50 years later in *Brown v. Topeka Board of Education*.[55]

Aristotle tried to immunize *nemesis* from its dark shadows, tying the emotion to a continuous effort for calibration against despicable excesses such as envy and malice. The philosopher may have underestimated *nemesis*' dark sides, for indignation does often cross its moderate borders to become a snobbish attitude on the one hand, and an irrational form of protest on the other. Aristotle's analysis, however, maintains an immense value for it sheds lights on *nemesis*'s ambivalence and as a consequence illuminates on law and politics' ambivalence towards privilege and power. On the one hand, *nemesis* invigorates the typical legal preference for status quo. On the other, however, it opens up the doors for protest and social equality.

11.7   Conclusions

Aristotle's analysis helps us to capture an element, which is usually disregarded when addressing the role that indignation may play in law and politics. Today there are two common attitudes towards this emotion: either it is associated with negative sentiments such as envy or excessive anger, or, on the contrary, it is elevated to the noble attitude of the moral man able to detect any injustice. Aristotle tells us that neither approach is fully appropriate: for *nemesis* on the one hand seems to prove that human beings may be driven by a moral impulse; however, on the other hand, he consolidates the opinion that even benign emotions are rooted in human psychology as well as being culturally conditioned. *Nemesis* as pain at unmerited good fortune exemplifies the idea that moral inclinations are based on psychological mechanisms, which experience and education may mold but not eradicate.

---

[54]163 U.S. 537 (1896).
[55]347 U.S. 483 (1954).

References

Abrams, Kathryn. 2011. Emotions in the Mobilization of Rights. *Harvard Civil Rights-Civil Liberties Law Review* 46: 551–589.

Adkins, Arthur W.H. 1960. *Merit and Responsibility: A Study in Greek Values*. Oxford: Clarendon Press.

Adorno, Theodor W., Else Frenkel-Brunswik, Daniel Levinson, and Nevitt Sanford. 1950. *The Authoritarian Personality*. New York: Harper.

Anderson, William Scovil. 2014. *Essays on Roman Satire*. Princeton, NJ: Princeton University Press.

Aristotle. 1907. *De Anima*. Translated by Robert D. Hicks. London: University of Toronto Press.

———. 1926. *Aristotle, with an English Translation: The "Art" of Rhetoric*. Translated by John Henry Freese. London and New York: W. Heinemann and G.P. Putnam's.

———. 1934. *The Nicomachean Ethics*. Translated by H. Rackham. Cambridge, MA and London: Harvard University Press and W. Heinemann.

Bandes, Susan A. 2009. Empathetic Judges and the Rule of Law. *Cardozo Law Review De Novo*: 133–48.

Burger, Ronna. 1991. Ethical Reflection and Righteous Indignation: Nemesis in the Nicomachean Ethics. In *Aristotle's Ethics*, ed. John P. Anton and Anthony Preus, 133–148. Albany: State University of New York Press.

Cairns, Douglas L. 2003. Ethics, Ethology, Terminology: Iliadic Anger and the Cross-Cultural Study of Emotions. In *Ancient Anger. Perspectives from Homer to Galen*, Yale Classical Studies, ed. Susanna Braund and Glenn W. Most, vol. 32, 11–49. Cambridge: Cambridge University Press.

Castelli, Laura M. 2015. Φθόνος· πάθος, ἦθος, Perception of Desert and the Place of Envy in Rhet. II. In *La Retorica di Aristotele e la dottrina delle passioni*, ed. Bruno Centrone, 221–248. Pisa: Pisa University Press.

Demosthenes with an English translation by A. T. Murray. 1939. Cambridge, MA and London: Harvard University Press and William Heinemann Ltd.

Dubreuil, Benoît. 2010a. *Human Evolution and the Origins of Hierarchies: The State of Nature*. New York: Cambridge University Press.

———. 2010b. Punitive Emotions and Norm Violations. *Philosophical Explorations* 13 (1): 35–50.

Elster, Jon. 2007. *Explaining Social Behavior: More Nuts and Bolts for the Social Sciences*. Cambridge and New York: Cambridge University Press.

Fitterer, Robert J. 2008. *Love and Objectivity in Virtue Ethics Aristotle, Lonergan, and Nussbaum on Emotions and Moral Insight*. Toronto, ON: University of Toronto Press.

Gastaldi, Silvia. 1990. *Aristotele e la politica delle passioni: retorica, psicologia ed etica dei comportamenti emozionali*. Turin: Tirrenia-Stampatori.

———. 1995. Il Teatro Delle Passioni. Pathos Nella Retorica Antica. *Elenchos* 16: 59–82.

Ginzburg, Carlo. 1998. Uccidere un mandarino cinese. Le implicazioni morali della distanza. In *Occhiacci di legno: nove riflessioni sulla distanza*, 194–209. Milan: Feltrinelli.

Haidt, Jonathan. 2003. The Moral Emotions. In *Handbook of Affective Sciences*, ed. Richard J. Davidson, Klaus R. Scherer, and H. Hill Goldsmith, 852–870. Oxford and New York: Oxford University Press. http://site.ebrary.com/id/10084743.

Hardie, W.F.R. 1975. Aristotle's Doctrine That Virtue Is a Mean. In *Articles on Aristotle*, ed. Jonathan Barnes, Malcolm Schofield, and Richard Sorabji, vol. 2, 33–46. London: Duckworth.

Harris, William V. 2013. How Strictly Did the Athenian Courts Apply the Law. The Role of Epieikeia. *Bulletin of the Institute of Classical Studies* 56 (1): 25–46.

Henderson, Lynne N. 1993. Legality and Empathy. In *Feminist Jurisprudence*, ed. Patricia Smith, 244–281. New York: Oxford University Press.

Hutchinson, Douglas. 1995. Ethics. In *The Cambridge Companion to Aristotle*, ed. Jonathan Barnes. Cambridge and New York: Cambridge University Press.

Kahneman, Daniel, and Cass R. Sunstein. 2007. Indignation: Psychology, Politics, Law. *John M. Olin Program in Law and Economics Working Paper* 346: 1–29.

Kant, Immanuel. 1963. The Idea of Universal History from a Cosmopolitan Point of View. In *On History*, ed. Lewis White Beck. Indianapolis, IN: Bobbs-Merrill.

Konstan, David. 2006. *The Emotions of the Ancient Greeks: Studies in Aristotle and Classical Literature*. Toronto, ON: University of Toronto Press.

Lysias. 1930. Translated by W. R. M. Lamb. M.A. Cambridge, MA and London: Harvard University Press and William Heinemann Ltd.

Maroney, Terry A. 2011a. Emotional Regulation and Judicial Behavior. *California Law Review* 99 (6): 1485–1555.

———. 2011b. The Persistent Cultural Script of Judicial Dispassion. *California Law Review* 99 (2): 629–681.

———. 2018. Judicial Emotion as Vice or Virtue: Perspectives Both Ancient and New. In *Aristotle on Emotions in Law and Politics*, ed. Liesbeth Huppes-Cluysenaer and Nuno M.M.S. Coelho. Dordrecht: Springer.

Mouchiroud, Christophe, and Franck Zenasni. 2013. In *The Oxford Handbook of the Development of Imagination*, ed. Marjorie Taylor. Oxford and New York: Oxford University Press.

Nagel, Thomas. 1979. *Mortal Questions*. Cambridge and New York: Cambridge University Press.

Nietzsche, Friedrich Wilhelm. 1994. *On the Genealogy of Morality*. Edited by Keith Ansell-Pearson and Translated by Carol Diethe. New York: Cambridge University Press.

———. 1998. *Beyond Good and Evil: Prelude to a Philosophy of the Future*. Translated by Marion Faber. http://search.ebscohost.com/login.aspx?direct=true&scope=site&db=nlebk&db=nlabk&AN=12317.

Nussbaum, Martha C. 1996. Aristotle on Emotions and Rational Persuasion. In *Essays on Aristotle's Rhetoric*, ed. Amélie Rorty, 303–323. Berkeley: University of California Press.

———. 2004. *Hiding from Humanity Disgust, Shame, and the Law*. Princeton, NJ: Princeton University Press. http://public.eblib.com/choice/publicfullrecord.aspx?p=445525.

———. 2013. *Political Emotions: Why Love Matters for Justice*. http://public.eblib.com/choice/publicfullrecord.aspx?p=3301331.

Ranulf, Svend. 1938. *Moral Indignation and Middle Class Psychology*. Copenhagen: Levin & Munksgaard.

Rapp, Christof. 2018. Dispassionate Judges Encountering Hotheaded Aristotelians. In *Aristotle on Emotions in Law and Politics*, ed. Liesbeth Huppes-Cluysenaer and Nuno M.M.S. Coelho. Dordrecht: Springer.

Ratnapala, Suri. 2009. *Jurisprudence*. Cambridge and New York: Cambridge University Press.

Rozin, Paul, Laura Lowery, Sumio Imada, and Jonathan Haidt. 1999. The CAD Triad Hypothesis: A Mapping Between Three Moral Emotions and Three Moral Codes. *Journal of Personality and Social Psychology* 76 (4): 574–586.

Sandel, Michael J. 2009. *Justice: What's the Right Thing to Do?* New York: Farrar, Straus and Giroux.

Scheffler, Samuel. 2000. Justice and Desert in Liberal Theory. *California Law Review* 88: 965–990.

Scheid-Tissinier, Évelyne. 2007. Le rôle de la colère dans les tribunaux athéniens. In *Athènes et le politique. Dans le sillage de Claude Mossé*, Collection "Bibliothèque Albin Michel Histoire", ed. Pauline Schmitt Pantel and François de Polignac, 179–198. Paris: Albin Michel.

———. 2012. Du bon usage des émotions dans la culture grecque. In *Anthropologie de l'Antiquité. Anciens objets, nouvelles approches*, Antiquité et Sciences Humaines. La traversée des frontières, ed. Pascal Payen and Évelyne Scheid-Tissinier, vol. 1, 263–289. Brepols Publishers: Turnhout.

Sherman, Nancy. 1993. The Role of Emotions in Aristotelian Virtue. *Proceedings of the Boston Area Colloquium in Ancient Philosophy* 9: 1–33.

Shields, Stephanie A. 2002. *Speaking from the Heart: Gender and the Social Meaning of Emotion*. Cambridge and New York: Cambridge University Press.

Slote, Michael. 2002. Justice as a Virtue. In *Stanford Encyclopedia of Philosophy*, rev. 2016. http://plato.stanford.edu/entries/justice-virtue/.

Smith, Angela M. 2013. Moral Blame and Moral Protest. In *Blame: Its Nature and Norms*, ed. D. Justin Coates and Neal A. Tognazzini. Oxford and New York: Oxford University Press.

Spinoza, B. n.d. *Political Treatise (Libro, 2000)* [WorldCat.org]. Translated by Samuel Shirley. Accessed May 14, 2016.

Strawson, G. 1962. Freedom and Resentment. *Proceedings of the British Academy* 48: 1–25.

Sunstein, Cass R. 2009. Some Effects of Moral Indignation on Law. In *Symposium: Emotions in Context: Exploring the Interaction Between Emotions and Legal Institutions*, 405–433. South Royalton: Vermont Law School.

Viola, Francesco, and Giuseppe Zaccaria. 2003. *Le ragioni del diritto*. Bologna: Il mulino.

Viola, F. 2014. Diritti umani e ragion pratica. *Metodo. International Studies in Phenomenology and Philosophy* 2 (1): 49–58.

Vromen, Jack. 2012. Human Cooperation and Reciprocity. In *Evolution and Rationality: Decisions, Co-operation and Strategic Behaviour*, ed. Samir Okasha and K.G. Binmore, 158–184. Cambridge and New York: Cambridge University Press.

Weiner, Bernard. 2006. *Social Motivation, Justice, and the Moral Emotions: An Attributional Approach*. Mahwah, NJ: Lawrence Erlbaum Associates.

Williams, Bernard. 1981. *Moral Luck: Philosophical Papers, 1973-1980*. Cambridge and New York: Cambridge University Press.

Cases

163 U.S. 537 (1896).
347 U.S. 483 (1954).

Chapter 12
Rethinking Legal Education from Aristotle's Theory of Emotions and the Contemporary Challenges of the Practical Realization of Law

Ana Carolina de Faria Silvestre

Abstract The traditional perspective on emotions assumes an unassailable dualism between emotions and reason. For common sense, including legal common sense, emotions are always dangerous and have nothing to do with rational decision-making. Nonetheless, the Aristotelian perspective regarding the relationship between emotions and reason is extremely enlightening. The relationship between emotions and law has been studied by a large range of scholars from different legal movements and with diverse objectives. This chapter is based on three theoretical pillars: Aristotle's theory of emotions as elaborated in Rhetoric and Nicomachean Ethics, Aristotle's view on the close relationship between reason, emotions and phronesis as elaborated in the Nicomachean Ethics, and a specific contemporary view: Jurisprudentialism. We assert that through a Jurisprudentialist analysis of Law as an open task and through Aristotle's account of emotions, the challenges of legal education could (and should) be more realistically reassessed.

12.1 Introduction

In the Western world, reason and emotion are traditionally assumed to be distinct universes where the one has nothing to do with the other. This vision of emotions as being divorced from reason goes back to classical Greek antiquity, particularly, to Plato. Although Aristotle was Plato's student and a member of the academy for 20 years, he advanced his own understanding of emotions and highlighted their cognitive character. According to Aristotle, emotions are not wild beasts, completely deprived of reason. When speaking of emotions, we are discussing a non-rational part of the human soul, which is able to listen to what the rational part of the soul says, but can impair our judgment as well.

A.C.d.F. Silvestre (✉)
Southern Minas Gerais Law School and Higher Education Center in Management, Technology and Education, Minas Gerais, Brazil
e-mail: fariasilvestre@yahoo.com.br

© Springer International Publishing AG 2018
L. Huppes-Cluysenaer, N.M.M.S. Coelho (eds.), *Aristotle on Emotions in Law and Politics*, Law and Philosophy Library 121, DOI 10.1007/978-3-319-66703-4_12

This chapter is divided into four parts. Initially, we present Aristotle's theory of emotions. Secondly, we will explore the relationship between emotions and reason in the practical world. Subsequently, we will present some core concepts of a legal philosophical approach on law and adjudication entitled jurisprudentialism, stressing how the Aristotelian perspective on virtues, phronesis and emotions can enrich this jurisprudentialism. Finally, we will provide a critical overview of the challenges of legal education under the assumption that law presents not mainly a theoretical problem but a practical one.

12.2 Aristotle and Emotions

What are emotions according to Aristotle? In Rhetoric,[1] Aristotle defines emotions as:

> all those feelings that so change men as to affect their judgments, and that are also attended by pain or pleasure. (*Rhet.* 1378a20–25, trans. Roberts)

In the Nicomachean Ethics he explains the meaning of passions/emotions as:

> appetite, anger, fear, confidence, envy, joy, friendly feeling, hatred, longing, emulation, pity, and in general the feelings that are accompanied by pleasure or pain. (*EN* 1105b20–25, trans. Ross/revised by Urmson)

These two definitions do not present a full account of emotions in Aristotle's thought, because the first one regards the specific aims of rhetoric, while the second one concerns a list of categories, together with the statement that they are accompanied by pleasure and pain. The decisive element of emotions does therefore not appear in the two previous definitions but is deeply explored in Rhetoric: emotions are based on thoughts, opinions or evaluative judgments. As Zingano formulates it:

> This element is not only a part of the emotions: it is the decisive element.[2]

If someone assumes there is a lion nearby, they will feel fear because the lion may attack them; however, if they also assume that the same lion is not dangerous, they may feel joy instead of fear.

> The agent has an opinion and the emotion is felt according to this opinion.[3]

Aristotle realized that emotions are not an auxiliary element of persuasion but are intimately connected with: (a) states of pleasure and pain; (b) our opinions and evaluative judgements and the objects at which they are directed; (c) our desires;

---

[1]Edition used: for all texts of Aristotle: *The Complete Works of Aristotle: The Revised Oxford Translation*, edited by Jonathan Barnes.

[2]Zingano (2009), p. 152. Free translation of "Na verdade, este elemento não é somente uma parte da emoção: ele é seu elemento decisivo".

[3]Zingano (2009), p. 152. Free translation of "O agente tem então uma opinião e a emoção é sentida conforme a esta opinião".

(d) certain cognitive efforts, such as having beliefs and making judgments.[4] Emotions express our evaluative judgments and can be educated but never (completely) eliminated from the decision-making process.

Plato studied emotions and realized that emotional responses are different from bodily sensations and bodily drives. In Philebus, Socrates distinguishes between three kinds of mixed pleasure and pain. There are mixtures which concern the body and are found in the body, those that belong to the soul itself and are found in the soul, and those that belong to the soul and to the body. Emotions such as anger, fear, lament, love, longing, emulation, envy etc. are understood to be mixed pleasures and pains belonging only to the soul.[5] Socrates is not clear, however, about the cognitive nature of emotional responses. In Philebus, Socrates and Protarchus discuss the relationship between emotions (and other kinds of pain and pleasure) and cognition. Protarchus understands that an opinion can be true or false but he is not ready to concede that pleasure and pain can be classified as true or false. Facing the provocative theme, Socrates points out the similarities between opinion, pleasure and pain. In order to establish that pleasure and pain can be true or false as opinion, he affirms that pleasure often occurs together with false opinion. According to Fortenbaugh, the use of "with" reflects a simple concurrence between opinion and pleasure. Opinion accompanies pleasure but is external to pleasure. It is clear that Plato understood that emotions and pleasure are closely related but it is not clear what kind of relationship exists between emotion and cognition, according to him.[6]

In Rhetoric, the relationship between emotion and cognition is much clearer than Aristotle's answer to this debate presented in Topics. In Rhetoric we can find an explicit relation between the thought of outrage (as an efficient cause) and the emotion of anger, for example.

> For Aristotle, the thought of outrage (. . .) [is] not merely characteristic of anger (. . .) [It is] necessary and properly mentioned in the essential definition of anger.[7]

That the thought of outrage is the efficient cause of anger[8] means that someone cannot be angry when she thinks herself treated justly. If a person did something wrong and knows it, she will not feel angry. In that case she can feel shame, fear, sadness or another emotion but never anger. There is a logical distinction between similar emotions. Anger, for example, is an emotion motivated by the thought of outrage. Someone said or did without any reason something outrageous to another

---

[4]Rapp (2015), pp. 443–444.

[5]Fortenbaugh (1975), p. 10.

[6]Ibid., p. 11.

[7]Ibid., p. 12.

[8]It is important to keep in mind that the Aristotelian notion of anger is different from the contemporary notion of anger. "The Greek word that is translated by "insult" implies acts of contempt, spite or belittling; such acts manifest someone's opinion that the affected person is worthless (. . .) Our anger reflects the fact that we think of ourselves as valuable persons who deserve to be treated with due respect. This is also Aristotle's justification of anger". Rapp (2018).

person herself or to those she cares about. Anger is directed at an individual who is perceived as outrageous because of excessive abusive and insulting behavior. Hate is distinct from anger. When hate occurs it is not necessary to believe that the person who is hated acted outrageous. It is sufficient to think he or she is a certain kind of person.[9] (*Rhet.* 1382a). Aristotle realized that at least some emotions are based on impressions, thoughts or opinions and these can be altered by arguments. The good speaker should take this into account. The study of emotions is also reflected in the need to rethink the role of tragedy and music. It gives rise to the development of a theory of benefits through purgation (katharsis)[10] and, with regards to our main concern in this chapter, its culmination in an enlightened approach to ethics.

12.3 The Education of Desire Through Reason and Practical Deliberation

Book VI of the Nicomachean Ethics is dedicated by Aristotle to the reflection on the fair mean between excess and deficiency in practical deliberation. Aristotle begins his reflection stating that there are two dimensions of the human soul: one which engages in reasoning and one which cannot itself reason but can listen to the reason. The first may be split into two: (a) a contemplative part, which studies the invariable truths of mathematics and metaphysics (scientific faculty); and (b) one that deals with the practical matters of human life (calculative faculty) (*EN* 1139a 5–10). In the other part of the human soul there are irrational elements, which are shared with animals and are contributive to nutrition and growth (vegetative part) or emotions and desires (appetitive part). Animals, like humans, experience emotions connected with desires, albeit different from humans. Animals cannot develop the ability to properly control moral virtue. Phronesis is the excellence of the calculative faculty of the soul (*EN* 1140b 25–30). Virtues are not given by nature but are the result of a practical effort which starts in childhood, acting in one way rather than another. It is not exclusively obtainable for philosophers but can be reached by everyone.[11]

The only way to overcome the challenges of deciding well in the practical world is deciding or, in other words, the only way of becoming a phronimos person is being a phronimos one. A courageous person is one who acts in a courageous way, which does not mean that she does not feel fear. A courageous person will feel fear

---

[9]Notwithstanding the importance of efficient cause for the definition and distinction of one emotion from another, Aristotle is not exclusively concerned with this kind of cause. His scientific purposes move him toward the identification of other causes such as the material and final cause Fortenbaugh (1975), p. 15.

[10]See especially, Fortenbaugh (1975).

[11]Berti (1997), p. 280.

because he/she is a human being, limited by this condition, but the more she acts as a courageous one, the more willing she will be to act in a courageous way.

> Having the virtues of character implies that one always has the right emotions when one should, toward whom one should, and so on.[12]

The courageous act is not experienced by the courageous person as burdensome but as enjoyable.[13]

Habituation precedes the development of the virtues of the autonomous individual. From childhood on we start to do what is right, as long as we are raised in well-ordered cities with good laws and are influenced by parents, teachers and friends who do the right thing. This precedes the autonomous reflection on what is good and bad in a specific situation; it precedes deliberation. As we grow older and face on our own the concrete problems of daily life, which demand a solution, we need to evaluate what is the right thing to do and to decide what is the right decision to make in a specific situation (*EN* 1106b5).

Habituation and deliberation will not solve the real problem of doing the right thing in the right moment and in the right way—this remains a great challenge for every moral agent. Nevertheless, the more people act in one way and not in another, the more disposed they will become to act in that way. This means that each person is, in a certain way, responsible for the dispositions, which constitute its second nature.[14] As we can decide and act according to a previous process of habituation and decision-making we can be held strongly morally responsible for our virtuous or vicious dispositions of character.[15]

There is an inversion in Aristotle's ethics, according to Zingano.[16] Desire is the starting point of the deliberative process. Reason is called upon to find the means to reach an end posed by the desire. However, it is in deliberating about how to get that previous "end" that reason exerts its guidance and makes the decision appropriate, i.e., when the reason evaluates the end and makes the living being consider its capacity to even refuse it. Acts in the sphere of "what is, but could be otherwise" constitute the dispositions and the virtues of character of the non-rational part of the soul. The virtuous person tends to feel appropriate emotions in different situations. That is the reason why Aristotle is not concerned about appropriate or inappropriate

---

[12]Rapp (2015), p. 444.

[13]Kraut (2014).

[14]Zingano (2009), p. 163. "Once we are the masters of each action and once our dispositions are built according to the repetition of the acts, then somehow we are responsible for our dispositions. These dispositions constitute what we can call the second practical nature of the moral agent" (free translation). "Já que somos senhores de cada ação e dado que as disposições se criam com base na repetição de atos em uma mesma direção, em certa medida somos responsáveis de nossas próprias disposições. Estas disposições constituem o que podemos chamar de uma segunda natureza prática do agente".

[15]Zingano (2009), p. 163. "Aristotle sustains a strong moral responsibility thesis in regard to virtuous and vicious acts" (free translation). "Aristóteles [sustenta] uma tese forte da responsabilidade moral a respeito dos atos virtuosos e viciosos".

[16]Zingano (2009), p. 164.

emotions but rather about the development of dispositions which will lead the moral agent to feel the appropriate emotions and act according to the good.[17]

This understanding of the challenges of practical life is very realistic because it is not focused on the avoidance or the rejection of emotions in practice, but on the education of desire by reason in a deliberative practice. Emotions express desires which can be educated by habituation and deliberation in practical matters. The goal of moral education is to educate desire in order to make it pursue what is good—and the good in practical issues, in general, is the middle ground between excess and deficiency.

> The whole problem lies exactly in the relation between the desire and the thinking in the concrete moment of decision. Moral virtue is a disposition concerning the choice/election (...) so the thought has to be right and the desire straight in order that the prohairesis is good. There has to be a coincidence between what reason says and the desire pursues which will make the prohairesis serious.[18]

The calculative faculty and desire are the bases of the choice.[19] The man constituted by thought and desire is the origin and the efficient cause of the action: good actions if you have true thought and right desire and bad actions if you have false thought and wrong desire.[20]

Good deliberation in practical life includes, almost all of the time, emotions. A wise person, rather than suffocating or avoiding its emotional experience, should be engaged in educating its own emotions. The wise man/woman feels emotions

---

[17]"Aristotle's interest in appropriate emotions cannot be separated from his interest in character virtues". See Rapp (2018).

[18]Coelho (2012), p. 97. Free translation: "Todo o problema radica exatamente na relação entre o desejar e o pensar no momento concreto da decisão. A virtude moral é uma disposição relativa à escolha/eleição (...) logo o pensamento tem que ser correto e o desejo reto para que a proairesis seja boa. Tem que haver coincidência entre o que a razão diz e o desejo persegue para que a proairesis seja séria".

[19]"Affirming that desire is persuaded by reason is different from affirming that desire is chosen by reason. If it could be chosen rationally in a deliberate way, then there would be no need for the habit as a formative practice of the desire. Desire cannot be immediately and directly determined by reason. It must be prepared, cultivated and used to obey reason". Free translation of. "Dizer que o desejo é persuadido pela razão é bem diferente de dizer que ele é escolhido por ela. Se pudesse ser escolhido racionalmente, i.e., deliberadamente, então não haveria necessidade do hábito como uma prática formativa do desejo. Ora, o desejo não pode ser imediata e diretamente determinado pela razão, pelo o que ela dita como certo. Ele deve ser preparado, cultivado, habituado a obedecê-la". Aggio (2010), pp. 6–7. For a detailed account on the relation between desire and pleasure in Portuguese language, see Aggio (2012).

[20]Coelho (2012), pp. 97–98. "The act gives the mobilization of the whole soul. The different dimensions of the soul (the rational or the irrational, each one with its different dimensions) are mobilized in the very act of the serious man particularly because only then he, while serious, constitutes his own character" (free translation). "No agir, dá-se a mobilização de toda a alma. As diferentes dimensões da alma (seja a racional, seja a irracional, cada qual também com suas diferentes dimensões) mobilizam-se no agir do homem sério até porque apenas assim é que ele, enquanto sério, constitui o seu próprio caráter".

at the right times, with reference to the right objects, towards the right people, with the right aim, and in the right way, is what is both intermediate and best, and this is characteristic of excellence. (*EN* 1106b20–25, trans. Ross/Urmson)

12.4   The Excellence of Phronesis and Law

Even in legal positivism Law is not perceived as a strictly theoretical science. It is a science which is called upon to solve problems arising in praxis, e.g. in the world of life, which is always in motion. There are cases in which the application of law[21] will generate injustice due to the abstract and general features of the law, while the situations of life are contingent. Law must rule a large range of different cases and sometimes it will be necessary, in order to reach practical justice, to correct law through equity (*EN* 1137a31–1138a3). However, equity is not the rule but the exception according to Aristotle. In Politics Aristotle states that the rule of law is better than being ruled by human beings who can be distorted by emotions (*Pol.* 1287a30–35). Rapp concludes from this that for Aristotle the rule of law is like:

> a divine and or well-reasoned governance, while the one who wants particular human beings to rule, also accepts that brutish element gains influence, as thumos (...) seduces even the best human beings.[22]

Aristotle's trust in the superiority of law is profoundly entrenched in his cultural, political and juridical background. As Rapp states, Aristotle's reflection on the role of judges is profoundly related to the Athenian legal system of his time in which it was more common to have some hundred democratic jurors than one judge and in which the judges had to decide as little as possible. As virtue is hard to achieve and the process of moral development strongly depends on each person's commitments, it was unrealistic to assume that the majority of the judges could be virtuous.

The contemporary judicial scenario in the occidental world is considerably different from Aristotle's Athenian legal system. These differences cannot be discarded, but must be taken into account in order to reach the main goal of this chapter, which is to reflect on the contemporary challenges for legal education on the basis of Aristotle's view on emotions. At this point we will remove ourselves from Aristotle's reflection on judges, legal judgment and law, while maintaining his general account on the relationship between emotions and reason in ethics and the challenge, which arises from this relationship concerning the moral virtues. This deliberate choice exposes us directly to Rapp's criticism but it seems to us that there

---

[21]However, what Aristotle thought about law? See in this volume Huppes-Cluysenaer (2018a, b).
[22]Rapp (2018).

are reasons[23] to face this challenge and move on even if, in the end, the result of this enterprise is worthless for enthusiastic Aristotelians.

12.5 The Juridical Decision as a Special Kind of Practical Decision

The wise man is the one who, in every situation of life, being invested with the task of figuring out what is good, will do the best thing to do in a concrete problem. On the dimension of "what is, but could be otherwise" (e.g. in the practical world) there will always be needed a decision. The judgment is the core of practical life and also the core of the adjudication:

> What characterizes the judgment is the resolution of a practical controversy.[24]

According to Castanheira Neves, law is an incomplete task because between the legal system and the legal case there exists a dialectical relationship, meaning that the situated and singular problematic intentionality of the legal case asks for the normative intentionality of the legal system to reach an adequate legal answer. At the end of the methodological search for an adequate legal answer for a specific case, the legal system can also appear to have been normatively redefined.

Scientific knowledge about law, principles, doctrine and jurisprudence is not enough to solve a legal problem because the question posed by the legal case is always unique and the legal system needs to reflect on the right legal answer to the problematic intentionality of the legal case.

> The intentionality of the question influences the intentionality of the answer, at the same time the intentionality of the answer influences the intentionality of the question.[25]

The judge must know the law well and have a general knowledge of the legal material. However, the judge must keep in mind that there is a circular relationship (or a hermeneutic circle) between the legal system and the legal problem. In short, the understanding of the legal problem presupposes the understanding of the legal system, at the same time the understanding of the legal system presupposes the pre-understanding of the legal problem. The goal of the methodology of the legal

---

[23]The most prominent ones are the differences between the very meaning of law under Greek world and the role of judges roughly pointed out in the text. We do not intend to analyse these differences but to assume them in order to reflect on legal education in the occidental world in general. In the next section we will work with a contemporary approach to adjudication called jurisprudentialism which emphasizes the element of decision in the practical realization of law. Decision, in this legal approach, is a decisive part of the process of adjudication.

[24]Castanheira Neves (1993), p. 31. Free translation: "O que caracteriza o juízo é a resolução de uma controvérsia prática".

[25]Simioni (2014), p. 443. Free translation of: "A intencionalidade da pergunta já influencia a intencionalidade da resposta, ao mesmo tempo em que a intencionalidade da resposta já influencia a própria intencionalidade da pergunta".

decision is to accomplish adequate mediation of this hermeneutic circularity through the determination (selection) of the juridical norm, which can be assumed in abstract to be the adequate legal answer for the legal case.

In some cases there will be no norms which provide the abstract answer for the legal case but this does not mean there is no answer for the legal case. In cases like this, analogy is the standard and the communal values and the principles of law[26] are the bases.[27] Analogy is neither deductive nor inductive, it is intuitive. In the approach to law and adjudication of jurisprudentialism, analogy is the essence of the practical realization of law and that which differentiates the equal from the different in analogical terms is a choice. The assumption of an analogical rationality of law implies the recognition of the role of choice in the practical realization of law.

In judgment there is decision (What is the juridical problem of the concrete case? What can be assumed as the abstract adequate norm of the legal case? Can the abstract norm be confirmed in a concrete case as the adequate norm for the legal case?). The methodological dimension of the practical realization of law aims to establish the conditions, the assumptions and the requirements of this exercise. Notwithstanding, this does not suffice to solve the practical realization of legal challenges. We understand that the crossbreeding of jurisprudentialist methodological concerns with the Aristotelian virtue ethics can lead to a more adequate practical realization of law which rightly acknowledges the uniqueness of the legal case.

In order to answer the questions presented by the legal case in its historical-cultural context it is necessary to have more than scientific knowledge of law; it is necessary to have juridical virtues and phronesis. The prudent judge clearly comprehends that establishing the law in a case is much more complex than accomplishing a jurisdictional function only. She takes seriously into account the human dimension of adjudication because she is able to understand that the legal process is about human dramas, which can be experienced by any human being and that the way the judge conducts the process, the audience and, in general, the way she judges marks her as moral agent. The judge is not the moral agent par excellence when judging a legal case, i.e. she does not make decisions concerning her own life and then acts on them according to the classical concept of the moral agent. However, deciding a case is not ruled by fixed norms and principles which are formulated in abstract, theoretical terms.

---

[26]Positive, transpositive and suprapositive principles. Castanheira Neves (1993), p. 155.

[27]"The problem of binding validity that the juridical thought is called to assume and to realise continually in concrete cases" (free translation). "O problema de uma validade vinculante, que o pensamento jurídico é chamado a assumir e continuamente a resolver em concreto" Castanheira Neves (2008), p. 385.

Since a judge has to reflect on what works and what doesn't in legal interpretation and application, the professional quality of phronesis is crucial.[28]

Let's imagine, for example, a judge who must decide an alimony case in which the ex-spouse asks for the continuation of a short-term financial support after its termination date because she hasn't been able to put her professional and personal life on track yet. What must the judge do? The answer is an open one—this does not mean that it is arbitrary. If it is true that the judge deals with factual questions of the past, it is also true that the legal answer for the case cannot be found in the past in an objective manner. The judge is engaged in the task of having to

bridge the gap between the generality of the rule and the particularity of the situation.[29]

The virtuous (phronimos) judge is concerned about good practical decisions in the future (prohairesis)[30] which can have impact for people who have a direct interest in the outcome of a legal matter (the parties).

In summary, the adjudication needs Aristotle's excellence of practical wisdom (phronesis) and other specific juridical virtues[31] to reach justice in practice. However, does legal education prepare the student of law for the practical realization of these legal challenges?

---

[28]Gaakeer (2015), p. 8.

[29]Ibid.

[30]Rapp sustains a different point of view for strong reasons. According to him, the *prohairesis* is always directed at things that are possible for the agent to do and that lie in the future. If the *prohairesis* is good, than it is the best contribution for the agent's life as a whole. "A judge, by contrast, does not make decisions that are expected to concern her own life or her own happiness directly (. . .) Whereas in the decision of moral agents the non-rational part of the soul (which, on Aristotle's account, is also responsible for the emotions) determines the goals of the virtuous conduct, there are no practical goals that the judge could realize (. . .) Since the judge is not herself about to undertake certain actions (apart from the formulation of the just judgement or sentence), the question of her motivation does not occur. In all these respects the situation of the judge is different from the moral agent who makes practical decisions and who is the subject of Aristotle's formula that one should have emotions in the right way". Rapp (2018), especially section 6.

[31]Iris van Domselaar states that the following judicial virtues are decisive for the moral quality in adjudication: judicial perception, judicial courage, judicial temperance, judicial justice, judicial impartiality and judicial independency. "On the basis of (my understanding of) these *endoxa* I propose the following judicial virtues as pertinent for our understanding of moral quality in adjudication: judicial perception, judicial courage, judicial temperance, judicial justice, judicial impartiality and judicial independency. Judges must have these virtues to a sufficient degree if adjudication is to be a morally justified practice and judicial decisions are to be right". van Domselaar (2014), p. 234. She refers in this respect to Aristotle (Nicomachean Ethics, trans. Sarah Broadie and Christoffer Rowe) and to Iris Murdoch's account of moral vision and other neo-Aristotelians. Jeanne Gaakeer states, in the same direction, that "despite their differences most legal systems share core values such as judicial impartiality, consistency and integrity which, not incidentally, are considered virtues in the Aristotelian sense". Gaakeer (2012), p. 21.

12.6 Legal Education: A Critical Reflection in the Light of Aristotle's Understanding of Emotions, Combined with the Contributions of Jurisprudentialism

In legal positivism Law is traditionally assumed as mainly a theoretical science. Nevertheless, the judicial decision is the result of a practical-prudential judgment (an adequate legal treatment of a concrete controversy which is a unique experience). In order to accomplish justice in a specific legal case, the legal professional must be more than a scientist of law. The person must be cultivated and seriously committed to find the unique significance in every legal case.

The cross-pollination between Castanheira Neves and the Aristotelian tradition leads us to affirm that legal education should be concerned with the moral improvement of law students. The more the legal student exercises the practical realization of law, the more she can improve her moral capacity and deal better with her emotions in law and in life, which is decisive for deciding in the sphere of "what is, but could be otherwise".

The student of law should participate in extra activities during the course, which offer hours of simulated or real practical legal activities. However, do these activities really reach the main goal of preparing law students for the practical realization of law?

12.6.1 A Re-Founder Reflection for a Renewed Law School

Law schools in Brazil and around the world should be able to prepare their students for the practical realization of the challenges of law. This means that the learning environment should be an open, creative and stimulating space where the law student feels compelled to reflect on the law and meet the challenges posed by the legal case.[32] This general concern may lead the professor to use other educational methods of teaching rather than the expositive classes in which student remains in a passive and receptive position during the classes. In environments of this kind, there is little space for critical reflection, for the development of the excellence of practical wisdom (phronesis) and other juridical virtues.

When we consider legal education we usually see the student of law as a faceless person. However, the real classroom is constituted of people with different characteristics, interests and objectives. Using multiple teaching strategies in the classroom can contribute to an effective teaching-learning process, which will benefit all

---

[32]For another perspective on how emotions could be taken into account in law schools.

and not only those who adapt best to the expositive classes.[33] In addition to this, and with regards to our research, it is important that the professor offers as many opportunities as possible to students to feel and live the law in practice. As we stated before, the practical realization of law demands more than knowledge about the law and the legal system. It is an open task accomplished by real people in the daily practice of law. Legal education should not be primarily concerned with the development of the scientific faculty, but more with the calculative faculty of the legal students's souls (in Aristotelian words), creating opportunities (inside and outside the classroom environment) for the development of the practical wisdom (phronesis) and other judicial virtues.

Inside the classroom, the law professor can use a lot of teaching strategies and she is free to decide which one can be assumed as the most appropriate for a specific purpose. The most important thing is not the learning strategy itself, as one isn't essentially better than another, but using it in order to create opportunities for a vivid experience with the living law. What is the best answer for a concrete legal situation? What would you do if you were the defendant's lawyer in this concrete case? Did the judge offer an adequate decision for the legal case under analysis? As Iris van Domselaar emphasizes, legal education can contribute to the development of judicial virtues[34] and each professor can accomplish this task in many different manners. If one is a philosophy of law professor engaged with the character building of her students, one can start thinking of this from the moment one starts to elaborate the curriculum. If one teaches constitutional law or another dogmatic discipline one is not so free as the philosophy of law professor to change the curriculum to make it fit for the moral building of ones students but one can integrate issues of ethics when discussing concrete legal cases, inviting students to conduct autonomous reflections about the juridical/moral decisions made by the legal actors and of the consequences of these for the parties, the society and for the judge's character building as much as one can.

Moreover and independent of the specific-discipline one teaches, one can choose what kind of relationship one would like to establish with one students inside and outside the classroom, either a hierarchical relationship or a horizontal person to person relationship. The first one stimulates students to completely accept the authority of the precedent, the law, the tradition, the legal doctrine, the professor, the judge and so on, instead of critically analyzing the concrete meaning, power and limits of the law in a concrete legal problem. This hierarchical relationship, based on the very idea that the professor should be regarded as a reliable source of truths,

---

[33]Pryal argues that the literature, for example, is able to provide to the legal pedagogy a variety of heuristics or learning tools that can give to the different students who enter annually in law courses learning tools that could be mobilized by them, considering their individual characteristics, for the construction of legal knowledge. See Pryal (2011).

[34]van Domselaar (2014), pp. 244–249.

closes, not completely but in a decisive way, the door for dialog and critique and opens it to surplus epistemic deference.[35]

The classroom must be a time for exercising concrete legal choices, but for that to occur we must give greater autonomy to the student in the classroom. The professor must resist the appeal of authority and should assume herself, whenever possible, as a facilitator of knowledge, which will be built by the student with her support. Immersed in the task of practical deliberation, looking for an adequate answer for the case, the student of law will have to deal with emotions. As we discussed above concerning Aristotle's understanding of emotions, emotions and sentiments are a constitutive part of the human soul which cannot be simply put aside. Law is a human task which involves emotions. This is the reason why legal education should be concerned with the moral education of the students in Aristotelian terms as well as with legal rules, precedents, doctrine and so on.[36] The professors should be aware of being an example of prudence to their students. We learn about prudence through example and the more the professors bear this in mind, the higher the chances to contribute to the moral building of her students.

Legal practice and legal training must also be rethought in order to create spaces which are as challenging as possible to engage the development of the excellence of phronesis and juridical virtues of the undergraduates. Students should be encouraged to participate in the largest possible number of practical activities throughout the law course in order to experience law and be challenged by the practical exercise. Autonomy should be given to the undergraduate student to enable her to experience law. Legal training should not only be a time for the technical application of knowledge learned in the classroom, or less than that: a place where the trainee is assumed to be merely an office assistant. Certainly, at the beginning of the training, the law students will occupy a more passive role, but gradually opportunities for acting and deciding in practice must be provided to them. The practical realization of law is an exercise of practical wisdom (phronesis) and an opportunity for developing juridical virtues rather than an intellectual search guided by the legal system. Law is an open task in which all of us are called to play an important role.

---

[35]Epistemic deference is, according to Buchanan: "the disposition to regard some other person or group of persons as especially reliable sources of truths. Social institutions that recognize some persons as experts encourage this sort of deference". Surplus epistemic deference occurs when this deference "is misplaced, as when a person or a group is regarded as a reliable source of truths about matters on which he or it is not, or excessive, as when there is an overestimation of a person's or group's reliability as a source of truths". Allen (2002), p. 136. All societies include hierarchical institutions and due to the division of labor they all recognize authorities. However, states Buchanan, "the right sort of deference to the right sorts of authorities is essential for the efficient creation, preservation, and transmission of true beliefs". Ibid., p. 137. "Education environment is replete with (. . .) surplus epistemic deference (. . .) [because] students have to internalize a specific ideologically laden view of law as 'true', simply because others tell them so". van Domselaar (2014), p. 248.

[36]For an interesting approach on emotional regulation for judges. See for all Maroney (2011).

12.6.2 Final Notes

The realization of the law is a practical task. If we assume Castanheira Neves's jurisprudentialism to reflect on law and adjudication, we will be urged to look to law as a task that is accomplished in practice by legal professionals.

Solving a legal problem implies much more than offering a legal answer for the legal case. It demands judges and more generally legal professionals who are really committed to the practical deliberation of law. The core of the realization of law is the legal case (assumed as a methodological prius) and the adequate answer for it is not available in the legal system but is, rather a human task. By exercising this task which holds at its core judgment and choice, the judge can develop and improve the excellence of practical wisdom (phronesis) and other juridical virtues which can alter the way she sees juridical cases and will decide them.

However, is legal education committed to this beautiful and challenging task? Is legal education, in the way it is configured, able to accomplish this task? According to our understanding, legal education should be more concerned with the moral building of the legal students. This claim does not mean that legal education is on the wrong track, but that it could be improved, from the curriculum definition to the interaction in the classrooms and the legal training/practice, but only if we all assume this general concern. The students of law must be given greater autonomy to reflect on what is the right response to the legal cases. The teacher must resist the appeal of hierarchical superiority and put herself before the student as a facilitator/ mediator of knowledge and as an example of phronesis. Whenever it is possible, freedom should be given to students to experience law in the deliberative practice, whether in real or simulated situations.

References

Aggio, Juliana Ortegosa. 2010. A Educação do Desejo Segundo Aristóteles. *Revista Do Seminário Dos Alunos Do PPGLM/UFRJ* 1: 1–12.
———. 2012. Prazer e Desejo em Aristóteles. University of São Paulo. http://www.teses.usp.br/teses/disponiveis/8/8133/tde-10082012-185037/pt-br.php.
Allen, Buchanan. 2002. Social Moral Epistemology. In *Bioethics*, vol. 19. Cambridge: Cambridge University Press.
Aristotle. 1984a. Nicomachean Ethics. In *The Complete Works of Aristotle: The Revised Oxford Translation*, ed. Jonathan Barnes and trans. W. D. Ross and J. O. Urmson. Princeton, NJ: Princeton University Press.
———. 1984b. Politics. In *The Complete Works of Aristotle: The Revised Oxford Translation*, ed. Jonathan Barnes and trans. B. Jowett. Princeton, NJ: Princeton University Press.
———. 1984c. Rhetoric. In *The Complete Works of Aristotle: The Revised Oxford Translation*, ed. Jonathan Barnes and trans. W. Rhys Roberts. Princeton, NJ: Princeton University Press.
———. 1984d. Topics. In *The Complete Works of Aristotle: The Revised Oxford Translation*, ed. Jonathan Barnes and trans. W. A. Pickard-Cambridge. Princeton, NJ: Princeton University Press.

Berti, Enrico. 1997. *Aristóteles No Século XX*. Translated by Dion Davi Macedo. São Paulo: Loyola.

Castanheira Neves, A. 1993. *Metodologia Jurídica: Problemas Fundamentais*, Vol. Boletim da Faculdade de Direito. Stvdia Ivridica. Coimbra: Coimbra Editora.

―――. 2008. O Sentido Actual Da Metodologia Jurídica. In *DIGESTA: Escritos Acerca Do Direito, Do Pensamento Jurídico, Da Sua Metodologia E Outros*, vol. 3. Coimbra Editora: Coimbra.

Coelho, Nuno Manuel Morgadinho dos Santos. 2012. *Sensatez Como Modelo E Desafio Do Pensamento Jurídico Em Aristóteles*. São Paulo: Editora Rideel.

Fortenbaugh, William W. 1975. *Aristotle on Emotion: A Contribution to Philosophical Psychology, Rhetoric, Poetics, Politics, and Ethics*. New York: Barnes & Noble Books.

Gaakeer, Jeanne. 2012. Configuring Justice. *No Foundations An Interdisciplinary Journal of Law and Justice* 9: 20–44.

―――. 2015. Practical Wisdom and Judicial Practice: Who's in Narrative Control? *ISLL Paper, The Online Collection* 8: 1–17.

Huppes-Cluysenaer, Liesbeth. 2018a. Introduction: A Debate Between Aristotelians and Neo-Aristotelians. In *Aristotle on Emotions in Law and Politics*, ed. Liesbeth Huppes-Cluysenaer and Nuno M.M.S. Coelho. Dordrecht: Springer.

―――. 2018b. Religion of Humanity: A Shift from a Dialogical to a Categorical Model of Rationality. In *Aristotle on Emotions in Law and Politics*, ed. Liesbeth Huppes-Cluysenaer and Nuno M.M.S. Coelho. Dordrecht: Springer.

Kraut, Richard. 2014. Aristotle's Ethics. In *Stanford Encyclopedia of Philosophy*. http://plato.stanford.edu/entries/aristotle-ethics/.

Maroney, Terry. 2011. Emotional Regulation and Judicial Behavior. *California Law Review* 99: 1481. http://papers.ssrn.com/sol3/papers.cfm?abstract_id=1785616.

Pryal, Katie Rose Guest. 2011. Law, Literature, and Interdisciplinary Copia: A Response to Skeptics. *SSRN Elibrary* 24. https://doi.org/10.2139/ssrn.1479270.

Rapp, Christof. 2015. Tragic Emotions. In *A Companion to Ancient Aesthetics*, ed. Penelope Murray and Pierre Destrée. Hoboken: Wiley-Blackwell. https://www.academia.edu/14898301/Tragic_Emotions.

―――. 2018. Dispassionate Judges Encountering Hotheaded Aristotelians. In *Aristotle on Emotions in Law and Politics*, ed. Liesbeth Huppes-Cluysenaer and Nuno M.M.S. Coelho. Dordrecht: Springer.

Simioni, Rafael Lazzarotto. 2014. *Curso de Hermenêutica Jurídica Contemporânea: Do Positivismo Clássico Ao Pós-Positivismo Jurídico*. Curitiba: Juruá.

van Domselaar, Iris. 2014. *The Fragility of Rightness: Adjudication and the Primacy of Practice*. Amsterdam: Universiteit van Amsterdam.

Zingano, Marco Antônio de Ávila. 2009. Emoção, Ação e Felicidade em Aristóteles. In *Estudos de Ética Antiga*, 2nd ed. São Paulo: Paulus Discurso Editorial.

Chapter 13
Remorse and Virtue Ethics

Humber van Straalen

Abstract At the center of many ethical theories is the question 'what we should do?'. This often goes hand in hand with a conceptual scheme in which the only thing which is morally evaluated, are the acts of the actor and their consequences. By first presenting a short analysis of two main texts in the debate on dirty hands, and secondly a swift presentation of Aristotle's virtue ethics as developed in the *Nicomachean Ethics,* a suggestion is made that human beings might care about more things than just the acts and their consequences. For instance, about the whole of their lives, about the opinions of others, about who they are becoming, and about the character which accompanies the act. These concerns might help to see feelings of remorse in the way that Walzer did, namely not as mere psychological facts, but as of the highest moral importance.

13.1 Introduction

The question at the center of many ethical theories is the question 'what we should do'. And so ethics is supposed to reason about the best options for action, which are open to us at any time. And doing this is important, because every situation allows for only one concrete action to actually take place. Thinking like this opens up a perspective on ethics in which everything turns around *weighing* different options and their consequences against each other. In this sense it seems a truism to say that morality is about realizing the best outcome.[1] This approach to ethics is theoretically understandable (because it is simple and plausible) and practically commendable (because a lot of people have taken moral inspiration from it).

Yet when it comes to cases of what has been called *dirty hands*, this approach seems to become problematic. For cases of dirty hands are cases in which the best outcome has been realized, but the actor still feels that he has done something terrible. That is, he knows he has done evil, even though he also knows that he did

---

[1]Christine Korsgaard complains that deontologists and utilitarians alike reason as if they are consequentialists (Korsgaard 2009, p. 8).

H. van Straalen (✉)
The Research Master Philosophy, University of Amsterdam, Amsterdam, The Netherlands
e-mail: H.vanStraalen@hotmail.com

© Springer International Publishing AG 2018   277
L. Huppes-Cluysenaer, N.M.M.S. Coelho (eds.), *Aristotle on Emotions in Law and Politics*, Law and Philosophy Library 121, DOI 10.1007/978-3-319-66703-4_13

the best he could. He is filled with an emotion which can—among other candidates—be described as remorse or pollution.

On the other hand it is easy to see why some commentators question whether 'making dirty hands' is even conceptually coherent. If the most important ethical question is what we should do, and the answer is found by weighing off the different consequences against each other, it seems utterly impossible for us to do the wrong thing if the best consequences are reached. My suggestion below will be that this is so, because within such a perspective, we only care about the *overall evaluation of an act.*[2]

In this chapter I will argue that the dirty hands debate might benefit from looking at human conduct through the eyes of a non-consequentialist ethics, which is less concerned with the question of *what we should do.* I will try to show how virtue ethics, with its emphasis on the question *who we should be,* can present different points of evaluation than the mere overall-evaluations of our acts.

To do this I will first present two important articles in the debate, namely the classical piece by Michael Walzer,[3] and a (in)famous critical article by Kai Nielsen.[4] Secondly I will present an interpretation of Aristotle's *Nicomachean Ethics,*[5] in which I will draw attention to the way in which eudaimonia, character, and upbringing work together to shape human practice. Thirdly, I will take the structure of human practice which Aristotle provides, and use it for my own purpose. This purpose is to pinpoint different things human beings might care about, aside from the mere overall evaluation of their acts.[6]

Doing so might help to broaden the scope of the debate on dirty hands. A part of this discussion might be about what our moral evaluations are directed towards (acts, characters, reputations, lives). Even if all of this is only a suggestion, perhaps it might help to think of feelings of remorse in the way that Michael Walzer did, namely not as mere psychological facts, but as of crucial importance to our moral practices. I will, however, end on a critical note.

13.2 Dirty Hands

In ethics, the notion of dirty hands popped up somewhere in the mid-seventies. (Incidentally around the time that crucial steps were being taken in the Vietnam War). One of the classical articles which further fueled and focused this debate was

---

[2]Compare De Wijze (2007).

[3]Walzer (1973).

[4]Nielsen (2007a).

[5]Edition used: Aristotle (1926), Loeb Classical Library.

[6]Aristotle himself however, might not provide the conceptual space required to think of cases of dirty hands. This has for instance been argued by Karen M. Nielsen, who makes it convincing that Aristotle himself would not think that cases of dirty hands could exist (Nielsen 2007b).

the article 'political action: the dilemma of dirty hands' by Michael Walzer.[7] In it, Walzer argued that our moral reality demanded us to have a notion of dirty hands in place.

For at first sight it seems our moral thinking can be quite linear. We should just try to do the good and avoid doing the evil. But of course, Walzer notices, it is not as easy as that for we do not live in a perfect world.[8] There is no complete absence of evil possible. And this also means that sometimes it is required of us to do the *lesser* out of two evils. Walzer argued that in these cases a stubborn form of absolutism is not acceptable.[9] That is, digging your feet down in the sand, and washing your hands in innocence, demanding to 'do only good by doing good',[10] is not the way to go. Sometimes we have to do wrong to do right.

Examples of dirty hands often repeated are situations in which a military official has a terrorist tortured in order to find out where the bomb is,[11] or in which the political candidate with great moral aspirations has to make a deal with a polluting company to acquire the funds to continue his campaign.[12] The thought being that *ordering people tortured* and *making dirty deals* might be necessary, but still remains *bad*.

So in cases of dirty hands, Walzer noticed a double bind or paradox. For even if it is morally required of us to do evil things to do good, these things do not thereby somehow lose their evilness. After doing evil, our hands become *dirty*. We truly *do* do evil to do good. And the recognition of this fact should make us feel certain things.

---

[7]Walzer (1973).

[8]Or in the poetic way that Walzer introduces his subject: "The argument relates not only to the coherence and harmony of the moral universe, but also to the relative ease or difficulty – or impossibility – of living a moral life." (Walzer 1973, p. 161). Compare De Wijze: "From a meta-ethical perspective, tragic-remorse confirms that we live in a world where our moral reality is nuanced and messy" (De Wijze 2005, p. 465).

[9]Walzer: "The notion of dirty hands derives from an effort to refuse "absolutism" without denying the reality of the moral dilemma." (Walzer 1973, p. 162).

[10]Ibid., p. 165.

[11]Ibid., pp. 166–167.

[12]Ibid., p. 165. In two later works (Walzer 1978, 2004), Walzer increasingly came to think of dirty hands as both a specifically political problem and one involving analyses of catastrophes. However, many commentators in the debate, for instance De Wijze (2007), Coady and O'Neill (1990) and Nielsen (2007a) have to a great extent interpreted cases of dirty hands as also occurring outside of the domain of politics, and outside of the domain of catastrophe. Compare: "As to the narrowly political, the fact that dirty hands problems are so consistently posed in terms of it should not blind us to the possibility that such problems can arise in other areas. Machiavelli and the modern Machiavellians do not explicitly deny this possibility but their emphases are such as to obscure it. My own view is that the necessities that give rise to dirty hands problems are part of the human rather than the specifically princely condition, but that the political milieu gives a particular focus and, sometimes, urgency to them" (Coady and O'Neill 1990, p. 264) and: "Dirty work goes on in the world (and not only in politics)" (Nielsen 2007a, p. 35).

In texts by Walzer and his commentators, the following feelings are taken into account: remorse, corruption, feeling unclean,[13] dirty, guilty,[14] shame,[15] anguish,[16] pollution,[17] being morally burdened,[18] the feeling of having lost innocence,[19] the feeling of giving up one's soul.[20] And as Walzer noted, we demand to see these feelings reflected on the face of the one who makes dirty hands. We only want the politician who will feel polluted, to make the deal with the polluting company, and no one else. Feeling terrible about making dirty hands is a qualification for being allowed to make them.

Contemporary scholars like Stephen De Wijze have tried to create more conceptual clarity in this issue, and came up with the following defining points of dirty hands. First of all, making dirty hands is not the same as doing evil, because one does the morally required thing to do. Secondly, having to make dirty hands is not like having to settle a moral dilemma, because in a moral dilemma, there is no preferable way out. In cases of dirty hands however, at least one option open to us is the morally right one to take[21] (De Wijze 2007, p. 9). To sum up, one gets one's hands dirty both *because* and *despite* of doing the right thing. Or as Stephen De Wijze notices, in cases of dirty hands we are still somehow willing to *do the same thing again.*[22]

13.3 Overall Evaluations

It is easy to understand that some think all of the above sounds too mysterious and paradoxical. For to speak with Walzer:

> how can it be wrong to do what is right? Or, how can we get our hands dirty by doing what we ought to do?[23]

And the easiest way out of this paradox is to state that, no, in fact we cannot possibly do evil by doing the right thing. We either do the right thing or we don't. We do not become dialetheists in ethics.

---

[13]Walzer (1973), p. 161.

[14]Ibid., p. 166.

[15]De Wijze (2005), p. 467.

[16]Ibid.

[17]Ibid.

[18]Walzer (1973), p. 167.

[19]Ibid., p. 161.

[20]Ibid., p. 176.

[21]Ibid., p. 178.

[22]De Wijze (2005), p. 468.

[23]Walzer (1973), p. 164.

This is the approach which Kai Nielsen takes in his article 'There Is No Dilemma of Dirty Hands'.[24] According to Nielsen there might very well be something like having dirty hands, but it can impossibly be the case that this means a decision has both been right and wrong. In cases of dirty hands we should not forget that—from the outset—we presuppose that there is one right thing to do. And when someone does this one thing, this is all that we can morally speaking hope for.

Nielsen's article contains three facts about or moral practice, which help to clarify this further. First of all, when it comes to the rightness of a particular act, for instance to torture someone, we should always consider the *context* of the act, because in, a certain way and up to a certain extent, in morality *it all depends* and the importance of circumstance and context is vital.[25] What is wrong in some cases might be right in others. Secondly, in every situation in which we can't do good only by doing good, we should *always try to do the lesser evil* and aim for the best outcome in the given circumstances.[26] And finally, we should never lose the fact out of sight that if everything goes right, this thing was *all things considered* the right thing to do,[27] and so in a strict sense no *moral wrong* has been done:

> Where whatever we do or fail to do leads to the occurrence of evil or sustains it, we do not do wrong by doing the lesser evil. Indeed, we do what, everything considered, is the right thing to do: the thing we ought – through and through ought – in this circumstance to do.[28]

And everything that Nielsen says makes good sense. However, the statement 'everything considered' is of crucial importance. For what Nielsen suggests, is only uncontroversial against a backdrop in which the *overall evaluation of an act as to its consequences in this specific context* gets the entirety of moral evaluative weight. It must be the only thing which we morally evaluate. It seems to me that if this focus on the specific act itself is admitted, everything that Nielsen says follows. And this also means that I think most people who do not agree with Nielsen (for instance Stephen De Wijze) do not agree with the basic point above. And in that case it might be worthwhile to wonder whether this makes sense, and whether human beings care about more than merely the overall evaluation of the consequences of their acts.

---

[24]First print in 1996, *South African Journal of Philosophy,* vol. 15, no. 1, pp. 1–7.

[25]Nielsen (2007a), pp. 26, 27, 34, and 35.

[26]Ibid., pp. 20, 21, 23, 34, and 35.

[27]Ibid., pp. 22, 26, 27, and 32.

[28]Ibid., p. 22. Compare Walzer: "it might be said that every political choice ought to be made solely in terms of its particular and immediate circumstances – in terms, that is, of the reasonable alternatives, available knowledge, likely consequences, and so on. [...] Even when he lies and tortures, his hands will be clean, for he has done what he should do as best he can, standing alone in a moment of time, forced to choose." (Walzer 1973, p. 169).

13.4 Dirty Hands According to Nielsen

Nielsen, by the way, nowhere states that he thinks cases of dirty hands themselves are impossible.[29] The above is a bit of a caricature. Indeed Nielsen explicitly recognizes that these cases of dirty hands exist, and gives a clear presentation of what a (part) of this experience entails according to him. Yet this presentation itself is telling, because it could be claimed that it corrodes the experience too much. For instance, Nielsen states that we get dirty hands by doing specific things which would under *normal circumstance*[30] be morally wrong to do. We break a *prima facie* duty in order to do our actual duty.[31]

This might sound like an appealing and clearheaded analysis of dirty hands cases, (and as I will argue below, it can even be called commendable), but it does have some difficulties. For instance, it seems to turn the remorse we feel into a feeling which is directed towards something other than the actual act we performed. After all, this act was the right one. If this is really all that matters, it seems dubious that talk of *prima facie* duties is even necessary. At most we feel bad because in *other* circumstances we would not have acted this way. But why should that be a good reason to feel bad now? Does it justify the moral importance of this feeling?[32] Would it not be better to have an actor who performs the same kind of acts without feeling anything at all?

Nielsen explicitly denies that people who make dirty hands are guilty, for "psychologically speaking, it is perhaps inevitable that he will feel guilty" but "to feel guilty is not necessarily to be guilty."[33] And of course this makes sense, for on the approach which focuses on what should be done, nothing has gone wrong. But we might wonder whether this does not spill over into the discussion on emotions. We can wonder whether the bad feelings caused by making dirty hands are not mere psychological *inertia*. That is, that they are feelings which psychologically speaking pop up, but which have no moral value of their own.

---

[29]Both De Wijze (1996) and the *Stanford Encyclopedia of Philosophy* (Coady 2014) seem to claim that Nielsen states that dirty hands are 'conceptually confused'. But he clearly does not do this (Nielsen 1996).

[30]Nielsen (2007a), pp. 20, 21, 22, 23, and 35; "[...] it is sometimes true that, to succeed in politics, political leaders, and frequently others as well, must get their hands dirty. That is, they will have to do things, or condone the doing of things, which in normal circumstances at least would be utterly morally impermissible" (Nielsen 2007a, p. 21).

[31]Nielsen (2007a), pp. 25 and 31.

[32]And Nielsen does care about this: "He [the one with dirty hands] should, I agree, feel pain, anguish and regret." (Nielsen 2007a, p. 30).

[33]Idem, p. 21.

13.5   Aristotle

So what is suggested above is that when you take an ethical perspective in which only the overall evaluation of an act counts, this makes it hard to fully make sense of everything Walzer said. It might even make it difficult to understand why the remorseful feelings in cases of dirty hands should get that much attention in both literature[34] and philosophy. If we feel that even in these cases, Walzer was on to something, a serious option might be to look at other kinds of concerns which human beings might have, outside of their concern with realizing the best outcome. And this might start with Aristotle. (Even if it is clear that Aristotle himself is not interested in the phenomenon of making dirty hands, and it is in fact likely that he would see no conceptual possibility to do so.[35] Still, Aristotle can be a stepping stone). So, what is ethics about according to Aristotle?

13.5.1   Eudaimonia, Function, and Soul

The *Nicomachean Ethics* starts with the remark that every action or art is directed towards the good. For actions, this partially means that it is constitutive of action that it has an end. Doing things in a random directionless way is not doing anything at all.[36] But it also means that every action aims to realize some highest good. Aristotle notes that there are vast differences in what people take this highest good to be, but that at least everyone agrees on the name:

> both the multitude and persons of refinement speak of it as happiness (*eudaimonia*). (*EN* 1095a1, trans. Rackham)

Everything a human being does is directed towards him obtaining eudaimonia. Yet as many years of Aristotle scholarship have made clear, eudaimonia is not a fleeting feeling of joy.[37] It is not so much a pleasant subjective experience (also known as 'philosophical hedonism') as an excellent continuous activity for a human being to be in.

It is therefore also specific to the species under investigation. That is, we can only judge whether a human being is in an optimal condition when we understand

---

[34]Sartre (n.d.).

[35]Compare the article by Nielsen (2007b).

[36]Christine Korsgaard: "in at least some cases an act is done for some specific purpose or end. For instance, Aristotle tells us that the courageous person who dies in battle lays down his life for the sake of his country or for his friends (*EN* 1169a17–31). In the same way, it seems natural to say that the liberal person who makes a donation aims to help somebody out (*EN* 1120b3), the magnificent person who puts on a play aims to give the city a treat (*EN* 1122b23), the magnanimous man aims to reap honors (*EN* 1123b20–21), the ready-witted man aims to amuse his audience in a tactful way (*EN* 4.8 1128a24–27), and so on." Korsgaard (2009), p. 9.

[37]Urmson (1988), p. 12.

what a human being is. This is why the discussion of eudaimonia in the first book of the *Nicomachean Ethics* seamlessly turns into a discussion of what the human soul is (*EN* 1102a5–3a10). In the *Nicomachean Ethics,* this is not supposed to be a different topic. The *human soul* is the *form* that determines *what* a human being is. Whoever knows what the human soul is, knows what a human being is, and therefore knows what is *good* for a human being. There is an interwovenness of what we might call anthropology, biology, and ethics. In the literature, this is sometimes called 'the function argument'.[38]

So calling someone eudaimon means that this individual is living an excellent human life. The big conclusion of the first book is therefore that we should investigate what the human excellence, or virtue (*arete*), looks like. And immediately Aristotle concludes that *eudaimonia* has an 'external' aspect. That is, to possess *eudaimonia* to the fullest extent, there are certain things which human beings need to have:

> there are certain external advantages, the lack of which sullies supreme felicity, such as good birth, satisfactory children, and personal beauty: a man of very ugly appearance or low birth, or childless and alone in the world, is not our idea of a happy man, and still less so perhaps is one who has children or friends that are worthless, or who has had good ones but lost them by death.[39] (*EN* 1099b1, trans. Rackham)

In general however, Aristotle is more concerned with the quality of the soul itself, instead of its possessions. This comment needs further qualification however, because Aristotle distinguishes three different parts of the soul. So more specifically, Aristotle's focus lies on the question of the quality of the *moral* part of the soul. Ethics has little to do with either the biological functions of the soul (the excellence of which is an object for biology or medicine) or the purely theoretical intellectual functions of the soul (the excellence of which is reached through philosophy and science). So the *Nicomachean Ethics* will only be a study of the excellence of the moral part of the soul, and the practical intelligence (*phronesis*) in as far as this is required to be moral.

To shortly note something which might already be obvious: this concern with realizing the specific human excellence is a different concern from those of the consequentialist. It is an approach which does not look at a human being like the arbitrary producer of acts, but rather as a growing being. Judging the quality of a being might not be the same as judging the quality of the acts it produces.

---

[38]Compare for instance in this volume the comments and further explanation on this in: de Matos (2018).

[39]Compare also Nussbaum (2001), p. 318.

13.5.2 Acquiring the Moral Excellence

When turning towards ethical excellence in the second book, the first question that Aristotle poses is how we come in possession of it. This already turns out to be a difficult topic.

For in most cases, Aristotle notices, the activity of a faculty only comes after the possession of the faculty itself. We already have the potentiality (*dunamis*) to do something and then we bring it into activity or actuality (*energeia*) by doing it. For instance, Aristotle notes that we can only see after we already possess the faculty of sight (*EN* 1103a27–31). Although this logic also applies to ethical virtue, there is a slight difference. For with ethical virtue, we only truly possess the potentiality to do virtuous things, when we have in a way already brought this potentiality to activity:

> The virtues on the other hand we acquire by first having actually practiced them [*energesantes proteron*]. (*EN* 1103a31–32)

And so in ethics, the activity comes before the potentiality. There are two reasons for this. First of all, Aristotle notes that being ethically virtuous means being a certain kind of person. We have to be someone with immediate tendencies and dispositions (*hexis*) to do certain things. But according to Aristotle, we only acquire these dispositions by acting. So Aristotle can write and repeat:

> For things that we have to learn to do, we learn them doing them: for instance, men become builders by building houses, harpers by playing on the harp. Similarly we become just by doing just acts, temperate by doing temperate acts, brave by doing brave acts. (*EN* 1103a33–5, trans. Rackham)
>
> some men become temperate and gentle, others profligate and irascible, by actually comporting themselves in one way or the other in relation to those passions. In one word, our moral dispositions are formed as a result of the same activities [homoion energeia]. (*EN* 1103b18–23, trans. Rackham)

The 'same' (*homoion*) between the disposition and the act in the second quote above, should probably be understood to signify the specific kind of disposition which is at stake, for instance justice and temperance. An act might be called a brave act and therefore suitable to perform to acquire the same kind of character. And I don't think this is meant to be mysterious in any way: one becomes such by acting such, and one becomes different by performing different kind of acts.[40]

It is also particularly clear that Aristotle (unlike perhaps the Stoic or Plato) sees no other way to become virtuous. Perhaps some people might suggest that virtue is like knowledge, and we should study hard, but in the case of moral virtue Aristotle denies this:

> But the mass of mankind, instead of doing virtuous acts, have recourse to discussing virtue, and fancy that they are pursuing philosophy and that this will make them good men. In so doing they act like invalids who listen carefully to what the doctor says, but entirely neglect to carry out his prescriptions. That sort of philosophy will no more lead to a healthy state of

---

[40]So someone with the bad luck of a bad upbringing might end up unvirtuous. I will come back to this in the paragraph on upbringing below.

soul than will the mode of treatment produce health of body. (*EN* 1105b13–18, trans. Rackham)

You have to *do* and *practice* the thing you want to become. And so in a way, the activity comes before the potentiality.

13.5.3 Performing the Moral Excellence

Secondly at least some form of activity needs to be in place to acquire virtue, because a fixed disposition needs to be in place before *real* virtue is possible. Aristotle thinks that there is an enormous difference between doing things and doing these things from an already acquired disposition. In fact, acting without a well-formed character is not real virtue at all. Real virtue only realizes itself as a realization of a disposition which one already possesses.

This points to one of the big differences between the arts and the virtues, namely that with the arts, all value attaches to the product itself, while with the virtues it is not only the 'product' also the one who acts needs to be in a certain condition. Aristotle writes:

> Moreover the case of the arts is not really analogous to that of the virtues. Works of art have their merit in themselves, so that it is enough if they are produced having a certain quality of their own; but acts done in conformity with the virtues are not done justly or temperately if they themselves are of a certain sort, but only if the agent also is in a certain state of mind when he does them. (*EN* 1105a26–32, trans. Rackham)
>
> Just and temperate, however, is not he who does these [just and temperate] things, but he who does them in the way that the just and temperate man does them.[41] (*EN* 1105b6–9, trans. Rackham)

For example, the applaudable way in which a generous man gives part of his money to a poor beggar, is very unlike the random way in which a child might reluctantly give a part of his money after instruction by his parents. Only the first can properly be called *virtue* in true actuality.

As commentators note, the particular acts which we perform could not have come about without obtaining a well formed character which provide us with the background required to face the particular situations in which we find ourselves:

> This continuous basis, internalized and embodied in the agent's system of desires, goes a long way towards explaining what that person can and will see in the new situation: an occasion for courage, for generous giving, for justice. [...] it is now time to say that the particular case would be absurd and unintelligible without the guiding and sorting power of the universal.[42]

---

[41] Also compare Nussbaum (2001), p. 308.

[42] Ibid., p. 306. Compare also Gadamer: "If man always encounters the good in the form of the particular practical situation in which he finds himself, the task of moral knowledge is to determine what the concrete situations asks of him – or to put it another way, the person acting must view the concrete situation in the light of what is asked of him in general." (Gadamer 1989, p. 311).

13.5.4 Community and Upbringing

Finally however, we could wonder, however, why we would even want to develop a certain character and perform certain acts. For perhaps in a common-sense way, a brave man will not think of doing cowardly things, and in this sense his bravery is motivated. But supposedly a young child is not yet brave, so where would this motivation come from?

Here Aristotle has an out however: the growing child is not alone. Perhaps the child can see no particular reasons for acting bravely, but definitely his parents, up-bringers, and perhaps also is neighbors and community members can. So Aristotle can say something like:

> Hence it is incumbent on us to control the character of our activities, since on the quality of these depends the quality of our dispositions. It is therefore not of small moment whether we are trained from childhood in one set of habits or another; on the contrary it is of very great, or rather of supreme, importance.[43] (*EN* 1103b20–26, and 1104b11–3 trans. Rackham)

In this sense Aristotle might, although it is a bit of a stretch, be called a communitarian, because the access of the individual to his virtues is through the community in which he lives.[44] The virtues which the virtuous man carries within himself are the virtues circulating within the community of which he is a part. It is tempting to say that the upbringing of the child into virtue is something like the child getting enveloped in the 'life form' of the community: he learns the significant stories and learns to recognize how to behave according to the customs of tradition. (Although as I will try to show below, there is an important sense in which this is not enough, and individuality plays a major role in Aristotle).

13.6 Being Concerned with Other Things

To be clear on this point, the above is a short interpretation of parts of the *Nicomachean Ethics*. What the interpretation shows—if we agree that my interpretation is to some extent correct and Aristotle himself is to the greatest extent right— is how human practice works. Talking about human action requires words like 'eudaimonia', 'soul', 'virtue', 'character', and comes with a particular story on how dispositions are obtained. The question I will consider now is whether this structure

---

[43]Compare Urmson: "If we are normal human beings and not naturally incapacitated by some abnormal defect, then whether we acquire a good or a bad character depends on the kind of upbringing we get. [...] Before one has acquired the art or skill one acts in accordance with the instructions of a teacher, who tells us what to do, and one does it with effort. Gradually, by practice and repetition, it becomes effortless and second nature." (Urmson 1988, p. 25).

[44]Many philosophers identified as 'communitarianists' also seem to have some appreciation for Aristotle on exactly this point, for instance, Alasdair MacIntyre and Charles Taylor. It is also interesting that Walzer mentions Charles Taylor in a footnote to his article Walzer (1973), p. 160.

of human practice might not give a way to conceptualize concerns and feelings which are directed towards other bits of this practice than merely the outcome of any particular act.

A note for the Aristotelians: this is not the same as saying that Aristotle himself is particularly concerned with this. Furthermore, to repeat a point already made above, it is very unlikely that Aristotle would for instance consider cases of dirty hands conceptually possible. Part of which might be explained by the limited attention the *Nicomachean Ethics* has for instances of 'failed' lives, and the largely automatic or 'deterministic' way in which it describes human conduct.

So the guiding question below will be to what kinds of reflections and feelings might the structure of human practice give rise, when we stop being Aristotelians on some points. That is, whether for instance the feelings stemming from a concern with our eudaimonia might not be distinguished from the feelings which stem from a concern with producing the best possible outcome.

So back to dirty hands. We have acted. We have ordered the terrorist tortured, we have made the dirty deal with the shady company, we have bombarded the civilians, we have pulled the trigger, and consequently we feel sick and stained. But we also realize that we have done the best we could. But then why might the mere thought of having done this and that cause such distress? What could this feeling be about?

13.6.1   Eudaimonia

First of all Aristotle could help us realize that an act is never just a random event in the world. An act is performed by an agent who remains the same throughout the performance of any number of acts. *Eudaimonia,* as noted before, is a term which has as its object the entire life of an individual (and also somewhat stretches beyond this). Every act of this individual is at the same time a part of its life. As Aristotle himself notes, not only does every act have a goal, but in a way this goals is also always eudaimonia. After all, every act is also to benefit the worth of one's entire life. But we might be concerned about the way specifically making dirty hands affects the 'value' of our life.

For first of all, not every single human life is such that it contains dirty acts. Certain circumstances are required for these acts to be called for.[45] And we might wonder whether the mere fact that we find ourselves in these circumstances does not somewhat detract from the choose worthiness of our life. At least in a common-sense way, no one would wish their child to face terrible circumstances.[46] And we

---

[45]Something also noted by De Wijze: "Tragic-remorse indicates recognition by an agent that she has been morally polluted by events and circumstances outside of her control" (De Wijze 2005, p. 464).

[46]Even if this does sound somewhat un-Aristotelian. After all, Aristotle claims that to 'some extent' bad circumstances can be handled in a beautiful way. For instance, military excellence is not merely reached when victory is obtained (*NE* 1101a3–5).

ourselves can curse the circumstances in which we are thrown. At least we can recognize that they are not *ideal*. A feeling which, with a reference to Walzer, can perhaps be called 'sadness about the circumstances'.

Secondly, perhaps making dirty hands does not sit in well with the particular *ideal* we have of what a practical human life should look like. Perhaps turning into someone whose life stories depict a lot of dirty deals is something which on its own makes us feel sick. The act itself might feel like something which should not be something which *is us*. We might feel that it hurts the value of our life.[47] A feeling which we could describe as 'sadness about the act'.[48]

In both (and other similar) cases, of course a healthy response to this stroke of moral bad luck could be to explicitly take a contextual approach like that of Nielsen: whether a life is being lived well or not is itself contextual. To judge what happens in our life we need to think of the specific options which were open to us at the time, and not compare it with circumstances which were not there.[49] Our dirty acts don't hurt our *eudaimonia*, if the latter is considered against the backdrop of the elements of chance which run their course with the world. (Strange enough, it is exactly by accepting this 'frailty', that our *eudaimonia* can seem a guaranteed thing). Yet it also seems fair to say that in fact we often do not judge our own lives in a contextual way like this.

13.6.2   Others

Secondly, the moral appreciation of our acts is not something which happens in isolation from others. Just as we as children had to be taught how to behave, so our acts always take place in a world which we already share with others.[50] This gives

---

[47]Although it seems a hard thesis to defend, Michael Stocker claimed that Aristotle explicitly thought that doing 'base' deeds would decrease our *eudaimonia*, even if these deeds were necessary: "Base deeds are among those severe disasters that can make eudaimonia difficult if not impossible. This is obvious in the case where there is no good reason for doing what is base. For only an evil or bad person could act that way, and such a person cannot have eudaimonia. But it also holds, I suggest, where a good person is morally compelled to do what is base. We can be helped in seeing why this is so by noting these points. Aristotle's ethics is importantly one of achievement. On his view, to be a eudaimon person, and in this sense a good person, one must have honour, pride, and self-esteem, which, in turn, require doing well at good and important activities (e.g. 4. 2–4, and *Rhetoric* 2. 2). Thus, again on his view, one cannot have eudaimonia, if one does what is base—even if one does it for the best." (Stocker 2004, p. 65).

[48]De Wijze calls this 'agent-regret' (De Wijze 2005, p. 461).

[49]This has a lot to do with the quote from footnote 9 above. In particular the 'standing alone in a moment of time, forced to choose' part.

[50]This is something which Walzer seemed to have felt acutely: "For while any one of us may stand alone, and so on, when we make this or that decision, we are not isolated or solitary in our moral lives. Moral life is a social phenomenon, and it is constituted at least in part by rules, the knowing of which (and perhaps the making of which) we share with our fellows. The experience of coming

an 'objective' side to our subjective decision. Our act is not merely there before us, and is not merely judged by the big objective moral standard in the sky. It is also there for the others to see. To act brave is also a claim to be that which Achilles was. To claim that one has done the right thing, is also to claim that others should agree this is so. It is easy to think of cases in which this might be felt as being risky business.

For instance, having done the best we could in terribly restrictive circumstances, we might still anxiously wonder whether others will even agree that what we have done was the right thing to do. And their opinion matters to us, because if they disagree, they might well be right. We might 'doubt our own judgement', and eagerly or anxiously wait to hear that of others.

Furthermore, when the stories of what we have done are reiterated, we might feel anxious that some elements of it will not remain quite the same in different contexts. For instance, the cruelty involved in torturing the terrorist can be taken out of context, so that when the story gets retold, we might be made out to look like monsters. And we don't want to be known as monsters! (Note that this is not the same as to say that 'we do not want to be known as monsters *because* of the bad consequences this has for us'). The dirt on our hands might make us 'fear for our reputation'.

Also, if the moral code of our society is 'objectively' contained in a set of legal or conventional laws, this might provide us with an unwelcoming prospect of punishment. It is unlikely that Aristotle himself would reason like this,[51] but it seems unproblematic to say that our decision was a good one, and yet the law just does not accommodate this. We might face punishment because we indeed *did* order the terrorist tortured, and torture indeed *is* illegal. Even within the domain of rights, we distinguish *positive law* from *natural law*, and *legal* law from *moral* law. Conflicts between these are possible. Walzer seems to be concerned with this when he writes: "In [cases of just assassination and civil disobedience] men violate a set of rules, go beyond a moral or legal limit, in order to do what they believe they should do. At the same time, they acknowledge their responsibility for the violation by accepting punishment or doing penance."[52] Crossing a limit is not necessarily as much a contextual term as 'doing the right thing'. A punishment might be

---

up against these rules, challenging their prohibitions, and explaining ourselves to other men and women is so common and so obviously important that no account of moral decision-making can possibly fail to come to grips with it." (Walzer 1973, p. 169).

[51]Compare the article of Saulo de Matos in this volume, in which the claim that *nomological approaches to ethics* only started with Christianity: de Matos (2018).

[52]Walzer (1973), p. 178. Stephen De Wijze points towards this passage of Walzer when he writes: "some understandings of dirty hands, the agent may need to be punished in order to emphasise the moral wrong, expiate the guilt and shame, and remove the moral pollution that adheres from certain actions. [...] Just what kind of punishment is appropriate is difficult to delineate. The difficulty is to find a balance that sends the appropriate signal that a moral wrong has been done with all the appropriate opprobrium attached to moral violation yet also acknowledge that it was necessary (if not obligatory) for the appropriate moral reasons." (footnote De Wijze 2005, p. 465).

'objectively' required, even if we (and even our entire community) agree that our 'legal evil' was 'morally' required.

13.6.3 Character

Most importantly however, an act is not performed by a faceless actor who has no particular personality traits, or does not have a specific relation to the act he performed. Acts come about through our character. In a way, every act *is* the realization of the kind of person which we are. And our character, who we are, itself might reflectively be a concern to us. It requires a certain kind of character to be expected to perform certain kinds of acts.

For a start—aside from what Aristotle himself might have to say about this issue—we can wonder whether it is utterly impossible for a kind man to do a cruel thing. It seems conceivable that in some circumstances the act of ordering a terrorist tortured is required. And it also seems conceivable that the act of ordering a terrorist tortured can be called 'cruel', even if it is required.[53] And it also seems conceivable that a kind man might realize that this act is required, and so be forced to do it even though it could still be called 'cruel'.[54] And surely such a discrepancy will make him feel uncomfortable, *because he is not like that*. Because being a certain kind of person makes it almost unthinkable to torture another human being, even if this person can still *do* that which he can hardly imagine himself doing.

Secondly, there is the issue of *corruption*.[55] Doing things which are 'normally' not allowed is *the* way to acquire a personality in which these things are not considered to be particularly bad things to do. For instance, pushing the red glowing iron rod against another human beings face is not easy to do at first, but every time you do it, it will become easier and easier to do so again. The screams that first cut through your soul somehow lose their edge when this process has been repeated thousands of times. And if it has not yet come to this, we might reflectively realize that *we don't want to be like that*. We might be disgusted with finding ourselves on a road with the prospect of turning into someone who will not have a hard time doing

---

[53]The objection to this thought of course being that one is not really, for instance, doing something 'cruel' when one whips or otherwise hurts another human being, if it is justified by the extraction of much needed evidence.

[54]After all, it seems unproblematic to say that someone learns to play the harp, learns to do so *by playing the harp*. Even if *truly* playing the harp requires the ability to do so skillfully. In the same way, it seems to be no paradox for a harp playing expert to *not* play the harp, or skip a specific note in a piece if this is required for external reasons.

[55]Coady writes: "What is at stake is the moral degradation of individual character or institutions or environments and this involves the prevalence of attitudes to what is acceptable conduct which have the effect of treating behaviour that is seriously immoral as normal." (Coady and O'Neill 1990, p. 265).

these kinds of things. Doing these kinds of things will, in a way, opens the perspective to *losing yourself.*

13.6.4 Walzer

The feeling accompanying making dirty hands might probably be attributed to any or any combination of the above. It can probably also be attributed to yet other kinds of evaluation or concern. The above is most of all suggestive, and I do not pretend to be complete. Still I think the above analysis might be promising when it comes to an interpretation of what Walzer was after.

For what is important to note here, is that some moral feelings we experience seem to be dependent on the kind of person we are. Especially in the case of concerns which have to do with the kind of character we possess. For as Aristotle himself puts it:

> We should consider the pleasure and pain of our deeds as signs (*semeion*) of our disposi-
> tions (*hexis*). (*EN* 1104b4, trans. Rackahm)

If we feel terrible about torturing another human being, this reveals something. Not merely something about the act and its consequences, but something about the actor as well. It shows that *he is the kind of person to feel bad about doing this.*

Sure enough this can be translated back into a consequentialist vocabulary (although the consequentialistic hedonist might be even more tempted to argue that it is advisable that torture be done by those who enjoy it most). Still we might wonder whether we do not directly care about the character of another person. I think this is partially what Walzer was after, when he wrote about the moral politician that:

> Surely we have a right to expect more than melancholy from him. When he ordered the
> prisoner tortured, he committed a moral crime and he accepted a moral burden. His
> willingness to acknowledge and bear (and perhaps to repent and do penance for) his guilt
> is evidence, and the only evidence he can offer us, both that he is not too good for politics,
> and that he is good enough. Here is the moral politician: it is by his dirty hands that we
> know him. If he were a moral man and nothing else, his hands would not be dirty; if he were
> a politician and nothing else, he would pretend that they were clean.[56]

The feelings that the moral politician shows are signs of the kind of person he is. And this is the kind of person who is able to recognize the wrong in the action, and is not oblivious to it.[57]

---

[56]Walzer (1973), p. 167.

[57]As de Silvestre notices in her contribution to this volume: "The good speaker can´t ignore the emotions because they are crucial lens through which we see the facts of the world. Emotions are cognitive even when we criticize a person's act moved by a specific emotion" Silvestre (2018), p. 7.

I think in this respect it is important to note that dirty hands do not just happen to anybody. Dirty hands are something which one has to bear. The feelings that accompany it are only available in certain kinds of people. And we might judge these people fit, exactly because they feel terrible about doing terrible things. We require them not only to be a cold and calculating functionary of our own demands, but we demand that they themselves are of a certain kind. For starters, we will have a hard time putting our trust in someone who is unable to even see any moral burden to carry.

13.7 Psychological Versus Moral

One final note: it might in fact be very arguable to care much about the character and dispositions of a fellow human being. And I think on this point there might be something very 'un-modern' in Aristotle (and possibly virtue ethics in general): Aristotle is concerned with *who we should be* and not merely with living a *correct* life. But for 'us' moderns, who know a difference between the good life and the law, this might not make much sense. We might think that morality is largely a private issue, and adherence to the public law merely demands rightness as a kind of correctness: 'you don't have to like it, but just don't break the rules, and don't run through any red lights'. Aristotle however, just doesn't agree:

> lawgivers make the citizens good by training them in habits of right action—this is the aim of all legislation. (*EN* 1103b2–3, trans. Rackham)

Because moral discourse posing the question 'what we should do' seems to be modeled on questions of correctness ('there is *one* right thing, you should find it, and are wrong if you do not do it'),[58] this might be a good reason to also think that feelings of guilt and a demand for remorse in cases of dirty hands are a bit of a dubious move. After all, in cases of dirty hands *there is no real possibility for anyone to demand that any more should have been accomplished*. The act itself is as correct as can be.

In this sense, the difference between Nielsen and Walzer (in my opinion) also seems to be one between on the one hand a normative-progressive perspective on ethics, which draws a distinction between moral reasons to feel guilty and 'valid' moral reasons to feel guilty, and on the other hand an approach which tries to lend words to the moral phenomenon as it is in fact found, whether this phenomenon is 'valid' or not. This, by the way, seems to be one of the points that Walzer himself makes, and which is largely neglected in the discussion of his article:

> It may very well be right to say that moral rules ought to have the character of guidelines, but it seems that in fact they do not.[59]

---

[58]Compare again de Matos (2018) in this volume, in which he discusses the influence of the 'nomological' view of rights, and reviews the question whether the nomological approach leaves any room for our moral emotions.

[59]Walzer (1973), p. 170.

It is telling, and we should take notice of how difficult it is for us to take this statement of Walzer seriously.

I don't really feel confident in elaborating on this too much, but there might be a kind of double bind here: perhaps our 'modern sensibilities' and clear-headedness make it impossible for us to explicitly discuss the wrong in breaking moral rules if this was required, while on the other hand the kind of explicating of our moral reality and our emotional life which is presented in Aristotle and Walzer tends to show us that this might *in fact* not be how our moral reality actually works.

References

Aristotle. 1926. *Nicomachean Ethics*. Translated by H. Rackham. Cambridge, MA: Harvard University Press.

Coady, C.A.J. 2014. The Problem of Dirty Hands. In *The Stanford Encyclopedia of Philosophy*, ed. Edward N. Zalta, Spring 2014 ed. http://plato.stanford.edu/archives/spr2014/entries/dirty-hands/.

Coady, C.A.J., and Onora O'Neill. 1990. Messy Morality and the Art of the Possible. *Proceedings of the Aristotelian Society, Supplementary Volumes* 64: 259–294.

de Matos, Saulo. 2018. Aristotle's Functionalism and the Rise of Nominalism in Law and Politics: Law, Emotion and Language. In *Aristotle on Emotions in Law and Politics*, ed. Liesbeth Huppes-Cluysenaer and Nuno M.M.S. Coelho. Dordrecht: Springer.

De Wijze, Stephen. 1996. The Real Problem of Dirty Hands—Reply to Kai Nielsen. *South African Journal of Philosophy* 15 (4): 149–151.

———. 2005. Tragic-Remorse—The Anguish of Dirty Hands. *Ethical Theory and Moral Practice* 7 (5): 453–471.

———. 2007. Dirty Hands: Doing Wrong to Do Right. In *Politics and Morality*, ed. Igor Primoratz, 3–4. Basingstoke and New York: Palgrave Macmillan.

Gadamer, Hans-Georg. 1989. *Truth and Method*. 2nd ed. New York: Crossroad.

Korsgaard, Christine M. 2009. *Self-Constitution: Agency, Identity, and Integrity*. Oxford and New York: Oxford University Press.

Nielsen, Kai. 1996. There Is No Dilemma of Dirty Hands. Response to Stephen de Wijze. *South African Journal of Philosophy* 15 (4): 155–159.

———. 2007a. There Is No Dilemma of Dirty Hands. In *Politics and Morality*, ed. Igor Primoratz, 20–37. Basingstoke and New York: Palgrave Macmillan.

Nielsen, Karen M. 2007b. Dirtying Aristotle's Hands? Aristotle's Analysis of 'Mixed Acts' in the 'Nicomachean Ethics' III, 1. *Phronesis* 52 (3): 270–300.

Nussbaum, Martha Craven. 2001. *The Fragility of Goodness: Luck and Ethics in Greek Tragedy and Philosophy*. Rev. ed. Cambridge and New York: Cambridge University Press.

Sartre, Jean Paul. n.d. *No Exit and Three Other Plays: Dirty Hands, The Flies, and The Respectful Prostitute*. New York: Vintage.

Silvestre, Ana Carolina de Faria. 2018. Rethinking Legal Education from Aristotle's Theory of Emotions and the Contemporary Challenges of the Practical Realization of Law. In *Aristotle on Emotions in Law and Politics*, ed. Liesbeth Huppes-Cluysenaer and Nuno M.M.S. Coelho. Dordrecht: Springer.

Stocker, Michael. 2004. *Plural and Conflicting Values*. Reprinted. Clarendon Paperbacks. Oxford: Clarendon Press.

Urmson, J.O. 1988. *Aristotle's Ethics*. Oxford and Malden, MA: B. Blackwell.

Walzer, Michael. 1973. Political Action: The Problem of Dirty Hands. *Philosophy & Public Affairs* 2 (2): 160–180.

———. 1978. *Just and Unjust Wars: A Moral Argument with Historical Illustrations*. London: Allen Lane.

———. 2004. *Arguing About War*. New Haven, CT: Yale University Press. http://public.eblib.com/choice/publicfullrecord.aspx?p=3420155.

Chapter 14
Virtue as a Synthesis of Extremes Versus Virtue as a Mean Between Extremes: A Comparison of Chesterton's Account of Virtue with Aristotle's

Wojciech Zaluski

Abstract Both Aristotle and Gilbert Keith Chesterton asserted that virtue can be analyzed by means of a 'tripartite' scheme, viz. as being opposed to its two 'correlated' extremes (the excess of or the deficiency in a passion or action to which the virtue refers). However, while according to Aristotle virtue is radically different from its 'correlated' extremes (is 'the mean' between them), according to Chesterton, virtue, rather than being radically different from extremes, is a paradoxical synthesis of them, holding them in an ethically creative tension. The paper aims at elucidating this—Chestertonian—account of virtue, providing examples of virtues which can be plausibly analyzed in accordance with it (including, for instance, courage, modesty, charity), and comparing it to Aristotle's account.

14.1 Introduction

The Aristotelian account of virtue assumes that virtue is a mean between its two 'correlated' extremes (i.e., the excess of or the deficiency in a passion or action[1] to which the virtue refers) and thereby is radically different from them. This account was criticized on many grounds, but, to my knowledge, no philosopher, with the exception of Gilbert Keith Chesterton,[2] raised an objection that it relies on a mistake consisting in radically opposing virtue to its correlated extremes. On Chesterton's own account, developed in his book *Orthodoxy* but invoked also in his other works (e.g. *Heretics*), virtue holds together in an ethically creative tension

---

[1] Of moral virtues, only justice has as its object actions (more specifically: actions by which we deal with external things in interpersonal relations); the object of the other moral virtues are passions. Cf. Aristotle (1947) (*EN* 1106b15).

[2] Gilbert Keith Chesterton (1874–1936), a Christian writer, essayist and philosopher, was one of the towering figures of the British intellectual life in the first half of the twentieth century.

W. Zaluski (✉)
Faculty of Law and Administration, Jagiellonian University, Kraków, Poland
e-mail: zaluskiwojciech@gmail.com

© Springer International Publishing AG 2018
L. Huppes-Cluysenaer, N.M.M.S. Coelho (eds.), *Aristotle on Emotions in Law and Politics*, Law and Philosophy Library 121, DOI 10.1007/978-3-319-66703-4_14

297

two apparently opposite extremes; it is therefore not radically different from them, but, rather, is the paradoxical synthesis thereof. In this paper we shall try to elucidate this—Chestertonian—account of virtue, provide examples of virtues (including, for instance, courage, modesty, charity) which can be plausibly analyzed in accordance with it, and compare it with the Aristotelian account.

14.2   The Chestertonian Account: Reconstruction

According to Aristotle, virtue does not embrace extremes but occupies a 'middle' place between them, while according to Chesterton virtue embraces—*synthesizes*—extremes. In this section we shall reconstruct the latter view by presenting its five crucial points; in the course of the reconstruction we shall follow the relevant passages of Chesterton's *Orthodoxy*.

(1) Virtue is not "in a balance" but "in a conflict"—it arises as a result of "the collision of two passions apparently opposite (...) of the still crash of two impetuous emotions."[3] The Chestertonian view implies that two passions whose "collision" gives rise to a virtue "were not really inconsistent; but they were such that it was hard to hold simultaneously."[4]

(2) The main argument of Chesterton for his account is that it makes virtue ethically more attractive: according to Chesterton, on his account virtue's ethical quality becomes unquestionable, whereas on the Aristotelian account its quality is dubious, because it leads, as Chesterton believed, to the view of virtue as mediocrity. He claimed that, on his account, the ethical quality of virtue becomes unquestionable because the opposite passions constituting a virtue are preserved "at the top of their energy."[5] Another argument he advanced for his account is that in some cases (especially in the case of courage) acting in accordance with the virtue understood as a synthesis of extremes is practically useful (we develop this point in Sect. 14.3.3). As we can see, Chesterton's arguments for his interpretation are ethical and pragmatic, not interpretative; in other words, Chesterton did not deem his account of virtue to be an interpretation of the Aristotelian doctrine of the mean, which is quite understandable given that his account differs from the Aristotelian one in crucial points, and draws on it only as far as the 'tripartite' scheme for conceptualizing virtue is concerned.

(3) According to Chesterton, the view that virtue is in a balance is characteristic for Paganism whereas the view that virtue is in a conflict is characteristic for Christianity.

---

[3]Chesterton (2010), pp. 85 and 86.

[4]Ibid., p. 85.

[5]Ibid., p. 88.

(4) The Chestertonian account of virtue is supposed, like the Aristotelian one, to explain the structure and essence of *all virtues*. Chesterton does not say so explicitly but this thesis can be inferred from the relevant passages in *Orthodoxy* (though whether he really claimed that he provides an account of *all* virtues is a moot point to which we shall return in Sect. 14.3.1).

(5) Chesterton analyzes at greater length the following virtues: courage, modesty (humility), charity, faith and hope.

   (a) Of courage, which concerns, basically, the fear of death, he writes as follows:

> Let us follow for a moment the clue of the martyr and the suicide; and take the case of courage. No quality has ever so much addled the brains and tangled the definitions of merely rational sages. Courage is almost a contradiction in terms. It means a strong desire to live taking the form of a readiness to die. He must seek life in a spirit of furious indifference to it; he must desire life like water and yet drink death like wine. No philosopher, I fancy, has ever expressed this romantic riddle with adequate lucidity, and I certainly have not done so. But Christianity has done more: it has marked the limits of it in the awful graves of the suicide and the hero, showing the distance between him who dies for the sake of the living and him who dies for the sake of dying (. . .) The Christian courage is a disdain of death; not the Chinese courage, which is a disdain of life (. . .); this duplex passion was the Christian key to others.[6]

Thus, on Chesterton's account, *courage is a paradoxical combination of a strong attachment to life and a disdain of death.*

   (b) As regards modesty, he claims that on the Aristotelian (or, as he prefers to say: 'Pagan') account of virtue, modesty is "the balance between mere pride and mere prostration"; and he provides the following profound analysis:

> The average pagan, like the average agnostic, would merely say that he was content with himself, but not insolently self-satisfied, that there were many better and many worse, that his deserts were limited, but he would see that he got them. In short, he would walk with his head in the air; but not necessarily with his nose in the air. This is a manly and rational position but it is open to the objection [that] being a mixture of two things, it is a dilution of two things; neither is present in its full strength or contributes its full colour. (. . .) It loses both the poetry of being proud and the poetry of being humble. Christianity sought by this same strange expedient to save both of them. It separated the two ideas and then exaggerated them both. In one way man was to be haughtier than he had ever been before; in another way he was to be humbler than he had ever been before. In so far as I am Man I am the chief of creatures. In so far as I am a man, I am the chief of sinners (. . .) Christianity got over the difficulty of combining furious opposites, by keeping them both, and keeping them both furious. The Church was positive on both points. One can hardly think too little of one's self. One can hardly think too much of one's self.[7]

---

[6]Ibid., pp. 85–86.
[7]Ibid., p. 86.

Accordingly, on Chesterton's account, *modesty is a paradoxical combination of high self-esteem ("thinking too much of one's self") and low self-esteem ("thinking too little of one's self")*.

(c) Of the so called theological virtues, faith, hope and charity, Chesterton wrote as follows:

> Charity is a paradox, like modesty and courage. Stated baldly, charity certainly means one of two things – pardoning unpardonable acts, or loving unlovable people. But if we ask ourselves (as we did in the case of pride) what a sensible pagan would feel about such a subject, we shall probably be beginning at the bottom. A sensible pagan would say that there were some people one could forgive, and someone couldn't: a slave who stole wine could be laughed at; a slave who betrayed his benefactor could be killed, and cursed even after he was killed. In so far as the act was pardonable, the man was pardonable. That again is rational, and even refreshing; but it is a dilution. It leaves no place for a pure horror of injustice, such as that which is a great beauty in the innocent. And it leaves no place for a mere tenderness for men as men, such as is the whole fascination of the charitable. Christianity came in here as before. It came in startlingly with a sword, and clove one thing from another. It divided the crime from the criminal. The criminal we must forgive unto seventy times seven. The crime we must not forgive at all (. . .) We must be much more angry with theft than before, and yet much kinder to thieves than before. There was room for wrath and love to run wild.[8]
>
> Charity means pardoning what is unpardonable, or it is no virtue at all. Hope means hoping when things are hopeless, or it is no virtue at all. And faith means believing the incredible, or it is no virtue at all (. . .) Charity is the power of defending that which we know to be indefensible. Hope is the power of being cheerful in circumstances which we know to be desperate (. . .) It is true that there is a thing crudely called charity, which means charity to the deserving poor; but charity to the deserving is not charity at all, but justice. It is the undeserving who require it (. . .) Charity forgives the sins that are like scarlet. Whatever may be the meaning of faith, it must always mean a certainty about something we cannot prove.[9]

Thus, *charity (in one of its aspects) is a paradoxical combination of forgivingness (towards the agent) and un-forgivingness (towards the deed), or wrath and love (i.e., wrath towards the deed and love towards the doer)*. Since Aristotle also claimed, as Cristina Viano and José Brito emphasize in the articles published in this volume,[10] that crime should be separated from the criminal, the very distinction in the moral or legal evaluation between the deed and the doer cannot be regarded as having been made by the Christian thinkers; the contribution of Christianity is that charity consists (among other things) in treating the doer with love (with forgivingness) even if his or her deed is morally atrocious (unforgivable). It is hard to disagree with Chesterton that charity understood as being forgiving towards people who did something unforgivable was unknown to the Pagan world, and that it has the paradoxical nature that can hardly be analyzed in the Aristotelian fashion. As for the two other theological virtues: according to Chesterton, *faith is a paradoxical*

---

[8]Ibid., p. 87.

[9]Chesterton (2009), pp. 80–81.

[10]Compare Brito (2018) and Viano (2018).

synthesis of a strong belief and the awareness of its un-provability; and hope is a paradoxical synthesis of having grounds for despair and looking serenely at the future.

Other examples of virtues analyzable in this fashion, provided by Chesterton himself, are the Christian combination (lacking a good name) of pessimism and optimism, opposed to "resignation", and the "prophetic virtue", which is a combination of "pure gentleness" (i.e. "being a lamb") and "pure fierceness" (i.e., "being a lion").[11]

14.3   The Chestertonian Account: Evaluation

The Chestertonian account has weak, strong, and unclear points; we shall discuss them successively.

14.3.1   Weak Points

Firstly, a weak point is Chesterton's misinterpretation (in one aspect) of the Aristotelian account of virtue. Chesterton writes of virtue, as understood by Aristotle, that "being a mixture of two things, it is a dilution of two things; neither is present in its full strength or contributes its full colour".[12] Accordingly, Chesterton suggests that on the Aristotelian account the mean is a *sui generis* compromise between the extremes, i.e., that the mean includes both extremes but includes them, as a result of their "mixing", in some "diluted" form. Thus, Chesterton can be ranked among those (numerous) critics of Aristotle's account who maintain that it purportedly recommends mediocrity. But this picture of this account is distorted, or, rather, simply false. Virtue, as understood by Aristotle, does not recommend mediocrity; quite the contrary: it recommends extremity as far as moral perfection is concerned; as Aristotle explicitly wrote about virtue:

> It is a mean state between two vices, that which depends on excess and that which depends on defect; and again it is a mean because the vices respectively fall short of or exceed what is right in both passions and actions, while virtue both finds and chooses that which is intermediate. Hence in respect of its substance and the definition which states its essence virtue is a mean, with regard to what is best and right an extreme. (*EN* 1107a2–7, trans. Ross)

Furthermore, virtues understood in the Aristotelian fashion need not issue in 'mediocre' behavior in the non-moral sense of 'mediocrity'; there seems to be nothing 'mediocre' in courage or generosity as they were understood by Aristotle.

---

[11]Chesterton (2010), pp. 85–86.

[12]Ibid., p. 86.

But, of course, the weakness of the Chestertonian objection to the Aristotelian account does not undermine Chesterton's account; it only undermines one of his arguments for the claim that on his own account virtue is ethically more attractive than virtue on the Aristotelian account. One may ask *en passant* what could have been the cause of the Chestertonian misinterpretation of the Aristotle's account. Arguably, the source of it might have been the confusion of Aristotle's "mean" with Horace's 'golden mean (*aurea mediocritas*)'. Horace did recommend moderation in the Epicurean sense (which is indeed close to mediocrity, for instance: in its requirement of limiting one's desires only to those which are natural and necessary), arguing that it ensures its possessor a calm life; as he writes in Ode II. 10:

> Better wilt thou live, Licinius, by neither always pressing out to sea nor too closely hugging the dangerous shore in cautious fear of storms. Whosoever cherishes the golden mean, safely avoids the foulness of an ill-kept house and discreetly, too, avoids a hall exciting envy.[13]

However, this view of virtue is essentially different from Aristotle's: as we see, the Aristotelian 'mean' and the Horacean '*aurea mediocritas*' are similar only in their name.

Secondly, in *Orthodoxy* Chesterton seems to defend the claim that his account can be universally applied, i.e., it is applicable to all virtues. However, in *Heretics* he asserts that his account of virtue refers only to the Christian virtues, such as faith, hope, charity or humility:

> The real difference between Paganism and Christianity is perfectly summed up in the difference between the pagan, or natural, virtues, and those three virtues of Christianity which the Church of Rome calls virtues of grace. The pagan, or rational, virtues are such things as justice and temperance, and Christianity has adopted them. The three mystical virtues which Christianity has not adopted, but invented, are faith, hope, and charity. Now much easy and foolish Christian rhetoric could easily be poured out upon those three words, but I desire to confine myself to the two facts which are evident about them. The first evident fact (in marked contrast to the delusion of the dancing pagan)--the first evident fact, I say, is that the pagan virtues, such as justice and temperance, are the sad virtues, and that the mystical virtues of faith, hope, and charity are the gay and exuberant virtues. And the second evident fact, which is even more evident, is the fact that the pagan virtues are the reasonable virtues, and that the Christian virtues of faith, hope, and charity are in their essence as unreasonable as they can be. As the word "unreasonable" is open to misunderstanding, the matter may be more accurately put by saying that each one of these Christian or mystical virtues involves a paradox in its own nature, and that this is not true of any of the typically pagan or rationalist virtues. Justice consists in finding out a certain thing due to a certain man and giving it to him.[14]

Now, the claim (let us leave aside the question of whether Chesterton really makes it or not) that each virtue can be interpreted as a synthesis of extremes does not seem convincing; it is by no means easy to interpret in the Chestertonian manner other virtues than those insightfully analyzed by Chesterton and presented in the

---

[13]Horace (1995), pp. 130–131.
[14]Chesterton (2009), pp. 79–80.

preceding section. The list of virtues that can be interpreted in the Chestertonian manner could, perhaps, be supplemented with romantic love and toleration. The former could be construed as a result of the "impetuous collision" of two "apparently inconsistent" emotions/attitudes, viz. the desire to possess the other person and the respect for her or his autonomy, whereas the latter could be construed not as neither too strong ('fanaticism') nor too weak ('indifference' or 'opportunism') attachment to one's views (as its construal on the Aristotelian account might look like), but as a result of the "impetuous collision" of a very strong attachment to one's views and an awareness of one's fallibility, or alternatively, as a result of the impetuous collision of two opposite attitudes, viz. disapproval of the other agent's view and respect for this agent. Toleration does seem to be more attractive on this interpretation than on the Aristotelian one which arguably assumes that it is a manifestation of a moderate (neither too strong nor too weak) attachment to one's views. As for romantic love, it seems that it can hardly be interpreted in the Aristotelian manner as the mean between extremes.

14.3.2 Strong Points

Firstly, this account provides a strong defence of virtue against the objection that it is tantamount to mediocrity; on this account virtues are anything but instances of mediocrity. As was argued above, the objection of mediocrity is not apt with respect to the Aristotelian account, but the adherents of this account refute this objection in a less evocative way than the adherents of Chestertonian account: the former account implies that virtue is an extreme in an ethical but not in an emotional sense; the latter implies that virtue is an extreme in both senses (since it is a synthesis of extremes, it preserves them both "at the top of their energy", as Chesterton put it in the already quoted passage).

Secondly, it should also be emphasized, that on Aristotle's account, reason is strongly connected with virtues: Aristotle stressed that the mean can only be reached by means of *phronesis* (practical wisdom); as he put it:

> virtue, then, is a state of character concerned with choice, lying in a mean, i.e., the mean relative to us, this being determined by a rational principle, and by that principle by which the man of practical wisdom would determine it. (*EN* 1106b36–1107a2, trans. Ross)

By contrast, the role of reason in the Chestertonian account is marginalized: virtue is defined only by means of "apparently inconsistent" emotions. This may be regarded as an advantage of this account, since, as is well known, one of the objections raised against the Aristotelian account is that it in fact reduces the description of virtue to rules to be discovered by reason (*phronesis*); these rules are to specify, for instance, when, towards which persons, to what degree one should experience fear, or towards whom, in what circumstances, and when a generous person should exhibit her or his generosity.[15] Accordingly, so this objection goes, the concept of virtue is in fact redundant or secondary because a given virtue can be defined only by invoking a set of rules that make precise what it means, e.g., to be courageous or generous[16]: it turns out that to be courageous or generous simply means to comply with a certain set of rules. If this objection is apt, the concept of virtue proves to be empty: it boils down to the requirement of doing the right thing; and it is only due to the considerations of linguistic economy that we use the language of virtues rather than the language of rules. This objection, however, does not apply to the Chestertonian account, which implies that virtue appears, so to speak, 'automatically'—as a result of the clash of opposite passions. Accordingly, whereas the role of deliberate choice (*proiaresis*) is central on the Aristotelian account, which implies that virtue is a disposition to make deliberate choices, and thereby does not exist without reason, it seems to be marginal on the Chestertonian one.

Thirdly, the Chestertonian account holds out against the objection raised by Rosalind Hursthouse to the Aristotelian account. The crux of her argumentation is contained in the following passage:

> The idea that the concept of the *right reason* could be captured by specifying it as a mean between too many and too few reasons has only to be stated to be seen as absurd. What I want to illustrate in what follows is that *right object* and *right occasion* [and *right amount*] similarly cannot be specified as means, and that, more generally, some vices that correspond to the virtues of temperance and courage (. . .) cannot be understood as dispositions to exhibit or feel an emotion (a *pathos*) too much or too little.[17]

Thus, Hursthouse's argument with respect to courage (and then generalized to all virtues) is that being cowardly or rash does not consist in *not being in the mean*, i.e., in fearing, respectively, too much or too little, or fearing too many or too few objects, but simply in fearing *wrong* objects, and whether objects are right or wrong cannot be defined by recourse to the category of the mean. She further argues that 'wrong occasion' and 'wrong amount' can be reduced to 'wrong objects', since "*any* time you fear a wrong object you have felt fear on a wrong occasion (. . .) We cannot maintain that fearing death etc. 'the right amount' is fearing them somewhere between too much and too little. What fearing death 'the right amount' comes to (. . .) is fearing an ignoble death but not fearing an honourable one".[18] To illustrate her point that the rightness of the objects cannot be defined in terms of the

---

[15]Cf. the following quotation: "Of the faults that are committed one consists in fearing what one should not, another in fearing as we should not, another in fearing when we should not, and so on; and so too with respect to the things that inspire confidence. The man, then, who faces and fears the right things and from the right motive, in the right way and at the right time, and who feels confidence under the corresponding conditions, is brave; for the brave man feels and acts according to the merits of the case and in whatever way the rule directs." (*EN* 1115b15–19, trans. Ross).

[16]This objection was raised, e.g., by Hans Kelsen; cf. Kelsen (1957), pp. 125–136.

[17]Hursthouse (1980), p. 61.

[18]Ibid., pp. 67–68.

mean, Hursthouse imagines a person who is fearless with two exceptions: the person fears only the dark, enclosed spaces and mice. She calls such a person a 'fearless phobiac' and claims that this person is regarded as cowardly not because she is afraid of too many objects (she fears only two objects) but because she fears *wrong* objects. The weakest point of Hursthouse's claim seems to be its assumption that when we fear right objects we *ipso fact* we fear them in the right amount. Now, one can plausibly maintain that fear (of death, wounds, or pain, or anything that can be regarded as a 'right object') can be too strong or too weak, or *at least that there is nothing unreasonable in the idea that it can come in degrees* (though, arguably, Hursthouse is right in treating as "absurd" the idea that 'right reason' for action could be captured as a mean between too many and too few reasons[19]). One must agree with Howard J. Curzer that Hursthouse's claim that the right amount of fear cannot be specified as the mean is "counterintuitive", because common sense says that 'fearing the wrong amount' is 'fearing too much or too little' and that 'the right amount of fear' is 'an amount of fear somewhere between too much and too little' (Curzer 1996, p. 133).[20] Accordingly, one must regard as untenable Hursthouse's claim that the doctrine of the mean is deeply flawed because acting wrongly is always being wrong with respect to objects (and thereby with respect to occasion and amount of one's passion), and not having too much or too little of a given passion. But, and here is my crucial point, *even if Hursthouse's claim were right, it would not apply to the Chestertonian account*, for this account does not imply that acting wrongly is feeling 'too strongly' or 'too weakly' a given passion; what it implies is that acting wrongly is not holding simultaneously two extreme passions.

Fourthly, Aristotle provides in fact negative definitions of particular virtues. He does not say, for example, what exactly courage is. He says only that it is neither cowardice nor rashness; the positive aspect of his definition is in fact blank: courage, for him, is a state of character concerned with choice, lying in a mean,

---

[19]Regarding Hursthouse's claim that "what fearing death 'the right amount' comes to (...) is fearing an ignoble death but not fearing an honourable one" Howard J. Curzer aptly remarked that "the courageous person fears both death and baseness. An ignoble death is a combination of these and so should be feared more than either, but even a noble death should be feared" (Curzer 1996, p. 133). It is also worth adding that Howard J. Curzer provides an interesting, even if slightly strained, argument in favour of such interpretation of right reason according to which it is a mean between too many and too few reasons; he writes as follows: "A person can have too many reasons for acting courageously by having all of the right reasons plus more. Tom typically stands fast in battle not only (a) to acquire or maintain his courage, and (b) to win the battle, but also (c) to win honour, and (d) to avoid penalties. Similarly, a person can have too few reason for acting courageously. Bill typically stands fast in battle only for the sake of (a) and not (b). Of course, it is possible to have the wrong reasons without having too many or too few reasons for acting courageously. Fred typically stands fast in battle only for the sake of (c) and (d) and not (a) or (b) (Ibid., pp. 134–135)." Regarding Hursthouse's claim that "what fearing death 'the right amount' comes to (...) is fearing an ignoble death but not fearing an honourable one" Howard J. Courzer aptly remarked that "the courageous person fears both death and baseness. An ignoble death is a combination of these and so should be feared more than either, but even a noble death should be feared" (Ibid., p. 134).

[20]Curzer (1996), p. 134.

i.e., the mean relative to us, this being determined by a rational principle, and the choice concerns matters engendering fear. This account does not specify what courage exactly is. Chesterton, by contrast, provides positive definitions of particular virtues, e.g., courage is for him a synthesis of a strong attachment to life and a disdain of death.

14.3.3 Unclear Points

14.3.3.1 Firstly

It is unclear whether the Chestertonian account makes sense only if one assumes the Christian worldview, or whether it can be upheld even if one assumes a naturalistic worldview. On the one hand, it is clear that in order to accept, for example, the Chestertonian construal of modesty, one must abandon the view of "merely rational sages"; on this view certain combinations of attitudes, e.g., being at the same time proud and humble, are not legitimate though paradoxical, as they are within the Christian worldview, but they are simply unthinkable, since, on the Chestertonian account, the grounds for both pride and humility are explicitly theological. The same point applies to the theological virtues, and the 'no-name' combination of pessimism and optimism. On the other hand, in the case of courage, the Chestertonian account seems to be plausible even if one rejects the Christian worldview. Chesterton seems to have admitted it himself, pointing at the positive practical consequences of combining the two opposite passions or attitudes constituting courage, viz. a strong attachment to life and a disdain of death:

> "He that will lose his life, the same shall save it", is not a piece of mysticism for saints and heroes. It is a piece of everyday advice for sailors and mountaineers (...) This paradox is the whole principle of courage; even of quite early or quite brutal courage. A man cut off by the sea may save his life if he will risk it on the precipice. He can only get away from death by continually stepping within an inch of it. A soldier surrounded by enemies, if he is to cut his way out, needs to combine a strong desire for living with a strange carelessness about dying. He must not merely cling to life, for then he will be a coward, and will not escape. He must not merely wait for death, for then he will be a suicide, and will not escape.[21]

The relation between the Chestertonian account and Christian doctrine should therefore be described as follows: the Chestertonian account implies the Christian doctrine in the context of the analysis of such virtues as modesty, faith, hope, and the 'no-name' combination of pessimism and optimism but not in the context of the analysis of courage, tolerance or romantic love. One may also argue that charity, understood as a combination of forgivingness (towards the doer) and unforgivingness (towards the deed), though discovered by Christianity, does not imply the specifically Christian assumptions in its Chestertonian analysis. It should also be noticed that (contrary to what Chesterton seems to have suggested) *Christianity*

---

[21]Chesterton (2010), p. 85.

does not imply the account of virtue as a synthesis of extremes. In support of this last claim, one may adduce the historical fact that the great Christian philosophers *did not* assume this account. Accordingly, the claim of Chesterton that his account of virtue is Christian must be weakened: the Christian doctrine had assuredly inspired him to propose the account of virtue as a synthesis of extremes, but does not entail it.[22] Consequently, the Christian doctrine admits of both accounts of virtue—the Aristotelian and the Chestertonian. It should be emphasized, however, that the theological virtues may also be interpreted in a different way—neither the Chestertonian nor the Aristotelian. This third interpretation, which boils down to the rejection of the tripartite structure with reference to these virtues, was proposed by Aquinas. Aquinas, in *Summa Theologica* (I–II, q. 59, a. 1) invokes approvingly Aristotle's definition of moral virtue as a mean, i.e., as

> a habit of choosing the mean appointed by reason as a prudent man would appoint it.[23]

and interprets in its light the moral virtues and the intellectual virtues. However, he encounters serious difficulties in applying this account to the theological virtues. When dealing in *Summa Theologica* with the question of whether the theological virtues observe the mean, he asserts that the measure, as applied to the theological virtues, may be twofold. The first one

> is taken from the very nature of virtue, and thus the measure and rule of theological virtue is God Himself: because our faith is ruled according to Divine truth; charity, according to His goodness; hope, according to the immensity of His omnipotence and loving kindness. (*ST* I–II, q. 66, a. 4, trans. Fathers of the English Dominican Province)

Now, according to Aquinas,

> this measure surpasses all human power: so that never can we love God as much as He ought to be loved, nor believe and hope in Him as much as we should. Much less therefore can there be in excess in such things. Accordingly the good of such virtues does not consist in mean, but increases the more we approach to the summit. (*ST* I–II, q. 66, a. 4, trans. Fathers of the English Dominican Province)

The second measure

> is by comparison with us: for although we cannot be borne towards God as much as we ought, yet we should approach to Him by believing, hoping, and loving, according to the measure of our condition. Consequently it is possible to find a mean and extremes in theological virtue, accidentally and in reference to us. (*ST* I–II, q. 66, a. 4, trans. Fathers of the English Dominican Province)

Thus, theological virtue, when "considered in itself", i.e., essentially rather than accidentally does not consist

> in a mean of reason by conformity with a measure that may be exceeded.[24]

---

[22]This remark only stresses Chesterton's originality, though it was not his intention to be original: he believed to only have made explicit what was implicit in the Christian ethics.

[23]Thomas Aquinas (1981), I–II, q. 59, a. 1.

[24]Ibid.

The definitions of faith, hope and charity which rely on the 'tripartite structure' (e.g., the definitions of hope as the mean between presumption and despair, or faith as the mean between contrary heresies[25]) are therefore only definitions "by comparison with us", because, essentially, there can be no excess of faith, hope or charity "in comparison with God". As we can see, Aquinas, like Chesterton, was skeptical towards the possibility of analyzing theological virtues in the Aristotelian manner. The basic difference between Aquinas and Chesterton is that Chesterton believed that the essence of these virtues can be captured by appealing to the tripartite structure, whereas Aquinas rejected this view. Furthermore, Chesterton believed that his account of virtue also provides a better interpretation of (at least some) moral virtues, whereas Aquinas analyzed moral virtues in accordance with the Aristotelian account. These considerations allow us to complete the above description of the relations between the Chestertonian account and Christianity: *Christianity does not imply the account of virtue as a synthesis of extremes but, arguably, it implies the rejection of the Aristotelian account as far as the theological virtues are concerned.*

14.3.3.2   Secondly

It is not entirely clear what, according to Chesterton, happens with the 'extreme' dispositions when they form a synthesis (i.e., a virtue). It would be rather odd to understand the Chesterton's account of virtues as implying, for instance, that courage is a simple combination or sum of cowardice and rashness (it would be odd because such a combination is by no means ethically attractive; in fact, it seems morally worse than any of its components). Two interpretations of Chesterton's view in this point seem to be possible, which salvage his view that the synthesis is ethically attractive. According to the first interpretation, virtue arises as a result of the 'collision' of two extreme dispositions (vices), and thereby is not a simple *sum* of them, in which sum these dispositions remain entirely unchanged: the creative tension between the extremes (vices) generates a unique virtue—a synthesis of the extremes, which cannot be called by their names (say, courage = cowardice + reck-lessness), because *within this synthesis they lose to some extent their original character* (one could see this process as a kind of the Hegelian *Aufhebung*). This interpretation, however, is vague because of the vagueness of the very process of synthesis understood as simultaneous losing and preserving by the vices their original character. According to the second interpretation (not only more clear than the first one but also, arguably, more consistent with Chesterton's intentions), *extremes fully preserve their original character within a virtue.* This interpretation makes sense only on the assumption that the extremes are not vices, and thereby

[25]Aquinas gives the example of faith "in one Person and two natures", saying that it is "the mean between the heresy of Nestorius, who maintains the existence of two persons and two natures, and the heresy of Eutyches, who held to one person and one nature" (Ibid.).

cannot be named by means of evaluative terms (e.g., cowardice or recklessness). To develop this interpretation, it is necessary to clarify the concept of 'extremes'. On the Aristotelian account a virtue and its correlated extremes refer to the same passion (e.g., to fear, or pleasure). The situation looks differently on Chesterton's account (on its second interpretation). His statement that dispositions giving rise to a virtue are "opposite" can be construed in this context in two ways: *it may mean either that (A) there are two different passions involved, or that (B) there is one passion involved but, for each of its 'extremes', the disposition relies on categorically different reasons.* On either construal extremes are not really vices.

Ad. (A) This construal suits, for instance, the interpretation of courage. Courage could not be a synthesis of excessive fear of death and insufficient fear of death—this would be blatantly inconsistent to define it in this way. Accordingly, courage is a synthesis of the extreme dispositions ("a strong desire to live" and a "disdain of death") referring to different passions or attitudes (an attitude to life and an attitude to death). These two dispositions are opposite, because otherwise they would not be capable of producing a creative tension, but they are not really inconsistent.

Ad. (B) This construal suits, for instance, the interpretation of modesty. Modesty could not be a synthesis of high self-esteem and low self-esteem if in both cases self-esteem were to rely on the same category of reasons (e.g., referring to the degree of sinfulness of human nature); such a synthesis would be really (and not "apparently") inconsistent. Modesty means possessing high self-esteem *because one has been created by God "in His image and likeness"* and at the same time possessing low self-esteem *because one is sinful.* Thus, the inconsistency here is a creative ("apparent") because of the differences in the category of reasons that stand behind differences in the 'level' of self-esteem.

14.4   Concluding Remarks

Chesterton provided an original and insightful account of virtue, which takes from the Aristotelian one only the claim that virtues can be analyzed by appealing to the 'tripartite' scheme (extreme—virtue—extreme). In the paper we have tried to reconstruct the Chestertonian account, provide some corrections to it, and compare it with the Aristotelian one. The corrections were as follows. We have rejected Chesterton's claim (raised in *Orthodoxy*, but not in *Heretics*) that his account is applicable to all virtues: arguably, not all virtues can be interpreted as embracing extremes (e.g., it is not easy to work out how generosity or temperance could be analyzed as being syntheses of extremes). We have also argued that Christianity does not imply the Chestertonian account, and that this account entails the Christian doctrine with regard to such virtues as faith, hope, modesty, the 'no-name' combination of pessimism and optimism, but not with regard to courage, toleration, romantic love, and charity (Chesterton seems to have maintained that his account is entailed by Christianity and entails Christianity with regard to all virtues). The main clarification provided in the paper concerned the very notion of a 'synthesis of extremes'; we have distinguished two interpretations of this notion: according to the first one, in our view less plausible, the synthesized extremes are vices (though they lose to some extent their original character when they become components of a synthesis), while according to the second one—they are not vices but just opposite and only apparently inconsistent dispositions (according to the latter interpretation extremes are therefore not extremes in the Aristotelian sense).

It was not our intention to decide which of the two account of virtue—the Chestertonian or the Aristotelian—is more convincing. It is worth noticing, however, that superiority of one account over the other could be analyzed in two dimensions: of *ethical attractiveness* and of *universality*. The question of whether a given virtue is ethically more attractive on a given account seems hard to decide on purely rational grounds. Chesterton claimed that virtues, on the Aristotelian account, recommend mediocrity, but, as we have argued, this claim is based on a misreading of *Nicomachean Ethics*. Thus, arguably, it is a matter of personal preferences whether we shall aim at developing, e.g., courage in the Chestertonian sense (as a synthesis of strong attachment to life and disdain of death) or in the Aristotelian sense (as the mean between cowardice and rashness). Both accounts seem ethically attractive and, since they are incompatible, one cannot develop in oneself a given disposition which would be a virtue both in the Chestertonian and in the Aristotelian sense (e.g., courage in the former sense would probably be viewed as rashness from the Aristotelian standpoint). As for the dimension of universality, let us recall that, arguably, not all moral virtues can be analyzed in the Chestertonian manner. The Aristotelian account seems to have an advantage in this point because it enables an analysis of all moral virtues. But the Chestertonian account seems to have an advantage over the Aristotelian one in the context of the theological virtues. As was argued by Aquinas, the essence of these virtues cannot be captured by means of the Aristotelian scheme. He did not consider the possibility of analyzing them as a synthesis of extremes, but this account seems to especially pertinent in this context.

There is no doubt that the two accounts of virtue analyzed in this paper are essentially different (virtue understood as a synthesis of extremes cannot be identified with virtue understood as a mean between extremes), and that Aristotle did not take into account the possibility of conceiving virtue in the Chestertonian manner. However, it is worth noticing at the end of our considerations that Aristotle made one remark that could be viewed as anticipating (though with a critical bent) Chesterton's account. In *Eudemian Ethics*[26] he writes as follows:

> And the mean is more opposed to the extremes than the extremes are to one another, because the mean does not occur in combination with either extreme, whereas the extremes often do occur in combination with one another, and sometimes the same men are venturesome cowards, or extravagant in some things and illiberal in others, and in general

---

[26]Edition used: Aristotle (1952).

not uniform in a bad way— for when men lack uniformity in a good way, this results in men of the middle characters, since the mean contains both extremes. (*EE* 1234a34–b6, trans. Rackham)

At the end this passage, in saying that "the mean contains both extremes", Aristotle makes a remark that may be viewed as formulating the Chestertonian-like account of virtue. However, as it seems, the passage should be interpreted as referring to persons combining extremes in their behaviour *at different times* ("venturesome cowards") or *with reference to different objects* ("extravagant in some things and illiberal in others"). Chesterton would have agreed with Aristotle's criticism of such persons, since, in Chesterton's view, a person is virtuous if she combines extremes *at the same time*. But even if we assume that Aristotle did mean persons combining extremes at the same time (the phrase 'venturesome cowards' undoubtedly allows both interpretations), it would still not be a real anticipation of Chesterton's view, since, as we have argued in Sect. 14.3.3, Chesterton did not mean by a synthesis of extremes a synthesis of vices understood in the Aristotelian manner (accordingly, courage, according to Chesterton, is not a synthesis of being cowardly and being venturesome).

References

Aristotle. 1947. Nicomachean Ethics. In *Introduction to Aristotle*, ed. Richard McKeon. New York: Modern Library.

———. 1952. Eudemian Ethics. In *Aristotle, The Athenian Constitution; The Eudemian Ethics; On Virtues and Vices*, Loeb Classical Library. London and Cambridge, MA: W. Heinemann and Harvard University Press.

Brito, José de Sousa e. 2018. Aristotle on Emotions in Ethics and in Criminal Justice. In *Aristotle on Emotions in Law and Politics*, ed. Liesbeth Huppes-Cluysenaer and Nuno M.M.S. Coelho. Dordrecht: Springer.

Chesterton, Gilbert K. 2009. *Heretics*. New York: Wilder Publications.

———. 2010. *Orthodoxy*. New York: Simon & Brown. https://www.worldcat.org/title/orthodoxy/oclc/49293360&referer=brief_results.

Curzer, Howard J. 1996. A Defense of Aristotle's Doctrine That Virtue Is a Mean. *Ancient Philosophy* 16 (1): 129–138.

Horace. 1995. *The Odes and Epodes*. Translated by C. E. Bennett. Cambridge, MA and London: Harvard University Press.

Hursthouse, Rosalind. 1980. A False Doctrine of the Mean. *Proceedings of the Aristotelian Society* 81: 57–72.

Kelsen, Hans. 1957. *What Is Justice?: Justice, Law, and Politics in the Mirror of Science: Collected Essays*. Berkeley: University of California Press.

Thomas Aquinas, Saint. 1981. *Summa Theologica*. Complete English Edition in Five Volumes. Translated by Fathers of the English Dominican Province. Westminster, MD: Christian Classics.

Viano, Cristina. 2018. Ethical Theory and Judicial Practice: Passions and Crimes of Passion in Plato, Aristotle and Lysias. In *Aristotle on Emotions in Law and Politics*, ed. Liesbeth Huppes-Cluysenaer and Nuno M.M.S. Coelho. Dordrecht: Springer.

Chapter 15
The Place of Slavery in the Aristotelian Framework of Law, Reason and Emotion

Peter Langford and Ian Bryan

Abstract This chapter considers the Aristotelian examination of slavery in Book I of the *Politics* in order to question the relationship between slavery and the wider Aristotelian framework of law, reason and emotion. A detailed analysis of Book 1 reveals that it is orientated by an appropriation and transformation of the Platonic conception of virtue and rulership. The Aristotelian response defines the slave as the particular determination of the connection between nature and necessity which, in turn, shape the notions of law, reason and emotion. The relationship between the slave and notions of law, reason and emotion are conferred after the initial determination of, and justification for, the division between (natural) master and (natural) slave. The division is a form of rulership within the household. The slave's subjection to the master determines that the relationship to law, reason and emotion is coextensive with household management. It is only the free population and, in particular, free men, who are capable of developing a political regime. The political regime is the sole form through which the relationship between law, reason and emotion is to be established in order to realize the ideal or good life. The further development of the *Politics* is predicated upon the simultaneous recognition and disappearance of a relationship of subjection.

15.1 Introduction

The Aristotelian framework, composed of the relationship between the notions of law, reason and emotion, retains a significant presence in contemporary legal and philosophical discourse. From the perspective of the recent Anglo-American development of virtue ethics,[1] the Aristotelian framework has been the background

---

[1]See, for example, Annas (1995, 2011), Hursthouse (2002), Russell (2009, 2012), Sloate (1995), and Swanton (2005).

P. Langford (✉)
Law and Criminology, Edge Hill University, Ormskirk, UK
e-mail: langforp@edgehill.ac.uk

I. Bryan (✉)
Law School, University of Lancaster, Lancaster, UK
e-mail: i.bryan@lancaster.ac.uk

© Springer International Publishing AG 2018   313
L. Huppes-Cluysenaer, N.M.M.S. Coelho (eds.), *Aristotle on Emotions in Law and Politics*, Law and Philosophy Library 121, DOI 10.1007/978-3-319-66703-4_15

against which a distinctive theory of practical reasoning has been elaborated. From the perspective of European or continental philosophy, in particular, the work of Giorgio Agamben, the Aristotelian framework has provided the interpretative resources for establishing a distinction between *bios* and *zoe*, and for undertaking a critique of the origins of both the political and natural law.[2]

In relation to these two dominant interpretations, this paper adopts an indirect approach, by concentrating upon the explicit presence of, and justification or explanation for, slavery in Aristotle's *Politics*.[3] Thus, it opens the question of the relationship between slavery and the wider Aristotelian framework of law, reason and emotion. For, it is this wider framework which provides the conceptual apparatus for the definition and justification of slavery. The placing of this relationship into question, therefore, also involves the wider understanding of the meaning, or sense, to be attributed to Aristotelian notions of law, reason and emotion.

This, in turn, necessitates a preliminary statement of the interpretative position adopted in Aristotle's textual treatment of slavery. The text is not considered to be merely or simply the direct reflection or expression of the predominance and acceptance of the institution of chattel slavery within Ancient Greece: Aristotle's philosophical approach is "a more philosophically sophisticated version of the cultural assumptions of [...] the slave-owning elite".[4] Hence, in opposition to this perspective, the structure and argumentation of Aristotle's text are, in themselves, considered to be centrally important in both the presentation of the justification for chattel slavery, and for the further development of the textual structure and coherence of the *Politics*. Here, however, a further distinction arises between the approach of this Chapter, and the work of Goldschmidt[5] and Brunschwig[6] who, while offering an exemplary and highly original interpretation/presentation of the importance of the textual structure and coherence of Aristotle's text, seek to 'depoliticize' Aristotle's approach to slavery, by insisting upon its purely 'economic' significance within this domestic sphere of the household.[7]

In contrast, in this Chapter, the structure and argumentation of Aristotle's text have importance precisely because the reflection upon, and justification of natural slavery, are intended to extend beyond the question of slavery itself in order to provide the philosophical framework for a distinctively Aristotelian discussion and delineation of political power[8] and rulership.[9] The notions or conceptions of

---

[2]See, Agamben (1998, 2013, 2016).

[3]Edition used: Aristotle (1998).

[4]Rosivach (1999). See, also, Schofield (2005) and Lévy (1989).

[5]Goldschmidt (1984).

[6]Brunschwig (2005).

[7]The chapter, therefore, considers the 'economic' arguments for slavery which Aristotle presents (Aristotle 1998, p. 14, 1253b37–1254a1) as secondary to the primarily political purpose of the discussion of slavery in the *Politics*.

[8]As emphasized by Pellegrin (2013).

[9]As emphasized by Deslauriers (2006).

political power and rulership are articulated at the intersection of law, reason and emotion; and it is the particular treatment of natural slavery, within Aristotle's consideration of the form of rulership which typifies the household, which facilitates this intersection.

The Aristotelian consideration of slavery is to be understood as an element within the wider philosophical project of the *Politics*. The wider project is itself a further development of the importance accorded to law and the study of legislation in the final chapter of the *Nicomachean Ethics*.[10] In this further development, the connection between Aristotelian ethics and politics becomes evident as the elements of a more general science of politics (*politike epistēme*) which are differentiated by their focus upon the individual (ethics) and the collective (politics) (*EN* 1094a26–b11).[11] The notion of a science of politics, orientated by a predominantly scientific method and principles, flows from the character of the potential addressee—the lawgiver[12]—who is not to be engaged through the form of rhetoric centred upon the influencing of emotions,[13] but educated through the methods of trained judgment (practical wisdom). Here, therefore, the methods of demonstration cannot attain the degree of exactness or precision (*akribeia*) of the subject matters of other sciences (*EN* 1094b11–14). This, however, is not to disqualify, from the outset, the scientific character of philosophical inquiry encompassed by Aristotelian ethics and politics, but to acknowledge its different purpose and orientation: "*practical* questions – questions about precepts rather than first principles".[14] Thus:

> practical wisdom falls apart into two sub-branches, which constitute the same epistemic state, but which are separable in being (*EN* 1141b23-33): one dealing with the individual good, also called practical wisdom (in the narrow sense), and one dealing with the good of the city, called political science. Political science itself consists of three sub-branches of knowledge: household science, legislative science and political science (in the narrow sense). Political science in this latter, narrow sense sub-divides into a deliberative and a judicial part.[15]

---

[10]Edition used: Aristotle (2000). See on this, Kamtekar (2014). The other aspect of this further development of the study of legislation is the collection and commentary upon the existing Greek constitutions of which only the Aristotelian commentary on the Athenian Constitution survives.

[11]See for a more extended delineation of this general science of politics, Schofield and Kraut (2006).

[12]The figure of the lawgiver is to be understood in relation to the ancient Greek notion of a constitution (*politeia*). The particular sense to be attributed to this term is that of the 'system of laws and practices in the civic community that constructs, educates and constrains a person's condition of citizenship' Harte and Lane (2013). Hence, the lawgiver is the individual whose character and education indicate their ability to promulgate laws which will fulfil this notion of a constitution. See, also, on the relation between law and constitution in *Politics*, Morel (2011).

[13]Here, following, John M. Cooper's account of Aristotle's treatment of emotions in the *Rhetoric*, and his reading of Aristotle (1991), 1.4.1359b2–18 with 1.2.1358a21–26, and the restriction of the premises of oratorical argument to plausible or reputable opinion (*endoxa*) and, therefore, its exclusion from the premises of political and ethical science (see, Cooper 1999, 408ff.). However, compare Garver (1995), who seeks to indicate a stronger degree of affinity between Aristotle's *Politics*, *Eudaimonian Ethics* and *Nicomachean Ethics* and the *Rhetoric*. See also, Rapp (2009).

[14]Henry and Nielsen (2015), p. 9. Emphasis in original.

[15]Leunissen (2015), p. 216, fn. 5.

The degree of exactness or precision common to these sub-branches of the science of politics is analogous to that of the inexact sciences, in particular, "the science of medicine and other stochastic arts".[16] Hence, it proposes a distinct relationship between the universal and the particular in which the premises of the science of politics have the status of generalizations which guide, but do not seek exhaustively to determine the particular action (*EN* 1179a16–22). It is this relationship which produces the combination of demonstration and training appropriate to the subject matter of the general science of politics.

The different character and subject matter of the Aristotelian general science of politics renders it open both to "a more than basic familiarity with theories from his natural treatises"[17] and to Aristotelian metaphysics.[18] For the parameters and content of the practical wisdom which are sought to be generated by the general science of politics operates upon a notion of life and nature derived from these other sciences.[19] The *Politics* exemplifies this relationship of the general science of politics to the broader Aristotelian notions of life and nature, through the examination of the definition and position of the slave. The examination establishes the extent to which slavery, and the character of the slave, are to be related to notions of law, reason and emotion. The analysis centres upon the absence or deficiency of practical wisdom which marks the position of the slave as the corollary of the position of the master as a rudimentary form of political power and rulership.[20] In the process, the *Politics* proceeds beyond the question of individual practical wisdom to the question of practical wisdom and its distribution within the initial part of the state (*polis*)[21]: the household (*oikos*). Hence, the education of the lawgiver, through the argumentative structure of the *Politics*, seeks to constitute the opinion of the lawgiver, in regard to slavery and the slave, based upon coherent, scientific reflection appropriate to the subject matter of this general science of politics.[22] The *Politics*, therefore, encompasses the definition and position of the

---

[16]Nielsen (2015), p. 47. The analogy is explicitly drawn by Aristotle, as Nielsen indications, for example, Aristotle (2000) (*EN* 1137a13–18; 10.9.1180b7–19).

[17]Leunissen (2015), p. 217.

[18]See, Gottlieb (2009).

[19]See, for the further detailed development of this argument, Leunissen (2015), pp. 218–231; and Leunissen (2017).

[20]On this, see, Frank (2005), pp. 17–53; Nichols (1992), pp. 13–51; Trott (2014), pp. 16–41 and 175–201.

[21]The translation of "*polis*" as state follows the interpretation of Hansen and the Copenhagen Polis Centre. On this interpretation, "*polis*" has the sense of both city and state. It is Aristotle's Book 1of the *Politics* which, for Hansen, exemplifies its use in the sense of state in which the initial "'atom' of the city-state is the household", Hansen (2009), p. 110.

[22]Here, it must be acknowledged that the education provided by the *Politics*, is necessarily partial and specific, as it exists as the corollary of, and compliment to, the education furnished by the ethical works of Aristotle (*Eudaimonian Ethics* and *Nicomachean Ethics*). For, following the analysis of Bodéüs (1993), the ethical works of Aristotle are to be grouped together with the *Politics*, as the ethical works and the *Politics*, in the distinctive knowledge which they impart, are both integral to shaping the formation of the potential lawgiver. Compare, however, the approach in Pangle (2013).

slave as part of the education of the lawgiver, and this education is a process of formation based upon its theoretical principles.

15.2   Excursus on the Position of the Slave

It is necessary, as a preparatory stage, prior to entering into the presentation and discussion of Aristotle's approach, to provide an outline of the position of an individual who has been determined as a slave. This is in order to comprehend, from a position outside Aristotle's text, the particular relationship between law, reason and emotion which the categorization of an individual as a slave involves. This position outside Aristotle's text is, in part, one of the theoretical interpretation of historical material[23] which seeks to provide a conceptual delineation or determination of the position of the slave, as a position within a wider system of social relations, political power and rulership. From this conceptual reconstruction, it is then possible to indicate the particular character of life or existence of this position of the slave and, thus, to emphasize the character of *bare life* that is attributed to this position. The position of the slave is a necessarily contrastive one, as it is part of a spectrum of positions within a social order the distinctiveness of which is reproduced through a system of identities and differences which are organized to maintain and reproduce a wider system of social relations, political power and rulership.

The central, organizing difference is between the positions of master and slave (*doulos*) in which the master is an exclusively male role, and that of slave a more general position capable of being attributed, without significant internal differentiation, to men, women and children. The slave is a position resulting from a process of enslavement, which effectively erases the previous identity of the individual, and marks them as unfree and *subject to* the master. The master is free (*eleutheros*) in the sense not merely of occupying the position of a non-slave, but through a more complex identity as part of a family in which he also occupies the position of husband in relation to the position of wife (and, therefore, the expression of the wider difference between men/women—sexual difference) and the position of father in relation to the position of the child or children (the expression of the wider difference between father and child). Both the wife/women and children are also free, but these positions are the expression of a limited freedom in relation to the full or exemplary freedom of the master/citizen/man.

The position of the slave, as *subject to* the master expresses a relation of *subjection* which is beyond or outside that of a notion of law predicated upon the definition of reciprocal rights and duties between citizens. For the slave, through the process initiated by enslavement, is devoid of legal personality, in relation to a master to whom the slave is without either legal rights or duties. Rather, any

---

[23]This is based upon the work of Rosivach (1999) and Vlassopoulos (2011).

semblance of rights or duties arise from the particular treatment—mastery—exercised by a specific master over a slave. Hence, it is a semblance because it is merely the effect of the repetition of a particular form of treatment of a slave by a master which, as the mere continuation of a particular form of mastery, is essentially contingent on the personal authority of the master.

For the process of enslavement, as the subjection to another's personal authority, also involves ownership—chattel slavery—the position of the slave is that of a human being who is unfree because he/she is the property of another. Enslavement is the reduction of a human being (*anthropos*) to the property of another—the master—and the position of the slave, is also located on the (unstable) boundary between the human and the non-human or animal. The reduction is the creation of the position or presence of *bare life*: the potential indistinction of the human and the animal.

The connection between the process of enslavement and the *bare life* of the slave creates the potential for the continual resurgence of the question of the origin of slavery and the position and condition of life of the slave. From the overt presence of violence/non-consensual force in the transformation of a human being into a slave, and the concomitant emergence of the position of the master, and the associated capacity to exercise mastership over the slave, the degree to which the *origin* of slavery is intrinsically and essentially one of violence and force is revealed.

Here, slavery, to the degree to which violence and force are not considered co-extensive with its origin, then becomes open to the question of justification or legitimation by a supplement to, or substitution of, the *origin* in violence and force. This, in turn, introduces a reflection upon the origin of slavery which has recourse to the conceptual resources offered, separately or in some form of combination, by law, reason and emotion in order to generate this supplement or substitution.

This reflection upon the origin of slavery is, however, despite any conscious or explicit consideration of its initial parameters, required to become a wider reflection upon the social order of which slavery is a part. For, both the process of enslavement and the creation of the positions of master and slave involve the maintenance and reproduction of a wider system of social relations, political power and rulership.

15.3   The *Politics*, Book 1

This preliminary excursus on the position of the slave, then leads to the examination of the distinctiveness of Aristotle's approach to the question of slavery. This will be undertaken through the analysis and interpretation of the argumentative structure of the sections within the *Politics* that attend most closely to slavery (*Pol.*, 1253b–2a–1260a). The *Politics* is not, however, confined to, nor exclusively centred upon, the justification of slavery. While Aristotle presents a particular justification for slavery in the *Politics*, this arises as an aspect of the wider philosophical purpose of the first book of the *Politics*, and beyond it, in relation to the further argumentative development of the subsequent books.

The position Aristotle accords to the justification of slavery derives from the opening statements and presentation of the philosophical approach in the first book of the *Politics*. This is a combination of a disagreement with an existing philosophical position with regard to forms of rule and the consideration of politics on the basis of a specifically Aristotelian philosophical method. The disagreement relates to a position which would differentiate forms of rule solely on the basis of the 'number of subjects' subject to this form of rule and, then, within this, to further distinguish the statesman from the king on the basis of personal and citizen rule. The Aristotelian method, applied to politics, separates the state or political community into its component parts:

> For, as in other cases, a composite has to be analyzed until we reach things that are incomposite, since these are the smallest parts of the whole, so if we also examine the parts that make up a city-state, we shall see better both how these differ from each other, and whether or not it is possible to gain some expertise in connection with each of the things we have mentioned.[24] (*Pol.* 1252a17–13 trans. Reeve)

The notion of examination should be understood entirely within the parameters of Aristotelian philosophy and, therefore, for its potential connection to relevant concepts and approaches articulated in the *Metaphysics* and *Physics* and other Aristotelian texts.[25] The potential for connection arises, in particular, with the introduction, deployment and differentiation of the notion of nature within the *Politics*.

The method commences by establishing the first growth or origin of the state (*polis*) which presupposes a metaphysico-historico-anthropological origin in the union of the male and female from which then there progressively emerges the family, the unity of several families in the first political association or society of the village which is

> constituted out of several households for the sake of satisfying needs other than everyday ones. (*Pol.* 1252b15–16 trans. Reeve)

The state (*polis*) itself arises from, and is

> "constituted out of several villages, once it reaches the limit of total self-sufficiency" at the stage at which "several villages are united in a single complete community, large enough to be nearly or quite self-sufficing." (*Pol.* 1252b26–27, with reference also to *Pol.* 1252a1–7. trans. Reeve)

---

[24]As C. D. C. Reeve adds in an accompanying footnote to this passage, 'That is to say, do household managers, masters, statesmen, and kings each employ a different type of technical expertise in ruling? Expertise (*technikon*) is technical knowledge of the sort embodied in a craft or a science' (Ibid., p. 2).

[25]On this question more generally, in relation to the notion of physis, see Ward (2005).

This stage marks the transition from the origin of the state (*polis*) in "bare needs of life [to its continued existence] for the sake of living well"; and this transition is also the comprehension of the state (*polis*) as *both* the end (*telos*), therefore, the nature—full development—of these earlier forms of society, and the best (*Pol.* 1252b30–1253a1). Hence, the notion of the state (*polis*) operates to connect and differentiate two conceptions of nature—the first growth or origin and the end—and, through this, to place the end at the origin. This has the effect of situating the origin of the state (*polis*) within the bare needs of life, but presenting its full development as entailing its passage beyond these initial limits of the bare needs of life.

The inclusion of these two conceptions of nature, within the notion of the state (*polis*), is accompanied by the assertion that this nature establishes that it is

> also prior in nature to the household and to each of us individually, since the whole is necessarily prior to the part. (*Pol.* 1253b19–20 trans. Reeve)

The *proof* for this necessary priority is that

> if an individual is not self-sufficient when separated, he will be like all other parts in relation to the whole. (*Pol.* 1253a25–26 trans. Reeve)

or, the individual is no part of a city-state, being unable to

> "form a community with others, or who does not need to because he is self-sufficient" (thus existing as) "either a beast or a god." (*Pol.* 1253a28–30 trans. Reeve)

The isolated individual, as separated from the state (*polis*), is, thus, separated from law and justice (*Pol.* 1253a31–32), because

> justice is a political matter; for justice is the organization for a political community, and justice decides what is just. (*Pol.* 1253a39–40 trans. Reeve)

The position accorded to the state (*polis*)—a creation of nature prior to the household and to the individual—constitutes man as,

> by nature a political animal. (*Pol.* 1253a5–7, our emphasis, trans. Reeve)

This, in turn, creates a distinction between speech—the articulation of what is beneficial or harmful, and hence also what is just and unjust and mere voice—the articulation of pleasure and pain—which is the political supplement or character-istic of man in contrast to animals. The attribution of speech, and the perception of good or bad, just or unjust from which it derives, exclusively to man, entails that

> it is the community in these that makes a household and a city-state. (*Pol.* 1253a17–18 trans. Reeve)

Aristotle, having established that the state (*polis*), as the whole, is in this conceptual position, then turns to the part of the state composed of the household, and, in particular the form of rule characteristic of household management (*Pol.* 1253b1–2). This, in turn, leads to the division of the household (the whole) into parts from which the household is constituted, and a complete household consists of slaves and free. (*Pol.* 1253b3–5 trans. Reeve)

However, this initial division must be preceded by the examination of

each thing in terms of its smallest parts, and the primary and smallest parts of the household are master and slave, husband and wife, father and children. (*Pol.* 1253b5–6 Trans. Reeve)

In relation to each of these smallest parts, the examination is directed by the requirement to

see what each of them is and what features it ought to have. (*Pol.* 1253b6–8 trans. Reeve)

Here, we leave unconsidered the other element of household management, wealth acquisition (*Pol.* 1253b13–14) to which Aristotle also devotes attention.

The methodological division and examination, based upon these primary and smallest parts, is the preliminary stage in Aristotle's distinction of his philosophical position from two predominant conceptions of the relationship of rule between master and slave. The first, which does not consider the relationship unjust, is the repetition, at the level of the relationship between master and slave, of the initial position, outlined at the outset of Aristotle's exposition, in which:

all forms of rule are merely distinguished by number. The second, in contrast, asserts that the relationship between master and slave is one in which it is contrary to nature to be a master (for it is by law that one person is a slave and another free, whereas by nature there is no difference between them), which is why it is not just either, for it involves force.[26] (*Pol.* 1253b19–23 trans. Reeve)

In relation to both these two predominant positions, Aristotle adopts a particular philosophical approach in which the examination of the relationship reverses the conventional understanding of Aristotelian scientific method.[27] In this reversal, the predominant positions are not examined immediately and directly (the examination of the prevailing opinions (*doxa/endoxa*)) as the initial, preparatory stage for the further examination of the matter or thing itself which is in question (the scientific examination). Rather, the scientific examination—what the relationship of slavery is, and, therefore, ought to be—is commenced immediately. By commencing in this manner, the nature of the slave, and the relationship of master and slave, is determined philosophically, and then, from this determination, the question is posed whether individuals can be held to exist who fulfil these definitions.

The household, as a component of the economy (*oikos*), provides for the continuance of life in the form of both the bare needs of life and the good life.[28] The satisfaction of these bare needs involves the science of property acquisition which is also a part of household management (*Pol.* 1253b23–24). Within the

---

[26]For the examination and identification of the opponents of slavery, see Cambiano (1980).

[27]Here, following the analysis of Goldschmidt (1984), which is cited and re-presented by Brunschwig (2005). Brunschwig, and cited with approval, by Garver (1994), p. 118, fn. 14. However, the reference to Goldschmidt is absent from Garver's subsequent book on Aristotle's *Politics* (Garver 2014).

[28]See, Nagle (2006).

science of managing the household, the slave is a part of the property of the household, and is defined as

"a piece of animate property of a sort" (*Pol.* 1253b32), "a tool for maintaining life" (*Pol.* 1253b31, trans. Reeve).

The slave is, therefore, to be considered a specific type of property—a living instrument or tool—but being unable to perform its task on command or by anticipating instructions, cannot relieve the master of the need for slaves (*Pol.* 1253b33, 1253b38).

Aristotle then introduces further precision to the definition of the slave as a tool. The precision is based upon the distinction between action and production in relation to which the slave, who is a piece of property, can only be related to action and not production. For the slave, as a piece of property which is animate, is an

assist[ant] in the class of things having to do with action. (*Pol.* 1254a7–8. trans. Reeve)

The slave, as a living instrument, is an instrument of action of the master and, as such, is also a possession. The status of a possession flows from the analogy between the definition of a part and a piece of property:

A part is not just a part of another thing, but is *entirely* that thing's. The same is also true of a piece of property. This is why a master is just the slave's master, not his simply, while a slave is not just his master's *slave*, he is entirely his (*Pol.* 1254a8–12. trans. Reeve, emphasis in original)

As a possession, the slave is both part of the master and wholly belongs to him, and this concludes the first stage of Aristotle's particular methodological approach to the two predominant approaches to slavery. The conclusion is reached with the attainment of clarity regarding

the nature and capacity of a slave. (*Pol.* 1254a13–14. trans. Reeve)

Thus, the term *natural slave* can be applied to a human being if the individual

is by nature not his own but someone else's [. . .] And he is someone else's when, despite being human, he is a piece of property; and a piece of property is a tool for action which is separate from its owner. (*Pol.* 1254a14–16. trans. Reeve)

Hence, the slave is to be contrasted with the master, as the other element of this relationship of rule. The master is a human being who is also the possessor of the slave, as a piece of animate property, and, therefore, exercises mastership over the possession and living instrument of action which is the slave.

With the conclusion of this philosophical definition of the relationship of master and slave, within the household, Aristotle then proceeds to the question of whether anyone is to be found who is a slave

by nature or not, and whether it is better or just for anyone to be a slave or not (all slavery being against nature) (*Pol.* 1254a17–18. trans. Reeve)

Hence, the examination moves from the question of *is* to *ought*—the justification for the relationship of master and slave within the household.

The justification remains philosophical, and concerns the foundation for a conception of natural slavery in which the incompletion or deficiencies of an individual render their presence, as a slave, within the relationship of master and slave, expedient and right. The conception of *natural slavery* operates to redefine the character of enslavement by centring the determination upon the intention of nature and, therefore, upon the examination of the particular individual's characteristics. This, in turn, displaces the forcible and non-consensual character of enslavement as an intrinsic element of slavery, and, redefines it as a separate form of slavery resulting from war.

The examination of the individual is undertaken in order to determine whether and to what extent nature intends that

> some things are distinguished right from birth, some suited to rule and others to being ruled. (*Pol.* 1254a20–22. trans. Reeve)

The determination of the intention of nature involves the introduction and reference to notions of reason (*logos*) and emotion (*thumos*), together with those of soul (*psyche*) and body (*soma*), as the elements through which to define the characteristics of the *natural slave*.

The incompletion or deficiencies of the individual, as the prerequisite of the natural slave, are the necessary counterpart of the completion and proficiency or perfection of the master. The relationship of master and slave is redefined as *natural* in the double sense of the presence of incomplete or deficient individuals in the position of the natural slave, and the relationship between master and slave expressing the natural rule of the superior over the inferior which is, also, the completion of the slave by the addition of the external rule of the master.

The exact operation of the notions of reason (*logos*), emotion (*thumos*), soul (*psyche*) and body (*soma*), in the determination of natural slavery, are the subject of continued academic dispute, and relate to the reflection upon, and reconstruction of, the internal coherence of Aristotle's justification of *natural slavery*.[29] Rather than assuming the parameters of this debate as the level at which to intervene in the further interpretation of Aristotle's method, it is possible to suggest that one can redefine these initial parameters through the work of Schütrumpf and Deslauriers.[30] From this perspective, the problems of coherence are the expression of a deeper level of philosophical engagement with the work of Plato in which Aristotle attempts to think with and beyond Plato.[31]

Before turning to this interpretation of Aristotle's text, it is necessary to outline the manner in which the philosophical justification of natural slavery responds to the two predominant conceptions of slavery with which Aristotle initiates his philosophical analysis. The conception of slavery as conventional and, therefore, unnatural and unjust, is confronted first, and is adapted, through the philosophical justification of natural slavery, to enable natural slavery, as expeditious and just, to be distinguished from a second form of slavery, resulting from war, which is, thus,

---

[29]See, for example, Ambler (1987), Dobbs (1994), Frank (2004), Garver (1994), Heath (2008), Levin (1997), Preus (1993), Smith (1991), Thornton (2007), and Veloso (2013).

[30]Schütrumpf (1993) and Deslauriers (2006).

[31]On Aristotle's critical engagement with Plato, see Cherry (2013) and Mayhew (1997).

characterized as unjust (*Pol.* 1255a3–1255b4). The qualified acceptance of this characterization of slavery serves to enhance the naturalness of natural slavery, because war *always* threatens to undermine the *natural* distinction between master and slave:

> otherwise, those regarded as the best born would be slaves or the children of slaves, if any of them were taken captive and sold. (*Pol.* 1255a26–28. trans. Reeve)

Beyond the potential critique that this position reflects in relation to the expansion of slavery, under Phillip of Macedon, to include Greeks,[32] it constitutes forcible enslavement as exclusively characteristic of war. Hence, natural slavery, as expeditious and just, can then enable this relationship between master and slave to be characterized as one in which

> there is a certain mutual benefit and mutual friendship. (*Pol.* 1255b12–13, trans. Reeve)

The predominant conception of slavery, in which the relationship between master and slave is merely defined by the number of subjects, is rejected by demonstrating that there is an intrinsic and distinctive nature which is characteristic of the relationship between master and slave. This enables Aristotle to distinguish the form of rulership which is characteristic of the relationship between master and slave from that form of rulership over equals which is constitutional (*Pol.* 1255b16–20). The distinction between rule over slaves and constitutional rule is also the depoliticization of this form of rulership in the household, because only those forms of constitutional rule over those who are free and equal are considered as political. Hence, the different relationships which are evident as parts of the household prefigure and facilitate the later discussion of different types of constitution and the further elaboration of the notions of law, reason and emotion within the structure of the *Politics*.[33]

15.4 The Platonic Background

The Aristotelian response to the predominant conception of forms of rulership, as distinguished merely by the number of subjects, represents a particular response to two, central philosophical positions of Plato. The first concerns the Platonic conception of virtue which, as Deslauriers emphasizes, citing Plato's *Meno* (71a–73d) and *The Statesman* (259b–c),[34] is held to be without intrinsic or natural distinction between individuals and this remains unaffected by its particular form of exercise. The general equality of distribution of virtue among individuals is the counterpart of the definition of

---

[32]See, Rosivach (1999).

[33]On this, see, Veloso (2011).

[34]Deslauriers (2006), pp. 55–57, together with the additional references, p. 58, fn. 19.

the virtue necessary for ruling [being] identified with an art or a kind of expert knowledge.[35]

Therefore, the philosophical method which Aristotle adopts to examine the household, as part of the state (*polis*), and with it the deployment of the notions of reason (*logos*), emotion (*thumos*), soul (*psyche*) and body (*soma*) in the determination of the character of the forms of rule within the household, reflects the

> differences […] in […] their claims about who can have such virtues, what the virtues amount to, and how distinct the intellectual virtues are from the moral virtues.[36]

The connection between the Aristotelian rejection of the virtue of ruling as an expertise and the justification of 'natural slavery' arises from the need:

> to show that [ruling well] involves virtues other than theoretical virtues, and to demonstrate the importance of the practical intellectual virtues to good rule, he needs to show that there are significant differences in the soul faculties of different kinds of people[37]

This, in turn, leads to the introduction and emphasis upon the distinction between science (theoretical intellectual virtue) and *phronesis* (practical intellectual virtue).[38] The distinction then enables the generation of two forms of difference: the difference between rulers and subjects (incapacity/capacity for *phronesis*) and the difference among subjects (degrees of incapacity for *phronesis*).[39] These two forms of difference are then deployed and operate to enable Aristotle

> to argue that there are naturally different kinds of persons, and hence that the possession of science is insufficient for being a good ruler because it fails to include the practical and moral aspects of character which distinguish the ruler from the subject.[40]

For Aristotle, natural slavery, as the relationship between master and slave, within the household, functions not simply to distinguish between slaves and free men, but also to indicate that there is a part of the household, as a relationship between persons, which is in nature a relation between equals.[41] This is prefigured in the relationship between husband and wife and, therefore:

> Aristotle must argue not only that natural slaves are different from free men, but also that women are different from men, and also different from slaves, and that children are different from adult free men, but also from women and slaves, in order to demonstrate the legitimacy (by way of naturalness) of constitutional rule and monarchy.[42]

The deployment and operation of these forms of difference also responds to a second Platonic philosophical position which emerges, following Schütrumpf,[43]

---

[35]Ibid., p. 58.

[36]Ibid., p. 55.

[37]Ibid., p. 60.

[38]Ibid., p. 61.

[39]Ibid., p. 62.

[40]Ibid., pp. 62–63.

[41]Ibid., p. 64.

[42]Ibid., pp. 64–65.

[43]Schütrumpf (1993).

326 P. Langford and I. Bryan

once we consider the response of Plato to the position of Thrasymachos in *The Republic* (338c). This position holds 'that every form of rule serves only the interests of the ruler',[44] and an essential part of Plato's argument in *The Republic* consists of its philosophical rejection. For Schütrumpf, an overt connection between the topic of slavery and Plato's refutation of Thrasymachos's views on justice is evident[45]:

> to ensure that men of this type [those who work with their hands] are under the same authority as the highest type, we have said that they should be slave of that highest type which is governed by its divine element. But, as we believe, this control should not be exercised, as Thrasymachos thought, to the detriment of the slave, but because it is better for every creature to be under the control of divine wisdom. That divine wisdom should, if possible, come from within, failing that it must be imposed from without.[46]

Here, as Schütrumpf emphasizes, the Aristotelian philosophical position

> that slaves serve their owners as tools [...] cannot be squared with that of Plato in the passage discussed here.[47]

The Aristotelian response to the challenge represented by the position of Thracymachos and, here, the argument in this Chapter proceeds differently from the further development of Schütrumpf's argumentation, is one which attempts to dissolve the challenge through the framework of the forms of difference between ruler and subjects and among subjects. The justification of natural slavery, as the relationship between master and slave, recognizes a despotic form of rule—mastership—within a part of the household. Thus, a form of rule which serves only the master appears to be present in the first growth or origin of the state. However, the further differentiation of forms of rulership within the household, as the corollary of the differentiation of forms of virtue, prevents the generalization of the position of Thrasymachos to encompass *all* forms of rule in the same manner that it operates to prevent the distinction of forms of rulership merely on the basis of the number of subjects. For, the form of rule which benefits the master—the relationship of master and slave—is confined to a relationship of natural inequality which is, in turn, only present in the household. The passage beyond the household to the wider realm of politics, and forms of constitution, is only possible if it is founded upon the relationship between equals. The differences between, on the one hand, the relationships *within* the household and, on the other, the household (*oikos*) as the realm of the economy and city-state (*polis*), thereby provide a distinctively Aristotelian response to the challenge of Thrasymachos.

---

[44]Ibid., p. 114.

[45]Ibid., p. 115.

[46]Plato (2000) Book IX 590c9. Quotation from Schütrumpf (1993), p. 115.

[47]Schütrumpf (1993), p. 115.

15.5   The Slave: Reason, Emotion and Law

The distinctiveness of Aristotle's approach to the question of slavery, in which Aristotle appropriates and transforms certain concepts from Plato, reveals the position of the slave as the particular determination of the relationship between nature and necessity. This, in turn, shapes the manner in which the slave is to be considered in regard to the notions of reason emotion and law.

While Aristotle does not deny the capacity to exercise reason to the slave, it is conferred after the initial determination of, and justification for, the division between (natural) master and (natural) slave. The division confers a minimal content to reason which is entirely encompassed by

> the distinctions to be made regarding slave and master. (*Pol.* 1255b40. trans. Reeve)

This reason is not recognized to be innate in the slave, but is to be given as a form of training—slave-craft—as exemplified by the training of boy slaves in routine services (*Pol.* 1255b23–25) and further differentiated and extended depending upon the tasks to which they are assigned. For Aristotle,

> [a]ll such sciences, then, are the business of slaves. (*Pol.* 1255b30. trans. Reeve)

The limitation of reason to the science of slave-craft is the corollary of the Aristotelian evaluation of the master's science of using slaves as one which is nothing grand or impressive: it is simply the master's knowledge of

> how to command things that the slave needs to know how to do. (*Pol.* 1255b32–33. trans. Reeve)

This evaluation derives from its comparison with the master's engagement in politics and philosophy, and Aristotle considers the conferral of exercise of the *science* of using slaves upon a steward, for those masters "who have the resources not to bother with such things", as the expression of the status of this science.[48]

Reason, as the combination of these two sciences—slave-craft and the science of using slaves—is coterminous with household management. It is a reason which can never attain the level of politics and philosophy, and it is only the master, as a free man, who has the capacity, to move from the science using slaves to the level of politics and philosophy.

The Aristotelian resolution of the question of reason within household management, leaves the question of virtue unresolved, until the further examination of household management demonstrates that it is

> more seriously concerned with human beings than with inanimate property [and, thus] with their virtue [...], and with the virtue of free people more than with that of slaves.(*Pol.* 1259b20–22. trans. Reeve)

---

[48]A further 'science', "the 'science of acquiring slaves'" is also distinguished by Aristotle, "and is a kind of warfare or hunting" Ibid., *Pol.* 1255b39.

The question of slaves returns as the question of whether they have some other virtue more estimable than those he has as a tool or servant, such as temperance, courage, justice, and other such states of character? Or has he none besides those having to do with the physical assistance he provides? (See *Pol.* 1259b23–25).

The similarity or difference in virtue between slaves and the free has the potential to destabilize the natural division between master and slave. For, if

> both of them should share in what is noble-and-good (*kalokagathia*), why should one of them rule once and for all and the other be ruled once and for all? (*Pol.* 1259b34–35. trans. Reeve)

The Aristotelian response is to prevent the potential for destabilization through an argumentative analogy with the *nature* of the soul.[49] The soul is composed of

> a part that rules and a part that is ruled, and we say that each of them has a different virtue, that is to say, one belongs to the part that has reason and one to the nonrational part. (*Pol.* 1260a4–7. trans. Reeve)

The analogy is then developed through its application within the household, in which,

> while the parts of the soul are present in all these people [slaves, females, children and men], they are present in different ways. (*Pol.* 1260a10–11. trans. Reeve)

The different presence of the parts of the soul reintroduces the *nature* of those within the household:

> [t]he deliberative part of the soul is entirely missing from a slave; a woman has it but it lacks authority; a child has it but it is incompletely developed. (*Pol.* 1260a9–14. trans. Reeve)

It is this spectrum of deficiencies, as differences in the presences of parts of the soul, which then reestablishes the *natural* rule of the free man over slaves, women and children within the household. For, the free man has the part of the soul which is reason in its full authority.

The resolution of the question of virtues is undertaken in the same manner—all must share them, but not in the same way (*Pol.* 1260a15)—with the differentiation based upon being enabled to perform his own task (*Pol.* 1260a16–17). The free man, as a master and, thus, a ruler must have virtue of character complete, whereas the slave

> is useful for providing necessities, so he clearly needs a small amount of virtue – just so much as will prevent him from inadequately performing his tasks through intemperance or cowardice. (*Pol.* 1260a34–35. trans. Reeve)

The slave's lack of deliberative capacity for the use of reason, established through the preceding analogy with the nature of the soul, entails both the dominance of the nonrational in the nature of the slave, and the absence of a connection

---

[49]For Fuselli, in this volume, the question of the contemporary relevance of Aristotle's notion of the soul is its conceptual superiority in comparison to the limitations of existing approaches to the emotions and their relationship to law and legal decision-making. Fuselli (2018).

between reason and emotion. The slave, therefore, has a nature which is incapable of producing virtue immediately from within itself, because the absence of the deliberative capacity for the use of reason removes the potential to direct, guide and shape emotion.[50]

This absence and, thus, the natural difference of the slave from the other human beings in the household, reveals that the virtue which the slave manifests has an *external* cause: the master (*Pol.* 1260a3), the only individual in the household who possesses the full deliberative capacity for the use of reason. The master completes the slave, and allows the slave to develop and share in virtue, but this share is necessarily limited. For, since it is introduced externally, it is shaped by the reason of the master, and calibrated to the successful performance of tasks, as a living instrument, within the household.

The essentially limited character of the virtue of the slave also defines the character of the law to which the slave is subject. The external introduction of virtue, through the reason of the master, is expressed in the form of orders and admonishment, and, for Aristotle, slaves should be admonished more than children (*Pol.* 1260b6). The character of the law, in relation to the slave, is the most prescriptive and coercive, because, in the contrast to the child of the master whose deliberative capacity is undeveloped, the slave lacks the deliberative capacity for reason. The prescriptive and coercive character is reinforced by the origin of the law in the master and his rulership within the household.

The law created for, and applied to, the slave is an integral aspect of household management: the norms of household management. The particular norms relating to the slave are, however, to be distinguished from those relating to the wife and child or children of the master. It is this distinction between those who are free and those who are slaves in the household with which Aristotle concludes his discussion of the slave. The conclusion—"we may take matters to be determined in this way" (*Pol.* 1260b7)—indicates that the law relating to the slave has no enduring interest as it can have no connection to the further development of the *Politics*. The commands and admonishment to which the slave is subject are never conceived to extend beyond the sphere of household management. The normativity of these commands and admonishments are not introduced and applied in order to shape the virtue of the free, but to inculcate the necessary forms of behaviour—limited virtue—for household management.

The continued reflection upon law relates only to those who compose the free population (*Pol.* 1260b17) of the household, and is confined to them alone because the virtue relevant to each of them requires an examination in connection with the constitutions (*Pol.* 1260b9–12).

---

[50]For Bombelli, in this volume, the examination of the Aristotelian relationship between reason and emotion indicates its continued pertinence in comparison with contemporary approaches to this relationship. Bombelli (2018).

15.6   Conclusion

The discussion of slavery in the *Politics*, marked by its philosophical examination and comprehension of slavery, provides the basis for the further books of the *Politics*. The preparation for the development and elaboration of the subsequent Books is predicated upon the presentation of the distinctiveness of the form of rule exercised in the household. This distinctiveness is derived from the response to the question of nature and its different determinations within those who compose the household.[51] The slave, as unfree, is an animate piece of property utilized, by the master, as a free man, for action within the framework of household management. The other humans who compose the household—a wife and a child or children—are free, but their freedom is qualified or limited in relation to the rule of the (natural) master. Those who are free continue, due to the inherent connection between their virtue and the constitution (*politeia*) of the state (*polis*), to be the focus of discussion in the *Politics*. The slave, however, remains confined to the domestic sphere,[52] for the virtue of the slave is coextensive with the household: it derives externally from the master who limits the virtues to those necessary for the continued operation of the household. The philosophical comprehension of the slave as coextensive with the household, and subject to the rule of the master, defines the necessarily limited relationship of the slave to reason, emotion and law. It is only the free population and, in particular, free men, who are capable of developing a political regime. The political regime, or community, is the sole form through which the relationship between law, reason and emotion is to be established in order to realize the ideal or good life. The further development of the *Politics* is predicated upon the simultaneous recognition and disappearance of a relationship of subjection.

---

[51]For a discussion of this argumentative use of the question of nature, see Annas (1997).

[52]The presentation of natural slavery, as confined to the household, indicates that this interpretation sees a disjunction, rather than any continuity with the later discussion of the slavish character of non-Greeks (Aristotle 1998, 1285a16–28). The re-emergence of this term is situated with the initial differentiation of types of kingship, and disappears in the subsequent discussion (*Pol.* 1285b33–1286a1–6). It is also to be differentiated from the further discussion of the 'natural qualities of citizens' (*Pol.* 1327b19) and the 'lack of spirit' of nations in Asia which makes them 'ruled and enslaved' (*Pol.* 1327b27–28). This relates to a susceptibility of those who are initially citizens, as is evident from *Politics* (1327b36–37), where the presence of both spirit and intelligence provides the legislator with an easier task in guiding these citizens to virtue. Hence, the presence of only one of the two simply makes any potential legislator's task more difficult, but not impossible. The whole discussion is further qualified in *Politics* (1328a19–20), where the degree of precision of theoretical discussion of these natural qualities of citizens is held to be lower than that provided by perception.

References

Agamben, Giorgio. 1998. *Homo Sacer: Sovereign Power and Bare Life*. Translated by Daniel Heller-Roazen. Stanford, CA: Stanford University Press.
———. 2013. *The Highest Poverty. Monastic Rules and Form-of-Life*. Translated by Adam Kotsko. Stanford, CA: Stanford University Press.
———. 2016. *The Use of Bodies*. Translated by Kevin Atell. Stanford, CA: Stanford University Press.
Ambler, Wayne C. 1987. Aristotle on Nature and Politics: The Case of Slavery. *Political Theory* 15 (3): 390–410.
Annas, Julia. 1995. *The Morality of Happiness*. Oxford: Oxford University Press.
———. 1997. Ethical Arguments from Nature: Aristotle and After. In *Beiträge Zur Antiken Philosophie: Festschrift Für Wolfgang Kullmann*, ed. Hans-Christian Günther and Antonios Rengakos, 185–198. Stuttgart: Steiner.
———. 2011. *Intelligent Virtue*. Oxford: Oxford University Press.
Aristotle. 1991. *On Rhetoric: A Theory of Civic Discourse*. Translated by George A. Kennedy. Oxford: Oxford University Press.
———. 1998. *Politics*. Edited and Translated by C. D. C. Reeve. Indianapolis, IN and Cambridge, MA: Hackett Publishing.
———. 2000. *Nicomachean Ethics*. Edited and Translated by R. Crisp. 2nd ed. Cambridge: Cambridge University Press.
Bodéüs, Richard. 1993. *The Political Dimensions of Aristotle's Ethics*. Translated by Jan E. Garrett. New York: State University of New York Press.
Bombelli, Giovanni. 2018. Emotion and Rationality in Aristotle's Model: From Anthropology to Politics. In *Aristotle on Emotions in Law and Politics*, ed. Liesbeth Huppes-Cluysenaer and Nuno M.M.S. Coelho. Dordrecht: Springer.
Brunschwig, Jacques. 2005. L'esclavage Chez Aristote. *Cahiers Philosophiques* Hors Série \September: 9–21.
Cambiano, Giuseppe. 1980. Aristotle and the Anonymous Opponents of Slavery. *Slavery & Abolition* 8 (1): 22–41.
Cherry, Kevin M. 2013. *Plato, Aristotle, and the Purpose of Politics*. Cambridge: Cambridge University Press.
Cooper, John M. 1999. An Aristotelian Theory of Emotions. In *Reason and Emotion. Essays on Ancient Moral Psychology and Ethical Theory*. Princeton, NJ: Princeton University Press.
Deslauriers, Marguerite. 2006. The Argument of Aristotle's 'Politics' 1. *Phoenix* 60 (1/2): 48–69.
Dobbs, Darrell. 1994. Natural Right and the Problem of Aristotle's Defense of Slavery. *Journal of Politics* 56 (1): 69–94.
Frank, Jill. 2004. Citizens, Slaves, and Foreigners: Aristotle on Human Nature. *American Political Science Review* 98 (1): 91–104.
———. 2005. *A Democracy of Distinction: Aristotle and the Work of Politics*. Chicago, IL: Chicago University Press.
Fuselli, Stefano. 2018. Logoi Enuloi. Aristotle's Contribution to the Contemporary Debate on Emotions and Decision-Making. In *Aristotle on Emotions in Law and Politics*, ed. Liesbeth Huppes-Cluysenaer and Nuno M.M.S. Coelho. Dordrecht: Springer.
Garver, Eugene. 1994. Aristotle's Natural Slaves: Incomplete Praxeis and Incomplete Human Beings. *Journal of the History of Philosophy* 32 (2): 173–195.
———. 1995. *Aristotle's Rhetoric: An Art of Character*. Chicago, IL: Chicago University Press.
———. 2014. *Aristotle's Politics. Living Well and Living Together*. Chicago, IL: Chicago University Press.
Goldschmidt, Victor. 1984. La Théorie Aristotélicienne D'esclavage et Sa Methode. In *Écrits I. Études de Philosophie Ancienne*, 63–80. Paris: Vrin.
Gottlieb, Paula. 2009. *The Virtue of Aristotle's Ethics*. Cambridge: Cambridge University Press.

Hansen, Mogens H. 2009. *Polis: An Introduction to the Ancient Greek City-State*. Oxford: Oxford University Press.

Harte, Verity, and Melissa Lane. 2013. Introduction. In *Politeia in Greek and Roman Philosophy*, ed. Verity Harte and Melissa Lane, 1–11. Cambridge: Cambridge University Press.

Heath, Malcolm. 2008. Aristotle on Natural Slavery. *Phronesis* 53 (3): 243–270.

Henry, Devin, and Karen Margarethe Nielsen. 2015. Introduction. In *Bridging the Gap Between Aristotle's Science and Ethics*, ed. Devin Henry and Karen Margarethe Nielsen, 1–25. Cambridge: Cambridge University Press.

Hursthouse, Rosalind. 2002. *On Virtue Ethics*. Oxford: Oxford University Press.

Kamtekar, Rachana. 2014. The Relationship Between Aristotle's Ethical and Political Discourses (NE X 9). In *The Cambridge Companion to Aristotle's Nicomachean Ethics*, ed. Ronald Polansky, 370–382. Cambridge: Cambridge University Press.

Leunissen, Mariska. 2015. Aristotle on Knowing Natural Science for the Sake of Living Well. In *Bridging the Gap Between Aristotle's Science and Ethics*, ed. Devin Henry and Karen Margarethe Nielsen, 214–231. Cambridge: Cambridge University Press.

———. 2017. Biology and Teleology in Aristotle's Account of the City. In *Teleology in the Ancient World: The Dispensation of Nature*, ed. Julius Rocca. Cambridge: Cambridge University Press.

Levin, Michael. 1997. Natural Subordination, Aristotle On. *Philosophy* 72 (280): 241–257.

Lévy, Edmond. 1989. La Théorie Aristotélicienne D'esclavage et Ses Contradictions. *Mélanges de Pierre Lévêque* 3: 197–216.

Mayhew, Robert. 1997. *Aristotle's Criticism of Plato's Republic*. Lanham, MD and Oxford: Rowman and Littlefield.

Morel, Pierre-Marie. 2011. Le Meilleur Et Le Convenable. Loi Et Constitution Dans La Politique D'Aristote. In *Politique d'Aristote: Famille, Régimes, Éducation*, ed. Emanuel Bermon, Valery Laurand, and Jean Terrel, 89–103. Bordeaux: Presses Universitaires de Bordeaux.

Nagle, D. Bernard. 2006. *The Household as the Foundation of Aristotle's Polis*. Cambridge: Cambridge University Press.

Nichols, Mary P. 1992. *Citizens and Statesmen: A Study of Aristotle's Politics*. Lanham, MD and Oxford: Rowman and Littlefield.

Nielsen, Karen Margarethe. 2015. Aristotle on Principles in Ethics: Political Science as the Science of the Human Good. In *Bridging the Gap Between Aristotle's Science and Ethics*, ed. Devin Henry and Karen Margarethe Nielsen, 29–48. Cambridge: Cambridge University Press.

Pangle, Thomas L. 2013. *Aristotle's Teaching in the Politics*. Chicago, IL: Chicago University Press.

Pellegrin, Pierre. 2013. Natural Slavery. In *The Cambridge Companion to Aristotle's Politics*, ed. Marguerite Deslauriers and Pierre Destrée, 92–116. Cambridge: Cambridge University Press.

Plato. 2000. In *The Republic*, ed. G.R.F. Ferrari. Cambridge: Cambridge University Press.

Preus, Anthony. 1993. Aristotle on Slavery: Recent Reactions. *Philosophical Inquiry* 15 (3/4): 33–47.

Rapp, Christoph. 2009. The Nature and Goals of Rhetoric. In *The Blackwell Companion to Aristotle*, ed. Georgios Anagnostopoulos, 579–595. Oxford: Blackwell.

Rosivach, Vincent J. 1999. Enslaving 'Barbaroi' and the Athenian Ideology of Slavery. *Historia: Zeitschrift Für Alte Geschichte* 48 (2): 129–157.

Russell, Daniel C. 2009. *Practical Intelligence and the Virtues*. Oxford: Oxford University Press.

———. 2012. *Happiness for Humans*. Oxford: Oxford University Press.

Schofield, Malcolm. 2005. Ideology and Philosophy in Aristotle's Theory of Slavery. In *Aristotle's Politics: Critical Essays*, ed. Richard Kraut and Steven Skultety, 91–120. Lanham, MD and Oxford: Rowman and Littlefield.

Schofield, Malcolm, and Richard Kraut. 2006. Aristotle's Political Ethics. In *The Blackwell Guide to Aristotle's Nicomachean Ethics*, 305–322. Oxford: Blackwell.

Schütrumpf, Eckart. 1993. Aristotle's Theory of Slavery—A Platonic Dilemma. *Ancient Philosophy* 13 (1): 111–123.

Sloate, Michael. 1995. *From Morality to Virtue*. Oxford: Oxford University Press.

Smith, Nigel D. 1991. Aristotle's Theory of Natural Slavery. In *A Companion to Aristotle's Politics*, ed. David Keyt and Fred D. Miller, 142–155. Oxford: Oxford University Press.

Swanton, Christine. 2005. *Virtue Ethics a Pluralistic View*. Oxford: Oxford University Press.

Thornton, Lockwood. 2007. Is Natural Slavery Beneficial? *Journal of the History of Philosophy* 45 (2): 207–221.

Trott, Ariel M. 2014. *Aristotle on the Nature of Community*. Cambridge: Cambridge University Press.

Veloso, Claudio W. 2011. La Relation Entre Les Liens Familiaux Et Les Constitutions Politiques. In *Politique d'Aristote: Famille, Régimes, Education*, ed. Emanuel Bermon, Valery Laurand, and Jean Terrel, 23–39. Bordeaux: Presses Universitaires de Bordeaux.

———. 2013. Aristote, Ses Commentateurs et Les Déficiences Délibératives de L'Esclave et de La Femme. *Les Études Philosophiques* 107 (4): 513–534.

Vlassopoulos, Kostas. 2011. Greek Slavery: From Domination to Property and Back Again. *Journal of Hellenic Studies* 131: 115–130.

Ward, Julie K. 2005. Aristotle on Physis: Human Nature in the Ethics and Politics. *Polis* 22 (2): 287–308.

Part IV
Legitimation

Chapter 16
Empathic Political Animal: What a North Korean Prison Camp Can Reveal About the Aristotelian Political Association

Tommi Ralli

> *Raised in a dysfunctional family in a secret prison, badly educated, and tortured, he is a flawed eyewitness to the savagery of the world's last totalitarian state. As he has often said of himself, he is an "animal" slowly learning how to be a human being*
>
> Harden, *Escape from Camp 14*

Abstract The memoir *Escape from Camp 14* tells the story of a camp-born North Korean prisoner. The deprived conditions in which he grew up give rise to hypotheses as to what must be present in our interactions as we are 'political animals'. The chapter argues that the story of a childhood in the camp makes us think in a new way about the 'capability of being partner in an association' that one who is without a city lacks. The chapter examines, in particular, what type of empathy could agree with Aristotle's statement that the city is by nature prior to individual. Projective empathy is discarded in this respect. Concepts close to empathy in Aristotle's works are surveyed: (1) feeling the same as a friend feels, (2) emotional contagion, (3) discernment, and (4) education from music. An Aristotelian concept of empathy is then defined. It is suggested in the chapter that in extreme cases the absence of empathy leads to the incapability of association, and an individual who lacks a minimal sense of empathy becomes an *apolis*.

T. Ralli (✉)
Centre of European Law and Politics, University of Bremen, Bremen, Germany
e-mail: ralli@uni-bremen.de

© Springer International Publishing AG 2018
L. Huppes-Cluysenaer, N.M.M.S. Coelho (eds.), *Aristotle on Emotions in Law and Politics*, Law and Philosophy Library 121, DOI 10.1007/978-3-319-66703-4_16

16.1 Introduction: The Memoir of Shin Dong-hyuk[1]

The memoir *Escape from Camp 14* tells the story of a camp-born North Korean prisoner. It says that children who grow up in the camp are untrustworthy and abusive. They report to guards and teachers what all the others are eating, wearing, or saying, in an attempt to win extra food rations. The narrator survived like the others by informing on all of them. As a young child, he even saw his mother, whom he lived with and depended on for meals, as competition for survival. After his escape, he associates his past with a low sense of animal. He says, 'I am evolving from being an animal'.[2]

In this chapter, I raise the possibility that a prison camp in North Korea has become a concrete laboratory for the identification of those elements, whose absence would prevent the development of a full-blown Aristotelian political association. The deprived conditions in which a child grows up in the camp give rise to hypotheses as to what needs to be present—or is very important to be present—in our interactions as we are 'political animals'. Put another way, the camp has created a control situation and a complementary group (born in the camp), a comparison that allows us a chance to understand better our own human condition, free from idealising elements.

I stress the aspect of knowing our own condition better. As the memoir demonstrates, children born in the camp know only what they can experience in their surroundings, like we do as well. The narrator discovered loneliness, regret, longing and anger only after signs from the outside, such as his conversation (in whispers) with an old man in one of the prison chambers of Camp 14.[3] Even after this encounter, he never contemplated suicide. He describes a difference between prisoners:

> There was a fundamental difference, in his view, between prisoners who arrived from the outside and those who were born in the camp: many outsiders, shattered by the contrast between a comfortable past and a punishing present, could not find or maintain the will to survive.[4]

Born in the camp, he purely followed the rules and obeyed the guards. He was not ashamed to beg a guard for forgiveness, and it did not trouble him, in the day-to-day competition for food, to betray another person; these were, for him, 'survival skills'.[5]

---

[1]The memoir of Shin Dong-hyuk was written by American journalist and author Blaine Harden. It is based on interviews and the narrator's Korean language book 'Escape to the Outside World', published in 2007, 2 years after his escape. In 2015, Harden released a new 'Foreword': his source had altered parts of his story. Despite the altered story, the essentials for us in this chapter remain: the narrator was born and raised in a high-security prison camp, in conditions seeped in selfishness.

[2]Harden (2012), p. 207.

[3]Ibid., p. 84.

[4]Ibid., p. 86.

[5]Ibid.

The difference between growing up in the camp and being sent there is the reason to revisit Aristotle's *Politics*[6] where household is key to the nature of a human as a political animal. Furthermore, the examination of ancient Greek figures such as Philoctetes (who was abandoned on a desolate island and so 'citiless' by bad fortune)[7] and the Cyclopes (possibly citiless by nature)[8] is an established part of *Politics* scholarship to determine what Aristotle means when he says that the city is by nature prior to individual (*Pol.* 1253a20–29). No one has yet, to my knowledge, utilised a contemporary example in the last area, such as birth in the camp. Thematically, both Aristotle's polis and household and the dark twentieth-century invention of the camp have been investigated by Agamben.[9] Nevertheless, his work differs from ours methodologically[10] and also focally: our focus, as bears repeating, is on a person born and raised in the camp.

The chapter will, to begin, pick up the Aristotelian political angle (Sects. 16.2 and 16.3), in particular his city-individual priority (Sect. 16.4). Two new themes emerge, when people are born in the camp (Sects. 16.5 and 16.6): First, the camp might show us what follows from the fact that an individual grows up under circumstances where there is competition for survival rather than social bonding. Second, we should seek clarity as to what level of selfishness—this is posed as a question—would no longer support a political association. The main question is then whether a sense of empathy should be added to the characteristics of Aristotle's political animal (Sect. 16.7). I differentiate projective empathy from the desired characteristic (Sect. 16.8) and examine concepts close to empathy in Aristotle (Sect. 16.9). I close with an Aristotelian definition of empathy (Sect. 16.10).

16.2 The First Line of Inquiry in *Politics* I.2

The union of male and female must exist for generation and the relationship of master and slave for foreseeable security; from both of these relations is first formed household, the naturally arising association for everyday purposes. So begins the first line of inquiry in *Politics* I.2, the so-called genetic[11] analysis of polis. The next association, formed from several households, is village, or a colony, for the sake of more than daily needs. The most autarkic association, polis, is composed of several villages. While coming into existence for the sake of living, it exists for the sake of living well (*Pol.* 1252a26–1252b30). At this point, Aristotle deems he has shown

---

[6]Editions used: Aristotle (1932); Aristotle (2013).

[7]Keyt (1987/1991), p. 139.

[8]Mayhew (1997), pp. 19–20.

[9]Agamben (1995/1998).

[10]See Sect. 16.2.

[11]For instance, Kullmann (1980/1991), pp. 95–96.

that polis exists by nature, in so much as the first associations do so, for polis has grown from them and exists for the sake of the end of associations, which he affirms is autarky: this is best in their case. The completed inquiry explains, in his view, that human is, by nature, a political animal, an animal living in a polis (*Pol.* 1252b31–1253a3).

We are not determining what kind of an association either North Korea or its camps are. We are trying to understand—from the bottom up—the conditions of an Aristotelian political association. Concerning such conditions, we need not seek classification of a camp starting from the top end of his scale. We analyse what is missing at the bottom.

This last task may be an insurmountable challenge, if polis is opposed to the earlier associations. As said by Arendt, the human capacity for political organisation 'stands in direct opposition to' the natural association experienced in household life.[12] Following Arendt, Agamben has contended that simple natural life was excluded from the polis and confined to the sphere of reproduction and subsistence in the household.[13] Instead of strict opposition, we need some sort of an 'onion-peeling' model, where the associations overlap, we grow up in a household, and household is the social foundation. In that manner, by working 'downwards' or backwards from Aristotle's historical or ideal comprehension of associations, we shall be able to discover an association-based reason for the deficient political nature of the camp.

I prefer, then, to conceive of Aristotle's associations as a 'scale of forms': each form of association is new in degree and new in kind compared to the last one, and each step sums up the scale to that point.[14] This arrangement makes sense of the circumstance that there are both differences of degree among associations, such as the number of people who are ruled, and, at the same time, differences which may best be considered differences in kind, between the management or ruling of a household and a polis, and perhaps between the ends that can be assigned to each association. The bottom of the line of associations is connected with the top, the categorical differences are not eradicated, but each difference is also not turned into an opposition. The result is a vividly Aristotelian picture.

Polis arises from household, and human is, by nature, a political animal living in the most complete or fully realised association at the top end of an inclusive[15] scale. In the camp, we are told, children and even a child and his mother are competitors for survival. Accordingly, where Aristotle's line of associations starts, there is competition for survival instead.

---

[12] Arendt (1958/1998), p. 24.

[13] Agamben (1995/1998), pp. 1–12. Agamben is adamant that opposition alone describes the relation of household and polis in Aristotle. Agamben (2007/2011), pp. 17 and 21.

[14] For the method of a scale of forms and Aristotle's use of it, see Collingwood (1933/2005), pp. 99–102.

[15] '[T]he community that [...] embraces all others [...] is called the city.' (*Pol.*, trans. Lord, 1252a5–6).

16.3 Two Lines of Inquiry Meet

We are more political than any gregarious animal, Aristotle argues. Speaking of this as the second line of inquiry in *Politics* I.2, and trying to bring it together with the first (the narrative of associations), I do not count Aristotle's arguments as discrete items with the first inquiry preceding several other arguments.[16] I concentrate on how the two inquiries coalesce (this section) and how a person who is least of all connected with polis is to be characterised (next section).

The two lines of inquiry would seem to belong together so that the more political human nature is marked with the associations of household and polis. This interpretation becomes evident at the end of the 'biological'[17] view that is announced by the comparative remark that a human is political to a greater degree than a bee or any gregarious animal.[18] The passage ends:

> it is peculiar to man as compared to the other animals that he alone has a perception of good and bad and just and unjust and the other things of this sort; and community in these things is what makes a household and a city. (*Pol.* 1253a15–19, trans. Lord)

For indicating these valuations, only humans have reasoned speech (*logos*, a.k.a. speech, language, discourse, reason). The relation between the quoted peculiar perception—'awareness', *aisthēsis*—and the reasoned speech that stands out among other communication is a perennial source of wonder.[19]

The peculiar awareness is necessary for both household and polis. This line of inquiry meets the first one. The development of the peculiar awareness through household and polis is not detailed by Aristotle in all the relations concerning perception and speech. Nevertheless, it is clear from his ethics that household is an environment of growth for, for instance, justice. He observes, in the *Eudemian Ethics*,[20] various relationships in household (friendships, the master-and-slave relationship). 'Hence,' he says,

> in the household are first found the origins and springs of friendship, of political organization and of justice. (*Eth. Eud.* 1242a40–1242b2, trans. Rackham)

This follows his declaration that human is not only a political but also a house-holding animal.[21]

---

[16]Cf. Keyt (1987/1991).

[17]'Aristotle's argument in the second chapter of his *Politics* arises from two quite different starting points. In the first part it proceeds from the social development of humanity, leading to the polis. [...] In the second part Aristotle clearly argues from a biological point of view.' Kullmann (1980/1991), p. 100.

[18]Aristotle, *Pol.*, trans. Rackham, 1253a8.

[19]See, for instance, the fascinating excavation into archives in Agamben (2002/2004), pp. 35–37.

[20]Edition used: Aristotle (1935).

[21]'[M]an is not only a political but also a house-holding animal, and does not, like the other animals, couple occasionally and with any chance female or male, but man is in a special way not a solitary but a gregarious animal, associating with the persons with whom he has a natural kinship; accordingly there would be partnership [*koinōnia*], and justice of a sort, even if there were no state.' (*Eth. Eud.*, 1242a23–27, trans. Rackham).

It is said that Aristotle assumed by and large favourable conditions for the early habituation and learning of a child.[22] In the camp, these circumstances do not exist, as the environment offers, instead, restricted communication and eye contact, competitiveness, lack of trust, distant guards, and the bizarre institution of 'reward' marriage—which we will look at below.

16.4   Is Incapability of Associating About Empathy?

The inquiries into the associations and the highly political human nature appear to meet in another respect. This concerns the position of one who is least of all connected with political association. That person is '*apolis*', without a city, by nature, or one 'not capable of community'[23] or 'being partner in (*koinōnein*) a community (*koinōnia*)'.[24] These remarks help us to refine the hypotheses about birth in the camp and the empathic character of the highly political animal.

The *apolis* makes an appearance as the account of associations ends, just before the biological inquiry:

> man that is by nature and not merely by fortune citiless is either low in the scale of humanity or above it (like the "clanless, lawless, heartless" man reviled by Homer, for he is by nature citiless and also a lover of war) inasmuch as he resembles an isolated piece at draughts. (*Pol.* 1253a3–8, trans. Rackham)

The word 'hearthless', quoted from Homer's *Iliad*, has been taken to mean that the *apolis* is 'without a household'.[25] Such a reference is consistent with Aristotle's emphasis on both household and polis, when speaking of what is human.

The attribute of being through nature *apolis* could bear on birth in the camp. Although people who are put in a political prison camp after they have lived outside may be citiless by bad fortune, they are different, as argued in the memoir, from people who are born there. Superficially, birth in the camp might translate into *apolis* by nature, which would bring into play such condemnations as 'low in the scale of humanity' (in Rackham's translation (1932) or 'a mean sort' (in Lord's translation (2013)). Yet the survivor's expression 'I am evolving from being an animal' as he is comparing his early life in the camps to life after them is usable in another way. It suggests an elevated hypothesis: not all that the camp brings forth in the human born there is inherently true nature.

Aristotle's claim about the one who is incapable of being partner in an association occurs in the context of a famous conclusion. He reasons that, by now, a fully

---

[22]Sherman (1989), p. 156.

[23]Kraut's translation of *Pol.* 1253a27–28. Kraut (2002), pp. 255 and 262.

[24]*Pol.*, trans. Lord, 5 (translator's footnote explaining 1253a27–28).

[25]Nagle (2006), pp. 89–90.

grown, autarkic polis has been shown to be by nature prior to each individual like the whole is prior to the part.[26] Aristotle says among other things that

> if each individual when separate is not self-sufficient, he must be related to the whole state as other parts are to their whole, while a man who is incapable of entering into partnership, or who is so self-sufficing that he has no need to do so, is not part of a state, so that he must be either a lower animal or a god. (*Pol.* 1253a25–29, trans. Rackham)

Commentators have illustrated—with such examples as an imaginary Greek child raised by wild animals—Aristotle's likely meaning that virtues cannot be acquired and life lived well without the environment of polis, family, education, and friendships.[27] I wish to pose a frankly anachronistic question. The question is about the incapability of associating. (Or 'entering into partnership' according to the quoted translation.) The description illuminates, by way of a contrary meaning, the sense in which polis is naturally prior to individual. I want to ask if this incapability could, in today's terms, imply inability for empathy.

An affirmative possibility would then open: some of our conceptions of empathy could capture the sense in which polis is by nature prior to individual. It is worth querying whether empathy—let us say, for now, as shorthand, the ability to see the view of other—underlies the classical priority. The development of empathy through household or family would come on top of those considerations. Regarding both family and the 'evolution from being an animal', we should next observe the North Korean camp in greater detail.

16.5 Reward Marriage as the Sole Association

The only association possible in the narrator's camp was 'reward' marriage.[28] 'Model' prisoners were allowed to couple with a mate selected by the prison staff. Instead of parents, guards had supreme importance for the children. The narrator's parents could not meet almost at all (only five nights after their marriage, and, following that, the father could visit the mother a few times a year).[29] The narrator, who hardly knew his brother and was indifferent to the vague intermittent presence of his father, looks back as follows:

---

[26]For different types of priority in Aristotle, see Keyt (1987/1991), pp. 126–127; Miller (1995), pp. 45–56; and Kraut (2002), pp. 255–267.

[27]The imagined case of a feral Philoctetes and the exemplified conditions for leading the good life are from Miller (1995), pp. 52–53.

[28]According to another ex-prisoner's testimony, men and women were allowed to choose their partners and live together in the neighbouring Camp 18. See Hawk (2012), p. 72.

[29]It is not known what the narrator's mother had been rewarded for. His father said that he had been rewarded for 'his skill in operating a metal lathe in the camp's machine shop'. Harden (2012), p. 24.

In the years after he escaped the camp, Shin learned that many people associate warmth, security and affection with the words "mother", "father" and "brother". That was not his experience. The guards taught him and the other children in the camp that they were prisoners because of the "sins" of their parents. The children were told that while they should always be ashamed of their traitorous blood, they could go a long way towards "washing away" their inherent sinfulness by working hard, obeying the guards and informing on their parents.[30]

While the narrator called the camp home,[31] family relations resembled competition for the scarce resource, food.[32] During school years, trust among friends was poisoned by the constant competition for food, the pressure to squeal, and the practice of collective punishment if a class failed to meet its daily work quota.[33] Later, he had difficulty in trusting his biographer, too, and the biographer found him an unreliable narrator of his own life.[34] 'As he readily admits, he struggles to trust anyone,' we read. 'Guards taught him to sell out his parents and friends, and he assumes everyone he meets will, in turn, sell him out.'[35]

The description of the environment—which includes also instances of helping and children treating a smaller boy as peer at school—makes one think of the early development of empathy. The young concept of empathy has both emotional and cognitive elements. For example, in the nineteen-eighties, a paucity of research on how our capacity for empathy develops in early childhood was attributed to 'the strong influence of cognitive-developmental theory of empathy research,' which required such 'role-taking' capacities that empathy was ruled out before the late pre-school years.[36] Yet when we speak of empathy in a non-fragmented sense, its developmental origins can be a matter of both middle and early childhood. In this period, the guards are the authority figures in the camp.

Rather than learning to understand others in household, the children learned to obey guards and follow the memorised camp rules to such an extent that, as said by the narrator, he was "more faithful to the guards than to my family. We were each other's spies."[37] The very thin association of reward marriage and the major importance of guards may undermine the foundation in household, which Aristotle built into his account of human nature.

---

[30]Ibid., pp. 24–25. Children brought to or born in the camps are 'indoctrinated to inform on other prisoners, even their parents'. Hawk (2012), p. 34.

[31]Harden (2012), p. 8.

[32]'When he was in the camp — depending upon [his mother] for all his meals, stealing her food, enduring her beatings — he saw her as competition for survival.' Ibid., p. 22.

[33]Ibid., p. 37.

[34]Harden (2015), pp. vii–xxiii and ix.

[35]Harden (2012), p. 15.

[36]Thompson (1987), pp. 120–121.

[37]Harden (2012), p. 58.

16.6   Developing a Scale of Selfishness

Another perspective on empathy provided by the camp is selfishness, which stands out at all levels: in the guards and teachers, and also the children, including the protagonist, who has related many details about his involvement in the events leading up to his mother's and brother's execution in the camp.[38] "Outsiders have a wrong understanding of the camp," he says. "It is not just the soldiers who beat us. It is the prisoners themselves who are not kind to each other. There is no sense of community."[39]

The theme of selfishness impresses itself upon our mind, when we hear the story of the camp, yet the question is how one might think it more deeply than as a motive. Aristotle looked beneath the surface of selfish motives. He argued in a deeper way when he denied that happiness is self-sufficient for a solitary human. Instead, he said, happiness is that which is sufficient for individuals with their parents, children, friends, and a somehow delimited group of others, because human is a political animal (*Eth. Nic.* 1097b9–13). Again, challenging the idea that individuals pursuing their own interest had wisdom, Aristotle made it clear that one's own good is inseparable from household management and dependent on political organisation (*Eth. Nic.* 1141b34–1142a9). The basis of these assertions by Aristotle seems markedly different from the minimised household and the individual pressure to report in the camp.

In some way, we are all selfish, we might argue, but there are varieties of selfishness that do not exclude each other. We begin to shed light on the subject of empathy by analysing these varieties. Let selfishness have four stages. The first is self-preservation. In this sense, we are all selfish. Nonetheless, we may, more narrowly, be self-interested by choice. Also, even more narrowly, egocentric (that is, in need of circulating any other views through our own experience). Finally, as the ultimate form of selfishness, totally incapable of empathy.

For example, we would be selfish if we could only understand other views by circulating everything through our own experience. In this case, we are only able to feel ourselves into a situation by putting our experience into the object of understanding. This is the first point illuminated by the arrangement of the senses of selfishness in a scale. (We are following the method that was ascribed to Aristotle in Sect. 16.2.) Imagine the various phases as concentric, nested circles.

---

[38]Reporting his mother's and brother's escape plan to the night guard of the school, he bargained with the guard for more food and the position of a grade leader at school in exchange for the information. The night guard told his superiors that he himself had discovered the plot. After returning to school, the narrator was bullied life-threateningly by his teacher, who blamed the boy for the lack of credit the teacher himself had got, when the scheme was uncovered. In the teacher's eyes, the youngster had, unjustly, informed the guard, and not the teacher, first. Ibid., pp. 59–81.

[39]Ibid., p. 58.

After self-preservation, rarer[40] cases pass into highly developed forms, which relate to empathy. The forms overlap, so it is true to say about the higher forms of selfishness that the person is trying to survive.

Aristotle differentiated between everyone's natural affection for oneself and selfishness that is justly blamed. The latter meant having more affection for oneself than one should (*Pol.* 1263b1–4). In a sense, the proposed scale makes further distinctions within the area of 'justly blamed' selfishness. One modern precedent to such distinctions would seem to be C. S. Lewis' contrast between a selfish and a self-centred life. In the first, one's mind is directed towards a thousand things (Lewis even denied that one's self was among those things), but in the second self-concern and self-pity fill people's thoughts.[41] Here, I call a person whose mind is directed towards others egocentric if everything about the others has to be circulated through his or her own self or ego. This type of 'empathy' is selfishness in a peculiar form, deeper than selfish motives because it concerns the very ability to be aware of others' situations. Theoretically, such egocentrism has been modelled as empathy and 'simulation' (see the discussion on projective empathy below).

Only when a self-centred person is altogether incapable of seeing the view of other, at the extreme exhibiting 'zero degrees of empathy' we would reach the end of the scale. The expression in quotation marks is borrowed from Baron-Cohen, who re-describes in these terms people who are so deeply self-centred that they are imprisoned in their own self-focus. That is the sole longer-term or permanent condition available to someone, whom others avoid meeting on the street, who accuses people close to him of being selfish, to whom what those people do is never enough, who switches on his charm with certain people while storing up information on how they might later be of value to him, and who discards people when they are of no use to him.[42] What causes such empathy deficits and how they should be conceptualised are among the major scientific questions of our age.

This four-part scale works, of course, only if many people think that selfishness is self-preservation, many think that it is self-interest by choice, many think it is egocentrism, and many that it is an inability to empathise. Here, these forms are simply included in an increasing scale.

The camp-born narrator escaped from the camps at the age of 23. The memoir attests to a long process of evolution after the escape. In the camp, there had been a lack of trust, absence of remorse, and also ignorance about sympathy. In one speech (which had been tailored to the audience), the memoirist said he 'had been bred in the camp to inform on family and friends and to feel no remorse': "I

---

[40]For example, Korsgaard contrasts to most of us 'a creature who lives in a state of deep internal solitude, essentially regarding himself as the only person in a world of potentially useful things'. 'It is absurd to suggest that this is what most human beings are like [...] beneath a thin veneer of restraint'. Korsgaard (2006), p. 102.

[41]'Either condition will destroy the soul in the end.' Lewis (1955/2002), p. 166.

[42]Baron-Cohen (2011), pp. 20 and 91–93.

did not know about sympathy or sadness[.]"[43] As described by a Western non-governmental organisation worker, he sees himself sometimes through the eyes of his new self and sometimes through the eyes of the guards in the camp.[44] In this last context, when asked if the description was true, the narrator articulated his approval by saying that he is evolving from being an animal.[45]

One is yearning to know how permanently the camp may have affected the development of emotions. There is evolution, and perhaps, we may speculate, only an extreme level of inability for empathy would be permanent. Testing the permanence of even the utter lack of empathy would require following individuals throughout their lives, it is said.[46] According to one host of the narrator from his post-escape years, "Shin shows real empathy for others". The narrator's self-report was, on the other hand, that he was surrounded by good people: "I try to do what good people do. But it is very difficult. It does not flow from me naturally."[47]

16.7   Towards Inferring Empathy in Aristotle

We have inquired whether authentic interest in another develops when one grows in an unloving environment. For Aristotle, the origins of friendship, political organisation, and justice are first found in the household (*Eth. Eud.* 1242b1). It is conceivable that, in a place like the camp, neither empathy nor friendship develops,[48] although a sense of justice may develop, even if it is different from ours.[49]

I have, specifically, inquired if there is a part for empathy in Aristotle's statement that polis is prior to each individual. Put negatively, the topic of this quest is the nature of one who is incapable of associating (Sect. 16.4). After posing the question of the place of empathy in the priority statement, we can embark on the interesting task of trying to infer empathy in Aristotle's oeuvre. A specific aim can now be set for this attempt. We have discovered the aim in the text of the *Politics*. Our aim shall be to explain, by empathy, the sense in which polis may be prior to each one of us.

---

[43]Harden (2012), p. 219.

[44]"He is kind of here and kind of there." Ibid., p. 207.

[45]Ibid.

[46]Baron-Cohen (2011), p. 97.

[47]Harden (2012), pp. 209–210.

[48]"Before, I thought like a prisoner in the labor camp and didn't really understand basic things like friendship and family." Ramstad and Shin (2012).

[49]For justice in the camp, see Harden (2012), pp. 79 (deserved execution) and 80–81 (the 'unjust' informing of one guard before another). Nevertheless, the track of a sense of justice is another question, not pursued here.

We must first probe the modern notion that we are only able to form a view of how another is affected if we imagine what our own impressions would be, if we were in the other's situation (Sect. 16.8). Past the paradigmatic assumption, we look into the ideas nearest to empathy in Aristotle: (1) feeling the same as a friend does; (2) emotional contagion; (3) discernment; and (4) education from music (Sect. 16.9).

16.8   The Preliminary Question of Projective Empathy

Empathy is a truly recent concept compared to such qualities as understanding, wisdom, or pity discussed by Aristotle. In fact, some of the earliest renditions of empathy have later seemed so distinctively 'modern' that they may not apply to Greek thinking. However briefly, we must look at these initial situations, where the concept of empathy was adumbrated (the concept of *Einfühlung*, or 'in-feeling', introduced by German aesthetician Robert Vischer in 1873), before we explore empathy more broadly than in the projective sense here. Imagining oneself 'in the shoes' of another is a means of understanding, that much can be acquiesced to, but this sort of empathising invites questions.

We can illustrate the kind of empathy that a professional, a spectator, or other recipient may use to 'feel into' (*einfühlen*) a work or a situation by a story about an actress. The actress invites her unassuming cousin to a summerhouse to observe her studiously, which is a ploy to get into her own leading role as an insignificant character that does not, in her opinion, suit her.[50] The manipulative actress succeeds in understanding the character. The character is not only insignificant, but has natural goodness. One may pick up things this way. Sometimes, we make a conscious effort to imagine another person's angle. This technique can be quite successful. We might succeed through imagination based on memory or, as the story highlights, even by manipulating others.

I take the method of putting oneself in another's situation to occur most naturally when the other is distant, even absent—such is a character in a work (the play's character in the story)—or when one is speaking with someone else in a setting which comprises the imagined party. Others have thought this method well suited to occasions where an observer cannot easily see the point of someone's doings, and so needs an aid to overcome the difficulty.[51] In any case, the method does not necessarily imply egocentrism in the sense of Sect. 16.6. We might just try to understand another person in this way.

In the early-modern 'sympathy' (the word empathy was not yet invented), imagining oneself in another's place was less a method than a theoretical assumption. 'By the imagination we place ourselves in his situation' was Adam Smith's

---

[50]Jansson (1978/2014).

[51]Blackburn (1992/1995), p. 278.

explanation of what must go on in us, whether we are aware of it or not, when we feel for others—including those 'heroes of tragedy or romance who interest us'.[52] At the start of the twentieth century, Theodor Lipps' explanation of *Einfühlung* terminated similarly in our own experiences and our imagination. In our imagination, Lipps explained, the movements of other's expressions are first imitated. Then, we reproduce what is evoked in our past experiences. Finally, we project those reproductions into other.[53]

Lipps' projective empathy—which in recent years has been revived within 'simulation theory'[54]—was criticised in its original era. In 1927, Martin Heidegger's *Being and Time* discussed the derivativeness of the account. Heidegger argued that, if we were as separate as the projective empathy model assumes, we might regard empathy as the 'first ontological bridge'[55] from one to another. Yet it was precisely this bridge that projective empathy could not give. The reason was that, according to Heidegger, our knowledge is grounded in being with others. As a result, the processes of projection are not what makes possible the being of each of us with one another.[56]

Heidegger's criticism would justify downplaying empathy in an Aristotelian context, if the criticised concept of empathy were the only or main concept available. The modern assumption of initially separate one and other—like a spectator and an artwork—reduces the usability of projective empathy as a template defining the contours of what to look for in ancient works as corresponding to empathy. Today, though, projective empathy is no longer empathy as a whole. Many theories rely on emotional contagion, and the subject of this debate is broader than the target of Heidegger's criticism. Again, a commonplace view is that empathy involves feeling what another person feels, and this aspect can also be appreciated without assuming that we know feelings only from our own case.

Besides the criticised separateness, the danger of a deluded understanding of other accompanies projective empathy; worse, the imaginer may act on his or her deluded understanding. The object or observer of such delusion and action may feel that this combination is among the worst things a person can do to another. In these

---

[52]Smith (1759/2007), pp. 1–2 and 3, respectively.

[53]Lipps' theory of 'projective "empathy"' based on its criticism in Scheler (1913/2008), pp. 8–12. The early-modern sympathy and Lipps' projective empathy have been counted as two concepts. The first developed in 'interpersonal' and the second in aesthetic context, and in the first the self remains more focal. Batson (2009), p. 7.

[54]'Lipps' account of empathy [...] has recently undergone something of a revival in the hands of contemporary simulationists.' Zahavi (2010), p. 285.

[55]'What "initially" presents phenomenally a way of being-with-one-another that understands — is at the same time, however, taken to mean that which "originally" and primordially makes possible constitutes being toward others. This phenomenon, which is none too happily designated as "*empathy*," is then supposed, as it were, to provide the first ontological bridge from one's own subject, initially given by itself, to the other subject, which is initially quite inaccessible.' Heidegger (1927/2010), p. 121 [A124].

[56]Ibid., pp. 114–122 [A117–A125].

cases, empathy proves to be the opposite of the sought-after basis for association. If, then, projective empathy is inserted into a wider, religious or non-religious, theory encompassing action, it must be given a subordinate place to some ethical notion. Thus, for example, when Martha Nussbaum turns to the emotion most frequently viewed with approval and taken to provide a good foundation for action in the philosophical tradition, compassion (or 'pity' before that term acquired its current associations of condescension and superiority to the sufferer, for which reason Nussbaum does not use this alternative), she stresses that projective empathy—like the mental preparation of a 'Method' actor—is not necessary for compassion.[57] According to Nussbaum, projective empathy can, in a non-necessary way, lead to compassion, which is the emotion that prompts a decision to act beneficently. When it fails to lead to compassion, projective empathy is not ethically important, she says, except in the sense that any use of it, even a playful one and without any concern for the other, counts as a recognition of the other's 'reality' or 'the other as a centre of experience'.[58]

When exclusively focused on, projective empathy is not necessary for political association—as Nussbaum's work makes clear—and we can proceed on the common ground that the imaginer may get things wrong, that projective empathy is an attempt to understand other, and that projection can be ethically relevant. Yet, while her work combines the criticised modern empathy with compassion from a long philosophical tradition, we shall map the nearest phenomena to empathy in Aristotle's philosophy.

16.9 Concepts Close to Empathy in Aristotle

Aristotle did not have the word empathy in our meaning. He uses the noun *empatheia* once, in the short work *On Dreams*. The word signified in Greek the heightened state of emotion. It comes from *pathos*, emotion or passion, with the prefix *em-* functioning as an intensifier. It did not mean any particular connection to other's feelings. In *On Dreams*, Aristotle speaks of emotions altering perceptions, and says that the coward may expect fearful things based on a mere slight resemblance between what is the case and his foes. The deeper this person is in his emotional state, the slighter the resemblance needed to spark the apprehension.[59] In other words, a person with a long-term disposition for cowardice will, in the grip of heightened fear, see enemies all around. This is a profound point, and may precisely be correlated with a low sense of empathy, but it shows that we must seek elsewhere

---

[57]Nussbaum (2001), pp. 297–353.

[58]Ibid., pp. 297–353; Nussbaum (2013), pp. 145–146 (the second direct quotation in the text at p. 146).

[59]On Dreams, 2. Edition used: Aristotle (1984).

in Aristotle's works for concepts close to present-day empathy. The nearest concepts are found in his ethics, his *Politics*, and the encyclopaedia *Problems*.

16.9.1 Feeling the Same as a Friend Does

Aristotle's remarks on feeling the same as a friend feels have two different contexts in his ethical works.[60] The first might be called the context of inner concord. It is illuminated by a comparison between our relationship with our own self and the shared feelings between true friends. In the second context, Aristotle ponders the maximum number of true friends. This is suggestive of the uncomfortable fact that, even between friends, there may be competition, so that one friend's joy is not met with the other friend's shared joy, but an opposite, perhaps envious, feeling.

We are looking for, in shared feelings between friends, an element of empathy. These feelings are, to begin with, a reference point for Aristotle's discussion on affection for oneself in a healthy, positive sense. Rather than being at odds with himself or herself, a decent person and a person who regards himself or herself as decent share their grief and joy with their own self. This absence of inner division is, Aristotle compares, similar to a friend feeling the same grief or the same joy as another friend feels, and feeling it absent any ulterior reason than because the other one feels it. As the reference point is put in the *Eudemian Ethics*:

> For a friend wishes most of all that he might not only feel pain when his friend is in pain but feel actually the same pain — for example when he is thirsty, share his thirst — if this were possible, and if not, as nearly the same as may be. The same principle applies also in the case of joy [. . .]. (*Eth. Eud.* 1240a36–39, trans. Rackham)

The contrast is with an evil person, in whom there is discord. The evil one is, Aristotle says, 'not a single individual but many, and a different person in the same day, and unstable' (*Eth. Eud.* 1240b20, trans. Rackham).

Most characteristically, friendship is sharing one's life, says Aristotle. Between friendlessness and excessively many friends, he says that an upper limit would presumably be the largest number of people with whom one could share one's life—which is not a large number. And, he reasons, it

> also becomes difficult to join intimately with many people in their joy and grief; for it is not unlikely that one would find oneself simultaneously sharing one friend's pleasure and another's sorrow. (*Eth. Nic.*[61] 1171a6–8, trans. Rowe)

---

[60]Compared to the ethical writings, the pared-down notes on friendship in the *Rhetoric* list many characteristics of friends and adversaries that are easily comprehended without empathy. The list is also clearly addressed to the orator: 'It is evident, then, [. . .] that it is possible to prove that men are enemies or friends, or to make them such if they are not; to refute those who pretend that they are, and when they oppose us through anger or enmity, to bring them over to whichever side may be preferred.' (*Rhet.*, Book II, Chapter 4, trans. Freese). Edition used: Aristotle (1926).

[61]Edition used: Aristotle (2002).

The context and shared feelings within it as an argument are familiar from everyday life. For example, we tend to doubt that a friend whose questions and wishes follow their own course when we are in grief is a true friend.[62]

Aristotle's notes hint nowhere at any concept of projection. It is unnecessary to interpret these comments on shared feelings through early-or-late-modern models. To understand how a friend feels from her point of view, it need not ultimately be my imagination that 'transport[s] me to her feelings.'[63] Quite apart from the likely fact that projection occurred long ago too, we can avoid anachronism by refusing to impose projective empathy on the ancient text as an interpretive scheme.

Indeed, the ability to feel the same as a friend does can be that fundamental element in friendship, which makes the layered, Aristotelian, political experience possible. The main argument here is that, without such an ability, one would be incapable of being partner in an association—'no part of a city' (*Pol.* 1253a28–29). The presence of the capacity for shared feelings would, then, give, for its part, meaning to the natural priority of the political community to individual. This interpretation is not about the extent of one's friends, nor is it about any discussion whether friends and acquaintances feel empathy more easily towards each other than do strangers. The question is about the capacity for living together, without which, Aristotle claimed, one would apparently be a beast (*Pol.* 1253a29). In the same vein, the question may be about the sense, in which childhood in the camps seems afterwards to be associated with a low sense of animal.

16.9.2 Emotional Contagion in 'Problems Arising from Sympathy'

Why, in response to others yawning, do people usually yawn in return? (*Problems*[64] 886a23–24, trans. Mayhew)

With this question opens the book 'Problems Arising from Sympathy' in the encyclopaedia *Problems* (or *Physical Problems Arranged According to Kind*), some parts of which are attributed to Aristotle. The contagious—in humans and in animals—is the topic of the book. It seeks explanations to problems including the frequently mentioned case of contagious yawning, consumption and other infectious diseases, and, in one section, the phenomenon that we suffer along in thought when we see another person 'being cut or burned or tortured or experiencing something else that's terrible' (*Problems*, 887a15–22). The word *sympatheia*

---

[62] Aristotle uses another kind of example to illustrate a similar discrepancy: 'Those who have many friends, and greet everyone in an intimate fashion, are thought to be friends to nobody, except in the way that fellow citizens are friends; in fact people call them obsequious.' (*Eth. Nic.* 1171a15–17, trans. Rowe).

[63] As contemplated by Sherman on the basis of Aristotle's observations. Sherman (1989), p. 136.

[64] Edition used: Aristotle (2011).

appears only in the title of the book. The noun 'sympathy' is, in fact, found nowhere else in any primary Aristotelian text.

Apart from new examples, new explanations, and a focus on facial expressions conspicuously absent in the ancient text, modern studies do, in certain respects, seem to take place in a changed world compared to the classical one.[65] On the other hand, even two millennia ago, the example of contagious yawning was prominent among the phenomena of contagion. Explanations were then sought under the heading 'sympathy'—connoting perhaps 'travelling together'—while the modern rubric is 'emotional contagion'.

At present, researchers still say that surprisingly little is known about what underlies the phenomenon of contagious yawning.[66] It is often linked to the capacity for empathy. It and other emotional contagion feature, for instance, in a 'Russian doll' model of empathy, as part of its hidden, inner core. This model is based on a wide survey of empathy research in the twentieth century. According to the model, the inner emotional core is needed for the development of outer layers, such as 'cognitive empathy' and 'adopting other's perspective'. Deficiencies in those outer layers could, it is suggested, go back to deficient inner layers.[67]

Regardless of the logic in the 'Russian doll' model, its core displays the hypothesis of a shared basis between emotional contagion and empathy. This contemporary association makes it relevant to consider if the ancient remarks on contagion and yawning should likewise be integrated into an Aristotelian notion of empathy. Against that mix, arguments by Max Scheler from the early twentieth century—against explaining 'fellow-feeling' by means of emotional contagion—show how strongly contagion differs from empathy. In contagion, Scheler says, nothing in my feeling points to its origin in another person or in the group. I take the experience to be my original experience, although it is later, *post hoc*, traceable to contagion from others.[68] That is, in contagion, the focus can be on oneself; in empathy, it is on another.

Attending to the state of other is of course part of the overlying phenomena in the many-layered model that surveyed current science. By including contagion among the phenomena that are close to empathy in classic Aristotelian works, we can acknowledge this debated subject. I stress, nevertheless, only the capacity of sharing a feeling and the next property, discernment. Looking at a photograph of a yawning person—or hearing the word yawning or even reading about yawning—and catching a yawn may be related to understanding others, but whether and how they are is left to today's science.

---

[65]For example: 'Why, when we stand near the fire, do we desire to urinate, and if we stand near water, for instance a river, we *do* urinate? Is it because all water reminds us of the moisture in the body, and the nearby (*water*) calls out for it? Further, the fire itself dissolves what is solidified in the body, just as the sun does the snow.' (*Problems*, 886a37–886b3).

[66]'Contagious yawning [...] is a well-documented phenomenon [...], but surprisingly little is known about the mechanisms underlying it.' Senju et al. (2007), p. 706.

[67]Preston and de Waal (2002); de Waal (2006), pp. 37–42.

[68]Scheler (1913/2008), p. 15.

16.9.3   Discernment and Understanding: Their Relation to Empathy and Sympathy

Discourses on putting oneself in another's shoes tend to get interesting when the speaker explains how we can avoid the figment that the other's view is as we imagine it. Presumed knowledge of other can be a self-deluded projection. The problem of inaccurate diagnosis is well expressed by Jodi Halpern in her plea for clinical empathy. Halpern advises doctors to be 'cautious about situations in which we experience emotional empathy for a patient going through a similar medical problem or personal loss to something that we ourselves have experienced. In such situations it can be tempting for the doctor to imagine *herself* in a patient's shoes and think that she knows how the patient feels because of how *she* (the doctor) would feel. Given that each person has a different personal history and personality and is likely to be affected by similar medical diseases in very different emotional ways, this is usually a clinical mistake.'[69] Instead, Halpern suggests that the doctor should be authentically curious to learn more about the patient's concerns. The doctor should also stay interested throughout the time that the patient attempts to correct and guide the doctor's initial understanding. In history-taking, the doctor should listen carefully and, crucially, listen in a nonverbally attuned way.[70]

The suggested empathic processes—at once professional and authentically individual—serve the doctor's cognitive ends. They show that empathy is related to understanding. So does Lauren Wispé's summary of empathy as a 'way of knowing'.[71] So does the above 'Russian doll' model of empathy, its outer layers addressing cognitive empathy research.[72] And so does Arne Johan Vetlesen's view that empathy discloses the other's emotional experience and is a necessary prerequisite for the development of an understanding of the other's emotions.[73]

This variegated and widely discussed aspect of understanding must be stated so that it is merely an aspect, not the whole, of empathy. It would also be desirable if this statement preserved the non-judgmental, not directly action-oriented, nature of empathy.[74] Neither should the overconfidence of those who think they know others well be built into the cognitive side of empathy. As we seek the aspect of understanding in Aristotle, we shall comply with these essentials.

---

[69]Halpern (2012), p. 237.

[70]For 'engaged curiosity' and 'nonverbal attentiveness' in clinical care, see ibid., pp. 236–237 and 234, respectively.

[71]Wispé (1991), p. 80.

[72]de Waal (2006), pp. 37–42.

[73]'In my view, empathy, being humanity's basic emotional faculty, contains a cognitive dimension by virtue of which it, and it alone, *discloses* to us something about another person — namely, his or her emotional experience in a given situation. Empathy is a necessary *prerequisite* for the development of an awareness and understanding of the emotions and feelings of another person.' Vetlesen (1994), pp. 204–205.

[74]The term 'non-judgmental' comes from Wispé, according to whose definition empathy refers to 'the attempt by one self-aware self to comprehend non-judgmentally the positive and negative experiences of another self'. Wispé (1991), p. 79.

The experience of understanding is addressed on the intellectual side of Aristotle's picture of the soul. The capacities there are not, of course, separate from the soul as a whole. The non-judgmental nature of empathy directs us to look at those capacities that do not, by themselves, prescribe any way to act or non-action, but help us discern particulars, so that we come to the practical judgments. There are two such virtues connected with practical wisdom: discernment (*gnōmē*, 'sense') and understanding (*sunesis*).

Discernment (*Eth. Nic.* 1143a19–24) seems to be an obvious candidate for the intellectual element of empathy. Empathic relationships with others cannot consist in the application of categories and stereotypes. Discerning the particulars of others is a natural cognitive side of empathy. Conversely, there are reasons to hesitate about incorporating correct understanding as part of empathy. These reasons show themselves, when we compare empathy with sympathy.[75]

Since debates on the moral value of literature in the nineteenth century, sympathy has so frequently been associated with an impulse to action and feelings for sufferers that its older connotation of a projection of imagination is currently called 'empathy'.[76] The closer connection of sympathy to action is one reason for concentrating on empathy rather than sympathy.

Besides, sympathy appears to presuppose further understanding of another's situation than empathy does. The empathiser is trying to understand another, while sympathy already supposes that we think we understand something about the other (and can then harmonise with him or her, like two strings tuned to an identical pitch). Our sympathy may disappear and be replaced by empathy, if we learn things about the person with whom we have originally sympathised. In this way, for instance, the director of a film can play with our sympathy. We sympathise with a character, then learn something about her or him, after which we try to understand the character more.

This empathic feature of trying to understand raises a question about the impulse, the emotion that makes us try to understand other. We may wonder if we are pushed by a desire. The desire to understand another could be the function of empathy.

On the other hand, a more demanding intellectual aspect of empathy than only trying to understand would seem to put empathy at the crossroads with regard to respect. Respect for other people limits attempts at 'solving' anyone in the sense of getting fully inside another mind. The question is not simply about the possibility of knowing others (whether we may only know our own inner lives), but also any 'over-figuring-out' of another ('I solved you') shows a lack of respect towards the

---

[75]The traditional exercise of comparing empathy and sympathy has yielded contrasts, such as reaching out for other (empathy) and being moved by other (sympathy), and having understanding (empathy) or other's well-being (sympathy) as one's object. Ibid., pp. 79–80.

[76]See, for instance, Mitchell (2014), pp. 121–134.

other person. Thus, having respect, the empathiser tries to understand the other without aiming at perfection.

Although we opt to discuss empathy rather than sympathy for the two reasons that sympathy is closer to action and presupposes more understanding, empathy has been taken to mean sympathy in everyday life[77] and they have been treated together in some scientific analyses.[78] Yet, we might be proud of being able to empathise or having discernment, while it is questionable whether someone is proud of sympathising. This brings us to a tentative divergence between discernment and understanding. The two virtues are both said to grow with age and to be found in the same individuals (*Eth. Nic.* 1143a25–29 and 1143b7–14). Discernment matures into a sense that is above all about the particular experiences of other people[79]; it is more about the other's situation than sympathy is. Whereas understanding (*Eth. Nic.* 1142b35–1143a18) makes one hesitate: as knowledge, it may, like sympathy, reflect less the other's and project more one's own situation. When a sympathiser says 'I know exactly what you are feeling', the knowledge may be delusive. Further, the claim makes it about the speaker, marginalising the other's experience. Still, as a virtue, understanding is exercised in situations where another person is speaking (*Eth. Nic.* 1143a12–15), and listening is an important empathic trait.

Understanding, when it pertains to listening, should not be overlooked as an empathic element. Nevertheless, the difference between conceived understanding and empathic listening is required for this purpose, and it does not necessarily come out if the meanings of empathy and sympathy align themselves. Although they are not separate in an either-or manner, ultimately I do not think that we can suspend differentiation between empathy and sympathy, at least in cases where one can take sides—conflicts, games, game-like disputes, contests of all kinds—and sympathy can be all that matters. In these cases, we see that, when there are two sides, empathy can be towards both, while sympathy moves us for one side. If, for instance, we are watching a match between two unknown sides and trying to figure out which side to support, empathy would be an underlying appreciation for both sides, while sympathy relates to which side we take. Empathy is part of our perception of what happens in the game in this way. Sympathy, by contrast, may develop towards one side and, while it lasts, tip us to this side.[80] In short, when there are sides to take, it is possible to have empathy for both sides, but sympathising— now something further appears to happen.

---

[77]Strayer and Eisenberg (1987), p. 390: 'Many persons outside the university had not heard of it, and most responded that it meant sympathy.'

[78]For example, Preston and de Waal (2002).

[79]See also *Eth. Nic.* 1143a20–24 (a reference to concepts analysed at the end of the book on justice).

[80]We are not refereeing the game, so sympathy can matter all the way. For an ancient illustration of a kindred situation, many Greeks believed that audiences are attracted by claims and people heard first. Aristotle gives the example of Theodorus, an actor who never allowed anyone else to appear on the stage before him, and continues: 'this happens alike in regard to our dealings with people and to our dealings with things — all that comes first we like better.' (*Pol.* 1336b31–33, trans. Rackham) This inclination, it is maintained in the text, is closer to sympathy, instead of empathy.

16.9.4 Education from Music

The early habituation in household is part of a broader education. Against the practices of his day, Aristotle defends common education, in the context of which he evaluates education from 'music'. Here, we discover something akin to empathy. Besides powers that relate to amusement and pastime, music has educational power, contributing to our character, he says. This power is shown in the ability of music to make soul inspired, and in the implicitly empathic engagement that

> all who listen to imitations come to experience similar passions, even apart from rhythms and tunes themselves (*Pol.*, 1340a12–14, trans. Lord)

What matters for us in this much-debated passage is that Aristotle focuses on the resonance of feelings, when speaking of the power of moulding a developing character. He is not here concerned with any targeted educational content or preaching. Instead, we may think, in line with the passage, of such experiences as listening to sounds that take us to another place. These engaged feelings as sources of education are consonant with today's research on the empathic effect of literature and fantasy. (Aristotle's theme, we must remember, is much broader in scope than the music of our time.) It is argued that mental visualising and immersion in another world can enhance the reader's empathy, and that an instruction to put oneself in the place of a character has no such effect.[81] Accordingly, immersion in other world, including a fictional world and its characters, can have an empathic dimension evocative of that of music in Aristotle's educational programme. One means of developing empathy missing in the camp was literature: the teacher had the only book at school, and the narrator had never learned what fiction or non-fiction was.[82]

16.10 Conclusion: An Aristotelian Concept of Empathy

The question as to whether empathy should be added to the characteristics of Aristotle's political animal was aroused by the discovery of selfishness in the regulated growth environment in a prison camp. The question was localised in the text of *Politics* I.2 by suggesting that empathy can be that individual capability of partnership, which supports Aristotle's thesis that polis is by nature prior to each individual. The initial discourses in the *Politics* give a beautifully orchestrated picture of the contribution of ancient household to political organisation. I read in the same vein the summary statement in the *Eudemian Ethics* that the origins and springs of friendship, political organisation, and justice are found in household. The particular ways in which this contribution of household is uncertain in the camp— the barriers to communication and eye contact, competitiveness, lack of trust, selfishness—were summed up succinctly by the narrator: no sense of community.

---

[81] Keen (2014), p. 25 (referring to her discussions with psychologist Dan R. Johnson).
[82] Harden (2012), p. 35; Harden (2015), p. xiii.

The story of a childhood in these conditions allows us to reflect on what someone who is not part of a city lacks: the capability of associating. The ability for empathy was regarded as that sense in which the political association is prior to an individual. According to Bombelli (2018), an Aristotelian notion of friendship expresses the emotive basis of political association. For Bombelli, Koziak, Coelho, and others, spiritedness (*thumos*) is also called for.[83] Like empathy, these notions illuminate emotions as a condition of political life.[84]

We inferred the requisite type of empathy from Aristotle's work. We drew on his notes on friendship to uncover one part of an Aristotelian concept of empathy: the ability to feel the same as a true friend does. We chose discernment as the intellectual element of empathy. Let us try and define an Aristotelian concept of empathy:

Empathy consists of trying to understand other. It comes from a desire or longing to understand, which can exist even without the ability for empathy, and its parts are the ability to feel the same as a friend does and a measure of discernment.

The last parts imply, to use the shorthand that conveys empathy in everyday life, that one is able to see the view of other—though never wholly, and one is only ever trying to understand other with respect. We left open whether the inability to see others' views except by imagining ourselves in their position would support living in a political association. An absolute inability for empathy would, it is assumed, preclude an individual's long-term contribution to living with other people. The absence of empathy leads, by implication, to the incapability of association, and the individual who lacks a minimal sense of empathy becomes an *apolis*.

Empathy composed of these basic elements is immune to Heidegger's criticism of projective empathy. The inferred concept does not make the modern assumption of separate one and other, in the style of a perceiver and a work. In the combination of an ability to feel the same as a friend feels and discernment, we have found a candidate for the capacity that a political association is at the deep level of individuals' connectedness. Freedom from the camp could mean evolution towards being this empathic political animal.

References

Agamben, Giorgio. 1995/1998. *Homo Sacer: Sovereign Power and Bare Life*. Translated by Daniel Heller-Roazen. Stanford, CA: Stanford University Press.
———. 2002/2004. *The Open: Man and Animal*. Translated by Kevin Attell. Stanford, CA: Stanford University Press.
———. 2007/2011. *The Kingdom and the Glory: For a Theological Genealogy of Economy and Government (Homo Sacer II, 2)*. Translated by Lorenzo Chiesa (with Matteo Mandarini). Stanford, CA: Stanford University Press.

---

[83]In this volume Bombelli (2018) and Coelho (2018); Koziak (1999), pp. 99–125.
[84]Bombelli (2018).

Arendt, Hannah. 1958/1998. *The Human Condition*. 2nd ed. Chicago, IL: University of Chicago Press.

Aristotle. 1926. *Art of Rhetoric*. Translated by John Henry Freese, Loeb Classical Library. Cambridge, MA and London: Harvard University Press and William Heinemann.

———. 1932. *Politics*. Translated by H. Rackham, Loeb Classical Library. Cambridge, MA and London: Harvard University Press.

———. 1935. Eudemian Ethics. In *The Athenian Constitution; The Eudemian Ethics; On Virtues and Vices*, trans. H. Rackham, Loeb Classical Library. London and Cambridge, MA: William Heinemann and Harvard University Press.

———. 1984. On Dreams. In *The Complete Works of Aristotle: The Revised Oxford Translation*, ed. Jonathan Barnes and trans. J. I. Beare. Princeton, NJ: Princeton University Press.

———. 2002. *Nicomachean Ethics*, ed. Sarah Broadie and Christopher Rowe. Translated by Christopher Rowe. Oxford: Oxford University Press.

———. 2011. *Problems, Volume I: Books 1–19*. Edited and Translated by Robert Mayhew, Loeb Classical Library. Cambridge, MA and London: Harvard University Press.

———. 2013. *Aristotle's Politics*. Translated by Carnes Lord. 2nd ed. Chicago, IL and London: University of Chicago Press.

Baron-Cohen, Simon. 2011. *The Science of Evil: On Empathy and the Origins of Cruelty*. New York: Basic Books.

Batson, C. Daniel. 2009. These Things Called Empathy: Eight Related but Distinct Phenomena. In *The Social Neuroscience of Empathy*, ed. J. Decety and W. Ickes, 3–15. Cambridge: MIT Press.

Blackburn, Simon. 1992/1995. Theory, Observation, and Drama. In *Folk Psychology: The Theory of Mind Debate*, ed. Martin Davies and Tony Stone, 274–90. Oxford and Cambridge, MA: Blackwell.

Bombelli, Giovanni. 2018. Emotion and Rationality in Aristotle's Model: From Anthropology to Politics. In *Aristotle on Emotions in Law and Politics*, ed. Liesbeth Huppes-Cluysenaer and Nuno M.M.S. Coelho. Dordrecht: Springer.

Coelho, Nuno M.M.S. 2018. Emotions: Impediment or Basis of Political Life? In *Aristotle on Emotions in Law and Politics*, ed. Liesbeth Huppes-Cluysenaer and Nuno M.M.S. Coelho. Dordrecht: Springer.

Collingwood, R. G. 1933/2005. *An Essay on Philosophical Method*. Edited by James Connelly and Giuseppina D'Oro. Oxford: Clarendon Press.

de Waal, Frans. 2006. Morally Evolved: Primate Social Instincts, Human Morality, and the Rise and Fall of "Veneer Theory". In *Primates and Philosophers: How Morality Evolved*, ed. Stephen Macedo and Josiah Ober, 1–80. Princeton, NJ and Oxford: Princeton University Press.

Halpern, Jodi. 2012. Clinical Empathy in Medical Care. In *Empathy: From Bench to Bedside*, ed. Jean Decety, 229–244. Cambridge, MA and London: MIT Press.

Harden, Blaine. 2012. *Escape from Camp 14: One Man's Remarkable Odyssey from North Korea to Freedom in the West*. Basingstoke and Oxford: Pan Macmillan.

———. 2015. Foreword. In *Escape from Camp 14: One Man's Remarkable Odyssey from North Korea to Freedom in the West*, updated ed, vii–xxiii. London: Pan Books.

Hawk, David. 2012. *The Hidden Gulag: Second Edition: The Lives and Voices of 'Those Who Are Sent to the Mountains': Exposing North Korea's Vast System of Lawless Imprisonment*. Washington, DC: Committee for Human Rights in North Korea.

Heidegger, Martin. 1927/2010. *Being and Time*. Translated by Joan Stambaugh. Albany: State University of New York Press.

Jansson, Tove. 1978/2014. A Leading Role. In *The Woman Who Borrowed Memories: Selected Stories*, trans. Thomas Teal. New York: New York Review Books.

Keen, Suzanne. 2014. Novel Readers and the Empathetic Angel of Our Nature. In *Rethinking Empathy through Literature*, ed. Meghan Marie Hammond and Sue J. Kim, 21–33. New York and London: Routledge.

Keyt, David. 1987/1991. Three Basic Theorems in Aristotle's *Politics*. In *A Companion to Aristotle's Politics*, ed. David Keyt and Fred D. Miller Jr., 118–41. Oxford and Cambridge, MA: Blackwell.

Korsgaard, Christine M. 2006. Morality and the Distinctiveness of Human Action. In *Primates and Philosophers: How Morality Evolved*, ed. Frans de Waal, Stephen Macedo, and Josiah Ober, 98–119. Princeton, NJ and Oxford: Princeton University Press.

Koziak, Barbara. 1999. *Retrieving Political Emotion: Thumos, Aristotle and Gender*. University Park, PA: Pennsylvania State University Press.

Kraut, Richard. 2002. *Aristotle: Political Philosophy*. Oxford: Oxford University Press.

Kullmann, Wolfgang. 1980/1991. Man as a Political Animal in Aristotle. In *A Companion to Aristotle's Politics*, ed. David Keyt and Fred D. Miller Jr., 94–117. Oxford and Cambridge, MA: Blackwell.

Lewis, C. S. 1955/2002. *Surprised by Joy: The Shape of My Early Life*. London: HarperCollins.

Mayhew, Robert. 1997. *Aristotle's Criticism of Plato's Republic*. Lanham, MD: Rowman & Littlefield.

Miller, Fred D., Jr. 1995. *Nature, Justice, and Rights in Aristotle's Politics*. Oxford: Clarendon Press.

Mitchell, Rebecca N. 2014. Empathy and the Unlikeable Character: On Flaubert's Madame Bovary and Zola's Thérèse Raquin. In *Rethinking Empathy Through Literature*, ed. Meghan Marie Hammond and Sue J. Kim, 121–134. New York and London: Routledge.

Nagle, D. Brendan. 2006. *The Household as the Foundation of Aristotle's Polis*. Cambridge and New York: Cambridge University Press.

Nussbaum, Martha C. 2001. *Upheavals of Thought: The Intelligence of Emotions*. Cambridge and New York: Cambridge University Press.

———. 2013. *Political Emotions: Why Love Matters for Justice*. Cambridge: Belknap Press.

Preston, Stephanie D., and Frans B.M. de Waal. 2002. Empathy: Its Ultimate and Proximate Bases. *Behavioral and Brain Sciences* 25 (1): 1–20.

Ramstad, Evan, and Soo-Ah Shin. 2012. A Conversation with Shin Dong-hyuk. *Wall Street Journal*, March 26.

Scheler, Max. 1913/2008. *The Nature of Sympathy*. Translated by Peter Heath. Rev ed. New Brunswick, NJ: Transaction Publishers.

Senju, Atsushi, Makiko Maeda, Yukiko Kikuchi, Toshikazu Hasegawa, Yoshikuni Tojo, and Osanai Hiroo. 2007. Absence of Contagious Yawning in Children with Autistic Spectrum Disorder. *Biology Letters* 3 (6): 706–708.

Sherman, Nancy. 1989. *The Fabric of Character: Aristotle's Theory of Virtue*. Oxford: Oxford University Press.

Smith, Adam. 1759/2007. *The Theory of Moral Sentiments*. New York: Cosimo.

Strayer, Janet, and Nancy Eisenberg. 1987. Empathy Viewed in Context. In *Empathy and Its Development*, ed. Nancy Eisenberg and Janet Strayer, 389–398. Cambridge: Cambridge University Press.

Thompson, Ross A. 1987. Empathy and Emotional Understanding: The Early Development of Empathy. In *Empathy and Its Development*, ed. Nancy Eisenberg and Janet Strayer, 119–145. Cambridge: Cambridge University Press.

Vetlesen, Arne Johan. 1994. *Perception, Empathy, and Judgment: An Inquiry into the Preconditions of Moral Performance*. University Park, PA: Pennsylvania State University Press.

Wispé, Lauren. 1991. *The Psychology of Sympathy*. New York and London: Plenum Press.

Zahavi, Dan. 2010. Empathy, Embodiment and Interpersonal Understanding: From Lipps to Schutz. *Inquiry* 53 (3): 285–306.

Chapter 17
Emotions: Impediment or Basis of Political Life?

Nuno M.M.S. Coelho

Abstract This chapter focuses on the emotional ground of politics in Aristotle's thought. The passages on "war lovers" and on the difference between Greek adult males (citizens by nature) and foreigners, slaves or women demonstrate that living in a *polis* as an equal and free partner requires a proper emotional temper. Aristotle's criticism of Platonic communism and of economic inequality shows that according to him emotions are necessary for stability of *polis*, but are also a source of instability. The way Aristotle describes the crowd as the best judge in real world situations shows how emotions help to establish and maintain the best regime. All of this helps to understand how emotions were seen as important for instituting, preserving and developing the *polis*—and how at the same time they could be their main obstacles.

17.1 Introduction

Passions, emotions and feelings (*pathe*[1]) are central in understanding the implementation, conservation and development of the *polis*, which is permanently at risk of dissolution or degradation. Aristotle's *Politics*[2] is not just a theoretical treatise

---

[1]In this chapter, we don't need to differentiate passions, emotions and feelings as phenomena in the semantic horizon of *pathos*. From *Nicomachean Ethics* we learn that *pathos* is a very important element of psychic and ethical life: "A state of the soul is either (1) an emotion, (2) a capacity, or (3) a disposition; (...). By the emotions, I mean desire, anger, fear, confidence, envy, joy, friendship, hatred, longing, jealousy, pity; and generally those states of consciousness which are accompanied by pleasure or pain. The capacities are the faculties in virtue of which we can be said to be liable to the emotions, for example, capable of feeling anger or pain or pity. The dispositions are the formed states of character in virtue of which we are well or ill-disposed in respect of the emotions; for instance, we have a bad disposition in regard to anger if we are disposed to get angry too violently or not violently enough, a good disposition if we habitually feel a moderate amount of anger; and similarly in respect of the other emotions." (*EN* 1105b20...).

[2]Editions and translations of Aristotle's works are listed in the references at the end of this text.

N.M.M.S. Coelho (✉)
University of São Paulo (USP), São Paulo, Brazil

University of Ribeirão Preto (UNAERP), Ribeirão Preto, Brazil
e-mail: nunocoelho@usp.br; nunommcoelho@yahoo.com

© Springer International Publishing AG 2018   361
L. Huppes-Cluysenaer, N.M.M.S. Coelho (eds.), *Aristotle on Emotions in Law and Politics*, Law and Philosophy Library 121, DOI 10.1007/978-3-319-66703-4_17

and therefore, its aim is not just to know about the good, but also to help people to make this real. Most passages on emotion (*pathos*) assume a clear practical sense, and must be read as counsels to be implemented in historical contexts in real world situations.

In this chapter we investigate the way emotions support some of Aristotle's political views—such as his defence of the multitude as the best judge in cases where laws are defective.

Emotions have recently become again a major theme in political philosophy, while in the last century attention to them was mostly avoided in positivist and behaviorist approaches.[3] The renewed contemporary attention for emotions in politics takes Aristotle and other ancient philosophers as a point of departure.[4]

At the same time, however, Aristotle also emphasizes the rational grounds of politics and law. Two very famous statements in *Politics* are exemplary in this respect, namely, the statement of the political animal as the only one who has reason (*logos*)[5] and the advocacy of the supremacy of laws instead of the rule of man.[6] Aristotle's definition of human beings as rational animals thus inspires rationalistic approaches. His suspicion regarding the role of emotion in judicial

---

[3]"It seems odd that, while acceptance of the role of the emotions in public and political life was once commonplace, it is only now being rediscovered after decades of neglect. The Greeks debated the role of the emotions in public rhetoric, Machiavelli analyzed the contribution of love and fear to the exercise of power, and Hume examined the contribution of the moral sentiments to human reason. But during the last century political studies mostly eschewed consideration of the emotions. It was assumed that political subjects were essentially rational actors busily maximizing their strategic interests even while sometimes constrained by their limited information-processing abilities. This strange and lopsided account of the political subject split cognition from emotion, and reason from passion. To some extent, what happened in political studies simply echoed what was going on elsewhere in the social sciences, where, throughout much of the period after the Second World War, the grip of positivism and behaviorism was powerful. Only slowly was this tide to be turned: first, through what has sometimes been referred to as the 'discursive turn' in the social sciences – that is, through the interest in language, meaning and discourse which gathered force in the 1980s; second, and more recently, through what is sometimes referred to as the 'affective turn' in the social sciences." (Hoggett and Thompson 2012, p. 1).

[4]Nussbaum's work is especially important in the "emotional turn." See for example Nussbaum (2004), Nussbaum (2010), and Nussbaum (2013). For emotions and Jurisprudence, see Maroney (2006).

[5]"Man alone of the animals possesses speech" (*logon de monon anthropos echei ton zoon*) (*Pol.* 1253 a). The verb "echo" means *I have, I hold, I possess*. Having the *logos*, here, does not simply mean it is something the human being holds: it is *the way he is*. *Logos* marks and confirms him in an essential sense.

[6]"Therefore it is preferable for the law to rule rather than any one of the citizens." (. . .) "He therefore that recommends that the law shall govern seems to recommend that God and reason alone shall govern, but he that would have man govern adds a wild animal also; for appetite is like a wild animal, and also passion warps the rule even of the best men. Therefore the law is wisdom without desire." (*Pol.* 1287 a).

rhetoric[7] and in political decision-making echoes in modern defenses of rationalized deliberation processes.[8]

However, it is actually also possible to understand these very same passages as explaining why emotions are important and an inevitable element of political life. We will recall their context in Aristotle's work in order to show the prominence of emotion (*pathos*) as a foundation of the *polis* and democracy.

When facing the question of emotions and the conditions of possibility of political life, we are reminded that the definition of citizen in *Politics* (1253 a 9–10) includes not only having reason (*logos*), but also a proper emotional condition of the soul that naturally enables one to live as a free and equal person. The emotional temper of the citizen will, therefore, be discussed.

Regarding the discussion about emotions and the best regime, it will be argued that democracy is the preferable regime for real people and real cities because, according to Aristotle, "the many" (the crowd) is (among other reasons) emotionally more capable of good judgment than "the few" (*Pol.* 1286 a 30–35).

This chapter will further clarify the political meaning of emotions with respect to other topics such as the study of the emotional links that connect people within a political community, as well as the emotions involved in our relationship to property. The passages pertaining to this will help us to understand how emotions may both guarantee and threaten the unity and the continuity of the *polis*.

In order to illustrate this, the emotional grounds of Aristotle's claim for limitation of economic inequality will be discussed.

By noting the way Aristotle fights the Platonic concept of political unity, it is evident that social cohesion does not exist without *pathos*—but also that *pathos* can destroy it. Love for money, love for other people and love for oneself are indispensable conditions of communitarian life, but also the primary bearers of trouble.

Through the analyses of these issues, it will be evident that *pathos* is not just an obstacle, but also a positive condition of communitarian life and good government. There can be neither *polis* nor good regime without certain emotional conditions and bases, while at the same time emotions can strongly harm regimes and even the very unity of *polis*. Hence, it is important to understand how emotions can be both an impediment as well as a basis of political well-being.

---

[7]"Now, previous compilers of "Arts" of Rhetoric have provided us with only a small portion of this art, for proofs are the only things in it that come within the province of art; everything else is merely an accessory. And yet they say nothing about enthymemes which are the body of proof, but chiefly devote their attention to matters outside the subject; for the arousing of prejudice, compassion, anger, and similar emotions has no connection with the matter in hand, but is directed only to the dicast. The result would be that, if all trials were now carried on as they are in some States, especially those that are well administered, there would be nothing left for the rhetorician to say." (*Rhet.* 1354 a).

[8]"At times, some of the more rationalist currents within political studies have tacitly assumed that if discourse is to be truly reasonable it should be free of passion. Indeed, we have argued that at times accounts of political deliberation have posited an ideal of communicative rationality shorn of the emotions (...). Of course such an ideal assumes that our reasoning capacities are enhanced when freed from emotion." (Hoggett and Thompson 2012, p. 4).

17.2   Natural Approach of Aristotle's Theory

Aristotle's reasoning in *Politics* rests strongly on nature.[9] His method of "examining the elements of which it [*polis*] is composed" (*Pol.* 1252 a) and "studying things in the process of development from the beginning"[10] (pursuant to the principle: "ex arches"[11]) (*Pol.* 1252 a 24), can be observed where Aristotle states (*Pol.* 1252) that familiar community (household) rises from the "natural instinct to desire to leave behind another being of the same sort as oneself"[12]; that master and slave are

---

[9]"Aristotle's politics may be characterized as 'naturalistic', in that it assigns to the concept of nature (*physis*) a fundamental role in the explanation and evaluation of its subject matter. Indeed, naturalism, in this sense, is a dominant theme throughout his philosophy." (Miller 2011, p. 195). Nature (*physis*) has many meanings in Aristotle: ""Nature" means: (a) in one sense, the genesis of growing things (...) (b) in another, that immanent thing from which a growing thing first begins to grow. (c) The source from which the primary motion in every natural object is induced in that object as such. (d) the primary stuff, shapeless and unchangeable from its own potency, of which any natural object consists or from which it is produced (...) (e) the substance of natural objects; as in the case of those who say that "nature" is the primary composition of a thing (...)" (*Met.* 1014 b). *Politics* mobilizes the concept of nature in different meanings. It is important to keep in mind "that the primary and proper sense of "nature" is the essence of those things which contain in themselves as such a source of motion; for the matter is called "nature" because it is capable of receiving the nature, and the processes of generation and growth are called "nature" because they are motions derived from it. And nature in this sense is the source of motion in natural objects, which is somehow inherent in them, either potentially or actually." (*Met.* 1015 a). This is the central idea: nature is an inner principle of change of the natural things.

[10]There is a clear link between (1) the method of understanding a composite thing (*sunthetos*) from dividing (*diaireo*) it into uncompounded things (*asunthetos*)—this means, from finding the least parts of the whole (*elachista moria tou pantos*)—and (2) the method of understanding how things (*pragmata*) develop (*phuo*) from an inner principle (*ex arches*). The passages are juxtaposed (the fact that some editors put these passages at the end and at the beginning of different paragraphs tells us little about Aristotle's argument), and they are both identified as a method used in other fields of study (*en tois allois*). Their link is especially clear from the strategy Aristotle follows next: he divides *polis* into its parts (families; tribes; men, women and children; slaves and free males) and wonders about the inner impulses that drive them to associate with each other. From this, Aristotle explains how political association develops (*phuo*) from forces which lie at the least parts (*asunthetos*) of community—at the origin (*ex arches*). Notice that also in *Metaphysics* Aristotle juxtaposes the passages about principle, cause, indivisible things and nature.

[11]"It is a common property, then, of all "beginnings" to be the first thing from which something either exists or comes into being or becomes known; and some beginnings are originally inherent in things, while others are not. Hence "nature" is a beginning (...)" (*Met.* 1013 a 15–21). In *Physics* we learn: "Of things that exist, some exist by nature, some from other causes. (...) All the things ['by nature'] mentioned present a feature in which they differ from things which are not constituted by nature. Each of them has within itself a principle of motion and of stationariness (in respect of place, or of growth and decrease, or by way of alteration). (...) they do have such an impulse, and just to that extent which seems to indicate that nature is a source or cause of being moved and of being at rest in that to which it belongs primarily, in virtue of itself and not in virtue of a concomitant attribute. (...) 'Nature' then is what has been stated. Things 'have a nature' which have a principle of this kind." (*Phys.* 192 b 8–35).

[12]See also *DA* 415 a 22.

"naturally ruler and naturally subjected"[13]; that "the female and the slave are by nature distinct" (as they have different "purposes"); that "the barbarians have no class of natural rulers" (...) "implying that barbarian and slave are the same in nature"; that household "comes about in the course of nature for everyday purposes" (reproduction, safety); that "village according to the most natural account seems to be a colony from a household", "for the satisfaction of not mere daily needs"; and that "every *polis* exists by nature". Furthermore (*Pol.* 1253), Aristotle states that "the impulse (*horme*) to form a partnership of this kind [*polis*] is present in all men by nature".

The naturalistic approach leads Aristotle to deconstruct *polis* into its smaller parts (tribes, families, free men, women, children, slaves) until reaching the human being's soul and the set of capabilities and needs that make *polis* possible and necessary for us.[14]

Rational capacity does not exhaust the set of human psychic principles from which *polis* develops. Political life unfolds from impulses that sprout (*phuo*) from needs (safety, procreation, food, ease, happiness). Humans are essentially needy beings, and that makes desire a strong factor in any association:

> every partnership is formed with a view to some good (since all the actions of all mankind are done with a view to what they think to be good). (*Pol.* 1252 1–5, trans. Rackham)

As we are not self-sufficient, associating turns into an end (a good) we seek—and living in communities into a necessary condition of good life.[15]

Necessity is the first of a set of causes that push human beings to *polis*. *Pathos* is also a principle responsible for human political nature. The reason why some human beings fail at this, such as those whom Aristotle call "war lovers" for instance, helps in understanding why not just reason, but also emotions act as conditions in the possibility of living well. This is the subject of the next topic.

---

[13]"(...) for he that can foresee with his mind is naturally ruler and naturally master, and he that can do these things with his body is subject and naturally a slave; so that master and slave have the same interest." (*Pol.* I, 1252 a).

[14]The methodic decomposition of *polis* into its simple parts (human beings) is a necessary step in the naturalistic approach Aristotle assumes in *Politics*. Their souls hold the principles, which drive them to associate, in order to face the needs whose satisfaction is good. Necessity and end are based on them. *Polis* is according to nature (*kata physin*) as it answers to the natural impulses present in the parts which compound it. Yack is right in denying that political naturalism is a biological kind, as many scholars defend: "For Aristotle the "impulse" to form political communities exists in human nature. It is the human being that is substance and "has a nature"; the polis exists "according to nature," a consequence of the natural behavior of human beings." (Yack 1993, p. 94).

[15]As Mary Nichols notes: "Implicit in Aristotle's presentation of the human good is our need for others, with whom we share our deliberations, choices, and actions. When Aristotle speaks of the human good as the end of our most authoritative association, he indicates that this good comes to us through association – not in isolation from others" (*Pol.* 1252 a 1–7). (Nichols 1991, p. 15).

17.3   Emotions as Condition of Possibility for Being a Citizen

The link between nature and emotions is that political life depends on adequate feelings and sentiments. Aristotle states in Politics that

> (...) the *polis* is a natural growth, and that man is by nature a political animal, and a man that is by nature and not merely by fortune citiless is either low in the scale of humanity or above it (like the "clanless, lawless, heartless" man reviled by Homer, for he is by nature citiless and also 'a lover of war') inasmuch as he resembles an isolated piece at draughts. (*Pol.* 1253 a 3–7, trans. Rackham)

And

> the state is also prior by nature to the individual; for if each individual when separate is not self-sufficient, he must be related to the whole state as other parts are to their whole, while a man who is incapable of entering into partnership, or who is so self-sufficing that he has no need to do so, is no part of a state, so that he must be either a lower animal or a god. (*Pol.* 1253 a 23–30, trans. Rackham)

Political community is prior to each part of *polis*. The priority of *polis* is teleological, and not chronological. *Polis*'s end is higher than the end of the household or the village. It is self-sufficiency, a chief good: good life, and not merely surviving or living comfortably. As the nature of something is that which each thing is "when its growth is completed", and "*polis* is a natural growth", "man is by nature a political animal" (*Pol.* 1252b30–1253a5). That does not mean that he inevitably lives in a *polis*.[16] It means that this is the good life of human beings. We are political by nature because we can only completely flourish when in association with others in the *polis*, wherein self-sufficiency is possible.

We are not gods. We need to associate in order to achieve self-sufficiency. This is a natural principle. As we have seen, "by nature" is what happens according to a principle that lies within the thing itself. Being needy *and* having the *logos* turns the human being into the political animal, because *logos* enables him to foresee what is indeed good for human life (*eudaimonia*) and thus allows him to accomplish his own nature.

17.3.1   The War Lover

Of course, not everything happens by nature. Other causes such as chance, for instance, can explain why something is the way it is, and can also intervene in natural processes in order to prevent something from realizing its own nature. The realization of the principle (nature) may be prevented by an external force. This

---

[16]Mary Nichols (1991, p. 17) remarks "Unlike the growth of other natural beings, however, the development of cities is not inevitable."

occurs when a human being is for example prevented to be a citizen merely because there is an oligarchy, in which he has no citizenship because he lacks enough wealth.[17] Also people that were prevented to partake in a family would probably never be able to accomplish their own nature.[18]

However, the complete flourishing of a human being can also fail due to natural reasons. The possibility to associate with others can simply not exist, as it happens to the one who "is by nature and not merely by fortune city-less". The "clanless, lawless, hearthless" human being is "by nature cityless and also a lover of war". He is "low in the scale of humanity" because he is incapable of association.

At the other extreme, gods are also cityless, not because of an inability to associate, but because they have no need to associate. They are self-sufficient, complete, while men need others (in families, tribes and cities) to face their natural deficiency.[19]

These first boundaries define our political nature and already disclose the role of emotions. The "man, who is incapable of entering into partnership" and "is no part of a state" for being "a lower animal", is prevented from doing so by a sort of emotional deficiency.

Although it is difficult to accurately state this, it is possible that the expression "war lover" (*polemou epithumetes*) refers to the emotional temper that renders one incapable to even live together and to partake in communities. He is unyoked (*azux*), unpaired, because he is "war lover" (*polemou epithumetes*). He doesn't even have the capacity of socializing, which is present in "any bee or any gregarious animal".[20]

Both scarcity (lack of self-sufficiency) and the capacity for living together bring us to associate. Both of these attributes clarify the communitarian nature of human beings. In spite of having the need (as they are not self-sufficient, for they are human beings), war lovers fail with regards to having the capacity to live in communities, because their emotions and character make them incapable of living

---

[17]"often somebody who would be a citizen in a democracy is not a citizen under an oligarchy" (*Pol.* 1275 a 5).

[18]See Ralli's "Empathic Political Animal", in this volume.

[19]"And inasmuch as it is rare for a man to be divine (. . .) so a bestial character is rare among human beings; it is found most frequently among barbarians, and some cases also occur as a result of disease or arrested development." (*EN*, 1141 a 30–35).

[20]Aquinas thinks it is incapability for philia, and suggests an emotional limit to exclude them from political life: "He [Aristotle] adds to this the saying of Homer, who condemned those who were solitary out of depravity. For he says that such individuals were unsocial because they were incapable of being bound by the bond of friendship, lawless because they were incapable of being bound under the rule of law, and criminal because they were incapable of being bound under the rule of reason. And those who are such by nature, being quarrelsome, as it were, and unrestrained, are at the same time necessarily disposed to be warlike. Just so, we see that solitary wild birds are predatory." (Aquinas 2007, p. 16). Actually, the deprivation which affects, according to Aquinas, the *polemou epithumetes* is not just emotional, but also ethical (as he cannot be just) and intellectual (as he cannot be bound under the rule of reason). However, for the argument we develop in this text, it is useful to note the reference Aristotle possibly makes, in this passage, to *emotions (pathos)* as a condition of possibility for political life.

together. Lovers of war cannot associate; they live the worst life possible for a human being to live, as their life totally denies human nature as a gregarious animal.

Nature makes the war lover at the same time needy (as they are not gods, who do not need to live in community) but incapable of association. It becomes by nature impossible for them to accomplish their own nature as human beings. How is this possible?

In order to understand this, we must considerer the term "nature" in Aristotelian terms. It may seem strange to modern readers, but "by nature" should not be read here as necessarily, it does not mean "unavoidable" or "inevitable."[21]

We have already seen that something natural can fail because of an external cause (someone can be cityless by fortune, for instance). But it can also fail as a result of internal reasons. Nature, as the process of development from the principle (*ex arches*) to the actualized state, does not mean the same in all situations.

In a very broad sense, the natural principle of a being refers to necessity, which pushes it to become what it is.[22] Necessity, however, does not drive things in identical ways. For example, there is a difference between saying that fire needs to burn, and that man needs to be happy. We can easily agree that, whilst the first is hard or impossible to avoid, the second is hard or even impossible to accomplish.[23]

These different meanings of nature deal with different domains of beings, in which necessity assumes different degrees of contingency and variability. This is a source of confusion for those who defend that natural law is immutable law, when they interpret the passages on it in the *Nicomachean Ethics* on Justice (*EN*, 1129a3–1138b14). In order to understand the concept of nature in the political field (natural justice), it is necessary to clearly understand that the movement it implies is not the same as that which is presented by fire, or celestial objects. It means

---

[21]For the many meanings of "nature" and "necessity", see *Metaphysics* V, 1014 b and 1015.

[22]"Nature, then, is what has been said, and anything which has a source of this sort, has a nature. Such a thing is always a reality; for it is an underlying thing, and nature is always in an underlying thing. It is in accordance with nature, and so is anything which belongs to it of itself, as moving upwards belongs to fire – for that neither is a nature nor has a nature, but is due to nature and in accordance with nature." (*Phys*. 192 b 30–35) "Again, nature in the sense in which the word is used for a process proceeds towards nature. It is not like doctoring, which has as its end not the art of medicine but health. Doctoring must proceed from the art of medicine, not towards it. But the process of growth does not stand in this relation to nature: that which is growing, as such, is proceeding from something to something. What, then, is it which is growing? Not the thing it is growing out of, but the thing it is growing into." (*Phys*. 193 a 10–20) "Further, it belongs to the same study to know the end or what something is for, and to know whatever is for that end. Now nature is an end and what something is for. For whenever there is a definite end to a continuous change, that last thing is also what it is for; whence the comical sally in the play 'He has reached the end for which he was born'—for the end should not be just any last thing, but the best." (*Phys*. 194 b 25–35).

[23]Necessity is a key concept to understand the diverse meanings of nature Aristotle employs in *Politics*. "*Necessary* (*anagkaion*) means: (a) That without which, as a concomitant condition, life is impossible; e.g. respiration and food are necessary for an animal, because it cannot exist without them. (b) The conditions without which good cannot be or come to be". Family and *polis* are certainly necessary in this last sense. However, fire burns necessarily in the sense that "what cannot be otherwise we say is necessarily so") (*Met*. 1015).

that natural (political) justice does not depend on opinion and that is refers to necessity as an end. But this does not mean that natural law is the same everywhere, nor in every time. Natural justice changes—and it is obviously absent when a written law is unjust according to nature (for instance: the law that allows the enslavement of people who are free by nature—*Pol.* 1255 b 15), or, even more obviously, when a particular human action fails in being just or fair according to nature.

The difference draws on deliberation. The fulfilment of the need may happen with or without deliberation.[24] Fire necessarily burns unless some external pressure prevents it from doing so. Human beings, however, do not depend solely on the absence of external obstacles to develop into perfect persons. They also need to deliberate, meaning they have to decide about what to do. In a human (ethical and political) horizon, an act of mediation is required from the being itself, without which the need will not be fulfilled (the principle does not actualize—and the nature does not become effective). This turns the actualization of human nature into a task, and the success in achieving it becomes meritorious. *Polis* does not simply happen, and that is why

> the man who first united people in such a partnership was the greatest of benefactors (*Pol.* 1253 a, trans. Rackham).

War lovers are by nature incapable of the act of decision and deliberation, which helps each one of us to live with others. They need others, but they cannot live together because the way they feel and desire makes them incapable of it.

Hence, this allows us to conclude that the investigation on the psychic grounds of political life shows nature as a complex set of principles that hold requirements as well as conditions for political life. Nature is the same in all human beings as necessity (no one can be self-sufficient without others, and therefore *polis* is the only possibility to achieve a good life (*eudaimonia*). Nature, however, is not the same in all human beings as capacity (not everyone is able to fulfill this need of self-accomplishment). This means that all men by nature need *polis* to be happy, but it is not possible for all of them to be happy, also by nature.

This is a first step to understand how *pathos* makes *polis* possible. Partaking in any association requires an emotional sociability, without which one is condemned to fail in realizing one's own human nature.

17.3.2 Women, Children and Slaves

War lovers are not the only ones who are incapable of partaking in a political community. There are also other human beings who are not citizens by nature. Once again, we discuss people whose soul prevents them from realizing human nature in its most complete form.

---

[24]"That is a rough enumeration of the things which are called causes. (. . .) The seed, the doctor, the man who has deliberated, and in general the maker, are all things from which the change or staying put has its source. And there are the things, which stand to the rest as their end and good; for what the other things are for tends to be best and their end." (*Phys.* 195 a).

In Politics (*Pol.* 1252 a 34) it is stated that the nature of the natural slave is determined by an intellectual deficiency. He is not capable of foresight, and this is why it is advantageous for him to associate to a free man as a master. Several pages later (*Pol.* 1260 a), Aristotle explains that slaves, by nature do not have the deliberative part of the human soul, even though they can reason.[25] The highest good life is not possible for them, as they are not capable of seeing what is truly good to them.

A similar argument explains why children and women are not citizens. The deliberative part of their soul is not (yet) developed in children, and is not sovereign in the women. They need to live in the *polis* to actualize their nature, but different kinds of deprivation create a natural deficiency which makes it impossible for them to partake fully in it. The psychic deficiency is not so severe as in the war lovers. Although incapable of self-sufficiency, women and slaves can associate in human communities. They can associate in families, in tribes and even in *poleis*—but not as citizens (free and equal), as their natural condition drives them to assume an inferior position. The citizen, by nature, in turn, holds the commanding position in his association over them, for he has the *logos* complete. Once again, we notice that nature varies in human beings.

Aristotle's investigations in this field allow even for a more definite and positive role for the emotions in the definition of the citizen by nature.[26] As we have seen, the citizen commands because he is rationally apt to deliberate. However, the psychic conditions which are foundational of polis and enable the citizen to command, are not just intellectual, but both rational and irrational.[27]

This is evident through the explanation Aristotle provides for the natural inferiority of Barbarians. Non-Greeks are by nature incapable of living as citizens.

---

[25]It is manifest therefore that the master ought to be the cause to the slave of the virtue proper to a slave, but not as possessing that of art of mastership which teaches a slave his tasks. Hence those persons are mistaken who deprive the slave of reasoning and tell us to use command only; for admonition is more properly employed with slaves than with children.

[26]Aristotle looks for the definition of citizen. The search of the citizen is quite congruent to the method of analysing the *polis* until its most simple parts. *Polis* is a community of citizens. "we now declare that one who has the right to participate in deliberative or judicial office is a citizen of the state in which he has that right, and a state is a collection of such persons sufficiently numerous, speaking broadly, to secure independence of life." (*Pol.* 1275 b 20) "For inasmuch as a state is a kind of partnership, and is in fact a partnership of citizens in a government." (*Pol.* 1276 b) To understand *polis* it is necessary to understand the citizens: "But a state is a composite thing, in the same sense as any other of the things that are wholes but consist of many parts; it is therefore clear that we must first inquire into the nature of a citizen; for a state is a collection of citizens, so that we have to consider who is entitled to the name of citizen, and what the essential nature of a citizen is." (*Pol.* 1275 a) The definition of human being is obviously not the same as the definition of citizen. There is a significant discussion about the criteria of citizenship in the fifth and fourth Centuries legal and political oratory. Aristotle recalls it in his dialectical effort to find the citizen by nature. Women, children, slaves are all human beings, but they fail in some aspect of reason (*logos*) or emotion (*pathos*) which is necessary to live as a citizen. The failure is explained above.

[27]In *Nicomachean Ethics* there is another important case of emotional incapacity to deliberating and acting well: "(c) that the unrestrained man does things that he knows to be evil, under the influence of passion, whereas the self-restrained man, knowing that his desires are evil, refuses to follow them on principle." (*EN*, 1145 b 10–15).

Some, such as the Asians are incapable because they are, in spite of their intelligence, not spirited enough. Others, such as the Europeans are incapable because they are too spirited.

After asking about the geographical traits a successful *polis* should display (after his "conclusions about the territories and harbors of cities, and the sea, and about naval forces"—*Pol.* 1327 b 16–18), Aristotle wants to know what kind of nature is required for the people in the city-state *polis*. The passage famously notes:

> The nations inhabiting the cold places and those of Europe are full of spirit but somewhat deficient in intelligence and skill, so that they continue comparatively free, but lacking in political organization and capacity to rule their neighbours. The peoples of Asia on the other hand are intelligent and skillful in temperament, but lack spirit, so that they are in continuous subjection and slavery. But the Greek race participates in both characters, just as it occupies the middle position geographically, for it is both spirited and intelligent; hence it continues to be free and to have very good political institutions, and to be capable of ruling all mankind if it attains constitutional unity. (*Pol.* 1327 b 23–33, trans. Rackham)

Greeks fit political life better, not because they are more intelligent, but because they combine emotions and rationality in the right way. It is not enough to be clever, it is also necessary to be adequately spirited.

> It is clear therefore that people that are to be easily guided to virtue by the lawgiver must be both intellectual and spirited in their nature. (*Pol.* 1327 b 36–3, trans. Rackham)

Anger (*thumos*)[28] supports freedom. Apathy (being *athuma*) leads Asians to be subjected and enslaved (*archomena* and *douleuonta*)[29]: spirit is a commanding and indomitable element (*archikon gar kai aetteton ho thumos*). "That power to command and love of freedom" (to archon de kai to *eleutheron*) have for principle (*huparchein*) the capacity to feel anger. If one's emotions do not react against subjection, one is not free by nature, but rather a slave.

This means that the natural capacity to be a citizen is not just the capacity of thinking correctly, but also a capacity of feeling correctly, which naturally enables one to partake in a political community as free and equal partners.[30]

---

[28] Anger (*thumos*) is a central emotional phenomenon both in ethics and in politics, as well as friendship (*philia*). See also *On the Soul* "If we consider the majority of them, there seems to be no case in which the soul can act or be acted upon without involving the body; e.g. anger, courage, appetite, and sensation generally" (*DA*, 403 a 16): "But we must return from this digression, and repeat that the affections of soul are inseparable from the material substratum of animal life, to which we have seen that such affections, e.g. passion and fear, attach, and have not the same mode of being as a line or a plane." (*DA* 403 b 16).

[29] See also *Politics*: "for because the barbarians are more servile in their nature than the Greeks, and the Asiatics than the Europeans, they endure despotic rule without any resentment." (*Pol.* 1285 a).

[30] Garver stresses the rational-deliberative incapacity that follows from emotional deficiency, and its political meaning: "*Thymos*, then, is not simply will, the will to put one's judgments into action. The European and Asiatic character flaws show that without the *thymos*, and, on my reading, without *eunoia*, certain cognitive capacities would be incomplete, and *phronesis* impossible. *Phronesis* is incomplete without citizenship, and citizenship impossible without *thymos*." (Garver 1994, p. 114).

All of this relates to the conditions of possibility of political life. Emotion is a specific psychic principle that enables some people to live as citizens, and precludes others (women and natural slaves) from this possibility.[31] Citizens are by nature different from war lovers (whose emotionality prevents all associating, as they are incapable of friendship (*philia*), and from natural slaves (whose servility or irascibility do not allow them to partake as an equal citizen in a *polis*).

Citizens are also different, by nature, from women. This shows that emotions play yet another role, in the reasoning concerning the natural differences between the citizen (male, adult) and the other members of the family. Women's incapacity to command does not follow from a lack of a certain psychic capacity. Women have the deliberative part of the soul, but it is "not sovereign":

> And all [children, slaves, women] possess the various parts of the soul, but possess them in different ways; for the slave has not got the deliberative part at all, and the female has it, but without full authority, while the child has it, but in an undeveloped form. (*Pol.* 1260 a, trans. Rackham)

That could very well mean that women do see the good and do even deliberate well—but that their opinion is naturally subjected to the deliberation of the male. This reading suggests that women have no deliberative deficiency. The lack of sovereignty of their deliberative capacity would not be an "intrapersonal phenomenon", but would rather be derived from the necessary structure of the household as a political organization in which the male presides and the woman is subjected. This description does not fit, however, the context of the investigation in which Aristotle inquiries into the nature of the citizen in view of the inner conditions that enable some people to command and others to obey. This context suggests that Aristotle does talk about an "intrapersonal phenomenon". In this sense, the lack of supremacy of women's deliberative part of the soul relates to their desires and feelings and the way these feelings relate to the rational capacity of women. In this sense, in spite of being able to see the good, women would be incapable of pursuing it, as they would be incapable of breaking free from their emotional constrains.[32]

All of this forms a wider picture where the naturalistic analysis of psychic principles aids in the understanding of how emotions and reason, and not reason alone, enable a human being to actualize its own nature.

Nature varies among human beings. Some (but not all human beings) are capable of political life, and it is considered that this capacity is also an emotional capacity.

---

[31]We cannot address here the question of the possibility of overcoming the psychic deficiency that prevents the natural slave from living as a citizen. That requires investigating whether this (both emotional and rational) capacity to deliberate is due to socialization processes. This possibility was certainly on the table: there were strong speeches against slavery. Aristotle demonstrates the controversy surrounding this topic, but there are probably no safe reasons to support that thesis in *Politics* (although this would make his position on slavery less confronting). In any case, it is important to notice that Aristotle's concept of nature involves comprehending things that usually (and not necessarily) happen. From this, it is not surprising that some Greek citizens think and feel as slaves, and that some Barbarians can deliberate well (*Pol.* 1254 b).

[32]For this important debate, see Fortenbaugh (1977), Dobbs (1996), and the bibliography debated in Deslauriers and Destrée (2013).

Being the animal who possesses *logos* also comprehends the capacity to feel correctly. Without the right measure of anger (*thumos*), one is not a citizen by nature.

These remarks are useful in order to understand everyday political life. They have more than just theoretical interest. The citizen's emotions are responsible for his political reactions. When aroused, they make it difficult for the citizen to simply remain silent and accept acts, which make him inferior.

17.4 Love as Social Bond

Our first topic focused on *pathos* as condition of possibility of political life. Integrating in a political community as a citizen requires emotional capacities that war lovers, slaves and women do not have. The emotional incapacity to feel friendship (*philia*) prevents the war lovers of any association; slaves have an emotional incapacity to live as free people (as they are too much or too little *thumos*) and women cannot live as equal people for their emotional incapacity to obey reason. From all of this we learn that the institution of political life requires emotional grounds.

The aim of the next section is to show that emotions play a decisive role in the preservation of *polis*, as they tie people together and help to avoid disaggregation.

17.4.1 Love of Family

Aristotle discusses in *Politics* the issue of what should be common in the political community. He criticizes Plato's surprising proposal, presented in *Republic*, that women and possessions should be common (*Pol.* 1260 b, 1261 a).

According to Socrates, the community of women would guarantee the strongest emotional ties among citizens. All people would regard the elder males as fathers and contemporaries would all love each other as brothers and sisters.[33] Emotional bonds would be strengthened, affection and attention would be maximized, and thus, *polis* would achieve the perfect unity.

---

[33] As he had done in Book 1, Aristotle starts Book 2 by analysing a Platonic thesis. The Platonic thesis presented in *Politics* II (women should be common as this would increase the emotional bonds among citizens) is congruous with the (also Platonic) thesis proposed in Book 1 (according to which there is no essential difference between domestic and political communities). To Plato, as both *polis* and family have the same nature, it is possible to achieve political unity by increasing familial love. Aristotle does not accept this notion. He believes that *polis* and family are essentially different, and then the bonds that unify each community must be different too. This way he distinguishes familial and political friendship.

Aristotle also thinks that friendship is the major blessing of *polis*, as it prevents dissolution and civil strife.[34] Plato's proposal, however, contradicts in practice the goal it aims to achieve, which is the unity of *polis*.[35] Aristotle attacks the Platonic position specifically because it weakens the emotional bonds among citizens. Instead of making people consider (*diaphrontizein*) each other and increasing attention and care (*epimeleia*), these feelings would actually decrease as a result of the community of women and children.[36] The same may be said for the communism of possessions. If everything belonged to everybody, then no one would take care of these possessions (*Pol.* 1262 b 20...).[37]

This passage closes Aristotle's counterargument to the two communist theses of Plato (community of women, and community of possessions). According to Aristotle, communism produces indifference and lessens social cohesion for it weakens the two major bases of caring (*kedestai*) and loving (*philein*): property and affection (*to te idion kai to agapeton*). Plato's proposal should ground (*huparchein*) the political community, but it fails to do so, in Aristotle's view (*Pol.* 1262 b 20). It is clear that love and affection are emotional foundations of *polis*. People treat others and objects with care because they love and regard them with affection. The absence of them would destroy *polis*.

Once again, emotions work as an unstable footing for political coexistence. In the first section of this chapter, we have explained that emotions are present in the roots of political life. The very definition of citizen includes a proper emotional

---

[34]Striving (*Stasis*) is a major theme in Greek political philosophy. Internal striving and external conflicts made Athenians anxious about the risk of destruction. There are some important reflections regarding how emotions play a role both in the destruction of and the preservation of *polis*: "friendship is the greatest of blessings for the state, since it is the best safeguard against revolution, and the unity of the state" (*Pol.* 1262 b 7–9). This perspective clearly shows *emotions (pathos)* as both a basis for, and a threat to *polis*' survival. "Instead of a view of politics that stresses the importance of regime legislation, Aristotle favors a view of politics which stresses preservation (...) This is a task that requires far more skill and wisdom (...) he [Aristotle] stresses the importance of preservation over founding in his political science." Bates (2016, p. 25); Bates (2015) offers an interesting table of emotions as causes of political stasis.

[35]This is an important *topos* in Aristotle's *Politics*, recurrently used in the problematization of city-states (*politeai*) and laws: the exam of conformity between their intended goals, and the results they actually achieve.

[36]Plato's proposal aims at increasing consideration (*diaphrontizein*). Nevertheless, it would lessen esteem (*oligoresousin*).

[37]Another methodical remark now to notice the use of *emotions (pathos)* by political philosophy as a criterion for choosing among disputant positions. In *Politics* Aristotle states that the Socratic thesis for the community of women is disgusting (*echei de duschereias*) (*Pol.* 1261 a 10). The expression is usually translated into "involves difficulties", consistent with the dialectical structure of Aristotle's political inquiry. However, the context suggests more than an intellectual obstacle, it indicates an emotional difficulty to the acceptance of the thesis. This is another basis for refusing Plato's thesis: it is repulsive. This shows the use of *emotions (pathos)* as a *topos* in (political) philosophical investigation and teaching. The emotional argument is quite familiar to the reader of *Rhetoric*. Its use in political research shows some rhetorical aspect, It is not surprising that political philosophy, as practical thought, uses rhetoric. Its aim is not only knowing about the good in common life, but making it real, we could state in analogy to *Nicomachean Ethics*.

condition (there must exist *thumos*). However, emotions can also make political coexistence impossible, as we are told by the references to war lovers and their antisocial life, to barbarians from Europe with their too spirited soul (which makes obeying impossible to them), to barbarians from Asia and their too little spirited soul (which makes them too servile), or to the women and their not sovereign (*akurion*) decision (which makes them incapable of submitting emotions and desires to rational deliberation).

Something similar happens when we focus on the role of love for family as ground of the social cohesion in the political community. In spite of being a guarantee of political unity, these emotions can also put the community at risk. Familiarity puts our capacity of discerning under pressure and causes us to judge poorly. It is hard to judge ourselves or people we love or hate because when we are "in *pathos*", we cannot find the middle point. Both friendship and enmity make us partial, and this supports the argument for the government of law instead of man.

17.4.2   Love for Money

Emotion (*Pathos*) also works to destabilize *polis* when we consider the possession of things. Aristotle's attack on Plato's communism of goods shows that emotions, in this field, are also ambivalent, as they are necessary but also dangerous for political life. *Polis* could not survive if people didn't care about things, but love for things is probably the most harmful threat to polis's unity.

Love for money both grounds and threatens political life. For the positive role of the love for money it must be remembered that human flourishing (*eudaimonia*) is not possible without external goods, both in personal and in communitarian perspectives. Money is not the cause of happiness, but rather an obviously necessary condition.

Possession of things is necessary to the accomplishment of the human end. This leads to the definition of *polis* as a system of exchange of goods, among people who could never achieve, alone or even in the close contexts of family or tribe, self-sufficiency.[38]

There are other arguments in favor of private property in Aristotle, which help to understand the positive role that the love for things plays in *polis*. From *Nicomachean Ethics* we learn that the one who does not care about his goods is

---

[38]*Polis* is also defined as a system of exchanges. We choose associating in *polis* because self-sufficiency can be obtained this way. Exchange makes an achievement of goods possible, which could never be obtained in the family or the tribe. If there were no love for things, would there be any exchange? Without love for things, would *polis* be possible as community wherein people interact to achieve autarchy and self-sufficiency? (*Pol.* 1321 b 10–20).

not virtuous, but lavish. In *Politics*, for instance, Aristotle defends private property because this is necessary to virtue: how can one be generous without possessions?

Nevertheless, the love for money and possessions can threat political life. In *Politics* I, Aristotle distinguishes between two techniques related to the gathering of possessions. It can be either according to or against nature. Aristotle strongly condemns chrematistics as unnatural. Wealth is a set of instruments, and its accumulation is good to the extent that the things collected maintain their instrumental purpose (*Pol.* 1256 b 41 and 1257 a 4). When money and things lose their instrumentality, they become subject to an unlimited pursuit with harmful consequences to the community. Too much love for things, thus, endangers political association.

Accumulation of money and possessions is unnatural as it perverts the soul's good order and prevents the accomplishment of human nature (*eudaimonia*). While pleasure seems to depend on the ownership of things, it easily leads people to infinite accumulation. Whoever seeks unlimited wealth seeks for unlimited pleasure.[39]

The difference between the natural art of acquisition of goods that family and *polis* need, and the unnatural and endless pursuit of wealth, illustrates how *pathos* can endanger political life.[40]

It is obvious that the confusion between good life and life of pleasure is the most common failure in the task of *eudaimonia*. Love of money (*philochrematia*) may have a negative effect on the individual, but it is potentially worse for a community. The greatest danger associated with wealth accumulation relates to the destruction of political equality. In contrast to Plato, Aristotle believes that *polis* is not an association of homogeneous people. Heterogeneity is essential as it makes the system of exchange possible through which we can get communitarian auto-sufficiency. If we were all identical in skills, goods and preferences, there would be no commerce for instance. There must, however, be limits to diversity. When people become heterogeneous to an exaggerated degree, it destroys political equality. This is why Aristotle and many other political thinkers of his time defended the limitations of economic inequality.

All considerations in *Politics IV* regarding the righteous regimes (monarchy, aristocracy and *politeia*) give place to historical reality, in which emotions play a

---

[39]Of course a life with no pleasure is not a good life: that's (also) why love for money can destroy eudaimonia both whether it is too big or too little.

[40]"Hence the business of drawing provision from the fruits of the soil and from animals is natural to all. But, as we said, this art is twofold, one branch being of the nature of trade while the other belongs to the household art; and the latter branch is necessary and in good esteem, but the branch connected with exchange is justly discredited (for it is not in accordance with nature, but involves men's taking things from one another)." (*Pol.* 1258 a–b).

role.[41] Aristotle seeks the best regime for peoples and persons who are not extremely virtuous. What is the best regime for most cities and normal people?

His answer should not be belittled or disregarded. Best is the life according to the middle, and this is the life accessible to the majority of people and peoples. This is the criterion for distinguishing the virtuous or vicious character of a city.

> It is clear therefore also that the political community administered by the middle class is the best. (*Pol.* 1295 b 35, trans. Rackham)

The good (real) city should have a strong middle class and not very much economic inequality[42], because people who find themselves in the extremes find it difficult to listen to and obey *logos*.

People who are too rich do not even know what obeying is[43]; actually, nor are they able to rule a political community, as they "only know how to govern in the manner of a master". On the other hand, extremely poor people are humble and obey as slaves. Neither of them are good citizens, because they are neither capable of ruling nor of being ruled as citizens.

Therefore, the association of free people requires limitations to be placed on the differences in wealth. Equality (isonomy) imposes limits to diversity (heterogeneity) among the associated parts. Exaggerated heterogeneity in property may destroy political isonomy. Citizens must not be too heterogeneous, in order to ensure the political nature of the association and prevent the *polis* from becoming an association between masters and slaves. Once again, there are important emotional reasons for this, which shall be highlighted before concluding this topic.

Exaggerated wealth or poverty makes it difficult to obey reason (*to logoi peitharchein*).

> For this degree of wealth is the readiest to obey reason, whereas for a person who is exceedingly beautiful or strong or nobly born or rich, or the opposite—exceedingly poor or weak or of very mean station, it is difficult to follow the bidding of reason; for the former

---

[41]This is central to understanding the whole *Politics*. Political philosophy has three different levels of inquiry and counsel. The analogy with a physical educator is elucidative. He masters an art able to give counsels to perfect bodies, to average and even to very bad ones. It is same for political philosophy: "so that the good lawgiver and the true statesman must be acquainted with both the form of constitution that is the highest absolutely and that which is best under assumed conditions, and also thirdly the form of constitution based on a certain supposition (for he must be also capable of considering both how some given constitution could be brought into existence originally and also in what way having been brought into existence it could be preserved for the longest time: I mean for example if it has befallen some state not only not to possess the best constitution and to be unprovided even with the things necessary for it, but also not to have the constitution that is practicable under the circumstances but an inferior one)" (*Pol.* 1288 b 24–30).

[42]Notice that Aristotle's perspective remains normative and not simply descriptive, but it is quite different giving counsels to normal people from counselling perfect ones.

[43]"and they have acquired this quality even in their boyhood from their homelife, which was so luxurious that they have not got used to submitting to authority even in school" (*Pol.* 1295b).

turn more to insolence and grand wickedness, and the latter overmuch to malice and petty
wickedness, and the motive of all wrongdoing is either insolence or malice. (*Pol.* 1295 b
5–6, trans. Rackham)

Bringing together the two criticisms by Aristotle (his censure of chrematistic as
unlimited accumulation of goods, and of exaggerated economic inequality) aids in
understanding how dangerous the love for things can be. The unnatural accumulation brings to the rich the incapacity to listen the *logos*, and the same emotional
impediment strikes the poor.[44]

17.4.3 Love for Oneself

People easily confuse "good life" and "bodily pleasures", and seek to accumulate
things as sources of pleasure.[45] Endless accumulation rises from excessively seeking pleasure, and this is rooted in the very love one feels for oneself.[46] Also love for
oneself (*to philei eauton*) is both natural and important, albeit dangerous.

When considering the emotions we feel about ourselves, including the emotions
we feel about money, the concept becomes relatively easy to understand in Aristotelian terms: neither too much, nor too little. It also helps us in understanding how
emotions make *polis* possible, despite threatening it.

---

[44]The best cities have a strong and dominant middle class. This realizes the equilibrium between
equality and heterogeneity: "But surely the ideal of the state is to consist as much as possible of
persons that are equal and alike, and this similarity is most found in the middle classes; therefore
the middle-class state will necessarily be best constituted in respect of those elements of which we
say that the state is by nature composed." (*Pol.* 1295b) The exaggerated heterogeneity threatens
polis also because it impedes friendship. Friends must have something in common. *Philia* is the
bond, which links people who aim at a same goal, and who are somehow similar. If diversity is
total—as it can be between the very rich and the very poor—there is no friendship but slightness
and envy—both "very far removed from friendliness, and from political partnership — for
friendliness is an element of partnership, since men are not willing to be partners with their
enemies even on a journey" (*Pol.* 1295b).

[45]"And even those who fix their aim on the good life seek the good life as measured by bodily
enjoyments, so that inasmuch as this also seems to be found in the possession of property, all their
energies are occupied in the business of getting wealth; and owing to this the second kind of the art
of wealth-getting has arisen. For as their enjoyment is in excess, they try to discover the art that is
productive of enjoyable excess; and if they cannot procure it by the art of wealth-getting, they try
to do so by some other means, employing each of the faculties in an unnatural way." (*Pol.* 1258 a).

[46]As Aristotle states in *Politics*, "to feel that a thing is one's private property makes an inexpress-
ibly great difference for pleasure; for the universal feeling of love for oneself is surely not
purposeless, but a natural instinct. Selfishness on the other hand is justly blamed; but this is not
to love oneself but to love oneself more than one ought, just as covetousness means loving money
to excess—since some love of self, money and so on is practically universal." (*Pol.* 1263 a
35–1263 b).

17.5 The Role of the Multitude for the Rule of Law

17.5.1 Rule of Law

Aristotle investigates in *Politics* III what the citizen is in an absolute sense (*haplos*), beyond any particular regime (*Pol.* 1275 a 20...).[47] The same Book IV presents the famous table of righteous (monarchy, aristocracy and *politeia* in a strict sense) and deviated (tyranny, oligarchy and democracy) regimes. The difference between righteous and deviated regimes lies in the end of the government.

> It is clear then that those constitutions that aim at the common advantage are in effect rightly framed in accordance with absolute justice, while those that aim at the rulers' own advantage only are faulty, and are all of them deviations from the right constitutions; for they have an element of despotism, whereas a city is a partnership of free men. (*Pol.* 1279 a, trans. Rackham)

In none of the deviated regimes there is a government "with regard to the profit of the community" (*Pol.* 1279 b 9–10). The opposition between ruling in the interest of oneself and of the whole *polis* is parallel with the opposition between the government of man and the government of law.

The criticism of Monarchy deals with this problem. Which is better, the government of man or of law? Aristotle recalls here the debate on the limits of written laws. The defenders of Monarchy argue that this regime is better because laws cannot rule over particular situations. Aristotle agrees that a rigid commitment to laws with no attention to the particularity of the case is not the best. Nevertheless, he distinguishes cases that can be adequately ruled by a general law, from cases that do not fit it.[48] To the first group, laws rule better than men do because laws are free of emotions

> a thing that does not contain the emotional element is generally superior to a thing in which it is innate; now the law does not possess this factor, but every human soul necessarily has it. (*Pol.* 1286 a 17–20, trans. Rackham).

Government of law is the government of reason and strives for the common good, and not for the officer's good:

> Therefore it is preferable for the law to rule rather than any one of the citizens. (*Pol.* 1287 a 18–20)
>
> (...)
>
> He therefore that recommends that the law shall govern seems to recommend that God and reason alone shall govern, but he that would have man govern adds a wild animal also;

---

[47]He concludes that "A citizen pure and simple is defined by nothing else so much as by the right to participate in judicial functions and in office." (*Pol.* 1275 b). It is not by chance that this definition of citizen (thought to stand for any regime, and not just relative to any specific model) fits the democratic regime better. It has to do with Aristotle's conception of democracy as the regime that better realizes, in the real world, the nature of the citizen and of the political community.

[48]The theme of *epieikeia* is familiar to jurists. It raises the task of being equitable.

for appetite is like a wild animal, and also passion warps the rule even of the best men. Therefore the law is wisdom without desire. (*Pol.* 1287 a 28–32, trans. Rackham)

The comparison between physicians and political functionaries highlights why the government of law is better. When one is personally involved, one loses impartiality. To be a judge of things close to us (*to krinein peri te oikeion*), makes it impossible to discern truly (*ou dunamenoi krinein to alethes*), because they are under the influence of feeling (*dia kai en pathei ontes*). This prevents the judge from finding the middle and being just (*Pol.* 1287 b 2–3).

In contrast to physicians, the political authorities usually act for reasons of friendship or hate, holders of political office usually do many things out of spite and to win favor. The context of struggle in which office-holders decide is quite different from the context wherein physicians work. Political fighting puts office-holders and judges under pressure and makes impartiality an important and difficult requirement. Difficultly increases exactly because conflict shakes the emotions.[49]

All of this leads to the conclusion that it is preferable to be judged by the law instead of by the emotional preferences of the judge.[50]

17.5.2   The Multitude

We have seen, however, that law cannot rule everything. There are cases in which law fails for being general.[51] Aristotle asks:

in matters which it is impossible for the law either to decide at all or to decide well, ought the one best man to govern or all the citizens? (*Pol.* 1286 a, trans. Rackham).

---

[49]"Yet certainly physicians themselves call in other physicians to treat them when they are ill, and gymnastic trainers put themselves under other trainers when they are doing exercises, believing that they are unable to judge truly because they are judging about their own cases and when they are under the influence of feeling." (*Pol.* 1287 a 25–30).

[50]Christof Rapp's defense, in this book, of judges' rationality ("Dispassionate Judges Encountering Hotheaded Aristotelians") brings clever warnings about the risks of partiality and probably portrays very well Aristotle's concerns on the topic.

[51]"(...) equity, though just, is not legal justice, but a rectification of legal justice. The reason for this is that law is always a general statement, yet there are cases which it is not possible to cover in a general statement. In matters therefore where, while it is necessary to speak in general terms, it is not possible to do so correctly, the law takes into consideration the majority of cases, although it is not unaware of the error this involves. And this does not make it a wrong law; for the error is not in the law nor in the lawgiver, but in the nature of the case: the material of conduct is essentially irregular. When therefore the law lays down a general rule, and thereafter a case arises which is an exception to the rule, it is then right, where the lawgiver's pronouncement because of its absoluteness is defective and erroneous, to rectify the defect by deciding as the lawgiver would himself decide if he were present on the occasion, and would have enacted if he had been cognizant of the case in question." (*EN* 1137 a 15–25).

This passage is important. Aristotle faces here the very dangerous situation, in which the office-holder does not have a legal criterion to decide.[52] This means that he does not find an accepted common rule or tradition which clarifies for him sufficiently what the right middle is or the common good. In such a situation there is an increased risk of deviation. The office-holder has to decide. How can it be ensured that he will not judge with regard to his own profit?

In *Nicomachean Ethics*, Aristotle says that in these cases the judge must decide "as the lawgiver would himself decide". This means that the judge must remain impartial even when there is no law to guide him. However, who is best prepared to do so? His answer is quite surprising:

> for this reason in many cases a crowd judges better than any single person.[53] (*Pol.* 1286 a 30, trans. Rackham).

Aristotle does not endorse the monarchical or aristocratic argument that one or a few wise men are the best judges to discern the just and fair in all circumstances. Instead, he offers logical,[54] ethical[55] and emotional reasons in favor of the crowd as the best judge in some situations.

He indicates several interesting factors regarding the emotional superiority of the many. Let us recall some of his arguments.

Aristotle states that the multitude should judge for being less corruptible. He puts it in emotional terms:

> Also the multitude is more incorruptible—just as the larger stream of water is purer, so the mass of citizens is less corruptible than the few; and the individual's judgement is bound to be corrupted when he is overcome by anger or some other such emotion, whereas in the

---

[52]"This is the essential nature of the equitable: it is a rectification of law where law is defective because of its generality. In fact this is the reason why things are not all determined by law: it is because there are some cases for which it is impossible to lay down a law, so that a special ordinance becomes necessary." (*EN*, 1137 b).

[53]"for where there are many, each individual, it may be argued, has some portion of virtue and wisdom, when they have come together, just as the multitude becomes a single man with many feet and many hands and many senses, so also it becomes one personality as regards the moral and intellectual faculties." (*Pol.* 1281 b 4–7). Once again, he seems to fight Plato.

[54]The crowd discerns better because it is rationally superior than one or a few man. Although separately the individual is immature in judgement (*ekastos ateles peri to krinein estin*) (*Pol.* 1281 b 38), "all when assembled together have sufficient discernment" (*Pol.* 1281 b 34–35). He challenges the *topos* about the superiority of the specialist: "for although each individual separately will be a worse judge than the experts, the whole of them assembled together will be better or at least as good judges" (*Pol.* 1282 a, 15–17).

[55]The crowd discerns better because it is ethically superior to one or a few man. The sum of virtues of the majority exceeds the virtue of any singular person. If there were someone who exceeded the sum of crowd's virtue, he should govern, Aristotle admits. But this is just for the sake of the argument—in reality, there is not such a man or a group. Actually, this would require virtue above the level of human nature (*Pol.* 1286 b 27) and it is not applicable to his own time: "But now that the states have come to be even greater than they were, perhaps it is not easy for yet another form of constitution beside democracy to come into existence." (*Pol.* 1286 b 20–22).

other case it is a difficult thing for all the people to be roused to anger and go wrong together. (*Pol.* 1286 a 30–35, trans. Rackham).

In defending the government by rule of law instead of men, Aristotle warns about the risk of *pathos*, stating that it deviates the functionaries (or office-holders) from acting impartially and truthfully. This turns laws into better rulers than men. In many cases, however, it is unavoidable that a man has to judge. In these cases, *pathos* is always there, and the emotional structure of the crowd makes it in some cases best prepared to perform the task impartially.

This is an important argument in favor of democracy. Aristotle states that for emotional reasons the crowd can work best as the legislator in particular cases.[56] The emotional argument is central in Aristotle's defense of democracy, which he believes to be the best regime for normal (we could say, for real and historical) communities. Democracy is the best regime because in the end the multitude is best (not only rationally and ethically, but also emotionally) conditioned to deliberate and judge according to the mean, and this makes living possible according to reason and law.

17.6 Conclusions

Notwithstanding the emphasis on reason as the human capacity, which substantiates the political nature of human beings, Aristotle's *Politics* offers several clues to understand that the citystate (*polis*) or political life would not be possible if men were not emotional. The very passage from which the emphasis on the rational nature of man as political human is derived, supports this assertion.

"Man alone of the animals possesses speech" (*logon de monon anthropos echei ton zoon*) is a definition.[57] It gives the essential property to distinguish the "human being" from all other species in the genus "animal".[58] The statements about *genera*, however, are also indicative of essential features of the beings these genera

---

[56]Actually, this is true also for deliberation: "For to lay down a law about things that are subjects for deliberation is an impossibility. Therefore men do not deny that it must be for a human being to judge about such matters, but they say that it ought not to be a single human being only but a number: (. . .) it would doubtless seem curious if a person saw better when judging with two eyes and two organs of hearing and acting with two feet and hands than many persons with many" (*Pol.* 1287 b 20–30).

[57]"A 'definition' is a phrase signifying a thing's essence." (*Topics* 101 b a 39–40).

[58]"The discovery of the differences of things helps us both in reasonings about sameness and difference, and also in recognizing what any particular thing is. That it helps us in reasoning about sameness and difference is clear: for when we have discovered a difference of any kind whatever between the objects before us, we shall already have shown that they are not the same: while it helps us in recognizing what a thing is, because we usually distinguish the expression that is proper to the essence of each particular thing by means of the differentiae that are proper to it." (*Top.* 108 a 38–b 6).

embrace. Everything that can be stated about the essence of the animal as a *genus*, can be stated about all species of animals[59], including human beings.

That is why grasping the essence of human being includes not only understanding his logical property, but also the features that mark animals in general.[60] Human beings are then marked by perception, emotions and desire, which belong to their very (animalistic) nature. Therefore, when Aristotle states political animals as logical animals, he is not talking about simply rational beings—because being "animal" includes much more than this.

Important passages in *Politics* display emotions as conditions of possibility of political life. Their absence, paucity or excess in people for whom social life or citizenship is impossible, shows that their presence, in a correct measure, makes polis and political life possible.

For sure emotions can also make political association impossible. War lovers simply lack the natural capacity to feel *philia*, and therefore they could never partake in any association for emotional reasons. Europeans and Asians do not have the right balance of intelligence and emotion, which makes them incapable of associating as equals. In particular, the Asians show that there is no *polis* without the emotion (*pathos*) of anger, because one needs to be somehow spirited in order to be a citizen.

Emotions can endanger the continuity of political life. In many cases, they cause striving. If people feel too much love for themselves or for things, for instance, they fight and endanger the very unity of *polis*. Nevertheless, if there were no love for oneself, for other people, or for things, *polis* would also be risked, because nobody would care about anything or anyone.

Finally, emotions are clearly bad for judgments and ruling, as it prevents impartiality. This supports Aristotle's defense of law's (reason's) government instead of man's. Nevertheless, when political philosophy focuses on the real world, it receives help from emotional traits of the crowd to state the superiority of democracy, because both the rationality and emotional temper of the crowd are needed for correct ruling and right judgement.

All of this leads to the conclusion that emotions do not play a simple role in political life. It is not something simply good, or simply bad, nor is possible to distinguish in an absolute sense between good and bad emotions for politics. They make *polis* possible, yet also endanger it.

References

Aquinas, Thomas. 2007. *Commentary on Aristotle's Politics*. Translated by Richard J. Regan. Hackett Publishing.

---

[59]"If, then, we render as the genus what is common to all the cases, we shall get the credit of defining not inappropriately." (*Top.* 108 27–28).

[60]The genus proposition also indicates the essence of things. "A 'genus' is what is predicated in the category of essence of a number of things exhibiting differences in kind." (*Top.* 102 a 31–32).

Aristotle. 1926a. *Art of Rhetoric*. Translated by John Henry Freese. Loeb Classical Library 193. Cambridge, London: Harvard University Press.

———. 1926b. *Nicomachean Ethics*. Translated by H. Rackham. Loeb Classical Library 73. Cambridge, London: Harvard University Press.

———. 1926c. *On the Soul. Parva Naturalia. On Breath*. Translated by W. S. Hett. Loeb Classical Library 288. Cambridge, London: Harvard University Press.

———. 1932. *Politics*. Translated by H. Rackham. Loeb Classical Library 264. Cambridge, London: Harvard University Press.

———. 1933. *Metaphysics. Volume I. Books 1–9*. Translated by Tredennick Hugh. Loeb Classical Library 271. Cambridge, London: Harvard University Press.

———. 1934. *Physics. Volume II. Books 5–8*. Translated by P. H. Wicksteed and F. M. Cornford. Loeb Classical Library 255. Cambridge, London: Harvard University Press.

———. 1935. *Metaphysics. Volume II. Books 10–14*. Oeconomica. Magna Moralia. Translated by Tredennick Hugh and G. Cyril Armstrong. Loeb Classical Library 287. Cambridge, London: Harvard University Press.

———. 1957. *Physics. Volume I. Books 1–4*. Translated by P. H. Wicksteed and F. M. Cornford. Loeb Classical Library 228. Cambridge, London: Harvard University Press.

Bates, Clifford. 2015. *Chart on Causes and Beginnings of Revolution and Stasis in Aristotle's Politics 5.3/5.4*. https://www.researchgate.net/publication/280978789_Chart_on_causes_and_beginnings_of_revolution_and_stasis_in_Aristotle's_Politics_5354.

———. 2016. *The Fundamental Political Problem of Legislators Addressed in Politics 2*, 6 June. http://www.academia.edu/784233/The_fundamental_political_problem_of_Legislators_addressed_in_Politics_2.

Deslauriers, M., and P. Destrée, eds. 2013. *The Cambridge Companion to Aristotle's Politics*. Cambridge: Cambridge University Press.

Dobbs, D. 1996. Family Matters: Aristotle's Appreciation of Women and the Plural Structure of Society. *American Political Science Review* 90: 74–90.

Fortenbaugh, W.W. 1977. Aristotle on Slaves and Women. In *Articles on Aristotle. Ethics and Politics*, ed. Jonathan Barnes et al., vol. 2, 135–139. London: Duckworth.

Garver, Eugene. 1994. *Aristotle's Rhetoric. An Art of Character*. Chicago: The University of Chicago Press.

Hoggett, Paul, and Simon Thompson, eds. 2012. *Politics and the Emotions: The Affective Turn in Contemporary Political Studies*. New York: Continuum.

Maroney, Terry A. 2006. Law and Emotion: A Proposed Taxonomy of an Emerging Field. *Law and Human Behavior* 30: 119–142.

Miller, Fred D. 2011. Aristotle's Political Naturalism. *Apeiron* 22 (4): 195–218.

Nichols, Mary P. 1991. *Citizens and Statesmen. A Study of Aristotle's Politics*. Savage: Rowman & Littlefield.

Nussbaum, Martha. 2004. *Hiding from Humanity Disgust, Shame, and the Law*. Princeton: Princeton University Press.

———. 2010. *From Disgust to Humanity: Sexual Orientation and Constitutional Law*. Oxford, New York: Oxford University Press.

———. 2013. *Political Emotions: Why Love Matters for Justice*. Cambridge, London: Harvard University Press.

Ralli, Tommi. 2018. Empathic Political Animal: What a North Korean Prison Camp Can Reveal About the Aristotelian Political Association. In *Aristotle on Emotions in Law and Politics*, ed. Liesbeth Huppes-Cluysenaer and Nuno M.M.S. Coelho. Dordrecht, Heidelberg, New York, London: Springer.

Rapp, Christof. 2018. Dispassionate Judges Encountering Hotheaded Aristotelians. In *Aristotle on Emotions in Law and Politics*, ed. Liesbeth Huppes-Cluysenaer and Nuno M.M.S. Coelho. Dordrecht, Heidelberg, New York, London: Springer.

Yack, Bernard. 1993. *The Problems of a Political Animal: Community, Justice, and Conflict in Aristotelian Political Thought*. Berkeley: University of California Press.

Chapter 18
Aristotle's *Rhetoric* and the Persistence of the Emotions in the Courtroom

Emma Cohen de Lara

Abstract This chapter investigates whether, according to Aristotle, participation in judicial practices promotes the development of the moral, intellectual or civic virtues of the rhetorician or the audience. A close reading of Aristotle's *Rhetoric* reveals that Aristotle did not understand the art of rhetoric as having an inherently moral purpose. Rather, for Aristotle the art of rhetoric in a judicial setting implied an understanding of the available means of persuasion and entailed the ability of appealing to the emotions of the audience in order to win a lawsuit. For this purpose the rhetorician may arouse emotions that, in themselves, are morally questionable. Therefore, Aristotle emphasized the need for laws that govern the judicial process and prevent or curtail corrupting practices. Based on a reading of Aristotle's *Rhetoric*, the chapter takes issue with the participatory democracy approach, which traces its roots to Aristotle's political thought, and presents the argument that political activity, including jury duty, necessarily constitutes an experience that promotes the moral or civic development of the citizen.

18.1 Introduction

Aristotle's ethical and political thought is considered to be an important source of inspiration for theories about citizenship that emphazise the active participation in the judicial and deliberative offices of the polity. Following Aristotle's claim that a human being is a political animal, the participatory democracy approach argues that human flourishing is achieved and the political system is enhanced when citizens participate in politics as much as possible. On this account, political participation allows the citizen to transcend from being a narrowly minded individual focused on his own desires and self-interest towards becoming a more creative and social individual who has learned to control his passions and to develop his interests with reference to the community. This transformation brings the human being closer to his genuine, more social nature and enables him to engage in meaningful relationships with others and to pursue justice in the community. Benjamin Barber,

E. Cohen de Lara (✉)
Amsterdam University College, Amsterdam, The Netherlands
e-mail: e.cohendelara@auc.nl

L. Huppes-Cluysenaer, N.M.M.S. Coelho (eds.), *Aristotle on Emotions in Law and Politics*, Law and Philosophy Library 121, DOI 10.1007/978-3-319-66703-4_18

for example, argues that in a participatory democracy the individual becomes receptive to change, cooperative and creative.[1]

As such, the approach places the transformation of the person into a citizen at the heart of the democratic process.[2]

In the participatory democracy approach, an important role is allocated to the jury system because it provides important opportunities for citizens to participate. Barber argues that there should be different forums of justice that empower citizens to engage in the mediation, arbitration, and settling of disputes.[3]

And Albert Dzur, in *Punishment, Participatory Democracy, and the Jury*, considers jury service indispensible because it nurtures the citizens' development in thinking about justice in impartial terms and their sense of social responsibility.[4]

Hence, the turn of the participatory democracy approach to ancient Athens as a source of inspiration is a natural one. Ancient Athens had a jury system and the city devoted a large part of its energies to the practice of jurisdiction. The Athenian legal system of the city was sophisticated and highly developed, which was a sign of the Greek passion for litigation.[5] In the Athenian courts, citizens prosecuted one another in both private and public cases and there were no professional lawyers and no public prosecutors, meaning that citizens would defend their own cases. Furthermore, the majority of judges were lay judges and most cases were prosecuted in front of large lay juries.[6] Rhetoric was an important art or craft; excelling at rhetoric boosted one's reputation and constituted a necessity when confronted with a lawsuit.

And, yet, we have to exercise caution in appealing to Aristotle as an authority on the transformative benefits of judicial participation. This chapter aims to provide an interpretation of Aristotle's *Rhetoric*[7] that seeks to inform and possibly adjust the argument that participating in judicial practices activates a sense of virtue or public spiritedness. The chapter does so by showing that even though Aristotle is well-known for his understanding in the *Nicomachean Ethics* and several sections of the *Politics*[8] that the engagement in the life of the city is essential for the moral development of the person, in the *Rhetoric* the connection between the art of producing persuasive arguments and the moral development of either the public speaker or the audience is rather tentative. Given the weak connection between rhetoric and morality, Aristotle displays an awareness of the need for rules and sanctions that regulate judicial discourse. This aspect of Aristotle's *Rhetoric*

---

[1]Barber (1984), p. 119.

[2]Ibid., p. 215.

[3]Ibid., p. 208.

[4]Dzur (2013), p. 66.

[5]Lanni (2006), p. 170. See also Christ (1998).

[6]Lanni (2006), p. 163.

[7]Edition used: Aristotle (1991).

[8]Editions used: Aristotle (1975) and Aristotle (1998).

deserves more attention in contemporary debates about participatory practices in the courtroom.

The argument of the current chapter centers on the idea that, for Aristotle, the emotions of people play an ambiguous role in judicial settings. I do not deny, as some in this volume have argued, that the emotions play a substantive role in the process of deliberation and, in particular, that *virtuous* emotions—meaning emotions that flow from a good character—are conducive to sound moral deliberation. But the emphasis, here, should be on the idea that only emotions that are habituated towards virtue promote moral choices. Just like Christof Rapp argues in his chapter "Dispassionate Judges Encountering Enthusiastic Aristotelians", I am reluctant to attribute to Aristotle the understanding that any emotion plays a consistently positive role in the deliberative process.[9] According to Aristotle, human emotions are not naturally, and therefore not automatically, virtuous. Indeed, in the *Nicomachean Ethics*, Aristotle focuses on the *habituation* of the emotions, which is done by practicing morally appropriate behavior. The question is whether, for Aristotle, the art of rhetoric provides for the moral education of the emotions.[10]

Furthermore, several chapters in this volume (Simão Nascimento; Bonanno and Corso; Maroney; Silvestre)[11] follow William Fortenbaugh[12] and Martha Nussbaum in arguing that the emotions can be trained to become obedient to reason because the emotions themselves actually have a cognitive dimension. This, purportedly, helps the emotions play a positive role in the deliberative process. As Nussbaum states specifically that emotions are closely akin to beliefs of some sort, which makes them responsive to reasoned change.[13]

My problem with this interpretation is that Nussbaum tends to underestimate Aristotle's commitment to the idea that the emotions should be habituated through moral practices in order to become constitutive of a good moral choice. For Aristotle, emotions do not so much embody thought as they become pliable to the dictates of reason through habituation. As such, emotions become intelligent in a derivative sense, that is, in the same way that a dog becomes intelligent once he is trained to listen to his master. A trained dog is not capable to rationally articulate why certain actions are good or not but will obey commands, just as emotions of people do not and cannot provide a rational discourse on the goodness or badness of a certain course of action but, when trained, will obey the reasoning part of the soul. An individual is virtuous if she experiences emotions at the right times, with reference to the right objects, towards the right people, with the right motive, and in the right way, and it is reason that comprehends what is right in each given circumstance (*EN* 1106b21–22). Moral virtue implies the habituation of emotion, especially of desire, and always involves prudential judgment about when it is right

---

[9]Rapp (2018).

[10]See also Garver (1994), p. 5.

[11]Nascimento (2018), Bonanno and Corso (2018), Maroney (2018), and Silvestre (2018).

[12]Fortenbaugh (2006).

[13]Nussbaum (1996), p. 303.

to indulge in a particular emotion. In other words, the emotions are not and cannot become independently virtuous—because they do not embody thought—but, instead, the emotions remain in need of the directive judgment of the reasoning or calculating part of the soul that possesses prudence. In short, I would argue that the emotions do not share in cognition, and here, again, I side with Christof Rapp who, in the chapter in this volume, argues that for Aristotle it would be ambiguous to call emotions rational.[14]

Given the argument about the need for habituating the emotions, the ambiguous and potentially volatile role of the emotions in the courtroom becomes more pronounced. Lacking a cognitive dimension, the emotions depend on proper habituation in order to make a positive contribution to moral judgment. The concerns that I have with opening up too much room for the emotions in the courtroom is that, for Aristotle, the art of rhetoric does not produce moral agents. Rather, the purpose of the art of rhetoric is to produce persuasion. For an explanation of what the art of rhetoric involves, an analysis of the emotions is essential, but this analysis is instrumental rather than normative; it is aimed at providing the rhetorician with the understanding of how the emotions of people influence their judgments, not at providing the rhetorician with the understanding of how the emotions should be appealed to in a morally appropriate way.

As such, in the *Rhetoric* Aristotle offers an account of the emotions that is very distinct from his account in the *Nicomachean Ethics*, a treatise that *is* focused on explaining moral and intellectual development. The argument permeating this chapter is that it is important to keep the different objectives of the two treatises—the *Rhetoric* and the *Nicomachean Ethics*—in mind and to read them on their own terms, in particular when it comes to evaluating the role that the emotions play or can play in judicial settings.

Several authors have interpreted Aristotle's *Rhetoric* from the perspective of the *Nicomachean Ethics*. Generally their reading results in the conclusion that the *Nicomachean Ethics* provides the ethical-political grounding for Aristotle's defense of the art of rhetoric as an art that harmonizes the emotions of the audience with the logic or facts of the case.[15] If we were to draw such conclusions, then there is a case to be made for the transformative effect of participating in the life of the city. Let us follow this line of argumentation for the moment. In the *Politics*, Aristotle states that human beings are political animals who belong in a city-state (*Pol.* 1253a1–2). The city-state is the natural habitat for human beings because, unlike other living beings, they possess the faculty of speech. Even though animals have a way of communicating pleasure and pain, only human beings use speech for indicating what is beneficial or harmful and what is just or unjust. For Aristotle, speech and moral deliberation constitute the specific activity of a human being, meaning that speech and moral deliberation are those actions which only human beings can perform, or which are best performed by them. Among living things, only human

---

[14]Rapp (2018).

[15]Becker (2013), p. 10. See also Cooper (1994), p. 206.

beings have the perception of good or bad, just or unjust, and so forth (*Pol.* 1253a15–7). In performing his function well, a human being develops the virtues or excellences that make him truly human. Now, as Aristotle explains in the *Nicomachean Ethics*, the moral virtues come about as a result of habit, which means that human beings have to practice the moral virtues in order to acquire them (*EN* 1103a31–32). Human beings learn to become courageous by performing courageous acts just as someone becomes a good lyre-player by playing the lyre. However, unlike the lyre-player who can practice the lyre on his own or with a teacher, a human being cannot fully develop the function of speech and moral deliberation in isolation. A human being needs others—he needs the community— to develop his speech to the fullest and to practice moral deliberation and *excel* at it. Consider, for example, justice. Of course, acting justly can be practiced in small, familial settings as one is expected to act justly towards one's wife and children. However, on Aristotle's account, just actions are more relevant in the social and political setting of the city in which one is confronted matters of justice on a grander scale, affecting a larger group of people. The same goes for courage. A human being practices courage in the face of poverty or disease, but a greater or more noble kind of courage is practiced on the battlefield where one faces the ultimate threat of death. Someone may properly be called brave who is fearless in the face of a noble death, which occurs most often in warlike circumstances (*EN* 1115a33–5). This makes the political community the natural place for a human being to live his life, for only in relationship to others he can develop his character fully.

In other words, based on the standard interpretation, participation in the life of the city is essential for a person's moral development and, hence, for his flourishing. Schofield, for example, reads Aristotle to mean that participating in the life of the city is important because it is the only way in which human beings can achieve their potential.[16]

But is this an accurate picture when it comes to Aristotle's understanding of judicial practices? When we read the *Rhetoric* on its own terms a different picture emerges. A rhetorician of good character is said to be more persuasive, but Aristotle does not elaborate on the implications of this for moral education. Nor does Aristotle explore the idea that the practice of rhetoric necessarily improves the audience in a moral way. In the *Rhetoric* we find an extensive analysis of the emotions that motivate human beings to make particular decisions. However, curiously absent from this analysis is a normative reflection on how the emotions should be managed, appealed to, or transformed.

I will argue that, as a result, reading Aristotle's *Rhetoric* has a sobering effect on those who connect Aristotle's understanding of the life of participation in politics and courtroom activities perhaps too closely to his ethics and who consider such activities to be morally transformative. Surprisingly scarce are Aristotle's remarks in the *Rhetoric* about the way in which the practitioner of rhetoric develops moral

---

[16]Schofield (2006), p. 321.

character. Instead, in the early parts of the *Rhetoric*, we find an emphasis on the rule of law, a principle that Aristotle advocates for judicial settings in particular in order to prevent the practice of rhetoric having a detrimental effect on justice and the common good.

Let us now turn to Aristotle's *Rhetoric*. Here, I want to make three points about Aristotle's understanding of the relationship between the art of rhetoric and the ethical life. First of all, Aristotle explicitly delineates the art of rhetoric as a field that does not necessarily have a moral purpose and that has a distinct function compared to ethics and politics. The rhetorician practiced in the art of rhetoric is able to be as successful as possible in persuading the audience, but not necessarily with moral effect. Secondly, Aristotle's elaborate analysis of the emotions in part two of the *Rhetoric* is focused on providing the rhetorician with insight into the emotions of the audience. But unlike in the *Nicomachean Ethics*, where Aristotle carefully considers the emotions in the context of the moral development of human beings, in the *Rhetoric* the analysis of the emotions is practically devoid of any moral consideration. Rather, the focus in the *Rhetoric* is to provide an understanding of the emotions so that the rhetorician becomes effective in arousing the emotions that best support his argument and help him to persuade the audience. Some of these emotions may even be inappropriate in a moral sense. Hence, the treatment of the emotions in the *Rhetoric* is instrumental instead of moral. Thirdly, we see in Aristotle's *Rhetoric* an emphasis on the rule of law and laws that help to curb the excesses of public speaking in the courtroom. This fits Aristotle's understanding that even though the art of rhetoric may involve an appeal to the emotions that is conducive to justice, it may also involve an appeal to emotions that disturbs the judgment of the audience and subverts the course of justice.

18.2 Defining the Art of Rhetoric

In the *Rhetoric*, Aristotle proposes that the art of rhetoric has a specific function or activity, namely, seeing the available means of persuasion in each case (1355b26–27). Aristotle considers the art of rhetoric or public speaking to be akin to dialectic, i.e. the art of logical discussion. Both make use of syllogistic reasoning; whereas dialectical reasoning is based on syllogisms, rhetorical reasoning is based on rhetorical syllogisms or enthymemes. But, according to Aristotle, there is an important distinction between rhetoric and dialectic. A rhetorician may be called a rhetorician simply because he possesses the knowledge of the technique of persuasion, even when a moral purpose is absent. Someone can be called a public speaker (*rhetor*) on account of his knowledge or on account of deliberately choosing misleading arguments. This is different from dialectic. A dialectician who deliberately employs plausible but wrong arguments and lacks a moral purpose can no longer be called a dialectician but, instead, is called a sophist (*Rhet.* 1355b18–20). As such, dialectic is defined as a technique that serves a moral purpose, whereas rhetoric, according to Aristotle, may actually be in part sophistical (*Rhet.* 1359b11).

Aristotle, thus, presents rhetoric as a useful technique that enables the speaker to become as successful as possible in public speaking, with or without a moral purpose. But also when rhetoric is without a moral purpose, he still calls it an art and not a fake copy of the art. It is correct, as Arnhart[17] has argued, that Aristotle considers rhetoric to be an art that is especially useful to make the true and just argument prevail. The just argument in most cases is by nature stronger, easier to prove, and more persuasive (*Rhet.* 1355a20–23). But Arnhart also admits that the art of rhetoric seems impartial when it comes to truth or falsehood, justice or injustice.[18]

In other words, the art of rhetoric does not only apply to true and just arguments but also to less true and just arguments in order to make these persuasive.

Aristotle also considers the art of rhetoric to be related to ethics and politics as a branch or offshoot (*Rhet.* 1354a1; 1356a26–27; 1359b10–11). Unlike ethics and politics, however, rhetoric is not a science of a specific subject matter and it does not produce substantive knowledge. Rather, rhetoric refers to the art of supplying arguments (*Rhet.* 1356a34). Some have argued that even though rhetoric is not part of ethical-political science, it does require knowledge that resembles scientific knowledge and, as such, is not qualitatively different from dialectic.[19] According to this interpretation, rhetoric operates based on accepted opinions that may not convey the whole truth but that are not nonsensical either. After all, there is generally speaking a commonsense wisdom in the collective judgment of the audience, and the rhetorician needs to appeal to this collective wisdom in order to be successful in his argumentation. Based on this reading, the difference between the art of rhetoric and a science is explained by the nature of the subject. The subjects of public speech are not the same as subjects of science because the former can be otherwise whereas the latter, i.e. the subjects of science, are not capable of being otherwise.

However, we should note that Aristotle sometimes uses opinion in a pejorative sense and in contrast to science. According to Aristotle, rhetoric *dresses itself up* as political science (*Rhet.* 1356a27–8). Whereas the sciences of ethics and politics truly yield substantive knowledge, the art of rhetoric pretends to generate knowledge but, effectively, it does not. In other words, the rhetorician—solely by nature of his art—does not possess nor produce genuine knowledge of ethics and politics, even though he does deal with the same topics, namely, human character, the emotions, and so forth. Even in his own time, Aristotle writes, people were confused about the distinction between the art of rhetoric and the science of politics. As it is, people allocate much more than its proper area of consideration to rhetoric (*Rhet.* 1359b8). The ethical-political sciences deal with true definitions and belong to a more real branch of knowledge (*Rhet.* 1359b5–6). These sciences deal with the topics of public speech in a more substantive way, that is, in a way that is more

---

[17]Arnhart (1981), p. 27.

[18]Ibid.

[19]Cooper (1994), pp. 205–206. See also Arnhart (1981), pp. 28–31.

instructive and fuller of understanding. The kind of knowledge implied in the art of rhetoric concerns the available means of persuasion (*Rhet.* 1355b-26–27). This is its specific function - and one that is more limited than people thought at the time - and to deny its specific function by turning rhetoric into a science, so Aristotle tells us, is to destroy its true nature.

18.3   The Role of the Emotions

Given that rhetoric as a technique does not necessarily have a moral dimension, the reader may wonder why Aristotle provides an extensive analysis of the emotions in book two of the *Rhetoric*. For Aristotle, the rhetorician must work to put the judges in the right frame of mind (*Rhet.* 1377b23–4). This is particularly important in lawsuits, when people's emotions are especially prone to affect their judgment. Aristotle points out that there is always an element of subjectivity involved; someone who is friendly and calm will judge a person less harshly compared to someone who is angry or hostile (*Rhet.* 1377b31). Overall, Aristotle understands the emotions as having a decisive impact on one's judgment and changing people's emotions oftentimes means changing their judgment (*Rhet.* 1378a20–41). A rhetorician who by nature of his art seeks the best means of persuasion needs to be able to effectively arouse or dispel emotions in anyone (*Rhet.* 1378a27). This is why the rhetorician needs to understand the state of mind of people experiencing emotions, the people towards whom an emotion is usually experienced, and on what grounds they experience the emotion towards these people. In other words, the emotions need to be analyzed and understood for the benefit of becoming as successful as possible at persuading an audience. The emotions are not analyzed in order to provide direction to moral development.

When we read part two of the *Rhetoric*, the absence of a moral analysis becomes apparent. Take, for example, the emotion of anger. According to Aristotle, the effective rhetorician must be able to recognize anger; he must be able to perceive who the people are with whom they usually get angry, and he must understand on what grounds they get angry with them (*Rhet.* 1378a22–6). Clearly, so Aristotle continues, it is helpful if one can put the audience in an angry state of mind while persuading them that one's opponent is the cause of what angers them (*Rhet.* 1380a2–4). The rhetorician, in other words, must be able to make emotional appeals to the audience when the situation demands it and when success in persuasion requires it. This includes the arousal of anger when necessary. Still, one may question the moral effect of such an arousal. In the *Politics*, Aristotle mentions anger as an emotion that enlists pain, which has the tendency to overpower reason and make rational calculation difficult (*Pol.* 1312b32–4). In other words, anger generally makes an audience less capable of judging accurately and, yet, it is part of the rhetorician's art to be able to arouse the emotion of anger when this suits his purpose of winning an argument.

In the *Nicomachean Ethics*, by contrast, Aristotle's focus is on mildness, which means that one experiences anger at the right moment, towards the right object, and in the right amount. Morally speaking, someone who is angry at the right things and with the right people, at the appropriate time and for as long as is appropriate, is praised (*EN* 1125b31–33). Giving in to anger at the appropriate times, for the right object, and so forth, is conducive to moral excellence. The rhetorician, however, aiming to be victorious in his argument, does not arouse anger for the purpose of moral education. Pedagogical concerns have no place here; the rhetorician does not learn about the emotion of anger in order to be persuaded or to persuade others to experience it in the right way. Instead, the purpose of the analysis in the *Rhetoric* is to explain that—realistically—anger is a passion that is easily aroused and that has a strong effect on the judgment or decision. To this effect, the rhetorician needs to understand how and why particular people or audiences get angry. A successful rhetorician is able to use this understanding to make his argument effective.

The discussion of anger also reveals Aristotle's awareness of the pettiness of human beings or, at the very least, of their moral imperfections. His claim is that anger is an emotion that people generally *like* to self-indulge in and he approvingly quotes Achilles in Homer's *Illiad* stating that anger is sweeter than honey (*Rhet.* 1378b6–7). The image of revenge arouses feelings of pleasure in an angry person. Furthermore, so Aristotle continues, people take pleasure in insulting others and saying things that injure, shame, or annoy someone. They also take pleasure in robbing others of the honor they are due. These things are pleasurable to the agent because they provide him with feelings of superiority (*Rhet.* 1378b27–8). People are particularly angered when their inferiors, or even their friends, slight them. Mildness, on the other hand, is said to stem from those who have men humble themselves before them. The proof of this, so Aristotle continues, is in the behavior of dogs that cease to bite those who sit down for them (*Rhet.* 1380a24–6).

Aristotle's analysis of fear likewise lacks a moral dimension. Fear is defined as a kind of pain or anxiety on account of imagining future bad things to happen (*Rhet.* 1382a21–2). Fear arises mainly when someone has power over another. Aristotle presents fear as an emotion that is or can be everywhere. Those who are physically more powerful are feared as well as those who have hurt people weaker than oneself (*Rhet.* 1382b16). Those who have been wronged or at least believe themselves to be wronged pose a threat because they are always looking for an opportunity to retaliate. Those who have wronged people in the past will use their power to preempt being retaliated against. Scarcity of goods also inspires fear because it turns people into rivals who are prone to hurt one another (*Rhet.* 1382b13–14). The effective rhetorician is expected to be able to make use of fear so that he knows how to arouse it in his audience (*Rhet.* 1383a8–12).

The discussions of anger and of fear show how, for Aristotle, the art of rhetoric is grounded in a realistic understanding of human nature, which effectively differs from the teleological understanding of human nature in the *Nicomachean Ethics*. In the *Rhetoric*, Aristotle states, rather bluntly, that most people are bad, greedy and cowardly, which is why being at the mercy of someone is almost always a cause of fear (*Rhet.* 1382b4–5). Being someone's inferior is a vulnerable position because human beings generally do wrong when they are able to do so (*Rhet.* 1382b10). Whereas in the *Nicomachean Ethics*, the focus is on human flourishing by means of practicing the virtues, in the *Rhetoric* Aristotle portrays human beings as they are and not as they may become.

Some have argued, based on a reading of the *Rhetoric*, that the passions such as anger and fear are "janus-like" in that they contribute to human happiness and the common good depending on the particular circumstances and the guidance of reason. Most emotions can be moderated into virtuous dispositions.[20]

Fear, on this reading, is conducive to courage when experienced at the right times, towards the right object and in the right amount. This is correct when one analyzes the ethical theory of the emotions in the *Nicomachean Ethics*, but it is a mistake to draw such conclusions from the *Rhetoric*. Instead of being presented as Janus-like and susceptible to moral development, the emotions are presented in the *Rhetoric* in a more factual and realistic way.

A third emotion that is illustrative of the realistic approach to human nature in the *Rhetoric* is shame. In comparison, let us first look at Aristotle's treatment of shame in the *Nicomachean Ethics*. Here, shame is not presented as a virtue but rather as a passion conducive to moral development, since it restrains the human being from performing morally bad and shameful actions (*EN* 128b10–11). Aristotle makes clear that shame should not be experienced by everyone, but only by the young (*EN* 1128b16). For the young, shame functions as a restraint on the many other passions that dominate their souls and on account of which they commit moral errors. Older people are, however, expected to no longer have these passions dominating their soul. Instead of shame causing them to restrain themselves, they are expected to have modified and trained their passions to such an extent that they are no longer problematic. Older men are not meant to need the passion of shame in order to act virtuously. In fact, we can say that for older people the expression of shame is a sign of moral immaturity. Aristotle also argues in the *Nicomachean Ethics* that experiencing a sense of shame is *not* the characteristic of a good man, for actions that cause a sense of shame simply should not be performed. And whether such actions are naturally disgraceful or merely conventionally disgraceful is irrelevant, because both kinds of actions should be avoided (*EN* 1128b22).

When we turn to the *Rhetoric*, however, the emphasis on shame being a passion that is appropriate to the young but not to mature human beings is lost. The *Rhetoric* describes several actions that are shameful and that are most often performed by adults, such as making a profit from a poor person, throwing away one's shield and fleeing in battle, praising people to their face, refusing to endure a hardship that is endured by others, or yielding to lust. People feel shame before those whom he respects, before those who admire him, before those by whom he wishes to be admired, before those to whose rank he aspires, and even before those whose

---

[20]Sokolon (2006), p. 5, cf. 164.

opinion he does not loath (*Rhet.* 1384a27–29). Shame in Aristotle's *Rhetoric* is, thus, presented as a common social emotion that realistically affects people's actions and judgment regardless of their age. As such, shame is an important emotion for the rhetorician to understand in order to arouse or dissipate it when necessary or useful for the argument.

Anger, fear, shame, and the other emotions should, of course, not be evoked indiscriminately. These emotions should be aroused in order to make the argument successful. An argument is successful if it helps to establish justice, if it persuades an audience that cannot be instructed, or if it helps to defend oneself in an argument (*Rhet.* 1355a18). Nowhere does Aristotle explicitly indicate that rhetoric is an art or technique that has as its characteristic function the moral education of the audience or the rhetorician himself. Justice may demand a correct appeal to the emotions of the audience, but there are also times when an appeal to the emotions blurs the judgment of the audience and sometimes this is necessary in order to win the case.

18.4 The Rule of Law

Once we see that, for Aristotle, rhetoric does not inherently promote a moral purpose or train the practitioner to become morally good, we grasp more easily why in the beginning parts of the *Rhetoric* he recommends measures that are meant to control the undesirable excesses of public speaking. This applies in especially to public speaking in law courts, because these are more susceptible to corrupt practices compared to the public assemblies (*Rhet.* 1354b28–30).[21] Whereas in the political arena the participants in the debate often reflect on prospective and general issues, the participants in a judicial arena deal with particular issues, which enable self-interest and the passions to affect the outcomes and decisions. Compared to the political arena, so Aristotle argues, the judicial arena is more prone to verbal attacks and personal appeals to the judges based on anger and pity together with an inattentiveness to the facts (*Rhet.* 1354a16–17). In forensic oratory especially it pays to sway the judges because they are susceptible to be placated or to be sweet-talked (*Rhet.* 1354b35).

Aristotle's response to the corrupting practices in law courts takes recourse in affirming the need for the rule of law. In general, good laws should define everything in an exact manner and leave as little as possible to the decision of the judges (*Rhet.* 1354a32–34). Aristotle provides three reasons why the rule of law is preferred over the judgment of men. First of all, the law is more aristocratic

---

[21]The Athenian law courts were known historically to be both democratic and chaotic, producing outcomes that were not always just (Lanni 2006, p. 168). Ehrenberg argues that centuries later, in the Hellenistic age, the city frequently called in foreign judges to decide even in private cases as a move to curtail corrupted practices at the law courts since a more impartial verdict was expected from external judges (Ehrenberg 1960, p. 79).

compared to a jury decision. Juries in an Athenian courtroom were numerous, ranging from 201 to 501 members.[22] By contrast, laws could be written by a small selection of people, and Aristotle argues that it is simply easier to find a few men who are capable and prudent in the framing of laws than it is to find a larger group of people who are capable and prudent judges (*Rhet.* 1354a34–b2). Secondly, Aristotle argues that the writing of laws is given more time compared to courtroom decisions and that justice requires extensive deliberation (*Rhet.* 1354b3–4). Thirdly, and most importantly, a legislator is detached from the particulars of the case and, therefore, likely to be rational and less excitable by passions that could influence his judgment. Law itself, on account of its general nature, is likely to be more reasonable. This is different for the jury, which is judging present and specific cases. For jury members, according to Aristotle, feelings of friendliness and hostility, and self-interest, more easily influence their judgment to the extent that they no longer see what is right (*Rhet.* 1354b5–11).

When it comes to specific laws that should govern judicial practices, Aristotle makes several suggestions. First of all, a good system of laws should ban argumentatively irrelevant appeals to emotion in the courtroom. Well-governed states have rules in courts that forbid talk about matters external to the subject and Aristotle approves of such laws (*Rhet.* 1354a23–25). Good laws are meant to prevent a speaker from manipulating the audience by drawing on arguments and emotions that are not relevant to the facts of the case. Furthermore, a judge or juror should have the authority to determine as little as possible and restrict himself to fact-finding, meaning that he knows whether something has happened or has not happened, will be or will not be, is or is not (*Rhet.* 1354b12). In a public assembly, Aristotle argues, the audience is more on guard against the rhetoric of a public speaker because the arguments raised before them may affect all of them and because people in an assembly are more numerous compared to a courtroom setting and hence less likely to be collectively manipulated into feeling or deciding one way or the other (*Rhet.* 1355a2–3). Jurors in lawsuits are more open to be manipulated and Aristotle seems keen to restrict their sphere of judgment. From the *Constitution of Athens*,[23] we know that there were other laws that applied to courtroom practices. In Aristotle's time, litigants were required to take an oath to speak to the point (*Const. Ath.* lxvii.1). Also, water clocks were used to limit the length of time for speeches, allowing an equal period of time for the prosecutor and the defendant (*Const. Ath.* lxvii.2).

In the context of the main argument of this chapter, Aristotle's emphasis on the rule of law at the start of his treatise on rhetoric should not come as a surprise. Since virtue cannot be relied upon in the courtroom, Aristotle's insistence upon the rule of law as a necessary constraint of rhetorical practices makes good sense. Good laws are meant to deter the rhetorician from excessively or inappropriately arousing the emotions of the jurors. Aristotle certainly does not exclude the possibility that a

---

[22]Lanni (2006), p. 166.

[23]Edition used: Aristotle (1975).

litigant uses emotions to make a just case to his audience. But it cannot be said that Aristotle *relies* on rhetoricians to make morally beneficial appeals to the emotions. Moreover, the art of rhetoric itself does not provide a kind of moral training for the practitioner. This is why an appeal to the rule of law becomes essential.

18.5   Conclusion

Participating in the judicial arena was an important part of what it meant to be a citizen in ancient Athens. What I have tried to show in this chapter is that, for Aristotle, participation in the judicial arena, whether as a litigant or as a juror member, meant that one participated in an arena where the emotions had an impact on judgment. According to Aristotle, the art of rhetoric consists of using the emotions of the audience to become effective in persuasion. In part, the moral character of the speaker and the moral rightness of his cause are to vouch for his persuasiveness, but, as mentioned earlier, Aristotle does not elaborate on the implications of this statement. Aristotle's understanding of the art of rhetoric seems to be grounded in a realistic understanding of human nature as it shows itself in settings where virtuous character cannot be counted on and, hence, where the emotions can both support but also derail rational deliberations towards just outcomes.

Are there, then, two Aristotles, namely, one of the *Nicomachean Ethics*, and one of the *Rhetoric*? I would argue that, in a way, the texts are premised on a similar psychology. In the *Nicomachean Ethics,* Aristotle emphasizes moral development because the emotions present a moral challenge for good decision-making. If moral habituation would have been easier, or if Aristotle would have considered the human emotions to be naturally good, then moral education would be superfluous. But it is not, and hence Aristotle's ethical theory revolves around the idea that a human being must habituate his emotions by engaging in morally good actions. At the same time, if Aristotle would have assumed that the human emotions are naturally moral, then the rule of law would *also* be superfluous. Good emotions that flow from a good character can enhance the cause of justice, but Aristotle knows that emotions that undermine justice in judicial discourse have a tendency to persist. The art of rhetoric itself does not contain internal mechanisms to prevent the abuse of justice and, therefore, rules, laws and restrictions remain essential to constrain the practice of rhetoric in the courtroom.

Furthermore, it is useful to keep in mind that the purposes of each treatise, the *Nicomachean Ethics* and the *Rhetoric*, are quite distinct. Whereas the first treatise seeks to answer the question of what constitutes human flourishing, the second treatise seeks to answer the question of what is the art of rhetoric. I do not see Aristotle making a strong effort to reconcile these two purposes as part of one coherent whole. Aristotle's strength as a philosopher often lies more in making perceptive distinctions between different beings, practices, or sciences instead of showing how everything relates as different parts of a connected whole. For

Aristotle, rhetoric does not produce moral education. Rhetoric could be said to depend on ethics and politics for its moral purpose but, on Aristotle's account, a rhetorician is still a rhetorician even if the moral purpose is lacking or misconceived.

This view of what the art of rhetoric as a political activity entails is possibly less naïve compared to those that arise from specific theories of participatory democracy. Whereas Barber defined politics as "the search for reasonable choices,"[24] Aristotle has a more realistic sense of the emotional ties, opportunism and self-interest that may affect one's judgment in the courtroom. And whereas Barber argues that the search for reasonable choices leads us towards a commitment to the common good, Aristotle is less confident that participation in courtroom practices produces moral development. Aristotle explicitly relies on external, legal checks and seems less inclined to put his trust in what Barber calls the "internal checks" on behavior, namely, a kind of commitment to the common good that naturally arises on account of participation.[25]

In light of our continuing efforts to read Aristotle as a source of inspiration for contemporary ethical and political thought, his understanding of the art of rhetoric and the emphasis on the rule of law may serve to enrich the discussion of the jury system as part of the attempt to promote participatory democracy, but may also temper the expectations of the benefits of such a system. If my reading of Aristotle holds, then we should seek to promote opportunities for engagement while continuing to pay close attention to the rule of law. Aristotle, in the *Rhetoric*, shows himself to be more of a realist about human nature compared to the Aristotle of the *Nicomachean Ethics*. In advocating participatory democracy we would do well to keep this tension in mind.

Acknowledgments The author wishes to thank Rafael Sanchez and two anonymous reviewers for their useful comments and Nathan Cooper for his valuable assistance.

References

Aristotle. 1975. In *The Politics and the Constitution of Athens*, ed. S. Everson. Cambridge: Cambridge University Press.

———. 1975. *The Nicomachean Ethics of Aristotle*. The World's Classics. New ed. Reprint. London and Indianapolis, IN: Oxford University Press and Hackett Publishing.

———. 1991. *Aristotle on Rhetoric. A Theory of Civic Discourse*. Oxford: Oxford University Press.

———. 1998. *Politics*. Translated by C. D. C. Reeve. Indianapolis, IN and Cambridge, MA: Hackett Publishing.

Arnhart, Larry. 1981. *Aristotle on Political Reasoning: A Commentary on the "Rhetoric"*. DeKalb, IL: Northern Illinois University Press.

---

[24]Barber (1984), p. 127.

[25]Ibid., p. 160.

Barber, Benjamin. 1984. *Strong Democracy. Participatory Politics for a New Age*. Berkeley: University of California Press.

Becker, Marcel. 2013. Aristotelian Ethics and Aristotelian Rhetoric. In *Aristotle and the Philosophy of Law: Theory, Practice and Justice*, ed. Liesbeth Huppes-Cluysenaer and Nuno M.M.S. Coelho, 109–122. Dordrecht: Springer.

Bonanno, Daniela, and Lucia Corso. 2018. What Does Nemesis Have to Do with the Legal System? Discussing Aristotle's Neglected Emotion and Its Relevance for Law and Politics. In *Aristotle on Emotions in Law and Politics*, ed. Liesbeth Huppes-Cluysenaer and Nuno M.M.S. Coelho. Dordrecht: Springer.

Christ, Matthew R. 1998. *The Litigious Athenian*. Baltimore, MD: Johns Hopkins University Press.

Cooper, John M. 1994. Ethical-Political Theory in Aristotle's Rhetoric. In *Aristotle's Rhetoric: Philosophical Essays*, ed. David J. Furley and Alexander Nehamas, 193–210. Berkeley: University of California Press.

Dzur, Albert W. 2013. *Punishment, Participatory Democracy and the Jury*. New York: Oxford University Press.

Ehrenberg, Victor. 1960. *The Greek State*. Oxford: Blackwell Press.

Fortenbaugh, William W. 2006. *Aristotle's Practical Side: On His Psychology, Ethics, Politics and Rhetoric*, Philosophia Antiqua. Vol. 101. Leiden: Brill.

Garver, Eugene. 1994. *Aristotle's Rhetoric: An Art of Character*. Chicago, IL: University of Chicago Press.

Lanni, Adriaan. 2006. *Law and Justice in the Courts of Classical Athens*. Cambridge: Cambridge University Press.

Maroney, Terry A. 2018. Judicial Emotion as Vice or Virtue: Perspectives Both Ancient and New. In *Aristotle on Emotions in Law and Politics*, ed. Liesbeth Huppes-Cluysenaer and Nuno M.M.S. Coelho. Dordrecht: Springer.

Nascimento, Daniel Simao. 2018. Rhetoric, Emotions and the Rule of Law in Aristotle. In *Aristotle on Emotions in Law and Politics*, ed. Liesbeth Huppes-Cluysenaer and Nuno M.M.S. Coelho. Dordrecht: Springer.

Nussbaum, Martha C. 1996. Aristotle on Emotions and Rational Persuasion. In *Essays on Aristotle's Rhetoric*, ed. Amélie Oksenberg Rorty, 303–323. Berkeley: University of California Press.

Rapp, Christof. 2018. Dispassionate Judges Encountering Hotheaded Aristotelians. In *Aristotle on Emotions in Law and Politics*, ed. Liesbeth Huppes-Cluysenaer and Nuno M.M.S. Coelho. Dordrecht: Springer.

Schofield, Malcolm. 2006. Aristotle's Political Ethics. In *The Blackwell Guide to Aristotle's Nicomachean Ethics*, ed. Richard Kraut, 305–322. Oxford: Blackwell.

Silvestre, Ana Carolina de Faria. 2018. Rethinking Legal Education from Aristotle's Theory of Emotions and the Contemporary Challenges of the Practical Realization of Law. In *Aristotle on Emotions in Law and Politics*, ed. Liesbeth Huppes-Cluysenaer and Nuno M.M.S. Coelho. Dordrecht: Springer.

Sokolon, Marlene. 2006. *Political Emotions. Aristotle and the Symphony of Reason and Emotions*. DeKalb, IL: Northern Illinois University Press.

Chapter 19
Rhetoric, Emotions and the Rule of Law in Aristotle

Daniel Simão Nascimento

Abstract This article argues that two of the three types of rhetorical speech conceived by Aristotle, namely, judicial speech and rhetorical speech, could be used by those wishing to assure that a well-ordered political community of a kind envisaged by Aristotle, was actually governed in accordance with what Aristotle took to be good governance, i.e. "the rule of law". In judicial settings, rhetorical speech can arouse emotions about the rule of law that may lead citizens to refrain from disrespecting it. In deliberative settings, it can create a kind of emotional involvement with our fellow citizen that seems to be required in order for a deliberative assembly to function well. If what is said here is correct, rhetoric as conceived by Aristotle would be a powerful tool in both the hands of the unjust and the just.

19.1   Introduction

Questions concerning the "rule of law" have drawn the attention of various classical scholars. In the *Politics*[1] Aristotle states that there are some forms of constitutions—the correct forms (kingship, aristocracy and politeia)—in which the governing is carried out according to laws and the interests of the whole community, and some forms—the deviated forms (tyranny, oligarchy and democracy)—in which the government may either not be carried out according to laws or be carried out according to laws that do not aim at the interests of the whole community (*Pol.* 1279a23–1279b10). The first group, says the philosopher, are the political communities that exist according to nature. As for the law, Aristotle thinks that it is proper for the laws, when rightly laid down, to be sovereign but he recognized that laws may be good or bad, just or unjust (*Pol.* 1262b1–13).

---

[1]Edition used: Aristotle (1977).

D.S. Nascimento (✉)
Pontifícia Universidade Católica of Rio de Janeiro's Nucleus of Estudies in Ancient Philosophy (NUFA), Rio de Janeiro, Brazil
e-mail: danielsimaonascimento@gmail.com

© Springer International Publishing AG 2018   401
L. Huppes-Cluysenaer, N.M.M.S. Coelho (eds.), *Aristotle on Emotions in Law and Politics*, Law and Philosophy Library 121, DOI 10.1007/978-3-319-66703-4_19

It would be easy to conclude, then, that for Aristotle "the rule of law" would be a neutral expression, neither good nor bad, since laws could be either just or unjust. What is truly important, it seems, is that a community is ruled in accordance with justice. Be that as it may, it is not this sense of the expression "rule of law" that will concern us here. Rather, I would like to say that in the deviated forms of regime the law does not perform its proper function and, consequently, that the proper meaning of the expression "rule of law" refers to the ways of governing that are both in accordance with law and the interests of the political community as a whole. In saying this, of course, I'm merely following those who—like Bates Jr.—say that the rule of law only takes place in the correct forms of government.[2] But even this interpretation, or at least so I'll argue, still leaves something to be said.

Indeed, although it suggests the type of constitution determines whether or not a given community is governed according to the rule of law, the fact that Aristotle foresees the possibility that even the correct forms of government might lose sight of their own laws in the activities of government should, by itself, be enough for us to recognize that, according to him, no form of constitution is enough to ensure that a given community will actually be governed in accordance with the rule of law. Having a correct form of constitution creates the political environment that makes the rule of law possible, but in order for it to be actual the activities of government have to be in accordance with it. This is something that comes out a lot more clearly in the *Rhetoric*[3] than in the *Politics*.

As we know, the study of rhetoric as the art of public speaking and persuasion began in Greece at a time when citizens were expected to take part in their own government. In the *Politics*, Aristotle distinguishes three 'parts of government'—namely, the part which deliberates about common affairs, the part concerned with offices or magistracies, and the judicial part (*Pol.* 1297b38–1298a3). In the *Rhetoric* he distinguished three kinds of rhetorical speech: judiciary, deliberative and epideictic (1358b7-9). According to Aristotle, then, both the judicial decisions and the decisions that issued from political deliberation were acts of government.[4]

Since the government in any correct constitution aims at the good of the whole of the community, it follows that both judicial decisions and political deliberations should also aim at this end. Although this is clearly the case with political deliberations, the primary aim of judicial decisions is not to decide what's best but to decide what's just (*Rhet.* 1358b20–30). It is because he believes that it is best for a community to live abiding by justice (*Pol.* 1282b14 sq.) that Aristotle says the judicial process aims at what is best. Nevertheless, since rhetoric is a form of discourse through which one can influence the judicial and political decision-making process of a political community so as to subvert or uphold its laws and its proper function, the task of ensuring that a given community will be governed in

---

[2]Bates (2013), p. 59.

[3]Editions used: Aristotle (1926, 1991).

[4]Although the conjunction of these two passages suggests a correspondence between epideictic speeches and the magistracies, I shall also refrain from commenting on this possible analogy since constraints of space make it impossible for me to treat epideictic speeches in this article.

accordance with the rule of law will need to be performed each time that a judicial or political decision is to be made.

Can rhetoric, as conceived by Aristotle, be a useful tool in accomplishing this? Can the emotions aroused by rhetorical speech actually be helpful to the well governing of a well ordered political community? As we know, there are some who deny Aristotle recognized any positive influence for the emotions in rhetorical speech.

Indeed, by the end of the twentieth century some scholars were moving away from an interpretation of Aristotle's *Rhetoric* that views the art of rhetoric as essentially amoral, towards one that attributes to Aristotle what Engberg-Pedersen called "an austere view of rhetoric."[5]

According to this interpretation, an austere view of rhetoric was to be found in Aristotle's *Rhetoric* as an ideal that can only be realized when it is directed at the best of audiences in the best of governments. These authors argue that according to Aristotle this ideal is the paradigm by which all other forms of rhetoric should be measured.

In order to make that clear, Engberg-Pedersen's first suggestion is that we should translate *peitho*—which Aristotle recognizes to be the business of the rhetorician in his *Topics*[6] (149b25) and *Rhetoric* (1355b26)—not as persuasion but as conviction. According to the author, the first translation causes us to forget that rhetoric is used within a setting where the main concern is the search for factual, ethical or political truth,[7] and the task of the austere notion of rhetoric is simply to show the facts of the matter. This is what Pedersen takes to be the point of Aristotle's criticism of his predecessors, in the *Rhetoric* (1354a11–1355a19), where he condemns the orators that speak outside the subject and introduces the "master of enthymemes" as the truly accomplished rhetorician.[8]

An austere rhetoric is a rhetoric that tries as best as it can not to make use of emotions when trying to persuade, that plays the truth-finding game by sticking to the facts. Engberg-Pedersen's analysis echoes Grimaldi's stance in his famous book titled *Studies in the Philosophy of Aristotle's Rhetoric* (1972) where the author argues that Aristotle's work reflects its antecedents, since the Greeks were of the opinion that rhetoric was an art whose object was the structure of language as the mode of human communication[9] and whose aim was the study of discourse in order to discover the most effective way in which to present problematic issues so that another person may reach an intelligent decision about it.[10]

---

[5]Engberg-Pedersen (1996), p. 122.

[6]Edition used: Aristotle (1997).

[7]Engberg-Pedersen (1996), p. 124.

[8]Ibid., p. 133.

[9]Grimaldi (1972), p. 2.

[10]Ibid., p. 3.

Although there's much to be said about such an austere conception of Aristotle's rhetorical teaching, what I argue in the following pages is that the austere conception of Aristotle's rhetoric has shortcomings when it comes to fitting his thoughts about both the judicial and the deliberative speeches.[11] I think this is also true of epideictic speeches, but constraints of space make it impossible to treat them here.

19.2   The Austere Conception of Rhetoric and Judicial Speeches

As Aristotle remarks, the judicial process aims at assuring a just decision (*Rhetoric* 1358b25–27). While in the *Rhetoric* Aristotle is exclusively concerned with giving advice on how to be persuasive when making judicial speeches, he never says what does it take for a decision to be just. Since my argument needs such a statement in order to move forward, I would like to define a just decision as a decision that (1) applies a given law to a given case in accordance with both the letter and the intention of that same law, (2) reaches a verdict for the right reasons and (3) is in accordance with the truth. I hope one example will help to clarify this definition and to give it a little context within the Greek legal system.

As we know, ancient Greek law recognized some possible excuses for cases of homicide. One of them is when the killing was in self-defense. As we also know, it is a matter of much debate how exactly that law was formulated.[12] What we do know, both from a speech called *Against Medias* (71–75) by Demosthenes[13] and from Antiphon's *Third Tetralogy*,[14] is that if someone was brought before the Aeropagus on a charge of murder it was possible to defend oneself arguing simply that the other man struck first, but it wasn't enough to prove that one was stricken first in order to be acquitted even though—from what we can infer from the defender's claims as they are reported by Demosthenes—it seems that this was the only demand formulated in the letter of the law.

In the case quoted by Demosthenes, we hear of a certain Euaeon who attempted such a defense when he killed a man called Boeotus, but ended up being convicted. The final vote count, which was 5 to 4, shows that the question was probably no easy matter to solve. According to Demosthenes, in the case in question Euaeon had multiple witnesses that could vouch for the fact he had been struck first, but since the blow was not meant as an attempt to kill, but to insult, he was convicted. What the majority of the jury found, then, was that the law was not to be applied in this case even though it seems the letter of the law did not make any specification on the contrary. In saying this, of course, I'm merely agreeing with the reading of the case

---

[11]For a recent defense of the opposing view see in this volume Rapp (2018).

[12]On this topic, see Gagarin (1978).

[13]Demosthenes (1935).

[14]Antiphon (1954).

that is provided by Demosthenes himself. I take this to be evidence of the fact that Athenian courts were sensitive to the fact that the application of a law must take into account both its letter and its intention.[15]

As for (2), all I mean is that it is not enough to convict someone of a crime one has indeed committed in order for the law to be properly applied. In other words, I take it to be the case that if a court ends up convicting a murderer not because it really was persuaded—by the proof, evidence, testimonies and speeches presented during the trial—that he committed the murder, but for some other reason, then the decision was not just. By now, it must be clear that (3) is made so as to cover the opposite case. When it comes to doing justice, it can't be enough to play by the rules and to make an honest and impartial decision in accordance with the appropriate procedures—one has to actually get it right.

Once we accept this definition it might seem that if a decision was reached because of an emotion then it couldn't possibly have been reached for the right reasons. Indeed, a superficial reading of Aristotle's *Rhetoric* may give us the impression that the whole point of stirring feelings in a judicial context is to manipulate the judge's emotions so as to do away with the need for the rational work that would actually satisfy (2). Aristotle does state both that passions can modify judgments and that the orator has to know how to inspire them adequately without ever bothering to consider in which cases should one try to modify an opinion by inspiring a passion (*Rhet.* 1378a20–30). After considering love, hate, friendship and enmity, he does conclude that it is possible to prove that men are enemies or friends, or to make them such if they are not; to refute those who pretend that they are, and when they oppose us through anger or enmity, to bring them over to whichever side may be preferred (*Rhet.* 1382a17–20). That being said, it is important to be clear about what we mean when we say someone was moved to a decision by an emotion.

As has been remarked by many, when it comes to Aristotle's philosophy it is a mistake to see emotions as simply opposed to reason. Anger, for example, is defined as a desire for vengeance (accompanied by pain) for some undeserved slight to oneself or one's own (*Rhet.* 1378a30–31). According to Aristotle, to feel anger is to feel and to be moved by the judgment that some such slight has occurred, and at least some of Aristotle's recommendations on how the orator should deal with anger presuppose that if one can somehow modify this judgment one can also modify the feeling. Indeed, according to Aristotle one will be angry only if one believes such a slight has been voluntary and will be calm if he thinks it is involuntary (*Rhet.* 1380a5 sq.). This allows us to conclude that if somebody who thinks that a slight was voluntary can be convinced that it was actually involuntary he will cease to be angry and become calm.

---

[15]Whether or not Euaeon was actually convicted because of this, of course, is an entirely different matter. Nevertheless, the fact that Demosthenes interprets the case in this way in order to support his argument shows that he believed that the judges he was addressing would recognize and accept this reading.

Having recognized that, it is not at all a stretch to say that Aristotle's analysis of emotions clearly shows that he believes them to be complex feelings that involve judgments, and that those judgments are what explains why some emotions simply cannot be felt at the same time and towards the same persons, like envy and pity for instance.[16] Some go even further, following Nussbaum, and recognize that according to Aristotle the belief that certain judgments are not only external, necessary—and sometimes even sufficient—conditions for eliciting some emotions, but that they are at least part of what individuates the different emotions.[17]

Since in some cases some such emotion might be the appropriate feeling for those who hear a truthful and impartial description of a given case, it may as well be the case, for instance, that one of these emotions was aroused precisely because the jury believes that (2) was satisfied. In such cases emotions will be present together with the rational argument that would satisfy (2) without harming the audience's cognitive capacities or being a cause to their decision. This is a welcome result: a lot of times emotions simply cannot be avoided if we are to look at the cold and hard facts of some cases that are judged in a court of law, and an orator who tried to avoid them would have to avoid the facts.

So far we have considered how a rhetorician might, by describing the case or his opponent, arouse emotions in the jury. But there is nothing that prevents this same orator from addressing the jury about the jury's own emotional state during a judicial speech. That such a task might prove necessary follows from the assumption that, since emotions are composed of judgments that do not admit of their contraries while the emotion is in place, we might have to change an audience's pathological state *before* addressing it with a contrary rational argument.

The most obvious case is the case of the angry mob serving as jurors. Suppose that someone of influence has been known to make insulting comments against a class of citizens and is now being accused of a crime in front of a jury that is mostly composed of that same class of citizens. Feeling wrath at being slighted, they are more than ready to take revenge. Having been the target of injustice, they don't see anything wrong with paying the man back with injustice themselves. This is a mob that needs to be calmed down and reminded of the actual purpose and importance of law before being addressed with any austere judicial argument. Any argument that tries to dissuade them from acting so because such behavior would be unjust has very little hope of being successful. If the man is actually innocent of insulting them and if he can somehow show that to the audience he may, it is true, appease them. But what if he isn't innocent or cannot convince them? How can he be expected to have a fair trial?

This example is important because it points towards an oversimplification in the austere interpretation of Aristotle's rhetoric. It is true, of course, that the judicial apparatus is concerned with truth finding. But it is not at all true that every time this apparatus is being used everyone who is using it is concerned with finding the truth.

---

[16]Leighton (1996), p. 210.

[17]Nussbaum (1996), p. 309.

Defenders of the austere interpretation have a ready answer for this line of argument. According to them, the austere conception of rhetoric can only be realized if its target is the most perfect of audiences, namely, an audience that is composed entirely of fully knowledgeable and virtuous individuals, which is the audience that characterizes the perfect political community.

This ideal conception of rhetoric, then, is closely connected with a very specific form of community, namely, the best possible form. This connection can be found, for example, with Reeve,[18] Engberg-Pedersen[19] and Kennedy.[20] For the purposes of this paper, it will be enough to point out that, given the definition of the rule of law adopted here, what is of interest for the present investigation is not only the rule of the ideal political community but the rule that takes place inside every well-ordered political community when they are ruled in accordance with their laws and their proper function.

In other words, if we accept the definition proposed above then we have no reason to believe that being a community that is governed in accordance with the rule of law is the same as being a community composed entirely of virtuous and knowledgeable citizens. We are, then, still free to conceive a use of rhetoric that manipulates the emotions of the audience in order to influence the jury to make a decision that is in accordance with the rule of law inside a community that is governed in accordance with nature.

Such use of rhetoric will not be confined to the calming down of mobs. Its purpose may very well be to remind an audience of the actual purpose of law and of the importance of sticking to it. This means using rhetoric in much the same way as Aristotle envisions it being used in the *Rhetoric* but, instead of arousing emotions in the audience that have to do mostly with how they feel about the individuals directly involved in the trial, the objective would be to arouse emotions that have to do mostly and firstly with how they feel, or should feel, about the law. By that I mean that a good orator can and should arouse in his audience the feelings of respect towards the law and the intention which guides it, shame at the thought of its distortion, pride in the striving for its good use, fear of its perversion and, consequently, love towards those who strive to uphold it and hate towards those who try to pervert it.

This would be very much in line with the idea, also previously stressed by Bates Jr., that the laws of any given community express the notions of this community about what justice is and how to live by it.[21] According to Aristotle, the constitutional laws determine the kinds and functions of the magistracies of each political community (*Pol.* 1278b09–12) as well as its most important aims and values (*Rhet.* 1336a4 sq.), while all the other various laws set the rules of behavior that each community takes to be in its own interests for the citizens and the magistracies to

---

[18]Reeve (1996), p. 199.

[19]Engberg-Pedersen (1996), p. 122.

[20]Kennedy (1991), p. 18.

[21]Bates (2013), p. 62.

follow (*EN* 1129b11 sq. and *Pol.* 1289a10–20). In this light, it seems natural to say that those trying to pervert the laws are trying to pervert the very ideas around which the way of a life of a given community is organized. A citizen for whom this way of life has any merit at all should be open to feeling these kinds of emotions, whether or not he can be called virtuous in the fuller sense of the word.

As I hope to have made clear, even when it comes to the judicial speeches we can find some shortcomings with the austere approach to Aristotle's rhetoric. That being said, these shortcomings are a lot less serious than the ones we will find in the deliberative speech. This is because even if we accept all that was said above, it still remains true that the main goal of a judicial process is finding the truth about something that happened in the past and that a judge is expected to reach a judicial decision by sticking only to the pertinent facts and the letter and meaning of the law. On the other hand, Aristotle recognized not only that deliberation aimed at the future and concerns itself with things of which knowledge is lacking but also that it draws on an inseparable mix of desire and intellect, emotion and reason (*EN* 1113a8-12, 1139b4-5), and there is no reason to believe this should be any different when it comes to political deliberation.

This is why the shortcomings of the austere conception of rhetoric become more serious when we consider deliberative speeches.

19.3   The Austere Conception of Rhetoric and Deliberative Speeches

According to Aristotle deliberative speeches have to do with what is expedient or harmful (*Rhet.* 1358b25sq). But expedient and harmful for whom? As we have said before, according to Aristotle a community is only governed in accordance with nature when it is governed with a view to the benefit of the political community as a whole as opposed to the benefit only of its ruling body (*Pol.* 1279a17–32).

We have seen that according to Aristotle a community is only governed in accordance with nature when it is governed with a view to the benefit of the political community as a whole and that the deliberative body is a governing institution. It follows that the decision reached by an act of deliberation of the deliberative body will be an act of government, and that political deliberation will only be done in accordance with both nature and justice when it aims at the good of the whole community. Also, since the laws of a political community are supposed to say how the citizens, the ruling body and all the magistrates should behave (*Pol.* 1289a10–20), it follows that any deliberative body is supposed to behave according to those laws.

These statements fit well with what we find in the passage of the *Rhetoric* where Aristotle tells us what he thinks are the five most important subjects on which people deliberate and on which deliberative orators give advice in public, namely, finances, war and peace, national defense, imports and exports, and the framing of laws (*Rhet.* 1359b22sq). It is with "the city" (*polis*) taken as a whole, as he refers to it several times in this passage, that Aristotle takes political deliberation to be primarily concerned.

This is why, as has also been remarked by Yack, the pursuit of the common good structures political deliberation in a number of significant ways, the most important of which might very well be the fact that it rules out explicit recourse to self-serving arguments.[22] But while Yack believes that this means that anybody who tries to persuade an assembly to do something in his own interest will have to find a way of portraying what is good for him as good for the other members of the community as well,[23] it seems all he would really have to do is to portray his suggestion as good for his target audience, which is composed of the persons who are actually taking part in that one specific act of political deliberation.

This is in line with Yack's suggestion that this limitation is 'structural.'[24] An even better word, and perhaps more Aristotelian too, would be 'functional'. Indeed, this limitation seems derived from what Aristotle takes to be *the function* of political deliberation. The importance and weight of this limitation must be well understood. Aristotle does say that political leaders can admit that a proposed plan of action is unjust and dishonorable because, as long as they can show that it will ultimately serve the common good of the community, their speech might still be effective (*Rhet.* 1358b35sq). Even so, it seems excessive to follow Yack when he claims that "whatever else they promise to us, political proposals cannot be persuasive unless they appear to promote the common good or advantage."[25] From the fact that there are rules we cannot conclude that people are playing by them.

Be that as it may, for the purposes of our present argument it is even more important to ask how one is supposed to balance the different interests of the different citizens and groups of citizens inside of a political community when deliberating. This is a question that finds little treatment in Aristotle's *Rhetoric*.

Although when giving us advice about deliberative speeches Aristotle does give us some pointers on how to compare different goods and evils, when it comes to evaluating different courses of action most of the time he seems to assume that their relative value will be one and the same for the whole political community and that the problem is figuring out exactly what is that value. The exception, of course, is when he states that what the majority wants may be said to be good, because what everybody wants is surely good and

> the majority may almost stand for all. (*Rhet.* 1363a13–15, trans. Freese)

The key in the last sentence, of course, is the word "almost". Political deliberation poses a special challenge because every individual that takes part in it needs to balance the different interests of the different groups and/or individuals that are a

---

[22]Yack (2006), p. 422.

[23]Ibid.

[24]Ibid., p. 423.

[25]Ibid., p. 424.

part of the political community in order to reach a decision on the course of action that is best for the whole community. In order for individuals to form a well-functioning deliberating assembly they must hear arguments for all the open courses of action and to consider the impacts they will have not only on their lives but on the lives of the other citizens and of the community as a whole. In the following pages, I argue that this task requires some emotional involvement with our fellow citizens if we are both to make that evaluation and to give it its proper weight in our deliberation.

19.4   Judging What Is Best for the Whole in Political Deliberation

According to what was said above, everyone that takes part in a political deliberation is supposed to consider the costs and benefits of the possible courses of action in order to decide what is the best course of action for the political community as a whole. But it may very well be the case that either, or both, the costs and the benefits involved in the different possible courses of action are not equally distributed amongst the different parts of the political community. When that is so, it may be particularly difficult to make certain individuals or groups of individuals concede the same value to interests that are indifferent or opposed to their own as they do to their own interests. Let's call this the "problem of evaluation".

This problem would, of course, be greatly mitigated if we accept a now famous interpretation of the idea of civic friendship in Aristotle's philosophy. The interpretation I'm referring to was most famously defended by John Cooper during the *XI Symposium Aristotelicum*.[26] In his article, Cooper argues that being a political animal means having an '*ergon*' that is performed in common with other animals of the same species, and that in the case of men this *ergon* is the political activity performed inside a political community. In a political community worthy of its name, says Cooper, every citizen is united by a bond of civic friendship, which consists in an emotional bond that extends to a whole city the kind of emotional bond that exists in a family.

According to Cooper, just as inside a family each family member participates in the good of the others because of the friendship that binds them together, so in the political community where there is civic friendship every citizen participates in the good of each other.[27] Last but not least, civic friendship makes it so that fellow citizens worry about each other's well-being in and for itself, which means worrying for them for their own sake. It is because of friendship, says Cooper, that Aristotle thinks that whatever a human being's happiness ultimately turns out to consist of, it must be something that suffices not just for his own individual good but also somehow includes the good of his family, his friends, and his fellow citizens.[28]

---

[26]Cooper (1990).

[27]Ibid., p. 236.

[28]Ibid., p. 220.

If we conceive of an assembly where everyone involved was united by the bond of friendship as Cooper conceives it, the problem of evaluation diminishes considerably. In such a case, all someone would have to do is explain the benefits or inconveniences of a given course of action for himself to his fellow citizens in order for them all to feel his anxiety, his fear or even his pain, just like they would do if they were listening to a son or a father. Although the assumption that there is a kind of friendship that unites all the citizens of a political community in such a way has been questioned by many, my aim here is to explore the insufficiency of this interpretation for the problem I'm trying to pose even if we concede that such friendship exists. In order to achieve this purpose, it will be enough to highlight a few passages from books VIII and IX of the *Nicomachean Ethics* that shed sufficient light on the insufficiency of Cooper's hypothesis when it comes to the problem of evaluation.

I'll start with a passage from book IX where Aristotle discusses the possible conflict presented by competitive claims of different friends over the same individual[29] (*EN* 1164b23–1165a35). At first, the questions presented are (1) whether a man owes unlimited obedience to his father or if (a) he, when sick, should follow the advice of his doctor; (b) when electing a general should he vote for the best soldier—as opposed, of course, to voting for his own father; (2) whether he ought to do a service to a friend rather than to a virtuous man and (3) whether he ought to repay his obligations to a benefactor, who is a friend, rather than perform a service to a comrade, who is also a friend.

Although Aristotle goes to the trouble of reminding us that there can be no exact rule for these matters, the philosopher does feel confident enough to mention three criteria that we should keep in mind—the importance, the nobility and the urgency of the claim. In general, says the philosopher while answering question (3), it seems one ought to repay favors before doing a favor. But even this rule admits of exceptions.

Suppose, says Aristotle, that one has been ransomed from brigands. In principle, one would be obliged to ransom one's ransomer in turn if need be or to repay the price of the ransom to the friend who spent it. But if our father needs to be ransomed

---

[29]The interpretation defended here does not need to claim that any cases where this conflict presents itself is a case of what van Straalen in this volume calls 'the dilemma of dirty hands'. In order to support such a claim, we would have to show that Aristotle thought that even the best way out of at least some episodes of this conflict would involve the commission of an act that is both right and shameful, and that would involve an independent argument against Nielsen (2007) which would take us too far from our subject. However, insofar as the interpretation proposed here shows that Aristotle not only conceived of possible cases of that dilemma that are not considered either by van Straalen or by Nielsen but also provided us with recommendations on how to act on these cases that neither author mentions, this interpretation does give us reasons to at least reassess the claim first made by Nielsen (p. 273) and reaffirmed in this volume by van Straalen, according to which Aristotle did not recognize any cases that would qualify as cases of 'the dilemma of dirty hands'.

at the same time and we are forced to choose, then according to the philosopher the man should give his father priority. This means that he believes the balance of nobility, urgency and utility points that way, and although by the end of his discussion Aristotle reaffirms the need for us to struggle in order to give everyone their due it is clear that his own answer accords some sort of priority for the family. There are two passages from book VIII that explain why it is that Aristotle answers the problem he raises in book IX as he does and what exactly justifies this priority.

According to the philosopher:

> The claims of justice (ta dikaia) also differ in different relationships. The mutual rights of parents and children are not the same as those between brothers; neither are those between members of a comradeship and fellow-citizens; and similarly with the other forms of friendship. Injustice, therefore, also is differently constituted in each of these relationships; wrong is increasingly serious in proportion as is done to nearer friend. For example, it is more shocking to defraud a comrade of money than a fellow-citizen; or to refuse aid to a brother than to do so to a stranger; or to strike one's father than strike anybody else. Similarly, it is natural that the claims of friendship also should increase with the nearness of the friendship, since friendship and justice exist between the same persons and are co-extensive in range. (*EN* 1159b35–1160a9)

> The affection of children for their parents, like that of men for the gods, is the affection for what is good, and superior to oneself; for their parents have bestowed upon them the greatest benefits in being the cause of their existence and rearing, and later for their education. Also the friendship between parents and children affords a greater degree both of pleasure and of utility than that between persons unrelated to each other, inasmuch as they have more in common in their lives (*EN*, 1162a4–9, trans. Rackham).

As we can see, in the first passage Aristotle claims that injustice is more serious when it is done against nearer friends and in the second passage he states that the friendship between parents and children is superior to the others in terms both of pleasure and utility because they have more in common in their lives. It seems natural, then, to infer that this friendship will hold a special place amongst all the others and so will the claims of justice that come from it. All this is confirmed when we read the previous mentioned passage from book IX where Aristotle analyzes the possibility of conflict between competitive claims of friendship.

Even though we cannot possibly answer all the questions aroused by these passages, I believe it is clear from what was said above that the existence of a bond of civic friendship would not be enough to insure that every citizen gives equal thought and value to the interests of all his fellow citizens. Although I see no need to argue that this might be the case even when someone is taking part in political deliberation, it doesn't seem to be as clear that Aristotle thinks that even in this case one should give priority to one's family.

After all, the decision of who to ransom is a private one and the fact that Aristotle thinks it right to settle a private decision in the way described above does not mean that he also believes that when taking part in political deliberation one should also put the interests of those closer to oneself above the rest. Indeed, such a consideration would be contrary to what he takes the function of political deliberation to be. Nevertheless, there is a passage of the *Politics* where Aristotle does recognize some cases in which that tends to happen. In discussing those cases, the philosopher proposes a solution for the problem they create which, in my mind, has not received the attention it deserves (*Politics* 1330a9–25).

In the passage in question, Aristotle makes a point of saying that in his perfect political community every citizen would receive a portion of land in the center and a portion of land near the the frontiers. In proposing that, Aristotle says he wishes not only to make a just and equitable distribution of land but also to avoid what he takes to be a perennial problem in many cities, namely, that when it comes the time to deliberate about war with a neighbor the people who live in the center are a lot more willing to go to war than the people who live near the frontiers with said neighbor. According to the philosopher, this is why many cities passed laws prohibiting those who lived near the frontiers to deliberate about any war near that same frontier.

As we know, the property of land in ancient Greece was strictly tied to the family, which means that Aristotle's considerations here show us just how preoccupied he was in aligning the interests of the families with the interests of the political community. What the pattern of choice mentioned by Aristotle reveals is that, when pressed to choose, the individual sometimes does choose the well being of his family over the interests of his political community. Could such behavior be *always* described as *simply unjust or imprudent*? There are some passages in Aristotle's works which seem to indicate otherwise.[30]

When criticizing monarchy in the *Politics*, Aristotle raises a difficulty concerning this type of government when it comes to the transmission of power. According to the philosopher, it is not reasonable to expect a king *not to* give the throne to his kids in case they are not worthy of ruling because this would be an act of virtue above human nature (*Pol.* 1286b23–28).

In the Nicomachean Ethics, when he is analyzing the so called "mixed actions", Aristotle states that (a) some deeds though not praised are condoned, when a man does something that he shouldn't through fear of penalties that impose too great a strain on human nature and, when it comes to draw the line between what is reasonable to do under coercion and what is not, that (b) it is ridiculous when Alcmaeon, a character in a play by Euripides, is compelled by certain threats to murder his mother (*EN* 1110a20–1110b1).

Now, a most intuitive reading of the passage will take (a) as referring to the example of the man whose family is under the power of a tyrant who threatens to bring harm to them unless he performs some vicious action. And it is very peculiar that, when it comes to drawing the line between what is reasonable to do under coercion and what is not, Aristotle does not simply say that one should not murder

---

[30] As De Lara remarks in this volume, many authors seem to believe that according to Aristotle living in a *polis* and engaging in political participation can cause a subjective change in men that transforms individuals who are guided by self-interest into individuals who are guided by the pursuit of the common good. The interpretation offered here is in accordance with and complements the critique of this position offered by De Lara.

even under coercion—even though he takes murder to be an action that is always vicious (*EN* 1107a9-18)—but that one shouldn't murder *one's own mother*.

The reading of Aristotle's theory of friendship provided here is in line with these passages. According to the interpretation defended here, the alignment of the interests of the political community with the interests of the different families that are a part of it is itself something fragile that can in no way be guaranteed just by the distribution of property.

By now, I think we can understand what I meant by emotional involvement when I mentioned political deliberation a while ago. Indeed, what is needed in order for a given body to deliberate well is for everyone not only to *understand* the costs and benefits involved in every possible course of action for each and every part of the political community but also *for everyone to give everyone else's interests their due weight in their own deliberation*. It is for this second step that emotional involvement seems to be required.

According to the interpretation delineated here, it is only to the extent that we can expect the citizens of a given community to give each other's interests their due weight in political deliberation that we can expect a political community to deliberate well. By this point, it should be clear that the above criticism was not made in order to reject the importance of the idea of civic friendship. On the contrary, I believe that this bond does provide us with the kind of emotional involvement that can ultimately explain why it is that anybody should take their fellow citizen's interests into account. It is only when it conflicts with other bonds of friendship that civic friendship proves to be, by itself, insufficient.

If this is correct, then it does seem plausible to say that friendship—whatever its kind—is the emotional bond that according to Aristotle makes us care for each other's interests and well-being. Without it, it is hard to see how political deliberation can regularly be successful. Can rhetoric help us achieve that? I believe we have good reason to answer affirmatively. Although when talking about Aristotle's theory of friendship most interpreters confine themselves to discussing the books devoted to it in both ethics, we will do well to remember that Aristotle does talk about friendship in the *Rhetoric* as one of the emotions that the orator must be capable of instilling. When he does instill it, it is supposed to make us not only desire the good of those towards whom we are so disposed for their own sake (1380b34-1381a2) but also feel pleasure in their fortune and sorrow in their distress (1381a4–6).

Since, as I said in the beginning, the expression "rule of law" is used here to refer to the ways of governing that are both in accordance with law and the interests of the political community as a whole, it follows that if rhetoric can inspire friendship so as to diminish or do away with the problem of evaluation, than the use of rhetoric in deliberative speeches can be instrumental to the actualization of the rule of law by inspiring an emotion—friendship—which is of great importance to the well-functioning of any deliberative body.

19.5   Conclusion

If what was said above is correct, we can conclude that rhetoric as conceived by Aristotle can make a positive contribution to the activity of governing in accordance with the rule of law by inspiring emotions that are conducive to the well governing of a political community both in judicial and deliberative settings.

In a judicial context, or so I have argued, rhetoric can serve a positive function not only by describing a case or an opponent in order to arouse emotions in the jury but also by addressing the jury about the jury's own emotional state during a judicial speech. Although the judicial apparatus is concerned first and foremost with truth finding, it is not at all true that every time this apparatus is being used everyone who is using it is concerned with finding the truth of the case in question even if we consider only political communities whose constitution is according to nature.

This is why it makes sense to say that, as conceived by Aristotle, rhetoric can be used to manipulate the emotions of the audience in order to influence the jury to make a decision that is in accordance with the rule of law inside a community that is governed in accordance with nature. It can do so, or so I have argued, by stirring in his audience the feelings of respect towards the law and the intention which guides it, shame at the thought of its distortion, pride in the striving for its good use, fear of its perversion and, consequently, love towards those who strive to uphold it and hate towards those who try to pervert it.

As for deliberative speeches, I emphasized the fact that Aristotle himself recognized that deliberation draws on an inseparable mix of desire and intellect, emotion and reason (EN 1113a8-12, 1139b4-5), and that political deliberation poses a special challenge because in order for individuals to form a well-functioning deliberating assembly they must hear arguments for all the open courses of action and to consider the impacts they will have on their lives, on the lives of the other citizens and on the political community as a whole.

The task of political deliberation requires not only intellectual capacities but also some emotional involvement with our fellow citizens if we are both to evaluate what our decisions mean for him and to give this evaluation its proper weight in our deliberation. This emotional involvement is what Aristotle calls friendship, and friendship is one of the emotions that the orator is able to inspire in his audience. It follows that by doing so in a deliberative setting an orator might contribute to the establishment of the emotional bond ideal for successful political deliberation and hence for the actualization of the rule of law inside a deliberative setting.

References

Antiphon. 1954. *Discours: suivis des fragments d'Antiphon le sophiste.* Translated by Louis Gernet. Paris: Les Belles Lettres.

Aristotle. 1926. *Aristotle, with an English Translation: the "Art" of Rhetoric.* Translated by John Henry Freese. Loeb Classical Library. London and New York: W. Heinemann and G.P. Putnam's.

———. 1947. *The Nicomachean Ethics.* Translated by Harris Rackham. Loeb Classical Library. London: W. Heinemann.

———. 1977. *Politics.* Translated by H. Rackham. Loeb Classical Library. Cambridge, MA and London: Harvard University Press and W. Heinemann.

———. 1991. *On Rhetoric: A Theory of Civic Discourse.* Translated by George A. Kennedy. New York: Oxford University Press.

———. 1997. *Posterior Analytics; Topica.* Translated by E. S. Forster and Hugh Tredennick. Loeb Classical Library. Cambridge, MA: Harvard University Press.

Bates, Clifford Angell. 2013. Law and the Rule of Law and Its Place Relative to Politeia in Aristotle's Politics. In *Aristotle and the Philosophy of Law: Theory, Practice and Justice*, ed. Liesbeth Huppes-Cluysenaer and Nuno M.M.S. Coelho, 59–75. Dordrecht: Springer.

Cooper, John. 1990. Political Animals and Civic Friendship. In *Aristoteles "Politik": Akten Des XI. Symposium Aristotelicum*, ed. Günter Patzig, 221–242. Göttingen: Vandenhoeck & Ruprecht.

Demosthenes. 1935. *Demosthenes III: Meidias, Androtion, Aristocrates, Timocrates, Aristogeiton 1 and 2, XXI-XXVI.* Translated by J. H. Vince. Loeb Classical Library. London: Harvard University Press.

Engberg-Pedersen, Troels. 1996. Is There an Ethical Dimension to Aristotelian Rhetoric? In *Essays on Aristotle's Rhetoric*, ed. Amélie Rorty, 16–141. Berkeley: University of California Press.

Gagarin, Michael. 1978. Self-Defense in Athenian Homicide Law. *Greek, Roman and Byzantine Studies* 19 (2): 111–120.

Grimaldi, William M.A. 1972. *Studies in the Philosophy of Aristotle's Rhetoric.* Wiesbaden: Franz Steiner Verlag GMBH.

Kennedy, George A. 1991. Introduction. In *On Rhetoric: A Theory of Civic Discourse.* New York: Oxford University Press.

Leighton, Stephen R. 1996. Aristotle and the Emotions. In *Essays on Aristotle's Rhetoric*, ed. Amelie Oksenberg Rorty, 206–237. Berkeley: University of California Press.

Nielsen, Karen M. 2007. Dirtying Aristotle's Hands? Aristotle's Analysis of 'Mixed Acts' in the Nicomachean Ethics III, 1. *Phronesis* 52 (3): 270–300.

Nussbaum, Martha Craven. 1996. Aristotle on Emotions and Rational Persuasion. In *Essays on Aristotle's Rhetoric*, ed. Amelie Oksenberg Rorty, 303–323. Berkeley: University of California Press.

Rapp, Christof. 2018. Dispassionate Judges Encountering Hotheaded Aristotelians. In *Aristotle on Emotions in Law and Politics*, ed. Liesbeth Huppes-Cluysenaer and Nuno M.M.S. Coelho. Dordrecht: Springer.

Reeve, C.D.C. 1996. Philosophy, Politics and Rhetoric in Aristotle. In *Essays on Aristotle's Rhetoric*, ed. Amélie Rorty, 191–205. Berkeley: University of California Press.

van Straalen, Humber. 2018. Remorse and Virtue Ethics. In *Aristotle on Emotions in Law and Politics*, ed. Liesbeth Huppes-Cluysenaer and Nuno M.M.S. Coelho. Dordrecht: Springer.

Yack, Bernard. 2006. Rhetoric and Public Reasoning: An Aristotelian Understanding of Political Deliberation. *Political Theory* 34 (4): 417–438.

Chapter 20
Aristotle's Political Friendship (politike philia) as Solidarity

Misung Jang

Abstract Aristotle's concept of friendship (philia), in particular the friendship between citizens, has had a significant impact on modern political philosophy. In a just state, citizens experience friendship with each other in that they wish each other well for their own sake and do things for each other even though they do not know each other. An important idea that runs throughout Aristotle's ethical and political works is that citizens aim at promoting the common good. Aristotle defines political friendship as a concord (homonoia) which is a friendship of utility that comprises legal friendship and moral friendship. Political friendship is elaborated in the different constitutions (*EN* VIII.10, *Pol.* III.5, IV.2) and can concern different relationships—between citizens, between cities, and among human beings (*EN* VIII and IX). Political friendship creates concord in society and prevents violence and strife. Aristotle's concept of political friendship could thus serve as model for contemporary communities, satisfying a growing need for social and global unity beyond liberty or justice. Aristotle insists that friendship (philia) is virtue, and concerns emotion and noble actions aimed at living well together. Therefore, political friendship is the greatest of blessings for the state, since it is the best safeguard against revolution and preserves the unity of the state (*Pol.* 1262b7–8).

20.1 Introduction

Political friendship plays an important role in Aristotle's *Politics*,[1] which aims at the public good among citizens. For the modern reader it is challenging to realize that Aristotle is emphasizing the need in political life for friendship as a bond of citizens beyond mutual interests. "Solidarity", "Tolerance", "Recognition", "Benevolence", "Love" or "Humanism" have currently become of main importance in the field of politics, esteemed by all citizens to the same degree and understood as

---

[1]Edition used: Aristotle, *The complete works of Aristotle: the Revised Oxford Translation.* Edited by Jonathan Barnes. Three works are especially relevant for Aristotle's political theory: *Nicomachean Ethics, Eudemian Ethics*, and *Politics.*

M. Jang (✉)
Faculty of Philosophy, Soongsil University, Seoul, South Korea
e-mail: misung91@gmail.com

© Springer International Publishing AG 2018   417
L. Huppes-Cluysenaer, N.M.M.S. Coelho (eds.), *Aristotle on Emotions in Law and Politics*, Law and Philosophy Library 121, DOI 10.1007/978-3-319-66703-4_20

an interactive relationship in which subjects mutually sympathize with each other's various different ways of life. These terms are rooted in the way Aristotle develops the concept of friendship (philia) in the *Nicomachean Ethics*[2] (*EN* 1155a22–27). In a just state, citizens experience friendship for each other in that they wish each other well for their own sake, do things for others even though they do not know each other, and aim at the common good. This is one of the most important issues running throughout Aristotle's ethical and political works. Aristotle insists that:

> Moreover, friendship would seem to hold cities together, and legislators would seem to be more concerned about it than about justice. For concord (homonoia) would seem to be similar to friendship, and they aim at concord among all, while they try above all to expel civil conflict, which is enmity. Further, if people are friends, they have no need of justice, but if they are just they need friendship in addition; the justice that is most just seems to belong to friendship. (*EN* 1155a24–29, trans. T. Irwin)

Modern scholars, such as M. Nussbaum[3] and R. Mulgan[4] are wont to recruit Aristotle for the contemporary political discussion, and core ideas of it, as "sharing the common good", "how to live as a citizen with others", "emotional bonding among citizens" or "personal virtue and social justice," lead to ongoing contestation in interpreting Aristotle's Ethics and Politics.

In this manner, solidarity, which refers to the concept of citizenship in a moral community, has become a famous term in contemporary political philosophy; it translates the ideal political norm of liberty and equality and discusses the emotional bonding among members beyond justice.[5] The concept of solidarity was in fact, introduced into the field of sociology by David Émile Durkheim with the publication of *The Division of Labour in Society* in 1893,[6] in which he presents an empirical approach to solidarity. He differentiates between two concepts of solidarity: for primitive societies a mechanic solidarity and for developed societies an organic solidarity. Lawrence Wilde uses a normative definition of human solidarity as a feeling of sympathy shared by subjects within and between groups.[7] In Jacques Derrida's *The Politics of Friendship* (1997),[8] the problem of relating intimate emotional bonds to a wider social and political commitment i.e., to solidarity, is discussed, and for Erich Fromm loving one's neighbor does not involve

---

[2]Editions used: *Nicomachean Ethics*, edited by Terence Irwin and Nicomachean Ethics, Clarendon Aristotle Series.

[3]Especially, see Nussbaum (1986, 2001, 2013).

[4]Mulgan (1977).

[5]Other scholars, especially Michael Sandel, Michael Walzer, and Amitai Etzioni are often faulted for undermining community feeling (or political affection or friendship), even though they insist they inherit Aristotle's viewpoints, especially justice as a virtue.

[6]Durkheim (2014).

[7]For the history of solidarity, see Wilde (2013).

[8]Derrida (1997).

transcending human nature but something that radiates from it.[9] Jill Frank emphasizes political friendship as sharing in the benefits of an effective practice, and in this sense, politics involves using others to promote collective aims.[10] Hannah Arendt, however, rejects this kind of view which is based on utilitarianism, claiming that the kind of love that citizens feel for each other means having respect and closeness.[11]

In this chapter it will be concluded that Aristotle's political friendship should specifically be understood to mean both political and moral solidarity. It will study how Aristotle developed the ideal city-state (*polis*) through friendship (*philia*) and concern with each other's goodwill in a manner that can also inspire modern thinking. The spotlight will be turned on Aristotle' notion of political friendship (*politike philia*): Can citizens reciprocally like and act in the interest of fellow citizens whom they do not personally know and whose existence even may be unknown to them? Is a state, animated by political friendship, an ideal? Can we choose to live together as rational actors, while we would not have chosen to do so if we did not already had some sort of affection for each other as an irrational disposition? How can the city have a foundation, which appears to be irrational and at the same time rational?

To answer those questions, we should examine Aristotle's conception of the political friendship in the *Nicomachean Ethics, Eudemian Ethics*, and *Politics*. Among the different interpretations of the political friendship, we will examine firstly, how the features of political friendship are different from personal friendship and next, concord (*homonoia*) as political friendship, specifically (Sect. 20.3) regarding the question whether political friendship is a friendship of utility or perfect friendship. Then the inquiry will turn to the way Aristotle differentiates between various political friendships in different constitutions (Sect. 20.4) and in relation to different objects (Sect. 20.5). Finally, it will be explained how according to Aristotle political friendship can be achieved and maintained as the greatest of blessings for the state, since it is the best safeguard against revolution, and creates the unity of the state (*Pol.* 1262b7–8). I shall argue that Aristotle's concept of political friendship as solidarity is the precondition for the state and that through it citizens do not merely live in the same place, but all participate in the state's common goods, and this way ensure the state's continued existence. By extension, interpreting Aristotle's work on friendship in this light, it is hoped that this paper offers a contribution to a contemporary understanding of Aristotle's political friendship as solidarity.

---

[9]Humans find fulfilment and happiness only in relatedness and solidarity' with their fellow humans. Humanistic ethics affirms life through the unfolding of human powers, provided that this empowerment is not at the expense of others, for this would be tantamount to evil. In this conception, virtue is regarded as self-responsibility and vice as irresponsibility. See Fromm (2003).

[10]Frank (2005), pp. 150–151 and 161–163.

[11]Bryan (2009), pp. 758–759.

20.2 Personal Friendship (philia) and Political Friendship (politike philia)

Philia is not easy to translate into English, since *philia* as such means the relation between friends as well as the emotion for ones friends or the disposition to make friends. *Philia* is usually translated as friendship, but: one can love or hold dear everything, from a cup of coffee to friends or God. For Aristotle, *philia* indicates the relations between marriage partners, parents and children, siblings, lovers, and even fellow citizens. Aristotle specifies the core common to all these relationships in the *Rhetoric*[12] (*Rhet.* 1380b–1381a) and especially in the *Nicomachean Ethics* (*EN* 1155a1–1172a15), presenting a list of various features by which *philia* is said to be defined: (1) Wishing and doing good or apparent good for the sake of the other; (2) Wishing the other to exist and to live for his own sake (which is what mothers, and friends who have quarreled, experience); (3) Spending time together and choosing the same things; (4) Experiencing pain and pleasure together with one's friend (which happens most of all in the case of mothers).[13]

These features of *philia* show us that Aristotle's *philia* is understood not as emotion, but as action or as a state related to a virtue. According to Aristotle *philia* is a virtue, or involves virtues (*EN* 1155a4):

> Friendship, then, consists more in loving; and people who love their friends are praised; hence, it would seem, loving is the virtue of friends. (*EN* 1159a35–1159b1, trans. T. Irwin)

Love is, of course, emotion, since the opposite of love, hate, is emotion, too,[14] but Aristotle focuses more on actions and states to explain *philia*, since *philia* is worth choosing and is related to virtuous activity and happiness.

> Loving (philesis) would seem to be a feeling, but friendship (philia) is a state. For loving is directed no less toward inanimate things, but reciprocal loving requires decision, and decision comes from a state; and [good people] wish good to the beloved for his own sake in accord with their state, not their feeling. (*EN* 1157b30–33, trans. T. Irwin)

---

[12]Edition used: *The Complete Works of Aristotle: the Revised Oxford Translation.* Edited by Jonathan Barnes.

[13]Cooper (1980, p. 300) explains that *philia* is (1) mutual awareness and liking, (2) a reciprocal wishing the other well for the other's sake, and (3) a reciprocal, practical "doing" of things for that other may be considered the denominators common to all friendships throughout Aristotle's works. Here we must notice friendship is not merely an emotion; it requires "actual social interaction," active engagement in one another's lives (*EN* 1157b, 1171b–1172a, and *Pol.* 1280b). But Price (1989), chapter 5 who is another expert of Aristotle's *philia* disagrees with Cooper. For more explanation, see Schwarzenbach (1996), p. 100.

[14]Aristotle emphasizes friendship as 'feeling' in the friendship of pleasure between young people. He says "for their lives are guided by their feelings, and they pursue above all what is pleasant for themselves and what is at hand...Young people are prone to erotic passion, since this mostly accords with feelings, and is caused by pleasure; that is why they love and quickly stop, often changing in a single day" (*EN* 1156a32–1156b4). I think that Aristotle believes the love for feeling is the main characteristic aspect for erotic love (*eros*) as the one of kinds of the friendship of pleasure, instead of *philia*.

Like a virtue, friendship is associated with a mean state and a praiseworthy activity as Aristotle already mentions in the doctrine of the mean in the *Nicomachean Ethics*. Living together (*suzen*) is the chief characteristic of friendship (*EN* 1157b21).

In order to explain a variety of friendships, Aristotle categorizes friendship according to what friends would give and take, differentiating between three kinds (for pleasure, utility or virtue) which are more or less concurrent with life-stages (youth, prime of life, and old age). Friendship for virtue is the most perfect (*teleia*) and long lasting form (*EN* 1156b7), but Aristotle emphasizes that even in both less perfect types of friendship for pleasure and advantage the friendship (*EN* 1157a15ff) has some resemblance to the friendship for virtue:

> Friendship for the sake of pleasure bears a resemblance to this complete sort, since good people are also pleasant to each other. And friendship for utility also resembles it, since good are also useful to each other. (...) Friendship has been assigned, then, to these species. Base people (phauloi) will be friends for pleasure or utility, since they are similar in that way. But good people (agathoi) will be friends because of themselves, since they are friends insofar as they are good. These, then, are friends without qualification (haplos); the others are friends coincidentally (sumbebekos) and by being similar to these. (*EN* 1157a1–b5, trans. T. Irwin)

This is the main concept of Aristotle's friendship (*philia*): every friendship involves equality and reciprocity between friends, and friendship is not only necessary, but also fine (*EN* 1155a30). After explaining the features and the kinds of personal friendship (*philia*), Aristotle moves on to the political friendship. In a community, Aristotle claims:

> Further, if people are friends, they have no need of justice, but if they are just, they need friendship in addition; and the justice that is most just seems to belong to friendship. (*EN* 1155a27–29, trans. T. Irwin)

If justice is the common arbiter, friendship lessens the need for it because friends are willing to compromise with and love each other. Consequently, on this reading, friendship makes law or justice less necessary. Nevertheless, when Aristotle connects friendship and justice together, they are not antithetical; in all communities, the purpose of justice is to negotiate conflict, and friendship also serves to unify people, to realize living together and acting together with the help of affective bonding.

In this sense, political friendship is the necessary resource for politics. It makes the political community more secure, more permanent and more prudent in seeking the political good. For Aristotle, a state without political friendship can never be a truly just one. Friendly political relations are a necessary component or constitutive element of a just state, and all members in a state—just like in any community—should be friends because of their citizenship, according to Aristotle. But, how can citizens be friends even though they never see each other?

Political and personal friendship have the following different features: it is true that (1) among political friends intimate knowledge and a close emotional bond are absent; (2) political friends have a general concern (*EN* 1167a28–29); (3) the core of political friendship is *homonoia* which is tied to the mind and is translated into English as "agreement," "unanimity," or "concord"; (4) it appears in different forms in different political communities such as city-states and households; and (5) it needs a public educative process. We will focus in this chapter on the third and fourth aspect i.e. on *homonoia* as political friendship and its features connected to the three different kinds of friendship belonging to six different political systems as distinguished by Aristotle.

20.3 Homonoia (Concord)

Aristotle explains that good will (*eunoia*) and concord (*homonoia*) appear to be features of friendship in the *Nicomachean Ethics*. Good will is not identical with friendship as good will would not elicit cooperation with others in any action, although it would seem to be a beginning of friendship (*EN* 1166b30–1167b3–4). Concord, however, seems to be political friendship, since it is concerned with advantage and with what affects life as a whole (*EN* 1167b3–4). According to M. Pakaluk,[15] concord (*homonoia*) can be understood as (1) practical agreement between citizens in city-state (*EN* 1167a22–b4), (2) the ability, peculiar to good persons, to get along well generally with other good persons (*EN* 1167b6–9), and (3) as what might be called self-concord, some kind of consistency and steadiness of purpose over time (*EN* 1167b5–7).

Homonoia means like (homo)—mindedness (nous), and unlike the term "stasis" it was a new word, which despite its frequent use made its appearance only late in the fifth century.[16] Political friendship occurs when each has the same opinion about things to be done; for instance, when both the common people and the decent party want the best people to rule, since when that happens both sides get what they seek (*EN* 1167a26–33). Aristotle devotes only nineteen lines of text in the *Eudemian Ethics*[17] (1241a15–33) to *homonoia*[18]; and thirty lines in the *Nicomachean Ethics* (1167a22–b16),[19] The two texts run parallel and cover much of the same ground. However, *homonoia* is not mentioned in *Politics* (related terms in *Pol.* 1261b32, 1306a9, 1330a18).

Antiphon, a Sophist, wrote a tract *On Homonoia*[20] in which he suggests that *homonoia* is the political reconciliation between opposing factions to live together.

---

[15] Aristotle (1998).

[16] Kalimtzis (2000), pp. 51–52.

[17] Edition used: *The Complete Works of Aristotle: the Revised Oxford Translation.* Edited by Jonathan Barnes.

[18] Here Aristotle mentions that "*homonoia* is the friendship of fellow citizens" (*EE* 1241a33).

[19] Here Aristotle mentions that "homonoia also appears to be a features of friendship" (*EN* 1167a22) and "homonoia, then, is apparently political friendship" (*EN* 1167b3).

[20] Antiphon (2002).

According to Xenophon,[21] (*Memorabilia* 4.4.16. 5–10), *homonoia* is essentially obedience to the laws, while Plato identifies concord, friendship, and internal harmony[22] (*Rep.* 351d5, 432a7, *Polit.* 311b9). Cicero points out that *homonoia* lies in a balance of interests. In the *De Amicitia* XII.40[23] he discusses the conflicts of loyalties generated by political obligation and private friendship. In this sense, Aristotle's thoughts form part of a long tradition.[24]

Therefore, the first feature of concord is connected with factions, conflicts, or wars; concord is not just solid, but it combines opposites, contradictions, and differences. This is why Aristotle criticizes Plato's utopian proposal in the Republic (462c); he claims that it is not the goal of the state to seek a perfect unity among the citizens, since a city-state is a complex and mixed whole by nature. He insists that when all the citizens call the same thing theirs, this may in a certain sense be a fine thing, but it is impracticable; for that which is common to the greatest number has the least care bestowed upon it (*Pol.* 1261b30–34). Aristotle always considers concord in relation to the plurality in a state, saying that

> The error of Socrates must be attributed to the false supposition from which he starts. Unity there should be, both of family and of the state, but in some respects only. For there is a point at which a state may attain such a degree of unity as to be no longer a state, or at which, without actually ceasing to exist, it will become an inferior state, like harmony passing into unison, or rhythm which has been reduced to a single foot. The state, as I was saying, is a plurality, which should be united and made into a community by education. (*Pol.* 1263b30–37, trans. B. Jowett)

Aristotle presents the ideal city-state not as a conflict-free perfect unity or harmony, but as a concord through conflicts or factions of the whole.

Next, Aristotle uses three different terms (1) political friendship (politike philia), (2) legal friendship (*nomike philia*), and (3) concord (*homonoia*). Unfortunately, Aristotle does not explain each clearly, and sometimes he regards political friendship as legal friendship, but at other moments, he regards political friendship as concord (*EN* 1167b2–3, *EE* 1241a32–33). Not all legal friendships entail concord (*homonoia*), but all political friendships require advantage, meaning that they aim at a legally bound "thing."

> But the bad prefer natural goods to a friend and none of them loves a man so much as things; therefore they are not friends. The proverbial 'community among friends' is not found among them; the friend is made a part of things, not things regarded as part of the friend. (*EE* 1237b31–34, trans. J. Solomon)

Aristotle thinks that in every community there is some form of justice and friendship, and that the extent of the association is the extent of the friendships, and the extent to which justice exists between them. The claims of justice, like

---

[21]Xenophon (2013).

[22]Plato (1997).

[23]Cicero (1887).

[24]Recitation in Stern-Gillet (1995), p. 149.

friendship, are between brothers different from those between parents and children for example. So all forms of community are alike:

> All communities [mentioned], however, would seem to be parts of the political community. For people keep company for some advantage and to supply some contribution to their life. And the political community as well [as the others] seems both to have been originally formed and to endure for advantage, for legislators also aim at advantage, and the common advantage is said to be just.[25] (*EN* 1160a8–14, trans. T. Irwin)

This is the second feature of the political friendship and justice as well; concord is concerned with advantage and with what affects life as a whole (*EN* 1167b3–4).

20.4   Political Friendship for Utility or for Virtue?

Aristotle classifies political friendship between citizens as concord which is a form akin to advantage friendship in his texts (*EE* 1242b22, *EN* 1161b13) and he never mentions that it is like the friendship of virtue. Should it not be concluded that political friendship could not be friendship for virtue? But another problem arises: right after Aristotle mentions that concord is political friendship, since it is concerned with advantage (*EN* 1167b3–4), he seems to contradict himself by saying that this sort of concord (*homonoia*) is found in decent people (*EN* 1167b5). Furthermore, political friendship seems to be more powerful than just use-friendship; in *Politics*, in fact, Aristotle explicitly emphasizes that the political bond is not merely a contractual arrangement for the purpose of utility (*Pol.* 1280a9–13), but is concerned with making citizens good (*Pol.* 1280b24). If political friendship is characterized by both virtue and utility, the political union must be one in which members are virtuous. Most people, however, are not decent people, and therefore according to the latter meaning of concord, it would not be possible for them to participate in political friendship. In this sense, Kouloumbaritses[26] could be right when he laments that political friendship would thus become limited to a few noble persons who have a virtuous character, and thus would lose its democratic character.[27]

Then, the only solution of this problem is to imagine that Aristotle is suggesting a utopian ideal that lacks any empirical basis. This would mean that his view on Ethics has little practical use for political friendship, but this is not Aristotle's manner.

In order to approach this riddle of the inconsistency between the friendship for utility and for virtue concerning political friendship, many commentators have tried to give plausible answers. On the one hand, Ernest Barker[28] and Anthony

---

[25]This idea is also mentioned in 1162a20–22: "For the other animals, the community goes only as far as childbearing, but also for the benefits in their life."

[26]Kouloumbaritses (1981), pp. 198–199.

[27]Recitation in Kalimtzis (2000), pp. 63–64.

[28]Barker (1959).

Kronman[29] insist that political friendship equates with virtue friendship; political friendship would be an extension of virtue friendship. They argue that political friendship is found in decent people, and it aims at noble actions which every citizen has to do as a virtue.

> Hence there arise in cities family connexions, brotherhoods, common sacrifices, amusements which draw men together. But these are created by friendship, for to choose to live together is friendship. The end of the state is the good life, and these are the means towards it. And the state is the union of families and villages in a perfect and self-sufficing life, by which we mean a happy and honourable life. Our conclusion, then, is that political society exists for the sake of noble actions, and not of living together. (*Pol.* 1280b36–1281a4, trans. B. Jowett)

This way it even could exclude the less virtuous members of the community from citizenship. Justice concerned with negotiating differences of opinion is less necessary if political friendship is robust and makes political friends agree with each other.

On the other hand, Bernard Yack[30] insists that the political friendship is a friendship for utility; Aristotle never classifies political friendship as virtue friendship, but as utility friendship.[31] Cities may be concerned with virtue and virtue friendship may evolve among the citizens, but the genesis of political friendship is utility.[32]

> But civic friendship is that resting on equality; it is based on utility; and just as cities are friends to one another, so in the like way are citizens. (*EE* 1242b23–24, trans. J. Solomon)

John Cooper[33] has challenged these suggestions by arguing that the friendship of utility is divided into two different friendships—legal friendship (*nomike philia*) and moral friendship (*ethike philia*). For instance, political friendship is the legal friendship that is based on contracts or agreements,[34] but it is the moral friendship if it is based for example on the belief that my friend will pay the money back. Cooper cites the following passage:

> Political friendship, then, looks to the agreement and the thing, moral friendship to the choice; here then we have a truer justice, and a friendly justice. The reason for quarrel is that moral friendship (ethike philia) is more noble, but useful friendship more necessary; men start, then, by proposing to be moral friends, i.e. friends through excellence; but as

---

[29]Kronman (1979).

[30]Yack (1993), p. 105.

[31]Cartland says that Yack does not consider the question of whether political pluralism (i.e., differences of opinion regarding moral dilemmas) is compatible with prudence and, therefore, whether the polity can achieve eudaimonia. Cartland (2011), p. 40.

[32]But Yack (1985) insisted that political friendship has the double meanings, both friendship for utility and for virtue in his older article, "Community and Conflict in Aristotle's Political Philosophy".

[33]Cooper (1980), p. 305.

[34]Stern-Gillet (1995), p. 149 confirms the rational meaning of political friendship, saying that "concord (homonoia) or friendship inevitably prevails between those who obey reason and recognize the irrelevance of such contingent factors as custom, ethnicity, and geography."

soon as some private interest arises, they show clearly they were not so. For the multitude aim at the noble only when they have plenty of everything else; and at noble friendship similarly. (*EE* 1243a33–1243b1, trans. J. Solomon)

Aristotle, in fact, does not explain clearly what moral friendship is and what the relationship between legal friendship and moral friendship is. I agree with Cooper when he points out that there are two different kinds of friendship for utility and explains political friendship in opposition to other scholars who try to separate friendship for utility from friendship for virtue. Aristotle even claims that people want to have both friendships.

Civic friendship, then, claims to be one based on equality. But of the friendship of utility there are two kinds, the strictly legal and the moral. Civic friendship looks to equality and to the object as sellers and buyers do; hence the proverb 'a fixed wage for a friend'. When, then, this civic friendship proceeds by contract, it is of the legal kind; but when each of the two parties leaves the return for his services to be fixed by the other, we have the moral friendship, that of comrades. Therefore recrimination is very frequent in this sort of friendship; and the reason is that it is unnatural; for friendships based on utility and based on excellence are different; but these wish to have both together, associating together really for the sake of utility, but representing their friendship as moral, like that of good men; pretending to trust one another they make out their friendship to be not merely legal. (*EE* 1242b35–1243a1, trans. J. Solomon)

This passage shows that according to Aristotle political friendship as legal friendship is based on the utility of friendship and that it operates on the principle of interests and concerns things. However, the passage shows also that Aristotle confirms that even in the context of friendship for utility people also try to reach moral or character friendship, which is based on trust and are also concerned with virtue and wish to share all goods in common. As a result, there are mostly two types of friendship comprised in the friendship for utility, while people are on the one hand acting as seller and buyer by contract and on the other as comrades and citizens by trust and choice (*prohairesis*) (*EE* 1243a33). Both—legal and moral— are therefore forms of political friendship, when they are oriented at utility.

For the next step, we must illuminate political friendship in complex situations and within various scales, insofar as political friendship incorporates the dual nature of philia, both legal and moral friendship. Our main questions have to do with how the polity achieves the political good, not merely economic harmony, and whether the friendship that supports the search for the political good allows for differing points of view. Aristotle says that

In the deviation, however, justice is found only to a slight degree; and hence the same is true of friendship. There is least of it in the worst deviation; for in a tyranny there is little or no friendship. (*EN* 1161a31–34, trans. T. Irwin)

Aristotle tries to illustrate the complex concept of political friendship in practical life in *Nicomachean Ethics* and in *Politics*. His examples are filled with contradictions which explain the different role of political friendships in six constitutions.

20.5 Political Friendship (politike philia) in Different Constitutions

Aristotle suggests a sixfold scheme of constitutions (*EN* 1160a32–1161a9). The six regimes are envisaged in a way analogous to friendship in the household: monarchies are characterized by parental friendship, aristocracies by marital friendship, and polities by brotherly friendship. The analogy between the household and the city that Aristotle uses, leads one to believe that the household and the city have a great deal in common. Aristotle claims that the household provides models for the kinds of friendship in the city (*EN* 1160b24).

Politeia	Good	Bad	Household
Ruled by one	Kingship	Tyranny	Father–Son
Ruled by a few	Aristocracy	Oligarchy	Wife–Husband
Ruled by the many	Polity	Democracy	Brothers

In the view of Aristotle, politics is considered an extension of household management. He writes that in the household first we have the sources and springs of friendship, of political organization, and of justice (*EE* 1242b1). The community of a father and his son has the structure of kingship, insofar as the father takes care of his son, since kingship is said to be paternal rule. However, the father's rule is tyrannical, when he treats his son as slave, as if the master's advantage is achieved in it. The community of wife and husband appears aristocratic, when the husband commits to his wife what is fitting for her, but if the husband controls everything, then he changes it into an oligarchy. The community of brothers is like a timocratic system, since they are equal except insofar as they differ in age. Democracy appears most of all in dwellings without a master and also in those where the ruler is weak and everyone is free to do what he likes (*EN* 1160b24–1161a9).

For Aristotle, therefore, political friendship cannot be a fixed one, but is diversified for each of the political systems. Aristotle insists that:

> all these definitions are appropriate to some friendship, but none to a single unique thing, friendship. Hence there are many definitions, and each appears to belong to a single thing, viz. friendship, though really it does not, e.g. the purpose to maintain the friend's existence. (*EE* 1244a25–28, trans. J. Solomon)

20.6 Political Friendship (politike philia) in Relation to Different Objects (Especially Between Human Beings)

Beyond the different types of friendship in different constitutions, we must consider additionally three different kinds of political friendship in different objects: among citizens, among cities and among human beings. The first two are already explicitly considered by Aristotle,[35] while the question whether Aristotle also considered the latter is the specific interest of many scholars, who currently study the boundaries of solidarity in political philosophy. The three objects of political friendship, especially friendship between cities and among human beings, have not been studied before, but these studies seem inevitable to bring some connections between modern views of solidarity and Aristotle's political friendship. This is relevant because Aristotle's method in ethics and politics is to examine various cases and common opinions (*endoxa*) as the starting-point of inquiry (*EN* 1145b2–7), and in the beginning of *Politics* he suggests political friendship has many aspects;

> As in other departments of science, so in in politics, the compound should always be resolved into the simple elements or least parts of the whole. We must therefore look at the elements of which the state is composed, in order that we may see in what the different kinds of rule differ from one another, and whether any scientific result can be attained about each one of them. (*Pol.* 1252a18–23, trans. B. Jowett)

Aristotle employs this mode of inquiry in *Physics*[36] (*Phys.* 187b11–13) and in Poetics, for example in his analysis of tragedy[37] (*Poet.* 1450a7–15). In *Politics* the state may be divided into parts in several different ways:

> For sometimes all of these parts participate in the constitution and sometimes a smaller or a larger number of them. It is clear therefore that there must necessarily be several forms of constitution differing in kind from one another, inasmuch as these parts differ in kind among themselves. (*Pol.* 1290a5–8, trans. B. Jowett)

After Aristotle has examined political friendship among citizens, which I call the first and central object of political friendship, he considers the function of friendship between cities to hold states together (*EN* 1155a24–25). This I will call the second object of political *philia*; for people include among friends also those who are friends for utility, as cities are—since alliances between cities seem to aim at expediency (*EN* 1157a 26–27). Aristotle insists:

> For if one were actually to bring the sites of two cities together into one, so that the city-walls of Megara and those of Corinth were contiguous, even so they would not be one city; nor would they if they enacted rights of intermarriage with each other, although intermarriage between citizens is one of the elements of community which are characteristic of states. And similarly even if certain people lived in separate places yet not so far apart as not to have intercourse, but had laws to prevent their wronging one another in their interchange of products...nevertheless they had no mutual dealings in anything else except such things as exchange of commodities and military alliance, even then this would still not be a state. (*Pol.* 1280b13–22, trans. B. Jowett)

---

[35]"But civic friendship is that resting on equality; it is based on utility; and just as cities are friends to one another, so in the like way are citizen." (*EE* 1242b24, trans. J. Solomon).

[36]Editions used for *Physics* and *Poetics*: *The Complete Works of Aristotle: the Revised Oxford Translation.* Edited by Jonathan Barnes.

[37]"There are six parts consequently of every tragedy, that make it the sort of tragedy it is, viz. a plot, characters, diction, thought, spectacle, and melody; two of them arising from the means, one from the manner, and three from the objects of the dramatic imitation, and there is nothing else besides these six..." (*Poet.* 1450a7–15 Trans. I. Bywater).

In order to make an alliance between cities or states, it is not enough to connect them only in relation to place, intermarriage or law. It is clear that besides having things in common between two cities such as alliance and trade, something else is needed. The city and its citizens is not the sharing of a place or a thing such as trade or marriage, but it should have the necessary conditions to be a city for the sake of the good life in common. This is not just living together in the same place, but good practices through political friendship for the common good. These would contribute most to such a state, and also to an alliance between states. One could think here of things such as celebration or thanksgiving festivals among all citizens in a dual alliance (*EN* 1160a19–28).

> But if it is pleasant for a man himself to live well and also his friend, and in their common life to engage in mutually helpful activity, their partnership surely would be above all in things included in the end. Therefore, men should contemplate in common and feast in common, only not on the pleasure of food or on necessary pleasure; such society does not seem to be true society, but sensuous enjoyment. (*EE* 1245b2–6, trans. J. Solomon)

Aristotle explains in the *Nicomachean Ethics* how the true society could be possible through fine actions in common, claiming that virtuous citizens are always eager to act just or temperate in accord with the virtues, as a moral competition in their common life (*EN* 1168b20–1169a8). This competition is different from other competitions in which one person's gain is another's loss; one man wins the competition about doing fine things, and others also benefit from this.

Furthermore, concerning friendship between human beings, Aristotle writes:

> Members of the same species and human beings most of all, have a natural friendship for each other; that is why we praise friends of humanity. And in our travels we can see how every human being is akin and beloved to a human being. (*EN* 1155a20–23, trans. T. Irwin)

Several lines above this passage Aristotle has argued that friendship (*philia*) occurs not only among human beings, but also among birds and most animals, and [among] those belonging to the same clan (*tois homothnesi*), especially human beings; whence we praise those who are lovers of humankind (*philanthropous*). I think that this is the third object of political *philia* as outlined, but Aristotle does not discuss it in detail in the *Nicomachean Ethics*.

Actually, Aristotle calls this natural friendship instead of political friendship. This friendship (*philia*) represents the cosmopolitan outlook that was first developed by the Cynics and Stoics in the Ancient Greek world of the fifth century BC, and got its full development in the late eighteenth century by the work of the great Enlightenment philosopher Immanuel Kant (1724–1804). The Cynics took their inspiration from Socrates, reputed to be the first to claim to be a citizen of the world. Cosmopolitanism became a significant political doctrine through the latter teachings of Stoics, who held that human beings all belong to the same species and should be thought of as living in a world community, governed by natural law and pursuing a goal of harmony. Zeno and the Stoics think that this sort of community is in the heavens, where only sages are one with themselves, with the universe, and with the gods as true friends.[38]

Today's cosmopolitanism holds the idea that we have a moral obligation to care for all human beings without any preference toward national, religious, or group affiliations and each human being has equal moral worth and moral responsibility in a universal scope. Especially M. Nussbaum connects this idea with Aristotle's work i.e. with

what humans share in being human and what is required for humans to flourish.[39]

We therefore now want to examine whether Aristotle's political friendship can be extended towards the relation between human beings.

Political friendship indeed comprises various aspects of friendship. It emerges as benevolent feeling, sympathy, or mercy toward one's friends, but this not a sufficient condition, since it also requires concord based on intelligence and even virtue as the mean state. Aristotle insists that friendship (*philia*) is a state (*hexis*) (*EE* 1234b28, 1237a34), e.g. a virtue or that it implies virtue, and that it is very necessary with a view to living (*EN* 1155a1–2). Aristotle describes love as a passion and friendship as a state, because love may be felt just as much towards lifeless things, while mutual love involves choice and choice springs from a state. Men wish well to those whom they love, for their sake, not as result of passion, but as a result of being in a state (*EN* 1157b29–32).

Certainly, Aristotle also sees the need for a social bond in the state and thinks that it can be created by festivals:

But all these communities would seem to be subordinate to the political community, since it aims not at some advantages close at hand, but at advantage for the whole of life. [We can see this in the arrangements that cities make for religious festivals. For] in performing sacrifices and arranging gatherings for these, people both accord honors to the gods and provide themselves with pleasant relaxation. For the long-established sacrifices and gatherings appear to take place after harvesting of the crops, as a sort of first-fruits, since this was the time when people used to be most at leisure [and the time when relaxation would be most advantageous for the whole life]. (*EN* 1160a22–29, trans. T. Irwin)

Besides, Aristotle indicates the need in the state for living well together and for noble actions, such as the pursuit of political excellence. These, then, are the possibilities Aristotle has in mind to realize the necessary unity in a political community. It is clear that Aristotle focuses more on the shared fine actions aiming at the common good, which arise from festivals or religious worship, than on the emotional bond created by these (*Pol.* 1280b36–1281a7).

---

[38]See more in Heater (2002), pp. 22–30 and Kalimtzis (2000), p. 66.
[39]Recitation Wilde (2013), pp. 3–6.

20.7 Public Education

Aristotle explains that friendship is revealed in different types, with each their own type of conduct: personal friends share something—pleasure, utility or virtue—for the sake of others; political friends exchange their things and achieve concord as solidarity. The relationship between political friendship and perfect friendship is no doubt complex. As Aristotle shows in *Politics*, political friendship as a friendship, which is both legal and moral, can be achieved by public education. Aristotle requires in this respect that we train our mean states including emotions and actions toward others, and he argues that this will generate good politics based on the foundation of friendship i.e. by sharing emotion, action, and virtue. Political friendship is seen by him as the cement in every state and even in the world.[40] Political friendship is a virtue for doing fine actions.[41]

This is the way Aristotle answers the questions he posed in *Politics*, i.e., what makes a city different from a chance gathering of people and from a group of persons who enter into trade relationships? What holds political community together? What makes it possible for human beings to live together and to take a noble action together? Aristotle points out that city-making is a matter of choice and friendship, saying that city-states are created by friendship, because friendship means rather to choose to live together than that it is a matter of justice and law (*Pol.* 1280b37). Friendship (*Philia*) is the greatest of blessings for the polis because it is the best safeguard against faction (*stasis*). The unity of the state, which Socrates praises most highly, appears to be, and is stated to be, the result (*ergon*) of friendship (*philia*) in various forms of relations (*Pol.* 1262b7–10).

In Aristotle's view, the political life of the city is centered on one effort; to achieve the political good which is the common life of a whole, which aims at self-sufficiency. The purpose of the city-state is not just living together but the conduct of noble actions (*Pol.* 1280b30–1281a3). And the state should be united and made into a community by education (*Pol.* 1263b37). This is why Aristotle mixes politics with ethics: good citizens working together in doing good actions will contribute to the good political life of all. In this manner, friendship is said to be a foundation for today's democratic practices.

Modern scholars, such as Jürgen Habermas, John Rawls, and Hannah Arendt, suggest a "post-westphalian" project to envision a globalizing world with solidarity, publicity, and a democratic framework as a key theme in political philosophy. Wendy Brown argues that tolerance is generally regarded as an unqualified achievement of the modern West to defuse conflict in contemporary struggles over identity, citizenship, and civilization and thus to realize a unity between

---

[40]Hutter (1978), p. 110.

[41]Schwarzenbach regards political friendship as 'care'; Aristotle repeatedly urges a "common care" (*koinon epimeleian*) when advising his statesmen in the *EN* 1180a2, and he uses the term 'care' (*epimeleia*) in a political context throughout his *Politics* (1261b27, 1263a27, 1293b13, 1299a20, 1300a5, 1325a7, 1328b12, 1335a7, 1395b20).

human beings. Nancy Fraser and Axel Honneth examine social justice issues as redistribution versus recognition to find out how to reduce the inequality, exploitation, and subordination that individuals and groups face in the contemporary world.[42]

Along with these movements, however, we need to reflect on discussions about common bonds between citizens in a state or among all human beings in a globalizing world and the role political friendship can play in holding together the more encompassing political communities. Aristotle does not think that we could have feelings of friendship for people who are remote from us or for people we know nothing about. His attention is focused rather on advantage friendship based on concord (*homonoia*) and virtue. This bond of friendship creates a concord in society that prevents violence and strife. In this sense, Aristotle's political friendship could serve as model for contemporary community, satisfying thus its ever growing need for social and global unity beyond liberty or justice. This will help us realize in what sense approaching each other as friends contributes to the political good life of the present in states as well as in the world.

References

Antiphon. 2002. In *The Fragments*, ed. Gerard J. Pendrick. Cambridge and New York: Cambridge University Press.

Aristotle. 1984a. Eudemian Ethics. In *The Complete Works of Aristotle: The Revised Oxford Translation*, ed. Jonathan Barnes and trans. J. Solomon. Princeton, NJ and Guildford, UK: Princeton University Press.

———. 1984b. Physics. In *The Complete Works of Aristotle: The Revised Oxford Translation*, ed. Jonathan Barnes and trans. R. P. Hardie and R. K. Gaye. Princeton, NJ and Guildford, UK: Princeton University Press.

———. 1984c. Poetics. In *The Complete Works of Aristotle: The Revised Oxford Translation*, ed. Jonathan Barnes and trans. I. Bywater. Princeton, NJ and Guildford, UK: Princeton University Press.

———. 1984d. Politics. In *The Complete Works of Aristotle: The Revised Oxford Translation*, ed. Jonathan Barnes and trans. B. Jowett. Princeton, NJ and Guildford, UK: Princeton University Press.

———. 1984e. Rhetoric. In *The Complete Works of Aristotle: The Revised Oxford Translation*, ed. Jonathan Barnes and trans. W. Rhys Roberts. Princeton, NJ and Guildford, UK: Princeton University Press.

———. 1998. *Nicomachean Ethics. Books VIII and IX Books VIII and IX*. Translated by Michael Pakaluk. Oxford and New York: Clarendon Press and Oxford University Press.

———. 1999. *Nicomachean Ethics*. Translated by Terence Irwin. Indianapolis, IN: Hackett Publishing.

Barker, Ernest. 1959. *The Political Thought of Plato and Aristotle*. New York: Dover Publications.

Bryan, Bradley. 2009. Approaching Others: Aristotle on Friendship's Possibility. *Political Theory*, September 25.

---

[42]Fraser and Honneth (2003).

Cartland, Jenifer. 2011. *Aristotle's Liberalism of Virtue: Unity, Disorder and Friendship*. Saarbrücken: LAP LAMBERT Academic Publishing.

Cicero, Marcus Tullius. 1887. In *Ethical Writings of Cicero: Cicero De Officiis, Cicero De Senectute, Cicero De Amicitia, Scipio's Dream*, ed. Andrew P. Peabody. Boston, MA: Little, Brown.

Cooper, John M. 1980. Aristotle on Friendship. In *Essays on Aristotle's Ethics*, ed. Amélie Rorty. Berkeley: University of California Press.

Derrida, Jacques. 1997. *Politics of Friendship*. London and New York: Verso.

Durkheim, Émile. 2014. *The Division of Labor in Society*. Edited by Steven Lukes and Translated by W. D. Halls. New York: Free Press.

Frank, Jill. 2005. *A Democracy of Distinction: Aristotle and the Work of Politics*. Chicago, IL: University of Chicago Press.

Fraser, Nancy, and Axel Honneth. 2003. *Redistribution or Recognition?: A Political-Philosophical Exchange*. London and New York: Verso.

Fromm, Erich. 2003. *Man for Himself: An Inquiry into the Psychology of Ethics*. London: Routledge.

Heater, Derek. 2002. *World Citizenship: Cosmopolitan Thinking and Its Opponents*. London: Continuum.

Hutter, Horst. 1978. *Politics as Friendship: The Origins of Classical Notions of Politics in the Theory and Practice of Friendship*. Waterloo, ON: Wilfrid Laurier University Press.

Kalimtzis, Kostas. 2000. *Aristotle on Political Enmity and Disease: An Inquiry into Stasis*. Albany: State University of New York Press.

Kouloumbaritses, L. 1981. Political Friendship in Aristotle. In *Aristotle and Politics*, ed. P. Demake, 198–199. Athens: Panteios School of Political Science.

Kronman, Anthony. 1979. Aristotle's Idea of Political Fraternity. *American Journal of Jurisprudence* 24 (1): 114–138.

Mulgan, R.G. 1977. *Aristotle's Political Theory: An Introduction for Students of Political Theory*. Oxford and New York: Clarendon Press.

Nussbaum, Martha Craven. 1986. *The Fragility of Goodness: Luck and Ethics in Greek Tragedy and Philosophy*. Cambridge and New York: Cambridge University Press.

———. 2001. *Upheavals of Thought: The Intelligence of Emotions*. Cambridge and New York: Cambridge University Press.

———. 2013. *Political Emotions: Why Love Matters for Justice*. Cambridge, MA: The Belknap Press of Harvard University Press.

Plato. 1997. *Complete Works*. Edited by John M. Cooper. Indianapolis, IN: Hackett Publishing.

Schwarzenbach, Sibyl A. 1996. On Civic Friendship. *Ethics* 107 (1): 97–128.

Stern-Gillet, Suzanne. 1995. *Aristotle's Philosophy of Friendship*. Albany: State University of New York Press.

Wilde, Lawrence. 2013. *Global Solidarity*. Edinburgh: Edinburgh University Press.

Xenophon. 2013. *Memorabilia; Oeconomicus*. Edited by Jeffrey Henderson and Translated by E. C. Marchant and O. J. Todd. Cambridge, MA: Harvard University Press.

Yack, Bernard. 1985. Community and Conflict in Aristotle's Political Philosophy. *Review of Politics* 47: 92–112.

———. 1993. *The Problems of a Political Animal: Community, Justice, and Conflict in Aristotelian Political Thought*. Berkeley: University of California press.

Chapter 21
Between Nomos and Pathos: Emotions in Aristotelian Theory of Adjudication and the Dual Process Theory

Mariusz Jerzy Golecki and Mateusz Franciszek Bukaty

Abstract Emotions play an important role in the Aristotelian theory of action since emotions can trigger action, including the actions of the judge. Aristotle concentrates on training habits of action to reach a state of mind conducive to coping with passions in a virtuous way. At the same time Aristotle observes that it is important that the law should rule rather than people. This requires that the judicial process be based on rational evaluation of the merits of a given case and optimal understanding of laws. The focus of this paper is on the antinomy, which arises from this double role of decisions—the choice between action (emotion) and deliberation (practical reason). The authors first discuss the virtue-centered approach. They concentrate on potential threats to impartiality and rational justification posed by individually fair decisions in complex cases. This problem cannot be resolved and is unavoidable in a virtue-centered approach. The second point of criticism of this approach is that it pays no attention to the interaction of reason and emotion in the judicial process. The authors then proceed to give an overview of the dual process theory, which does pay attention to this interconnectedness.

21.1 Introduction

The main purpose of this paper is to compare both the virtue-centered theory of adjudication, in which emotions seem play an important role and the Aristotelian concept of "emotion in action", as presented in *Nicomachean Ethics*,[1] with the contemporary findings on the dual process theory (DPT) concerning the theory of decision-making. Therefore, the topic of this paper concerns the relationship between emotion-driven aspects of a particular decision and the requirements of impersonality and objectivity. The justifiability of judicial decisions on the

---

[1]Edition used: Aristotle (2000).

M.J. Golecki (✉) • M.F. Bukaty
Faculty of Law, University of Lodz, Łódź, Poland
e-mail: mjgolecki76@gmail.com; mateuszbukaty@gmail.com

© Springer International Publishing AG 2018
L. Huppes-Cluysenaer, N.M.M.S. Coelho (eds.), *Aristotle on Emotions in Law and Politics*, Law and Philosophy Library 121, DOI 10.1007/978-3-319-66703-4_21

435

application of general rules to particular cases is crucial for adjudication, which can be defined as a process of taking decisions which are guided by the requirements of law and practical reason. These decisions play a double role. Firstly, they offer ultimate and authoritative solutions to particular conflicts. Secondly, they provide a publicly accessible justification for the adjudication. Aristotle observed that in some cases it is impossible to apply general rules to individual cases without changing their content and in such cases fairness requires departing from formal rules rather than abiding by them.

The research question of this paper concentrates on the antinomy between emotion as a component of moral actions, including adjudication, and the requirements of practical reason and justifiability. Firstly the question will be treated how a virtue-centered adjudication, controlled by reason, could possible and how it could be achieved according to Aristotle. The second part of the paper will confront the Aristotelian theory with the contemporary dual-process theory (DPT), which is widely accepted in cognitive psychology and some other contemporary psychological theories of law. It should be observed that both Aristotelian theory and the DPT underline the close relationships between reason and emotions. Emotions play an important role in the Aristotelian theory of action, since they are incentives for action and Aristotle does not associate them with any virtue or vice. The excellence of human life is based on a proper response to the emotions rather than on being affected by proper emotions.[2] Aristotle defines emotions (*pathe*) in *Nicomachean Ethics* as;

> feelings accompanied by pleasure or pain, listing appetite, anger, fear, confidence, envy, joy, love, hatred, longing, emulation, and pity as examples. (*EN* 1105 b 21 trans. Roger Crisp)

Those emotions seem to be a necessary part of a thought process concerning any moral action, as they will surely affect the feelings of an involved individual. The same applies to the actions of the judge, who should take the consequences of a particular judgement into account. The question remains whether, and to what extent, judges may control their emotions. Aristotle seems to give a partial answer, suggesting that there is an essential difference between feeling emotions and acting upon them. The relationship between action and feelings in a general sense (*pathe*) seems to be crucial for some dispositions of the character such as vices and virtues. Aristotle does not separate deliberation and emotions, concentrating rather on their moral importance and a proper disposition for certain types of acts. The influence of emotions upon moral agent seems to be shaped by habits. The dispositions to feel particular kinds of *pathe* on certain occasions refer to states (*hexeis*). Those states can be understood as

> the things in virtue of which we stand well or badly with reference to the passions. (*EN* 1105 b 26 trans. Roger Crisp)

---

[2]In this volume Bombelli (2018), pp. 41–48.

21.2 Virtue Centered Theory of Justice as a Union of Legal Rule (*nomos*) and Fairness (*epieikeia*)

Emotions play an important role in Aristotelian ethics, psychology and rhetoric. However, it seems that there is a problem with virtue-centered adjudication, namely the influence of emotions upon judges. In this respect a few questions arises: (1) How do reason and emotion interact with the judicial process?; (2) To what extent is it possible for the judge to remain neutral and objective and to resist strong emotions?; (3) Why should the judge remain unaffected by emotional components and how is this possible?

The judicial independence and rationality are deemed to be the most important characteristics of any judge. It is widely believed and commonly accepted that the judicial process should be based on the rational evaluation of the merits of any given case, on the best understanding of the legal acts and related precedents and on the most comprehensive and coherent justification for the judicial decision. This proposition was in fact initially formulated by Aristotle, who observed that:

> This is why it is not a person that we allow to rule, but rather law, because a person does so in his own interests and becomes a tyrant. (*EN* 1234 a 35 trans. Roger Crisp)

Aristotle offered a comprehensive theory of adjudication, which is strongly connected with his theory of justice in general, and the practice of doing justice (equalizing) in particular. Concerning the latter, Aristotle applied the concept of corrective (rectificatory) justice, which was focused on the restoration of the initial balance between parties. The compensation for wrongful acts was thus based on a principle of arithmetic proportionality. The damage which was being committed by the wrong-doer and the damage which was suffered by the victim, were not necessarily identical, according to Aristotle. Therefore there exists a wide scope of indeterminacy between the subjective nature of an act of injustice and the actual consequences of this act (*EN* 1133 a). The "virtue-centered" theory of adjudication sketched by Aristotle has recently been both elaborated and reaffirmed by L. Solum.[3] According to Solum, the virtue-centered theory of justice is based on five concepts: *a judicial virtue, a virtuous judge, a virtuous decision, a lawful decision* and *a just decision*. The starting point for further evaluation of a judicial decision should be associated with the first concept, namely *a judicial virtue*, in respect of, inter alia: "temperance, courage, good temper, intelligence, wisdom and justice." As Solum observes

> The central normative thesis of a virtue-centered theory of judging is that judges ought to be virtuous and to make virtuous decisions.[4]

---

[3]Cf. Solum (2013), pp. 12–30.
[4]Ibid., p. 26.

Then he proposes to confront this concept of virtuous decisions with cases, in which the degree of complexity would require a high level of knowledge and expertise pertaining to both, law and facts:

> When the facts are complex, other intellectual skills, e.g., a highly developed situation sense, may be required to see what even relatively simple legal rules require. Thus, in complex cases, it may be the case that only someone with sufficient legal knowledge and in possession of a high degree of judicial virtue will be able to fully grasp which outcome is just and why this is so.[5]

Complex cases contain two potential threats to the impartiality and soundness of the rational justification of decision. Firstly, they may result in a misapplication of complex rules flowing from errors in the interpretation of complicated relations between different rules. Secondly, they may result in systematic errors concerning the facts and causal links, which are caused by intellectual limits of human cognitive capacities.

Some problems such as the over and under-inclusiveness of legal rules and the significance of conscience (*synderesis*) and fairness (*epieikeia*) are notorious and extensively discussed in both philosophical and legal literature. By reading carefully the relevant part (*EN* 1137b–1138a) of the *Nicomachean Ethics* one can debunk some problems and shortcomings pertaining to the virtue-centered theory of adjudication.

Criteria based on the personal view of an individual should not play an important role in adjudication because the application of this would result in undermining the rule of law as such. Therefore the question arises how to reconcile the application of general rules to particular cases in extreme situations, where it is agreed that the sheer application of the black letter rules does not lead to a fair solution. Many judges may agree on the fact that the rule-based solution is deficient in a particular case and at the same time disagree on the remedy. The problem concerns the fact that in the long run any departure from rules results in arbitrariness and tyranny, replacing the rule of law with the rule of judge. How then the discrepancy between a fair decision for a particular case and the commonly accepted, impersonal requirements of justice could be, if at any rate, overcome by virtuous judges?

The proponents of virtue jurisprudence seem to rely on the difference between proper rules reflecting socially acceptable and stable legal norms continuously applied as properly so called legal standards (*nomoi*) and decrees (*psephismata*), which are referring to episodic enactments that are only applied in particular cases. Therefore it could rightly be concluded: firstly that legal standards (*nomoi*) have a broader scope than decrees (*psephismata*) and secondly, that legal standards (*nomoi*) have a general nature, while decrees (*psephismata*) are episodic in a sense that they apply only to specific situations. In particular R. Kraut suggests that Aristotle understood justice as an equivalent of a broader concept of lawfulness based on a coherent legal code that is not altered furiously and unpredictably, and

---

[5]Ibid., p. 26.

functions as a stable system of rules and laws.[6] It seems, however, that even if this wider concept of law (*nomos*) is accepted and contrasted with black letter rules that result from unpredictable and episodic alterations decrees (*psephismata*) this does not solve the problem. On the one hand, the formalistic application of the episodic black letter rules might be called tyranny. On the other hand, it does not mean that the application of legal standards (*nomoi*) could be based on some unspoken, implicit understanding of law by judges. Aristotle himself objected to such solution, stating clearly that:

> What is equitable, therefore, is just, and better than one kind of justice. But it is not better than unqualified justice, only better than the error that results from its lacking qualification. And this is the very nature of what is equitable- a correction of law, where it is deficient on account of its universality. (*EN* 1137b trans. Roger Crisp)

Aristotle emphasized the problem that even if we apply the wider concept of law based on legal rules (*nomoi*) there is still a real tension between them and the solution that is fair for individual cases, constituting fairness (*epieikeia*). Actually it seems that the requirements of *epieikeia* are of a higher authority that the laws and hence they are really significant for the judicial process. At the same time Aristotle distinguished between the act of judging in particular case (an act of fairness) and the requirement of fairness, since the latter is not based on a single decision. The collection of fair decisions leads to creation of fairness (*epieikeia)* rather than other way around.

21.3 Dual Process Theory Within the Light the Theory of Legal Decision

The influence of emotions upon the adjudication process has been traditionally stressed in legal theory by the supporters of American realism, who emphasize that judicial decisions are always indeterminate. Indeterminacy of decisions means that their content depends not only on legal rules or legal reasons but also on elements of an unconscious character, such as: emotions, impulses and intuition. These explanatory attempts were purely speculative at first, because they were not empirically verified or because the proposed verification was incorrect or unsatisfactory in the light of later achievements in the field of cognitive psychology or cognitive sciences. Currently, however, a change has been brought about by the research of behavioural law and economics which modifies the analysis of classical economics by taking into consideration the limits of cognition (bounded rationality) in order to examine the consequences of the so-called duality of cognitive processes (DPT).

The concept of bounded rationality has been introduced in cognitive psychology, and is later on successfully applied in economics and legal theory.[7] The theory of

---

[6]Kraut (2002), p. 106.
[7]Cf. Jolls et al. (2000) and Vermeule (2006).

bounded rationality supplements at least to some extent the traditional rational choice theory. It takes into account the fallibility of human cognitive abilities. Due to the fact that their cognitive abilities are not unlimited, human agents including judges and officials have limited computational skills and memory. This observation is supported even by some classical authors within the mainstream of analytical legal theory and jurisprudence. According to the literature of behavioural economics, agents often take their cognitive limitations into account, attempting to minimize the costs of decision-making process and at the same time trying to diminish the rate of errors.[8]

This state of affairs leads to wide usage of mental shortcuts and rules of thumb in some specific contexts. The problem remains however, that in some cases because of these tools, human behaviour differs in systematic ways from that predicted by the standard economic model, namely the rational choice theory. Therefore, it should be emphasized, that the use of these tools may result in predictable and repetitive mistakes. Those errors can generally be divided into two categories: judgmental and decisional processes.[9] Judgments and decisions demonstrate systematic departures from the rational choice model in both legal and non-legal contexts. It has been observed that judges are prone to both types of systematic errors.[10] This phenomenon can be partly explained by observing the way in which actors apply the so called rules of thumb.[11] In the context of adjudication those rules of thumb are very often based on the "availability heuristics", where the frequency of some event is estimated by judges, by thinking about similar instances of a given phenomenon. Thus the approach adopted by the proponents of the DPT is based on two crucial observations.

Firstly, the effects of the application of this heuristics are predictable, which means, that the rate of error is potentially controllable, which gives potential space for regulatory, institutional and practice-oriented improvements. Those improvements could be reflected in normative models of the application of law.

Secondly, it is assumed that in some contexts the use of this heuristics is useful and approximately provides a sound basis for decision. At the same time, however, they lead to errors in particular situational contexts and circumstances. This means that legal theoreticians should certainly pay more attention to the nature of the interplay between intuition and deliberations, since those relations are of complex nature. It is possible, however, to discover some properties of these processes and to distinguish between their respective application.

Concurrently it seems important to identify the situations, in which agents typically make mistakes and in which a clear reference to the used heuristics (which can turn out to be inadequate e.g. based on an incorrect assessment of

---

[8]Kahneman (2003) and Guthrie et al. (2001).

[9]Jolls et al. (2000).

[10]Kahneman (2003) and Vermeule (2006, 2009).

[11]Cf. Kahneman (2011).

probability) seems to be not only feasible, but also necessary for a sound model of applying law.

However, this does not necessarily mean that legal theory should uncritically adopt the findings proposed by cognitive psychology or behavioural law and economics. The complexity of the needed cognitive processes may require a more independent approach, based on the findings of empirical studies conducted in legal contexts. Those studies should include some experiments designed to examine certain theoretical assumptions concerning the application of law. The application of law is understood as a specific type of decision-making, followed by a justification which is aimed at a particular case and is understood to contribute to a general practice of legal discourse. Such a justification in the institutional sense reflects the reasons (arguments) supporting the judicial decision of a given case.

These reasons (arguments) may belong to two different contexts. Firstly, if the reasons (arguments) were formulated by the decision-maker post factum, i.e. after the decision has been made, they belong to the "context of justification" of this specific case. They constitute the rationalization of a decision that has been made and serve to persuade the auditorium of the rightness of it. They do not expose, however, the actual premises (reasons) by which the decision-maker was directed. Secondly therefore, if the reasons (arguments) provided in the justification are the expression and documentation of the actual premises by which the decision-maker was directed at the moment of decision-making, they belong also to the "context of discovery" of this specific case.

The concept of legal coherence is traditionally related to the "context of justification" of the judicial decision. It is used to evaluate the internal or external rationality of the justification and thus serves as a criterion to determine whether the given justification (arguments provided in it) constitutes a coherent whole. However, the idea of coherence may also be applied to determine the relation between the arguments given in the context of justification and the reasons in the mind of the decision-maker while "discovering" his or her decision. This type of coherence would not only serve as an indicator of the rationality of the justification, but would also indicate the external relation between the arguments provided to justify the decision in a specific case and the reasons occurring in the "discovery" of it. The proposed research strategy concentrates on the latter aspect of the application of law, namely the reconstruction of the dynamics of the cognitive process associated with the discovery of a decision-making.

The model of dual process theory (DPT) explains the complex character of cognitive processes by assuming that alongside conscious (deliberative—so called System 2) activities there are also unconscious (intuitive—so called System 1) activities. The functional complexity is being analysed within the DPT with regard to evolutionary psychology as well as experimental cognitive psychology. The delimitation of both systems: intuitive System 1 and deliberative System 2 is based on the purely functional character of cognitive processes. The cognitive operations and activities may therefore, to some extent, correspond with the activity of relevant parts of human brain, but it should be observed that intuitive processes are also connected with emotions.[12]

However, to avoid confusion, it is important to emphasize that intuition and emotions, while being closely connected, are two separate processes of the human brain. Intuition affects only fast, System 1 thinking, while emotions can affect thought processes both under System 1 and System 2.

The DPT leads theoreticians to being sceptical about the commonly accepted assumptions concerning the deliberative character of the decision-making process within the field of application of law. According to some versions of dual-process theory, a clear distinction between intuition and deliberation is possible. Intuitive processes are described as unconscious, automatic, fast, parallel, effortless, and having a high capacity. On the other hand, deliberate decisions are thought to be accessible to conscious awareness, slow, sequential, effortful, rule-governed and having a limited capacity.[13] This proposition, commonly known as the strong separation thesis, has been offered by Sloman, who claims that intuition and deliberation are completely distinct and separable processes, since they are:

two systems, two algorithms that are designed to achieve different computational goals.[14]

Sloman's hypothesis has not been unanimously accepted among psychologists, and some theories propose a very weak or even "no separation" thesis, as an alternative view based on the adoption of the, so called, integrative model of automatic and deliberate decision-making. The Integrative approach is based on the assumption that every decision relies heavily on automatic cognitive processes.[15] This theory has been endorsed by A. Glöckner who was convinced that

people can integrate a multitude of information in a weighted compensatory manner within a short time frame due to automatic-intuitive processes. However, these automatic-intuitive processes can be supervised and modified by additional operations of the deliberate system.

It is a great challenge for both scholars and regulators to develop some experiments in a legal context, which can provide empirical support for the separation thesis.[16] Generally speaking, the role of intuition and emotion in a judicial setting seems to be twofold: on the one hand, it is a condition (considered even to be a necessary condition) for initiating a decision-making process[17] and for coping with problems such as an information deficit, time horizon, the need to act within uncertainty. On the other hand, one may observe several other factors linked to the influence of intuition upon the process of law application. One of those factors

---

[12]Damasio (1994).

[13]Kahneman (2003).

[14]Sloman (2002).

[15]Cf. Glöckner (2008) and Glöckner and Ebert (2011).

[16]This aspect has also been stressed by A. Damasio and is rediscovered in context of Aristotelian philosophy. Cf. Fuselli in this volume (2018), pp. 8–10.

[17]This suggestion clearly coincides with Aristotelian model of *pathos* as incentive for action in *Nicomachean Ethics*. Cf. In this volume Bombelli (2018), pp. 57–58.

concerns legal institutions, which can be understood as sets of formal and informal rules, which may successfully shape the motivation of decision-makers. This leads to the following question: Does the negligent attitude toward intuition and its non-inclusion, as a factor co-shaping the content of decision, may lead to the introduction of inefficient regulations? It could lead to a sub-optimal level of the allocation of resources, due to unrealistic assumptions concerning the cognitive processes that play a role in the decision-making process. Within this context one may imagine an increased number of legal conflicts, putting high costs on the participants of legal proceedings or increasing the costs of the functioning of the judicial system or administration. In American jurisprudence, especially within the analysis of law by behavioural economics, it has been pointed out that regulations which do not take into consideration the significance of intuition tend to lead to inefficient allocation of resources.[18]

In the literature of behavioural economics it has been pointed out that heuristics and biases may lead to systemic problems and inadequacies which are strongly influencing the application of law. A notorious example of such a phenomenon can be found in research concerning the quality and capacity of jury members during tort and criminal law trials. In these trials the jurors generally have to determine the probability of an event that occurred. Within the context of American tort law this problem refers to negligence standards. Judgment of the jurors can easily be obscured and weakened by a so called hindsight bias i.e. thinking that since an event has occurred, its occurrence was highly probable and could have been predicted. That leads to the jury holding the defendant to a higher standard, than they should. As a result plaintiffs have better chances of winning such cases.

Secondly, the ignorance about the complex and limited character of the cognitive process can lead to the adoption of too rigorous requirements for the recipients of norms by the organs dealing with the application of law. Such an attitude is ineffective, because it is based on the assumption of a purely deliberative and rational character of the decision-making process. Moreover, within the prescribed conditions it will not be possible to achieve an institutional point of equilibrium as long as the participants of a legal discourse still accept unrealistic assumptions concerning a uniquely deliberative character of the decisions that concern the application of law. This attitude is reflected in systemic flaws committed during the process of applying of law. Within this context many different errors can be pointed out, such as: too rigorous standards of diligence in regard to civil and criminal liability (the problem of overdeterrence), systemic flaws in adjudication in relation to the evaluation of the rationality of actions; those, which are based on the delusion of hindsight bias. The origin of all these flaws is linked to the influence of heuristics and rules of thumb on the decision-making process of judges and officials.

The influence of intuitive processes on the application of law is visible within the heuristics which are gradually recognized (discovered), classified and explained as part of cognitive processes (cognitive aspect) as well as in regard to their effect on

---

[18]Jolls et al. (2000).

the process of law application (institutional and legal aspect). These intuitive processes consist of the following heuristics: availability, representation, anchoring and adjusting. Heuristics of availability is linked to a thought process where individuals perceive some specific situations as more important just because they are familiar to them and they can be easily recalled.[19] A particular type of availability heuristic is a delusion of hindsight bias which occurs when individuals assign higher than usual probability to situations which they known already have happened. Heuristics of representation can be observed within the process of categorization of objects with regard to their similarity to a prototype (exemplary, prototypical categorization). This type of categorization differs from a theoretical categorization, which is based on a rule by which the object is categorized in conformance with a precise definition of its characteristics.[20] Anchoring and adjusting heuristics can be observed when individuals rely too heavily and without any reflection on the first piece of information they obtain and it is very difficult for them to adjust their further thought process to more detailed information they subsequently get.

The catalogue of heuristics is not a finite list. Law application may be accompanied by some *sui generis* heuristics which are not yet identified or thoroughly examined. In this respect it is worthwhile to pay attention to certain intuitively appropriate moral rules, advanced by C. Sunstein, such as: "do unto others as you would have done unto you", "treason should be severely punished", "action is more conducive to damage than omission". It seems obvious that such a heuristics may influence the decisions concerning the acceptance of particular legal consequences within the process of law application (e.g. the amount of fee, compensation).[21]

21.4 DPT and the Adjudication Under the Shadow of Emotions

One of the best representations of the adjudication process from the perspective of the DPT has been offered by Chris Guthrie, Jeffrey Rachlinski, and Andrew J. Wistrich. They address the question to what extent it is possible to defend the rational character of judicial process on the one hand and to take into account the influence of emotional responses to cases on the other hand. They offer an extensive model of adjudication under the shadow of emotions (the "intuitive-override model of judicial decision-making - IOM").[22]

According to this model judges firstly make their initial, intuitive decision under the System 1 thinking, and then control it as far as possible, contemplating the result of the first stage and comparing it with the results of the deliberative and conscious

---

[19]Kahneman (2003).

[20]Allen and Brooks (1991).

[21]Sunstein (2005).

[22]Guthrie et al. (2007).

cognitive processes of System 2. Decisions are thus firstly based on intuition and then, in some cases, corrected by the operation of a cognitive, rational process which is based on valid reasons rather than on hints or gut feelings. The case with emotions is even harder, because emotions can influence decisions made under System 2 without discernible symptoms, and their role may be unknown to the decision-maker. It is therefore of crucial importance to identify situations in which intuitions or emotions systematically override deliberative decisions rather than the other way around.

> To illustrate the DPT consider a following question:
> A bat and a ball cost $1.10 in total. The bat costs $1.00 more than the ball.
> How much does the ball cost? _____ cents
> For most people the intuitive answer to this question is 10 cents., however, upon further reflection individuals realise that it is wrong. If the ball would cost 10 cents, then the bat would have to cost $1.10 and together they would cost $1.20, instead of $1.10. The correct answer, can be reached by analyzing the aforementioned question with System 2 thinking. The ball costs 5 cents.[23]

The IOM is inarguably a powerful extension of the DPT. Additionally Guthrie, Rachlinski and Wistrich interpret the DPT in such a way that they encapsulate the *nomos/pathos* antinomy including emotions into operations of the System 1. Thus they come to the conclusion, that an absolute suppression of emotion is impossible due to the complexity of the cognitive operations of the human mind. In other words, rational decisions not influenced by intuitive processes and emotions do not exist. From the psychological point of view the relationships between deliberative and intuitive processes are inevitable, because in many cases the System 2 deliberative decisions could not have been reached without the assistance of the System 1 and its overwhelming influence upon cognition and decisions. Modern explanations of the judgmental process should not be blind in this respect and should take the complexity of the reason-emotion, deliberation-intuition pairs into consideration. Moreover, looking at the process of judging from the perspective of the "enlightened" legal theory, which takes the DPT for granted, it is possible to reduce the irrationality of decisions by making them rather well informed and justified than absolutely isolated from emotions or intuitions.

Some judicial decisions may be based on emotions because these cannot be controlled by the System 1 components, as has been demonstrated by neurobiological research.[24] Because intuition is automatic, quick, and easily invoked, it can easily dominate deliberation as decision-makers simply rely on a quick, intuitive response or as intuition affects the judgments that follow. Intuition can be surprisingly accurate, but sometimes good judgment will require that the deliberative process is purged from these intuitional influences. Intuitive responses can also emerge from the repetition of a certain deliberative procedure. Furthermore, some decisions might require to shift back and forth between both systems.[25]

---

[23]Frederick (2005).

[24]Bennett and Broe (2010), p. 16.

[25]Guthrie et al. (2007), pp. 7–8.

The application of DPT to the explanation of the judgmental process concentrates on the presence of emotional components in judicial decisions and runs as follows: Emotions are related to the System 1 intuitive processing. The crucial role of intuition in the decision-making process brings emotion into the process itself and enables it to influence the final, allegedly rational, decision. Additionally it is obvious, especially looking from the Aristotelian or virtue-centered perspective that emotional responses are not only important, but sometimes even a necessary condition for reaching any reasonable (System 2 shaped) conclusion.[26] Accordingly, Wistrich, Rachlinski and Guthrie observe that the presence of emotions does not create a serious danger for the rule of law.[27] However, an excessive reliance on them may lead to erroneous judgements and may create a serious threat for the judicial system. Given the fact, that emotions or affective responses to stimuli are an aspect of System 1 intuitive processing, it should be observed that emotional responses, like other System 1 responses, are not always wrong, but that they should be carefully observed, monitored and controlled. Especially in situations where they are likely to lead to systemic errors or grounding judicial decisions on criteria which are explicitly prohibited. According to the IOM, the potential ways in which the operations of System 1, such as emotional impulses or intuitions, lead to systemic errors of undue influence upon the judicial decisions can be generally classified. Those situations and criteria constitute a list of judicial vices, which might be treated as opposite to the judicial virtues as perceived by L. Solum. The list of such vices based on the unacceptable influence upon emotions includes the affect heuristic and the motivated cognition. As somewhat opposed to the concept of judicial virtue, the modern IOM model based on the insights of the DPT theory seems to be unable to constitute a catalogue of the positive interactions of reason and emotion.

The affect heuristic pertains to the situation in which emotions appear rapidly and automatically, excluding the capacity of System 2 to take control over System 1.[28] This heuristic has been described by D. Kahneman in the following way:

> The affect heuristic is an instance of substitution, in which the answer to an easy question (How do I feel about it?) serves as an answer to a much harder question (What do I think about it?).[29]

Motivated cognition refers to a process of accepting an intuitive preference as the most logical option, excluding counter arguments or other possible reasons to such an extent that the decision-makers even in the deliberate process reach the same conclusion. This phenomenon has been described and explained by Z. Kunda,

---

[26]For a strong argument in favor of indispensable character of emotions cf. Damasio (1994).

[27]Guthrie et al. (2015).

[28]The concept of affect heuristic has been introduced in Slovic (2002), p. 397.

[29]Kahneman (2011), p. 139.

who suggests that the so called motivated cognition leads to such a high preference for a particular option, that it

> "triggers the operation of cognitive processes that lead to the desired conclusions" (so that) "goals enhance the accessibility of those knowledge structures – memories, beliefs, and rules – that are consistent with the desired conclusions."[30]

As A. J. Wistrich, J. Rachlinski, and C. Guthrie observed:

> Emotions influence how people perceive others, what they remember about others, and how they process information about others. Emotions guide "people's attitudes, beliefs, and inferential strategies."[31]

Therefore individuals affected by this bias may even perceive people they like as having positive qualities, and people they do not like as possessing negative ones. Consequently, even deliberative reasoning can be influenced by intuitive, emotional reactions.

This analysis leads to the question if and eventually how the judicial vices of both emotion-based heuristics could be eliminated from the judicial process. This problem has been convincingly demonstrated by T. Maroney, who emphasizes that it is possible and necessary to embody the sphere of emotions into the institutional framework of the judiciary.[32] Moreover, that the concept of righteousness derived from the Aristotelian theory of virtue provides sufficient guidelines for the strategy of emotional control, particularly in the case of anger, which thus could be transformed from an emotional vice into a righteously applied instrument of judicial behaviour and in this manner become a virtue. As Maroney observes, Aristotle concentrates on the requirements of the righteously angry person. Anger is righteous and becomes a judicial virtue if it complies with the following requirements: it is applied "with reference to the right objects, towards the right people, with the right motive." As Maroney observes:

> The justification inquiry is logically precedential, as if anger is unjustified no experience or expression of it is proper. If the anger is justified, we when ask whether its manifestation comports with the expectation that judges be fair and dignified—again in Aristotle's terms, whether it is shown at the right times, and in the right way." (. . .) "Judicial anger is justified if it rests on accurate premises; is relevant; and reflects worthy beliefs and values."[33]

The only reservation about the plausibility of this proposition refers to the presence of the heuristic of affect. If the emotional response creates bias in some situations, it remains outside the scope of control of the System 2, because it simply creates a cognitive illusion. It should be stressed that the motivated cognition leads to a preference for a particular option inducing by this the operation of cognitive processes which eventually lead to the solution as already initially preferred, being dressed up as a justification on an intellectual basis. In other words, the decision is

---

[30]Kunda (1990), pp. 493–494.

[31]Guthrie et al. (2015), p. 869.

[32]Maroney (2018), p. 206.

[33]Cf. Ibid., pp. 212–213.

no longer justified in Aristotelian terms, but the agent is not capable of recognizing the problem. This situation requires the intervention of an impartial spectator, who is not involved in the process of judgement in a specific case, but rather in the whole decision-making process, so that the bias could be identified, and the heuristics of affect eliminated.

In general Aristotle and the proponents of the DPT actually could agree on this point. However, the Aristotelian concept of the judicial virtue as a mean between both ends of an equilibrium between two extreme positions seems to be too imprecise. From the perspective of the current debate on the interaction between reason and emotion, two possible solutions are available. The first one is based on the assumption that legislation can prevent the unacceptable influence of emotions upon litigation and may thus effectively prevent affect heuristic and motivated cognition. It seems, however, that this institutional response is weakened by the flaws of legislation, as the application of general rules to particular cases can turn out to be deficient. The other solution would be based on the possibility of publically accessible justification based on rational presumptions or, at least, on persuasive argumentation (*topoi*). Both alternatives may justly be discussed from the perspective of an Aristotelian model of adjudication as it is presented in *Nicomachean Ethics* as well as the concept of persuasion that can be found in *Rhetoric*.

21.5 Conclusion

It seems that the interrelation between reason and emotion plays an important role in understanding reason-based and irrational decisions alike, however, one could ask the following question: can a decision be purely rational—not based on any emotions? The assumption that the decision is a derivative of either reason or emotion is probably in practice impossible. The DPT states that a "clear" cut distinction between reason and emotion may be too crude. Besides that, in some cases emotions cannot be controlled by reason. They are then not controlled by the System 2 operations and thus still may influence the output of decision-making process. This, however, does not necessarily mean that this concerns all decisions or that irrationality cannot be controlled. Even if a complete separation between System 1 and System 2 is in practice impossible, there can still be two potential solutions. Firstly, the legal process may be designed to limit the number of weak decisions, where the judges rely too heavily on emotions. This will not be possible through the self-constraint of judges, because they may well be unaware of the influence of emotions on their decisions? It is therefore important to design an institutional environment and procedural safeguards protecting judges from the uncontrolled influence of their emotional reactions. Knowing in advance that some incentives may strongly affect judges, the legislator may simply limit the number of such incentives or create procedural limitations restricting their exposure to some emotion-sparking information such as some sensitive personal details of the perpetrator or the victim. Generally it is an art of virtue-driven legislation to prevent the potential consequences of excessive emotion and the reliance on intuition and to prohibit these factors well in advance. This approach albeit being promising, has some limits. It does not address the problem of particular biases and emotion-based judgments as there are no clear rules concerning the degree of justified or accepted influence. In other words, a more precise tool is needed to overcome this problem, but this solution will rather shift the problem on the higher level of abstraction than solve it. As Aristotle pointed out, any general rule will have to face the problem of under or over-inclusiveness, leaving only fairness (*epieikeia*) as a mean to solve individual problems within the context of general rule and judicial impartiality. A second potential solution can be offered, here, in accordance with the distinction Aristotle makes between the ethical approach as presented in the *Nicomachean Ethics* in which he explains the basic dilemmas about the application of law, referring to fairness (*epieikeia*) as a higher form of justice and the instrumental approach of the Rhetoric. Aristotle does not explain how a decision is reached, referring in the Nicomachean Ethics only to some form of intuition in the application of the demands of practical reason. What is important, however, is that Aristotle does refer to the justification of those decisions in *Rhetoric*, demonstrating the ways in which the legal argument should be presented in order to be effective. Therefore the insights of contemporary psychology, such as discovery of dual nature of human cognition, could be used to affirm Aristotle's view, that on the level of public debate and exchange of arguments, rationality requires some kind of rational justification for judgment. Aristotle himself outlines the nature and limits of such justification. When analysing the phenomenon of fairness and unsatisfactory application of general rules to some particular cases he admits that:

> it is right (. . .) to correct the omission. This will be by saying what the lawgiver would himself have said had he been present, and would have included within the law had he known. (*EN* 1137b trans. Roger Crisp)

This operation of explaining on behalf of the legislator may well be treated as a kind of rationality standard, which has to be provided with legitimate and universal justification for any given judgment rather than just the judgement itself.

References

Allen, Scott W., and Lee R. Brooks. 1991. Specializing the Operation of an Explicit Rule. *Journal of Experimental Psychology: General* 120 (1): 3–19.

Aristotle. 2000. In *Aristotle: Nicomachean Ethics*, ed. Roger Crisp. Cambridge: Cambridge University Press.

Bennett, Hayley, and G.A. Broe. 2010. Judicial Decision-Making and Neurobiology: The Role of Emotion and the Ventromedial Cortex in Deliberation and Reasoning. *Australian Journal of Forensic Sciences* 42 (1): 11–18.

Bombelli, Giovanni. 2018. Emotion and Rationality in Aristotle's Model: From Anthropology to Politics. In *Aristotle on Emotions in Law and Politics*, ed. Liesbeth Huppes-Cluysenaer and Nuno M.M.S. Coelho. Dordrecht: Springer.

Damasio, Antonio R. 1994. *Descartes' Error: Emotion, Reason, and the Human Brain*. New York: Putnam.

Frederick, Shane. 2005. Cognitive Reflection and Decision-Making. *Journal of Economic Perspectives* 19 (4): 25–42. https://doi.org/10.1257/089533005775196732.

Fuselli, Stefano. 2018. Logoi Enuloi. Aristotle's Contribution to the Contemporary Debate on Emotions and Decision-Making. In *Aristotle on Emotions in Law and Politics*, ed. Liesbeth Huppes-Cluysenaer and Nuno M.M.S. Coelho. Dordrecht: Springer.

Glöckner, Andreas. 2008. How Evolution Outwits Bounded Rationality: The Efficient Interaction of Automatic and Deliberate Processes in Decision-Making and Implications for Institutions. In *Better than Conscious? Decision-Making, the Human Mind, and Implications for Institutions*, ed. Christoph Engel and Wolf Singer. Cambridge: MIT Press. http://public.eblib.com/choice/publicfullrecord.aspx?p=3338898.

Glöckner, Andreas, and Irena D. Ebert. 2011. Legal Intuition and Expertise. In *Handbook of Intuition Research*, ed. Marta Sinclair. Cheltenham, UK: Edward Elgar.

Guthrie, C., J.J. Rachlinski, and A.J. Wistrich. 2001. Inside the Judicial Mind. *Cornell Law Review* 86: 777–830.

———. 2007. Blinking on the Bench: How Judges Decide Cases. *Cornell Law Review* 93 (1): 1–44.

———. 2015. Heart Versus Head: Do Judges Follow the Law or Follow Their Feelings? *Texas Law Review* 93 (4): 855–923.

Jolls, Christine, Cass R. Sunstein, and Richard Thaler. 2000. A Behavioral Approach to Law and Economics. In *Behavioral Law and Economics*. Cambridge and New York: Cambridge University Press.

Kahneman, Daniel. 2003. A Perspective on Judgment and Choice: Mapping Bounded Rationality. *American Psychologist* 58 (9): 697–720.

———. 2011. *Thinking, Fast and Slow*. London: Penguin Books.

Kraut, Richard. 2002. *Aristotle: Political Philosophy*. Oxford and New York: Oxford University Press.

Kunda, Ziva. 1990. The Case for Motivated Reasoning. *Psychological Bulletin Psychological Bulletin* 108 (3): 480–498.

Maroney, Terry A. 2018. Judicial Emotion as Vice or Virtue: Perspectives Both Ancient and New. In *Aristotle on Emotions in Law and Politics*, ed. Liesbeth Huppes-Cluysenaer and Nuno M.M.S. Coelho. Dordrecht: Springer.

Sloman, Steven. 2002. Two Systems of Reasoning. In *Heuristics and Biases: The Psychology of Intuitive Judgement*, ed. Thomas Gilovich, Dale W. Griffin, and Daniel Kahneman. Cambridge and New York: Cambridge University Press.

Slovic, Paul. 2002. Affect Heuristic. In *Heuristics and Biases: The Psychology of Intuitive Judgement*, ed. Thomas Gilovich, Dale W. Griffin, and Daniel Kahneman. Cambridge and New York: Cambridge University Press.

Solum, Lawrence. 2013. Virtue Jurisprudence: Towards an Aretaic Theory of Law. In *Aristotle and the Philosophy of Law Theory, Practice and Justice*, ed. Liesbeth Huppes-Cluysenaer and Nuno M.M.S. Coelho. Dordrecht: Springer. http://public.eblib.com/choice/publicfullrecord.aspx?p=1083709.

Sunstein, C.R. 2005. Moral Heuristics. *Behavioral and Brain Sciences* 28 (4): 531–542.

Vermeule, Adrian. 2006. *Judging Under Uncertainty: An Institutional Theory of Legal Interpretation*. Cambridge, MA: Harvard University Press.

———. 2009. *Law and the Limits of Reason*. Oxford and New York: Oxford University Press.

About the Editors and Contributors

Giovanni Bombelli graduated in Philosophy and Law (PHD) at the University of Padua, Italy. Currently he teaches philosophy and theory of law at the Catholic University of Milan. His research interests include the Western model of community and the multicultural question. Among his publications: *Occidente e 'figure' comunitarie. I Un'ordine inquieto: koinonia e comunità "radicata". Profili filosofico-giuridici* (2013) and *Toward a New Lexicon and a Conceptual Grammar to Understand the "Multicultural Issue"* (2015).

Daniela Bonanno teaches Greek History at the University of Palermo. Her research interests are the Greek history of the Archaic and Classical period, the history of religion in the Classical world and the reception of the Antiquity. She was A.v. Humboldt Fellow at the Max-Weber-Kolleg, Universität Erfurt and at the Westfälische Wilhelms Universität Münster working on a research project about the role of the goddess Nemesis in the Greek World. She is author of several articles and of a book on *Ierone il Dinomenide: storia e rappresentazione* (Pisa-Roma 2010) and recently co-edited with P. Funke and M. Haake the proceedings of the conference held in Palermo, *Rechtliche Verfahren und religiöse Sanktionierung in der griechisch-römischen Antike* (Stuttgart 2016).

José de Sousa e Brito is Justice (emeritus) of the Constitutional Court, Lisbon, Portugal, and Professor at Universidade Nova, Lisbon. Former visiting Professor at the University of Munich, President of the European Consortium of Church and State Research and President of the International Society for Utilitarian Studies, he is since 2008 President of the Portuguese Society for Legal Theory, Philosophy of Law and Social Philosophy. He has published in English, German, French, Italian and Portuguese on ethics, philosophy of law, criminal law, constitutional law, and law on religion. He published recently *False e vere alternative nella teoria della giustizia. Lezioni napoletane di filosofia del diritto*, Napoli: Editoriale Scientifica, 2011.

© Springer International Publishing AG 2018
L. Huppes-Cluysenaer, N.M.M.S. Coelho (eds.), *Aristotle on Emotions in Law and Politics*, Law and Philosophy Library 121, DOI 10.1007/978-3-319-66703-4

Ian Bryan, School of Law, Lancaster University, UK. His research and publication activities span a wide range of fields, including the Administration of Criminal Justice, Criminal Law, the Laws of Evidence, Legal History, Human Rights and Legal Theory. In legal theory, his publications include *The Reconstruction of the Juridico-Political: Affinity and Divergence in Hans Kelsen and Max Weber* and *Kelsenian Legal Science and the Nature of Law*.

Mateusz Bukaty is a PhD candidate in legal sciences at the University of Lodz. He obtained an European Masters in Law and Economics at Erasmus University of Rotterdam. He studied behavioral law and economics at the University of Haifa (Israel) and law and economics at University of Bologna (Italy). His scientific interests include law and economics and behavioral analysis of law.

Nuno Coelho teaches law, ethics and philosophy of law in Brazil (USP, UNAERP, USU). He published articles and books on Aristotle's Ethics and Politics, such as "ἕτεροι καὶ ἴσοι: Aristotle on Diversity and Equality in the Constitution of Polis" and "Aristotle and The Philosophy of Law: Theory, Practice and Justice".

Emma Cohen de Lara is lecturer in political theory at Amsterdam University College, where she teaches courses on classical and modern political thought. As part of her involvement with Amsterdam University College, which is the liberal arts and sciences college of the University of Amsterdam, she takes an active interest in the topic of education as character formation in the history of philosophy. Emma is also affiliated with the Amsterdam Institute for Social Science Research. In her current research, she analyses the extent to which Aristotle's political science is rooted in his conception of the good life, and how this ethico-political approach relates to Aristotle's practical insight into the constitutional arrangements that benefit the stability of the regime. Emma is co-editor of *Back to the Core. Rethinking Core Texts in Liberal Arts & Sciences Education in Europe* (2017) and is co-editor of *Aristotle's Practical Philosophy: On the Relationship Between His Ethics and Politics* (forthcoming).

Lucia Corso teaches philosophy of law, legal reasoning and bioethics at the University of Enna, Kore (Faculty of Economics and Law). LLM at New York University school of law School, PhD at University of Naples, she is currently a member of the doctoral school run through the University of Enna. Her research interests range from legal sentimentalism to the relationship between constitutional law and legal theory, to the role of religion in the context of legal and political philosophy. She conducted her research studies at Yale University, at Columbia Law School and at Cambridge University. She has authored four books and several essays. Her latest work "I due volti del diritto. Élite e uomo comune nel costituzionalismo americano" explores among other things the role of emotions in constitutional theory.

Stefano Fuselli teaches Philosophy of Law, Legal Argumentation and Legal Logic at the University of Padua. His main research fields are Hegel's logic and philosophy of punishment; Theory of evidence and legal reasoning; Law and Neuroscience. In this field, he edited the volume: "Neurodiritto. Prospettive epistemologiche, antropologiche e biogiuridiche", 2016.

Mariusz Jerzy Golecki teaches legal logic, comparative law and law and economics at the University of Lodz, where he obtained his PhD, which concentrated on Aristotelian foundations of contract law. He earned an LLM at Cambridge University writing on law and economics. His research concerns Law and Economics, with special regard to Behavioral Law and Economics, Jurisprudence and Comparative Law. He is the author of 5 monographs and about 80 articles and chapters, including; "New York Times v. Sullivan in European Context" in *European Perspectives on Behavioural Law and Economics*; "Translation vs. Decoding Strategies in Law and Economics Scholarship" in *Ashgate Handbook of Legal Translation* and "Synallagma as a Paradigm of Exchange: Reciprocity of Contract in Aristotle and Game Theory" in *Aristotle and The Philosophy of Law: Theory, Practice and Justice.*

Liesbeth Huppes-Cluysenaer has a guest-appointment at the Faculty of Law of the University of Amsterdam to 2020 in order to complete a project about leading Dutch legal theorist Paul Scholten (1875–1946). Before she retired she taught legal philosophy and legal sociology at the same faculty. Since 2009 she and Nuno Coelho have convened a special workshop at the bi-annual conferences of the IVR on the philosophy of Aristotle, which resulted in the edited volume *Aristotle and the Philosophy of Law Theory, Practice and Justice* in 2013. For free downloadable publications in English see https://www.researchgate.net/profile/Liesbeth_Huppes-Cluysenaer2.

Misung Jang graduated with a degree in philosophy from Soongsil University and was a research professor at Inje University, South Korea. She was awarded a research grant for Argumentation in Western Antiquity (2011–2012) and Medical Practice and Humanities (2014–2016). Misung is currently (to June 2018) a visiting scholar at SUNY (State University of New York) and teaches ancient philosophy, ethics, eastern philosophy, ancient Greek and Roman mythology and philosophy of sexuality at Soongsil University, in Seoul. Her dissertation "Aristotle's Doctrine of the Mean" was published in 2009 at SUNY Buffalo. She has published in Korean about "A Justifiable Homicide in Adultery - Lysias 1. Killing of Eratosthenes", "Can Aristotle's Virtue Suggest an Alternative Idea for the Treatment of Depression?" and "Aristotle's Eros and Philia".

Peter Langford, Department of Law and Criminology, Edge Hill University, UK. His research focuses on the areas of legal theory and human rights. In legal theory, his publications include *Roberto Esposito: Law, Community and the Political* and

The Foundation of the Juridico-Political: Concept Formation in Hans Kelsen and Max Weber.

Terry Maroney teaches law at Vanderbilt University, where she also is affiliated with the program in Medicine, Health, and Society. She gives classes related to criminal law, particularly focusing on juvenile justice and wrongful convictions, areas in which she also writes and maintains an active advocacy practice. She was selected as a Fellow of the Center for Advanced Study in Behavioral Sciences at Stanford University (2016–2017) to pursue a theoretical and empirical investigation on the role of emotion in judicial behavior and decision-making; she will continue that work as a 2017–2019 Vanderbilt University Chancellor's Faculty Fellow. *Emotional Regulation and Judicial Behavior* and *Angry Judges* are two publications which exemplify well her interest in emotion and law.

Saulo de Matos currently teaches philosophy of law at the Faculty of Law of Federal University of Pará, Brazil, where he also obtained his bachelor's degree in law. He got his master's degree in philosophy of law in Heidelberg, where he specialized in Gadamer's philosophical hermeneutics and obtained his PhD in philosophy of law in Göttingen, with the dissertation "Zum normativen Begriff der Volkssouveränität" ("On the Normative Concept of Popular Sovereignty") (Nomos, 2015).

Daniel Simão Nascimento studied philosophy at the Pontifical Catholic University of Rio de Janeiro (PUC-RJ). During his doctorate he spent a year teaching philosophy of education at the State University of Rio de Janeiro (UERJ) and a year researching under the supervision of prof. Annick Jaulin at the Sorbonne. From 2013 to 2016 he was post-doctorate researcher in philosophy at Federal University of Pelotas (UFPEL). Currently he is associated researcher at the Nucleus of Ancient Philosophy (NUFA) at PUC-RJ) and post-doctorate researcher at the Federal University of Santa Maria (UFSM). His main areas of interest are ancient philosophy and contemporary meta-ethics. He is the author of "On the normative consequences of virtue and utility friendships in Aristotle" (forthcoming in Revista Latinoamericana de Filosofía) and "Akrasia e irracionalidade em Eurípides: notas sobre Hipólito e Medéia" (Revista Hypnos, v. 35).

Fabiana Pinho is PhD candidate in Legal Theory and International Law in a double degree program between the University of São Paulo (USP), Brazil, and the University of Kiel (CAU), Germany. She is a recipient of fellowship grants from the Research Foundation of the State of São Paulo (FAPESP) and the German Academic Exchange Service (DAAD). She also earned a Bachelor of Law degree from the University of Sao Paulo in 2011. Her research interests cover topics in philosophy of law, legal argumentation, rhetoric, human rights and international courts.

Tommi Ralli graduated in law at Helsinki University and holds a PhD from the European University Institute in Florence. His thesis 'Justice Through Legal Dispute' focused on issues of natural justice, judicial attention, and dispute resolution. His research interests include virtue ethics and conflict resolution. He is the author of a number of articles, including 'Intellectual Excellences of the Judge', and participates in European comparative research projects, such as 'Cross Border Acquisitions of Residential Property in the EU: Problems Encountered by Citizens'.

Christof Rapp teaches philosophy at the Faculty of Philosophy of the Ludwig-Maximilians-University in Munich, where he is Chair of Ancient Philosophy. He is conducting research on Aristotle's moral psychology, on Aristotle's dialectic, on Aristotle's metaphysics and on the use of the concept of 'nature' in ancient political theory. He is author of: Aristoteles, Rhetorik, 2 Vols., Berlin: Akademie Verlag 2002, Metaphysik, Munich: C. H. Beck 2016.

Ana Carolina de Faria Silvestre teaches philosophy of law at the Faculty of Law of Southern Minas Gerais and philosophy at the Higher Education Center in Management, Technology and Education in Brazil. She is currently a PhD student in law and emotions at the University of Coimbra (Portugal). Co-author of the books *Vidas à Venda* (Lives for Sales) and *Cidades Impossíveis* (Impossible Cities) published in Brazil and *Fiscalidade: outros olhares* (Taxation: Other Points of View) published in Portugal.

Humber van Straalen followed the research-master program for philosophy at the University of Amsterdam (2015). Current research interests include meta-ethics, action-theory, phenomenology, naturalism, and the history of Dutch philosophy. He teaches philosophy classics (a.o. Popper's *Logic of Scientific Discovery* and Camus' *Myth of Sisyphus*) at the extra-curricular program of the Technical University Delft, and is currently doing a post-master to acquire a teaching degree in educational philosophy.

Cristina Viano is *Directeur de Recherche* at the French National Center for Scientific Research (CNRS), Léon Robin Center, Paris-Sorbonne. Her field of research is history of philosophical and scientific thought in antiquity. Main topics are: Aristotle: natural philosophy, ethics and rhetoric; theories of causality (Project AITIA/AITIAI, CNRS); ancient theories of matter from Presocratics to Neoplatonists; Alexandrian alchemy and the relationship with Greek philosophy.

She has published the book *La matière des choses. Le livre IV des Météorologiques d'Aristote, et son interprétation par Olympiodore*, with the Greek text and a translation of Olympiodorus' commentary to book IV (Vrin 2006) and has edited three books in the collection of AITIA/AITIAI Project: *with* C. Natali and M. Zingano, *Aitia I. Les quatre causes d'Aristote: origines et interpré tations*, Peeters Louvain, 2013; with C. Natali, *Aitia II. Le débat sur les cause à l'âge hellénistique et impérial* Peeters Louvains, 2014, *Materia e causa materiale in Aristotele e oltre (AITIA III)*, Edizioni di Storia e Letteratura, Roma, 2016.

Glossary

A

absent *pros ten elleipsin*
absolute sense *aplos*
absurd *atopon*
accepted opinions *endoxa*
account *logos*
accused *pheugon*
accuser *diokon*
acquiring knowledge *manthanein*
acting first *energesantes proteron*
activity of sense-perception *aisthanesthai*
actuality *energeia, entelecheia*
adikia injustice, unjust act
adikon unjust
adjudicate by dividing in equal parts *dichastes*
adulterer in the act *hoion moichon labon*
adultery *graphe moicheias, nomos moicheias*
aetteton ho thumos indomitable element
affections *pathemata*
affections of the soul *pathe tes psuches*
against a person *eis to soma*
aganaktein anger
agathoi good people
agathos good
agnoia ignorance
agreement *homonoia*
aidos self-respect, shame
aischune shame

L. Huppes-Cluysenaer, N.M.M.S. Coelho (eds.), *Aristotle on Emotions in Law and Politics*, Law and Philosophy Library 121, DOI 10.1007/978-3-319-66703-4

aisthanesthai activity of sense-perception
aisthesis sensation
aisthetike mesotes sensitive mean
aitios responsible
akon involuntary
akousia involuntary acts
akrasia lack of control
akribeia exactness or precision
akurion not sovereign, incapable
alogon ditton irrational element
alogon irrational
amphisbetountes opposing parties in a lawsuit
anagkaion necessary
andreia courage
anger *orge*, *thumos* and *aganaktein* are considered to be synonym
anthropokoteron gar to timoreisthai natural and positive
anthropos human being
aorgesia spiritlessness
apainetes laudable
apathy being *athuma*
aplos absolute sense
apolis without a city
appetite *epithumia, orexis*
appetitive *epithumetikon*
aprobouleutos without deliberate intention
apsuchon soulless, without soul
arche cause, source, principle
archikon commanding
archomena subjected
archon to command
arete virtue
argument *ergon*
armotton standard of appropriateness and convenience
arouse (emotion) *paraskeuazein*
art of politics *politike*
art *techne, technikon*
asomaton incorporeality
association *koinonia*
asunthetos uncompounded
at liberty *eleutheros*
at the origin *ex arches*
athuma apathy
atimia disrespect, a form of *hubris*
atimois ergois harm the honour

atopon absurd
azux unyoked

B

bare life *zoe*
base people *phauloi*
belittle certain things *peri to medenos axion*
belittling *oligoria*
belong to *huparchein*
belonging to the same clan *tois homothnesi*
biaion kai sumphanon violent and being publicly committed
biazetai element of violence
bios political life or existence
blabai harmful acts
blabe damage
body soma
boulesis volition, wish

C

calculative *logistike*
calm *praotes*
calmness *praotes*
care *epimelia*
caring *kedesthai*
catharsis *katharsis*
cause *arche*
chalepoi diorizein difficult to classify
character ethos
charan joy
charis kindness
choice *prohairesis*
citizen *polites*
city-state *polis*
close embrace *epi damarti*
command *to archon*
commanding and indomitable element *archikon gar kai aetteton ho thumos*
common *koinon*
common opinions *eudoxa*
common sense *koine aisthesis*
community *koinonia, kononia*

compassion *eleos*
composite thing *sunthetos*
composition of parts *sunthesis ton meron*
concerned about good practical decisions in the future *prohairesis*
concord *homonoia*
confidence *tharros, tharsos*
conscience *synderesis*
consider *diaphrontizein*
consisting of many varieties *polumeres*
constitution *politeia*
contempt *kataphronesis*
contributions *ta eisenechthenta*
controller *kurios*
convention *kata suntheken*
courage *andreia*
courageous *thumoeideis*
craft *techne, technikon*
custom ethos

D

damage *blabe*
decrees *psephismata*
dei shall
deinotate hubris or megiston ton adikematon exceptional seriousness
desire *epithumia*, oregesthai, *orexis*
desiring element *orektikon*
develop *phuo*
di' hosa metaballontes diapherousi pros tas kriseis reasons which change the
   judgments of people
dia kai en pathei ontes under the influence of feeling
diaireo dividing
dialectician *dialektikos*
dialektikos dialectician
dianemetikon dikaion distributive justice
dianoia intelligence, thought
diaphrontizein consider
dicha equal parts
dichastes adjudicate by dividing in equal parts
difficult to classify *chalepoi diorizein*
dihairesis division
dikaiosune justice in the complete and whole sense
dikon just

diokon accuse
discernment *gnome*
disposition *hexis*
disrespect *atimia, which is a form of hubris*
distributive justice *dianemetikon dikaion*
dividing *diaireo*
division *dihairesis*
douleuonta enslaved
doulos slave, someone who belongs to another
doxa opinion, prevailing opinions
dunamis potentiality, power

E

echei de duschereias involves difficulties
echthra hatred
education *paideia*
eidos form
eie logos single definition
eis adoxian loss of reputation
eis to soma against a person
ekastos ateles peri to krinein estin separately the individual is immature in judgment
elachista moria tou pantos smallest parts of the whole
element of violence *biazetai*
eleos compassion, pity
eleutheron love of freedom
eleutheros free, unrestrained, at liberty
emotion *pathos, thumos*
emotions *pathe, ta pathe*
empsuchon ensouled, what has soul in it
emulation *zelos*
en intrinsic
en hule in matter
en tois allois other fields of study
end telos/skopos
endoxa accepted opinions, prevailing opinions
energeia actuality, energy, activity
energesantes proteron acting first
energy/activity *energeia*
enmattered forms *logoi enuloi*
enslaved *douleuonta*
ensouled *empsuchon*

entelecheia actuality
envy *phthonos*
epereasmos spite
eph'emin it depends on us
epi damarti close embrace
epieikeia equity, fairness
epieikes esti [...] kai epieikon typical of virtuous men
epigramma qualification
epimeleia care
epimelia care
episteme science or knowledge
epithumetikon appetite
epithumia desire, appetitive, sensual desire
equal parts *dicha*
equity *epieikeia*
ergon argument, function, the result
eros erotic love
erotic love *eros*
ethike philia moral friendship
ethos character; custom/character; one of the three Aristotelian rhetorical means of
    persuasion, which is bound to the character of the speaker and, according to a
    legal perspective, to the authority of normative sources as well. In this paper, it is
    also a category of the rhetorical empirical method on the analysis of judicial
    decisions proposed by K. von Schlieffen
eudaimonia good for human life, human flourishing
eudaimonia happiness
eudoxa common opinions
eunoia good will, goodwill
evil *kakos*
exactness akribeia
ex arches at the origin, inner principle
exceptional seriousness *deinotate hubris* or *megiston ton adikematon*
exempted from the crime *katharos en to nomo*
exercising knowledge already acquired *theorein*

F

faction *stasis*
faculty of appetite *orektikon*
fairness *epieikeia*
fear *phobos*
feeling pity *to eleein*
feelings in a general sense *pathe*

forces *rhomai*
form *eidos*
free *eleutheros*
friendly feeling *to philein*
friends coincidentally *sumbebekos*
friends without qualification *haplos*
friendship *philia*
function *ergon*

G

gentleness *praotes*
gnome discernment, sense
gnome dikaiotate most just understanding
goal *telos*
good *agathos*
good for human life *eudaimonia*
good people *agathoi*
goodwill *eunoia*
graphe hubreos public outrage
graphe moicheias adultery
greediness *pleonexia*

H

haplos friends without qualification
happiness *eudaimonia*
harmful acts *blabai*
harm the honour *atimois ergois*
has difficulties *echei de duschereias*
hate *misos*
hatred *echthra*
hedone pleasure
hekousia voluntary, voluntary acts
hekousios phonos voluntary homicide
hek pronoias premeditated
hetton aischra less shameful
hexeis states
hexis disposition, state
hoion moichon labon adulterer in the act
homoion 'same'
homoion energeia the same activity

homoioteta metaphor
homonoia agreement, concord, sociability, steadiness of purpose, unanimity
horme impulse
house oikos
household *oikos*
hubris outrage
hule matter
human being *anthropos*
human feeling *philanthropon*
human flourishing *eudaimonia*
huparchein belong to
hupo te tou hubristhentos bia sexual abuse

I

ignorance *agnoia*
image/appearance *phantasma*
imagination *phantasia*
imitation *mimesis*
impossible to discern truly *ou dunamenoi krinein to alethes*
impulse *horme, thumos*
impulsive desire *thumos*
incapable *akurion*
incite anger in the judges with lies and devices *orgas tois akouousi...
  paraskeuazousi*
incorporeality *asomaton*
indication *semeion*
indignation *nemesan,* nemesis
in identical conditions *isos kai homoios*
injustice *adikia*
inner principle *ex arches*
in matter *en hule*
intellect *nous*
intellective faculty *noetikon*
intelligence *dianoia*
intentional action *prohairesis*
intermediate level between voluntary acts and involuntary acts *metaxu de pou
  tou te hekousiou kai akousiou*
in the shadow and by fraud *meta skotous kai apates lathraios*
intimation *semainein*
intrinsic *en*

involuntary acts *akousia*
involuntary *akon*
irascibility *orgilotes*
irrational element *alogon ditton, alogon, alogos*
isos kai homoios in identical conditions
it depends on us *eph'emin*

J

joy *charan*
judge of things close to us *to krinein peri te oikeion*
judgement *krinetai*
judgments *kriseis*
just *dikon*
justice *dikaiosune*
justice in the complete and whole sense *dikaiosune*

K

kakos evil
kalokagathia that which is noble and good
kataphronesis contempt
kata suntheken convention
kata tous nomous timoria requital accorded by our laws
katharos en to nomo exempted from the crime
katharsis catharsis
kedesthai caring
kindness *charis*
kinesis movement
knowing how to decide or how to act *phronesis*
knowing how to make things *techne*
knowledge *episteme*
koine aithesis common sense
koinon common
koinonein partner in
koinonia association, community, political community
krinetai judgement
kriseis judgments
kurios controller

L

lack of control *akrasia*
laudable *apainetes*
legal friendship *nomike philia*
legal rules, legal standards *nomoi*
less shameful *hetton aischra*
life *to zen*
living together *suzen*
logistike calculative
logographes speechwriters
logoi enuloi enmattered forms
logon de monon anthropos echei ton zoon Man alone of the animals possesses
   speech
logon echon rational
logos account, rational, rationality, ratio, reason, speech, one of the three Aristotelian rhetorical means of persuasion, which is meant to build an argument. In
   this paper, it is also a category of the rhetorical empirical method on the analysis
   of judicial decisions proposed by K. von Schlieffen
logos thes mixeos ratio of mixture
longing *pothos*
loss of reputation *eis adoxian*
love for oneself *to philei eauton*
love of freedom *eleutheron*
lovers of humankind *philanthropous*
love of money *philochrematia*
loving *philesis*

M

manthanein acquiring knowledge
man alone of the animals possesses speech *logon de monon anthropos echei ton
   zoon*
matter *hule*
mean *mesotes*
meaning *sematikon*
me hek pronoias without malice aforethought
mesotes mean
meta epiboules premeditated homicide
metaphor *homoioteta*
meta skotous kai apates lathraios in the shadow and by fraud
metaxu de pou tou te hekousiou kai akousiou intermediate level between
   voluntary acts and involuntary acts

mimesis imitation
misos hate
modes of persuasion *pisteis*
moral friendship *ethike philia*
moral purpose *prohairesis*
morphe shape
most just understanding *gnome dikaiotate*
most perfect *teleia*
movement *kinesis*

N

natural and positive *anthropokoteron gar to timoreisthai*
necessary *anagkaion*
nemesan indignation
nemesis *indignation*
noble and good *kalokagathia*
noein thinking
noetikon intellective faculty, thinking
nomike philia legal friendship
nomoi legal standards, legal rules
nomos moicheias adultery
nomos wider concept of law
not sovereign akurion
not to be indignant *ou nemesan*
nous intellect, thought
nutritive faculty *to threptikon*

O

obey reason *to logoi peitharchein*
offensive words or dishonorable acts *propelakisthentes logois kai atimois ergois*
oikos house, household
oligoresousin will esteem little
oligoria belittling
other fields of study en tois allois
opinion *doxa*
opposing parties in a lawsuit *amphisbetountes*
oregesthai to desire
orektikon desiring element
orexis (faculty of) appetite, the desire

orgas tois akouousi...paraskeuazousi incite anger in the judges with lies and devices

orge anger

orgilotes irascibility

ou dunamenoi krinein to alethes impossible to discern truly

ou nemesan not to be indignant

ouk epiboulos...alla phaneros which operates always openly

outrage *hubris*

P

paideia education

paraskeuazein arouse (emotion)

partner in *koinonein*

passion *pathos, thumos*

passions, emotions and feelings *pathe*

pathe emotions, feelings in a general sense, passions, emotions and feelings

pathemata affections

pathe tes psuches affections of the soul

pathos emotion or passion; one of the three Aristotelian rhetorical means of persuasion, which is meant to provoke emotional effect in the audience. In this paper, it is also a category of the rhetorical empirical method on the analysis of judicial decisions proposed by K. von Schlieffen

perceiving *aisthanesthai*

peri to medenos axion belittle certain things

peri tou dikaiou rightness or justness of the act

persuasive argumentation *topoi*

phantasia image/appearance, imagination

phantasma imagination

phauloi base people

pheugon accused

philanthropon human feeling

philanthropous those who are lovers of humankind

philesis loving

philia friendship

philochrematia love of money

phobos fear

phonos ek pronoias premeditation

phronein understanding

phronesis knowing how to decide or how to act/ product of practical reasoning, practical intellectual virtue, practical intelligence, practical wisdom

phronimos virtuous

phthonos envy

phuo develop, sprout

phusikos physicist

physicist *phusikos*

pisteis entechnoi technical means of persuasion

pisteis modes of persuasion

pity *eleos*

pleasure *hedone*

pleonexia greediness

ploutos wealth

polemou epithumetes war-lover

polis city-state

polis city-state, state

polis koinonia political community

politeia constitution

polites citizen

political community *koinonia, polis koinonia*

political friendship *politike philia*

political life or existence *bios*

politike science or art of politics

politike philia political friendship

polumeres consisting of many varieties

potentiality *dunamis*

pothos longing

power *dunamis*

practical intellectual virtue *phronesis*

practical intelligence *phronesis*

practical wisdom *phronesis*

pragmata things

praotes calm, calmness, gentleness

precision *akribeia*

premeditated *hek pronoeas*

premeditated homicide *meta epiboules*

premeditation *phonos ek pronoias*

prevailing opinions *doxa, endoxa*

principle *arche*

prohairesis choice; choice or intentional action; concerned about good practical decisions in the future; moral purpose; sagacity, proper deliberation designed to unify thought and desire

propelakisthentes logois kai atimois ergois offensive words or dishonorable acts

proper deliberation *prohairesis*

property and affection *to te idion kai to agapeton*

proportion *sumphonia*

pros ten elleipsin absent

psephismata decrees

psuche soul
psyche soul
public outrage *graphe hubreos*
public speaker *rhetor*
purpose *telos*
qualification *epigramma*

R

ratio logos
ratio of mixture *logos tes mixeos*
rational *logon echon*
rationality logos
reason *logos*
reasons which change the judgments of people *di' hosa metaballontes diapherousi pros tas kriseis*
requital accorded by our laws *kata tous nomous timoria*
responsible *aitios*
result *ergon*
rhetor public speaker
rhomai forces
rightness or justness of the act *peri tou dikaiou*

S

same *homoion*
same activitity *homoion energeia*
science *episteme*
science of politics *politike*
self-respect *aidos*
semainein intimation
sematikon meaning
semeia signs
semeion indication, sign
sensation *aisthesis*
sense *gnome*
sensitive mean *aisthetike mesotes*
sensual desire *epithumia*
separately the individual is immature in judgmenent *ekastos ateles peri to krinein estin*
sexual abuse *hupo te tou hubristhentos bia*
shall *dei*

shame *aidos, aischune*
shape *morphe*
signs *semeia, semeion*
single definition *eie logos*
skill *technikon*
skopos end
slave *doulos*
smallest parts of the whole *elachista moria tou pantos*
sociability *homonoia*
soma body
sophrosune wisdom
soul *psuche, psyche*
soulless *apsuchon*
source *arche*
speech *logos*
speechwriters *logographes*
spirit *thumos*
spiritlessness *aorgesia*
spite *epereasmos*
sprout *phuo*
standard of appropriateness and convenience *armotton*
stasis faction
state *hexis, polis*
states *hexeis, poleis*
steadiness of purpose over time *homonoia*
subjected *archomena*
sumbebekos friends coincidentally
sumbola symbols
sumphonia proportion
sunesis understanding
sunthesis ton meron composition of parts
suntheton composite thing
suzen living together
symbols *sumbola*
synderesis conscience

T

ta eisenechthenta contributions
techne art or craft, knowing how to make things
technical means of persuasion *pisteis entechnoi*
technikon skill, art or craft
teleia most perfect

telos end, goal, purpose
temper *thumos*
tharros confidence
tharsos confidence
thaumazein wonder
theorein exercising knowledge already acquired
things *pragmata*
thinking *noein, to noein, to noetikon*
thought *dianoia, nous*
thumoeideis courageous
thumos anger, impulsive desire, emotion, impulse, passion, spirit, temper
to desire *oregesthai*
to eleein feeling pity
to krinein peri te oikeion judge of things close to us
to logoi peitharchein obey reason
to nemesan unmerited fortune
to philei eauton love for oneself
to philein friendly feeling
to te idion kai to agapeton property and affection
to threptikon nutritive faculty
tois homothnesi those belonging to the same clan
topoi common places; topos in plural, persuasive argumentation, commonplaces
topos common place, commonplace
typical of virtuous men *epieikes esti [...] kai epieikon*

U

unanimity *homonoia*
uncompounded *asunthetos*
under the influence of feeling *dia kai en pathei ontes*
understanding *phronein, sunesis*
unjust *adikon*
unjust act *adikia*
unmerited fortune *to nemesan*
unrestrained *eleutheros*
unyoked *azux*

V

violent and publicly committed *biaion kai sumphanon*
virtue *arete*
virtuous *phronimos*

volition *boulesis*
voluntary *hekousia*
voluntary acts *hekousia*
voluntary homicide *hekousios phonos*

W

war-lover *polemou epithumetes*
wealth *ploutos*
what has soul in it *empsuchon*
which operates always openly *ouk epiboulos...alla phaneros*
wider concept of law *nomos*
will esteem little *oligoresousin*
wisdom *sophrosune*
wish *boulesis*
without a city *apolis*
without deliberate intention *aprobouleutos*
without malice aforethought *mē hek pronoias*
without soul *apsuchon*
wonder *thaumazein*

Z

zelos emulation
zen live
zoe bare life